SYSTEMATIC ANALYSES OF LEARNING AND MOTIVATION

SYSTEMATIC ANALYSES OF LEARNING AND MOTIVATION

FRANK A. LOGAN
DOUGLAS P. FERRARO
University of New Mexico

Published in Association with
Lawrence Erlbaum Associates.

JOHN WILEY & SONS

New York · Santa Barbara
Chichester · Brisbane · Toronto

Cover photos:
Top: The New York Times
bottom: Kathy Bendo

Library of Congress Cataloging in Publication Data:

Logan, Frank A
Systematic analyses of learning and motivation.

Bibliography: p.
Includes index.
1. Learning, Psychology of. 2. Motivation in education. 3. System analysis.
I. Ferraro, Douglas P., joint author.
II. Title.

LB1051.L77 153.1'5 78-6870
ISBN 0-471-04130-0

Printed in the United States of America

10 9 8 7 6 5 4 3 2 1

PREFACE

This book is an outgrowth of over ten years of joint-teaching a course in theories of learning. We accepted this as an exciting challenge because one of us began as a staunch empiricist and the other as an equally staunch theoretician. Over the years, we (and we hope our students) have profited from our divergent points of view, because we were both committed to a constructive and critical study of all systematic analyses of basic learning and motivational processes. By "basic" we mean simply those processes that we hold to apply to all animals, including humans. The experimental analyses of these processes have been largely conducted in animal laboratories and, hence, our focus will be in the laboratory context. However, we fully realize that the *issues* that we have chosen for discussion continue to be significant not only in the systematic analyses of animal learning and motivation, but also in a wide variety of human affairs. We recognize that additional principles are involved in human action and thought, and that only the systematic analysis of a variety of behaviors would lead to a complete understanding of behavior, but we have found that the student or researcher can profit significantly from the perspective and types of analyses that we have included in this book.

Our general purpose has been to acquaint the reader with the nature of systematic analyses, their role and possible value, the spirit of the debates in the field at the systematic level, and the interplay between systematic analyses and experimental analyses of behavior. This objective might be accomplished in any of several areas of psychology, but the area considered here is the richest that is currently available for the purpose.

We have as a more specific objective to review the systematic analyses that have been proposd by one scientist or another at one time or another; these have been included to illustrate the various ways in which an objective understanding of behavior has been attempted in the past and how it has changed. We do not propose to resolve any of these issues in this book. Instead, we hope to sample the experimental foundations upon which systematic analyses have been based, to consider various conceptual systems that appear to us to provide useful insights into the nature of the issues, and insofar as possible, to integrate these in terms of their relative strengths and weaknesses.

Some may feel that we overemphasize the role of historical antecedents, but it is our firm belief that the issues keep reappearing—often in somewhat different garb—and a solid foundation in the thinking of the many systematists who have wrestled with these issues is essential for a scholarly and dynamic understanding of ideas of more recent vintage.

We realize all too well that it is difficult to assimilate from the original publications the enormous scope of the literature that is relevant to our subject. Fortunately, there are excellent secondary sources, and we will freely refer to them. However, we have attempted to provide something of a compendium not only in the text itself but in a substantial bibliography and in a selection of pertinent abstracts at the close of each chapter. These are not substitutes for reading the original literature, but they are an introduction to the original works in an effort to familiarize the reader with primary sources.

Finally, we hope that our excitement about the subject matter and our conviction about its importance are reflected in the following pages. For us, the evolution of this book and its goals has extended our initial limited preconceptions; the result is clearly the joint effort of an empiricist and a theoretician.

Frank A. Logan
Douglas P. Ferraro

TO THE READER

The era of the big theories of behavior coincided with the era of the big bands. Theorists of the 1920s, 1930s, and 1940s, including Guthrie, Hull, Pavlov, Skinner, Thorndike, Tolman, and Watson, together with many of their followers, set out to follow the footsteps of the other natural sciences and develop a set of basic principles predicated on simple behavior situations that could be elaborated to encompass all forms of behavior—from individual personality to sociocultural phenomena. This youthful enthusiasm resulted from the acceptance of the thesis that behavior is a legitimate object of scientific inquiry and obeys laws that can be unraveled by experimental analysis. But theories on a "grand scale" were destined to run their course and, by the middle of the twentieth century, these big theoretical enterprises began to die of their own weight. Soon, few people even aspired to emulate their lofty goals.

However, these theories are more than historical relics; they illuminate the contemporary scene. Many of the issues that perplexed these psychologists can be traced still further back to the writings of the great philosophers and the early mentalists. Yet, interesting as a detailed study of each of these may be from the point of view of the history of psychology, we believe that a better approach focuses on the issues or topics that have persisted through these recent historical developments. In this way, we can gain a richer comprehension of the contemporary scene—its miniature theories, isolated conceptual ideas, and systematic analyses of narrowly circumscribed areas.

Our concentration on conceptual issues is an approach different from the traditional survey of systematic analyses that often are treated separately. Although we believe that the specialist must have a complete understanding of each of the separate approaches that has proven to have an influence on contemporary thinking, we also believe that a more meaningful approach to these systematic analyses considers the types of questions raised, the alternative answers that have been proposed, and the problems involved.

This approach has one major drawback for which we can only partially compensate: a systematist's answer to one question may constrain answers to other questions or, at least, favor certain alternatives in preference to others. For example, Pavlov was a physiologist who won a Nobel Prize before he seriously embarked on the studies of what we now call classical conditioning. He viewed the analysis of the conditioned response, which he initially referred to as a psychic reflex, as a means of determining both the structure and the function of the nervous system. In other words, he was not so much motivated by an interest in conditioning, in its own right, as in experimental operations that might lead to insights about the brain. Consider the following quotes (Pavlov, 1927):

In astounding contrast with the unbounded activity of the cerebral hemispheres stands the meagre content of present-day physiological knowledge concerning them (p. 1). This complex structure which is so rich in function . . . has never been adequately explored (p. 2). It is still open to question whether psychology is a natural science, or whether it can be regarded as a science at all (p. 3). There is no need for the physiologist to have recourse to psychology (p. 4). We continue to adhere strictly to the physiological point of view, investigating and systematizing the whole subject by physiological methods alone (p. 7). I must again emphasize how important it is to compile a complete list comprising all the reflexes with their adequate classification. For, as will be shown later on, all the remaining nervous functions of the animal organism are based on these reflexes (p. 12).

If one attempts to identify with the orientation implied by these quotes, it is easy to see why Pavlov was perplexed when a dog began to struggle against the ropes restraining it in the experimental apparatus; Pavlov's insightful solution was to posit a freedom reflex. He also proposed an investigatory reflex that, in humans, is the parent of the scientific method. Clearly, a bland reporting of a systematist's explicit statements may not capture the ever-present, personal style of the individual.

It is partly for this reason that publications such as *A history of psychology in autobiography* (Boring & Lindzey, 1967) and *Psychology: A study of a science* (edited by Koch, 1959) were conceived. Tolman's approach was commonsensical; for example, "What would I know if such and such happened to me, and what would I do if I knew those things?" Skinner tended to disregard behavioral research that did not involve response rate as measured in an operant chamber. And Hull not only believed in evolution but was guided by the resulting thesis that all principles of behavior must have, on balance, adaptive survival value. Spence thrived by discovering how to accommodate his protagonists' evidence within his own basic system. Devoted empiricists are embarrassed when they find themselves uttering hypothetical constructs; devoted theorists are equally embarrassed when one of their pet constructs proves to be superfluous. A very provocative exercise is to approach a problem with: "How would so-and-so handle this?"

We shall try to include our perceptions of as many of these styles as possible, since we believe they enrich one's understanding of the systematist qua person. We also unreservedly list in the bibliography a number of books dealing with the systematists from which we have learned. This textbook is conspicuously different from these works in that it is organized around systematic issues rather than around systematists. We are hopeful that it provides the reader with some useful ideas.

NOTES We have included many notes throughout the book. These are more in the nature of asides than core subject matter, and the reader can readily follow the text without reference to them. Accordingly, these are placed at the end of each chapter in order not to distract the reader.

Our principle purpose in including these notes is to further enrich our discussions and the text material with thoughts and information that we see as pertinent and necessary for a fuller understanding of the issues or methods involved. We hope that these brief notes will enrich the reader's appreciation of the scope of the issues with which we are dealing and will add to the reader's overall view of the complexity and nature of this field.

BIBLIOGRAPHY AND In the back matter of the book is a bibliography of relevant books and articles
ABSTRACTS that encompasses the topics of the chapters. We have tried to include most of the literature that is important to the study of systematic interpretations of

learning and motivation. Any oversights reflect the enormous body of literature that may be considered appropriate to the issues.

In compiling and listing the bibliography, we have used a format that will enable the interested reader to locate a book or article in any reasonably well-stocked library. Our goal has been to limit a listing to a single line of type, thus allowing us to provide a substantial bibliography within a reasonable space. The price of doing so, however, is to resort to various abbreviations and shorthand expressions that violate accepted practices. Our ground rules for abbreviations are described in the note on the bibliography.

We do not expect that many people will be able to read and study all of the books and articles listed in the bibliography. We certainly do not claim to have assimilated them all. However, the specialist in any particular subject field will want to be familiar with these publications, and the bibliography may prove useful in constructing relevant literature surveys. We have also listed publications at the end of each chapter.

These end-of-chapter listings include publications to which explicit mention is made in the chapter. For each, we have given the traditional reference listing and a brief abstract. The abstracts are either written by the author or are abstracted from the author's writing. In the latter case, of course, considerable text is omitted. We apologize to all authors for our shorthand presentation of their writings, but we feel the abstracts will lead readers to further study.

EXAMINATION ITEMS AND ANSWERS

Most people dislike examinations; indeed, they dislike being graded. However, we disagree with those who would dispense with examinations. Our performances are always being graded or judged by ourselves and others, and the important issue is not whether to engage in this activity but how to devise an appropriate examination that will honestly measure a person's understanding of the subject matter. Equally important are the criteria against which performance is assessed. Certainly one may legitimately complain about unfair examinations, but this is a commentary on the examiner and not on the examination process itself.

There is yet another important function of examinations: they may serve as very useful pedagogical devices by drawing on the reader's knowledge and leading toward new perspectives of the subject. A text, even one supplemented as this one is with notes, abstracts, glossary, and bibliography, cannot provide a concise, coherent organization of the relevant material and, at the same time, include all of the nuances and implications of the subject matter. A truly good examination should cause one to think and reason rather than simply to repeat and memorize text material.

In this spirit, many of the items included in the items-and-answers section at the end of each chapter are difficult and may sometimes seem elusive in their objective. These are made more elusive, because other items have been written in a more conventional question—answer style. We provide both types of questions, because we prefer "power tests" to "speed tests"; the power test provides time to study each item and reflect its purpose as well as its answer. We encourage the reader to use these examination items, not so much as an examination of the material, but as a means of further enriching one's understanding of the subject matter.

In scoring an examination, it is important to recognize that all psychological measurement is relative. There is no way that anyone can measure, on an absolute scale, the amount of knowledge a person has about the subject matter of this or any other textbook. Even being able to quote every word by page number would not, in itself, indicate real understanding. The best that one can do in evaluating a performance is to compare it with other performances.

RECOMMENDATIONS TO THE READER

We have prepared the text material and back-matter in a manner that we hope will facilitate the reader's appreciation of the systematic analyses of basic learning and motivational processes. Although each chapter is not completely self-contained, the reader who wishes may deal with each chapter separately and in whatever order. Nevertheless, the authors recommend that the book be read in the order presented. With respect to dealing with a particular chapter, it is our recommendation that the notes and relevant entries in the glossary be read in conjunction with a first reading of the chapter. Next, one should read the abstracts that, in many cases, are sufficient for the purposes of this book; in most cases, it will not be necessary to read the originals. In combination, these materials should give the reader a good initial overview of the subject matter of the chapter. Thereafter the text proper can be reread without diverting attention to these supplementary materials.

We recommend that as many of the listed books and articles be read as possible. Doing so will give one the flavor of the presentation in the original source and a better feeling for the authors' writing. In classroom situations, particular readings may well be assigned by an instructor, and this may preclude more leisurely study of the literature. However, the materials included here are archival and are available for future study should the occasion arise.

With respect to the examination items, we recommend that marginal notes be made where it is believed that an item is ambiguous or dependent on a particular interpretation. In this way, one may choose an alternative answer that is keyed as being "incorrect," but may display a good understanding of the subject, an understanding, perhaps, not thought of by the authors. Furthermore, it should be clear that the value of the examination items would be seriously diminished if the reader were to do a "sneak preview" of our answers. It is essential that you take the examination first, and only refer to the answers after you are convinced that you have done the best you can. In the process, you also should not refer back to the text while taking the examination. The test should be reserved for a time when you believe that you have completed your study of the chapter—only then can you benefit most from studying our answers and relating them to the discussions.

ACKNOWL-EDGEMENTS

During the writing of this book, we received the generous cooperation of several people. Indeed, much of what is presented here should be credited to the students in our Theories of Learning classes who shaped our ideas and our writing over the past ten years. Equally important has been the expert production assistance received from Mrs. Eleanor Orth and Mrs. LaNelle Ruebush who have been a great help from the beginning of our project. We have also been fortunate to have a stimulating environment in which to work—the University of New Mexico—and in which to live—thanks to Julie A. Logan and Sandra J. Odell-Ferraro.

We also acknowledge the cooperation of the following publishers who have granted us permission to use abstracts from their published materials: Academic Press; American Association for the Advancement of Science; American Psychological Association; Dalhousie University Press; Duke University Press; Harper & Row; Harvard University Press; Holt, Rinehart and Winston; J.B. Lippincott; *Journal of the Experimental Analysis of Behavior;* Journal Press; Macmillan; McGraw-Hill; Methuen and Company; National Academy of Sciences; Prentice-Hall; Psychological Reports; University of Illinois Press; University of Nebraska Press; John Wiley & Sons; and Yale University Press. Specific author and publisher credits are presented in full in the Abstract Credits at the end of the book.

CONTENTS

42674

I dedicate this book to my wife, Julie.

F.A.L.

I dedicate this book to my parents, Edith and Peter, and to my children, Kim and Craig.

D.P.F.

SYSTEMATIC ANALYSES OF LEARNING AND MOTIVATION

CHAPTER ONE

THE CONCEPTS OF LEARNING AND MOTIVATION

The capacity to learn—to modify future behavior as a result of past experience—is one of the most fascinating yet perplexing properties of organisms. It is fascinating because it reveals itself in virtually limitless variety, from the simple muscle twitches involved in blinking an eye to the complexity of charting the path of a spaceship embarking for a distant planet. It is perplexing because scholars and scientists believe that, in spite of the myriad complexity of the products of learning, the process or processes involved must be based on a finite, comprehensible set of fundamental principles. Yet years of inquiry have failed to provide a systematic analysis of learning with anything approaching the elegance of the laws of motion in physics or the periodic table of elements in chemistry.

This is not to say that these inquiries have been for naught—very much the contrary. An enormous inventory of knowledge has been accumulated from the experimental analysis of learning in various contexts, and many promising efforts toward systematizing this knowledge have been elaborated. This book is about these latter efforts and is directed primarily toward the issues that have emerged as a result of this endeavor. As background for this mission, it may be useful to review the most common learning paradigms that have been employed and a few of the phenomena that have been discovered.

It should be understood, however, that this review is not a substitute for a reasonably solid background of study of the empirical domain known as the "psychology of learning." The primary goal is to refresh the reader's memory and thereby to establish a set for the detailed analyses to follow. Second, but still of vital importance, is the need to appreciate the relevance of the subject matter. We will necessarily become engrossed in the fine details of issues that are most clearly formulated in highly artificial laboratory situations, which frequently involve the use of animals as subjects. It is our contention that these apparent minutia will ultimately become integral parts of a comprehensive, systematic analysis of learning. Toward this end, we have chosen the educational context as one in which to illustrate the applicability of these basic processes.

OVERVIEW OF THE PSYCHOLOGY OF LEARNING

For our immediate purposes, we shall follow conventional terminology and suppress many of the uncertainties and conflicts that appear in the literature of the psychology of learning. Very few of the phenomena have enjoyed the support of unquestioned reproducibility. But let us look beyond these subtleties for the major outlines of current empirical knowledge about the learning process. These are most conveniently organized around the classes of experimental operations that have been employed.

Classical Conditioning

Classical conditioning is generally regarded as the simplest of the learning paradigms and, indeed, it is from an operational point of view. A stimulus (unconditioned stimulus, US) with the existing, usually innate capacity to elicit some measureable response (unconditioned response, UR) is regularly preceded by some other stimulus (conditioned stimulus, CS) that is typically neutral vis-à-vis that response. A quite imaginative array of events have been used as the US for an impressive array of behaviors by organisms, ranging from paramecia to man. Pavlov elicited salivation in dogs as an alimentary response to food and a defense reaction to acid in the mouth, and most studies of classical conditioning with humans involve comparable unlearned reflexes. An airpuff to elicit an eyeblink, a shock to elicit finger withdrawal, a loud noise or a sexy word to elicit minute sweating in the palm of the hand illustrate very common US events. The basic phenomenon is that a response (conditioned response, CR) roughly corresponding to the UR comes to antedate the occurrence of the US thereby suggesting some kind of learned associative process involving the CS and the US-UR events.

Effective classical conditioning requires that the CS precede the US with the optimal interstimulus interval usually being found to be about one second or slightly less. The greater the intensity of the CS or the US, the greater the amount of conditioning observed and, generally speaking, relatively long intertrial intervals lead to more rapid conditioning. The CS may be momentary (trace conditioning) or may continue throughout the interstimulus interval (delayed conditioning). In either case, the latency of the observed CR ultimately becomes adjusted to this interval such that the maximal respose occurs just prior to the occurrence of the US. There are substantial individual differences in conditionability, and conditioning is significantly influenced by the instructions given to human subjects. It is important to recognize, however, that classical conditioning is automatic and not dependent on a voluntary set to give anticipatory responses. Conditioning can be obtained against a deliberate inhibitory set.

Of greatest practical significance is the fact that autonomic responses associated with emotions such as fear, anxiety, arousal, excitement, hope, relaxation, and even sleep fall within the purview of classical conditioning. A good teacher does more than present material in an organized manner; a major aspect of a teacher's job is the conditioning of attitudes toward the subject matter. Although we may debate the reason for the effect, everyone recognizes that students are more likely to study and learn material they like, enjoy, and find some value in learning. Attitudes are classically conditioned, including one's feelings about writing papers and taking tests. This fact alone would justify extensive experimental analysis of classical conditioning and efforts to develop a systematic understanding of the processes involved.

Operant/Instrumental Conditioning

The distinguishing feature of operant/instrumental conditioning from classical conditioning is that, in the latter, the occurrence of the US is completely independent of the organism's behavior while, in the former, the US (be it a reinforcer or a punisher) is dependent on the emission of some designated response. Whereas Pavlov administered food or acid regardless of whether or not his dogs salivated, Thorndike gave food or a slap only when his cats pulled a string or pressed against a lever. The distinction between operant and instrumetal conditioning is based on whether the designated response is freely available to the organism (operant) or is only periodically enabed for discrete trials (instrumental). This distinction in no way alters the fundamental principles that responses followed by a reinforcer reveal an increased probability of recurrence and responses followed by a punisher show a decreased probability of recurrence. This is the familiar empirical law of effect.

Although there are good reasons to question the symmetry of the effects of reinforcement and punishment, let us proceed on that presumption to review some of the phenomena in operant/instrumental conditioning. It should first be noted that reinforcement may be occasioned by the occurrence of an emotionally positive event such as food to a hungry organism (positive reinforcement) or by the termination of an emotionally negative event, such as an electric shock (negative reinforcement.) In general, performance is an increasing function of the quality, quantity, and immediacy of the reinforcer but is also importantly dependent on the schedule of reinforcement. The simplest case, of course, is continuous reinforcement (CRF) in which each emission of the response is immediately followed by reinforcement. However, only some portion of the responses may be reinforced (partial reinforcement, PRF). Although such a schedule produces a slower rate of learning, it may ultimately produce a higher level of operant/instrumental performance.

When the response is freely available to the organism, the occasions on which it will be reinforced may be scheduled in various ways. If several responses are required, a response/reinforcement ratio is imposed that may be fixed or varied. The behavior generated by such schedules is characterized by a pause after each reinforcement that is followed by a rapid run through the number of responses requisite to obtaining the next reinforcer. The major effect of the length of a fixed ratio is that longer ratios lead to longer postreinforcement pauses. Alternatively, if only one response is required for reinforcement, but the time at which a response will be reinforced is determined experimentally, an interval schedule obtains. When this interval is fixed, such that reinforcement is available at regular points in time, the postreinforcement pause tends to adjust to the length of this interval and is followed by an accelerating rate of responding up to the time of the next scheduled reinforcement. When the reinforcement interval is varied, such that there are not even temporal cues to determine when reinforcement is available, responding tends to be relatively steady over time at a rate inversely related to the length of the average interreinforcement interval.

Of greatest practical significance in an educational context is the fact that feedback about the adequacy of a student's performance constitutes a potential source of reinforcement or punishment. So long as the behavior being emitted by the student is desirable, the principles of reinforcement can be employed to schedule these reinforcers optimally for both learning and performance.

When however the feedback is punitive, undesirable behavior may indeed be suppressed, but there is no guarantee that the result will be the emission of desirable behavior. One of the major challenges to the educator is, therefore, to arrange the learning environment such as to foster correct responses and to arrange the contingencies of reinforcement so as to enhance their performance. Concurrently, it must be recognized that these events are also serving as unconditioned stimuli for the classical conditioning of emotional attitudes about the system itself.

Avoidance Conditioning   As previously defined, negative reinforcement refers to the termination of an aversive event and leads to defense or escape learning. Avoidance conditioning refers to the arrangement of contingencies, such that the emission of a designated response will preclude the scheduled occurrence of the aversive event. In classical conditioning, for example, withdrawal of a finger in response to a CS, which precedes an electric shock, removes the finger and prevents the shock. In an operant context, shocks that are scheduled for regular occurrence, unless a key is pressed, can be postponed by periodically pressing the key. In an instrumental context, a warning signal that a shock is about to occur in this compartment can be avoided by moving to another compartment. In all of these cases, organisms readily learn to emit the requisite avoidance response and even become quite adept at waiting almost until the last second before responding just in time to avoid the aversive event.

Avoidance conditioning is not always so straightforward. When the response required to escape from the aversive event (should it occur) is incompatible with the response required to avoid its occurrence, conditioning is difficult. Avoidance conditioning may be virtually impossible in organisms who have previously been exposed to unavoidable aversive events. There are also paradoxical effects, for example, the fact that rats may better avoid mild shock than intense shock; apparently, the innate freezing response to strong fear interferes with actively responding. Nevertheless, the fundamental phenomenon of avoidance conditioning is quite ubiquitous.

Insofar as an educational environment entails aversive events, students will learn to avoid them. Unfortunately in many cases, such avoidance responses engage a vicious circle; avoiding a class out of fear of doing poorly and being reprimanded serves to increase the likelihood of even stronger unpleasantries in the future—hence even stronger avoidance tendencies. The ultimate avoidance response is, of course, dropping out of school altogether.

Experimental Extinction   Regardless of the paradigm employed to produce conditioning, the removal of the terminal unconditioned stimulus results in a decrease in the performance of the conditioned response. Experimental analysis has revealed that there are many factors that determine the rate at which experimental extinction of a conditioned response will occur. The most pervasive of these is the schedule of reinforcement that obtained during original learning; responses that are most persistent are those acquired under irregular conditions of partial reinforcement. It is also the case that responses that received small rewards or even encountered occasional punishment are highly resistant to extinction. Where learning is generally facilitated by distributed practice, extinction is faster with massed practice.

Another phenomenon that must be appended to the principle of experimental extinction is spontaneous recovery; that is, extinguished responses are likely to reappear after a lapse of time following extinction. It should also be noted that extinguished responses can be reconditioned, typically very rapidly. If acquisition and extinction are alternated sufficiently often, a single reinforcement may be all that is required to reinstate the conditioned response completely.

Although there are many cases in which extinction might be appropriate in an educational context, such as undesirable habits learned outside of school, the principal importance of this phenomenon is that correct responses learned in a classroom are likely not to be explicitly reinforced outside the classroom. This means that the training program must be designed to enhance the persistence of such desirable behavior. On the other hand, if undesirable attitudes have been conditioned or avoidance responses have been acquired, then they may be extremely persistent in future situations. In such cases, extinction must be supplemented with counterconditioning, that is, the reinforcement of desired responses concurrent with the nonreinforcement of undesired responses.

Stimulus Generalization   Responses conditioned to a particular stimulus also tend to occur in the presence of similar stimuli in gradient fashion, that is, the greater the similarity, the greater the likelihood of the response. There are a number of factors that affect the extent of generalization and these are roughly the same ones that affect the overall persistence of a response. Specifically, irregular conditions of partial reinforcement increase generalization and large consistent rewards decrease generalization. The context in which learning occurs is a part of the total stimulus complex such that ostensibly the same stimulus may provoke a weaker response if encountered in a different context. As a general rule, experimental analysis suggests that the poorer the conditions for learning, the greater the persistence and generalization of that learning in the future.

Among the many phenomena that illustrate the principle of stimulus generalization is external inhibition. This refers to the fact that the occurrence of an unusual event in the environment leads to a decreased occurrence of a conditioned response. The counterpart phenomenon, disinhibition, describes an unusual event that may lead to an increase in the occurrence of an extinguished response. This latter phenomenon suggests that the effects of extinction also generalize in gradient fashion.

From an educational point of view, the objective is to train responses in the classroom that will generalize to the everyday environment outside the classroom. The educator is thus faced with an optimization problem: arrange the contingencies such as to promote persistent, generalizable responses without too severe a deleterious effect on the learning process itself. This is one direction for applied research that is suggested by the experimental analysis of basic learning phenomena.

Differential Conditioning   Any of the three basic conditioning paradigms, classical, operant, or instrumental, can be modified so as to include two (or more) different stimulus events that are presented in an irregular order and that are correlated with different conditions/schedules of reinforcement/punishment. Under most of the experimental conditions that have been studied, one of the stimuli is correlated with nonreinforcement (i.e., extinction) and the problem could be described as a go-no-go discrimination. But the more general expression is differential conditioning because the basic outcome is that the organism comes to respond differentially to the two stimuli more or less in accord with the condition/schedule prevailing in each. When one of the conditions is nonreinforcement, appropriate behavior is to respond in the presence of the reinforced stimulus (S+) and not in the presence of the nonreinforced stimulus (S−).

As would be expected from the principle of stimulus generalization, the major difficulty encountered in obtaining differential conditioning relates to the similarity of the stimuli. When the stimuli are sufficiently different to mediate differential performance, the phenomenon of contrast frequently is obtained. Performance is higher to the more highly reinforced stimulus than would be expected solely on the basis of the condition/schedule of reinforcement, and conversely. Among the many other phenomena observed in differential conditioning is the easy-to-hard effect: differential performance to two highly similar stimuli may be more rapidly obtained by starting with more disparate stimuli along the same stimulus dimension, and then shaping in toward the ultimate problem.

The basic operation of differential conditioning is pervasive throughout an educational program. More commonly, however, each stimulus has an appropriate response. For example, the visual stimulus "p" leads to the verbal response of "pea," whereas the visual stimulus "q" leads to the verbal response "queue." Illustrative of the implications of this view is the distinction between "p" and "q" that could be most readily acquired by making them highly discriminable at first (e.g., different sizes and colors) and then fading out these ultimately irrelevant features.

Information Processing   Stripped to its basics, learning involves bringing behavior under the control of informative stimuli. Even in classical conditioning, the CS informs the organism of the impending occurrence of the US. However, more demanding evidence that organisms process information being transmitted by environmental events is obtained when complex stimuli are employed in the learning situation. Again, for example, in classical conditioning the word "blue" printed in red letters is relatively ineffectual. In differential classical conditioning, a CS involving a correct mathematical equation such as $2 + 2 = 4$ can be distinguished from comparable, but incorrect equations, within the fraction of a second that is involved in emitting or not emitting the CR.

When a complex stimulus contains elements that are differentially informative about the impending occurrence of emotionally significant events, behavior comes predominantly under control of the most reliable elements. Even when the elements of a compound CS are equally informative, one element may overshadow the other either because of its innate perspicuity or because of its earlier history of reinforcement. More generally, organisms code complex stimulus events in various ways, and the amount of generalization to other complex stimuli depends upon the way the original stimulus has been encoded. Learning can thereby be equally viewed as memory with the invocation of various storage and retrieval processes.

Since the stimuli involved in most educational contexts are indeed complex, it is evident that the experimental analysis of information processing is especially relevant. Learning programs explicitly fostering efficient and effective codes, including mnemonic devices, certainly can improve memory. An important process in this regard is the organization of information into meaningful chunks that can be easily learned and retained.

Discrimination Learning   The operational difference between differential conditioning and discrimination learning is that, in the latter, the stimuli are presented concurrently and the organism is given a choice between them. In the prototypical case, one of the stimuli is associated with nonreinforcement such that discrimination learning entails choosing the correct stimulus. When two nonzero values of reinforcement are employed, we can determine, after the fact, which the organism prefers and then use this information to gain insight into the organism's motivational processes.

As with differential conditioning, stimulus similarity is a major factor in determining the ease of discrimination learning and, indeed, most of the phenomena are directly comparable in the two paradigms. However, more abstract stimulus features can be used in discrimination learning. For example, the oddity problem entails selecting the stimulus that is different from all of the rest in any dimension. Discrimination learning also gives rise to the phenomenon of transposition, that is, the selection from among a new array of stimuli on the basis of the same relationship among them that obtained for previously learned arrays.

For most practical purposes the distinction between discrimination learning and differential conditioning is unimportant; the organism must learn to distinguish between similar stimuli in both cases. Even on a multiple-choice examination, for example, the alternatives are given concurrently but the student must decide for each of these whether or not it is correct. However, much finer discriminations are possible by the simultaneous presentation of the alternatives and may well improve one's understanding of abstract notions. It is also important to note that organisms can learn to learn discrimination problems of a particular type such that there may be nonspecific positive transfer from early learning experiences to later studies.

Differentiation Learning   Where discrimination learning refers to stimulus selection on the basis of differential reinforcement of responding to somewhat different stimuli, differentiation learning refers to response selection based on differential reinforcement of responding in somewhat different ways. Responses may differ qualitatively (topographically) in ways characterized as form and style, or quantitatively in ways such as speed and amplitude. Generally speaking, differential reinforcement of particular ways of making a response leads to increasingly fine differentiations among responses. Such learning is presumably based on the difference in the kinesthetic and proprioceptive feedback generated by responses.

Response differentiation appears to follow very much the same principles that hold for stimulus discrimination, except that the cues involved are largely interoceptive. Operationally, however, responses can only be reinforced that are actually emitted and, accordingly, some degree of shaping of responses by means of reinforcing successive approximations is typically required. There is also evidence that organisms learn to perform the particular response that was reinforced, regardless of whether explicit differential reinforcement is imposed. However, there is a process of response generalization comparable to that of stimulus generalization.

Response differentiation arises in any educational context in which specific motor responses are required. Writing is an obvious case in point; learning to write is accomplished by differential reinforcement of relatively precise movements of the fingers and hand in accordance with symbolic conventions. The clarity and style of one's writing are, therefore, largely dependent on the extent to which response differentiation has increasingly required legibility. Writing speed is also a part of what is learned in practice. Of course, all skills, be they athletic or occupational, invoke the principles of differentiation learning.

Spatial Learning   Spatial leaning is a composite of discrimination learning and differentiation learning that involves the locomotion of the organism through space. The discrimination aspect refers to approaching and avoiding stimulus objects in the environment, and the differentiation aspect refers to making particular kinds of moving and turning responses coincident to getting from one point in space to another. Generally speaking, there is a goal location, and spatial learning is reflected in increased proficiency of getting from a starting location to the goal.

Spatial learning has typically been studied in the context of complex mazes, and many factors influence the ease of such learning. The most significant factor is the availability of distinctive cues in the environment that inform the organism of present location and the direction of the goal. As in all situations involving a chain of behaviors before a goal is reached, learning is facilitated by concentrating first on the last link of the chain and working progressively backward. Indeed, there is typically a goal gradient indicating that both learning and performance improve progressively as the organism gets closer and closer to the goal.

Although explicit spatial learning is probably not a major factor in most classroom situations, there are important analogous situations in the larger educational context. For example, learning to use a library effectively entails a form of spatial learning in locating a particular reference book. And some subjects, such as geography, involve spatial learning in symbolic form.

The Higher Mental   The preceding topics cover the domain of experimental analyses that have
Processes   generated the systematic issues to be discussed in this book. However, the total domain of the psychology of learning continues on well beyond those limits.

There are many highly relevant topics that involve characteristically human learning; that is learning that is unique to humans by virtue of the fact that we have an incomparable verbal language. Although humans learn effectively in all of the situations that we have described, and although verbal stimuli may be used with humans in each of those contexts, language learning itself and learning to use language in contexts (such as concept formation, thinking, reasoning, and problem solving) are generally thought to entail new processes not uncovered by the types of experimental and systematic analyses that will occupy us in this book.

Actually, the extent to which systematic analyses based on principles of conditioning will contribute to an understanding of the complex higher mental processes is an empirical issue. Certainly we would not contend that extant analyses are directly applicable to even so commonplace a process as our ability to transform sentences into different grammatical structures with the same interpretive meaning. But then, neither are extant analyses yet capable of dealing with the entire range of phenomena within the various conditioning situations themselves; it would be premature to state what can or cannot be done by future analysts. But we can assert that conditioning processes are quite pervasive throughout almost every facet of human behavior and that the systematic analysis of them, therefore, must be relevant to the overall mission of psychology as the science of individual behavior.

Summary It should be clear that these first few pages are not intended to provide an exhaustive or intensive review of the domain known as the psychology of learning. Our presumption is that the reader has already been exposed to a reasonably detailed study of at least the empirical foundations deriving from the experimental analysis of the learning process. If this is the case, this brief overview will have served the purpose of reinstating a preparatory set for the subsequent content. Furthermore, we recommend that the reader review the introductory-level examination items given at the end of this chapter, which provide a somewhat more complete survey of the fundamental concepts. As yet a further basis for review, we have provided a listing of the most relevant concepts and included a brief definition of each of these in the glossary. With these, students can best judge for themselves the adequacy of their preparation.

If our review is insufficient, we recommend a basic introductory text in the psychology of learning. (For continuity with the terminology used in this book, the text by Logan, 1976, may be most appropriate.) Although we have defined each concept introduced in the text, we have generally assumed that the reader is already reasonably familiar with the relevant types of experimental operations that have been employed and the nature of the empirical outcomes that result from the exposure of organisms to these operations. By way of contrast, the remainder of this chapter is devoted primarily to illustrating ways in which our conventional approach to thinking about learning in general poses many problems that are all too easily ignored by texts written at a more introductory level. We wish also to illustrate how any analysis of learning processes must equally encompass motivational processes.

The definition of learning as a hypothetical process, resulting from practice and reflected in a relatively permanent change in performance, is reasonably adequate only because of our personal familiarity with the meaning of the term. Our definition is improved somewhat by explicitly excluding from the concept other processes, such as fatigue and sensory adaptation.[1] Nevertheless, many confusions remain and some are quite subtle.

For example, one may question whether the phenomenon of imprinting should be included within the rubric of learning. It is now well established that the object to which a duckling is exposed during the period between sixteen and twenty hours after hatching becomes an object of attraction (e.g., Hess, 1959). Not only will the duckling follow the object around during its early life, but it will tend to select a similar object with which to attempt to mate as an adult. Here, certainly, is a relatively permanent change in performance resulting from experience, but should this example be conceptualized as an instance of learning?

In a somewhat similar fashion, an animal may watch the baiting of one of two currently inaccessible goal cups. When the animal is released after some period of time, he may correctly choose the baited cup (e.g., Berkson, 1962). Other examples are those organisms (both human and infrahuman) that appear to learn from simply observing another organism perform a response (e.g., Eron, Huesmann, Lefkowitz, & Walder, 1972). And yet another example is that a single experience with a particular taste and a subsequent bout with very severe sickness produces aversion to the taste, even if the sickness occurs several hours after the taste and is unrelated to it (e.g., Revusky & Garcia, 1970). The question again arises as to whether these phenomena, and others that could be cited, are to be identified as forms of learning.

Considerable importance centers on the answer to this question. If the answer is affirmative, the implication is that a general theory of learning should be able to encompass these phenomena. If the answer is negative, then the theorist is free to ignore the evidence about them when constructing and evaluating a theory. Unfortunately, our definition of learning does not provide a definitive answer nor is there a general concensus among learning theorists about the relevance of these phenomena.[2]

Of course, as we will discuss in the next chapter, a theorist can establish any boundary conditions desired. Briefly, boundary conditions specify the limits of the empirical domain to which a theory applies and may be quite encompassing or quite narrow. For example, one could build a theory of human paired-associates learning and attempt to account for the various facts in that area without recourse to any other empirical domain. But even such boundaries may become somewhat fuzzy upon close inspection, and they are especially suspect if the boundaries are established specifically to exclude evidence that does not fit the theory. In any event, our immediate goal is to identify the various experimental conditions that are generally accepted as producing some form of learning, restricting our consideration to those that have generated the most basic principles of behavior.

As with learning, we all have a personal familiarity with the concept of motivation, which is defined as a hypothetical state resulting from deprivation or stimulation and reflected in a relatively transitory effect on performance. In this case, we have a number of everyday words that refer to this state: need, desire, urge, want, intent, crave, and many others. But as prolific as our vocabulary may be in this regard, a rigorous delineation of the various motivational conditions is difficult.

Consider, for example, the concept of "instinct" (Beach, 1955). Birds migrate, bears hibernate, monkeys imitate, and all mammals copulate. These, and many other marvels of nature have been studied scientifically with the clear indication that hormonal balance and other biochemical states significantly affect the behavior of organisms. Should these states be viewed as motivational states, impelling moths to fly into a fire, whales to cast themselves upon the shore, and people to make sacrifices to gods of various ilks?[3]

A previously baffling and still perplexing area of interest concerns dreaming. People have long been fascinated by dreams, especially their sometimes bizarre nature, and Freud proposed an interpretation of dreams based on unconscious motivation. More recently, techniques have been developed that demonstrate that dreams occur during a paradoxical stage of sleep in which the body is very much asleep but the brain is very active. Dement (1960) has shown that dreaming is an important part of normal life. Thus, we need to sleep not only to restore the body but also the mind.[4]

Another example is the apparent need for comfort and affection (Harlow, 1959). At least we know that contact comfort is an important feature of the environment of well-adjusted infant monkeys, and that they also display clear affectional responses. In a similar fashion, female dogs will accept the sexual advances of some males, but not others (Beach, 1976). In this latter case, we might more appropriately talk of appetites rather than drives; you may crave one type of food, hungry or not. Should all such phenomena be placed under the rubric of motivation and, hence, be considered relevant to our mission?

Accordingly, we are in a somewhat uncomfortable position at the outset by having to admit that the very concepts that we are to consider are surprisingly vague. There is no point in trying to camouflage the problem by resorting to esoteric language and deceptive rhetoric. The plain truth of the matter is that we will have to proceed without all inclusive definitions of our basic terms. We can illustrate the various ways in which the terms have been used, and hopefully, thereby gain some understanding of the relevant domain. But we must always be cognizant of this fundamental difficulty.

THE CLASSICAL DISTINCTION BETWEEN LEARNING AND MOTIVATION

There were several bases on which it was presumed that the effects of various operations could be dichotomized into those affecting learning and those affecting motivation. Perhaps the most basic was the assumption that learning represents associative processes whereas motivation reflects nonassociative or state properties of the organism.[5] Related to this basis for the distinction was the assumption that learning is situational and motivation nonsituational. That is, learning requires exposure to the situation of interest while motivation can be affected elsewhere. For example, a rat can only learn the correct path through a maze by running the maze; his state of motivation can be determined by deprivation in his home cage.

In addition, it was generally agreed that learning is a gradual process but motivation can change rapidly. Furthermore, learning is relatively permanent while motivational states are more transitory. Now it is true that not all psychologists studying learning and motivation ascribed all of these characteristics to the concepts. Some contended that learning is a perceptual reorganization rather than an associative process; some thought that learning involved general principles that transcended the specific situation; some held that learning could be sudden and insightful; and some argued that phenomena, such as forgetting, indicate that learning is not permanent. To complicate the issue, hypotheses were advanced that either learning could be subsumed within motivation or that motivation could be subsumed within learning. Accordingly, the characterization of learning as associative, situational, gradual, and permanent, and motivation as nonassociative, nonsituational, rapid, and reversible is, at best, a simplification of the classical views concerning these concepts.

In spite of this simplification of the classical distinction between learning and motivation, there are reasons to question whether the distinction ever could be formulated in precise operational terms. A sufficient example is the very concept of learned motivation, such as fear. Into which category should fear be placed? We might call it learning, because it is associative and situational, that is, based on aversive experiences in particular situations. You are only afraid of social situations, if you have been exposed to unpleasant experiences in such situations. However, it is also somewhat nonsituational because it can be reduced by drugs, such as alcohol, outside the social setting; it is thus reversible and rapid. These should qualify it as being motivational in character. Clearly, fear has elements of both learning and motivation, no matter how well we conceptualize these terms.

We might attempt to weasel out of this dilemma by saying that you first learn the fear, and once having learned it, fear then serves as a source of motivation. But even this trick is not as neat as it sounds. What, we may ask, motivates fear? Fear itself? Even so, we would have to initiate fear and then stabilize it at some appropriate level. The reader is encouraged to think through this problem. Take a person who, at the moment, is under a very minimal state of motivation. Present a stimulus to which fear has been associated. If you energize the fear association with the initial level of drive, you will produce only a small amount of fear. But if you let that fear serve further to potentiate the association, it will feed upon itself progressively. You will soon see why one of the worst things of which to be afraid is fear itself. At the slightest provocation, it turns into terror.[6]

Accordingly, we shall continue to use the terms learning and motivation only as a matter of convention. Learning refers, generally, to knowledge and skills; motivation refers, generally, to the activation of knowledge and skills into performance. We will be safe in these usages only if we are constantly aware that they are more in the nature of givens than well defined concepts.

THE MUTUAL INTERDEPENDENCE OF LEARNING AND MOTIVATION

We have seen that the basic concepts of learning and motivation are on somewhat shaky ground with respect to formal definitions that separate them from other possible factors that affect behavior. Placing that quandary in limbo, we next encountered the problem that the concepts themselves could not readily be visualized as dichotomous categories with separate operations affecting learning and other, distinct operations affecting motivation. We now wish to complicate the matter still further by noting that these concepts may be viewed as mutually interdependent. It is for all of these reasons that we have chosen to include systems dealing with basic processes of both learning and motivation in this book; trying to separate them simply does not do justice to their natures.

Two or more variables are said to be *mutually interdependent* not only when the state of one determines the state of the other, but also vice versa. It is conceptually easier to think of a unidirectional causal chain: if A then B. To be sure, *A* has its own determinants and *B* has its own further effects, and so on both backward and forward in time. But at the moment of concern, *B* happened because *A* happened.[7] A banal example is the assertion that "He is wealthy because he is well educated."

We can use this same example to enhance our understanding of mutual interdependence. More often than we might wish to admit, wealth begets a good education. In order to sum up our results with more than the vacuous statement, "He is wealthy because he is wealthy," we have to devise an analysis of a mutually interdependent system in terms of its inner dynamics. Wealth may enable a good education, which may enable further accretion of wealth. In many situations, learning and motivation must be conceived of as interacting dynamically over time.

Let us illustrate the nature of this image of learning and motivation in the context of the familiar law of effect. This law, which might better be called the principle of reinforcement, states simply that a response that is followed by a reinforcing state of affairs[8] will have a greater likelihood of recurrence in the future. It is assumed that this increase in likelihood represents learning and, further, that performance of the response depends jointly on learning and the incentive motivation provided by the reinforcement.

Let us consider in this light a condition called correlated reinforcement. Now all conditions of reinforcement involve some correlation between response and reinforcement, even if that correlation be adventitious. Nevertheless, we can still think of a direct causal chain: a rat runs through a maze because he receives reward at the goal, and the larger the reward, the faster he runs. This is interpreted as demonstrating that performance, as measured by speed, depends on learning the correct route to the goal and the amount of reinforcement received.

Conditions of correlated reinforcement change the situation to one in which the amount of reinforcement depends on the rat's speed of running. Consider conditions of negatively correlated reinforcement (Logan, 1966), such as giving a rat a number of pellets at the goal equal to the number of seconds he takes to get there. This rat can, of course, run very fast but he will only receive a very small reward for his efforts. Conversely, the rat may run very slowly in order to receive a very large reward, but in the process, he significantly delays receipt of that reward. Although such conditions may sound somewhat diabolical, they are not at all uncommon in everyday life. For example, advanced education delays the presumably greater satisfaction of one's eventual career.

How, then, can we handle a situation that involves mutual interdependence? We know that the rat's speed depends on how much reward he gets, and we have devised conditions in which how much he gets depends on his speed. The conventional approach, borrowed from Economics, is to search for an *equilibrium solution*. The reasoning can be explained in this way. If the rat runs very slowly, he will receive a large reward. Large rewards induce him to run fast; therefore, his speed will increase. However, if he runs very fast, he will receive only a small reward, and since a small reward induces him to run slowly, his speed will decrease. By a series of successive approximations, the rat should arrive home at a speed that produces precisely that amount of reward which produces precisely that speed. This is a stable equilibrium, because any time he runs a bit too fast, he doesn't get quite enough. Any time he runs a bit too slow, he gets a bit too much. Hence, he settles into a more or less constant speed where both learning and motivation are in equilibrium.

As it happens in this particular case, the solution does not fit the facts (see Logan, 1960, and the micromolar approach). But the logic is, nevertheless, a useful one in conceptualizing how learning and motivation may combine in determining performance. For example, much of the research that has formed the basis for the systems that we will study involves subjects (usually animals) whose drive motivation is rigidly controlled by the experimenter. A rat, for example, may be maintained at some percent of its free-feeding body weight by being given a restricted diet.[9] Using this procedure, we can readily determine the effect of drive on learning and performance by varying the percent body weight imposed experimentally. Conversely, we can hold drive constant and vary conditions presumed to affect learning in order to observe their effects on performance. In a more advanced design of this type, we may vary both learning conditions and motivational conditions factorially in order to determine not only the main effects of each, but also their possible interaction. Such an approach has certainly served experimental psychology in good stead.

However, consider a rat which, instead of being placed in an operant-conditioning box daily for a session of responding under some programmed schedule of reinforcement at some predetermined level of drive, is allowed to live in that box and work for all of his food by pressing the bar. This is called a *free-behavior situation* (Logan, 1964). In this situation, we can no longer simply view the rat's level of drive as affecting his level of performance, because his level of performance determines how much food he receives each day and, hence, his level of drive. In this case, rats do appear to come into some kind of equilibrium in which the level of performance is commensurate with the resulting level of drive. If the conditions are changed so as to require more work for the food, the rat works harder but not hard enough to maintain the previous level of food intake. He, therefore, maintains himself under a higher drive sufficient to motivate a higher rate of responding.

Clearly again, many everyday situations are of this nature, although people are usually involved concurrently with a larger number of drives requiring a large number of responses. You could spend all of your money on food, but then you would have no place to live nor anything to wear. You can, of course, work harder, but then you have less time for leisure activities. In spite of these complexities, the experimental and conceptual analyses of behavior require their solution for really meaningful applications to human affairs.

Let us give but one final example: the behavior of you, as a student assigned this text. Without establishing priorities to the concepts, we can say that how much you learn will depend on how much you study. We can also say that how much you study depends on your motivation to learn. Your motivation, however, importantly depends on how much you are learning. Of course, how much you learn depends on the quality of this text in relation to your capabilities and background, and your motivation also depends on factors such as your goals in life. But in microcosm, to learn you must study; to study you must be motivated; to be motivated you must learn. Accordingly, learning and motivation are inextricably linked in a condition of mutual interdependence.

SUMMARY AND CONCLUSIONS

At this juncture, the reader might reasonably conclude that we are in a pretty sorry state of affairs! We cannot rigorously define either learning or motivation. We cannot clearly distinguish them one from the other. And under the circumstances, neither can we isolate learning and motivation from other possible causal factors in behavior. It might even appear to be somewhat presumptuous to attempt to proceed with systematic analyses of processes that are so poorly identified. This feeling will only be exacerbated when we encounter similar difficulties with defining critical concepts, such as reinforcement, punishment, and even the terms stimulus and response.

Yet the reader must be impressed by the enormous wealth of knowledge that has been amassed in spite of these fundamental deficiencies. We have focused on the deficiencies lest the reader relax serenely in the belief that the foundations of our science are solid. The basic data are there, to be sure, and vastly more must be acquired, but their systematic analysis also must be undertaken with caution. It is simple enough to utter the sentence, "Responses that are followed by reinforcement display an increased likelihood of recurrence," but it is quite another matter to examine that statement so as to evaluate its implications. How many parents of incorrigible children have said, "But we tried to give them everything."

At best, we can say that psychologists have a large degree of tolerance about the types of ambiguities that we have discussed, and an even larger degree of intolerance for those who would belabor these problems at the expense of getting on with the business of science. The approach is about as simple as this: Give me an organism, an apparatus, some procedures by which to control stimulus presentation, and some techniques for recording the behavior of that organism—then let me set about the task of finding out how what I do affects what the organism does. In the process I may, for convenience, refer to some of the operations that I perform as involving what I will call learning, others as affecting what I will call motivation, and still others not within the scope of the allowable operations. Such a scientist has a faith that order will emerge from a sufficient body of empirical data.

Indeed, to some extent it has. Given the infancy of psychology as a science, we might even profess amazement at the progress that has been made in ordering the domain of the behavior of organisms. At least this progress is sufficient to warrant enthusiasm for the future of such endeavors. We may ultimately abandon such terms as learning and motivation as having been borrowed from the vernacular and based on an intuitive understanding of behavior rather than a scientific one. Even so, the most promising avenue to any new conceptualization starts with a thorough study of systematizations that have already been attempted. It is toward that mission that this book has been written.

NOTES   1. Although learning theorists have been quite willing to state exclusions, such as fatigue and sensory adaptation, these terms are also subject to the need for independent definitions. If, for example, the definition of fatigue excludes learning, then we are actually no better off by exluding fatigue from learning.

2. Consensus is not required; nor must a theorist embrace all or none of the phenomena. However, a theorist should have good reason for rejecting any discrepant facts, preferably by relegating them to some other existing domain of analysis. That is, one should attempt to answer the question, "If it is not learning, what is it?"

3. Instinct doctrines saturated the field of psychology for many years prior to behaviorism and the advent of the experimental analysis of behavior. Well over a thousand instincts were proposed at one time or another, including for example, a dog's instinct to chase cars even though cars were only recently invented. Less subject to ridicule are the maternal instinct, the flight instinct, and the vocalizing instinct.

4. We will typically avoid the use of the term, "mind," because it is frequently used in an existential sense. It is a legitimate term, however, if used simply to summarize the myriad psychological factors that importantly affect behavior.

5. We will typically refer to learning as a process, and to motivation as a state. Of course, one's state of motivation results from the process of utilization of food substances in the case of hunger, but we can think of the state of hunger as the setting operation preceding an analysis of the situation in which the learning process is presumed to take place.

6. This paragraph is a good one to reread in the context of the reification of hypothetical constructs. We have followed conventional usage and referred to fear as an "it." But fear does not really exist as an entity, although our natural way of speaking tends to imply its existence.

7. One can also arrive at statements of the if A then B form from simple correlations. We are here referring to a causal inference based on experimental analysis rather than a correlation.

8. Although we shall follow convention and typically use the word "reinforcement," a more appropriate expression is a "reinforcing state of affairs." Negative reinforcement, namely the termination of an aversive state, is more aptly characterized by the longer expression.

9. A really provocative question is why the subjects continue to play the game when they actually have nothing to gain from doing so in terms of their total life economy. Apparently, obtaining a little bit of food immediately is sufficiently compelling to warrant engaging in the experimental task.

ABSTRACTS Beach, F.A. The descent of instinct. *Psychological Review,* 1955, *63,* 401–410.

The concept of instinctive behavior seems to have originated in antiquity in connection with attempts to define a clear-cut difference between man and all other animals. Human behavior was said to be governed by reasoning, and the behavior of animals to depend upon instinct. In his possession of the unique power of reason, man was elevated above all other creatures, and, incidentally, his use of them for his own purposes was thus morally justified.

The concept gained a central position in scientific thinking as a result of the Darwinian movement. Proponents of the evolutionary theory accepted uncritically the assumption that all behavior must be governed by instinct or by reasoning. Their aim was to demonstrate that animals can reason and that men possess instincts.

No such classification can ever be satisfactory. The analysis that is needed involves two types of approach. One rests upon determination of the relationships existing between genes and behavior. The other consists of studying the development of various behavior patterns in the individual, and determining the number and kinds of factors that normally control the final form of the response.

Beach, F.A. Sexual attractivity, proceptivity, and receptivity in female mammals. *Hormones and Behavior,* 1976, *7,* 105–138.

Attractivity refers to the female's stimulus value in evoking sexual responses by the male. Proceptivity connotes various reactions by the female toward the male which constitute her assumption of initiative in establishing or maintaining sexual interaction. Receptivity is defined in terms of female responses necessary and sufficient for the male's success in achieving intravaginal ejaculation.

Two types of evidence show that sexual attractivity depends upon more than the female's hormonal condition. In the first place, even when several ovariectomized females are treated with equal amounts of estrogen some consistently evoke more sexual responses than others. In the second place, males often exhibit individual preferences for particular females in contrast to others which are also in estrus and equally receptive.

Measurement of the visiting behavior shown by male dogs to different estrous bitches tethered in an open field revealed clear-cut individual preference patterns. Some males consistently visited certain females for 80–90% of their test time and spent 20% or less of the test with other bitches. Other males showed equally strong biases, but preferred females which had proven relatively unattractive to the first males.

Individual differences in attractivity are reflected in accounts of sexual "favoritism" shown by male monkeys and apes. Some rhesus males caged continuously with the same females copulate predominantly or even exclusively with one of two equally available partners. The attractivity of a favorite, or unattractivity of the nonfavorite may be so strong that the former is preferred even during periods when she is not in estrus and the latter is stimulated by estrogen treatment.

Berkson, G. Food motivation and delayed response in gibbons. *Journal of Comparative and Physiological Psychology,* 1962, *55,* 1040–1043.

The gibbon has special significance for comparative psychology because, as the most primitive of the anthropoid apes, it represents an evolutionary level between the catarrhine monkeys and the great apes. In these studies, food preferences were applied in investigations of motivational variables affecting performance on a delayed response task.

The foods used were raisins, raw sweet potato, and celery (the latter two being cut to the size of raisins). These foods had been ranked as the most, middle, and least favored foods, respectively. Each trial began with a transparent screen down. One of the three foods was placed in the center of a tray. As soon as the subject looked at the food, the food was transferred to a position six inches to the right or left of where it had been; it was then covered with one of the funnels. After 0, 5, 10, or 20 seconds, the transparent door was raised permitting the subject to displace one funnel. A noncorrection procedure was used.

Percent correct responses decreased with increasing delays. Preferred foods resulted in a greater number of correct responses at all delays. There was no interaction of food preference and delay interval. Food deprivation can result in improved performance for a nonpreferred incentive.

Dement, W. The effect of dream deprivation. *Science,* 1960, *131,* 1705–1708.

Dreaming occurs during periods of rapid eye movements. The directional patterning of these eye movements and the associated dream content suggests that the eye movements represent watching the events of the dream.

In undisturbed sleep, the eye movement periods occur regularly throughout the night in association with the lightest phases of a cyclic variation in depth of sleep, as measured by the electroencephalograph. The length of individual cycles averages about 90 minutes, and the mean duration of single periods of eye movement is about 20 minutes.

Dreaming appears to be an intrinsic part of normal sleep and, as such, although the dreams are not usually recalled, occurs every night in every sleeping person. A rather fundamental question is whether or not this amount of dreaming is in some way a necessary and vital part of our existence. The obvious attack on this problem was to study subjects who had been deprived of the opportunity to dream. This was done by awakening sleeping subjects immediately after the onset of dreaming and to continue this procedure through the night.

The results have been tentatively interpreted as indicating that a certain amount of dreaming each night is a necessity. It is as though a pressure to dream builds up with the accruing dream deficit during successive dream-deprivation nights—a pressure which is first evident in the increasing frequency of attempts to dream and then, during the recovery period, in the marked increase in dreaming. There is a more-or-less quantitative compensation for the deficit. It is possible that if the dream suppression were carried on long enough, a serious disruption of personality would result.

Eron, L.D., Huesmann, L.R., Lefkowitz, M.M., & Walder, L.O. Does television violence cause aggression? *American Psychologist,* **1972,** *27,* **253–263**

Among the results of a large-scale survey study of aggressive behavior in third-grade school children had been the findings that children at that age who preferred violent television programs were more aggressive in school as rated by their peers than children who preferred less violent programs. In a 10-year follow-up study, 427 of the original 875 subjects, including 211 males and 216 females, were interviewed as to their television habits. They again rated their peers on aggressive behavior. It was found that the violence of programs preferred by the male subjects in Grade 3 was even more strongly related to aggression 10 years later. By the use of correlation techniques, it was demonstrated that there is a probable causative influence of watching violent television programs in early formative years on later aggression. The effect of television violence on aggression explains a larger portion of the variance than does any other single factor which was studied including IQ, social status, mobility aspirations, religious practice, ethnicity, and parental disharmony.

Harlow, H.F. The development of affectional patterns in infant monkeys. In B.M. Foss (Ed.), *Determinants of Infant Behaviour.* **London: Methuen & Co., 1959.**

In our original experiment, eight newborn rhesus monkeys were separated from their mothers and placed in individual cages with access to two inanimate mother surrogates. Both surrogates were made of welded wire, but one was covered with a terry-cloth sheath. Half the monkeys received milk from a small nursing bottle in the wire mother's body, and half the monkeys received milk from the cloth-covered mother. All the babies, regardless of nursing condition, came rapidly to spend most of their time on the cloth mother. Not only did it seem that contact comfort was a system completely superordinate over activities associated with nursing, but there was no evidence that nursing, through the mechanism of secondary reinforcement, became an affectional variable of any real importance.

An efficient test for measuring infant–mother affection is the open-field situation, which consists of a room six feet by six feet by six feet containing a number of unfamiliar objects such as a small artificial tree, a crumpled piece of paper, a folded gauze diaper, a wooden block and a doorknob. When the cloth mother was present, the infant would rush wildly to her, climb upon her, rub against her, and cling to her tightly. However, when the cloth mother was absent, the infants would rush across the test room and throw themselves face downward, clutching their heads and bodies and screaming their distress.

Love of mother alone is not enough. The feral rhesus mother guides the infant through two kinds of affectional stages. First, it provides nutritional and comfort needs upon which are formed affection and security, and it safeguards the infant until danger signals are recognized. The second guided affectional pattern consists of the gradual relaxation of these affectional bonds; this is an essential stage for the subsequent development of normal infant–infant affection.

Hess, E.H. Imprinting. *Science,* 1959, *130,* 130–141.

Three statements are usually made about the effects of early experience. The first is that early habits are very persistent and may prevent the formation of new ones. The second statement is that early perceptions deeply affect all future learning. The third statement is simply that early social contacts determine the character of adult social behavior. This is the phenomenon of imprinting.

Lorenz was the first to call this phenomenon "imprinting." He was also the first to point out that it appeared to occur at a critical period early in the life of an animal. He postulated that the first object to elicit a social response later released not only that response but also related responses such as sexual behavior. Imprinting, then, was related not only to the problem of behavior but also to the general biological problem of evolution and speciation.

What can we say about the general nature of imprinting? Our best guess to date is that it is a rigid form of learning, differing in several ways from the usual association learning which comes into play immediately after the peak of imprintability. In other words, imprinting in our experiments results in the animal learning the rough, generalized characteristics of the imprinting object. Its detailed appreciation of the specific-object comes as a result of normal conditioning—a process which in the case of these animals takes a much longer time and is possible days after the critical period for imprinting has passed.

Logan, F.A. *Incentive.* New Haven: Yale University Press, 1960. (Ch. 7.)

The condition used to illustrate the equilibrium model is "controlled interval of reinforcement," which is the time between the occurrence of the stimulus and the receipt of the reward which, in the present studies, refers to the time between the opening of a start door in a runway and the delivery of food to rats. The subject has nothing to gain from running faster than the prevailing interval and the procedure involves a correlation between response speed and the delay of reinforcement. With a 10-second controlled interval, if the rat runs in 1 second, the delay will be 9 seconds; if it runs in 2 seconds, the delay will be 8 seconds; etc. It is, therefore, a condition of negatively correlated delay of reinforcement.

The incentive function shows how performance depends upon reward; in general, speed is slower the longer the delay of reinforcement. The terms function shows how reward depends upon performance; in this case, the increasing function would be linear if plotted against time, but is curvilinear when plotted against speed. The incentive and terms functions together determine the equilibrium level of performance. There is only one speed (where the incentive and terms functions intersect) which receives just that delay which provides incentive for that same speed. It, therefore, represents a stable equilibrium.

Because the equilibrium model can be used within conventional macromolar theories to provide predictions over a wide range of conditions from a relatively few estimated incentive functions, it deserves to be seriously tested. Only the consistent failure of this model would justify adopting the more complicated micromolar approach.

Logan, F.A. The free behavior situation. In M.R. Jones (Ed.), *Nebraska Symposium on Motivation.* Lincoln: University of Nebraska Press, 1964.

In a free behavior situation, a subject must work on some specifiable terms for his entire ration of some commodity. Unless the terms are so hard that even continuous work can not produce satiation, the organism himself controls his level of drive. That is to say, the subject determines how much of the commodity he obtains by how much work he does to get it. Thus, in contrast to typical research on motivation where drive is the independent variable whose effects on performance are studied, in free behavior research, drive can also be viewed as a dependent variable affected by various aspects of the terms.

Rats live in a box in which they have to work for any food and/or water they receive by pressing a bar. The terms are manipulated by varying the force required to depress the bar, the number of times the bar has to be pressed to get reward, and the size of the reward. It was found that intake is a negatively accelerated increasing function of amount of reward, that intake is a positively accelerated decreasing function of response ratio, that intake is a linear decreasing function of the force requirement, and that these latter two variables combine multiplicatively and then their combination additively with the first variable.

The results have been stated in terms of intake but total response output may be of interest. If the rat were "working" for the experimenter, conceivably even producing useful output, one might be interested in maximizing the number of responses made each day. In general, increasing the terms increases response output while reducing intake. Within the limits of survival, the harder the terms the more the output and the less the cost.

Logan, F.A. Continuously negatively correlated amount of reinforcement. *Journal of Comparative and Physiological Psychology,* **1966,** *62,* **31–34.**

When the number of pellets at the end of an alley on any trial equaled the number of seconds consumed in traversing the alley on that trial, the modal response time for 6 rats yielded 3 pellets. When the number of pellets equaled half the number of seconds, the modal response time for 5 rats yielded 2 pellets. These results, which were unaffected by moderate variations in drive level, conformed to quantitative predictions from micromolar theory.

Revusky, S., & Garcia, J. Learned associations over long delays. In G.H. Bower (Ed.), *The psychology of learning and motivation* **(Vol. 4). New York: Academic Press, 1970.**

An animal is made to consume a flavored substance, such as saccharin solution, and is later subjected to toxic aftereffects produced by such independent means as injection of poison or X-irradiation. After it has recovered from the toxicosis, the animal will avoid consuming the flavored substance. The animal behaves as though it thinks that consumption of the substance had made it sick. This phenomenon is best categorized as instrumental learning, but the temporal properties pose a serious problem for the traditional learning psychologist. These aversions occur even when the punishment of toxicosis follows ingestion by a number of hours.

Rats which had consumed about six times as much saccharin solution as water prior to irradiation preferred water to saccharin after irradiation. This changed preference was still apparent after a month of continuous access to both flavors. Delays of up to six hours produced maximal aversions, with less aversion if the delay was 12 or 24 hours. The more intense the irradiation, the greater the aversion. Aversions display repeated acquisitions and extinctions. (These phenomena were also obtained with other species and various methods of inducing sickness.)

Flavored water leads to reduced consumption if followed by toxicosis, but not if followed by shock. Conversely, when licking is accompanied by a flash of light and a click, consumption is reduced by subsequent shock but not by toxicosis.

A unique incentive theory is developed based on the following chain:

$$S_d \text{ —— performance —— } S_d \text{ —— ingestion —— } R_a$$

where S_d refers to drive stimuli resulting from deprivation, and R_a refers to need reduction following ingestion. This theory is described in a later chapter.

EMPIRICAL TERMS   This is a list of empirical phenomena and experimental operations that will be encountered in subsequent chapters of the book. The reader is presumed to be familiar with these terms, each of which is elaborated in the glossary.

  Act
  Act, pure stimulus
  Alternation
  Avoidance conditioning, cued-
  Avoidance conditioning, noncued-
  Behavior
  Behavior chain
  Blocking
  Centrifugal swing
  Compounding
  Conditioned emotional response procedure
  Conditioning, classical
  Conditioning, classical defense
  Conditioning, classical differential
  Conditioning, classical excitatory
  Conditioning, classical higher-order
  Conditioning, classical inhibitory
  Conditioning, classical omission
  Conditioning, classical temporal
  Conditioning, differential instrumental/operant
  Conditioning, instrumental
  Conditioning, operant
  Conditions, punisher
  Conditions, reinforcer
  Conditions, response
  Context
  Contiguity
  Contingency

Contrast, behavioral
Contrast, incentive
Contrast, negative
Contrast, positive
Contrast, simultaneous
Contrast, successive
Correction procedure
Counterconditioning
Cue
Cue reliability
Cue validity
Cue value
Differentiation
Discrimination
Discriminative differentiation
Disinhibition
Escape conditioning
Extinction
Extinction, latent
Extinction, resistance to
Feedback
Feedback, informative
Feedback, negative
Feedback, positive
Fixation
Frustration
Frustration effect
Generalization decrement
Generalization, phonetic
Generalization, response
Generalization, semantic
Generalization, stimulus
Gradient, generalization
Gradient, inhibition
Gradient, postdifferential-conditioning
Gradient, primitive
Gradient, relative
Imitation
Inhibition
Inhibition, conditioned
Inhibition, external
Inhibition, internal
Inhibition, reactive
Initial nonreinforcement effect on extinction
Insight
Intertrial reinforcement effect on extinction
Learning, differentiation
Learning, discrimination
Learning, observational
Learning, reversal
Learning, selective

Learning set
Massed-trials extinction effect
Movement
Noncorrection procedure
Operant level
Overshadowing
Overtraining extinction effect
Overtraining reversal effect
Partial punishment effect on extinction
Partial punishment effect on punishment
Partial reinforcement effect on acquisition
Partial reinforcement effect on extinction
Partial reinforcement effect on extinction, generalized
Partial reinforcement effect on extinction, interpolated
Partial reinforcement effect on generalization
Partial reinforcement effect on punishment
Peak shift
Punisher
Punisher, negative
Punisher, positive
Punisher, primary
Punisher, secondary
Punishment
Punishment, consistent
Punishment, correlated
Punishment, differential
Punishment, nondifferential
Punishment, partial
Punishment, principle of
Punishment, schedule of
Putting through
Reaction time
Reaction time, choice
Reinforcement
Reinforcement, consistent
Reinforcement, correlated
Reinforcement, differential
Reinforcement, nondifferential
Reinforcement, partial
Reinforcement, principle of
Reinforcement, proportional
Reinforcement, schedule of
Reinforcement, terminal
Reinforcer
Reinforcer, generalized
Reinforcer-magnitude-extinction effect
Reinforcer, negative
Reinforcer, positive
Reinforcer, primary
Reinforcer, secondary
Respondent

Response
Response, anticipatory
Response, avoidance
Response, conditioned
Response, consummatory
Response, emotional
Response, escape
Response, fear
Response, incompatible (competing)
Response, instrumental
Response, operant
Response, referent
Response, relief (relaxation)
Response, unconditioned
Satiation, need
Satiation, response
Satiation, stimulus
Schedule
Schedule, chain
Schedule, complex
Schedule, fixed-interval
Schedule, fixed-ratio
Schedule, fixed-time
Schedule, mixed
Schedule, multiple
Schedule, tandem
Schedule, variable (random) interval
Schedule, variable (random) ratio
Schedule, variable (random) time
Spontaneous recovery
Stimulus
Stimulus, aversive
Stimulus, compound
Stimulus, conditioned
Stimulus, discriminative
Stimulus, eliciting
Stimulus, emotional
Stimulus, exteroceptive
Stimulus, informative
Stimulus, interoceptive
Stimulus, maintaining
Stimulus, neutral
Stimulus, proprioceptive
Stimulus, redundant
Stimulus, reinforcing
Stimulus, response-produced (feedback)
Stimulus, safety
Stimulus, unconditioned
Stimulus, warning
Transposition
Varied reinforcement effect on extinction

EXAMINATION ITEMS

1. A scientific method is objective if
   a. any trained person using the method gets the same result
   b. the concepts involved are operationally defined
   c. it restricts the alternatives to a small, finite number
   d. it has previously produced verifiable implications

2. An event is explained to a scientist when
   a. it has been correctly deduced from a theory
   b. another event has been correlated with it
   c. the conditions necessary for its occurrence have been described
   d. it has been shown to be consistent with an established model

3. Which of the following is not included in the basic definition of learning?
   a. it results from practice
   b. it results in a change in performance
   c. it is relatively permanent
   d. it is directly observable

4. Which of the following is characteristic of all learned acts?
   a. they are accompanied by awareness of improvement in ways of responding as learning progresses
   b. they are acquired by a gradual process of conditioning
   c. they enable the organism to deal effectively with new situations
   d. they represent changed ways of responding to stimulus situations

5. The principal basis for distinguishing between learning and motivational factors is their relative
   a. importance
   b. complexity
   c. permanence
   d. separability

6. The belief that learning is an associative process is characteristic of the
   a. behaviorist approach
   b. cognitive approach
   c. behaviorist and cognitive approaches
   d. more true of the behaviorist approach than the cognitive approach

7. Which of the following would provide the weakest stimulus?
   a. a decrease in energy
   b. no change in energy
   c. an increase in energy
   d. an energy level related to the sensitivity of the receptor

8. The ability of a child to pick the largest piece of pie indicates that
   a. certain abilities are uniquely human
   b. desserts provide positive feedback for the child
   c. relationships may function as a stimulus
   d. the child was very hungry

9. Similarity among stimuli depends in part on
   a. the sensory modality involved
   b. the response system involved
   c. the number of dimensions involved
   d. experience

10. Stimulus satiation is a
    a. physical process
    b. physiological process
    c. psychological process
    d. psychiatric process

11. Experimental evidence indicates that organisms prefer
    a. constancy of stimulus and constancy of response
    b. constancy of stimulus and some variety of response
    c. some variety of stimulus and constancy of response
    d. some variety of stimulus and some variety of response

12. The most critical component of the definition of a response is that it is
    a. a glandular secretion
    b. a muscular action
    c. objectively identifiable
    d. importantly related to survival

13. In the psychology of learning, an act is defined
    a. by its consequences on the environment
    b. by its success
    c. as a part of a larger behavior scene
    d. as a make-believe performance

14. Responses are considered incompatible when they interfere with each other
    a. physically
    b. psychologically
    c. physically or psychologically
    d. physically and psychologically

15. Which of the following is not a correct fact of conditioning?
    a. the strength typically increases gradually
    b. the limit of strength is greater for strong stimuli
    c. the rate of conditioning is slower with faster occurrence of trials
    d. the optimal condition is when the CS and US occur simultaneously

16. In temporal conditioning there is
    a. a preceding stimulus
    b. not a preceding stimulus
    c. irregularity in time
    d. not any way to understand the phenomenon

17. The experimenter who wished to establish a higher-order conditioned response in an animal would encounter difficulties because of
    a. external inhibition
    b. extinction
    c. spontaneous recovery
    d. disinhibition

18. A dog has been trained to salivate to the flash of an electric light. This morning you discontinued giving him food after the light flashed, during which the amount of saliva produced over consecutive trials was 10 drops, 9 drops, 8 drops, 7 drops, 6 drops. After a delay (during which the experimenter goes out for a beer) another five trials without meat powder are run. The best guess as to the number of drops of saliva produced on these trials is

a. 8, 6, 5, 4, 4
b. 5, 4, 3, 2, 1
c. 6, 7, 8, 9, 10
d. 6, 6, 6, 6, 6

19.′ Having been bitten by laboratory rats on several occasions, you find that the cage also elicits fear. This would illustrate the concept of
a. temporal conditioning
b. experimental extinction
c. higher order conditioning
d. external inhibition

20. Differential conditioning necessarily involves
a. reinforcement
b. nonreinforcement
c. punishment
d. stimulus intensity

21. Counterconditioning involves
a. extinction
b. punishment
c. acquisition and extinction
d. acquisition and punishment

The next five questions are based on the following three assumpions: (1) Awakening is a response that can be elicited by strong stimuli such as an alarm clock. (2) Awakening is a learnable response; that is, it can be conditioned to initially neutral stimuli. (3) People contain an "internal clock" that provides stimuli to the person telling, with quite remarkable accuracy, what time it is.

22. Suppose that your alarm clock awakens you at the same hour each morning in spite of moderate variations in the hour at which you go to bed. We can view this, then, as a classical conditioning situation in which the relevant elements are your internal clock time, your alarm clock time, awakening to your internal clock time, and awakening to your alarm clock time. In the order given, these events can be identified as
a. CS, US, CR, UR
b. CS, US, UR, CR
c. US, CS, CR, UR
d. US, CS, UR, CR

23. You are awakened by a thunder storm one morning shortly before your normal time to get up and, after checking the windows, you turn off your alarm clock but go back to bed for the few minutes remaining. If you go back to sleep, you might not awaken on time because of
a. negative reinforcement
b. external inhibition
c. spontaneous recovery
d. failure to reset your internal clock

24. During exam week, you stay up extremely late at night studying and repeatedly fail to awaken either to your internal clock or to your alarm clock. You can expect this to result in some
a. extinction

   b. disinhibition
   c. experimental neurosis
   d. generalization

25. While on a visit, you discover that you have forgotten your alarm clock, but are confident of your ability to awaken on time anyway. You might fail in this new context because habits show gradients of stimulus generalization.
   a. True
   b. False

26. If you are unhappy about awakening so early on Saturday and Sunday mornings, you might consider differential conditioning by means of
   a. sleeping in a different bed on Friday and Saturday nights, without the alarm clock
   b. using the alarm clock on an irregular schedule
   c. refusing to get up on Saturday and Sunday mornings
   d. arranging to disinhibit the habit on Saturday and Sunday mornings

27. For rewards to be effective, they must
   a. be an effect of the response
   b. be apparent to the person
   c. occur shortly after the response
   d. result in drive reduction

28. Discrete trials or intertrial intervals are characteristic of
   a. classical and instrumental conditioning
   b. classical and operant conditioning
   c. instrumental and operant conditioning
   d. instrumental conditioning only

29. Treating "good" and "bad" behavior as alternatives, a student who leaves home for college is more likely to exhibit good behavior in that new environment if, during earlier years
   a. good behavior was rewarded
   b. bad behavior was punished
   c. good behavior was disinhibited
   d. bad behavior was inhibited

30. When a response is followed by negative reinforcement, the probability of that response occurring in the future is
   a. increased
   b. decreased
   c. unchanged
   d. dependent on the emotions produced by the negative reinforcer

31. Which of the following statements about delayed reward is false?
   a. delayed reward is inferior because it rules out the development of secondary reinforcement
   b. delayed reward may strengthen a wrong response
   c. verbal cues may alter the effects of delayed reward
   d. animals other than man can develop a tolerance for delayed reward

32. To predict whether a larger amount of reward will lead to higher instrumental peformance, you need to know the
   a. nature of the reward

    b. amounts of reward involved

    c. nature of the response

    d. amount of response required

33. After several years of attending both circus shows that visit your home town for one week each year, you decide in the future to go to one but not the other. This learning represents

    a. differential classical conditioning

    c. multiple operant conditioning

    c. multiple instrumental conditioning

    d. generalized classical conditioning

34. Grades in school are intended to provide

    a. correlated reinforcement

    b. correlated punishment

    c. increased learning

    d. increased drive

35. Negative contrast refers to

    a. the comparison between secondary and primary reinforcers

    b. the subject's response to reduced reward

    c. a type of discrimination task

    d. the shape of the goal gradient in continuous reinforcement

36. An ambiguous goal is one that is associated with both reward and punishment and, hence, has both approach and avoidance tendencies. As one gets near to the goal in such a situation, the net tendency (approach minus avoidance)

    a. decreases

    b. increases

    c. remains unchanged

    d. cannot be described without knowing the absolute strengths of the approach and avoidance tendencies

37. In a behavioral context, positive feedback refers to a situation where the response-produced stimuli

    a. serve further to accentuate the response

    b. have positive secondary reinforcing value

    c. have negative secondary reinforcing value

    d. are associated with competing responses

38. One primary difference between operant and instrumental conditioning is that

    a. in operant conditioning the response is freely available, in instrumental conditioning the response is enabled by discrete trials

    b. in instrumental conditioning the response is freely available, in operant conditioning the response is enabled by discrete trials

    c. the effects of reinforcement are exhibited in instrumental conditioning and the effects of punishment are exhibited in operant conditioning

    d. the effects of reinforcement are exhibited in operant conditioning and the effects of punishment are exhibited in instrumental conditioning

39. The operant level is the rate of occurrence of a freely available response with

    a. reinforcing but not punishing consequences

    b. punishing but not reinforcing consequences

    c. both reinforcing and punishing consequences

    d. neither reinforcing nor punishing consequences

40. The most effective way to shape a behavior chain is to begin with
    a. the first component
    b. the weakest component
    c. the last component
    d. each component equally

41. The most important ingredient in combining S-R associations into a continuous chain of behavior is
    a. stimulus trace
    b. relationships
    c. context
    d. feedback

42. The rate at which reinforcement is received is more dependent on the
    a. person in ratio schedules and the environment in interval schedules
    b. person in interval schedules and the environment in ratio schedules
    c. person in the day and the environment in the night
    d. person in the night and the environment in the day

43. A pause followed by a high steady rate of responding is characteristic of
    a. fixed-interval and fixed-ratio schedules
    b. variable interval and variable ratio schedules
    c. fixed-interval and variable interval schedules
    d. fixed-ratio and variable ratio schedules

44. When an instructor schedules an exam every four weeks of the semester, the student would be expected to
    a. study at a steady rate over time
    b. pause after an exam, then study harder as the time for the next exam approaches
    c. pause after an exam, then study at a high and steady rate until the next exam
    d. study at a decreasing rate over the time following each exam

45. A person who starts wearing a seat belt only after being injured in a car accident is exhibiting
    a. discrimination behavior
    b. differentiation behavior
    c. escape behavior
    d. avoidance behavior

46. The principal operational distinction between escape and avoidance learning is the presence of
    a. incompatible behavior in escape
    b. incompatible behavior in avoidance
    c. a warning signal in escape
    d. a warning signal in avoidance

47. An important distinction between escape and avoidance learning is
    a. escape learning refers to unconditioned responses, avoidance refers to conditioned responses
    b. escape learning refers to conditioned responses, avoidance refers to unconditioned responses

    c. the organism has no control over the occurrence or nonoccurrence of the aversive US in escape

    d. the organism has no control over the occurrence or nonoccurrence of the aversive US in avoidance

48. Escape learning is most rapid if the reflexive reponse to the aversive stimulus
    a. terminates the stimulus
    b. does not terminate the stimulus
    c. is incompatible with the escape response
    d. is not incompatible with the escape response

49. Well learned avoidance responses are difficult to extinguish partly because they prevent discovering that the situation is no longer aversive. The "reality testing" procedure is to restrain the organism in the situation, but you would correctly doubt the value of this procedure because the organism is eventually likely to
    a. get too emotional to learn anything
    b. learn incompatible responses
    c. discriminate the testing procedure from the regular situation
    d. become neurotic

50. A psychologist once advocated the following technique for breaking bad habits: perform the response continuously until it becomes painful. He correctly reasoned that this punishment would "suit the crime." However, he failed to attend to the nature of the specific S-R habit being punished and hence the effects of
    a. stimulus-generalization decrement
    b. counterconditioning
    c. secondary reinforcement
    d. secondary punishment

51. An example of negative reinforcement is
    a. taking a child's balloon away when a response is made
    b. giving a child candy when a response is made
    c. removing clothing from a child that is uncomfortably warm when a response is made
    d. spanking a child's hand when a response is made

52. The maxim that the punishment should suit the crime is based upon principles of
    a. partial reinforcement
    b. counterconditioning
    c. negative punishment
    d. nonreinforcement of responses

53. The phenomenon of fixation (persistence of previously punished behavior) suggests that punishment is
    a. worse then nonreinforcement
    b. similar to nonreinforcement
    c. better than nonreinforcement
    d. a special case of nonreinforcement

54. One of the important principles concerning the use of punishment is to
    a. keep it mild
    b. wait until a better time
    c. give rewards to counter the emotion produced

    d. provide an alternative response

55. Punishment is most effective in eliminating a habit when
    a. the punished response and the response to punishment are incompatible
    b. a discriminable cue immediately precedes the punishment
    c. the UR to punishment has positive transfer to the punished response
    d. the punishment is applied in the same modality as the reward

56. A normally responsible person would be most likely to become irresponsible when drunk if he had been taught responsibility using
    a. reinforcement training
    b. extinction training
    c. omission training
    d. punishment training

57. Organisms that have been exposed to aversive events over which they have no control or to problems that they cannot solve may, as a result,
    a. adjust more rapidly to future learning situations
    b. fail to adjust to future learning situations
    c. show better retention of prior learning
    d. show poorer retention of prior learning

58. Resistance to extinction is measured by
    a. how often a response is made after all reinforcement for that response has ceased
    b. the GSR indicating frustration
    c. the strength of the response under the reinforcement conditions
    d. the amount of stimulus variability

59. Among the factors that increase response persistence is
    a. large rewards
    b. extended training
    c. response specificity
    d. punishment

60. If, during an extended period of training, reward for the correct response is not given on every trial but is given haphazardly on only half of the trials, the result is that the correct response
    a. extinguishes slowly if no further reward is given
    b. is rarely learned
    c. is likely to be replaced by experimental neurosis
    d. is more susceptible to external inhibition

61. Among the factors that decrease response persistence is
    a. small rewards
    b. extended training
    c. response variability
    d. punishment

62. A mother can best train her child to persist in having good table manners by reinforcing the child
    a. constantly in the same situation
    b. intermittently in the same situation
    c. constantly in various situations
    d. intermittently in various situations

63. The principle of generalization says that learning constitutes habits formed between
    a. one stimulus and one response
    b. several stimuli and one response
    c. one stimulus and several responses
    d. several stimuli and several responses

64. The degree of generalization to similar stimuli is increased by
    a. constant rewards
    b. large rewards
    c. punishment
    d. extensive training

65. The easiest and quickest way to teach a person to make a fine discrimination between two highly similar colors would be to
    a. present one of the colors a large number of times, always giving reinforcement, then test for discrimination
    b. present the colors alternately, always reinforcing one and never reinforcing the other
    c. begin by presenting one color, always reinforcing it, and with another very dissimilar color, never reinforcing it, and then gradually changing the latter to the former
    d. reinforce both colors for awhile, then begin discrimination

66. Learning the proper way in which you should stand when hitting a backhand stroke in tennis is an example of
    a. stimulus generalization
    b. discrimination
    c. differentiation
    d. satiation

67. Transposition is concerned with the fact that
    a. the organism will only respond to the position of a stimulus
    b. relationships may be learned
    c. differential reinforcement is not operating
    d. learning will not transfer in certain cases

68. If a primate learns a sequence of 20 two-choice discriminations, the number of trials required to learn the twentieth discrimination will be
    a. smaller than the number to learn the first
    b. equal to the number required to learn the first
    c. larger than the number required to learn the first
    d. unrelated to the number required to learn the first

69. Which of the following procedures is most likely to retard subsequent discrimination learning?
    a. nondifferential reinforcement
    b. transposition
    c. transfer
    d. learning to learn

70. The behavioral principles most involved in understanding the development of racial prejudice are
    a. operant conditioning and discrimination

    b. operant conditioning and generalization
    c. classical conditioning and discrimination
    d. classical conditioning and generalization

71. If two events with different affective values (for example, food and shock) occur repeatedly in the same temporal order
    a. the first will come to dominate the second
    b. the second will come to dominate the first
    c. the stronger will come to dominate the weaker
    d. the weaker will come to dominate the stronger

72. Concerning the effect of motivational level on performance, the optimal level of motivation is
    a. higher the harder the task
    b. lower the harder the task
    c. higher for physical than intellectual tasks
    d. lower for physical than intellectual tasks

73. The psychological drives of hunger and thirst
    a. are based on the stomach and the mouth, respectively
    b. are based on the blood and the brain
    c. are based on the eyes and the skin, respectively
    d. actually have no known biological bases

74. One of the notable features of pain is that it
    a. only energizes instinctive responses
    b. is not a good guide to behavior
    c. has little bearing on reinforcement
    d. varies across regions of the body

75. Two drives are considered to be incompatible when the
    a. strength of one affects the strength of the other
    b. consummatory responses cannot be made simultaneously
    c. conditions which give rise to the drives are different
    d. reduction of one also reduces the strength of the other

76. If you have trained your dog to perform tricks when he is only slightly hungry, and then his performance goes down when he is much hungrier
    a. this is not predictable by theories of learning
    b. this is probably a result of generalization decrement
    c. he probably did not learn the trick well
    d. the high-drive level reduced the habit strength

77. An irrelevant drive is one which
    a. has no biological significance
    b. does not vary with deprivation
    c. is not related to the reinforcement
    d. is a secondary drive based on the primary drive present during original learning

78. The consummatory responses for hunger and thirst, namely eating and drinking, are
    a. instinctive and learnable
    b. instinctive but not learnable
    c. not instinctive but learnable

d. neither instinctive nor learnable

79. Drinking milk is reinforcing to a hungry rat. Injecting milk directly into the stomach is
    a. reinforcing
    b. punishing
    c. satiating but not reinforcing
    d. painful but not punishing

80. The effects of early social isolation of monkeys indicate that
    a. sexual behavior does not occur until physical maturity
    b. learning is involved in sexual behavior
    c. the older the monkey the greater the effects of isolation
    d. this research does not apply to human sexual behavior

81. Drive motivation and incentive motivation differ in that
    a. drive is hypothetical and incentive is observable
    b. drive is temporary and incentive is permanent
    c. drive is based on deprivation and incentive is based on reward
    d. drive is necessary for performance and incentive is not

82. Which of the following is not taken as evidence that reward affects motivation?
    a. performance improves gradually over rewarded trials
    b. learning occurs during nonrewarded practice
    c. changes in reward lead to changes in performance
    d. organisms can learn about the presence or absence of reward without making the response

83. Which of the following functions best describes that of incentive motivation?
    a. initiating behavior
    b. maintaining behavior
    c. guiding behavior
    d. terminating behavior

84. A drive is called "secondary " when it is
    a. weaker than the other drives present
    b. inappropriate to the reward
    c. not necessary for survival
    d. based on learning

85. The basic mechanism for secondary motivation is assumed to be
    a. hunger
    b. sex
    c. fear
    d. thirst

86. For a stimulus to acquire secondary motivating properties, it must be
    a. paired with an emotionally positive stimulus
    b. paired with an emotionally negative stimulus
    c. contingent on a positively rewarded response
    d. contingent on a negatively rewarded response

87. Fear and frustration differ primarily in the
    a. aversive conditions on which they are based
    b. types of feedback stimuli they produce

    c. types of responses they produce

    d. situations in which they may be aroused

88. Dealing with personal fears, such as failure and insuperiority, is more difficult than dealing with fears of external objects, such as snakes and airplanes, because

    a. they are more intense

    b. they involve the sympathetic rather than the parasympathetic system

    c. the stimuli eliciting them are more difficult to avoid

    d. their feedback is less distinctive

89. In dealing with one's fears, it is important to know that they can

    a. be extinguished and voluntarily controlled

    b. be extinguished but not voluntarily controlled

    c. not be extinguished but can be voluntarily controlled

    d. not be extinguished nor voluntarily controlled

90. With respect to adaptive behavior, fear is

    a. beneficial

    b. detrimental

    c. beneficial or detrimental depending on the source of the fear

    d. beneficial or detrimental depending on the responses made to the fear

ANSWERS TO EXAMINATION ITEMS

1. a	19. c	37. a	55. a	73. b
2. c	20. a	38. a	56. d	74. d
3. d	21. c	39. d	57. b	75. a
4. d	22. a	40. c	58. a	76. b
5. c	23. b	41. d	59. d	77. c
6. c	24. a	42. a	60. a	78. a
7. b	25. True	43. d	61. b	79. a
8. c	26. a	44. b	62. d	80. b
9. d	27. c	45. d	63. d	81. c
10. c	28. a	46. d	64. c	82. a
11. d	29. a	47. c	65. c	83. c
12. c	30. a	48. d	66. c	84. d
13. a	31. a	49. c	67. b	85. c
14. c	32. b	50. a	68. a	86. b
15. d	33. c	51. c	69. a	87. a
16. a	34. a	52. b	70. d	88. c
17. b	35. b	53. b	71. b	89. a
18. a	36. a	54. d	72. b	90. d

CHAPTER TWO

THE NATURE OF EMPIRICAL AND THEORETICAL SYSTEMS

The word "theory" has many usages both in the vernacular and in science. It always carries a connotation of providing an explanation of prior events or predicting future events, or both. In everyday langauge, you may say that you have a theory about who committed a crime, and you may say you have a theory about which horse is going to win the next race. A scientist may refer to the molecular weights of physical elements as a theory, the laws of motion as a theory, and relativity as a theory. Multiple usages of the same word often cause confusions, unless the particular meaning intended is clear in the context. We wish to develop the meaning of theory as we will use the term throughout this book and to distinguish it from an empirical system.

This development will rely heavily on the concept of *abstractness*. An abstraction, as it is commonly understood, is a summary, a condensation, an inclusive term or set of terms that encompasses some domain. The smallness of the abstraction relative to the size of the domain determines the level of abstractness. To give a simple example, the words chair, furniture, household goods, and worldly possessions, illustrate progressively more abstract concepts. Similarly, in science, a major goal is to subsume a large body of knowledge under a relatively small number of statements. Naturally, scientists are attracted to simple, concise abstractions involving fewer assumptions than the information to be summarized. The ratio of these determines the *parsimony* of the system. At any level of abstraction, a system in science always implies more knowledge than is currently available. This feature leads to predictions concerning future tests of the system, the outcomes of which help serve as confirmation or disconfirmation.

As is true with respect to all chapters of this book, there is a very substantial literature that we must draw on, thus, a review of that entire literature would be well beyond the scope of this book. We do not wish to debate issues within the philosophy of science nor to proclaim the ultimate virtue of any particular point of view. Indeed, the philosophy of science is not a prescriptive discipline, except insofar as logical consistency is involved; instead, its goal is to describe the ground rules according to which some groups of scientists play the game of science. Our purpose is primarily epistomological: to define various terms and elaborate their conceptual interrelationships as we will apply them in this book. Although these are consistent with the views of many experimental psychologists, it is by no means implied that the present formulation is rigidly fixed or universally accepted.[1]

DATA, FACTS, AND CONCEPTS

The subject matter of psychology begins at the common-sense, immediately observable level where words stand for physical or directly identifiable objects, properties, and relations. Scientists presume the existence of a real world without entering into metaphysical debates. But we must, nevertheless, be aware that our experiences are restricted by the sensitivity of our receptors, as these may be augmented by various physical devices, and that further selectivity results from the orientation of our receptors within the real world. Accordingly, our experiences are inherently an abstraction of events that occur in the total environment.

The experiences of a scientist, qua scientist, are transformed into *data*, namely verbal and numerical protocols of observations. Data represent a further abstraction of the real world, because the scientist cannot enter into a protocol everything that was actually observed. More importantly, data words are themselves influenced by the scientist's language system, which may itself be viewed as based on a kind of "theory" of the world. For example, given the identical event in the real world, a typical Hullian protocol would record that the rat "turned right," while a typical Tolmanian protocol would record that the rat "chose white." However, so long as there is intersubjective reliability, in the sense that trained observers agree, data become *facts*. If the facts are replicable, they become the foundation upon which science is built.

Scientific *concepts* are either defined by words at the physicalistic verification basis or are defined by other concepts that are, in turn, defined by words at the physicalistic verification basis. That is, scientifically useful concepts are *operationally* defined (Bridgman, 1956). The number of successive statements (often called "reduction sentences")[2] that must be traced in order to reduce a concept to this verification basis measures its degree of abstractness. Furthermore, to be scientifically interesting, concepts must not only be adequately defined but they must appear in some lawful relationship with other concepts.[3]

LAWS AND PRINCIPLES

The next level of abstraction in science is the formulation of empirical *laws*. These are generalizations, typically of an if-then nature, induced from the facts. Although induction, that is, going from the specific to the general, is conceptually the opposite of deduction, there are no formal, logical rules to constrain the inductive process. The only restriction in formulating empirical laws is that the facts can be deduced logically from the laws. Laws can themselves vary in abstractness. For example, the statement, "hungry hooded rats run mazes faster the greater the number of food pellets in the goalbox," is an abstraction in that it implies results in different mazes and the use of different food rewards. The statement, "performance is an increasing function of amount of reward," is more abstract because it not only implies the preceding statement but also the results using different species of organisms, different measures of performance, and different types of reward. Scientists strive to formulate highly abstract laws that will subsume large numbers of facts, although one can never be certain of their correctness. Our confidence in a law directly depends on the number of its implications that have been verified, but there is always the possibility of disconfirmation in a future test.

When a law is highy abstract and has been repeatedly verified in a wide variety of situations, it is called a *principle.* In formulating principles of behavior, the empiricist may introduce what we will call *hypothetical concepts.* (These are substantially what MacCorquodale and Meehl, 1948, have termed, "intervening variables.") Consider, for example, the word "learning." It is hypothetical because we can not see or uniquely point at learning; learning is inferred from the observation of a relatively permanent change in performance resulting from practice. It is, however, a concept in that it can be reduced to empirical observations. In this sense, nothing more is meant by the term, learning, than the functional relationships that obtain between various experimental operations and various measures of behavior. Similarly, the empiricist may use a term, such as "drive," as a convenient summary of the various deprivation or stimulation conditions that constitute the setting operations for an experiment. Again, this use of the term remains empirical, because it is reducible to explicit operations.

EMPIRICAL SYSTEMS The ultimate goal of atheoretical scientists is the development of an *empirical system.* Such a system constitutes interrelated sets of empirical laws and principles that, collectively, generate more implications than each in isolation. For example, one may assert that, "the greater the variability in behavior reinforced by a set of acquisition conditions, the greater the persistence of that behavior." Taken alone, this statement implies only that a correlation will be found between some measure of variability reinforced during acquisition and some measure of persistence. Add to it, however, the statement, "response variability is a decreasing function of the amount of reward," and we are in a position to predict that larger amounts of reward will lead to less persistence.

Although empirical systems are tied directly to operations and observations, it is not necessarily the case that there is one and only one empirical system that could be generated from the same data base. This is because any system is arrived at by a process of induction from that data base, and since there are no formal rules for induction, not all systematists will arrive at the same generalizations. In the last analysis, it is likely that all systems of this type would converge on the same set of very general principles, but at any particular moment in time differences are to be expected. One of the major differences would concern the level of abstractness at which an empirical system is cast. As will equally be true of theoretical systems, empirical systems may attempt to encompass ever wider ranges of behavior phenomena and, in the process, introduce ever more abstract concepts.

The example given above is a somewhat narrow one, pertaining quite uniquely to emission of a response during experimental extinction. It might be instructive to trace some of this development from its inception with the publication of *Behavior of Organisms* (Skinner, 1938). We had classified Skinner at that time as a reductive theorist, although a decade later he contended that such theories were unnecessary and favored the use of an empirical system (which he calls a theory when it is sufficiently abstract) in the prediction and control of behavior. But even early Skinner was a reluctant theorist.

He began with an experimental analysis of the behavior generated by various schedules of reinforcement. In doing so, he was not really interested in learning per se. It is true that the operant behavior of concern (at that time, uniquely the bar-pressing performance of rats) had to be shaped into the organism's repertoire, but this was almost as much a setting operation as was food deprivation. His approach would be termed by economists as a static one, because it addressed itself primarily to a steady-state rate of responding. The nature of the experimental analysis was primarily, given a hungry rat which has somehow learned to press a bar, what is the stable level of performance produced by one or another schedule of reinforcement? In the extreme, one can simply invent any conceivable schedule, run a rat under that schedule for a period of time, and observe the resulting performance.

For this purpose, Skinner contended that he did not need a theory. The behavior appeared before his very eyes in the form of a cumulative record of the rat's performance; there was no need to speculate about what is going on inside the rat when you already have the information of interest in the data. The snag that arose in this approach occurred when the rat was placed under a schedule of continuous nonreinforcement, namely extinction. Rats emit some number of responses during extinction, even though these are not being maintained by reinforcement. Thus emerged the reflex reserve as a reductive theoretical term. Skinner assumed that a schedule of reinforcement not only generated the observed rate of responding, while that schedule was in force, but built up some kind of reservoir of response strength that would reveal itself during extinction. This is not a very abstract construct, since the number of responses in extinction is eventually observable, but interest now centers not only on the rate during acquisition and maintenance, but also on using that empirical information to predict resistance to extinction.

Although this approach seemed to work reasonably well at first, Skinner abandoned it in part because of his personal predilection against introducing any imaginary properties in the organism, and in part because of difficulties in finding a simple relationship between rate during acquisition and rate during extinction. In this context, the reader may wish to review the miniature empirical system given as an illustration at the beginning of this section. This analysis assumes that the rate of extinction of any subclass of the molar bar-press response, such as force, duration, interresponse time, topography, and so on, is always the same, regardless of the schedule of reinforcement. However, different schedules of reinforcement lead to different amounts of variability in the number of such subclasses reinforced during acquisition, and hence the number of them that must be extinguished before the molar response itself no longer occurs.

This illustration not only shows how empirical systems may themselves vary, in this case by attention to response variability rather than simply response rate, it can also be used to show how novel predictions can be derived from an empirical system. Suppose, for example, that instead of simply letting response variability be reinforced as it naturally is by any schedule of reinforcement, we design a schedule that specifically reinforces variability. This can readily be done by differentially reinforcing that aspect of behavior. The result should be an extremely persistent molar response. Indeed, a very creative, empirical systematist might develop that theme into an understanding of optimal training conditions for creativity itself. People who have been selectively reinforced for trying out new ways of achieving the same goal should be more persistent in their efforts when faced with future failures and explore novel approaches as a result of generalization from the wide range of responses that could be produced.

MODELS   There is a tangential step between empirical systems and theoretical systems called a *model*. The approach of the model builder is to determine whether one set of interesting facts can be adequately described by the laws and principles already established in another, otherwise unrelated area of study. For example, a hydraulic model of electricity might assume that electricity flows like water. Now the model builder does not really propose that electricity is conducted through wires the same way that water flows through pipes, but the model is based on hypothesized correspondences, such as the diameter of the wire and the diameter of the pipe. Since we know that larger pipes can carry more water, we would predict that larger wires can carry more electricity.

Consider in this image a mathematical model of learning. There is no presumption that the model implies any basic, underlying processes. The question is only whether behavioral data can be adequately and efficiently described by a system developed by mathematicians. Markov, for example, worked out in a purely hypothetical sense the way in which a system would operate if it had a finite number of states and there were specific transition probabilities of moving from one state to another. Many psychologists have borrowed this model as well as other mathematical models in an attempt to describe the changes in behavior that constitute learning,[4] and the effects on that behavior that constitute motivation (see Levine & Burke, 1972).

THEORETICAL SYSTEMS   The inductive leap to theory is not a small step because the theorist introduces hypothetical constructs in an effort to "explain" behavior. As distinct from hypothetical concepts, *hypothetical constructs* are inventions of the theorist that cannot be reduced to empirical terms. Instead, a hypothetical construct constitutes a guess, a speculation, a conceptualization of the possible underlying mechanisms determining the observed phenomena. A *theory* (more fully, a *reductive theory*) attempts to move toward what is going on inside the organism that produces the observed behavior. There are, indeed, some ground rules for playing this game, but basically the theorist is free to postulate any processes with any deterministic properties within reason.

Perhaps the easiest way to get a feel for theory construction is again to leave the behavioral area and consider the molecular theory of gases. Boyle had shown empirically that there was a consistent relationship between the temperature, volume, and pressure of a gas. The theory postulated was that a gas is made up of molecules moving through space at a speed determined by the temperature. Boyle's law could be "explained" by the presumption that a gas constrained in a restricted space would exert increased pressure as a result of increased temperature, because the hypothetical molecules were ascribed the property of moving faster at higher temperatures and, hence, were bombarding the container more frequently and with greater force. This example is especially interesting because it illustrates the possibility that fact may overtake theory. Molecules are no longer hypothetical, but theoretical physicists continue to speculate about their internal processes.

With this background, consider the distinction between the hypothetical concept, learning, and the hypothetical constructs that have been invented to account for learning. Pavlov (1927) proposed "excitatory processes," Thorndike (1911) proposed "associations," Tolman (1932) proposed "sign-gestalt expectations," Guthrie (1935) proposed "S-R connections," Skinner (1938) proposed "reflex reserve," and Hull (1943) proposed "habit strength." These theorists were doing more than simply describing empirical laws. They were speculating about the *nature* of learning and about the underlying processes that they conceptualized as accounting for the observed changes in behavior. These conceptualizations, although derived from quite similar initial data, differ importantly in their implications. We shall be exploring these differences throughout the text.

The distinction between hypothetical concepts and hypothetical constructs is so critical to our mission that it deserves to be belabored. Return to the term "drive." We have indicated that this term can be used as a hypothetical concept, serving as nothing more than a shorthand expression for the various experimental operations that set the subject to participate in an experiment. When the term is used in a theory such as Hull's, however, it has a very different meaning. Hull postulated that deprivation produces a state in the organism that serves to potentiate habits. In this sense, drive has additional properties ascribed to it by the theorist. Hull assumed that drive states generate hypothetical drive stimuli, which are discriminable and which can gain control over behavior. He assumed that a drive state serves as a general energizer of all extant habits, that there is generalization between drive stimuli, and that the reduction of drive stimulation constitutes reinforcement. These are all statements about processes hypothetically taking place within the organism that have no direct empirical referents.

This is not to say that the theorist is completely free to let the imagination run wild. Foremost, theoretical postulates should be internally consistent.[5] For example, Hull assumed that habits are permanent. He also assumed that "conditioned inhibition" was a habit of not responding but that that habit could somehow be removed. Furthermore, he assumed that "reactive inhibition" was a kind of negative drive, but instead of energizing habits of not responding, it simply summated with them. These and other internal inconsistencies in Hull's 1943 theory have been elaborated extensively by Koch (1954).

The theorist also is required to anchor theoretical constructs to both antecedent and consequent variables. This is *not* the same as reducing concepts to an empirical level, because the theorist is allowed to ascribe to hypothetical constructs any deterministic properties whatsoever. But if they are not properly anchored, they have no predictive value. For example, Tolman was criticized for leaving his "animals buried in thought," because he originally failed to specify how expectancies, need pushes, and sign-gestalt expectations are translated into behavior. (Tolman, 1955, subsequently tried to correct this deficiency.) That is, Tolman specified what the subject was supposed to know from various past experiences, but did not state what the subject was supposed to do under the immediate circumstances. At the other extreme, Freud has been criticized for his failure adequately to anchor his constructs to antecedent conditions. It is easy enough to infer a presumed conflict between the id and the superego from observed behavior, but it is not possible to predict behavior unless these constructs are adequately anchored to their determinants.

Contrast Tolman and Freud with Hull. Hull specified that habit strength is an increasing function of the number of reinforced trials, that drive is an increasing function of hours of deprivation, that habit strength and drive combine in a multiplicative manner to determine excitatory potential, which is then translated into various performance measures such as latency. Whereas habit and drive remain as hypothetical constructs, they are adequately anchored to enable predictions and, hence, experimental tests of their implications. In a similar manner, Skinner related reflex reserve to the initial schedule of reinforcement and proposed that this reserve would reveal itself in the number of responses emitted during extinction.

Accordingly, we will use the term "theory" for any system that includes the introduction of hypothetical constructs that, while anchored to antecedent and consequent variables, are speculations about the conceivable inner workings of the organism. It must be made clear that the theorist is not liable for the reality of these speculations at a directly observable level. It is not necessary that a physiological psychologist locate a source of habit, drive, incentive, sign-gestalt expectation, association, or superego. On the contrary, physiological localization is quite irrelevant. A psychological theory is judged by its ability to predict behavior correctly. Some theorists (e.g., Hebb, 1951) argue that a theory should also be consonant with physiological knowledge, and so much the better if this is true. But the heuristic value of a theory lies in its ability to explain behavior in terms of hypothetical constructs that may or may not bear any resemblance to the actual nature of the organism.

ARGUMENTS AGAINST THEORIZING

There are some (e.g., Skinner, 1950) who eschew theory construction as it is defined here. Their arguments deserve notice. The first argument states that the theorist unnecessarily complicates the description of behavior. For example, we may begin with an empirical law that relates hours of deprivation to some measure of performance. The theorist introduces "drive" to "explain" this relationship. But one may reasonably question whether the introduction of a hypothetical construct has really accomplished anything helpful. If all that the theorist can say is that deprivation produces drive, and drive in turn produces increased performance, the theory has added nothing other than a complication in an already established empirical law. Deprivation admittedly does something to the organism; still, all that the behaviorist can observe is the empirical relationship—no real explanatory value is added by the term "hunger." Why indulge in useless fantasy?

Furthermore, a theoretical construct may be basically trivial in a quantitative sense. Suppose that we know that performance increases in a negatively accelerated manner with hours of deprivation, and we are attempting to develop a reductive theory. It might be satisfying to postulate that drive increases in a negatively accelerated fashion with deprivation, and that performance is in turn a linear function of drive. But it would be mathematically equivalent to assume that drive is an increasing linear function of deprivation, and that performance is a negatively accelerated function of drive. It requires no great talent to bifurcate an empirical relationship into any number of hypothetical subfunctions that regenerate the original information.

There are more serious reasons to resist the temptation to indulge in theory construction. One is the probability that the theorist will consciously or unconsciously reify hypothetical constructs. *Reification* denotes that the theorist believes that hypothetical inventions really exist. The theorist may become enamored of them and defend them as children of a fertile imagination. Where Skinner was able to allow reflex reserve to succumb to contradictory evidence, Hull was unable to disavow reinforcement as a necessary condition for learning. Spence's (1956) protestations notwithstanding, Hull believed that there are stimulus traces, drives, and habits buried in the organism. It may ultimately be proven that Hull was on the right track, but the fact remains that many theorists are inclined to adopt hypothetical constructs and to protect them with an unscientific zeal.

An even stronger argument against those who indulge in theory construction is that it is a luxury leading to countless hours spent in search for a "crucial" experiment. None has yet to occur in the literature of the experimental psychology of learning. We shall be reviewing a number of the classical controversies that erupted in the history of learning theory and will generally conclude that the published experiments were not as crucial as they were then thought to be. We also hope to show that these theoretical issues remain unresolved and that contemporary theorists are still grappling with them.

ARGUMENTS FOR THEORIZING   There are counterarguments favoring the step toward reductive theory. One of these is simply an admission: the personal style of some scientists includes speculating about why organisms behave the way they do. Now theorists know full well that science cannot, even in principle, answer the ultimate question, "Why?" That question can be repeated interminably, but the theorist is permitted to answer the question, by theoretical ground rules, only once. If it is asked, "Why do rats run faster the longer they have been deprived?" the theorist is willing to answer, "Because they are under higher drive motivation; they are hungrier." But if it is then asked, "Why does the rat get hungrier the longer the deprivation?" the theorist has to answer, "I don't know." Alternatively, the theorist might say that this is a problem at another level of discourse and that there are physiological psychologists studying that question. Nevertheless, some people simply feel more comfortable if they have reduced their observations at least one step toward understanding the underlying processes.[6]

This human trait was evident throughout ancient history in, for example, the invention of "gods" who were presumed to control natural phenomena such as rain. The difference between Greek mythology and scientific theory is in the ground rules by which the scientist must play the game. We have already noted several: hypothetical constructs must be anchored securely to both antecedent and consequent variables and the temptation to reify them must be resisted. Furthermore, hypothetical constructs cannot be given capricious capabilities, because the hallmark of science is determinism. It was quite appropriate for Hull to attempt to account for variability in behavior by assuming that excitatory potential oscillates from moment to moment according to specified mathematical rules, but it would have been quite inappropriate for him to have assumed that excitatory potential has the whimsical property of deciding whether or not to rise above the threshold. Nevertheless, one of the reasons that many scientists indulge in theory construction is a universal desire to understand, and possibly control, one's environment in terms of underlying processes.

A more substantive reason for attempting to develop theories is that they may be efficient. Earlier, we noted that simply inventing a hypothetical construct to intervene between an independent and dependent variable does nothing but add a complication to a known empirical relationship. But consider the case in which the theorist is able to relate a hypothetical construct to several antecedent conditions. For example, "hunger" can be related to hours of deprivation, amount of food given on a maintenance schedule, percentage of normal body weight, and even the injection of hormones into appropriate areas of the brain. Suppose further that the hypothetical construct is also anchored to several dependent variables. For example, "hunger" may affect not only latency, but also speed, vigor, variability, and persistence. Under such a circumstance, hypothetical constructs may provide a parsimonious account and integration of otherwise disparate empirical relationships. (See Miller, 1959, and also Skinner, 1938.)[7]

In a similar manner, we can agree that the breakdown of one function into two or more subfunctions is mathematically trivial, but it is not a trivial exercise to summarize a large number of empirical functions within a set of internally consistent subfunctions. The point is that theory construction is truly interesting when one is attempting to deal with a wide range of behaviors that are observed in a wide range of situations and can be accounted for with a relatively small number of hypothetical constructs.

The final and, perhaps, the most important justification for theory is its value in making predictions. This is not to say that one cannot make predictions from empirical systems; consider, for example, that a law generates predictions at least about future replications. As we have seen, an empirical system that integrates highly abstract laws can lead to much more novel predictions. But theorists contend that they can carry this goal of science a significant step forward. Let us give one example, albeit a somewhat specialized one.

Suppose we run rats under the following conditions. There are two runways, one of which is black and the other white. The rats are deprived of food, and there is an equal reward in each runway. The arrangement is such that the rat runs twice as often in one alley (let us say, the black one) as the other. This is accomplished by giving the rat a choice between the runways on the first of three trials a day. If he chooses the white alley, then the following two trials will be forced in the direction of the black alley. If he chooses the black alley on the first trial, then the remaining two trials will be forced, one toward one alley and one toward the other. In sum, the rat receives three trials a day, the first of which is a choice trial with the remaining trials forced to insure that black is encountered twice as often as white.

The question of interest is whether there will be a preference between the alleys. There are three alternative outcomes, each of which can be stated in informal terms. The rat might prefer the black alley, because he is more accustomed to it. He might prefer the white alley, because he is bored with the black alley. Or, he might be quite indifferent, because they both yield the same reward and there is no reason for him to be bemused by the experimenter's manipulations. Spence was able to make a more formal prediction from among these alternatives.

We will be discussing this theory in greater detail later, but suffice it to say here that there are three fundamental theoretical constructs relevant to the derivation. One is habit strength, which is based on the number of exposures to a stimulus-response sequence, and which grows in a negatively accelerated fashion toward an upper limit of unity. The second is drive motivation, which is based on the conditions of deprivation. The third is incentive motivation, which is based on the conditions of reinforcement. It is important to note that neither of these motivational variables leads to predictions of preference. Drive motivation is the same for both alleys, because the rat is equally deprived in each, and incentive motivation is the same because the reward conditions are identical. Accordingly, the only possible basis for a preference rests with the habit strength factor.

According to Spence, habit strength should grow at the same rate in both alleys as a function of the number of times the rat has encountered those alleys; it would grow differentially if plotted against days of training. The rat is getting twice as many trials per day in the black alley. This means that, as a result of the faster growth of habit over days, the rat will develop a preference for the black alley. However, this preference should be temporary. After the habit strength toward the black alley has reached its asymptote, it can gain no more in strength while the habit strength for the white alley, slowly but surely, is gaining daily. Ultimately, they will be equal, and the preference should disappear. Accordingly, the curve showing choice of the black alley should begin at chance, increase over days, and then decrease again to chance. Spence obtained at least some support for this prediction.

This example admittedly concerns a relatively narrow context; except for its illustrative value, one might evince little interest in the choice behavior of rats. But this was one of a number of studies that led Spence to accept the thesis that learning, in the sense of habit strength, results solely from the number of repetitions of a response in the presence of a stimulus. Consequently, this thesis has many implications of practical significance. For example, the student who studies in the presence of auditory stimulation from a record player, radio, or television for a number of times develops the habit of turning such instruments on even though it is known that they disturb total concentration. The person who languishes in bed instead of getting up to face the challenges of that day, develops a self-destructive habit. In a more positive vein, the person who practices fastening a seat belt, comparing the number on the speed-limit sign with that on the speedometer, and watching for erratic driving both in front and behind, is more likely to survive the mania of the modern highway. Spence's theory implies that if people will simply engage in these behaviors for some time, they will become habitual with no further ado.

The important thesis to the theorist, in both the narrow and the very general contexts, is that such predictions cannot be derived from an empirical system, because they invoke habit as a hypothetical construct. This is not to say that an empirical system could never deal with these implications, only that theorists can, in the present, project further ahead of the existing empirical domain. The

DISTINCTION BETWEEN THEORETICAL AND EMPIRICAL QUESTIONS

An *empirical* question is one in which all terms can be directly related to specific operations. Although such questions may be quite abstract, in that they require a number of reduction sentences in order to relate the terms to the immediately observable level of experience, the reduction is noncontroversial within the language system of the scientist. In short, empirical questions are, at least in principle, unambiguously answerable.

For example, we may ask whether an overt, unconditioned response is necessary to produce the change in performance customarily observed from pairing two stimuli in temporal sequence (classical conditioning). In a leg-flexion conditioning situation, for example, a light may be paired with a shock to the hindpaw of a dog that is hanging in a sling. The shock elicits leg flexion that ultimately becomes conditioned to the light as evidenced by anticipatory responding. It may be technically difficult to try to answer our empirical question, since it is necessary to prevent the leg-flexion response from occurring during the pairing operation. We might tie the dog's leg down, pair the light with shock when he is thus restrained, and then test for response to the light after the leg is released. The fact that a conditioned leg-flexion response is observed answers one empirical question: the complete overt response is not necessary for conditioning.

Even so, one may question whether the procedure of preventing the response was adequate for a more refined empirical question. The dog certainly flexed the muscles in response to the shock even though the restraining ropes prevented the leg from actually flexing. And so we might explore other techniques. For example, we might have the dog stand with the other hind leg tied up so that he must keep the tested leg straight to maintain balance; in this pose, we could pair a light with a shock. Subsequently, the dog's other leg is released so he can now flex the tested leg. Again, the observed conditioned flexion response indicates conditioning.

With further technological advance, the dog may be placed under curare, a drug which completely blocks the neural transmission to the striate muscles of the leg. Now the dog lies unrestrained (but respirated) in the sling and is presented with the light-shock pairing in a state in which leg flexion is physiologically impossible. When the dog is tested after recovering from the drug, the occurrence of a flexion response to the light still more definitely answers the empirical question concerning the necessity of the overt response for conditioning.

A *theoretical* question is one which includes one or more hypothetical constructs that, while anchored to both independent and dependent variables, are not directly reducible to observable operations. These refer to postulated states or processes. In short, answers to theoretical questions may be inferred from empirical observations, but cannot be unambiguously answered.

For example, one of the theoretical questions with which we will be concerned is, "What is learned?" We may pose this question in a classical conditioning context. If a light is paired with a shock to a dog's paw, does he learn an association between the light and the flexion response elicited (normally) by the shock, or does he learn an association between the light and the shock, for which anticipatory leg flexion is a natural response? Clearly, both alternatives are equally tenable from the original observation of unrestrained pairing operations. The S-R approach may be somewhat more questionable because restraining the flexion response during the pairing still leads to conditioning, since the actual unconditioned response could not occur. But if the S-R theorist claims that the association is with the muscular contraction, rather than with the overt response, the S-R approach is saved. This is also true with the finding of conditioning under curare, but now the S-R theorist must move the associative construct back still further into the nervous system, so that "response" becomes the firing of the appropriate motor centers in the brain. The fact that these are blocked from producing the overt response under curare still does not prevent the association from being formed and later revealed after the drug has worn off.

Many of the questions with which we will be concerned are theoretical questions. Indeed, some argue that these are the questions in which we are really interested. Although the answers to such questions are inherently inconclusive, the skilled theorist is one who can translate theoretical questions into empirical ones so that the answers to the latter constrain speculation and lend credence to the theoretical answers proposed. We hope to illustrate this interplay between empirical and theoretical questions.

SUMMARY AND CONCLUSIONS

We can summarize the principal substance of this chapter with the aid of Figure 2.1. No matter what the nature of the system, the science of psychology begins with some set of antecedent conditions that act on an organism, which in turn displays some consequent behavior. Boundary conditions may be imposed by the systematist with respect to any of these, that is, the allowable antecedent conditions, organisms, and appropriate consequent behaviors. It is important to note that both the empiricist and the theorist not only begin at the same point, but proceed from there in the development of facts and laws. It is possible, of course, that these latter may be directed to some extent by the nature of the system, but so long as they fall within the stated boundary conditions, they are grist for both empiricist and theorist.

Although the theorist may bypass intermediate steps, in principle, all scientists may introduce hypothetical concepts as convenient shorthand expressions for classes of operations, attempt to formulate general principles, and integrate these into an empirical system. For an empiricist, this is the end of the line: all terms are reducible directly (albeit sometimes circuitiously) to operationally

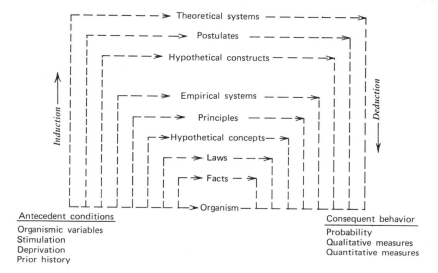

FIGURE 2.1.

Summary of Levels of Abstraction in the Conceptual Analysis of Behavior. Progressively Higher Levels of Abstraction Are Achieved by the Process of Induction, Returning to the Empirical Base Through Deduction. There Are Degrees of Abstractness in each of the Levels; the only Point at which the Boundaries Are Clear Is Where the Introduction of Hypothetical Constructs Moves Toward the Development of a Theoretical System.

defined terms. Certainly, creativity is importantly involved in the inductive process, which leads to progressively more abstract levels, but the hallmark of empiricism is that everything is not only based on data but tied to those data without encumbrances.

In contrast, the theorist proceeds to invent hypothetical constructs and ascribes to them any desired properties provided they are rigorously anchored in a causal, deterministic chain to both the antecedent conditions and the consequent behavior. The constructs are interrelated by means of postulates, and a set of postulates comprises a theory. It is this unique feature of introducing hypothetical constructs that sets a theorist apart from an empiricist.

Empiricists and theorists share many things in common in addition to having the same point of origin in the facts and laws of behavior. As indicated in Figure 2.1, both use inductive processes to arrive at ever higher levels of abstractness, and both use deductive processes to return with implications about behavior. Both have the same goal, namely the prediction and control of behavior in terms of some parsimonious system that can be stated explicitly and subjected to empirical tests. Indeed, it is quite possible that progressively more abstract empirical systems will begin to supplant existing theoretical systems.

Meanwhile, it is important to recognize the differences. On the one hand, the empiricist is secure in the knowledge that everything is tied down to observable events. The only possible arguments concerning correctness (the inductive process) relate to whether a statement is a gross overgeneralization. The only arguments concerning validity (the deductive process) relate to whether all of the necessary conditions have been included in the premises. Even these, however, are subject to direct empirical verification.

In contrast, the theorist is not secure because imaginary constructs may begin to take on some semblance of reality; their properties and interrelationships are subject to change at the whim of the theorist; and they may be ascribed surplus meanings by the theorist or by others. Furthermore, there is always the danger that the theory will become so unwieldy that the tracing of a logical chain between antecedent conditions and consequent behaviors will break down of its own weight.

Nevertheless, there need be no confrontation between empiricist and theorist. In some cases, the empiricist may properly claim to be able to get to the same implications without the introduction of needless hypothetical constructs; when this is the case, the theorist can only admit to a preference to play the game of science by inventing constructs as personally satisfying explanatory devices. In other cases, the theorist may properly claim to be able to derive implications from a theory that would not be subsumed under any extant empirical system; when this is the case, the best the empiricist can reply is that the system will eventually reach that level of abstractness when the necessary data base has been researched. Each may benefit from the other by focusing on repeated points of contact as well as divergencies.

One way to gain an understanding of the difference in the approaches of an empiricist and a theorist is to assign them both the task of designing an optimal society. (We do not necessarily favor actualizing such a society, even were it possible and practicable. We do contend, however, that our behavior is inevitably being affected by many influences, including persons who are often not well versed in the science of psychology. Hence, we view this only as a pedagogical exercise.) For this assignment, we find no theorist secure enough to venture an ideal, hypothetical society, but we can refer to Skinner (1969) as an empiricist spokesman. Let us, therefore, modify the assignment to ask the empiricist to describe aspects of an empirical design and then ask the theorist to critique them according to theoretical conceptualizations. Space limitations permit only a few illustrations. We begin by quoting Skinner.

Walden Two describes an imaginary community of about a thousand people who are living a Good Life. They enjoy a pleasant rural setting and work only a few hours a day, without being compelled to do so. Their children are cared for and educated by specialists with due regard for the lives they are going to lead. Food is good and sanitation and medical care excellent. There is plenty of leisure and many ways of enjoying it. Art, music, and literature flourish, and scientific research is encouraged. Life in Walden Two is not only good, it seems feasible. It it within the reach of intelligent men of goodwill who will apply the principles which are now emerging from the scientific study of human behavior to the design of culture.

We ''like'' a way of life to the extent that we are reinforced by it. We like a world in which both natural and social reinforcers are abundant and easily achieved and in which aversive stimuli are either rare or easily avoided. Unfortunately, however, it is a fact about man's genetic endowment and the world in which he lives that immediate rewards are often offset by deferred punishments, and that punishments must often be taken for the sake of deferred rewards. To maximize net gains we must do things we do not like to do and forego things we like. A culture cannot change these facts, but it can induce us to deal with them effectively. Indeed, that is its most important function.

It is not too often successful. The problem, in short, is not to design a way of life which will be liked by men *as they now are,* but a way of life which will be liked by those who live it. The concept of contingencies of reinforcement has led to a much more effective technology of behavior, a few examples of which may be cited.

Education. Teaching is the arrangement of contingencies of reinforcement which expedite learning. A student learns without being taught, but learns more effectively under favorable conditions. Programmed instruction is a technique taken directly from the operant laboratory; it is a set of contingencies which shape topography of response and bring behavior under the control of stimuli in an expeditious way. An equally important advance is the arrangement of contingencies of reinforcement in the classroom which take over the function of "discipline."

Psychotherapy. The often bizarre behavior of the psychotic naturally attracts attention. The problem is not to find in the structure of the observed behavior some hint as to how it may be made to disappear, but rather to build up the behavior which is missing. When the psychotic shows an insensitivity to normal contingencies of reinforcement, an environment must be designed to which he is likely to respond. In the "token economies" used in ward management, for example, a token has a clear-cut physical status, it becomes a powerful conditioned reinforcer when exchanged for other reinforcers, and it can be made immediately contingent on desired behavior.

Any theorist, commenting on these assertions by Skinner, would most probably begin by also proclaiming a commitment to an experimental analysis of contingencies of reinforcement. The theorist would chuckle only briefly over a cartoon inspired by Skinner's early work; it depicts one rat boasting to another rat, "Boy, have I got this human conditioned! Every time I press this little bar, he drops in a pellet of food." The typical theorist would then quickly agree that the rat is controlling the behavior of the scientist every bit as much as the scientist is controlling the behavior of the rat. Skinner's approach carries this connotation of mutual contingencies of reinforcement.

Thus, any theorist would contend that everything that is firmly rooted in empirical knowledge is equally within the province of theory. There is no monopoly involved in that. The important question is whether the introduction of hypothetical constructs in any way influences, in a useful way, one's approach to dealing with the types of issues considered by Skinner. Actually, the answer to this question rests, in part, on the particular hypothetical constructs introduced. For our didactic purpose, we will assume the general point of view of an S-R theorist, although this does not imply that this type of theory is any better or more successful in the present task than any other type of theory.

Pursuing the "what's yours is mine" approach, the S-R theorist would point out that programmed instruction hardly resulted from the experimental analysis of contingencies of reinforcement. Teachers throughout the ages have at least attempted to sequence the study of a subject by a shaping process. Using an example employed by Skinner, we may view a piano as an eighty-eight key Skinner box, but no piano teacher ever started a pupil with a Rachmaninoff Concerto. The critical issue resides in the design of the program: what are the rules which optimally match the requirements of the task with the potentials of the student? Neither empiricist nor theorist would expect the answer to this question to be the same for all students. Each can, however, attempt to assert several guidelines for the design of educational programs.

Skinner, for example, favors programs that do not involve errors. A basis for this is the empirical observation that errors may generate frustration (here used as an empirical concept defined by overt displays of aggression or withdrawal), which can interfere with effective learning. A second basis is Skinner's belief that performance is controlled by response-reward contingencies and that reinforcement should only be contingent on correct responding. Ideally, every student should learn according to a self-paced program that progresses in steps only as large as that individual student could readily take by inference from previous steps so that no mistakes are made in the process. The observation that many students become bored with extant programs of this sort is a commentary on the program itself, not on the principles underlying its construction. Brighter students can be challenged by being exposed to larger steps.

The theorist also may have objections to errors, but for quite different reasons. Many contemporary S-R theorists now believe that learning results simply from the temporal contiguity of the events to be associated. This implies that we inevitably learn our mistakes. We may be frustrated (here used as a hypothetical construct), but this is not inherently deleterious to learning the correct responses. The theorist would want to include contingencies of non-reinforcement.

In doing so, the S-R theorist would contend that contingencies of nonreinforcement can be profitable provided that the correct response is within the learner's repertoire and a correction procedure is used. A correction procedure does more than simply say "Wrong"; it permits the learner to engage in a process of trial and error and, thereby, learn which responses are wrong and which responses are right. Learning is sharpened in the process.

The empiricist would, of course, agree. Research has shown that generalization gradients (here used as a hypothetical concept in reference to response rate in an operant situation) sharpen as a result of discrimination training[8] and display a number of phenomena that are relevant. But the theorist will contend that these phenomena can be derived from generalization gradients (here used as a hypothetical construct in reference to underlying learned associations) that have heuristic value in designing educational programs.

Our goal is not to prejudice the reader in one direction or the other. Instead, we are trying to illustrate the types of interchanges that might take place between an empiricist and a theorist. Simply as a matter of empirical fact, the empiricist appears to be more facile in dealing with immediate practical applications to education, whereas the theorist is more inclined to plead inadequate knowledge for the development of an appropriate theory. (The reader might wish to contrast the papers prepared by Skinner and Spence, 1954, on this point.) The theorist is most frequently in the role of "Yes, but . . . ," while the empiricist is more inclined to get on with the problem of trying to do better than what hunches and intuitions, instead of scientific knowledge, have been able to do in the area of education to date.

With respect to psychotherapy, no one can deny the useful results that have been obtained by the use of contingencies of reinforcement (rather than punishment) in the control of psychotic behavior. Never mind if these results are largely confined to institutional conditions; patients who will at least engage in their biological functions in socially reasonably ways make life on a ward more pleasant for everyone involved. Further experimental analysis of behavior modification techniques will surely increase their value.

The issue that has most pervaded this area can be stated in medical terminology: behavior modification may be viewed as a symptomatic treatment that leaves the underlying sickness still festering, perhaps to reappear in still worse forms of behavior than that which was modified. This is an appeal to one view of motivation: drives continually goad the organism to do something in their service. The theorist believes that no behavior occurs without some motivating force. (Freud contended that usually trivial things, such as slips of the tongue, reflect unconscious motivation that is sometimes made conscious by the slip!) It is for this reason that a theoretically oriented therapist may use behavior modification techniques in order to have a manageable patient; hypnotism, drugs, or any other devices may also be used. But the theoretically oriented therapist will still insist on the necessity of determining the hypothetical causes of maladaptive behaviors in order to devise contingencies of reinforcement that encourage adaptive behaviors.

We could go on with other topics that are relevant to the general mission of designing an optimal culture and, indeed, Skinner has addressed himself to many of these. But we will encounter his empirical system in some detail later in this book, and our immediate purpose has been merely to illustrate the kinds of interplay that take place between empiricists and theorists, or for that matter, within the same individual when shifting gears from the purely empirical level of analysis to the more theoretical stance. Our general proposition is this: the burden of proof rests squarely with the theorist. For whatever purpose, the utility of hypothetical constructs must be convincing, if they are to be more than verbal machinations about one's intuitions. Because of the volume of theoretical work available in the literature, it is apparent that many scientists consider this endeavor worthwhile. But as we will see immediately in the next chapter, theoretical issues in learning and motivation have not been resolved by presumably crucial experiments and, as a result, there is very little in the way of unanimity of opinion.

NOTES   1. The approach taken in this section could be characterized as an "empiricist" one, deriving from conceptual analyses of the physical sciences as represented by Bridgman. We have also leaned heavily on what is known as "logical positivism" as represented by Bergmann, Carnap, and others. This approach assumes that all sciences are ultimately reducible to point-at-able events in the real world and, hence, are inherently subject to eventual unification. This is, in effect, a denial of "emergentism," which contends that the whole may be more than the sum of its parts. This philosophy has been challenged by a number of behavior scientists who contend that an organism is more than a bundle of muscles, nerves, and integrating tissue. Indeed, some argue that modeling behavior science on natural science is fallacious, that we need a less deterministic model that incorporates control by internal feedback systems. Our purpose here is not to dwell on the philosophy of science, interesting and challenging as that topic is. Instead, our goal is to set some ground rules and make some distinctions so as to proceed apace with classical and contemporary theoretical and empirical analyses of behavior.

2. Care must be taken to distinguish between "reduction sentences" and "reductive theory," since we will encounter this distinction in the pages that follow. Abstract concepts are still empirical so long as they can be reduced by a series of operational definitions. Constructs in a reductive theory cannot be so reduced, although they must be anchored to empirical concepts in order to be useful.

3. The point, as emphasized by Bergmann (1944), is that one can generate an indefinitely large number of operationally defined concepts, but they would have no other meaning and attract no scientific interest unless they are related to some other concepts. For example, response rate is interesting not because it is readily defined in operational terms, but because it varies systematically with the schedule of reinforcement.

4. This brief description is not intended to imply that models have no bearing on future theory construction. For example, in the context of human paired-associates learning, one may compare a model that assumes that changes in performance are all or none in character with others that assume various numbers of intermediate states. Although the model only provides a description of the data, the best-fitting model may help a theorist draw inferences about the underlying processes.

5. Internal inconsistencies are not always easy to detect. An ideal theory would be one that could be entered into a computer that would flash "error" if a postulate is made that is not consistent with ones that have already been entered. Even so, logical inconsistencies would not be detected. For example, Hull constrained excitatory potential to a scale between zero and one, yet allowed oscillation to subtract a larger number and generate, at random, negative values. Such an assumption works mathematically but is neither logical nor elegant.

6. This personal predilection may, however, be contaminated by the theorist's pretheoretic intuitions about the conceivable structure and function of the system of interest. For example, Hull did not disagree with Tolman that behavior "reeks of purpose"; instead, he contended that purpose was not a fundamental explanatory construct but was to be derived from more basic processes. And in this context, the following quote from Spence (1956) is also relevant:

[There is] a tendency to criticize theoretical concepts in this field as being too elementaristic, too mechanistic, and as failing to portray the real essence or true nature of man's behavior . . . . Thus they talk about such things as the impoverishment of the mind and object to what is described as a lack of warmth and glowing particulars in the behaviorist's account of psychological events.

To the writer such criticisms reflect essentially a lack of appreciation as to the difference between scientific knowledge of an event and other kinds of knowledge, e.g., the kinds of knowledge the novelist and poet portray. Either by reason of their training or because of their basically nonscientific interests these critics have apparently never really understood the abstract character of the scientific account of any phenomenon . . . . The difficulty, in part, is that too many individuals whose interests are not those of the scientists have become psychologists. If these persons were aware of their different interests and were appreciative of what the behavior scientist is attempting to do, the kinds of knowledge he is attempting to build, much needless controversy would be eliminated.

7. Miller and Skinner agree that a term is useful when introduced between a number of antecedent operations and a number of consequent behaviors. If no further properties are ascribed to such terms, then they are hypothetical concepts (intervening variables). They become hypothetical constructs when properties are ascribed to them and when they are imbedded in a theory containing other hypothetical constructs. At this level of discourse, the issue becomes whether these properties and interrelationships provide a more parsimonious account of the relevant phenomena than their exclusion.

8. It should be noted in this context that Terrace (1963) has described a procedure by which a discrimination may be learned with very few, if any, errors. The conceptual significance of this procedure will be discussed in a later chapter. The important point here is that generalization gradients can be sharpened without the presumed aversive consequences of nonreinforcement and punishment.

ABSTRACTS   **Hebb, D.O. The role of neurological ideas in psychology.** *Journal of Personality,* **1951, 20, 39–55.**

It is my conviction that we have no choice but to physiologize in psychology, overtly or covertly. It is only with the rubble of bad theories that we shall be able to build better ones, and without theory of some kind, somewhere, psychological observation and description would at best be chaotic and meaningless. Psychology has repeatedly anticipated neurophysiology, the purely behavioral evidence indicating the existence of neural processes not known at the time but discovered independently by the physiologist later. I do not suggest any subordination of psychology to physiology, but only that psychology must be influenced by physiological evidence, as neurophysiology is influenced by psychological evidence.

It appears that S-R theory is not merely physiological in descent, but by its persistent exclusion of psychologically justified conceptions it also shows that it is still essentially physiological. If we must be chained to physiological ideas, we should at least choose the modern ones that allow more freedom of movement. There appears to be a left wing and a right wing in psychology, and the activity of the Left cannot be understood if one does not see that the only continuity in its behavior is in being against the Right. The Right favors parsimony of explanatory ideas, a simple or mechanistic account of behavior, and definiteness even at the cost of being narrow. The Left is prepared to postulate more freely and can better tolerate vagueness and a lack of system in its account of behavior.

The argument is (a) that some scheme or model is necessary in practice, if not logically; (b) that the S-R model has served well and (with alterations) is the base of further theorizing; and (c) that psychology eventually will be using a "real" neurological model. Physiologizing is not a substitute for psychology but an aid to it.

Hull, C.L. *Principles of behavior.* New York: D. Appleton-Century, 1943, (Ch. 1.)

Men are ever engaged in the dual activity of making observations and then seeking explanations of the resulting revelations. Here we have the two essential elements of modern science: the making of observations constitues the empirical or factual component, and the systematic attempt to explain these facts constitutes the theoretical component.

In science an observed event is said to be explained when the proposition expressing it has been logically derived from a set of definitions and postulates coupled with certain observed conditions. The subsumption of a particular set of conditions under a category involved in a previously made empirical generalization is not exactly what is regarded here as a scientific theoretical explanation. The propositions required by an explanation are those stating the relevant initial or antecedent conditions and a set of statements of general principles. The concluding phase of a scientific explanation is the derivation of the answer from the conditions and the principles, taken jointly, by a process of inference or reasoning.

The deductive nature of systematic scientific theory closely resembles mathematics: its definitions, its primary principles, and the meticulous step-by-step development of the proof of one theorem after another, the later theorems depending on the earlier ones in a hierarchy of derived propositions. Theoretical "truth" appears in the last analysis to be a matter of greater or less probability. By successive agreements under a very wide variety of conditions, a theory may attain a high degree of justified credibility, but never absolute certainty.

Logan, F.A. The Hull-Spence approach. In S. Koch (Ed.), *Psychology: A study of a science* (Vol. II). New York: McGraw-Hill, 1959. (Pp. 298–309.)

Empirical generalizations organize the facts from behavior research into statements typically of the form "If S then R" from which predictions can be made about future instances of that S. Such laws may vary in their level of generality, i.e., in the range of phenomena to which they are relevant. Further generality may be gained by bringing several higher-level laws together into a system integrated by their relevance to the same behavior variables.

The postulates of a Hullian-type theory are around the level of physiological laws. However, physiological implications may be disregarded because the theory is properly evaluated only by the correctness of its psychological implications. The purpose of the theory is to mediate predictions over a specifiable range of phenomena. The postulates do not purport to describe the structure of the "real" organism. Instead, they describe a "model" organism whose input-output properties are the same as those of the real organism.

The method of postulate construction is analogous to induction. The only rule is that the postulates must imply the original statements deductively. Other constraints are parsimony and plausibility. Theorems are implied by the entire theory, not by any segment of it separately. Derivations may be made using illustrative numbers, but the theorems are stated in a greater-than language. When different illustrative numbers give different answers, the theory can be tested by a detailed study of the relevant variable. Only a fully quantified theory can yield exact predictions and therefore permit really rigorous tests.

MacCorquodale, K., & Meehl, P.E. On a distinction between hypothetical constructs and intervening variables. *Psychological Review,* 1948, *55,* 95–107.

Intervening variables seem to be identifiable by three characteristics. First, the statement of such a concept does not contain any words which are not reducible to the empirical laws. Second, the validity of the empirical laws is both necessary and sufficient for the "correctness" of the statements about the concept. Third, the quantitative expression of the concept can be obtained without mediate inference by suitable groupings of terms in the quantitative empirical laws.

Hypothetical constructs do not fulfil any of these three conditions. Their formulation involves words not wholly reducible to the words in the empirical laws; the validity of the empirical laws is not a sufficient condition for the truth of the concept, inasmuch as it contains surplus meaning; and the quantitative form of the concept is not obtainable simply by grouping empirical terms and functions.

It is suggested that the only rule for proper intervening variables is that of convenience, since they have no factual content surplus to the empirical functions they serve to summarize. In the case of hypothetical constructs, they have a cognitive, factual reference in addition to the empirical data which constitute their support. Hence, they ought to be held to a more stringent requirement in so far as our interests are theoretical. Their actual existence should be compatible with general knowledge and particularly with whatever relevant knowledge exists at the next lower level in the explanatory hierarchy.

Seligman, M.E.P. On the generality of the laws of learning. *Psychological Review,* **1970,** *27,* **406–418.**

That all events are equally associable and obey common laws is a central assumption of general process learning theory. A continuum of preparedness is defined which holds that organisms are prepared to associate certain events, unprepared for some, and contraprepared for others. A review of data from the traditional learning paradigms shows that the assumption of equivalent associability is false: in classical conditioning, rats are prepared to associate tastes with illness even over very long delays of reinforcement, but are contraprepared to associate tastes with footshock. In instrumental training, pigeons acquire key pecking in the absence of a contingency between pecking and grain (prepared), while cats, on the other hand, have trouble learning to lick themselves to escape, and dogs do not yawn for food (contraprepared). In discrimination, dogs are contraprepared to learn that different locations of discriminative stimuli control go-no go responding, and to learn that different qualities control directional responding. In avoidance, responses from the natural defense repertoire are prepared for avoiding shock, while those from the appetitive repertoire are contraprepared. Language acquisition and the functional autonomy of motives are also viewed using the preparedness continuum. Finally, it is speculated that the laws of learning themselves may vary with the preparedness of the organism for the association and that different physiological and cognitive mechanisms may covary with the dimension.

Skinner, B.F. *The behavior of organisms.* **New York: D. Appleton-Century, 1938. (Ch. 1.)**

The important objection to the vernacular in the description of behavior is that many of its terms imply conceptual schemes. The only way to obtain a convenient and useful system is to go directly to the data. We need to establish laws by virtue of which we may predict behavior, and we may do this only by finding variables of which behavior is a function.

The following are the static laws of the reflex: threshold, latency, magnitude of response, after-discharge, temporal summation. There are two dynamic laws related to elicitation of a reflex: refractory phase, and fatigue. There are also two dynamic laws involving a second stimulus which has no control over the response: facilitation, inhibition. There are then the dynamic laws of conditioning and extinction of Type S (classical). There are other dynamic laws related to operant (Type R) behavior that is emitted by an organism as measured by response rate: conditioning, extinction, which occur, respectively when a reinforcing stimulus does or does not follow an operant.

The operations characterizing drive involve concurrent changes in groups of reflexes. We must deal with drive as a "state" of a group of reflexes. This is done by introducing a hypothetical middle term between the operation and the resulting observed change. "Hunger," "fear," and so on, are terms of this sort. The notion of an intermediate state is valuable when more than one reflex is affected and when several operations have the same effect. No other properties are assigned to such hypothetical middle terms ("states").

The relation between strength and previous elicitation is such that we may speak of a certain amount of available activity, the reflex reserve. In one sense the reserve is a hypothetical entity, but it is very near to being directly treated experimentally. There is a relation between the number of responses appearing during the extinction of an operant and the number of preceding reinforcements.

Skinner, B.F. *Contingencies of reinforcement: A theoretical analysis.* New York: Appleton-Century-Crofts, 1969. (Preface.)

One sort of theory means any explanation of an observed fact which appeals to events taking place somewhere else, at some other level of observation, described in different terms, and measured in different dimensions. I have argued that theories of this sort had not stimulated good research on learning and that they misrepresented the facts to be accounted for, gave false assurances about the state of our knowledge, and led to the continued use of methods which should be abandoned.

However, a theory is essential to the scientific understanding of behavior. We need another kind of theory. Theory in the first sense can be replaced by an analysis of contingencies of reinforcement. Such a theory can be used to interpret cultural practices and in the prediction and control of human behavior. Such a theory takes up the nature and dimensions of behavior, the ontogenic and phylogenic variables of which it is a function, and the contingent relations among those variables.

The achievements of the hypothetico-deductive method, where appropriate, have been brilliant, but their significance has probably been exaggerated. Behavior is one of those subject matters which do not call for hypothetico-deductive methods. Both behavior itself and most of the variables of which it is a function are usually conspicuous.

Some of the questions to which a different kind of theory may be addressed are as follows: what aspects of behavior are significant? Of what variables are changes in these aspects a function? How are the relations among behavior and its controlling variables to be brought together in characterizing an organism as a system? What methods are appropriate in studying such a system experimentally? Under what conditions does such an analysis yield a technology of behavior and what issues arise in its application? These are not questions to which a hypothetico-deductive method is appropriate. They are nevertheless important questions, for the future of a science of behavior depends upon the answers.

Tolman, E.C. *Purposive behavior in animals and men.* New York: Century, 1932. (Ch. 1.)

(Preface: I wish now, once and for all, to put myself on record as feeling a distaste for most of the terms I have introduced. I especially dislike the terms *purpose* and *cognition* and the title *Purposive Behavior*. I do not mean entities that are ultimately subjective and metaphysically teleological; actually, I have used the terms in a purely neutral and objective sense.)

For the behaviorist, animal psychology plays into the hands of human psychology. "Behavior-acts," though no doubt in complete one-to-one correspondence with the underlying molecular facts of physics and physiology, have, as "molar" wholes, certain emergent properties of their own. Behavior always seems to have the character of getting-to or getting-from a specific goal-situation. There is a selectively greater readiness for short (i.e., easy) means activities as against long ones. Behavior as behavior reeks of purpose and cognition, be it that of a rat or a human being. A purpose is defined by the behaving organism's readiness to persist through trial and error and the tendency on successive occasions to select the easiest and quickest path (docility). The contingencies in the continuance of any given behavior-act upon environmental characters actually proving to be so and so define an act's cognitive aspects.

The behavior-determinants are subdivisible into three classes: (a) immediately "in-lying" objectively defined purposes and cognitions, i.e., the "immanent determinants"; (b) the purposive and cognitive "capacities" of the organism; (c) "behavior adjustments," which are produced by the immanent determinants in place of actual overt behavior and which serve to act back upon immanent determinants and correct them. These all intervene in the equation between stimuli and initiating physiological states on the one side and behavior on the other.

EXAMINATION ITEMS   **Topics for thought and discussion**

1.   Sociologists often reject psychological explanations of their data because of emergentism. A group, they say, is not just a collection of individuals but possesses properties which reveal that the whole is more than the sum of the parts. An analogous physical illustration is that water is composed of hydrogen and oxygen, but the properties of water could never be completely understood by studying those elements separately. Evaluate this argument and its impact on theories of learning and motivation.

2.   Think through the implications of physiological evidence that may contradict a postulate in a behavior theory.

Objective items

1. As concepts, learning and motivation are
    a. facts
    b. laws
    c. empirical
    d. hypothetical

2. Laws differ from hypotheses in that we are certain that laws are true, whereas hypotheses are not yet verified.
    a. True
    b. False

3. Empirical systems cannot include physiological terms.
    a. True
    b. False

4. Spence thinks that there is too much use being made of artificial, nonlifelike conditions in the study of behavior.
    a. True
    b. False

5. Acceptable hypothetical concepts must be "anchored" to both independent and dependent variables. Acceptable hypothetical constructs must be anchored to
    a. independent and dependent variables
    b. independent and organismic variables
    c. organismic and dependent variables
    d. independent, organismic, and dependent variables

6. The ultimate objective of Skinner's theoretic approach would be an exhaustive catalogue of the empirical relationships between independent and dependent variables.
    a. True
    b. False

7. Skinner has conceptualized drive as a
    a. stimulus
    b. state of strength
    c. relationship
    d. physiological state

8. In spite of more general implications of a theory it can properly be tested only within its stated boundary conditions.
    a. True
    b. False

9. Which of the following is not a critical property of the postulates of a theory?
    a. that they be as few as possible
    b. that they be consistent with each other
    c. that they be necessary
    d. that they be sufficient

10. As regards the controversy between empiricists and theorists, we have placed the burden of proof on the theorist because
    a. everything available to the empiricist is also available to the theorist
    b. everything available to the theorist is also available to the empiricist

c. theoretical systems are based on empirical knowledge

d. empirical systems are intrinsically proven because of the use of objective operational definitions

ANSWERS TO OBJECTIVE ITEMS

1.   (d) There are factors of learning and motivation and laws of learning and motivation, and these are all empirical. The generic terms "learning" and "motivation" however are hypothetical even when used as nothing more than shorthand expressions for the conditions that produce learning and motivation.

2.   (False) We are never certain of the truth value of laws. It is true that there may be some evidence concerning the truth of a law, whereas a hypothesis may at the time have no supporting empirical evidence. But one might have more confidence in a hypothesis derived from a generally sound theory than a generalization based on limited observations.

3.   (False) The source of the terms in an empirical system is not relevant; they may be drawn from physics, chemistry, physiology, psychology, sociology, or any other scientific domain. The only necessary condition is that they be empirical in the sense of being directly reducible to observations with no other properties stated or implied.

4.   (False) Very much on the contrary. Just as the laws of gravity required the study of falling objects in a vacuum, so too would Spence argue that the basic laws of behavior will best reveal themselves from the study of artificial and rigorously controlled environments.

5.   (a) Both hypothetical concepts and hypothetical constructs must be anchored to independent and dependent variables—the former through reduction sentences and the latter through the postulation of the necessary and sufficient antecedent and consequent conditions. Organismic variables are here thought of as biophysical/biochemical properties of the organism and need not be included in a theory of behavior. (However, they could be included.)

6.   (False) It is true that Skinner's approach leads to an exhaustive (and potentially exhausting) catalogue of empirical relationships, but this is not the ultimate objective. The goal is to subsume these laws under a parsimonious set of abstract principles.

7.   (c) To Skinner, drive is a hypothetical concept that summarizes various operations such as deprivation and stimulation which have similar effects on behavior. Only as a hypothetical construct can it be viewed as a stimulus or state of strength, and possibly even an underlying physiological condition.

8.   (True) Even though it might be fun to imagine a football game with no sidelines and the goal lines encircling the globe, the realistic game is played on a circumscribed field. In like fashion, although one may attempt to draw implications of a theory beyond its stated boundary conditions, even if these are confirmed and lead to an extension of the boundaries, any legitimate test of a theory must stay in bounds.

9.   (c) The postulates of a theory should be parsimonious, internally consistent, and sufficient to mediate predictions. They may not be necessary, however, because another theory may omit one or more of them and still deal effectively with the empirical phenomena of interest.

10. (a) The theorist must prove the utility of adding hypothetical constructs; these are not available to the empiricist. Alternative (c) is true, but equally true of empirical systems. Alternative (d) is false, because empirical systems involve induction and, hence, are still subject to disconfirmation.

CHAPTER THREE

THE NATURE AND CONDITIONS OF ASSOCIATIONS

Although systematic analyses of behavior have proceeded apace, systematists have often paused in order to join battle over controversial issues of learning and motivation. Historically, differences in data protocols have arisen because of differences in language systems, and the nondirective process of induction has yielded different abstract concepts for different systematists. But these sorts of differences are not the substances of controversial issues among theorists. Instead, controversy has centered around the underlying processes used to explain behavior. Just as the hypothetical construct is the mark of a reductive theory, so the nature and conditions of hypothetical constructs are the substance of theoretical issues.

For example, behavioristically oriented theorists have had no major quarrel with conceptualizing learning as an associative process that is reflected in a change in performance. However, the hypothetical nature of the associative process has been an open field for theoretical speculation and debate. Some believe that this associative process results in potentials, while others favor expectancies, readinesses, or dispositions. Furthermore, there are grounds for disagreeing about what is associated with what in this associative process. Consider the possibilities. Stimuli may become associated with subsequent stimuli or responses, and responses may become associated with subsequent responses or stimuli. The issue focuses on the hypothetical *nature* of associations: What is learned in learning?

Assume for the moment that the issue of "what is learned?" is resolved to the satisfaction of all theorists. Even so, other issues regarding the hypothetical associative process would emerge. For example, one would want to specify the necessary and sufficient *conditions* for the formation of associations. And, almost certainly, theorists would take exception to any other theorist whose specification of the conditions of association formation differed from their own. A controversial issue of learning would thereby be created—alternatives defined, experiments run, resolutions sought, and theoretical analyses altered.

The purpose of this chapter is to consider the theoretical issues regarding the nature of associations in learning and the conditions for establishing these associations. In order to prevent the reader from being misled, it needs to be noted at the outset that these two issues have threaded their way through most systematic analyses. They are historic and contemporary. They have been formulated and reformulated. They are important and unresolved.

THE NATURE OF ASSOCIATIONS

The "what is learned?" question has been variously answered in terms of stimulus-response (S-R) associations, stimulus-stimulus (S-S) associations, response-stimulus (R-S) associations, and combinations thereof (see, e.g., Spence, 1951). The possibility of response-response (R-R) associations has not been consistently advocated by theorists of learning. The sharpest lines of debate can be drawn among those theorists who argue that associations are formed to antecedent stimuli. The point of debate is whether antecedent stimuli are associated to subsequent stimuli or to subsequent responses. These S-S and S-R positions have historically been referred to by the rubrics of cognitive approach and behavioristic approach, respectively.

The general theme of the cognitive approach is that organisms tend to organize the stimulus environment perceptually and store the organized stimulus information according to some meaningful stimulus schema. Thus, learned associations occur among stimuli. More specifically, learning represents an acquired tendency to expect the occurrence of particular subsequent stimuli whenever a particular stimulus situation arises. In short, the hypothetical learning construct for cognitive psychologists becomes a form of expectancy or readiness regarding stimulus occurrence.

The cognitive learning construct, expectancy, was formalized by Tolman (e.g., 1948) who is now recognized as having been the most effective early spokesman for the cognitive position. Given the sequence of events, S_1-R_1-S_2, Tolman argued that organisms become aware of the significance of S_2 and that S_1 becomes a sign for its subsequent occurrence. Organisms learn the meaning of the stimulus sequence; that is, they acquire an expectancy that certain stimuli are followed by (i.e., associated with) certain other stimuli. A rat presented with the choice point in a maze, S_1, acquires an expectancy for the occurrence of food, S_2, provided he goes to the goal box, R_1. Actually, Tolman thought that families of expectancies arise in the organism's environment and that the totality of expectancies is perceptually reorganized into a field or cognitive map of the environment.

It is particularly important for our purposes here to note that a purely S-S cognitive position rejects any notion that organisms acquire a tendency to respond in a particular way when confronted with a particular stimulus situation. The nature of response occurrence is determined by the cognitive mapping of the environment. Behavior is flexible and varies to suit the situation rather than being fixed and invariable. The notion that behavior is typified by organism-environmental interactions instead of specific response sequences is central to the cognitive position.

In actuality, Tolman's early theoretical writings contained no specification of the relationship between expectancies or cognitive maps and the actual performance of a response. How expectancies produce behavior, or if they can, is unclear. Predictions regarding the occurrence of behavior could only be made at an intuitive level. Tolman eventually directed himself to the task of anchoring his S-S associative process to behavior changes by specifying certain principles of performance (Tolman, 1955). It is characteristic of the cognitive position, however, that even in this instance, the determinants of performance are described in only a general way. Predictions about the occurrence of specific responses seemingly are not of concern; they appear to be mere peripheral phenomena to the cognitive psychologist.

The behavioristic approach to the nature of associations differs in several ways from that of the cognitive approach (Spence, 1950). Most importantly, of course, behaviorists assert that associations between stimuli and responses are learned. For the S-R psychologist then, learning represents an acquired tendency to respond in a particular way when confronted with a particular stimulus situation. Again, given the sequence of events, S_1-R_1-S_2, a hungry rat at the choice point in a maze, S_1, develops a tendency to turn left, R_1; this response is followed by food, S_2. Various S-R systematists have proposed different hypothetical constructs to represent the learned tendency to respond. None, however, has been more rigorously formulated than the hypothetical construct of habit strength put forward by Hull (1930). Hull not only posited the habit construct, but he eventually identified those variables that determine the strength of S-R associations, defined the equation describing the rate of growth of habit and, most important, specified how habit is transformed into performance of the organism.

It is clearly important for S-R theorists to be able to predict correctly the occurrence of particular responses in particular stimulus situations. If what is learned is a tendency to respond in particular ways, then the most straightforward prediction from the S-R position is that the response that occurred previously in the situation will reoccur. It should be emphasized, however, that the S-R theorist's answer to the question "what is learned" is association, and *not* response. Particular responses are not learned[1]; instead, they occur because a tendency (or association) to make them has been acquired.

Response Definition

The language system used by S-S cognitive psychologists to describe the behavior of organisms typically implies that behavior is purposeful with respect to some significant stimulus event. Responses are defined in such molar terms as "approaches to goal objects" or "finding the path to a particular stimulus situation." Molar response definitions, in which all topographically different behaviors that result in the same consequence are aggregated, suit the purposes of the cognitive theorist quite well.[2] On the other hand, somewhat more molecular response definitions seem better suited to the behavioristic theory. However, there is nothing inherent in the behaviorist's theoretical approach to what is learned that requires that a particular definition of the response be adopted. The behavioristic approach can be both purposeful and molar with respect to response definition. It is the case that many (but by no means all) of the early behaviorists adopted quite molecular definitions of the response, such as glandular secretions, muscular contractions, or invariant muscle movements. Still others defined the response in terms of more molar acts, such as running, escaping, bar pressing, and so on. Whereas a response definition framed in more molar terms of organism-environmental interactions might be sufficiently molar to challenge the usefulness of S-R predictions made in such terms, the assumption that responses become associated to stimuli cannot predetermine the definition of the response any more than the assumption that stimuli become associated to stimuli.

The definition of a response that the theorist adopts must be internally consistent with the theory and must also provide for lawful relations in experimental investigations. Within these guidelines, there is wide latitude for the S-R theorist to specify the molar-molecular nature of the response that gets associated to stimuli. Thus, another form of the what-is-learned question arises for the S-R theorist: What is the nature of the response that gets associated in learning?

This new form of the what-is-learned question can be raised with respect to quantitative properties of the response, as well as with respect to the qualitative response properties that are represented by the molar-molecular distinction. There are two distinguishable S-R positions regarding the quantitative nature of the response that gets associated in learning. The macro position is that responses which differ quantitatively represent different strengths of the same response. Thus, as learning progresses and the associative strength increases, there should be a corresponding increase in the quantitative properties of the response, such as its speed or amplitude. The alternative answer to this aspect of the what-is-learned question is the micro approach (Logan, 1956), which assumes that quantitatively different behaviors represent different responses rather than different strengths of the same response. Part of what gets learned, then, is a tendency to make responses with particular quantitative properties.

Although concern about the molar-molecular, macro-micro nature of the associative response is most conspicuous in S-R theories,[3] it should be recognized that similar distinctions regarding the nature of the stimulus (or stimuli), which get associated, are pertinent to both S-S and S-R theorists. Another form of the what-is-learned question is then possible. Specifically, what is the nature of the stimuli that get associated in learning? Although differences in the molar-molecular nature of the stimulus have arisen between systematists, these differences do not always fall nicely along the lines of debate as defined by the nature of associations.[4] Even the early cognitive theorists' reliance on perceptual reorganization of the stimulus environment did not preclude a behavioristic analysis of these same phenomena. It does seem in this latter instance, however, that the S-S approach had a catalytic effect on the S-R approach. That is, S-S theorists challenged the S-R theorists to develop and specify new theoretical constructs. Witness, for example, that the S-S emphasis on perceptual organization stimulated S-R theorists to analyze the role of receptor orienting acts in perception (Spence, 1950).[5]

Issues concerning the nature of the response and the stimulus are quite interesting in their own right. However, these latter issues are derivative issues of the more fundamental what-is-learned issue. That is, they derive from the fundamental issue but do not lend to its resolution. It is in the empirical arena that the most earnest attempts to resolve the what-is-learned theoretical issue have been made. It is to these empirical attempts that we turn next.

Place-versus-Response Learning

Several experimental manipulations have been proposed as appropriate to the theoretical what-is-leaned issue, but the most influential one has been the "place versus response" learning paradigm. There are several variations of this general paradigm (e.g., Tolman, Ritchie, & Kalish, 1946), but the essential idea is first to train rats to run a maze to a goal object and then either to block the original path to the goal or to change the orientation of the rat with respect to the goal in some manner. For example, after rats have been trained to run consistently to the right side of a T maze, where food is located, the maze can then be rotated 180° so that it becomes a ⊥ maze for a test trial.

Under the test condition, the rat can do one of two things: it can either make the same right turn it has been making or go to the same place it has been going. Presumably, if the rat continues to perform the previously acquired response sequence, its behavior would suggest that what was learned was an S-R association, that is, a tendency to respond in a particular way. Alternatively, if the rat modifies its behavior to take a new but direct path to the original stimulus location, such behavior would be interpreted as supporting "place" learning and would suggest that what was learned was an S-S association, that is, an expectancy of a subsequent stimulus situation. Thus, the issue of "what is learned?" is reduced to the specific empirical question of whether organisms are "place" learners or "response" learners.

The bulk of the relevant experimental literature regarding place-versus-response learning was reviewed by Restle (1957). The large quantity of this literature exhibits that theoretical analyses of learning and motivation can be productive in generating empirical questions and related research. Indeed, theoretical analyses can be helpful in this way—even if the theoretical question, which the research is designed to answer, is inappropriately stated. At least in the present literature, no resolution to the what-is-learned question or even to the more specific place-versus-response issue has emerged.

It is instructive to analyze the place-versus-response issue more closely, since one can gain from it an understanding of the nature and pitfalls of controversial issues that exist in the systematic analysis of learning and motivation. First of all, the place-versus-response paradigm is predicated on the assumption that S-R theory necessarily implies the occurrence of limb or body-consistent responses and that S-S theory exclusively implies that organisms can shift their behavior to correspond to shifts in the environment (Campbell, 1954). In terms of the response-definition language used above, the assumption is that S-R theories are inherently molecular and S-S theories are inherently molar. Although such proclivities exist, they are not necessary, and place-versus-response procedures as well as other types of response transposition procedures are better viewed as being indicative of the molarity of the learned behavior. The results do not resolve the basic theoretical issue but do serve to constrain *both* conflicting views that describe the nature of learned associations.

Unfortunately, the results appear to be quite contradictory; it appears as if rats can become place learners or response learners at the whim of the experimenter. However, Restle (1957) has shown that the presence of large amounts of relevant extramaze stimulation results in place learning, whereas response learning occurs when only response-produced kinesthetic and proprioceptive cues are available. In one sense, this generalization can be accepted as an empirical resolution of the place versus response question. However, this empirical question is of theoretical interest only to the extent that its answer contributes to the resolution of the more general what-is-learned issue. In retrospect, it is doubtful that the place-versus-response issue can ever make such a contribution. The essence of the experimental paradigm is that it yields data pertaining to the molarity of the behavior learned by an organism. Given abundant extramaze cues, rats learn the molar concept of "where the goal is"; in a more impoverished environment, they learn the molecular concept of "how to get there." Both S-S and S-R theorists must accommodate to these facts, but neither approach is uniquely better suited for the purpose. Hence, the fundamental issue survived the flurry of place-versus-response studies and remains unresolved.

OPERATIONAL APPROACH

The what-is-learned question provides much fodder for the antitheoretical appetites of more operationally minded empirical systematists (e.g., Kendler, 1952). In general, the argument made is that the quesion of "what is learned?" and other similarly formulated theoretical questions are unanswerable and, therefore, are meaningless. In part this is because all theoretical constructs must be response inferred. Furthermore, no amount of reification or intuitive support can establish the existence of a hypothetical construct nor, for that matter, can any amount of experimental work. Only hypothetical concepts that are directly related to observables and that are given no meaning other than that which is given by the experimental variables can be so described. According to the argument, attempts to establish empirically the nature of a hypothetical construct or to determine which of two hypothetical constructs is to be preferred are doomed to failure.

Given the definitional, empirical, and operational objections of the place-versus-response issue, it is improbable that it will again be raised in the same fashion. It is also improbable that the larger question of the nature of associations will be quieted. It is far more likely that an apparently spent theoretical issue will reappear, perhaps in some new form, as theoretical analyses proceed. To be sure, the context may be different and the issue may be more indirect, but the fundamental theoretical question is likely to recur.

One can gain an appreciation for this by considering the nature of learned associations in the operant conditioning paradigm. Skinner (1937) uses the term operant behavior to describe responses that occur, seemingly spontaneously, in the absence of stimuli identified as being correlated with the instance of response occurrence. Note that Skinner never assumes that it is impossible to identify the stimuli correlated with operant responses. Instead, it is simply the case that no correlated stimuli are yet identified at the time the operant response occurs. Accordingly, the operant conditioning paradigm is simply defined operationally as a response-reinforcement contingency. That is, the presentation of a reinforcing stimulus is made contingent on (i.e., shortly follows) the emission of an operant response. It is an indisputable empirical fact that performance changes occur as a result of response-reinforcement contingencies. But what is the theoretical nature of learned associations in operant conditioning?

Before proceeding to a consideration of the question posed, it will be noted that Skinner sidesteps this theoretical question by adhering to a strictly operational approach. Learning as a hypothetical concept summarizes the changes in probability of operant-response occurrence that emerge as a result of empirical response-reinforcement contingencies. No separate hypothetical learning construct is entertained by Skinner to explain operant conditioning.

The scene for much of the preceding discussion, regarding the nature of associations, has been the runway or maze—a setting potentially rich with environmental stimuli and supportive of perceptual constructs. Neither the cognitive nor the behavioristic theorist has any difficulty conceptualizing that learning in this context represents the formation of associations to antecedent environmental stimuli. The nature of the associative process seems less obvious in the operant conditioning context where antecedent stimuli are unidentified. One could argue that antecedent stimuli are unimportant and that stimuli become associated to antecedent responses—an R-S learning construct. If one were to do so, then the problem would be to specify how this association becomes manifest in performance. This is the very problem faced by cognitive S-S theorists who also have a stimulus on the consequent side of the hypothetical association.[6] Alternatively, one could attempt to maintain the integrity of S-S and/or S-R associative constructs by postulating stimulus events correlated with either the response or the reinforcement. In actuality, theorists of learning, particularly S-R theorists, have been quite facile at maintaining that learning constructs represent associations to antecedent stimuli. Response-produced stimuli, time-dependent stimuli, reward stimuli, and their respective stimulus traces have in various instances been supplied by theorists in order to preserve the learning construct (e.g., Logan & Ferraro, 1970).

The operant conditioning context also provides a specific instance of the what-is-learned issue as it reappears in a slightly modified form: operant conditioning of verbal behavior. In a typical experiment (Greenspoon, 1955), an experimenter-specified aspect of a speaker's verbal behavior is correlated with reward. The speaker is not told the nature of the response-reinforcement contingency. One result is an increase in the performance of the specified aspect of verbal behavior. This result also occurs without the speaker being able to state the nature of the response-reinforcement contingency that produced the changes in the speaker's verbal behavior. To the strict operationalist, the situation is completely described in terms of changes in the probability of emission of the experimenter-specified response as it is a function of the response-reinforcement contingency.

As the reader may have already anticipated, this operant conditioning situation is not particularly pleasing to cognitive theorists. First, the specific verbal responses are surely not learned from the point of view of S-S learning constructs. Second, it would be appropriate to infer from the vantage point of the cognitive psychologist that the emitted verbal responses are overt manifestations of some underlying hypothetical associative process represented by, say, an idea, a hypothesis, or an expectancy of the experimental situation. One specific suggestion in this regard was made by Spielberger (1962) who argued that what is learned in verbal operant conditioning is an awareness of the response-reward contingency. Moreover, he stated that verbal conditioning should occur only for verbal behavior of which the speaker is aware.

The reader is reminded at this point of the original formulation of the "what is learned?" question. The similarities between the earlier approaches to the nature of associations and those within the later verbal conditioning context seem apparent. In both contexts, the cognitive approach assumes that the organism somehow behaves adaptively because of knowledge about environmental contingencies, whereas the behavioristic approach assumes that responses are emitted automatically as a result of these contingencies. Given the recurring nature of theoretical issues in learning and motivation this is not particularly surprising. It would be far more surprising if a question regarding the nature of learned associations, in some form or context, were never to appear again.

THE CONDITIONS OF ASSOCIATIONS

From the point of view of a theorist of learning, it is not enough just to specify what is learned, that is, to specify the *nature* of the hypothetical associative learning construct. In addition, the theorist must specify how this associative process results from experience. The necessary and sufficient *conditions* of association formation must be specified for the construct to be useful.

There has been no disagreement among the classic theorists of learning about one necessary condition for association formation. Cognitive theorists and behavioristic theorists alike have agreed that in order for associations to form, be they S-S, S-R, or even R-S in nature, there must be a temporal and spatial contiguity between the elements of the association. To be sure, various quantitative and topographical limits have been placed on the contiguity construct by various theorists. Nevertheless, there has been no challenge to the notion that contiguity is a necessary condition for the formation of associations.

Note that in the context of our present discussion, the term contiguity represents a hypothetical construct. Because our concern is with the hypothetical associative process, learning, the contiguity of interest is that one which occurs at a reductive level. Empirically, it is possible to arrange for the spatial and temporal contiguity of stimulus events, but this operational contiguity does not necessarily ensure the hypothetical contiguity to which the theorist has reference. Indeed, the theorist needs to specify how the empirical relationships between events are represented at the reductive level. This has been done variously in terms of perceptual organizations, receptor-orienting acts, stimulus traces, and the like (Hull, 1943; Miller & Dollard, 1941; Spence, 1937; Tolman, 1932). On the other hand, the lack of a clear spatial/temporal contiguity at the empirical level does not preclude the occurrence of a hypothetical contiguity at the reductive level. For example, it is quite theoretically possible for contiguity to occur between hypothetical stimulus traces or memorial representations of stimuli in the absence of immediately present stimuli in the environment.

The agreement among theorists that contiguity is a necessary condition for the formation of associations has not precipitated agreement of whether it alone is a sufficient condition for learning to occur. Indeed, the issue of whether or not contiguity is a sufficient condition for learning has divided theorists as much as has the what-is-learned issue. There is nothing vague about the contiguity issue; either contiguity is sufficient for learning to occur or it is not. If it is not, of course, then something else in addition to contiguity is necessary.

One additional necessary ingredient is reinforcement, which is discussed in the next chapter.[7] For our immediate purposes, we can stick with known reinforcers, such as food to a hungry organism. The "reinforcement-contiguity" issue reduces the theoretical question about the conditions of association to: Is contiguity alone sufficient for learning to occur or is reinforcement also necessary?

The reinforcement-contiguity issue may be alternatively viewed as an issue about the theoretical status of reinforcement. In one sense, all theorists of learning may be considered as reinforcement theorists; that is, all theorists agree to the empirical validity and efficacy of reinforcement in the control of behavior. In other words, there is general acceptance of the principle of reinforcement. In theory construction, this means that theorists have to state how it is that reinforcement functions theoretically with respect to their reductive hypothetical constructs. One alternative is to assert that reinforcement is necessary for learning in that it strengthens hypothetical associations of contiguous events. An alternative position, of course, is that reinforcement plays no role in the associative process and, thereby, is not necessary for learning. If the latter position is adopted, it is still necessary for the systematist to specify the theoretical status of reinforcement. As we shall discuss subsequently, reinforcement has been assigned various theoretical roles in the control of behavior other than that of strengthening associations. We will turn first, however, to an elaboration of the position that reinforcement is necessary for learning.

Although not the first,[8] perhaps the most influential statement of the reinforcement position was labeled the "Law of Effect" by Thorndike in 1911; we quote him briefly:

Of several responses made to the same situation, those which are accompanied or closely followed by satisfaction to the animal will, other things being equal, be more firmly connected with the situation, so that, when it occurs, they will be more likely to recur; those which are accompanied or closely followed by discomfort to the animal will, other things being equal, have their connections with that situation weakened, so that, when it recurs, they will be less likely to occur. The greater the satisfaction or discomfort, the greater the strengthening or weakening of the bond.

Another statement of the reinforcement position, which rivals that of Thorndike's in influence, was presented in 1943 by Hull as his fourth postulate regarding the principles of behavior (symbols here omitted):

Whenever an effector activity and a receptor activity occur in close temporal contiguity, and this is closely associated with the diminution of a need or with a stimulus which has been closely and consistently associated with the diminution of a need, there will result an increment to a tendency for that afferent impulse on later occasions to evoke that reaction. The increments from successive reinforcements summate in a manner which yields a combined habit strength which is a simple positive growth function of the number of reinforcements. The upper limit of this curve of learning is the product of (1) a positive growth function of the magnitude of need reduction which is involved in primary, or which is associated with secondary, reinforcement; (2) a negative function of the delay in reinforcement; and (3) (a) a negative growth function of the degree of asynchronism of S and R when both are of brief duration, or, (b) in case the action of S is prolonged so as to overlap the beginning of R, a negative growth function of the duration of the continuous action of S on the receptor when R begins.

It will be noted that the establishment of S-R associations does not guarantee response performance in this version of Hull's system. In order for habits to become manifest in performance, it is necessary that they be activated or energized by motivation. Hull's motivational construct, Drive, is anchored on the antecedent side to hours of deprivation and is assigned the properties of being nonassociative, nonsituational, temporary, and readily and rapidly modifiable. In contrast, the learning construct established by reinforcement, Habit, has the properties of being associative, situational, gradual in formation, and relatively permanent.

Furthermore, it is worthwhile to see certain communalities between the positions of Hull and Thorndike, since they typify one version of the general reinforcement theory of association formation. First, the nature of the association strengthened by reinforcement is a tendency to respond in a particular way in a particular stimulus situation; that is, reinforcement is necessary for S-R associations to form. To date, no systematist has come forth to propose alternatively that reinforcement is necessary for S-S associations to form. There is nothing inherent in the reinforcement side of the reinforcement-contiguity issue that necessarily links S-R associations with the necessity for reinforcement. However, given the sequence of events, environmental stimulus-response-reinforcing stimulus, there may be something theoretically unsatisfying about proposing that reinforcement is necessary to establish an S-S association of which the reinforcing stimulus itself is an integral part.

Both Thorndike and Hull adopted *uniprocess* positions with respect to learning: Reinforcement is necessary (in addition to contiguity) for associations to form in all stimulus situations, for all forms of response, and under all motivational conditions. Moreover, both theorists initially argued that not only is reinforcement necessary to strengthen associations but that the strength of an association is determined, in part, by the conditions of reinforcement: the stronger the satisfaction, the stronger the association; the larger the amount and the shorter the delay of reinforcement, the stronger the habit. For the sake of exposition, the "pure" reinforcement position will be the position that holds that the conditions of reinforcement, as well as the number of reinforcements, determine the strength of learned associations. The alternative position that some reinforcement is necessary but that the strength of an association is determined solely by the number of such reinforcements will simply be referred to as the reinforcement position (without the modifier "impure"). Note, in passing, however, that if it is assumed that the conditions of reinforcement do not affect the strength of associations, some other specification of their effects is theoretically required. This is akin to the point made above that if reinforcement is deemed unnecessary even for association formation, then some other reductive theoretical role needs to be assigned to it.

The argument that contiguity is sufficient for learning has been made by both S-S and S-R theorists. Moreover, contiguity theorists have proposed various determinants of the strength of associations, not the least of which have been the recency and/or frequency with which the end terms of the association have occurred contiguously. As a prototype of the S-R contiguity approach, we may consider Pavlov's 1927 treatment of the formation of the conditioned reflex in classical conditioning.

The paradigm of classical conditioning is straightforward for the S-R view of contiguity. A neutral stimulus that is present at the time that an unconditioned stimulus elicits a response will, on future occasions, evoke that response. The paradigm implies substitution of the conditioned stimulus for the unconditioned stimulus in eliciting the response. Classical conditioning is probably a more complex phenomenon than is implied by stimulus substitution. Consider, for example, that the conditioned response is often qualitatively different from the response evoked by the unconditioned stimulus. Nevertheless, Pavlov assumed that a hypothetical S-R association is based solely on contiguity. According to him, reinforcement is neither necessary for the association nor does it affect the strength of the association. Reinforcement has no theoretical associative influence. Instead, reinforcement is simply identified with the occurrence of the unconditioned stimulus and given the role of initiating the response so that it occurs contiguously with the neutral stimulus.

A second instance of an S-R contiguity position with respect to the nature and conditions of association was provided by Guthrie (1934). The essentials of Guthrie's position are somewhat unique in that he assumed that a single contiguous pairing of a stimulus and response produces an association at full strength; he stated that associations are either formed completely or not at all. Learning is neither continuous nor gradual. Instead, it is discontinuous and immediate. Practice provides the opportunity for a number of different S-R associations to form in a situation, but it does not determine the strengths of these associations.

Guthrie further assumed that if a stimulus situation is maintained, there will be a constantly changing set of associations formed to the stimulus as one response replaces another in the S-R association. Reinforcement has no associative influence on the learning process. Reinforcement, however, is assigned an important function by Guthrie. The occurrence of reinforcement has the capacity of changing the stimulus situation so that there is no replacement of the particular S-R association formed immediately prior to reinforcement. Reinforcement, in effect, preserves the last association formed prior to its occurrence. Thus, this association will be available to reoccur when the original stimulus situation is reinstated.[9]

Although Guthrie's S-R contiguity position has much intuitive appeal, it has never stimulated a large amount of research primarily because it is difficult to make predictions from the theory. For one thing, it is difficult to gain experimental control of the stimulus situation since, according to Guthrie, this consists of whatever the subject is noticing at the time. For another, because S-R associations are readily replaced, it is not possible to infer what S-R associations are actually formed, except for those protected by reinforcement.

As a final example of contiguity theory we may again consider Tolman's (1948) S-S learning theory. For Tolman, the formation of expectancies occurs solely because of the contiguity of sign and significate. Reinforcement serves to confirm an expectancy and can emphasize or change the meanings of expectancies, but reinforcement is not necessary in the formation of expectancies.

In Tolman's system, as in Hull's, learned associations are not automatically manifested in performance. Learned associations are used only when there is a justification for doing so. This justification is provided by motivation in the form of drive or in the form of reinforcement. Reinforcement then serves as a motivational variable that arouses responses to occur in a manner consonant with existing expectancies. In sum, expectancies are acquired on the basis of contiguity alone. Reinforcement is not necessary for learning, but instead is a motivational variable and, as such, is essential to performance.

DUAL-PROCESS APPROACH

The reinforcement-contiguity issue is precisely formulated, and the learning psychologist can completely embrace either reinforcement theory or contiguity theory and then apply this theoretical approach in a uniprocess fashion, that is, apply it equally well to all conditioning situations. A second alternative for the learning psychologist is to look for some compromise between contiguity and reinforcement. For example, one could finesse the reinforcement-contiguity issue somewhat by adopting a dual-process position and applying reinforcement notions to some situations and contiguity notions to others.

If one were to adopt a dual-process position, it would be necessary to identify explicitly those situations in which contiguity or reinforcement applies. In fact, precisely this has been done by those systematists of learning who have adopted a dual-process approach. For example, Skinner (1937) and Mowrer (1947) took the position that contiguity is sufficient for the establishment and strengthening of S-R associations in classical conditioning, whereas reinforcement is essential in the operant-instrumental conditioning context. Skinner made a further distinction between the nature of responses (autonomic versus skeletal) that are conditioned by contiguity or by reinforcement, and still other systematists (e.g., Spence, 1956) have made similar distinctions in terms of the type of motivation controlling behavior (appetitive versus aversive).[10]

As a digression note that neither the classical conditioning paradigm nor the operant-instrumental conditioning paradigm can specifically exist in the total absence of the other. This overlap between the paradigms can be appreciated if it is recognized that no matter how the experimenter arranges for the occurrence of stimuli and responses, organisms will continue to behave freely over time and always do so in a stimulus environment. The existence of this paradigmatic overlap has enabled psychologists to contend that behavior engendered under either one or the other of these conditioning procedures is an artifact of the overlap between them. For example, Smith (1954) argued that classically conditioned visceral responses are nothing more than innate corollaries of skeletal responses conditioned by an instrumental-operant reinforcement contingency. Although this implies a uniprocess approach, it must be recognized, in this context, that the existence of an overlap in the experimental paradigms for the two conditioning procedures by no means requires an overlap (or lack thereof) between reductive hypothetical associative processes.

LATENT LEARNING   Although a dual-process approach may be viewed as a theoretical compromise of the reinforcement-contiguity issue, it is not a very effective one. This can be quickly appreciated at a trivial level when it is realized that dual-process theorists disagree, although at different times, with both contiguity and reinforcement theorists! It would seem far more satisfactory if an empirical resolution to the issue could be obtained. In fact, several types of experiments have been run with the objective of distinguishing between reinforcement and contiguity theory. The primary, immediate objective of the research has been to determine if learning occurs without reinforcement. For example, a response might be elicited a number of times in the presence of a stimulus, but in the absence of known reinforcements, to see if any performance change results (e.g., Loucks & Gantt, 1938). Actually, the prognosis of whether these experiments can yield a satisfactory empirical resolution to the reinforcement-contiguity issue is quite poor. This is, in part, because it is extremely difficult, if not nearly impossible, to create a situation that does not contain a potential source of at least secondary reinforcement.

This gloomy prognosis, regarding an empirical resolution, has not curtailed the vigor of those seeking to find empirical support for one side of the theoretical issue at the expense of the other side. Nowhere has this vigor been more apparent than within the empirical domain known as latent learning. Just as the place-versus-response procedures may be conceptualized as constituting an empirical test for the what-is-learned question, latent learning procedures may be conceptualized as constituting an empirical test for the reinforcement-contiguity issue.

Several different varieties of latent learning procedures have been used, although two in particular have been most popular. In one, trials under a strong irrelevant drive, with respect to a goal object, are followed by trials in which the drive state is shifted to the relevant drive (e.g., Kendler, 1947; Spence & Lippitt, 1946). No explicit reinforcement for the behavior appropriate to the task is provided.

This procedure was originally thought to be a rigorous test of S-S contiguity theory, since it is assumed that learning should occur in the original situation through contiguity, regardless of the irrelevant drive state. When the drive is made relevant to the reinforcement, the learning that had occurred previously and that until then had not been manifest (latent), should occur. Generally, learning is not evident in these experiments and, thus, the reinforcement position is supported. But as has so often been the case when empirical questions have been formulated to resolve theoretical issues, unequivocal resolutions are not and probably cannot be forthcoming. In this particular instance, an S-S contiguity theorist, such as Tolman, could contend that learning does not take place, because the organism does not attend to the stimulus due to the absence of a drive that would make the stimuli relevant or emphasize the stimuli. Once again an attempt at an empirical resolution is foiled by the agility of the theorist's hypothetical constructs.

A second form of the latent learning procedure was conceived by Tolman to challenge pure reinforcement positions, such as Hull (1943). Under this general procedure (e.g., Tolman & Honzik, 1930), trials without any explicit reinforcement are followed by the introduction of a reinforcement relevant to the organism's motivtion. According to Tolman's contiguity position, learning should occur on all trials, but it should only become obvious in performance when the reinforcement is introduced to motivate the organism to perform. Moreover, since learning occurs prior to reinforcement (even though it is latent), the introduction of reinforcement should bring about a rapid change in performance. A large majority of studies using this procedure supports the contiguity position. But as might be expected, these results do not actually defeat the alternative reinforcement position.

If these latent learning experiments were indeed carried out in the complete absence of reinforcement during the early trials, the reinforcement position would be strongly challenged. Thus, it behooves the reinforcement theorist to suggest possible sources of, say, secondary reinforcement in the latent learning procedure. And this they have done with sufficient success so that even Tolman was willing to concede, without further argument, that some "slightly effective reward" might be operative in these studies.

Whether or not reward is present in the early trials, a pure reinforcement theorist has difficulty accounting for the rapid shift in performance that occurs with the introduction of (a larger) reward. Recall that a pure reinforcement theorist contends that the conditions of reinforcement, in part, dictate the strength of acquired associations. Recall further that learned associations are only gradually modified in strength. Adherence to a pure reinforcement position is incompatible with the rapid improvement in performance observed in the latent learning experiments, since the learned association should approach its new limit of associative strength gradually.

In challenging a pure reinforcement position, latent learning experiments do not challenge a reinforcement position that holds that learning is unaffected by the conditions of reinforcement. Indeed, the latent learning data are quite consistent with a reinforcement position that holds that the conditions of reinforcement affect performance through motivation, while the simple occurrence of reinforcement alone (no matter what the conditions) determines learning.

Both Thorndike (1931) and Hull (1952) eventually abandoned the pure reinforcement position but continued to maintain that reinforcement is necessary for learned associations to form. For Thorndike, the strength of the association bears no relation to the intensity of the satisfier, and for Hull, the strength of habits is not affected by the amount or delay of reinforcement. These latter conditions of reinforcement affect performance in their capacities as motivational variables. Thus, S-R reinforcement theory comes to treat the conditions of reinforcement in a manner similar to that of S-S contiguity theory. Hence, some of the differences between the theories are muted.

But what of the original question regarding the conditions of association formation? Latent learning procedures no more provide the answer they were intended for than do the place-versus-response procedures. Whether or not reinforcement is necessary for learning to occur remains a theoretical issue to be debated by systematists of learning and motivation. The issue may not continue to appear in the same form or in the same contexts, but it is reasonable to expect that the issue of the conditions of association, along with the issue of the nature of associations, will continue to demand the theorist's attention.

SUMMARY AND CONCLUSIONS

The essence of controversy in theories of learning and motivation results from different theorists proposing different hypothetical constructs in an attempt to explain the behavior of organisms. Several factors combine to determine the nature of the hypothetical construct put forth by a particular theorist. Obviously, the theorist is influenced by the data at hand, by historical factors, and by the theorist's best guess of what will be a fruitful approach to future events. The theorist's personality and style also contribute to the nature of hypothetical constructs. Hypothetical constructs always seem to have the property of "feeling right" to the originator, but not necessarily to other theorists.

Theorists who differ in these various ways construct different theoretical constructs; thus, there is ground for controversy. As we have seen in the controversial issues concerning the nature and conditions of learned associations, there are three basic types of controversy. At issue is whether the particular hypothetical constructs proposed are: (1) necessary, (2) useful, or (3) correct.

The issues regarding the necessity and usefulness of hypothetical constructs are mainly fought between empirical and theoretical systematists. Actually, these issues are no longer particularly fought with vigor. Both empiricist and theoretician now agree that hypothetical constructs are not necessary to explain behavior but may often be useful to the pursuits of the theoretician. In spite of this apparent agreement, theoreticians still need to resist the temptation of reifying their constructs (which they do with varying degrees of success) and to defend against feeling offended when systematists fail to appreciate their constructs (which they do as a matter of individual personality). On the other hand, empiricists still need to recognize that no matter how unreal hypothetical constructs may be, they do generate otherwise unanticipated predictions and stimulate empirical research. (Some empiricists seem particularly disturbed when predictions made from hypothetical constructs are confirmed.)

The crux of the contemporary controversy centers on the correctness of hypothetical constructs. This issue is engaged solely by theorists, particularly by ones who have alternative constructs to propose. Let us return to the specifics of the controversies discussed in this chapter. One issue discusses the nature of the hypothetical associative processes that define learning. To be sure, learning represents the associations between events, but for the cognitive theorist these associations are between stimuli, and for the behavioristic theorist, these associations are between stimuli and responses. A second issue concerns the conditions that are necessary for the formation of associations, whatever their nature may be. For the contiguity theorist, pure contiguity is both necessary and sufficient to support association formation. For the reinforcement theorist, contiguity is necessary, but not sufficient, for learning to occur; in addition, reinforcement is necessary for learning.

Each of these major theoretical issues has generated spin-off issues that have become important theoretically. For example, if stimuli are associated with responses then the macro-micro, molar-molecular nature of the associated responses becomes important. Either the quantitative properties of the response indicate the strength of the molar response, as is argued by macromolar theorists, or responses that differ quantitatively represent different responses, as is argued by micromolar theorists. Similarly, regardless of whether or not the occurrence of reinforcement is assumed to be necessary for learning, the role of the conditions of reinforcement becomes important. Either the conditions of reinforcement determine the strength of learned associations, as is argued by *pure* reinforcement theorists, or the conditions of reinforcement affect motivation, as is argued by reinforcement and contiguity theorists.

Both the "what is learned?" and "reinforcement-contiguity" issues also generate predictions of the outcome of experimental manipulations. To the S-S contiguity theorist, there is little doubt that organisms should be "place" learners in spatial response experiments and "latent" learners in experiments run without reinforcement. It seems equally clear to the S-R pure reinforcement theorist that organisms are "response" learners and that learning would not be "latent" in a situation without reinforcement, because it would not occur at all. Indeed, the predictions that are made from the various theoretical positions are so straightforward, clear cut, and opposite that it would seem relatively easy to determine the correctness of the hypothetical constructs from which the predictions are made. Presumably, all we must do is run the experiments, analyze the results, and then declare correct that hypothetical construct that is consonant with the data.

The developments of the place versus response and latent learning empirical issues serve to illustrate a general dictum regarding theoretical analyses and controversies. Specifically, the acceptability of a theory cannot be definitively established with data; the only way to overthrow a theory is by the creation of another (better?) theory (Conant, 1947). Empirical questions formulated to determine the correctness of a hypothetical construct can sometimes be declared to have been incorrectly drawn, as in the place-versus-response context. Alternatively, extant theory can sometimes be revised around a hypothetical construct so that the essence of the hypothetical construct is preserved, as in the latent learning context. More generally, where empirical data do not conform to a theory either the data may be considered inappropriate to the theory or a theory may be revised to encompass the data. In short, the very hypothetical nature of constructs prevents a decision as to the correctness of constructs from being made empirically.

This point is not peculiar to the empirical issues already discussed in this chapter. Other forms of the theoretical questions exist and other empirical contexts have been generated in which to test them. The outcome is the same. Perhaps it would be useful to describe one other of these instances. The context of sensory preconditioning will be appropriate for our purposes, since it relates to both the nature and conditions of association.

As has so often been the case, S-S contiguity theorists present the experimental paradigm of sensory preconditioning as a challenge to S-R reinforcement theorists. Under sensory preconditioning two neutral stimuli are first paired $(S_1 - S_2)$. One of the stimuli, say S_2, is then conditioned to a US $(S_2 - US)$. Sensory preconditioning is said to occur when in a third phase, S_1 elicits a response appropriate to the US used to condition S_2. This paradigm challenges S-R reinforcement theory, since in the first phase ($S_1 - S_2$) an apparent association is learned, although no response is evident nor is any obvious reinforcement delivered. Nevertheless, the empirical demonstration of sensory preconditioning does not negate S-R reinforcement theory. Instead, theorists sympathetic to the latter position tend to hypothesize the existence of first-phase responses that enter into associations with S_1 and S_2 and to assert that the first-phase stimuli have drive properties (however slight) that can serve to mediate reinforcement. The essence of the theory remains intact, despite apparent empirical evidence to the contrary.

Controversial issues in learning not only generate still other theoretical issues and differential empirical predictions, but they also yield differential implications in more applied contexts. Clearly the nature of psychotherapy is different depending on whether the therapist assumes the responsibility of modifying the meaning and significance of stimuli in a cognitive sense or of modifying behavioral responses to stimuli in a behavioristic sense. The parents' reaction to a crying child is not the same if the intensity of the cry is considered to have been learned rather than considered as a direct indication of the severity of a learned fear. The police officer's directions to a wayward motorist differ if the motorist is a place rather than a response driver, and so on. Examples of this sort can be generated in large numbers. Let it suffice for our purposes here to return to the instance of programmed instruction discussed in Chapter 2 and to review in some detail the implications suggested by S-R reinforcement theory and S-S contiguity theory.

The particular theoretical approach adopted has implications for both the formal construction of programs and the behavior of the learner. Since the S-S contiguity theorist is so often the plaintiff, empirically and theoretically, let's turn the coin and begin with the S-R reinforcement theorist. Learning is presumed to occur to antecedent stimuli. Thus, the S-R theorist would want to sequence carefully arranged bits of stimulus material (here called frames). Similarly, an S-R theorist's program would require that a response be executed contiguously with the stimulus material. Furthermore, the particular response to be executed would be the exact response that was intended to be associated. For example, if it were desired that the learner be able to write a word correctly, the word would be required to be written and not simply chosen from among several alternative words. Since the response called for is specific to particular stimulus material, only the stimulus material to which the response is to be associated would be presented in the frame. This would imply that a number of small-step frames should be constructed where the size of the step is measured in terms of the amount of stimulus material presented. Further restrictions on the nature of the response would be determined by the nature of the response definition adopted. A micromolar S-R theorist would require, for example, that desired quantitative properties of the response be made in the stimulus situation. From the point of view of the reinforcement theorist, only those contiguously occurring stimulus and response events, which are shortly followed by reinforcement, would be learned. Thus, the theorist would want to arrange for each correct response to be followed by reinforcement, ideally, to have every response be correct, so that every response can be reinforced.

Other characteristics could be identified, but it is convenient now to summarize the above points to make comparisons with S-S contiguity theory. In essence, S-R reinforcement theory would require that programmed instruction consist of small frames of stimulus material to which the learner would overtly respond by making the particular response to be learned and that each of these responses be followed by reinforcement.

The S-S contiguity theorist would also want to sequence carefully arranged bits of stimulus material. However, since stimuli are associated to other stimuli through contiguity, and since these stimulus-stimulus associations become organized according to some scheme, the S-S theorist would want to present relatively large amounts of stimulus material to the learner at any one time. That is, the S-S theorist's program would be characterized by large-step frames. No particular concern would be shown for the form of the response. The response required would be one which is consistent with respect to the organized S-S associations. Multiple-choice responses would, therefore, be acceptable as would any other form of the response. In fact, a response would be asked for only as a means of inferring that correct S-S associations were formed. Finally, reinforcement would play no role other than to confirm that a consistent response had been executed. Errorless responding would be of no major significance, since an "error" can serve effectively as a disconfirmation, just as a "correct" response can serve as a confirmation. Summarizing the essence of an S-S contiguity program, the program would consist of large frames of stimulus material to which the learner can respond by making any form of response consistent with the material that may or may not receive confirmation.

NOTES   1. The notion that associations rather than responses are learned does not mean that particular responses are not learnable. In fact, it is probably the case that all observable responses are learnable in the sense that they can be relatively permanently associated with stimuli as the result of practice.

2. Actually, the flavor of the cognitive style is not adequately captured by molar-response definitions. The cognitive theorist is not inclined to refer to concrete responses but rather thinks of behavior in terms of performances. A performance is a behavioral disposition that only can be specified by observing two or more concrete responses in different situations, so that the essence of the organism's behavior can be extracted.

3. Although S-S theorists do not contend that a response gets associated to stimuli during the learning process, the cognitive theorist must still deal with the nature of the response that occurs at the empirical level. That is, different quantitative responses do occur and do appear to be learnable. The cognitive theorist needs to account for such data. To date, no such formulation in cognitive terms has been offered.

4. The molar-molecular distinction with respect to the stimulus is analogous

to the distinction made between wholistic descriptions and elementaristic descriptions of the stimulus. Furthermore, the micro approach to the response, which treats different quantitative responses as different, is in agreement with the typical practice of specifying different intensity stimuli as different stimuli.

5. Actually, a large measure of the research generated by early S-S cognitive psychologists was directed against S-R theory rather than being designed to support a formalization of S-S theory. As a consequence of the empirical aggressiveness of S-S psychologists, S-R theory has been stimulated into further elaboration and continual modification. It is now generally acknowledged that the greatest impetus to the development of S-R theory has been the empirical battles fought along several fronts with S-S theory. Furthermore, as S-R theory evolves, the differences between S-S and S-R theory diminish. For example, S-R theorists' evolution of an incentive construct increasingly incorporates S-S-like expectancy notions. Of greatest significance is the fact that cognitive-type theories have been formalized at an increasing rate during the past decade with the result that S-R theorists are now in a position to challenge cognitive interpretations of learning and motivation.

6. The reader should not be misled by this statement. It is not necessary that each hypothetical construct in a theory be *directly* related to performance, not even so-called learning constructs. Indeed, hypothetical constructs would be expected to interact in a theoretical system to determine performance. Thus, it is no less likely a priori that an R-S construct can be related to performance than can an S-R learning construct.

7. Reinforcement is clearly the ingredient most often suggested as being necessary, in addition to contiguity, for learning to occur. However, it has not been the only suggested ingredient. For example, in other contexts, awareness is considered by some as a necessary ingredient for learning.

8. Reinforcement theory had its prescientific beginnings in Greek philosophy, as exemplified by the teleological concept of hedonism and the notion of catharsis. The biological basis of reinforcement theory began with Darwin's 1859 theory of evolutionary adaptation and was extended in 1870 by Spencer who asserted that an organism would tend to repeat actions that had brought pleasure and desist from those that brought pain. A later biologist, Jennings, first coined the term, "trial and error behavior" when observing that the behavior of paramecium was not random but instead was controlled by its effects.

9. Guthrie placed a heavy emphasis on the formation of associations of responses to maintaining stimuli that are those stimuli associated with biological drives in the organism. Reinforcement theorists, particularly drive-reduction reinforcement theorists, could argue that Guthrie's mechanism for reinforcement is drive reduction. That is, the most effective way to protect the association between the maintaining stimuli and the correct response is to remove these stimuli by reducing drive. Although drive-reduction theorists could thus assimilate Guthrie into their camp, regarding the mechanism of reinforcement,

Guthrie could still maintain that drive-reduction reinforcement was not necessary for the formation of associations per se.

10. Distinctions made along these lines are not essential to the fundamental reinforcement-contiguity issue, which is of primary concern here. Saying that contiguity is sufficient in only some situations does not resolve the issue vis-à-vis uniprocess-reinforcement theorists, any more than saying reinforcement is only sometimes necessary appeases the uniprocess-contiguity theorist.

ABSTRACTS   **Campbell, D.T. Operational delineation of "what is learned" via the transposition experiment.** *Psychological Review,* 1954, *61,* 167–174.

All perceptual, cognitive, and learning theories are response theories. Neglect of this point has led to a tendency to overlook the possibility of functional equivalence between perceptually stated intervening variables and those formulated in response terms, and thus in a number of instances has led to the generation of pseudo problems. But there still remains the possibility that two theories of learning, both utilizing response-inferred intervening variables, would differ in an experimentally meaningful fashion in terms of their specifications of "what is learned." The basic difficulty centers around a generally unrecognized ambiguity in the term "response." There is a tendency to choose one of several possible definitions of the response as the "obviously" correct one not recognizing that there are operational ways of determining which is the most appropriate. Possible interpretations of what is learned are experimentally confounded in all learning experiments in which the habit is tested only in the situation in which it was originially acquired. It behooves the learning theorist to set up experimental situations in which these possible interpretations are disentangled and unconfounded. Such experiments may be called "transposition experiments." These have in common the attribute that they modify the conditions under which the habit is executed in such a fashion that a muscle- or body- consistent definition of the learned response in the habit cannot be held if the animal continues to perform adequately.

Guthrie, E.R. Reward and punishment. *Psychological Review,* 1934, *41,* 450–460.

The future response to a situation can be best predicted in terms of what an animal has done in that situation in the past. Stimuli acting during a response tend on later occasions to evoke that response. I would not hold that all satisfiers tend to fix the associative connection that just preceded them. The influence of the stimuli acting at the time of either satisfaction or annoyance will be to reestablish whatever behavior was in evidence at the time. The something that the satisfier causes the animal to do on the second occasion is the repetition of its behavior on the first occasion—always allowing for possible new elements that may interfere. Punishment achieves its effects by forcing the animal or child to do something different, and thus establishing inhibitory conditioning of unwanted habits.

There is nothing in this discussion which should deprive punishment and reward of the place they hold in public favor. But we shall have a much better insight into the uses of punishment and reward if we analyze their effects in terms of association and realize that punishment is effective only when it reconditions new responses to the cues for unwanted behavior and reward is effective only through its associations. Punishment and reward are essentially moral terms and not psychological terms. Theory stated in their terms is bound to be ambiguous.

Hull, C.L. Simple trial-and-error learning: A study in psychological theory. *Psychological Review,* 1930, *37,* 241–256.

There appear to be a number of fairly distinct types of trial-and-error learning. A simple type is where each trial act is reinforced, if successful, but is followed by no special stimulus (is merely unreinforced) if unsuccessful. In this type of situation the organism persists in its attempts because the stimulus which evokes the attempts itself persists. The organism varies its reaction, when one reaction fails, because the consequent weakening of the primarily dominant excitatory tendency leaves dominant a second and distinct excitatory tendency conditioned to the same stimulus situation. That trial act is evoked at any given stage of the trial-and-error process which at that time is dominant, i.e., strongest.

The erroneous reactions become less and less frequent as the trial-and-error process continues because the basic superiority in the strength of the excitatory tendencies leading to erroneous responses become less and less dominant. This in turn owing (a) to the action of experimental extinction which continually weakens such erroneous reactions as chance to become functionally dominant, and (b) to the action of reinforcement which strengthens the excitatory tendency which, when dominant, evokes successful responses. From the foregoing, it is obvious that trial-and-error learning while "blind" in the sense that it is not assumed that there is available for its guidance and control any disembodied soul or spirit is not blind in the sense that it does not operate according to recognized principles.

Kendler, H.H. An investigation of latent learning in a T-maze. *Journal of Comparative and Physiological Psychology,* 1947, *40,* 265–270.

The present study examined the adequacy of Tolman's nonreinforcement learning theory. A single choice T-maze was used in which the left alley (painted black) led to water while the right alley (unpainted) led to food. During the training trials, six animals were thirsty but satiated for food while for four animals this motivational condition was reversed. All animals had equal experience with the contents of both goal boxes. During half of the test trials, the motivation of the animals was shifted to the drive which remained satiated during the training trials. During the test trials all animals continued to choose the side which had led to the appropriate reward object during the training series. These results were contrary to the expected results as deduced from Tolman's theory. They were in complete agreement with those of Spence and Lippitt (1946) and make less tenable the view that their results could be attributed to the poor differentiation between the signs of the two choice alleys of the maze.

Kendler, H.H. What is learned? A theoretical blind alley. *Psychological Review,* **1952,** *59,* **269–277.**

Contemporary learning theorists offer numerous and seemingly opposed answers to the question as to what is learned, the major difference among them being whether "cognitive maps" or "stimulus-response associations" are learned. The argument in this paper is that the problem of what is learned is a pseudo-problem. It stems from the methodological error or reifying theoretical constructs. This reification in turn is due to the failure to distinguish sharply and consistently between the operational meaning of intervening variables and the intuitive properties ascribed to these concepts. If we conceive the intervening variable as being an economical device by which experimental variables are ordered in relation to behavioral variables, then the confusion will not arise. The basic difference between such intervening variables as "habit" and "cognitive map" can be specified only in terms of their stated relationships to the observable variables, not in terms of the connotations they arouse.

Logan, F.A. A micromolar approach to behavior theory. *Psychological Review,* **1956,** *63,* **63–73.**

A discussion of the fundamental features of the classical macromolar approach to behavior theory, as exemplified by Hull, suggested that (a) the implications that all response dimensions should improve with practice and be highly correlated are not universally true, and (b) a new method of solution of the model is necessary for situations in which reward or drive depends differentially upon some response dimension, such as speed or amplitude. A micromolar approach was described, in which quantitatively different behaviors (e.g., different amplitudes) are viewed as different responses, rather than as different strengths of the same response. It is concluded that the micromolar approach is a potentially useful one, and deserves consideration alongside other theories of learned behavior.

Loucks, R.B., & Gantt, W.H. The conditioning of striped muscle responses based upon faradic stimulation of dorsal roots and dorsal columns of the spinal cord. *Journal of Comparative Psychology,* **1938,** *25,* **415–426.**

In summary, it appears that a conditional limb movement is readily established when based upon the stimulation of peripheral afferent neurones, as the unconditional stimulus, provided that nociceptive neural systems are activated. An unconditional stimulus which leads to reflex movement without exciting nociceptive neurones, or others of a similar category, seemingly constitutes an inadequate basis for establishing a conditional avoiding movement.

Mowrer, O.H. On the dual nature of learning: A reinterpretation of "conditioning" and "problem-solving." *Harvard Educational Review,* 1947, *17,* 102–148.

In the psychology of learning, there are three major traditions: hedonism, associationism, and rationalism. Many writers have attempted to base their understanding of learning exclusively upon one or another of these traditions; others have drawn unsystematically from all three. The position taken by the author of the present article is that there are two basic learning processes— "conditioning" (associationism) and "problem-solving" (hedonism)—and that rationality is a complex derivative of these other two.

If this type of formulation proves valid, it holds promise of not only resolving a number of theoretical paradoxes but of opening the way for new and important applications of the principles of learning in educational, clinical work, human relations, and other related fields.

Restle, F. Discrimination of cues in mazes: A resolution of the "place-vs.-response" question. *Psychological Review,* 1957, *64,* 217–228.

Consideration of early studies of the sensory basis of maze learning, and review of place-vs.-response experiments, indicate that there is nothing in the nature of a rat which makes it a "place" learner, or a "response" learner. A rat in a maze will use all relevant cues, and the importance of any class of cues depends on the amount of relevant stimulation provided as well as the sensory capacities of the animal. In place-response experiments, the importance of place cues depends on the amount of differential extra-maze stimulation. The writer's general conclusion is that further "definitive" studies of the place-vs.-response controversy, to prove that rats are by nature either place or response learners, would be fruitless since the issue is incorrectly drawn.

Skinner. B.F. Two types of conditioned reflex: A reply to Konorski and Miller. *Journal of General Psychology,* 1937, *16,* 272–279.

Different types of conditioned reflexes arise because a reinforcing stimulus may be presented in different kinds of temporal relations. There are two fundamental cases: in one the reinforcing stimulus is correlated temporally with a response and in the other with a stimulus. To avoid confusion and to gain a mnemonic advantage I shall refer to conditioning which results from the contingency of a reinforcing stimulus upon a *stimulus* as of Type S and to that resulting from contingency upon a *response* as of Type R. The correlation of the reinforcing stimulus with a separate term is here achieved. The solution depends upon the recognition that in the unconditioned organism two kinds of behavior may be distinguished. There is, first, the kind of response which is made to specific stimulation, where the correlation between response and stimulus is a reflex in the traditional sense. I shall refer to such a reflex as a respondent. But there is also a kind of response which occurs spontaneously in the absence of any stimulation with which it may be specifically correlated. It does not mean that we cannot find a stimulus which will elicit such behavior but that none is operative at the time the behavior is observed. I shall call such a unit an operant. All conditioned reflexes of Type R are by definition operants and all of Type S, respondents.

Operant behavior cannot be treated with the technique devised for respondents. The magnitude of the response in an operant is not a measure of its strength. Some other measure must be derived, and from the definition of an operant it is easy to arrive at the rate of occurrence of the response. Elaborate and peculiar forms of response may be generated from undifferentiated operant behavior through successive approximation to a final form. With a similar method any value of a single property of the response may be obtained. That responses of smooth muscle or glandular tissues may or may not enter into Type R, I am not prepared to assert. It is a question for experiment.

Smith, K. Conditioning as an artifact. *Psychological Review,* 1954, *61,* 217–225.

The case for a pure reinforcement theory of learning has been strongly put and it is difficult now to escape the conviction that such a view is essentially correct. In spite of its fundamental strength, however, reinforcement theory has remained weak in one respect. It has experienced continual difficulty in handling the problems of autonomic, visceral learning. One variant of reinforcement theory that is designed to meet the situation more adequately is the so-called two factor theory. The first factor refers to the process of learning by a stimulus-substitution, contiguity principle; the second term, to that of learning by a principle of reinforcement. Such incisive dualism has an undesirable appeal. It suffers, however, from a disquieting lack of parsimony. As it happens, there exists a rather simple way to save reinforcement, and parsimony with it. One can begin by accepting the notion that somatic learning is reinforcemental learning and expunge conditioning from the viscera. This procedure leaves the law of effect to rule in monistic majesty. Of course, it also makes the autonomic nervous system totally uneducable; but that, it can be asserted, is as it should be. For it can be argued that every "conditioned visceral response" is in reality an artifact, an innate accompaniment of the skeletal responses inculcated by the conditioning process.

Spence, K.W. Cognitive versus stimulus-response theories of learning. *Psychological Review,* 1950, *57,* 159–172.

The cognition, or S-S, theorists emphasize that learning involves the formation and modification of cognitive patterns representative of the relationships in the environment. The S-R learning theorists refer to such things as stimulus-response connections, bonds, associations, habits or tendencies. What are the main points of disagreement between these two theoretical positions?

With regard to the neurophysiological models favored by the two opposing camps, there undoubtedly is a considerable difference but one that has little or no significance so far as learning theory is concerned. Cognitive theorists appear to be quite united in the view that learning involves association of sensory or perceptual processes. S-R theorists have tended to hold to the conception that the association is between the stimulus and response mechanism. I do not find it difficult to conceive of both types of organizations or associations being established in learning.

Most cognition theorists emphasize what may be termed the intrinsic properties of their theoretical constructs, whereas the S-R theorist has tended to emphasize the properties of his concepts that are determined by antecedent experimental variables. Cognition theorists have been much more interested in the conditions that determine the reception of the stimulus events and that influence perceptual organization. The S-R psychologists, on the other hand, have been most interested in the effect of various temporal factors and in the motivational-reward conditions underlying learning. Unlike the S-S theorist, the S-R psychologist does not usually talk very much about such things as perception, meaning, knowledge, cognitive processes, etc. He has not, however, completely neglected the problem, and his point of view is not the naive one that it is usually represented to be in the writings of the cognitive theorists.

Spence, K.W., & Lippitt, R. An experimental test of the sign-gestalt theory of trial-and-error. *Journal of Experimental Psychology,* **1946,** *36,* **491–502.**

The present investigation attempted to arrange an experimental test of Tolman's sign-gestalt (non-reinforcement) theory of trial-and-error learning. The *S*s, 20 white rats, were given 12 days of experience under thirst motivation in a simple Y-maze in which one path led to water and the other to an empty box for half of the *S*s (Group O) and food in the case of the other half (Group F). The experimental test consisted in observing the performance of the *S*s under hunger motivation. On the first trial under hunger motivation, all *S*s continued to go down the water alley. Furthermore, comparison of the two groups (O and F) in learning to go to the left alley for food showed no difference.

The results are interpreted as being in disagreement with the Tolman-Leeper theory and as supporting the stimulus-response reinforcement theory of trial-and-error learning. The difficulties encountered in the testing of the two theories are discussed at some length.

Spielberger, C.D. The role of awareness in verbal conditioning. In C.W. Eriksen (Ed.), *Behavior and awareness.* **Durham: Duke University Press, 1962. (Pp. 73–101.)**

The general goal of this paper was to examine the role of awareness in verbal conditioning. The concepts of learning and awareness as employed in investigations of verbal conditioning were analyzed and the results of four verbal-conditioning experiments were reported. In these studies, a sentence-construction task was employed as the conditioning procedure and "food" was the reinforcing stimulus. Awareness was inferred on the basis of subjects' responses to a detailed postconditioning interview conducted immediately following conditioning trials.

The results of the four experiments were interpreted as supporting the hypothesis that "what is learned" in verbal-conditioning experiments is awareness of a response-reinforcement contingency. The extent to which subjects acted upon what they had learned seemed to depend upon how much they wanted to receive the reinforcement. Interpretation of the results of the four studies within the framework of cognitive-learning theory appeared to be most useful for generating specific hypothesis which led to observations in the data of previously unreported relationships between performance on the conditioning task and different aspects of the subjects' awareness.

Tolman, E.C. Cognitive maps in rats and men. *Psychological Review,* **1948,** *55,* **189–208.**

All students agree as to the facts. They disagree, however, on theory and explanation. First there is a school of animal psychologists which believes that the maze behavior of rats is a matter of mere simple stimulus-response connections. We believe that in the course of learning something like a field map of the environment gets established in the rat's brain. And it is this tentative map, indicating routes and paths and environmental relationships, which finally determines what responses, if any, the animal will finally release. It is also important to discover in how far these maps are relatively narrow and strip-like or relatively broad and comprehensive. The differences between such strip maps and such comprehensive maps will appear only when the rat is later presented with some change within the given environment. Then, the narrower and more strip-like the original map, the less it will carry over successfully to the new problem.

Narrow strip maps rather than broad comprehensive maps seem to be induced: (1) by a damaged brain (2) by an inadequate array of environmentally presented cues, (3) by an overdose of repetitions on the original trained-on path, and (4) by the presence of too strongly motivational or of too strongly frustrating conditions.

Tolman, E.C., & Honzik, C.H. Introduction and removal of reward and maze performance in rats. *University of California Publications in Psychology,* **1930,** *4,* **257–275.**

1.   Rats run with food reward at the end of the maze showed, when reward

was removed, large increases in both time scores and error scores, which could not be accounted for by chance factors alone.

2. Rats run without reward, when reward was introduced, showed large decreases in both time scores and error scores, which also could not be accounted for by chance factors alone.

Tolman, E.C., Ritchie, B.F., & Kalish, D. Studies in spatial learning. II. Place versus response learning. *Journal of Experimental Psychology,* **1946,** *36,* **221–229.**

1. The results of a previously reported experiment suggested the hypothesis that what is learned in T-mazes, where choices must be made, is *not* a disposition to make certain responses (e.g., right turns) but rather is a disposition to orient towards the location of the goal.

2. The experiment reported in the present paper tests this hypothesis. Two groups of rats were trained on a single unit maze, in which the starting path led into the choice point sometimes from the east and sometimes from the west. The Response-Learning Group (N = 8) was required to learn to turn always right. The Place-Learning Group (N = 8) was required to learn to go always to the same place, half the time turning left and half the time turning right.

3. Only three rats in the Response-Learning Group reached the criterion (10 successive errorless runs) while the rest developed consistent habits of going always to the same place. All of the rats in the Place-Learning Group reached the criterion within eight trials or less.

4. We conclude that in situations where there are marked extra-maze cues, place-learning is simpler than response-learning.

EXAMINATION ITEMS   **Topics for thought and discussion**

1. Consider the way you would approach the question, "Where is learning?" and relate this to the questions, "What is learning?" and "What is learned?"

2. Compare and contrast the possible role(s) of awareness from a cognitive point of view and from a stimulus-response point of view.

3. Since all theorists must specify the conditions that are necessary for learning to occur, a definition of "reinforcement" as those necessary conditions would lead to the classification of all theories as "reinforcement theories." Why, then, the reinforcement-contiguity issue?

4. Critically evaluate the notion of "contiguity" and its implications for acquisition and extinction under various types of learning theories.

Objective items

1. The question "What is learned?" is a(n)

    a. empirical question
    b. operational question
    c. systematic question
    d. theoretical question

2.   The cognitive approach to the question, "What is learned?" can best generate behavioral predictions from which of the following assumptions?
    a. S-S-S
    b. S-S-R
    c. S-R-S
    d. R-S-S

3.   There are four logically possible combinations of the components of associations: S-S, S-R, R-S, R-R. Both behavioristic and cognitive approaches would accept all four possibilities.
    a. True
    b. False

4.   Skinner believes that the two types of (operationally defined) conditioned reflexes are
    a. fundamentally the same
    b. fundamentally different
    c. superficially the same
    d. superficially different

5.   The most basic assumption of a micromolar theory is that
    a. learning is either an S-S or an S-R association
    b. learned associations are permanent
    c. the quantitative properties of the response are learned
    d. the qualitative (topographical) properties of the response are learned

6.   Which of the following statements is least true?
    a. even a presumed micromolecular theory could be viewed as micromolar
    b. even a presumed macromolar theory could be viewed as micromolar
    c. the distinction between molar and molecular is continuous
    d. the distinction between macro and micro is discontinuous

7.   Restle showed that learning may be cognitive or S-R depending on the nature of the stimulation in the situation.
    a. True
    b. False

8.   A Kendler-type analysis of the "What is learned?" issue would not include the argument that hypothetical constructs are
    a. always response inferred
    b. often the objects of reification
    c. always shown to be unnecessary
    d. always considered useless

9.   Campbell's operational delineation of "What is learned?" via transposition would suggest that we can determine what you learned from reading the abstract of his article by
    a. an item on the question, "What is learned?"
    b. an item on operationalism

    c. an item on the meaning of transposition
    d. this item

10. Contemporary cognitive theory stressing awareness as necessary, at least for adult human behavior, implies that we would have no
    a. superstitions
    b. unconscious mannerisms
    c. self-control
    d. emotional problems

11. The sense of "contiguity" that would most likely be generally accepted as a necessary condition for learning is
    a. spatial contiguity of the events to be associated
    b. temporal contiguity of the events to be associated
    c. spatial contiguity of the associated events with reinforcement
    d. temporal contiguity of the associated events with reinforcement

12. One relationship that serves to distinguish reinforcement theories from pure reinforcement theories is the relationship between operant learning and the
    a. schedule of response contingent reinforcers
    b. density of noncontingent reinforcers
    c. magnitude of noncontingent reinforcers
    d. overall frequency of contingent and noncontingent reinforcers

13. That a pupillary response produced by shock seems to be conditionable, whereas a similar response produced by light does not, challenges contiguity theory.
    a. True
    b. False

14. Guthrie considered reinforcement to be necessary for the repeated performance of an instrumental response.
    a. True
    b. False

15. Dual-process learning theorists have not used a basic distinction between classes of
    a. stimuli
    b. responses
    c. drives
    d. learning paradigms

16. With respect to dual-process theories of learning, recognizing the existence of an "operant-classical" overlap suggests that
    a. dual-process theories are, in fact, uniprocess theories
    b. the classical process is an artifact of the operant process
    c. the operant process is an artifact of the classical process
    d. the overlap need not be of consequence for dual-process theory

17. By accepting the fact that reinforcement was always present to some small degree in the initial phases of latent learning experiments, Tolman somewhat compromised his position that the magnitude of reinforcement did not determine the strength of learned associations.
    a. True
    b. False

18. Hull's primary problem in interpreting the Tolman and Honzik latent learning experiment was that he believed
    a. reinforcement was necessary for learning
    b. learning required practice
    c. the amount learned was linked directly to the amount of reward
    d. learning was relatively permanent

19. In the classical conditioning situation, the conditioned response often differs qualitatively, as well as quantitatively, from the unconditioned response. For which type of theory is this fact most problematic?
    a. S-S contiguity
    b. S-R contiguity
    c. S-R reinforcement
    d. S-R pure reinforcement

20. In a developmental context, the reinforcement-contiguity issue would be especially interesting in the area of
    a. imitation
    b. maturation
    c. specialization
    d. inspiration

ANSWERS TO OBJECTIVE ITEMS

1. (d) The question only arises for a theorist who introduces a hypothetical learning construct. Empirical, operational, and systematic approaches may be used in attempts to answer the theoretical question.

2. (c) A cognitive theorist could accommodate any of the listed alternatives, and each can be related to behavior. The one that most simply generates behavioral predictions is the expectation that a response in the presence of a stimulus is followed by an emotionally–significant stimulus.

3. (True) Most difficult for the cognitive approach, would be S-R, but subjects should still learn about exteroceptive-proprioceptive S-S associations. Most difficult to the behaviorist approach would be S-S, but subjects should still learn components of the response to the second S. The answer is true, since the same logic can be applied to the two other possible associations (e.g., R-R associations to an S-S theorist become proprioceptive-proprioceptive associations).

4. (b) Skinner believes that respondent and operant conditioning are fundamentally different in the sense that they obey different laws. Theorists who treat them as the same are held to be in error or superficial, and Skinner contends that there is nothing superficial about their differences.

5. (c) A micromolar theorist need not be restricted to either S-S or S-R associations, nor need these necessarily be permanent. The critical point is that quantitative properties of a response are inevitably learned. Qualitative properties also may be learned, in the approach of molecular theorists.

6. (b) Recognizing that (c) is true, since behavior always could be described in even finer detail, also makes (a) true. Recognizing that quantitative properties cannot both be learned and a measure of strength makes (d) true and (b) false.

7. (False) Restle did not resolve the S-S versus S-R controversy. Instead, he argued convincingly that the place-versus-response learning issue was a poor arena in which

to wage battle because the outcome depends on the perspicuity of extramaze cues. Both types of theories can accommodate to such an analysis, S-S contending that extra-maze cues are necessary to orient the organism's cognitive map and S-R contending that more perspicuous stimulus elements gain greater control.

8. (d) An operationalist-positivist approach would agree with all of the listed criticisms of a reductive theory, except with respect to their usefulness. This latter factor is a characteristic of the user (theoretician) and not the theoretical constructs.

9. (d) In some sense, items of the first three types might be somewhat different from the actual content of the abstract, but would not be likely to delineate whether you learned that content or whether you learned to apply the reasoning in new situations. This item was intended to tap the latter.

10. (b) This item is a giveaway because we could obviously not have unconscious mannerisms of which we are aware. It was included to emphasize that the foils can be made to fit with cognitive theory. For example, a "superstitious" pigeon could be "aware" that stretching his neck is followed by reward, even though there is no actual dependency relationship.

11. (b) Spatial contiguity may have some relevance to a Gestalt theory of a stimulus complex, and there is some evidence that the spatial contiguity of the reinforcer with the response is important. However, primary concern has centered on temporal contiguity. Although immediate reward is superior to delayed reward, the temporal contiguity of S and S or S and R is the most critical and generally accepted necessity for the formation of associations.

12. (c) The primary distinction between a pure reinforcement theory and a reinforcement theory is that only in the former do the conditions of reinforcement determine, in part, the strength of a learned association. Otherwise, the two types of theories are quite in agreement that learning is a function of the number of reinforcements, regardless of whether this number is specified in terms of frequency, density, or schedule of reinforcements.

13. (True) It may be presumed that shock has motivational properties, whereas light does not. The difference thus could be attributed to some form of reinforcement. A contiguous occurrence of S and R should be sufficient for a pure contiguity theory, regardless of how the response is elicited.

14. (True) According to Guthrie, if reinforcement were not continued, new responses would be learned to replace the originally reinforced response.

15. (a) Skinner has proposed that respondent and operant responses obey different principles; Spence has suggested that appetitive and aversive drives obey different principles; and Mowrer has contended that classical and instrumental conditioning paradigms follow different principles. No one has (yet) considered different principles for different classes of stimuli (although there is some evidence that different modalities are differentially conditionable depending on the motivational conditions).

16. (d) The operant-respondent overlap has been used by proponents of uniprocess theories to support their position vis-à-vis dual-process theories. However, the overlap is one of experimental paradigms, not of theoretical constructs and, thus, it is of little consequence to a theoretical position regarding the formation of associations.

17. (False) It is false to assume that Tolman ever compromised on his position that reinforcement was not necessary, no matter what the amount, for learning to occur.

By admitting to the presence of reinforcement, Tolman helped to focus the latent learning experiments on the motivational versus the associative aspect of magnitude of reinforcement, as opposed to the necessity versus nonnecessity of reinforcement for learning.

18. (b) Hull believed in all four statements, but it was the belief that learning resulted from practice that made it difficult for him to account for the rapid decrease in errors, which occurred subsequent to the introduction of food reward. Had this occasioned a gradual decrease in errors, Hull would have had no difficulty in interpreting the data.

19. (b) S-S contiguity theory is not bounded by response characteristics, and reinforcement positions, pure or not, may lean on differential reinforcement as an explanatory device. S-R contiguity theory will, however, have difficulty explaining how different responses occur to a stimulus than those that initially were contiguous. All positions can rely on generalization principles.

20 (a) Imitation is an important activity of the developing child, for example, in learning to talk. The issue is important because it reflects on the necessity of reinforcement for learning to imitate other people in appropriate situations. The other alternatives have no particular bearing on the issue.

CHAPTER FOUR

IDENTIFYING EMOTIONALLY SIGNIFICANT EVENTS

Environmental events can be classified into those that have unlearned emotional significance to particular organisms and those that do not. Events having unlearned emotional significance can be further dichotomized into those with positive effects and those with negative effects. Presumably there exists a continuum of emotionality from positive through neutral to negative. Here, we are concerned with the momentary emotional value of an event that may be determined, in part, by setting operations or boundary conditions. The essential distinction between emotionally positive and emotionally negative events is the distinction between events that are pleasant or unpleasant, satisfying or annoying, desirable or undesirable, beneceptive or nociceptive, and reinforcing or punishing.

The identification of emotional events is accomplished functionally; that is, responses are reinforced by the onset of emotionally positive events and by the termination of emotionally negative events. Alternatively, responses are punished by the onset of emotionally negative events and by the termination of emotionally positive events. In short, emotional events are identified as events that function as such under the empirical law of effect.[1] Because of this and in order to avoid any possible implication about the internal processes that may be coincident with emotional events, we will refer to them simply as reinforcers and punishers.

EMPIRICAL LAW OF EFFECT

The most influential statement of the empirical law of effect was made by Thorndike in 1911. Although this statement was presented in a previous chapter, its importance can be best attested to by representing it here (bracketed phrases added):

Of several responses made to the same situation, those which are accompanied or closely followed by satisfaction [reinforcers] to the animal will, other things being equal, be more firmly connected with the situation, so that when it recurs, they will be more likely to recur; those which are accompanied or closely followed by discomfort [punishers] to the animal will, other things being equal, have their connections with that situation weakened, so that when it recurs, they will be less likely to occur.

Several points are worth noting about the law of effect as stated by Thorndike. First, despite his use of hedonic-type terms, such as satisfaction-dissatisfaction and comfort-discomfort, Thorndike intended a law of consequent effect and *not* one of affect. Indeed, Thorndike defined his terms simply in relation to the organism's behavior. For example, satisfaction represents a situation that the "animal does nothing to avoid, often doing such things as attain and preserve it." Similarly, annoyance is a situation that the animal commonly "avoids and abandons." Accordingly, the law of effect in this form is empirical and essentially states that when reinforcers are closely associated with responses, the likelihood that those responses will recur in the future is increased. The law of effect also states that when punishers are closely associated with responses, the likelihood that those responses will recur in the future is decreased. Without exception, systematists of learning and motivation have accepted some such statements of the empirical effects of reinforcers and punishers. The empirical law of effect has, in fact, received sufficient empirical verification and has been shown to possess sufficient generality to be elevated, without argument, to the status of a principle rather than a law in the senses of these terms intended here.

It is usually inferred that Thorndike had reference to events that produced their respective reinforcing and punishing effects when being *presented* to the organism. If so, then Thorndike expressed the principles of positive reinforcement and positive punishment. The converse principles that pertain to *removing* events from the organism, namely, the principles of negative reinforcement and negative punishment, are equally well accepted by empiricists and theorists. Furthermore, note that the presentation or removal of events under all of these principles is response contingent in the sense of being correlated with (shortly following) response occurrence, but not response dependent in the sense that the occurrence of the response necessarily produces the presentation or removal of the event.

The principles of reinforcement and punishment, as usually written, are deficient in at least two respects. First, there is typically a lack of specificity regarding the qualitative and quantitative aspects of the events. For example, little recognition is given to the fact that behavior depends importantly on the amount, delay, quality, and distribution of reinforcers and punishers. More complete statements of these empirical principles would include the specification that the future occurrence of responses depends on the conditions and schedules of reinforcers and punishers associated with those responses.

A second deficiency is that rarely, if ever, is there an explicit statement made regarding the setting operations or boundary conditions necessary for an event to serve as a reinforcer or punisher according to the principles of effect. The precedent for this was evidently established by Thorndike who originally had nothing more explicit to say, regarding setting operations, than "other things being equal." Thorndike did subsequently (1913, 1932) describe some factors that affect the satisfaction of an event, such as the neurological state of "readiness" and the "belongingness" of responses. However, he did not describe these factors in operational terms and, hence, they have no empirical utility. We now know, of course, that food is or is not a reinforcer as a function of the setting operation of food deprivation and that electric shock is or is not a punisher depending on the part of the organism's anatomy to which it is applied. In short, events serving in the capacity of reinforcers and punishers are always restricted in generality to some degree.

An early objection to the empirical law of effect, as stated by Thorndike, held that the law seems to imply that reinforcers and punishers act in a retroactive manner (Postman, 1947). That is, a reinforcer that follows a response is apparently required to work backward in time to strengthen the association between the stimulus and response that preceded the reinforcer. Various theorists have attempted to resolve the presumed problem of retroaction in a manner consistent with their theoretical proclivities. For example, Tolman (1932) indirectly dismissed the problem by asserting that the responses preceding reinforcement do not enter into associations (all associations being cognitive in nature) and, thus, no retroaction of reinforcers on preceding responses need be involved. More behaviorally minded theorists (e.g., Thorndike, 1913) are inclined to postulate neurophysiological type constructs that have the effect of prolonging the representation of the S-R association in the organism so that the occurrence of the reinforcer is simultaneous with the association it is to strengthen. Probably the most theoretically useful construct of this type has been Hull's (1943) molar afferent trace. Briefly, the reception of a stimulus by an organism sets up an afferent trace of that stimulus in the organism that decreases as a function of time. If the reinforcer is not delayed too long following the response, the reinforcer and stimulus trace occur simultaneously.

Actually, the apparently retroactive nature of reinforcers and punishers is only a problem for those who are concerned with the theoretical nature of learned associations. Empiricists dismiss the logical problem of retroaction by pointing out that, operationally, the effects of reinforcers and punishers are always assessed on behavior that follows. As this argument states, it is not the preceding response as a particular instance that is changed but, instead, the future probability of responses in the same class as the preceding response (Skinner, 1953). So stated, the action of reinforcers is conceptualized as proactive.

To summarize, the empirical law of effect or, better still, the empirical principles of effect (principles of positive reinforcement, positive punishment, negative reinforcement, and negative punishment) are stated functionally, that is, in terms of behavior changes. Reinforcement involves the occurrence of a reinforcer following a response, and a reinforcer is an event the presentation or removal of which increases the future probability of the response it follows. Punishment involves the occurrence of a punisher following a response, and a punisher is an event the presentation or removal of which decreases the future probability of the response it follows. In both instances, the critical element is the change in future response probability rather than the dependency relationship between the response and the reinforcer or punisher. However, setting operations and boundary conditions need to be specified along with parametric values for the conditions and schedules of the events in order to define the limits of generality around the proactive changes in response probability.

Now if reinforcers and punishers are *defined* functionally, in terms of their effects on behavior, we must decide the issue of how to *identify* which events are reinforcers and which are punishers. There have been a variety of empirical and theoretical approaches to this. One approach has been to identify, as well as to define, reinforcers and punishers functionally.

EMPIRICAL IDENTIFICATION OF REINFORCING AND PUNISHING EVENTS

Functional Approach

The essence of the functional approach to identifying reinforcers and punishers is to identify these events in terms of their effects on behavior within the principles of effect. For example, a reinforcer is identified as an event that functions as a reinforcer according to the principles of (positive or negative) reinforcement. If a reinforcer is defined as increasing the probability of the future occurrence of a response it follows, then any event that increases the future occurrence of a response it follows is identified as a reinforcer. Similarly, a punisher is identified as an event that functions as a punisher according to the principles of (positive or negative) punishment. If a punisher is defined as decreasing the probability of the future occurrence of a response it follows, then any event that decreases the future occurrence of a response it follows is identified as a punisher. Thus, reinforcers and punishers are inextricably linked to changes in behavior, specifically those changes in behavior specified by the principles of effect.

Since in the functional approach it is not possible separately to identify reinforcers and punishers without testing to see what effects the events produce on behavior, the functional approach contains an inherent circularity. This circularity is of no major consequence to the empirical systematist who is inclined to identify events at a descriptive level. After all, behavioral changes that serve as the criteria for identification are both objective and empirical. And, indeed, the functional approach has exhibited great efficacy in identifying new and often unexpected reinforcers and punishers as is attested to by many of the abstracts included for this chapter. However, the functional approach is not devoid of limitations and shortcomings.

One type of limitation is technically empirical and concerns the interpretation of what is meant by changes in behavior. Take as an example an instance in which an operant response increases in frequency up to a reasonably high and stable level when followed by food. Functionally, food in this situation is identified as a reinforcer. Now water is substituted for food, and let us assume, for the sake of issue, that no change, increase, or decrease occurs in the frequency of the operant response. Functionally, is the water a reinforcer in this situation? Alternatively, the original amount of food can be replaced by a smaller amount of food. This time, let us assume that the frequency of the operant response *decreases* somewhat under the smaller amount of food, but not so much to return to the frequency that pertained prior to the delivery of any food. Functionally, is the smaller amount of food a punisher in this situation? Before dealing with these questions one other example (of many empirically possible) will be given to add to the flavor of the problem.

Take for this example the experimental situation in which a mild electric shock is made to occur shortly following every occurrence of an established response. Assume the introduction of shock produces a decrease in response frequency and, thus, the shock is functionally identified as a punisher. Empirically, it is now reasonably well established that if the shock condition is maintained, responding will increase in frequency (Azrin & Holz, 1966). At least, it would seem that response recovery in the presence of the shock nullifies the functional identification of the shock as a punisher, but has the shock now become a reinforcer functionally?

What these questions suggest is that the functional approach to identifying reinforcers and punishers is deceptively complex, even for the empirical systematist. Boundary conditions need to be specified; changes in behavior, relative to what ongoing behaviors, need to be defined. Setting operations need to be elaborated, and parameters of the events need to be stated: food given a history of a larger amount of food or shock given a history of prior shock. Clearly, the functional approach is not as neatly related to changes in behavior as it seems to be on first reading. Limitations on the nature of behavioral changes abound for any particular situation. A means of identifying reinforcers and punishers independent of the empirical principles of effect might be helpful in this regard, although such an approach would be unacceptable to strict empirical functionalists (Skinner, 1953).

Transsituational and Transprocedural Approaches

The circularity in functionally identifying reinforcers and punishers is evident, because this approach does not allow such events to be identified independently of the principles of effect. Although this circularity is not necessarily problematic at the empirical level, it does represent a logical flaw in the identification of reinforcers. The two empirical approaches that have attempted to attenuate this problem, the transsituational approach and the transprocedural approach, are fundamentally functional in nature, but they share the characteristic of being, to some degree, removed from the principles of effect.

The transsituational approach (cf. Meehl, 1950) predicts that a functionally identified reinforcer will serve as such for other behaviors in other situations. In essence, this approach states that although the initial functional identification of a reinforcer or punisher is dependent on the principles of effect (and hence, circular), the prediction that the event is transsituational is independent of these principles (noncircular). Now if reinforcers and punishers are further defined absolutely as transsituational, such that only events which function as reinforcers and punishers across all situations are reinforcers and punishers, then it may be asserted that any logical circularity is broken whenever the prediction of transsituationality is confirmed.

Nevertheless, it must be recognized that the *identification* (not the definition) of transsituational reinforcers and punishers is still a functional matter because such events are still identified as ones that function as such in the principles of effect. At best, this approach yields a catalogue of empirically identified transsituational reinforcers and punishers. Such a catalogue is of value in the control of behavior, but the absolute definition of reinforcers as transsituational requires that the catalogue contain provisions for making changes (both additions and, importantly, deletions) as dictated by future empirical evidence. And yet there is the problem of what to do with those that have been deleted.

The transprocedural approach (cf. Keller & Schoenfeld, 1950) is similar to the transsituational approach but identifies reinforcers and punishers functionally under one procedure (circular), and then predicts that the event will have the same function under some different procedure (noncircular). The transprocedural approach was anticipated by Thorndike (1911) when he suggested that reinforcers (satisfiers) were events that organisms do not avoid; functionally identify an event that organisms do nothing to avoid, and then predict that this event will be a reinforcer when it is made shortly to follow a response.

Although applicable to both reinforcers and punishers, the transprocedural approach has more often been used to identify punishers. Let's take as an instance the identification of a positive punisher. Under a strictly functional approach, a positive punisher is identified as an event that functions as such in the principle of positive punishment so that its presentation decreases the probability of a response it follows. Under a transprocedural approach, a positive punisher might be identified as an event the removal of which increases the probability of a response it follows. That is, a positive punisher would be identified as an event that supports learning in an escape (negative reinforcement) procedure. Alternatively, a positive punisher might be identified by using a simultaneous choice procedure. Given the alternatives of choosing either an event or nothing, a positive punisher would be identified by the choice of nothing. In either case, once a positive punisher has been procedurally identified, the prediction is then made that this event will decrease the probability of a response it follows in a punishment procedure.

Although this empirical approach to identifying reinforcers and punishers is attractive, it shares the limitations of any basically functional approach. Parameters limitations and setting-operation restrictions apply. For example, while two different intensities of electric shock may support escape learning, only the higher intensity shock may suppress behavior in a punishment procedure. Consider as well that organisms may choose nothing over electric shock in the simultaneous choice situation, but they also may choose nothing over food in this situation when satiated. This latter outcome would identify food as a positive punisher, perhaps an embarrassing outcome unless setting operations are specified.

In spite of the restrictions that apply to basically functional approaches that identify reinforcers and punishers, these approaches provide for an appealing amount of generality and utility in relation to more limited systematic conceptualizations. For example, Sheffield and Roby (1950) proposed that the elicitation and performance of consummatory responses serve to identify reinforcers. The identification of a reinforcer as a consummatory response has the advantage of being independent of the principles of effect, but it lacks generality with respect to punishers, in general, and to reinforcers that do not apparently involve a consummatory response. Identifying punishers as events that are painful, nociceptive, or fear producing, as done by other systematists (e.g., Mowrer, 1939), again has the advantage of being independent of the principles of effect. However, this latter approach is of minimum utility, since it is regressive; it creates the new problem of identifying what events are painful, nociceptive, or fear producing.

Relational Response Approach   Thus far, a characteristic shared by all the approaches discussed is that reinforcers and punishers are always identified absolutely. Events are identified dichotomously as being reinforcers or not or as being punishers or not. This characteristic results primarily because the empirical principles of effect are stated in absolute terms.

An alternative set of empirical effect principles has been stated in relational, rather than absolute, terms by Premack (1959). The primary assertion states that any response (or any stimulus governing the response) can affect any other response depending on the relative probabilities of the responses. Any response (R_1) will reinforce any other response (R_2) provided that the independent probability of R_1 is greater than that of R_2. Any response (R_1) will punish any other response (R_2) provided that the independent probability of R_1 is less than that of R_2. Since at any point in time a given response will reinforce (punish) some responses but not others, events are relational and not trans-situational or transprocedural. An event identified as a reinforcer or punisher in one situation need not function as such for any other response in any other situation.

This raises the issue of how to measure relative probability of response. Premack has suggested that independent rates of responses be obtained in free-response situations, while others have proposed that some preferential method of choice be used to index response probabilities. The matter of methodology is important in the likely case that different measures yield different rankings. It should also be recognized that two responses have to be observed in order to determine which one will reinforce the other and, symmetrically, which one will punish the other. And even then, no generality can be asserted regarding either response vis-à-vis still another response until their relative probabilities are observed.[2] Even though events are not categorized absolutely as being reinforcers or punishers, their status remains to be determined according to relational principles of effect. This is most conspicuously true of responses whose probabilities have been changed by prior experiences. No truly independent identification of reinforcement seems possible under any of these functional empirical approaches.

Summary   We consider the circularity of the law of effect as inescapable and simply inherent in a science of behavior. Viewed as an interrelated set of empirical principles, reinforcement and punishment have the status of hypothetical concepts. In the nature of the case, we can never be certain about the truth of even a law, much less a highly abstract principle. The task of the empiricist is to refine the formulation of these principles in order to specify the conditions under which they appear to hold. And there is no recourse but to a functional approach.

The functional approach asserts that there are two important classes of events that alter the probability of occurrence of a response. Reinforcers lead to high probabilities, punishers to low probabilities, and some events are fundamentally neutral in this regard. The goal is to categorize events into these classes in the most parsimonious, abstract way possible at any moment in time. Although straightforward in conception, that goal is still illusive. With the possible exception of unnatural events, such as electrical stimulation of the brain, it is not the case that we can isolate an event and declare once and for all and forever that that is definitely a reinforcer or a punisher.

Both the transsituational and transprocedural approaches are based on such a premise and are doomed to failure. At the same time, when adorned with detailed specifications of the setting operations and the particular conditions of the events, these approaches do enjoy a very substantial measure of success. However, we have seen that the reinforcing or punishing properties of events may be transitory, perhaps related to satiation or habituation. We have also seen that the properties of one event must be considered relative to those of other events. These issues reveal some of the complexities involved in attempting to formulate abstract empirical principles.

Accordingly, the empiricist may take either or both of two paths for research. One is to settle upon several well-established reinforcers and punishers about which the setting operations and boundary conditions are known and systematically study the additional principles involved in the various schedules and conditions of these events. The other is to attempt to do research aimed at sharpening the statements of the most abstract principles themselves. In either case, circularity may be a cross to bear, but it is not a major detriment to the pure empiricist. As we will see, this is not true of the theorist.

THEORETICAL IDENTIFICATION OF REINFORCING AND PUNISHING EVENTS

A theoretical identification of reinforcers and punishers not only implies that these events are identified apart from the empirical principles of effect, but also that the hypothetical mechanism(s) underlying the actions of reinforcers and punishers are specified. Theoretical identification attempts to answer the question of *why* certain events function as they do according to the principles of effect. Indeed, we are now talking about the *postulates* of reinforcement and punishment and may, in the case of many theories, refer to hypothetical affect as well as empirical effect. Of course, the answer to the question of why is given in terms of hypothetical constructs. An early example of a theoretical approach is Thorndike (1913). He identified satisfaction as conduction along a neuron that is in a hypothetical state of readiness. Thus, satisfiers are linked directly to the hypothetical construct readiness. It follows that annoyers are identified as conduction along neurons that never exist in a state of readiness.

Those theorists who adhere to a strictly contiguity approach to learning have done little by way of attempting to identify reinforcers and punishers theoretically. For example, Tolman (1932) accepted the empirical principles of effect and theoretically equated reinforcers and punishers with confirmations and disconfirmations. However, Tolman never separately identified the hypothetical mechanism underlying the process of confirmation. Furthermore, theorists who accept the necessity of reinforcement for only some forms of learning tend to be entirely content with a strictly empirical approach to identifying reinforcers and punishers (e.g., Spence, 1956). It also seems that more theoretical energy has been expended on identifying reinforcing events than on identifying punishing events. Indeed, punishing events have a somewhat meager theoretical heritage as compared to reinforcing events. For this reason, the remainder of the immediate discussion will emphasize the theoretical identification of reinforcing events that function in the postulate of positive reinforcement.

Biological Need Approach

This approach is generally characterized by identifying reinforcers in terms of physiological tensions, homeostasis, or biological survival needs. Basically, the mechanism of positive reinforcement is a reduction in a tension or need state that is of biological significance to the organism. The most systematic and influential identification of reinforcers under this approach is that elaborated by Hull (1943). Essentially, Hull proposed that reinforcers be identified absolutely as need reductions. A strong form of this postulate is that *all reinforcers entail need reduction.*

For Hull, bodily needs arise from deficiencies of substances necessary for the survival of the organism or from excesses of substances inimical to survival. Needs are anchored on the antecedent side to deprivation operations or to the presentation of events that produce tissue injury to the organism. Such bodily needs serve as the conditions for the establishment of the hypothetical motivational constructs of primary drive (D) and its consequent drive stimuli (S_D). Indeed, primary drives and drive stimuli are uniquely associated with need states so that whether a reinforcer is identified as a reduction in need, as a reduction in drive, or as a reduction in drive stimuli, it is of no major consequence to the need-reduction approach to identifying reinforcers. Increases in drives serve to instigate behavior and reductions in drives serve to reinforce behavior that they follow. But in order to reduce a drive, a reduction in the need, which gives rise to the drive, is necessary.

The strong form of the need-reduction approach to identifying reinforcers, specifically that all reinforcers involve need reduction, has some empirical support. However, it also runs afoul of a sufficient amount of contrary empirical evidence to compromise its theoretical utility. For example, although it can be shown that food injected directly into the stomach (a need reduction) is a reinforcer, food ingested normally is a more effective reinforcer (e.g., Miller & Kessen, 1952). Apparently, taste stimulation or other concomitants of the normal ingestion process also are reinforcers even though they are not interpretable as need reductions. Still other experiments show that the ingestion of nonnutritive substances (Sheffield & Roby, 1950), the onset of external stimuli (Kish, 1955), electrical stimulation to the brain (Olds & Milner, 1954), and manipulation of puzzles (Harlow, Harlow, & Meyer, 1950), serve as reinforcers. Once again these reinforcers are not readily interpretable as involving need reductions. Obviously, a complete reliance on need reduction as the identifying characteristic of reinforcers falls short of its intended objective. Although need reductions seem to function satisfactorily as reinforcers, not all reinforcers seem to involve need reduction. To identify all reinforcers theoretically, something else in addition to need reduction is apparently necessary. One very successful approach in this regard is the drive-reduction approach.

The Nature and Conditions of Drive Motivation

Before directly discussing the drive-reduction approach to identifying reinforcers, it behooves us briefly to describe the nature and conditions of drive motivation in the context of theoretical analyses of behavior. Beyond the possible role that motivation may play theoretically in the identification of reinforcers and punishers, drive motivation is usually assigned the theoretical task of energizing and/or directing behavior.[3] More generally, drive motivation is most often considered to be nonassociative, nonsituational, relatively temporary, and easily modified. We have already discussed the difficulties and corresponding inappropriateness of characterizing either the constructs of motivation or learning in such general terms (cf. Chapter 1). Consequently, only specific theoretical elaborations of primary drive-motivation constructs will be considered here. Primary drive motivation is that unlearned motivation that develops from deprivation operations or the occurrence of external stimuli. Secondary drive motivation, based on learning, will be considered in a subsequent section of this chapter. Incentive motivation, based on reinforcement, will be considered in the following chapter.

Since a portion of Hull's drive construct has already been introduced, it will be convenient to elaborate first on this conceptualization of drive motivation. Briefly in review, deprivation establishes a biological need in the organism that in turn gives rise to a hypothetical drive and its associated drive stimuli.[4] Drives and drive stimuli are persistent and activate responses. However, the responses activated are not necessarily specific to the need that give rise to the drive. According to Hull, a specific drive, no matter what its origin, contributes to a generalized drive state, and it is this latter generalized drive that evokes activity and energizes whatever habits are associated to the situation. Although drive energizes habits into performance, it is assumed that the acquisition of habit is independent of this energizing property of drive. In other words, *what* the organism learns does not depend on its drive motivation during learning.

At this point in the narrative of Hull's drive construct, two potential theoretical issues have been uncovered regarding drive motivation. The first is the issue of how many drives there are. Is there a drive for each deprivation operation or is there, as Hull assumed, only one generalized drive? The second issue involves the relationship of drive and habit. Does what is learned depend on the drive motivation at the time of learning or is learning independent of drive as Hull assumed?

As is the case with any theoretical issue, empirical evidence can be brought to bear on the present issues in the hopes of resolving them. In the instance of Hull's generalized drive construct, two experimental paradigms have been used. Both paradigms are predicated on the notion that if there is only one final generalized drive (D), which activates behavior, then all sources of D should be interchangeable in terms of their contribution to D. A habit learned under one source of drive should be energized by any other source of drive, even if this other source was irrelevant at the time of learning. Sources of drive should be mutually substitutable. Furthermore, all sources of drive should summate indiscriminately so that increasing one source of drive is equivalent to summing two or more different sources of drive. Both drive substitution experiments in which one source of drive is substituted for another (e.g., Brandauer, 1953; McFarland, 1964; Webb, 1949) and drive summation experiments in which an irrelevant source of drive is added to a relevant source (Danziger, 1953; Kendler, 1945; Levine, 1956) have been run. Yet, neither experimental paradigm has yielded data consistent enough to make a convincing argument that there is a single generalized drive or multiple specific drives. Either approach is somewhat uncomfortable with the data, but methodological problems abound. Consider the difficulties involved in determining whether hunger can be substituted for thirst, or vice versa, given that hunger and thirst cannot normally be independently manipulated.

Turning to the issue of the independence of drive motivation and habit, there are also two experimental paradigms that can be brought to bear. Organisms can be required to learn under different intensities of drive (Barry, 1958; Perin, 1942; Ramond, 1954). If no differences in the rates of learning occur, then the independence of habit from drive is supported. Alternatively, organisms can be required to learn under one drive level and then experience a shift in drive level (Finan, 1940; Kendler, 1945; Theios, 1963). If behavior attunes completely (and, ideally, immediately) to the shift in drive level, showing no residual influence of the original drive level, then no dependence of habit on drive is evidenced. Some measure of empirical support for the independence assumption can be gained from these experimental paradigms.[5] Nevertheless, the empirical data remain equivocal, since the outcomes depend on, among other things, the response measures used.

The reader has probably already anticipated that the theoretical issues, regarding the generality and independence of drive, are not likely to be resolved by experiment. The position adopted by the theorist, regarding the nature of drive motivation, is as much determined by the requirements of other constructs in the theory as it is by empirical evidence that is presumed to apply. This point can be emphasized by a brief description of Tolman's (1932) initial treatment of the nature of drive motivation within his cognitive theory.

Tolman accepted that deprivation operations and external stimuli give rise to biological needs in the organism and that these needs give rise to drives. Now at this point it is difficult for Tolman to argue that drive directly activates habits and remain true to his S-S cognitive approach to learning. Instead, Tolman proposed that drives arouse demands for goal objects and that organisms behave in a manner consistent with their demands. Thus, drive cannot be general, nor can sources of drive be intersubstitutable.[6] Drives must be specific to the need states that give rise to them in order that the organism can behave in a manner that is consistent with the demand for a specific goal object, which the drive produces.

Postulating specific drives implies that there will be a multiplicity of drives and this, in turn, requires that some ground rules be specified for invoking drives. Otherwise, there is no constraint, other than the dictum of parsimony, to prevent a new drive from being invoked in order to explain any behavioral occurrence. Such unconstrained explanations are as vacuous as early instinct theory. On the other hand, if specific drives are appropriately anchored on the antecedent and consequent sides,[7] specific drives may be used to explain the empirical fact that behavior quite often is appropriate to the source of drive (or is directed or purposeful). This advantage is a natural by-product of postulating specific drives.

Tolman also differs from Hull with respect to the dependence of learning on drive motivation. Drive motivation determines the broadness of the cognitive map acquired. The more intense the drive, the narrower or more striplike is the map. The mechanism for this dependency of learning on drive motivation is that of emphasis. Drive motivation emphasizes certain features of the environment and, thus, limits the features to which the organism pays attention. In other words, drive partially determines which cognitions are perceived and, hence, which are learned. Again, as expected, Tolman's position on drive motivation is affected by the other constructs of his theory. If organisms behave in a manner that is consistent with their acquired cognitions, and if behavior is more energetic and seemingly directed when motivated, then drive must contribute to the determination of cognitions. Thus, we can reaffirm that the theoretical issue of whether drive and learning are dependent or independent cannot be resolved by any amount of experimental evidence directed at the issue per se. A theoretical resolution is the only potential type of solution to be realistically considered.

It is appropriate now to consider the issue of whether it is in the nature of drive motivation to be directive as well as arousing. Clearly, generalized drive, itself, cannot be directive in Hull's theoretical system or, for that matter, in any theory that ascribes to a unitary drive. Nevertheless, empirically, behavior is often appropriate to a specific source of drive. Some theoretical construct must be imbued with the property of directiveness in order to account for the apparent purposefulness of behavior. As the next chapter reveals, this theoretical construct has quite often been an incentive-motivation construct rather than a drive-motivation construct. However, in Hull's theory drives give rise to specific drive stimuli. Accordingly, drive stimuli are available to enter into habit associations with responses appropriate to specific sources of drive. The establishment of a drive will then give rise to drive stimuli to which specific responses have been learned. To complete the picture, drive also will contribute to generalized drive that energizes the habit based on drive stimuli. In short, specific behaviors occur in the presence of specific drive stimuli, if the learned habits are energized by generalized drive.

Hull is not the only theorist to conceptualize drive in terms of stimuli. Quite notably, Miller (e.g., 1959; Miller & Dollard, 1941) completely relies on the stimulus properties of drive. For Miller, all stimuli have drive properties. The amount of drive possessed by a stimulus is directly related to the intensity of the stimulus. Importantly, because any stimulus can activate behavior, particularly if it is made strong, the source of the stimulus, external or internal, is of no particular consequence.[8] Obviously, since drive is so intimately equated with stimuli for Miller, drives possess distinctiveness or cue value and can enter as the antecedent condition in habit associations.

Miller does not embrace a generalized drive notion. Drives retain their cue distinctiveness in all situations. But this position creates a problem for the theoretician who maintains it. Some explanation needs to be given for the types of data that support the generalized drive construct; for example, there is empirical evidence that exhibits some degree of drive intersubstitutability. Miller's approach to this problem is to postulate drive (stimulus) generalization. Drives substitute for other drives to the extent that there is stimulus generalization between them.[9]

Miller's conceptualization of drive as intense stimulation accredited drives with the property of being noxious or aversive. A one-time professor of Miller's, Guthrie, also ascribed to a stimulus interpretation of drives. However, for Guthrie, drives are more associative than motivational.

Within Guthrie's systematic approach (e.g., 1940), drives are persistent stimuli that activate or excite the individual to respond; the drives are maintained until an act is executed that eliminates the maintaining stimuli. These maintaining drive stimuli are associated with the response that removes the stimuli, since this response enters into the last association formed in the presence of the stimuli. Motivation-specific behavior is associative. The recurrence of drive stimuli will evoke the act that previously removed the drive stimuli. Thus, the nature of drive motivation, per se, is not theoretically important in Guthrie's system. There is little concern with either the generality or the independence of drive motivation. What is important is what drives make the organism do (since what the organism does is what the organism learns) and, particularly, what drives make the organism do last (since what the organism does last is what the organism will do on the next occasion when the maintaining stimuli are present). Although Guthrie eschewed any theoretical attempts to identify reinforcers and punishers, his conception of maintaining stimuli and the consequences of their reduction or elimination are closely aligned with the drive-reduction approach to identifying reinforcing and punishing events.

Drive-Reduction Approach

The strong form of the biological need-reduction approach to identifying reinforcers is clearly wanting, because several reinforcers have been identified that do not involve need reduction. The drive-reduction approach to identifying reinforcers is closely allied with the biological need approach, but differs in one very essential way. As explicated by Hull (1951), all reinforcers are identified as drive-stimulus reductions. In the earlier biological need formulation, need reduction is accompanied by drive-stimulus reduction, since need and drive stimuli are perfectly correlated. In the drive-stimulus reduction approach, need reduction is still accompanied by drive-stimulus reduction but, and here is the key, *drive-stimulus reduction also may occur without need reduction.*

An important distinction is then made between biological need reduction and psychological drive-stimulus reduction. By identifying reinforcers as reductions in psychological drive stimuli, reinforcers may be identified that are not need reducing. Whereas the finding that food ingested normally is a more effective reinforcer than food injected directly into the stomach (Miller & Kessen, 1952) is a problem for a need-reduction approach, it is quite consistent with a drive-stimulus reduction approach. Obviously, appetitional factors surrounding the oral ingestion of food can be assumed to be drive-stimulus reducing.

More generally for Hull, reinforcement is identified as the occurrence of an event that reduces the drive stimuli occasioned by its absence or the removal of an event that reduces the drive stimuli occasioned by its presence. But no matter whether the reinforcement is positive or negative, all reinforcers involve drive-stimulus reduction.

Several of the theorists we discussed when elaborating on the nature of drive motivation either explicitly embraced a strong drive-stimulus reduction approach to identifying reinforcers or may be interpreted as implicitly doing so. We may place Miller in the former category, since reinforcement for him consists of drive-stimulus intensity reduction. In the category of implicit drive-reduction theorists, we may place Guthrie and, possibly, Tolman (although neither of these theorists would have been particularly pleased with being so categorized). In the instance of Tolman, reinforcers serve to satisfy demands aroused by drives. In the instance of Guthrie, reinforcers serve to remove maintaining stimuli that conceptually represent drives.

Although the drive-stimulus reduction approach has had its proponents (both real and imagined), it also has had its opponents who have come forth to challenge both the generality and utility of the approach. The most effective means of challenging the strong position that all reinforcers involve drive-stimulus reductions is functionally to identify reinforcers that do not involve any apparent drive-stimulus reduction. Historically, many such challenges have failed to distinguish between a need reduction and a drive-stimulus reduction identification of reinforcers and have consequently and exclusively attacked the former (e.g., Kish, 1955; Sheffield & Roby, 1950; Sheffield, Wulff, & Backer, 1951; Whalen, 1961). As one specific example, Kish (1955) functionally identified the onset of illumination as a reinforcer and correctly concluded that this functional identification poses a challenge to a theoretical need-reduction identification of reinforcers. The important point here, however, is that it does not necessarily pose a challenge to a theoretical drive-stimulus reduction identification of reinforcers.

Actually, the importance of the distinction made above is somewhat moot for a drive-stimulus reduction identification of reinforcers. If a reinforcer is identified functionally in the absence of a need, and if drive stimuli result directly from needs, then a reinforcer has also been identified, *pari passu,* in the absence of any possible drive-stimulus reduction. The appropriate conclusion is then that not all reinforcers involve drive-stimulus reductions. The drive-stimulus approach of Miller is less challenged by empirical demonstrations of this type, since it is not rigorously tied to biological need. For example, one of Miller's persuasion could argue in the case of the Kish (1955) experiment described above that rats experience intense fear stimulation when in the dark. The onset of illumination (although it constitutes an increase in stimulation) reduces the intense fear stimuli and, thereby, is reinforcing. Nevertheless, for any functionally identified reinforcer, whether it be as obvious as food or as intuitively remote as electric shock to the septum (Olds & Milner, 1954), there must be specified a corresponding theoretical reduction in drive stimuli if the strong form of this approach is to prevail. The burden of proof rests continuously on the shoulders of the sympathetic theorist.

Drive-stimulus reduction theorists have been remarkably facile in postulating sources of drive stimuli. Demonstrations that organisms will learn a response in order to get into a situation where they can explore (Montgomery, 1954) or learn to manipulate puzzles in the absence of obvious reinforcers (Harlow, Harlow, & Meyer, 1950) or solve discrimination problems in order to view the extra-cage environment (Butler, 1953), functionally identify the existence of reinforcers in these situations. But these, in turn, require drive-stimulus reductions and, therefore, the existence of drives. In the present instances, the requirement for drives is satisfied by postulating an exploratory drive or a manipulation drive that can be reduced, respectively, by exploration and manipulation. A corollary of postulating these drives is that some drives can be externally elicited. But this consideration raises the issue of how *drives* should be identified.

Obviously, if the drive-stimulus reduction approach to identifying reinforcers is to have any substance, there must be some criteria specified for the identification of drives. Otherwise, the theoretical position is beyond challenge, and the unrestrained creation of drives in order to satisfy a limited situation becomes an exercise in futility. Drive is a theoretical (hypothetical) construct requiring appropriate anchoring. In order for the postulation of a new drive to be useful, it must be accompanied by a specification of drive that establishes operations and of the relationship that pertains between the establishing operations and the drive. For example, in identifying a drive it should be shown that the drive is functionally related to deprivation operations, that it can be satiated, and that its reduction is reinforcing. Typically, considerations of drive satiations have been ignored, and the functional relationship to deprivation operations have been assumed when not otherwise empirically demonstrated. Consequently, the hallmark of postulating new drives is that their reduction is reinforcing.

Among the more compelling of the hypothesized drives that result from this line of reasoning is curiosity (e.g., Berlyne, 1960). This is not an unreasonable proposition for humans as well as cats; perhaps, there is merit in postulating some generic type of additional drive motivation that leads to exploratory behavior, manipulating objects, looking around, seeking some degree of novelty, or generally just being curious about the world in which we live. Recognizing the dangers of proliferation with respect to the postulation of drives, many theorists have been reluctant fully to embrace such notions. Their reticence also can be attributed to the fact that these developments do not settle neatly into the type of conceptualization of drive motivation, which was earlier described. The underlying characteristic of those views is that all drive stimuli are fundamentally aversive—they are states from which organisms seek relief. We work for food in order to relieve the uncomfortable feeling of being hungry. Much of the rebellion against this classic view is that it appears to paint a very dreary picture of life in which survival is so paramount as completely to overshadow any positive virtues of existence. Whether the anchoring operations that involve deprivation and satiation effects are necessary or whether some different approach will prove to be necessary, remains to be determined. In any event, there clearly are reinforcing states of affairs that do not follow directly from a classical drive-stimulus reduction point of view.

Summary   To the theorist, the empirical principles of reinforcement become theoretical postulates of reinforcement, and the problem of identifying reinforcers becomes one of "explaining" why certain events have their observable effects on behavior. The inherent circularity at the empirical level is not so easily shrugged off by the theorist, because reinforcing states of affairs have to be ones that fit conceptually within the theoretical approach. The theorist assumes that there has to be a reason.

To a cognitive theorist, what better reason could there be than confirmation or disconfirmation of one's expectancies. And to a behavioristic theorist, what better reason could there be than reduction of recurrent needs. In either case, these are the things adaptive organisms ought to learn and perform when appropriate. In the case of the cognitive approach there is little to challenge, but the behavioristic approach can be relentlessly assaulted.

The reaction has been to retreat into a weak form of the need-reduction hypothesis in which need reductions are reinforcing but not all reinforcers necessarily reduce needs. This leads to postulating drive motivation that is based primarily on needs but with more degrees of freedom. Specifically, a reduction in drive stimuli is assumed even though neither the need nor the concomitant drive is reduced. But as serviceable as this latter approach has been, it too appears destined to retreat still further. In is weak form, need reductions are certainly reinforcing, and so are drive-stimulus reductions, but there are still other reinforcing states of affairs that cannot be readily accomodated. It appears that the essence of reinforcement, as a construct, has not yet been captured and remains a theoretical enigma.

THE BEHAVIORISTIC-COGNITIVE ISSUE

Although we have yet many more theoretical issues to encounter, this appears to be a good point both to review the basic controversies and to organize them for future reference into the behavioristic-cognitive issue. To these ends, we will orient the discussion around the theories of Hull (1943) and Tolman (1932), but we will deliberately characterize them with extreme interpretations of their positions. The reader must recognize that neither theorist actually adhered rigidly to these extremes, but our intent is to magnify the differences in order to draw into sharp focus the nature of the larger issue. The component issues are listed in Table 4.1; let us briefly review each of them.

The first of these issues is essentially a matter of pretheoretic conceptions. It encompasses the basic orientation of the theory, its style, its character, and its fundamental nature. A truly mechanistic theory views an organism as a kind of machine or apparatus that simply receives various kinds of input and produces the appropriately programmed output. Such an organism is frequently characterized as being "passive," although a better term would be "reactive." That is, the organism does neither more nor less than continually react to the environmental events that are taking place. It is a completely determined system with no degrees of freedom in behavior. This orientation to behavior theory predisposes one to think in terms of mechanical models, physiological mechanisms, biochemical processes, or any system that is conceived in the image of the physical sciences.

A purposive theory is basically the antithesis of each of these characteriza-

TABLE 4.1.
**Summary of the Major Theoretical Issues and the Poles of the Resulting
Controversies.**

THEORETICAL ISSUE	BEHAVIORISTIC THEORY	COGNITIVE THEORY
Nature of the theory	Mechanistic (passive organism)	Purposive (active organism)
Nature of behavior	Molecular responses	Molar performances
Nature of the stimulus	Sensory processes	Perceptual processes
Nature of learning	S-R associations	S-S organizations
Conditions of learning	Pure reinforcement	Pure contiguity
Nature of reinforcement	Need/drive reduction	Confirmation/emphasis
Role of reinforcement	Learning	Motivation
Primary motivation	Biological needs	Psychological demands
Is motivation general?	Yes	No
Does motivation affect learning?	No	Yes

tions of a mechanistic theory. Most particularly, the organism is viewed as being active rather than reactive. A purposive organism is not constrained to behave reflexively and automatically but, instead, takes some initiative in controlling its destiny. The physical sciences are considered to be a poor model for behavior; the mind works on quite different principles.[10]

Let us reemphasize that neither Hull nor Tolman, nor perhaps any other theorist, explicitly ascribes to the extreme of these positions. Certainly, Hull acknowledged the fact that behavior appears to be purposive, and he entertained various methods of self-control by the organism. On the other hand, Tolman fully accepted the apparently reflexive nature of much behavior. But Hull still believed that the higher mental processes are ultimately to be understood in basically mechanistic terms, and Tolman viewed automatic behavioral mechanisms as an adaptive means of freeing the cognitive processes from routine biological activities. Such fundamental differences in the way of thinking about learning and motivation pervade many of the controversies from the inception of behaviorism to the present.

The effect is evident in the contrasting approaches to the nature of behavior. Behavioristic theorists tend to view behavior in terms of molecular responses, or at least as being ultimately describable in such terms. It is true that Hull explicitly defined responses in relatively molar terms, and this is compatible with an S-R approach, but a "response" could never be so molar as a "plan" (Miller, Galanter, & Pribram, 1960). And while there are permissible variations in molarity among cognitive theorists, adherents to that approach do not wish to deal with muscle twitches as being of intrinsic interest. Thus, Hull's theory can be just as molecular as one wishes, but it is somewhat constrained as to how molar it can be interpreted; Tolman's theory can be just as molar as one wishes, but it is somewhat constrained as to how molecular it can be interpreted. Very comparable reasoning applies with respect to the views about the nature of the stimulus. For Hull, stimuli impinge upon the organism's sensorium and elicit historically adaptive responses. For Tolman, the organism selects from the stimulus environment, processes the information received, and behaves adaptively in relation to the resulting analysis.

Because of these different understandings of the nature of stimuli and of behavior, the nature of learning inevitably becomes a focal controversy. S-R associations quite accurately capture the essence of learning from the behavioristic point of view; Hull explicitly postulated habit strength as a reflection of the tendency for a stimulus to elicit a response. But a cognitive theory is not so well described as a simple S-S association. There are situations in which one stimulus may become associated with another stimulus, as in classical conditioning; but more generally, learning is an organization of the environment, including events whose occurrence depends on the performance of some response. Tolman used hyphenated terms in an effort to convey this view; a sign-gestalt–expectation conveys that an environmental stimulus may serve as a sign to reconstruct from memory a gestalt image of the entire situation in which there may be expectancies of consequent events of significance to the organism's purposes.[11]

In the context of the behavioristic-cognitive issue, it is really impossible to separate the issue of the conditions of learning from the preceding one about the nature of learning. Among theorists who agree that learning is of an S-R nature, we can legitimately distinguish Hull (1943) as a pure reinforcement theorist for whom the conditions of reinforcement affect the amount learned; Hull (1952) as a reinforcement theorist for whom some reinforcement is still necessary for learning to occur; Guthrie (1935) for whom pure contiguity is sufficient for the establishment of S-R associations. But a quite different set of alternatives applies within the cognitive approach. Although we have identified Tolman as a pure contiguity theorist, the contiguity is a hypothetical one that assumes that the organism attends to the relevant stimulus events and, in the case of Spielberger (1962), is also aware of the contingency relationships in the situation. A more recent version of cognitive theory (Bower, 1975) proposes that organisms could not possibly learn everything that happens contiguously in space and time, as would presumably be the case for a pure contiguity theory, and only those features are learned that are selectively rehearsed. Accordingly, as soon as one leaves the pure contiguity S-R or S-S positions, the kinds of additional necessary conditions are quite different.

This fact makes the further issue of the nature of the reinforcement also one of dubious virtue. Note carefully that we are, for this moment, using "reinforcement" as a hypothetical construct referring to a postulated process within the theory as it affects learning within that theory. To Hull, drive reduction was a beautifully adaptive mechanism; organisms who learn to engage in behaviors that satisfy their needs are likely to survive. To Tolman, in contrast, the more the organism learns about the environment, the more likely that adaptive behavior will be forthcoming, particularly in an ever-changing world. Accordingly, reinforcement means quite different things to the two types of theorists, simply because learning means different things to them.

The role of reinforcement, as the term is used here, is a hypothetical concept and refers to the pervasive effects of certain emotionally significant events on behavior. As we have previously stated, both types of theorists must come to grips with the principles of reinforcement, and the distinction that we have made in Table 4.1 does, indeed, pertain to Hull (1943) and Tolman (1932). Hull assumed that reinforcement affects habit strength, and this position is not yet to be totally discounted. However, as we will discuss in the next chapter, most contemporary theorists have fallen in line with some version of Tolman's contention that reinforcement has a motivational effect on performance and that it affects learning only in the sense that the organism learns about the reinforcement.

Hull's notion of primary motivation was based heavily on Darwin's theory of evolution and survival of the fittest. His original version stated that biological needs goad the organism into action as if in search of some relief. Consistent with this approach was his view that there is a general motivational factor—generalized drive—that combines all sources of needs into an overall activation, arousal, and general activity. In many cases, this activity might well be directed by unlearned dispositions to make responses with greater-than-chance likelihood of servicing the prevailing needs; learning becomes important only when such innate response tendencies are inadequate. Thus, Hull's theory can be characterized as an interlocking set of biological survival mechanisms.

In contrast a cognitive theory, such as Tolman's, considers survival to be merely a prerequisite for more interesting aspects of behavior. There are many other possible sources of motivation available to a cognitive theorist and, quite naturally, these are kept separate in order to interact only with relevant types of behavior in appropriate types of situations. Most critically, there are positive sources of motivation, such as curiosity, social approval, and love.

Finally, the approaches differ in their positions concerning the role of motivation in learning. To Hull, any such effects are indirect. The organism clearly must be motivated in order for drive-reduction reinforcement to be possible; the organism must be motivated in order to engage in operant/instrumental acts and, thereby, encounter the reinforcement; and drives have characteristic drive stimuli that enter into learned associations with appropriate responses. However, learning itself is automatic; any responses followed by reinforcement enjoy an increment in habit strength to the prevailing stimulus complex. For Tolman, however, what an organism learns depends on the state of motivation. High drive may actually interfere with seeing all of the interrelationships among the events in the environment, and it is perfectly compatible with this approach to assume that the organism actively selects the material that will be learned.

With the summary of the issues that we have discussed thus far in Table 4.1, we would underscore again the fact that *none* of these issues is resolved. Indeed, their nature is such that they cannot be amenable to direct empirical resolution. This will equally be true with most of the issues that are reviewed in the remaining chapters of this book. But empirical research will undoubtedly continue to refine both approaches, and new innovations will make one or the other approach appear to be more attractive at least temporarily. At present, neither approach is as well organized as once seemed to be the case; there are about as many isolated conceptual ideas of a behavioristic nature as there are of a cognitive nature. It behooves contemporary psychologists to be well informed about the nature of these theoretical systems, their strengths and weaknesses, and their potential for an improved understanding of learning and motivation.

SECONDARY EMOTIONAL EVENTS
The Nature of Secondary Emotional Events

Underlying secondary emotional events is the basic assumption that originally neutral stimuli can acquire reinforcing or punishing value through classical conditioning. That is, neutral stimuli can acquire secondary emotional significance by virtue of being appropriately paired with primary reinforcers and primary punishers. The term secondary is not intended to convey any notion that such events are of lesser stature than are primary events. The term secondary is used simply to indicate that the reinforcing or punishing value of these events is based on the primary events.[12]

Both secondary positive and secondary negative reinforcers and punishers are logically possible in that the requisite operations can be identified.[13] These are displayed in Table 4.2 together with the resulting terminology. (In order not to complicate the diagram, we have omitted the fact that the innately neutral event can be either the onset or the offset of some neutral stimulus.) There are four potential ways to obtain secondary reinforcers and four potential ways to obtain secondary punishers—the method is based on whether the innately neutral event is first paired with the onset or the offset of an innately reinforcing or punishing event that, after the pairing operation, is either presented or removed. A particular example that we will encounter most often in the context of aversive control is of this type: a secondary negative reinforcer (type on-off) is the offset of a stimulus (e.g., a light) that has been paired with the onset of a primary punisher (e.g., electric shock). The off-off type of secondary negative reinforcement would be the termination of a signal (e.g., a light) that has been paired with the offset of a primary reinforcer (e.g., food). Of course, the matrix could be further expanded in recognition of higher-order conditioning.

This logical classification of possible secondary emotional events has not been completely supported empirically. Although the evidence seems strongly to suggest that secondary reinforcers can be based on primary positive reinforcement, there is no truly unequivocal evidence that secondary reinforcers can be formed using a primary negative reinforcer, such as the termination of an electric shock. The operations necessary for the formation of a secondary positive reinforcer of this type appear to be simple and obvious enough: subjects are occasionally subjected to an aversive state of affairs and, shortly preceding the termination of that state, a stimulus is presented. Subsequently, if presentation of this stimulus supports new learning, affirmative evidence is obtained. Actually, it is somewhat more difficult than this to study the effects of stimuli associated with primary negative reinforcement (cf. Beck, 1961; LoLordo, 1969; Siegel & Milby, 1969). But even when appropriate procedure

TABLE 4.2.

Matrix of Logically Possible Operations Involved in Secondary Reinforcement and Secondary Punishment
(An innately neutral event is paired with primary positive or negative reinforcers or punishers.)

Innately reinforcing event	Onset = Primary positive reinforcer	Onset = Secondary positive reinforcer (Type on-on)
		Offset = Secondary negative punisher (Type on-off)
	Offset = Primary negative punisher	Onset = Secondary positive punisher (Type off-on)
		Offset = Secondary negative reinforcer (Type off-off)
Innately punishing event	Onset = Primary positive punisher	Onset = Secondary positive punisher (Type on-on)
		Offset = Secondary negative reinforcer (Type on-off)
	Offset = Primary negative reinforcer	Onset = Secondary positive reinforcer (Type off-on)
		Offset = Secondary negative punisher (Type off-off)

are employed, the majority of studies in the literature report failures to obtain secondary reinforcers. In summary, although some positive results have occasionally been reported (e.g., Dinsmoor & Clayton, 1966; Lawler, 1965; Murray & Strandberg, 1965; Wagman & Allen, 1964), the present studies indicate that primary negative reinforcement is not capable of transferring reinforcing properties to an initially neutral stimulus.

Generally, secondary reinforcers and punishers are less readily formed when paired with the removal than with the presentation of a primary event. Secondary punishers are quite readily formed when paired with the presentation of primary aversive events.[14] However, in spite of some suggestive supporting evidence (e.g., Ferster, 1958; Wagner, 1963), there are no conclusive demonstrations of secondary punishers that are based on the removal of a reinforcer, such as the availability of food (cf. Leitenberg, 1965). Thus, secondary reinforcers and punishers seem by nature to be based on the *presentation* of primary reinforcers and punishers.

As we will elaborate later in this chapter, secondary reinforcers and punishers need to be identified, empirically and theoretically, in a manner analogous to primary reinforcers and punishers. We may anticipate the subsequent discussion somewhat by noting that functionally identified secondary reinforcers and punishers have the important characteristic of being both transsituational and transprocedural, because they function as such in a variety of situations and procedures that depart considerably from those in effect at the time they were established. This is, of course, as it must be, if the concepts of secondary reinforcement and punishment are to have any useful substance. If secondary events only function in the precise situation in which they are presumably formed, the concepts of secondary reinforcement and punishment would be superfluous, because the primary emotional event would still be present. Needless to say, there are innumerable everyday occurrences where individuals behave without obvious dependence on primary emotional events

Nevertheless, the extent of the independence of secondary reinforcers and punishers from the establishing situation has not been delimited completely. Certainly, boundary conditions must come to bear to specify how considerably the situations in which secondary events function can depart from the establishing situation. One aspect of the establishing situation that relates to this issue of independence and is of empirical and theoretical interest, in its own right, is the question of whether secondary reinforcers function independently of the drive motivation present at the time the originally neutral stimulus was paired with the primary reinforcer.

Recall that the independence of habit from specific drive motivation was empirically investigated by varying the level of drive during habit acquisition and by interchanging sources of drive. A similar empirical approach is used to investigate the relationship between secondary positive reinforcement and drive motivation. In general, it has been found that secondary positive reinforcement is somewhat independent of drive intensity during acquisition (e.g., Brown, 1956; Wike & Farrow, 1962) and that sources of drive are reasonably intersubstitutable with respect to the functioning of secondary reinforcement (e.g., Estes, 1949; D'Amato, 1955). These studies of Estes and D'Amato, again, involve only thirst and hunger. Can a secondary reinforcer, based on food, function as a reinforcer for an organism under thirst motivation, and vice versa? The affirmative answer to these questions obtained from drive-substitution studies is again compromised because of the interdependence of thirst and hunger (Grice & Davis, 1957; Verplanck & Hayes, 1953).

A related question regarding the nature of secondary reinforcers is whether secondary reinforcers involve drive reduction; does a secondary reinforcer actually reduce drive? A direct approach to an answer of this question becomes exceedingly difficult to implement, but it is generally found that secondary reinforcers do not reduce drive (at least, not hunger or thirst drive—Calvin, Bicknell, & Sperling, 1953; Miles & Wickens, 1953). An indirect approach to the same question may investigate whether secondary positive reinforcers function in the absence of drive motivation (minimal drive). The evidence on this point is mixed. In some situations secondary reinforcers are effective in satiated organisms (Gilbert & Sturdivant, 1958; Seward & Levy, 1953), whereas in other situations they are not (Cowles, 1937; Platt & Wike, 1962). No generalization regarding the necessity of drive for secondary positive reinforcement to operate is appropriate here, given the conflicting nature of the evidence. [15]

Our final topic, which relates secondary positive reinforcement to motivation, is that of generalized secondary positive reinforcers. It is Skinner's (1953) contention that if an originally neutral stimulus is paired with a variety of primary reinforcers under appropriate drive conditions, the secondary reinforcer then becomes completely generalized. It should function effectively in a variety of situations, regardless of how they differ from the original establishing conditions. Moreover, generalized reinforcers should be very durable even in the absence of the original drive and primary reinforcement. Skinner's notion of generalized reinforcers has intuitive appeal, since everyday counterparts to laboratory demonstrations of secondary reinforcers are often associated with a wide variety of reinforcers; money, for example, is associated with a wide range of goods and services. Appealing as this notion may be, there are no data that compel the conclusion that pairing a stimulus with more than one primary reinforcer enhances its durability or generality (Kanfer & Matarazzo, 1959; Nevin, 1966; Wike & McNamara, 1955).

To summarize the nature of secondary emotional events, as we know it to this point, we can conclude that secondary emotional events are based on the classical conditioning situation in which two stimuli are temporarily presented. Justification for this assertion comes from accumulated evidence that we have not reviewed here; this evidence reveals that variables, such as stimulus intensity, interstimulus interval, partial reinforcement, and so on, have the same general effects on secondary reinforcers and punishers as on directly measured conditioned responses. Stimulus pairing is necessary for secondary reinforcers to form, and both primary positive reinforcers and primary positive punishers serve to establish secondary reinforcers (of the positive and negative types, respectively). Secondary reinforcers are transsituational and transprocedural, but they are not more general or durable when originally established with several different reinforcers. Finally, secondary reinforcers exhibit some independence from drive motivation and do not reduce primary drive motivation. Having an overview of the nature of a concept does not negate the necessity of demonstrating the viability of the concept. It is to the matter of identification that we turn next.

Identifying Secondary Reinforcing and Punishing Events

The empirical approach to identifying reinforcers and punishers, whether primary or secondary in nature, is always fundamentally functional (and, consequently, benignly circular). Given a stimulus paired with a positive reinforcer, the options are functionally to test the stimulus for its secondary reinforcing effects by presenting it or for its secondary punishing effects by removing it. Given a stimulus paired with a positive punisher, the comparable options are functionally to test the stimulus for its secondary reinforcing effects by removing it or for its secondary punishing effects by presenting it. By far, the option chosen most often has been to test stimuli for their functional reinforcing effects.[16]

In the instance of secondary negative reinforcement, the usual functional touchstone for identification purposes is successful avoidance learning. When an organism learns to respond in the presence of the CS (and, thereby, terminates the CS) prior to the occurrence of an aversive US, the termination of the CS is identified as a secondary negative reinforcer. To be sure, there is circularity inherent in asserting that avoidance learning occurs because of secondary negative reinforcement and that we identify secondary negative reinforcement in terms of successful avoidance learning. Clearly, some independent identification of secondary negative reinforcers is desirable. And not surprisingly, such an identification has been provided in terms of theoretical drive constructs (e.g., fear—Miller, 1948; Mowrer, 1939).

The reader may perhaps experience a sense of déjà vu with respect to the identification of secondary negative reinforcers, since its development so closely mimics that of identfying primary reinforcers. Nevertheless, there are some problems quite peculiar to the identification of secondary negative reinforcers (Bolles, 1967). For example, if avoidance learning functionally identifies a secondary negative reinforcer, then it needs to be determined how the stimuli constituting the secondary reinforcer should be identified in the absence of a discernable CS (e.g., Sidman, 1953). For the most part, issues regarding secondary negative reinforcers have been inextricably linked with avoidance learning. Consequently, we will postpone further discussion of secondary negative reinforcement until avoidance conditioning is considered in detail in Chapter 6.

With respect to the functional identification of secondary positive reinforcers, two procedures have been typically used. In one procedure a between-group comparison of relative resistance to extinction is employed (e.g., Bugelski, 1938; Miles, 1956). Briefly, the procedure is to train an instrumental-/operant response (say, a bar press) that is followed by a neutral event (say, a click) and also a primary reinforcer. Following such training, extinction is begun by removing only the primary reinforcer for one group and both the primary reinforcer and the click for the other group. It is reasoned that if the click has acquired secondary reinforcing value by virtue of being paired with the primary reinforcer, then it should maintain the bar-press response longer during extinction—an expectation clearly confirmed in the large majority of instances using this procedure.

Note, however, that this type of functional identification of secondary reinforcers is not unequivocal. If the results from this procedure can be accounted for by appeal to other principles than secondary positive reinforcement, then the necessity of even invoking the concept of secondary reinforcement is doubtful. There have been three, more or less, formal objections to the notion that secondary reinforcement is necessary to explain the results from extinction procedures of the above type; some of these objections are more generally opposed to the concept of secondary reinforcement as identified under any procedure.

One objection to the extinction procedure can be described under the rubric of the discrimination hypothesis. Essentially, this hypothesis states that responding during extinction is directly related to the similarity between the training and extinction conditions (Bitterman, Fedderson, & Tyler, 1953). In the extinction test of secondary reinforcement, the click is one component of the total stimulus complex present during training; removing it, as in the control group, makes it easier to discriminate between extinction and training conditions and, thus, the control group stops responding sooner in extinction. The argument, in effect, is that the click group does not extinguish more slowly because of secondary reinforcement; instead, the no-click group extinguishes more rapidly, because it discriminates the extinction conditions more rapidly.

The second hypothesis, the elicitation hypothesis, has been proposed by Bulgelski (1956). It is his contention that stimuli serve only an eliciting function and not a reinforcing function. Eliciting stimuli become integrated into chains of behavior and, in that context, serve the function of simply eliciting the next response in the chain. To presume a stimulus reinforces, as well as elicits, behavior is for Bulgelski's hypothesis quite unnecessary. Again to return to the example of the extinction test of secondary reinforcement, the elicitation hypothesis views the click as a stimulus that elicits the response of going to the place where food had been delivered. This elicited response automatically puts the organism in a situation that elicits further pressing of the bar. The essentials of this argument are that the click group does not extinguish more slowly because of secondary reinforcement; instead, more responding is simply elicited by the click stimulus.

In contrast to the eliciting stimulus hypothesis, Wyckoff (Wyckoff, Sidowski, & Chambliss, 1958; Wyckoff, 1959) proposed a hypothesis that denies secondary reinforcement in favor of the discriminative effects of a stimulus. It is contended that what matters is what the organism does in the presence of the discriminative stimulus, not what the organism did prior to the occurrence of the stimulus. If the discriminative stimulus occasions behavior that facilitates further responding, then the outcome reported for our example-identification procedure will prevail. More specifically, this hypothesis, known as the facilitation hypothesis, states that the click in the example is a discriminative stimulus that does not directly elicit bar pressing but does occasion the response of approaching the reinforcer. This discriminative response places the organism near to the bar, so that further bar pressing is indirectly facilitated. In the absence of the click, there is no discriminative stimulus, which controls a response, that will facilitate bar pressing; therefore, extinction progresses more rapidly.

Less formally presented interpretations of the outcome to our reference experiment include the notion that the click may excite the organism or enhance activity, because of its association with the reinforcer, or that this nondirected behavior potentiates bar pressing. Alternatively, the occurrence of the click alone without reinforcement may elicit a frustrative effect of nonreinforcement, and the general activity characteristic of frustration may carry over to bar pressing.

The essential feature that causes us to collate all of these hypotheses into one category is that they deny the necessity of invoking a secondary reinforcement concept. Instead, some other function is attributed to the stimulus associated with primary reinforcement, be it discriminative, eliciting, facilitative, excitement inducing, or whatever. There is merit to the argument that studies using the extinction procedure functionally to identify secondary reinforcers do not demand an interpretation in terms of secondary reinforcement. That is not to suggest that any one of the alternative interpretations is demanded. To the contrary, these alternative hypotheses are only sometimes consistent with the obtained data and never totally impugn the concept of secondary reinforcement (cf. Kelleher, 1961; Kelleher & Gollub, 1962). On the other hand, we know that stimuli do have eliciting and discriminative functions. This fact prevents us from ever actually obtaining a completely pure measure of secondary reinforcement. Fortunately, a more convincing means of identifying secondary reinforcers than that provided by the extinction procedure is available.

The "new response" procedure uses the most fundamental functional property of reinforcers, namely, that their occurrence shortly following a response leads to an increase in the future likelihood of that response (e.g., Ratner, 1956; Saltzman, 1949). Under this functional identification procedure it is first established, either by the experimental subjects in a pretesting situation or by control subjects not given paired training, that the stimulus (say, a click) does not initially function as a reinforcer. Specifically, responses preceding the click do not occur more often. A pairing operation is then performed between the click and a primary reinforcer in the absence of the referent response (say, a bar press). Next, the click is shortly made to follow a bar press in the absence of the primary reinforcer, and an increase in the frequency of the bar press functionally identifies the click as a secondary reinforcer.

Although this new response procedure entails a strict functional identification of a secondary reinforcer, note that the identification is not pure in that discriminative, eliciting, or energizing functions of the click stimulus are not entirely ruled out. Actually, appropriate comparison groups are needed that control for these other functions of stimuli and permit a demonstration of secondary reinforcing effects over and beyond these other stimulus functions (e.g., Crowder, Gay, Fleming, & Hurst, 1959).

Note also that although the bar-press response is not undergoing extinction in this procedure, the secondary reinforcer is. In other words, the procedure is self-defeating. In order to be sure that the originally neutral stimulus is reinforcing, it is necessary to decontaminate the situation by omitting primary reinforcement. Thus, at the same time the bar press is receiving secondary reinforcement, the click stimulus is being rid of its reinforcing properties through extinction. Clearly, the effects of the secondary reinforcers are transitory.

Part of the inherent nature of any secondary reinforcer or punisher is that its effects are transitory when no longer paired with a primary reinforcer or punisher. Nevertheless, the effects of secondary positive reinforcers in many laboratory situations seem quite weak and very transitory—both on an absolute level and in comparison to the effects produced by secondary negative reinforcers (e.g., Solomon, Kamin, & Wynne, 1953). Those inclined toward criticism of the secondary reinforcement concept have not failed to note that the highly temporary nature of secondary reinforcers make them inappropriate for the persistent powers needed to explain everyday behavior. Proponents of secondary reinforcement counter by pointing out that procedures are available by which a very remarkable durability can be ascribed to secondary reinforcers (Saltzman, 1949; Zimmerman, 1959). Moreover, it is argued that secondary reinforcers in everyday life may not in themselves be very persistent. Their apparent durability results, because they are occasionally followed by primary reinforcement. In short, familiar everyday reinforcers that are not obviously related to primary reinforcement do not, in fact, encounter complete extinction as a rule; their persistence is illusory.

Procedures have been established for studying secondary reinforcement in situations where the pairing of the stimulus with a primary reinforcer is maintained. Most often these procedures for studying maintained secondary reinforcers involve a response chain terminating in primary reinforcement (Kelleher & Fry, 1962) or concurrent scheduling of primary and secondary reinforcement (Zimmerman, 1963). In the general chain procedure, a response that simply changes the stimulus in order to enable a second response that is given primary reinforcement is reinforced by the secondary reinforcing properties of this stimulus change. It needs to be recognized that maintained procedures provide a very useful method of studying the parameters of secondary reinforcers under reasonably stable conditions. However, it also must be conceded that these procedures do not serve well to identify nor to establish the necessity of secondary positive reinforcers: the first response is, after all, eventually followed by primary reinforcement and, hence, could be maintained by delayed reinforcement. Alternatively, the first response may be sustained due to generalization between the first stimulus and the stimulus immediately associated with primary reinforcement. Nevertheless, once the existence of secondary reinforcement is functionally identified, then it must follow that secondary reinforcement is involved in the chaining process.

The Conditions of Secondary Reinforcing and Punishing Events

Up to this point in our discussion of the nature and identification of secondary reinforcers and punishers, we have treated the conditions of these secondary events too lightly. We have adopted the position that a classical conditioning stimulus-pairing operation is the basis of this type of learning and, therefore, that simple stimulus pairing is the *necessary* condition for the formation of secondary reinforcers and punishers. And so it seems to be. But there exists the possibility that simple pairing, while a necessary condition, is not a sufficient condition for the formation of secondary reinforcers and punishers. Indeed, there have been several related hypotheses regarding the sufficient conditions for establishing secondary reinforcers that have asserted that contiguity of a neutral stimulus and a primary reinforcer is not sufficient. Before discussing these hypotheses, we will first recognize the alternative position that contiguity between a stimulus and a primary positive reinforcer or primary positive punisher is sufficient to produce a secondary reinforcer or punisher.

First, one must acknowledge that simple contiguity is accepted as sufficient by cognitive theorists. A stimulus that is associated with a primary reinforcing or punishing event will acquire the value of the subsequent event. The only restrictions that apply here are those that apply generally to the formation of expectancies. For example, stimuli that are emphasized and demanded will serve better as secondary reinforcers than will stimuli that are not.

Behavioral theorists of Hullian persuasion have also generally maintained that contiguity is a sufficient condition for imparting reinforcing or punishing functions to neutral stimuli. Hull's (1943, 1951) fundamental theoretical proposition is that a stimulus (actually, a receptor impulse) will acquire the power of acting as a reinforcing event, if it occurs repeatedly and consistently in conjunction with a reinforcing state of affairs. In order to accommodate higher-order conditioning, Hull presumes that the reinforcing state of affairs can be either primary or secondary. The theoretical mechanism underlying secondary reinforcement for Hull (1943) is response elicitation. It is assumed that at the time a stimulus is paired with a positive reinforcer, hypothetical fractions of the overt goal response and associated response-produced stimuli ($r_g - s_g$) become conditioned to the neutral stimulus because of the occurrence of drive-stimulus reduction. Indeed, the neutral stimulus acquires secondary reinforcing properties to the extent that it comes to elicit $r_g - s_g$; the more intense the occurrence of $r_g - s_g$ the greater the secondary reinforcing power of the stimulus. Thus, while drive-stimulus reduction is necessary for the establishment of a secondary reinforcer, it is not apparently involved in the functioning of a secondary reinforcer. Secondary reinforcement is a matter of eliciting a hypothetical component of the overt (consummatory) response associated with the primary positive reinforcer.[17] A similar mechanism based on primary positive punishment is postulated for secondary punishers, but instead of being mediated by a hypothetical goal response, secondary punishers are mediated by a hypothetical fear response and its associated response-produced stimuli ($r_f - s_f$). Thus, fear becomes conditioned to the antedating stimulus at the time of pairing with the primary punisher, and the antedating stimulus functions as a secondary punisher to the extent that it elicits $r_f - s_f$.

The elicitation of $r_g - s_g$ takes on an important incentive motivation function in subsequent developments of Hullian theory and will be more fully explored in the next chapter. Herein, we will note immediately the inconsistency, recognized by Hull, between his theoretical drive-stimulus reduction mechanism for primary reinforcement and his nondrive-stimulus reducing $r_g - s_g$ elicitation mechanism for secondary reinforcement. Actually, theorists sympathetic to Hull have suggested means by which this inconsistency can be lessened. For example, Mowrer (1960) proposed that all primary drives have an anxiety component that is reduced by secondary reinforcement, and Miller (1951) hypothesized an anticipatory relaxation mechanism. According to this latter hypothesis, drive-stimulus reduction involves hypothetical relaxation responses that become conditioned to antedating stimuli and, thus, become anticipatory.[18] The subsequent elicitation of anticipatory relaxation responses is reinforcing, because it reduces tension associated with drive stimuli. Hull (1951) incorporated much of Miller's thinking in his later development of secondary reinforcers. By hypothesizing that a secondary reinforcer is a learned source of drive reduction, Hull achieved a measure of internal consistency between his theoretical primary and secondary reinforcement mechanisms.

The proposed elicitation of hypothetical fractional goal responses, fear responses, or relaxation responses represents a theoretical mechanism for the functioning of secondary emotional events and is not a specification of the conditions necessary for secondary reinforcers or punishers to be established. As we have stated, the necessary and sufficient condition for establishing these mechanisms is assumed to be sheer contiguity between an innately neutral stimulus and a primary reinforcer or punisher.

The discriminative-stimulus hypothesis asserts that contiguity, while necessary in the formation of secondary reinforcers, is not sufficient.[19] In order for a stimulus to function as a secondary reinforcer, it must be established as a discriminative stimulus. That is, the stimulus must set the occasion for the execution of some instrumental/operant response—typically a response that leads directly to primary reinforcement[20] (Keller & Schoenfeld, 1950).

The discriminative-stimulus hypothesis was purportedly buttressed by early evidence that: a stimulus that occurs simultaneously with food, but does not precede food, does not function as a secondary reinforcer (Schoenfeld, Antonitis, & Bersh, 1950); a stimulus that sets the occasion for a bar press to produce food is equally effective in maintaining extinction responding, whether it occurs prior to or after a response (Dinsmoor, 1950); explicit discrimination training enhances the secondary reinforcing properties of a stimulus (Saltzman, 1949) or is necessary functionally to identify a secondary reinforcer (Ferster, 1951). The first line of evidence is important, since a stimulus needs to precede a reinforcer if it is to become a discriminative stimulus controlling a response that leads to reinforcement. The second line of evidence suggests that the discriminative and reinforcing properties of a stimulus are qualitatively and quantitatively interchangeable.

The third line of evidence is less direct and, perhaps, less applicable. This line of evidence essentially states that discrimination training enhances secondary reinforcers. Since discrimination training is the hallmark of forming discriminative stimuli, the data indirectly support the discriminative-stimulus hypothesis. However, the data do not directly support the notion that a stimulus must be discriminative for some response in order for it to be a secondary reinforcer. A number of empirical operations, among them discrimination training, affect the differential control exerted by stimuli over behavior. Demonstrating that an operation leads to stimulus control of behavior does not establish it as a necessary condition for the establishment of secondary reinforcers. For example, it is known that secondary reinforcers generalize (Thomas & Caronite, 1964) and that generalization is potentially quite broad in the absence of discrimination training (Jenkins & Harrison, 1960). Accordingly, it is difficult to separate directly whether discrimination training is necessary to establish secondary reinforcers or whether it simply sharpens the control exerted by otherwise established secondary reinforcers.

Nevertheless, numerous studies demonstrate a positive relationship between the discriminative and reinforcing functions of a stimulus. Indeed, this evidence led Wyckoff (1959) to propose that the strength of a secondary reinforcer is directly related to its cue strength, where cue strength is measured by the probability of response occurrence in the presence of the stimulus. However, a moment's thought will reveal the difficulty of demonstrating that a stimulus paired with a reinforcer without a response requirement can still become a secondary reinforcer. Most appetitive reinforcers require, at a minimum, some instrumental/operant approach or consummatory response. The demonstration necessary to disprove the discriminative-stimulus hypothesis was reported by Stein (1958) and extended by Knott and Clayton (1966). These researchers established a stimulus as a secondary reinforcer by pairing the stimulus with a primary reinforcer that can be delivered independently of the organism's behavior, namely, an electrical stimulation to the brain. No instrumental/operant response is necessary to approach or consume electrical brain stimulation and, consequently, it is concluded that a stimulus that does not exert discriminative control of a response can be established through contiguity as a secondary reinforcer. The occurrence of overt behavior in the presence of a stimulus is apparently not a necessary condition for making the stimulus a secondary reinforcer.

Although the research with electrical brain-stimulation reinforcement rules out the necessity of overt responses, it does not demonstrate by default that contiguity alone is both necessary and sufficient to establish secondary reinforcers. Another argument that contiguity is not sufficient has been made by Egger and Miller (1962, 1963). These researchers essentially retain the information-providing component, but not the response component, of the discriminative-stimulus hypothesis. Specifically, Egger and Miller hypothesize that a stimulus must be presented in such a fashion that it is informative with respect to the imminence of primary reinforcement. In order for a stimulus to become a secondary reinforcer, it is necessary that the stimulus be a reliable and nonredundant predictor of reinforcement.

Under the information hypothesis of secondary reinforcers, the informativeness and reliability of stimuli are not formally scaled. Instead, these properties are presumed to be evident from the relationship between the stimuli and reinforcement. For example, if two stimuli, S_1 and S_2, occur in fixed temporal order preceding primary reinforcement, the first stimulus, S_1, is said to be informative with respect to reinforcement. The second stimulus is redundant and conveys no new information not already foretold by S_1. Accordingly, S_1 and not S_2 should be established as a secondary reinforcer even though both stimuli are paired with primary reinforcement and even though S_2 is in closer proximity to reinforcement than S_1. Egger and Miller obtained the predicted results.[21]

Other researchers have specified parameter limitations to the basic finding (e.g., Thomas, Berman, Serednesky, & Lyons, 1968); while still others have shown that S_1 may not become a more effective secondary punisher than S_2 when the stimuli are paired with electric shock (Ayres, 1966). Additionally, there is no sound evidence that any systematic relationship exists between the effectiveness of a secondary reinforcer and the extent to which the stimulus reduces uncertainty about reinforcement (e.g., Berlyne, 1960; Bower, McLean, & Meacham, 1966). Nevertheless, Egger and Miller (1962, 1963) have effectively argued that it is not possible to predict whether a stimulus will become a secondary reinforcer simply from its contiguity with primary reinforcement. It is necessary as well to take into consideration the relationship that pertains between the stimulus in question and other stimuli currently in the situation and potentially more reliably correlated with reinforcement. In any event, the information hypothesis stands in defense of the position that something else in addition to contiguity is necessary for the establishment of secondary reinforcers.

Summary   It is easy to observe that individuals behave from day to day without a total dependence on primary reinforcers and punishers. Indeed, a portion of their behavior occurs, instead, in the context of stimuli that are innately neutral but that have a history of association with primary emotional events. When these originally neutral stimuli occur as the antecedent stimuli in a classical conditioning situation with primary positive reinforcement or primary positive punishment, it is often possible, functionally, to identify these stimuli as secondary reinforcers or secondary punishers. To be sure, these stimuli may control behavior to some degree by eliciting and facilitating or by suppressing behavior in their presence. But beyond these functions, the stimuli can come to function as reinforcers or punishers of behavior, which they shortly follow, by virtue of their being paired with the presentation of primary emotional events.

Secondary reinforcers and punishers are independent of their establishing conditions, because they function in a variety of situations apart from the presence of primary reinforcement or punishment. On the other hand, secondary reinforcers and punishers are dependent on their establishing conditions in that their effects are transitory in the complete absence of primary events. However, given that some pairing with a primary event is occasionally permitted to occur, secondary reinforcers and punishers can be made sufficiently durable to exert a meaningful amount of control over behavior in the absence of the primary event used to maintain them.

The nature of the neutral stimuli, which become secondary reinforcers and punishers after being paired with primary events, is not entirely clear. By some theoretical accounts any stimulus that comes to elicit hypothetical fractional goal, relaxation, or fear responses will serve as a secondary reinforcer or punisher, and any stimulus can acquire this eliciting property if appropriately paired with a primary event. By other more empirical accounts only stimuli that provide information about the occurrence of a primary event and/or that set the occasion for the occurrence of some response related to the primary event will become a secondary reinforcer or punisher. Presumably, the nature of secondary reinforcers and punishers will be better established after further study. In addition, further study may uncover secondary reinforcers and punishers that are based on the removal of primary reinforcers and punishers. If this is to occur, we may be assured that these secondary reinforcers and punishers will be identified functionally.

GENERAL SUMMARY AND CONCLUSIONS   To both empiricists and theorists alike, the principle that behavior is affected by emotional events is preeminent. There is simply no quarrel with the empirical principles of reinforcement and punishment. In a variety of organisms, and in a variety of places and ways, reinforcers increase the likelihood and punishers decrease the likelihood of responses they follow. To be sure, setting operations, parameter limitations, and boundary conditions may and do come into play in any particular instance. But the potential for control of behavior resides with the agent who has identified reinforcers and punishers for the behavior.

The application of the principles of reinforcement and punishment to everyday affairs appears on the surface to be quite straightforward; simply reinforce desirable behaviors and punish undesirable behaviors. Obviously, the application of these principles can be complicated by practical considerations, but the essence of the application remains true to the principle. Nevertheless, a major problem does arise and that is how to identify what is and what is not a reinforcer or punisher.

Some emotional events are primary, because they have reinforcing and/or punishing properties without special training. Other emotional events are secondary, because their properties are acquired by virtue of being associated with primary reinforcing and punishing events. In both instances, the matter of identification is paramount. By some empirical or theoretical device, it is necessary to identify reinforcers and punishers if, in fact, the principles of effect are to have an impact by their practical utility. On an empirical level, both primary and secondary emotional events are identified functionally; that is, identified as events that function as such events should. This is admittedly circular, and logically less than satisfactory, but it is practical. It may be reduced to a quite ordinary prescription: find out what works, then use it. It matters little whether an event is identified absolutely or relatively to other events, or whether an event is identified for one situation or across a variety of situations and procedures, a functional identification retains the characteristic of being directly useful.

Although practical and useful, a functional identification of emotional events is not necessarily flawless, nor is it always easy. Decisions have to be made establishing criteria for accepting when an emotional event is functioning as it should. In the specific instance of secondary reinforcers and punishers, distinctions need to be drawn and retained between the reinforcing and punishing properties of stimuli and other properties of stimuli, such as eliciting or discriminative properties. Furthermore, in the instance of secondary reinforcers and punishers, we should recognize that it is in the nature of these events to be transitory in the absence of their establishing conditions and that only the presentation, and not the removal, of primary reinforcers and punishers clearly serves as an establishing condition.

A further complaint to be registered with respect to functional identification is that it is in one sense inefficient. For the purpose of everyday application of the principles of effect, it is somewhat inefficient to have to first identify functionally the reinforcing or punishing event. An independent, and consequently *a priori,* identification of emotional events would have an advantage in this regard.

With respect to primary emotional events, the most widely acknowledged approach to specifying emotional events independently has been theoretically to relate such events to biological need states. Needs give rise to hypothetical drive stimuli. All primary reinforcers entail the reduction of drive stimuli. This and closely allied theoretical approaches have made an enduring impact, since they independently incorporate a large number of functionally identified reinforcers. Nevertheless, there exist primary reinforcers that do not appear to involve the reduction of drive stimuli. Although drive-stimulus reductions do identify reinforcers, some other theoretical mechanism is needed independently to identify reinforcers and punishers when drive-stimulus reduction is not applicable.

With respect to secondary emotional events, several attempts have been made to specify these events independently in terms of the conditions of the antecedent stimulus entering into an association with the primary emotional event. Often the condition prescribed for the stimulus is that it control a response. The response may be hypothetical, such as fractional goal or relaxation responses, or discriminative, such as operant/instrumental approach or consummatory responses. Other conditions prescribed are that the stimulus possess cue value or information value for an organism. It appears that the best independent identification of secondary reinforcers now available concentrates on stimuli that not only provide information but that also require some discriminative response. However, the boundaries and restrictions on this type of identification have not yet been adequately specified. Furthermore, we should anticipate much greater variability among individuals in the events that have secondary emotional value as compared with primary emotional events. This is a result of the inevitable variability in the learning histories of different people.

Accordingly, the empirical functional approach provides the most useful, practical, and general method of identifying the events that have reinforcing and punishing properties for particular people. It is true that both the need reduction and drive-stimulus reduction approaches can provide some guidance but, unfortunately, these approaches cannot encompass and predict all behavior—people who would rather be fed than feed themselves and others for whom pain is a source of pleasure. Some events may seem to have general secondary reinforcing value, but even money will not buy everything for everybody. If nothing else, the functional approach can strongly warn against the common misconception that other people are naturally reinforced and punished by events that reinforce and punish us individually.

NOTES 1. Emotionally positive and negative events may be either exteroceptive, interoceptive, or response-produced stimuli, or responses themselves. Most, but not all, systematists have assumed that emotional events are stimuli, and there is nothing inherent in the empirical law of effect that logically requires emotional events to be of one type or another.

2. Premack's relational approach should exhibit the property of transitivity. Having observed that R_1 will reinforce R_2 and that R_2 will reinforce R_3 in a particular situation, then it should be possible to predict correctly that R_1 will reinforce R_3 in that situation.

3. Hull apparently introduced the hypothetical construct, drive, because some needs are not associated with the instigation of behavior. Thus, although a need for oxygen may not directly instigate behavior, the hypothetical drive arising from such a need state can be assigned the property of behavior instigation. Similarly, increased deprivation leads to increased need, but it is not always continuously associated with increases in behavioral activation. Again, this lack of concordance can be handled theoretically by assigning behavioral instigation properties to hypothetical drives that usually arise from needs.

4. Presumably, motivation based on external stimulation also eventuates in drive stimuli, though Hull was never particularly explicit regarding the

theoretical mechanism for this. Spence (1956), who essentially followed Hull's lead regarding drive motivation based on deprivation, suggested that drive motivation based on external stimulation (specifically, aversive stimulation) is mediated by an emotional state that is aroused as a function of the intensity of the external stimulus.

5. This empirical support occurs primarily in the instance of appetitive drives that are based on deprivation operations. Indeed, the evidence concerning drives based on aversive stimuli can be interpreted as favoring the notion that what gets learned depends on drive motivation. But, once again, the theoretical interpretation of empirical data importantly depends on the theoretical assumptions made.

6. Tolman later (1951) proposed a generalized source of drive that was unrelated to any specific demand for a goal object but that could increase the demands for goal objects aroused by other drives. This "libido" drive concept of Tolman's is better thought of as one, nonspecific drive than as a generalized drive that incorporates all other sources of drive.

7. Tolman proposed that drives could be operationalized in terms of the readiness of individuals to exhibit consummatory responses toward a goal object or in terms of the vigor of approach/avoidance with respect to a goal object.

8. In Miller's writings, the intensity of stimuli appears to be thought of in a relative rather than an absolute sense. That is, drives are stimuli that are intense, relative to other existing stimuli. Thought of in this way, there is no need to identify, absolutely, intense stimuli that are associated with deprivation operations in order to account for drive motivation based on internal stimuli (as has been argued by some critics of Miller's position).

9. Miller predetermines the other theoretical issue of whether learning is dependent on primary drive motivation by asserting that learned motivation, like unlearned motivation, consists of strong stimuli. By equating learned and unlearned motivation in this manner, Miller is certain to find that drive and habit interact.

10. Pretheoretic orientations have no clearly defined source but are largely philosophic or religious. For example, a belief that humans are gifted with free will, personal responsibility, and awareness of right and wrong naturally leads to a purposive approach to an understanding of behavior; whereas a belief in continuity in nature, evolutionary doctrines, and relativity of good and bad inclines one toward a mechanistic approach. Regardless of the source, pretheoretical beliefs are indeed held to with religious zeal and render some conceptual issues beyond the pale of empirical resolution.

11. The controversy cannot be resolved simply by contending that conjuring up an image of an environmental gestalt is a response and that expecting reward is a response. Indeed, this would make such associations technically of an S-R nature, but then we would have to recognize the possibility of two

kinds of "responses"—those of a covert, cognitive nature and those of an overt, motor nature. However, this type of analysis may help clarify the distinction between the theoretical approaches. At issue would be whether these two kinds of "responses" obey the same laws and principles, as Hull would contend, or whether they are basically incommensurate, as Tolman would contend.

12. The term secondary is used synonymously in the literature with the terms conditioned, acquired, or learned. We prefer the term secondary, since it is the most specific and least interpretative of the alternatives. For instance, the term learned seems quite general, while the term conditioned seems to imply the underlying process.

13. By way of terminological interlude, it would be well to note at this point the influence of the drive-(stimulus)-reduction identification of reinforcement. Whereas, operationally, stimuli paired with primary punishers or aversive events become secondary punishers, or secondary aversive events, it is quite usual to hear such stimuli referred to as secondary (acquired, learned, etc.) drives. This results because the termination of a secondary punisher is reinforcing and because of the presumed interrelationship of drives and reinforcers. We will, therefore, use secondary drive as an equivalent term and understand it to mean the result of pairing a neutral stimulus with a primary drive arousing stimulus.

14. The evidence demonstrating the formation of secondary punishers, based on the onset of primary aversive events, has been primarily collected with the use of electric shock or the presentation of some other intense exteroceptive stimulus (e.g., noise). Attempts to demonstrate the formation of secondary punishers, based on deprivation of appetitive stimuli such as food and water, have generally failed (Cravens & Renner, 1970). One notable difference between electric shock and the onset of an appetitive drive is that the latter is relatively slow and gradual in occurrence, although there is no strong evidence that indicates this to be the critical factor accounting for the difference in formation of secondary punishers.

15. For secondary negative reinforcement, the operational equivalent of satiation is to withhold the primary punishing event. Demonstrations abound where a neutral stimulus is paired with shock and then shown to function as a secondary negative reinforcer in the absence of the shock. Apparently, then, the generalization that secondary reinforcers can function in the absence of primary drives can be made for secondary negative reinforcers but not (conclusively) for secondary positive reinforcers.

16. Not infrequently the secondary punishing effects of stimuli based on positive punishers have been tested in a conditional emotional response procedure (Hake & Azrin, 1965). A complete discussion of this procedure has been reserved for a later chapter on aversive control of behavior. However, secondary positive punishers are functionally identified as producing a decrease in ongoing behavior. Secondary negative punishing effects, based on the removal of a secondary positive reinforcer, have very rarely been functionally identified.

Experiments investigating the effects of response cost (Weiner, 1962) represent a positive instance where the removal of existing secondary reinforcers has been functionally identified as punishing.

17. Although not argued by Hull, it is possible to derive an explanation for the failure to obtain secondary positive reinforcement on the basis of primary negative reinforcement from the position that $r_g - s_g$ mediates secondary reinforcement. Typical negative reinforcers do not involve an overt goal response; shock termination is not, in any obvious sense, consumed. Since no consummatory responses occur (R_G), none is available for conditioning fractional parts. Hence, there is no $r_g - s_g$ conditioned to the antedating stimulus and, hence, no secondary reinforcement.

18. According to the anticipatory relaxation hypothesis, it should not be possible to establish secondary positive reinforcement based on primary negative reinforcement. This results because drive-stimulus reduction is necessary for learning. With negative reinforcement, the reduction in drive stimuli is rapid and precedes the occurrence of relaxation responses so that it is not available at the time of the relaxation responses to condition them to antedating stimuli. With positive reinforcement, the reduction in drive stimuli is more prolonged, occurs contemporaneously with relaxation responses and, therefore, serves to condition relaxation responses to antedating stimuli.

19. The reader is cautioned to maintain a distinction between the discriminative-stimulus hypothesis, which states necessary conditions for the formation of secondary reinforcers, and the discrimination hypothesis, which was earlier discussed as a challenge to the necessity of invoking the concept of secondary reinforcement, in order to explain data obtained using extinction procedures.

20. As typically run, experiments investigating the establishment of secondary reinforcers, based on primary negative reinforcers, simply allow the stimulus to precede the termination of the aversive state, so that no behavior is necessary in the presence of the stimulus. Similarly, in experiments investigating the establishment of secondary punishers, based on deprivation of appetitive stimuli, the potential secondary punisher is rarely made discriminative. In one study where this was done (Anderson & Larson, 1956), no evidence for a secondary punisher was obtained.

21. In the Egger and Miller experiments where S_1 onset preceded S_2 onset and both stimuli terminated together, S_2 during pairing always occurred in the context of S_1. During testing for secondary reinforcement effectiveness, S_1 and S_2 occurred separately. Thus, it can be argued that S_1 is more effective, because there is less generalization decrement to it inasmuch as it did, during training, occur for a time alone without the second stimulus. This argument has been at least somewhat vitiated by appropriate controls for stimulus change. Nevertheless, the data from these studies may be alternatively accounted for by a variety of stimulus-control phenomena, such as selective attention. We note these possibilities, not to detract from the potential contribution made by the information hypothesis, but to reemphasize that although

we discuss issues separately (e.g., the conditions of secondary emotional events), the various issues discussed throughout the book are interrelated.

ABSTRACTS Bitterman, M.E., Fedderson, W.E., & Tyler, D.W. **Secondary reinforcement and the discrimination hypothesis.** *American Journal of Psychology,* 1953, *66,* 456–464.

Rats were trained to traverse a runway and enter a goal box (black or white) under conditions of random 50% reinforcement. Group I was reinforced in a goal box of one color and nonreinforced in a goal box of the same color. Group II was reinforced in a goal box of one color and nonreinforced in a goal box of the opposite color. Then the animals were extinguished, half of each group with the reinforced color (Subgroup S) and half with the color not previously associated with reinforcement (Subgroup N). Group I-S extinguished less rapidly than I-N, and group II-N extinguished less rapidly than II-S. These results are discussed in relation to secondary reinforcement, stimulus generalization, and the discrimination hypothesis—the assumption that rate of extinction is inversely related to the similarity between conditions of training and extinction.

Bugelski, R. Extinction with and without sub-goal reinforcement. *Journal of Comparative Psychology,* 1938, *26,* 121–134.

Sixty-four albino rats were trained to press a bar to obtain food reward. Operation of the bar was accompanied by a sharp distinct click. After the animals had received 30 reinforcements of this habit they were divided into two groups and extinguished to a criterion of five minutes without a response. Half the animals were extinguished under the original learning conditions which included the sharp click. The other animals did not hear the click during extinction.

The results indicate that the animals who heard the click during extinction responded to the bar more often than did the animals who did not hear the click. The difference between the mean number of responses was over 30% in favor of the rats who heard the click. These results correspond with deductions drawn in advance of the experimental work.

After the first extinction the rats were divided into groups of 16: 32 rats now extinguished under reversed conditions of "click" or "no click." The remaining 32 rats extinguished a second time under the original conditions. The same general results followed: those animals who heard the click made more responses than those animals who did not hear the click. The results again corresponded to theoretical deductions drawn in advance of the experimental work.

On the basis of the results it appears fairly certain that the presence of the click during extinction was a partial or "sub-goal" to the animals and that its absence added more frustration to that resulting from the absence of the food reward. These findings offer an experimental demonstration of the sub-goal principle advanced to explain certain features of serial acts and the satisfying nature of anticipatory goal responses.

Butler, R.A. Discrimination learning by rhesus monkeys to visual-exploration motivation. *Journal of Comparative and Physiological Psychology,* **1953,** *46,* **95–98.**

Five rhesus monkeys learned a discrimination problem on the basis of a visual-exploration incentive. Efficient performance was maintained during the long daily sessions and throughout a series of daily sessions with little or no evidence of satiation.

A visual-exploration motive is hypothesized on the basis of the obtained data, and it is suggested that this motive is strong, persistent, and not derived from, or conditioned upon, other motivational or drive states.

Egger, M.D., & Miller, N.E. Secondary reinforcement in rats as a function of information value and reliability of the stimulus. *Journal of Experimental Psychology,* **1962,** *64,* **97–104.**

Albino rats ($N = 88$, male) were trained to press a bar for food and were then divided randomly into two groups and trained as follows for 135 trials in the same Skinner Boxes with the bars removed: two stimuli, when paired, ended together and always preceded food. For Group A, the second, shorter stimulus (S_2) was always redundant because the first stimulus (S_1) had already given reliable information that food was to come. But for group B, S_2 was informative, because for them S_1 also occurred sometimes alone, without food.

After the training sessions, the bars were reinserted; bar-pressing was retrained with food pellets, extinguished, and then retrained again, this time using 1 sec. of one of the training stimuli as a secondary reinforcer in place of the food. The total number of bar presses in 10 min. following the first occurrence of the secondary reinforcing stimulus was used as a measure of secondary reinforcing strength. The testing procedure was repeated after 48 hrs. using the other training stimulus as a secondary reinforcer, so that all *S*s were tested with both stimuli in a balanced sequence.

Control experiments were run to provide baseline levels for pseudoconditioned and unconditioned rates of pressing and for any activating effect of the stimuli.

As predicted, S_2 was a stronger secondary reinforcer when it was informative than when it was redundant; S_1 was a more effective secondary reinforcer than S_2 in that group for which S_2 was a redundant predictor of primary reinforcement. In addition, S_1 was a more effective secondary reinforcer when it had been a reliable predictor of food.

Estes, K.W. **A study of the motivating conditions necessary for secondary reinforcement.** *Journal of Experimental Psychology,* 1949, *39,* 306–310.

Previous experiments have shown that an originally neutral stimulus which has been associated with the presentation of water to thirsty animals will subsequently exert a reinforcing effect upon responses elicited when the animals are hungry but not thirsty. The present experiment was designed to verify that finding and to determine whether the presence of a strong hunger drive in the test period is a necessary condition for the transfer of secondary reinforcement.

Twelve albino rats were first pretested for rate of unconditioned barpressing. Next, the two experimental groups of four rats were subjected to repeated presentations of small quantities of water accompanied by a characteristic auditory stimulus under conditions of 23-hour thirst motivation. Four control rats did not receive this training.

In the test period, motivating conditions were as follows: control group and high-drive group: deprived of food for 23 hours, satiated on water; low-drive group; deprived of food for six hours, satiated on water. During the test, barpressing responses produced the auditory stimulus previously associated with water-reinforcement, but no other reinforcement. Rate of responding increased significantly over the pre-test rate for the high-drive group, but decreased for the other two groups.

It is concluded that a secondary reinforcing cue will be effective in strengthening new responses when the original drive has been eliminated by satiation, provided that some other source of motivation is present in strong enough degree to instigate activity. Presently available evidence does not require the introduction of a concept of secondary motivation to account for conditioning by secondary reinforcement.

Harlow, H.F., Harlow, M.K., & Meyer, D.R. **Learning motivated by a manipulation drive.** *Journal of Experimental Psychology,* 1950, *40,* 228–234.

Four rhesus monkeys were given 12 days' experience in manipulating a mechanical puzzle whose solution did not lead to any special incentive such as food or water. Four matched control subjects had the puzzles placed in their home cages the same period of time, but unassembled. The performance of the two groups was then compared by observing their responses to the assembled puzzle during five five-minute periods on Days 13 and 14.

The experimental monkeys were more efficient than the control monkeys in puzzle solution as measured by total number of solutions attained in 60 secs and the ratio of correct to incorrect responses. Subsequent introduction of food in the puzzle situation tended to disrupt, not facilitate, the learned performances of the experimental subjects.

A manipulation drive, strong and extremely persistent, is postulated to account for learning and maintenance of the puzzle performance. It is further postulated that drives of this class represent a form of motivation which may be as primary and as important as the homeostatic drives.

Kelleher, R.T. Schedules of conditioned reinforcement during experimental extinction. *Journal of the Experimental Analysis of Behavior,* 1961, *4,* 1–5.

Pigeons that had been trained on a 5-min. fixed-interval schedule of food reinforcement received three sessions of experimental extinction. During the extinction sessions, the birds could produce the sound of the food magazine according to different schedules. Schedules of presentation of the magazine sound was effective in controlling response patterns and response rates during extinction. Other investigators have suggested that the presentation of the magazine sound enhances resistance to experimental extinction only because the magazine sound is either a conditioned stimulus which elicits responding or a discriminative stimulus which controls a high rate of responding. The present experiment demonstrates that the magazine sound can control either a high or a low rate during experimental extinction. The magazine sound can be used as a conditioned reinforcer.

Kelleher, R.T., & Fry, W. Stimulus functions in chained fixed-interval schedules. *Journal of Experimental Analysis of Behavior,* 1962, *5,* 167–173.

Pigeons were required to complete three successive fixed-interval components to obtain food. When the same exteroceptive stimulus was correlated with the three components, responding was positively accelerated between food deliveries. When different exteroceptive stimuli were correlated with each component in a fixed sequence, prolonged pauses developed in the first component; low response rates developed in the second component; and responding was positively accelerated in the second and third components. When different exteroceptive stimuli were correlated with each component in a variable sequence, responding was positively accelerated in each component. Because the response and reinforcement contingencies were the same in all three procedures, the differences in performances must be due to the changes in the sequence of stimuli.

Kish, G.B. Learning when the onset of illumination is used as the reinforcing stimulus. *Journal of Comparative and Physiological Psychology,* 1955, *48,* 261–264.

Two groups of eight female C57 Black 10 mice each were tested in a modified Skinner box to examine the hypothesis that a perceptible environmental change which is unrelated to such need states as hunger and thirst will reinforce any response which it follows. The effect upon the emission rate of a bar-contact response of the onset of dim illumination which followed this response was tested.

Introduction of the stimulus significantly increased the rate of emission of this response. Significant extinction effects were also noted when stimulation was discontinued. The results were considered to be in agreement with the initial hypothesis that a perceptible environmental change unrelated to homeostatic needs will reinforce any response which it follows.

Knott, P.D., & Clayton, K.N. Durable secondary reinforcement using brain stimulation as the primary reinforcer. *Journal of Comparative and Physiological Psychology*, 1966, *61*, 151–153.

A tone and a brain shock were paired intermittently for 1 group and continuously for another. A control group received the tone only. After the pairings both the partial and continuous reinforcement groups exhibited a preference for a lever which produced the tone over a lever which did not. However, intermittent pairings produced a significantly stronger secondary reinforcing effect than continuous pairings. The results support the assertions that brain stimulation can serve as a primary reinforcer in secondary reinforcement training, and that partial reinforcement can produce a more durable secondary reinforcer than continuous reinforcement.

Landauer, T.K. Reinforcement as consolidation. *Psychological Review*, 1969, *76*, 82–96.

A theory of the nature of reinforcement is presented. It assumes that learning is essentially by contiguity, but that a hyperexcitable state exists in the nervous system following an experience, such that an ordinarily insufficient stimulus can reexcite all or part of the cells involved in a just prior learning experience. This reexcitation in turn generates additional consolidation and thus strengthens learning. The theory thus explains the retroactive effect of operant reinforcement. Coupled with an assumption of nonadditivity of two temporally overlapping consolidation processes, the theory predicts certain phenomena of temporal gradients of reinforcement. The predictions compare favorably with data.

Miles, R.C., & Wickens, D.D. Effect of a secondary reinforcer on the primary hunger drive. *Journal of Comparative and Physiological Psychology*, 1953, *46*, 77–79.

This experiment was designed to test the hypothesis that the occurrence of secondary reinforcement affects the magnitude of the primary drive as measured by consummatory behavior.

1. Sixteen rats were conditioned in a Skinner box with food as a reward and a click associated with the delivery of food.

2. Half the animals were given 20 extinction trials with click present and half without.

3. Immediately afterward food consumption was measured in a situation to which the animals had previously become habituated.

4. The test situation was repeated after reconditioning with groups reversed.

5. Test pairs were given under primary drive states of 22-hr. and 6-hr. deprivation.

6. In none of the four test situations is there any statistical evidence that the groups differed from each other.

Miller, N.E., & Kessen, M.L. Reward effects of food via stomach fistula compared with those of food via mouth. *Journal of Comparative and Physiological Psychology,* **1952,** *45,* **555–564.**

Albino rats had small plastic fistulas sewn into their stomachs. Then they were given training trials during which they received enriched milk when they went to the correct side of a simple T-maze and isotonic saline when they went to the incorrect side. They were divided into three groups trained respectively under the following conditions:

(a) The substances, 14 cc. of milk for a correct or saline for an incorrect choice, were injected directly into the stomach at the rate at which the animals normally drank.

(b) Dishes containing 14 cc. of milk for a correct or saline for an incorrect choice were inserted into the end of the goal box immediately after the animal had made its choice.

(c) Dishes containing 14 cc. of milk or saline were inserted into the end of the goal box after a delay of 7 min. 35 sec., the time required to complete an injection for the animals in *a.*

All animals were given two trials a day motivated by hunger. On the first trial the animal was free to go in either direction; this trial was used to measure correct choices. On the second trial, given four hours later, the animal was forced to go in the opposite direction and receive the other substance.

The animals which received injections directly into their stomachs learned to choose the milk side within 40 days of training. The animals which received milk by mouth, either immediately or after a delay, learned faster than those which received milk via fistula. The results confirm the prediction from the drive-reduction hypothesis and fail to confirm the prediction from the prepotent consummatory response hypothesis of reinforcement.

Olds, J., & Milner, P. Positive reinforcement produced by electrical stimulation of septal area and other regions of rat brain. *Journal of Comparative and Physiological Psychology,* **1954,** *47,* **419–427.**

A preliminary study was made of rewarding effects produced by electrical stimulation of certain areas of the brain. In all cases, rats were used and stimulation was by 60-cycle alternating current with voltages ranging from 1/2 to 5 v. Bipolar needle electrodes were permanently implanted at various points in the brain. Animals were tested in Skinner boxes where they could stimulate themselves by pressing a lever. They received no other reward than the electrical stimulus in the course of the experiments. The primary findings may be listed as follows:

(a) There are numerous places in the lower centers of the brain where electrical stimulation is rewarding in the sense that the experimental animal will stimulate itself in these places frequently and regularly for long periods of time if permitted to do so.

(b) There are also sites in the lower centers where the effect is just the opposite: animals do nothing to obtain or avoid stimulation.

(c) In septal area preparations, the control exercised over the animal's behavior by means of this reward is extreme, possibly exceeding that exercised by any other reward previously used in animal experimentation.

The phenomenon was discussed as possibly laying a methodological foundation for a physiological study of the mechanisms of reward.

Premack, D. Toward empirical behavior laws: I. Positive reinforcement. *Psychological Review,* 1959, *66,* 219–233.

This account of reinforcement is based upon a generalization, not a theory: Any response *A* will reinforce any other response *B,* if and only if the independent rate of *A* is greater than that of *B.*

Any stimulus to which the species responds can be used as a reinforcer, provided only that the rate of the *R* governed by the stimulus is greater than that of some other *R.* Because the generalization treats a rate differential as a sufficient condition for reinforcement, ranking the *R*s of an organism in terms of their independent rates should permit predicting which *R*s will reinforce which others. The function is nonspecific, however, in that it does not permit specifying the dependent rate that will be attained by the lower rate *R.*

Ratner, S.C. Reinforcing and discriminative properties of the click in a Skinner box. *Psychological Reports,* 1956, *2,* 332.

This study is concerned with the observation that bar pressing can be learned when followed only by a click, a secondary reinforcer. Specifically, it was designed to repeat that observation and determine if the reinforcing properties of the click are related to *S*'s going to the place of reinforcement, i.e., making a goal response.

Sixteen habituated rats on a 23-hr. water deprivation schedule were trained in modified Skinner boxes to approach the water tray at the sound of a click. Bars were removed but hinged panels were placed in front of the tray to measure goal-approach responses. The click-water sequence was presented 17 times per day for 6 days. Bars were then inserted and water removed for 2 days of testing. During testing 8 Ss received the click after each bar press, Click Group, and 8 did not, No Click Group. Bar pressing and goal approaching was recorded.

The means of the numbers of bar presses made during testing are 30.37 and 22.25 (Day 1), and 17.00 and 13.62 (Day 2) for the Click and No Click groups, respectively. The groups differed significantly on Day 1 but not on Day 2. The means of the number of goal responses are 40.12 and 27.37 (Day 1) and 16.75 and 31.37 (Day 2) for the Click and No Click groups, respectively. The groups did not differ significantly on Day 1 or on Day 2. Lastly, the numbers of bar presses followed by goal responses were obtained from the records as a more sensitive measure of the relationship between the reinforcing and discriminative properties of the click. The means are 8.50 and 5.00 (Day 1), and 1.00 and 1.00 (Day 2). Fs for both days are less than 1.00.

These results support the observation that novel responses can be established for a short time with a secondary reinforcer. However, this stimulus did not function as a discriminative stimulus for goal approaching any more than the general situation does. That is, bar pressing is significantly increased by the click, although goal responding, the discriminative response established by training, has a complex but nonsignificant relationship with bar pressing sequences.

Saltzman, I.J. Maze learning in the absence of primary reinforcement: A study of secondary reinforcement. *Journal of Comparative and Physiological Psychology,* 1949, *42,* 161–173.

In this study, as a whole, six groups of hungry rats (N = 72) were given 15 learning trials in a single choice U-maze where the only reward was a familiar goal box. Familiarity with the goal box had been established by having the rats traverse a straight runway to the goal box where food was presented. Three of the groups, in addition to the 15 trials on the maze, were given further runway trials along with the maze trials. Three different methods for establishing the familiarity with the goal box were studied. Each of the three methods was used with both the three groups which did not receive them.

Two groups of rats had received food reward on every trial during the runway training. Of these two groups, the one which had not received the extra runway trials during the maze learning gave little evidence of learning the maze. The behavior of the rats was characterized by improvement on the initial maze trials, followed by a rapid decline. For the 15 trials, as a whole, the elimination of errors was not significantly better than chance. The group that had the extra runway trials did not show the rapid decline, and genuine learning of the maze was indicated. The extra runway trials apparently served to prevent the rapid extinction of the acquired reward value of the goal box.

Two groups of rats had received food reward only on alternate runs on the runway. Both the group which did and the group which did not receive the extra runway trials learned the maze. Although the mean number of correct choices in the maze was greater for the group which had the extra runway trials, the difference was not statistically significant.

Two groups of rats had received differential training on the runway. The differential training consisted of alternate trials of food-in-black-box and no-food-in-white-box, or vice versa. . . .

The mean number of correct choices in the maze was greater for the former group, but the difference was not statistically significant. The mean number of correct choices in the maze was greater with differential reward training than with either regular or alternate reward training. This was true whether or not extra runway trials were given.

The conclusions drawn from the study are:

1. Rats are able to learn a simple maze when the only reward is an acquired secondary reward.
2. Secondary reward may be as effective as the primary reward of food in influencing the choices made in a maze.
3. Of the three methods studied for establishing secondary reward value, the most effective was the differential reward of positive and negative cues.
4. The effectiveness of acquired rewards for promoting learning may be prolonged by continuing the process of establishing the reward value during the actual learning tests.

Sheffield, F.D., & Roby, T.B. Reward value of a non-nutritive sweet taste. *Journal of Comparative and Physiological Psychology*, 1950, *43*, 471–481.

A non-nourishing but sweet-tasting substance was shown in three successive learning situations to be an effective reward for instrumental learning, its reward value depending on the state of hunger present. The possibility that the sweet taste was an acquired reward rather than a primary reward was shown to be extremely unlikely.

The findings demonstrate the expected limitations of Hull's molar "need reduction" theory of reinforcement and the necessity of exploring indirect reduction of striped-muscle tension as a drive-reduction factor in Miller and Dollard's theory of reinforcement. The results are consistent with Guthrie's last-response theory of reinforcement, and demonstrate that a sweet taste is "reinforcing" in Skinner's system, "satisfying" in Thorndikes's system, and "demanded" in Tolman's system.

It is suggested that elicitation of the consummatory response appears to be a more critical primary reinforcing factor in instrumental learning than the drive reduction subsequently achieved.

Skinner, B.F. *Science and human behavior.* New York: Macmillan, 1953. (Ch. 5.)

It is still commonly believed that reinforcers can be identified apart from their effects upon a particular organism. As the term is used here, however, the only defining characteristic of a reinforcing stimulus is that it reinforces. The only way to tell whether or not a given event is reinforcing to a given organism under given conditions is to make a direct test. There is nothing circular about classifying events in terms of their effects; the criterion is both empirical and objective. It would be circular, however, if we then went on to assert that a given event strengthens an operant *because* it is reinforcing.

There are, of course, extensive differences between individuals in the events which prove to be reinforcing. The fact that organisms evidently inherit the capacity to be reinforced by certain kinds of events does not help us in predicting the reinforcing effect on an untried stimulus.

Although it is characteristic of human behavior that primary reinforcers may be effective after long delay, this is presumably only because intervening events become conditioned reinforcers. A conditioned reinforcer is generalized when it is paired with more than one primary reinforcer. The generalized reinforcer is useful because the momentary condition of the organism is not likely to be important. Eventually generalized reinforcers are effective even though the primary reinforcers upon which they are based no longer accompany them.

When we reinforce a response and observe a change in its frequency, we can easily report what has happened in objective terms. But in explaining *why* it has happened we are likely to resort to theory. A biological explanation of reinforcing power is perhaps as far as we can go in saying why an event is reinforcing. Such an explanation is probably of little help in a functional analysis, for it does not provide us with any way of identifying a reinforcing stimulus as such before we have tested its reinforcing power upon a given organism.

EXAMINATION ITEMS   **Topics for thought and discussion**

1.   Distinguish between defining reinforcement and identifying reinforcers and consider the problems associated with each.

2.   Consider the problem of circularity with respect to the empirical law of effect and

how it may differ from the problem of circularity in the identification of reinforcers and drives in a drive-stimulus reduction approach.

3.   The fact that electrical stimulation of the brain may be reinforcing has been taken as a challenge to the strong form of the drive-stimulus reduction approach. Evaluate possible arguments and counterarguments.

4.   Would a contiguity theorist have any interest in the concept of secondary reinforcement?

5.   Relate the concept of secondary reinforcement to the reinforcement-contiguity issue of whether reinforcement is necessary for learning to occur.

6.   Discuss how one who adopted a relational approach to identifying reinforcers might answer the question of what conditions are necessary and sufficient for the establishment of secondary reinforcers.

Objective items

1.   Which of the following has not been considered to be a major objection to the law of effect as stated by Thorndike?
    a. it assumes that reinforcers act in a retroactive manner
    b. it lacks specificity about quantitative aspects of reinforcers
    c. it lacks an independent definition of reinforcers
    d. it assumes that associations are strengthened only by reinforcers

2.   The functional approach to identifying reinforcers is inherently
    a. circular
    b. transsituational
    c. relative
    d. physiological

3.   According to Meehl, a reinforcer is transsituational, if it functions
    a. in more than one situation
    b. in all situations
    c. more strongly in some situations than in others
    d. less frequently in somewhat different situations

4.   The primary difficulty with using the transprocedural approach to identifying reinforcers is
    a. that it is not transsituational
    b. parameter specificity
    c. that it may be reduced to a functional approach
    d. that it implies reinforcing effects are retroactive

5.   If Premack were to be consistent between primary and secondary reinforcement, then secondary reinforcement would have the characteristics of being
    a. relational and situational
    b. relational and transsituational
    c. situational and absolute
    d. transsituational and absolute

6.   Which of the following statements is most consistent with a drive-motivation approach to identifying emotional events?
    a. reinforcers involve both biological and psychological factors

    b. reinforcers involve biological factors

    c. reinforcers involve psychological factors

    d. reinforcers involve neither biological nor psychological factors

7. The weak form of the theoretical law of effect, that is, that not all reinforcers involve drive-stimulus reduction, implies that need-reduction reinforcement can occur without concommitant reductions in drive stimuli.

    a. True

    b. False

8. Which of the following approaches would be most likely to indicate a different procedure for identifying positive and negative reinforcement?

    a. functional approach

    b. drive-stimulus reduction approach

    c. stimulus-change approach

    d. consummatory response approach

9. One of the facts concerning the reinforcing effects of electrical stimulation of certain areas of the brain is that the subjects often need to be primed with a few shocks before they begin to respond. This fact is most compatible with which of the following approaches to identifying reinforcing events?

    a. drive-stimulus reduction approach

    b. consummatory response approach

    c. stimulus-change approach

    d. high-probability response approach

10. To a cognitive theorist, which of the following events would best identify a reinforcer?

    a. stimulus change

    b. confirmation

    c. exploration

    d. satiation

11. The expression "negative secondary reinforcement" refers to the

    a. onset of a stimulus previously associated with the onset of an aversive event

    b. offset of a stimulus previously associated with the onset of an aversive event

    c. onset of a stimulus previously associated with the offset of an aversive event

    d. offset of a stimulus previously associated with the offset of an aversive event

12. The best evidence that an originally neutral stimulus has acquired secondary reinforcing properties would exhibit that the stimulus

    a. is drive reducing

    b. is a discriminative stimulus

    c. retards extinction

    d. promotes new learning

13. Compared with primary reinforcers, one would expect that individual differences in the range of events, which have secondary reinforcing value, are

    a. less variable

    b. about equally variable

    c. more variable

    d. indeterminate

14. The major criticism of secondary reinforcement as a practical explanatory mechanism has concerned its

    a. demonstrability

b. durability
c. applicability
d. generality

15. If a secondary reinforcer is presented on an FR schedule for bar pressing, the resulting behavior occurs according to the same pattern as under a food reinforced FR schedule. This is least consistent with which hypothesis of secondary reinforcement?
    a. elicitation
    b. information value
    c. discriminative stimulus
    d. contiguity

16. A number of researchers have shown that the occurrence of anticipatory salivation has little or no correlation with the performance of food-oriented operant/instrumental responses. This fact has not deterred some theorists from assuming that the fractional anticipatory goal response is the mechanism of positive secondary reinforcement because
    a. secondary reinforcement is equally illusive
    b. secondary reinforcement is an artifact
    c. conditioned salivation has been found to be unstable
    d. conditioned salivation is not necessarily a measure of r_g

17. According to the discrimination-stimulus hypothesis, establishing an originally neutral stimulus as a discriminative stimulus is a
    a. necessary condition for secondary reinforcement
    b. sufficient condition for secondary reinforcement
    c. necessary and sufficient condition for secondary reinforcement
    d. sufficient but not a necessary condition for secondary reinforcement

18. As formulated, the perspicuity of a stimulus is not an important factor in the information hypothesis of secondary reinforcement.
    a. True
    b. False

19. The information hypothesis of secondary reinforcement implies that, under conditions of consistent reward, the amount of secondary reinforcement value accrued to feedback stimuli produced by the eating response will be (   ) that accrued to the goal-box stimuli.
    a. less than
    b. greater than
    c. same as
    d. indeterminable with respect to

20. Which of the following hypotheses of secondary reinforcement could Tolman most readily embrace?
    a. elicitation
    b. facilitation
    c. discriminative stimulus
    d. information value

ANSWERS TO OBJECTIVE ITEMS

1. (d) The first three objections have been raised repeatedly; they refer to its logical adequacy. The fourth was not actually assumed and would be grounds for research rather than objection.

2. (a) The functional approach, namely, that whatever events satisfy the definition are included, is inherently circular. Such events may prove to be transsituational, relative, and/or physiological, but none of these is presumed by the functionalist.

3. (b) According to the Meehl approach to the circularity of the law of effect, a reinforcer must function in more than just one other situation, and it does not (by its own nature) differ in strength or frequency. In short, "That that is, is."

4. (b) The transprocedural approach identifies whether an event is emotionally positive or emotionally negative by viewing performance in particular procedures. The problem is that the scale values that are obtained may vary between different procedures depending on the particular parameters of the event.

5. (a) For Premack, a reinforcer can be so identified only in relation to other responses and only with respect to the particular situation in which those responses occur.

6. (a) The drive-motivation approach states that all drive-stimulus (psychological) reductions are reinforcers. Since drive-stimulus reductions are sometimes produced by need (biological) reduction, the best statement would be that both biological and psychological factors are involved.

7. (False) Some reinforcers do not involve drive reductions and need reductions constitute reinforcers. However, drives are thought to be directly dependent on needs and, therefore, would be reduced whenever a need was reduced. On the other hand, drives could be reduced without reducing needs.

8. (d) The functional approach says only that whatever works, works. The drive-stimulus reduction approach is indifferent to whether the drive is appetitive or aversive. Similarly, the stimulus-change approach requires only that the last response is preserved. In contrast, it is difficult to conceptualize an organism consuming the termination of an aversive event, and even more difficult to imagine measuring the strength of such a consummatory response.

9. (a) If electrical stimulation of the brain was in some form consumed, if it was simply a stimulus change, or if it enabled high-probability responses, then it should be reinforcing without priming. The drive-stimulus reduction theorist could readily assume, admittedly post hoc, that the drive for ECS requires priming. For example, it could be thought of as something like an addiction, with reinforcement being the termination of withdrawal symptoms instigated by priming the organism with a few shots.

10. (b) A reinforcer in cognitive theory would be best identified in the context of expectancies. Although expectancies might involve stimulus changes or be influenced by exploration, the most likely mechanism by which reinforcers could affect behavior would be by confirming an expectancy of an emotional event.

11. (b) Used to specify an operation, the term negative refers to the offset of a stimulus.

12. (d) Just as primary reinforcement is identified by an increase in response probability, the same logic is the best one to use with respect to secondary reinforcement. The other properties may be true but are not as conclusive.

13. (c) Although there is some variability in primary reinforcing events, it is small compared with the variability associated with secondary reinforcement. This is because the conditions of learning vary widely and with them vary the conditions necessary for the establishment of secondary reinforcers.

14. (b) Critics contend that a process so fragile as secondary reinforcement could hardly sustain everyday behavior. It is clearly applicable, has wide generality, and has been adequately demonstrated.

15. (a) The pause following an FR schedule would not follow from the belief that the stimulus elicited more responding. The other hypotheses would have some difficulty but could be made to fit.

16. (d) It is true that theorists, such as Hull, have sometimes used salivation as an illustrative and possible component of the fractional anticipatory goal response. Since it is a hypothetical construct, there is no necessity for its physical identification. It would certainly have been encouraging if anticipatory salivation occurred in the manner postulated for r_g, but its failure to do so can be interpreted simply by concluding that it is not an appropriate measure.

17. (a) The hypothesis states that secondary reinforcing stimuli must have acquired discriminative properties also. However many stimuli, such as those signalling a period of nonreinforcement, are discriminative but not reinforcing.

18. (True) Although it is known that perspicuity can affect the control gained by a stimulus, this feature was not explicitly included in the information hypothesis. Indeed, such a complexity would be difficult to incorporate without an independent measure of perspicuity.

19. (a) Although the eating response is most closely associated in time with primary reinforcement, those feedback stimuli could be viewed as redundant, since the goalbox stimuli have already conveyed the information that reward is forthcoming.

20. (d) Tolman would probably not be overly anxious to embrace any of these, but the hypothesis most compatible with his scheme would be one that did not explicitly involve responding and one that took into account the significance of stimulus events, that is, the information hypothesis.

SYSTEMATIC ANALYSES OF REINFORCEMENT

As we have seen, the empirical law of effect or, more so, the principle of (positive) reinforcement is almost universally accepted in some form. It is true, as we will discuss in this chapter, there may be limitations on the generality of this principle. Furthermore, there may well be refinements concerning the optimal nature of reinforcers for particular motivational systems, stimulus conditions, and response systems. However, in the broad spectrum of the totality of mammalian behavior, the limitations on the generality of the principle of reinforcement are relatively small compared with the vast domains of data to which it demonstrably applies.

Our concern in this chapter is with the method in which various systematists have attempted to deal with the empirical evidence supporting this principle. For convenience, we will concentrate on emotionally positive events, such as defined in the previous chapter; aversive events will be considered separately in the next chapter.

EMPIRICAL REINFORCEMENT SYSTEMS

Unfortunately, we have been unable to find empirical reinforcement systems that have been stated in sufficient detail to illustrate the types of issues that may be involved in their construction. We do, however, find some programmatic approaches that will serve our immediate purposes. From the point of view of design or structure, an empirical system looks like a mathematical system,[1] except of course that the source is empirical reality. Behavioral laws are first organized into some coherent system. A few of these laws are considered to have such wide generality and to have received sufficient empirical verification in many situations that they are given the status of principles. Other laws may be viewed as amplifications of the basic principles, having more the status of corollaries. Some deductions may be so useful in further analyses that they may be called theorems. Finally, the totality of these are used deductively to arrive at implications concerning still lower-level laws and facts. We wish to illustrate the nature of such systems in the context of positive reinforcement.

Classical Conditioning: Operational Analysis

In classical conditioning "reinforcement" is not used in the same sense as we have used it in the preceding chapter. Although Hull did maintain that reinforcement entailed drive reduction in all situations, conventionally the term "reinforcement" in classical conditioning refers simply to the occurrence of an unconditioned stimulus following a conditioned stimulus. The ambiguity of the term can be tolerated only if the context provides a clear indication of its intended meaning. With this in mind, it seems appropriate to include classical conditioning in this chapter.

It is important that we do so not only because classical conditioning is a very significant learning process in its own right, but because it enters into almost any systematic analysis of motivation. We have already encountered this in the context of acquired drive motivation, and we will shortly reencounter it in the context of acquired incentive motivation. If a systematist asserts that learned sources of motivation result from classical conditioning, then clearly a systematic analysis of the process itself is indispensable in any comprehensive system. One way to approach this mission is by means of an operational analysis. This will at least serve its vehicular role in analyses of operant and instrumental conditioning.[2]

Operational analysis is a procedure of specifying the events experienced by an organism as programmed by an experimenter or the natural environment, without regard to the labels that are traditionally attached to the outcome. Verplanck (1971) and Snapper, Knapp, and Kushner (1970) have made four arguments favoring such an analysis. The first argument recognizes that analysis provides a systematic structure by which to organize the known laws of the domain of interest. Second, the all too frequent finding is that the same label is applied to operations that, upon analysis, differ in important respects; hence, the argument calls for stricter labels. Or, third, different labels may be applied to operations that, when examined without preconceptions, are functionally the same. And finally, such an analysis may well reveal gaps in existing knowledge and, therefore, suggest areas that appear promising for future research. Although the logic of this approach applies to all operations involved in the study of learning and motivation (e.g., Mechner, 1959; Skinner, 1958), we will here concentrate on the domain typically referred to as classical conditioning.

Disregarding this label and looking simply at what an experimenter does in such a situation, we first observe that it is a pairing operation involving two stimuli, one of which has the property of eliciting an observable response. Let us call this a "*pure stimulus operation,*" because the operation is completely independent of the subject's behavior. In order to generate a logical system of operations of this type, we might construct a display such as that shown in Table 5.1. There we give the possible sequences of four stimuli that occur or do not occur sequentially in time. Any number of these operations may be interspersed or sequenced in any way desired, and the number of occurrences of any operation or sequence of operations can be specified. The logic of the system assumes that if we know the conditions and parameters of the operations, we can then, through experimental analysis, specify the behavioral outcome.

Obviously the number of operations and sequences of operations is too large for us to consider in detail here, but a few examples should give the reader the flavor of this approach. Any of the two-stimulus operations could be considered an instance of classical conditioning, provided that the second one used in the sequence elicits an identifiable unconditioned response. However, some

TABLE 5.1.

Operational Analysis of the Possible Sequences of Four Stimuli Occurring or not Occurring Sequentially in Time, Reading from Left to Right. The Operations May Be Repeated, Interspersed, or Occur in Sequence.

PURE STIMULUS OPERATIONS

One-stimulus operations:	Op(1)	S1			
	Op(2)		S2		
	Op(3)			S3	
	Op(4)				S4
Two-stimulus operations:	Op(5)	S1	S2		
	Op(6)	S1		S3	
	Op(7)	S1			S4
	Op(8)		S2	S3	
	Op(9)		S2		S4
	Op(10)			S3	S4
Three-stimulus operations:	Op(11)	S1	S2	S3	
	Op(12)	S1	S2		S4
	Op(13)	S1		S3	S4
	Op(14)		S2	S3	S4
Four-stimulus operations:	Op(15)	S1	S2	S3	S4

Conditions of the operation:
1. Stimulus classes involved
2. Stimulus intensity
3. Stimulus similarity
4. Discrete or continuous stimuli
5. Response interactions

Parameters of the operation:
1. Interstimulus intervals
2. Time separating repeated presentations of the operation
3. Number of repeated presentations within a session
4. Time separating sessions
5. Number of sessions

may be more appropriate for indicating particular sequences of operations. For example, if we consider Op(8) (S2-S3) (with S2 an originally neutral stimulus, which precedes S3 as an effective unconditioned stimulus), we may ask the outcome of probing the process resulting from Op(8) with Op(11) (which entails another originally neutral stimulus preceding the continued pairing of

S2 and S3). This is the sequence of operations that is performed in the study of external inhibition.

Alternatively, we may begin with Op(11) again letting S3 be a US. This operation (S1-S2-S3) is the one used by Egger and Miller (1963), which they followed by Op(1) or Op(2), (S1 or S2 alone), for evidence that would indicate the importance of information value in conditioning. However, the time separating S1 and S2 is a parameter of the system. If this interval is indefinitely small, we have a compound of S1 and S2 as the CS. In this case, both stimuli become conditioned to the CR; and if we allow this interval to be rather long, then S2, albeit redundant, might be expected to gain more from original training with Op(11).

Let us give a few more examples of familiar sequences of operations. Op(8) followed by Op(2) is experimental extinction; Op(8) followed by Op(4) is stimulus generalization; Op(1) alone is habituation; Op(2) followed by Op(8) is preadaptation to the CS; Op(5) followed by Op(8) in turn followed by Op(1) is sensory preconditioning. Designating S4 as an effective US and using Op(10) (S3-S4) as the basic conditioning operation, Op(10) interspersed irregularly with Op(2) refers to differential conditioning. If we probe the processes resulting from these operations with Op(14) (S2-S3-S4), we observe conditioned inhibition; if we probe with Op(15) (S1-S2-S3-S4), we have external inhibition of conditioned inhibition. The reader is encouraged to define various other known phenomena, such as higher-order conditioning, disinhibition, spontaneous recovery, overshadowing, partial reinforcement, and generalized conditioning, in terms of the stated set of possible pure stimulus operations. The entire experimental literature of pure stimulus operations, which includes classical conditioning and related phenomena, could be subsumed under a specification of the operations that were performed, and the conditions and parameters of those operations.

Interesting possibilities begin to emerge from fitting known facts into this system. We have already indicated that Op(11) (S1-S2-S3) under the temporal parameters used by Egger and Miller led to greater conditioning to S1 than to S2. We have also noted that this same operation, when the interstimulus interval between S1 and S2 is zero results in compound conditioning. But we also know that if Op(11) under the latter parameter values is preceded by Op(8) (S2-S3), the phenomenon of blocking results (i.e., the added S1 shows little evidence of conditioning). We may reasonably ask: if Op(11) with the temporal parameters used by Egger and Miller is preceded by Op(8), would there be blocking of the conditioning of S1 even though S2 is now made redundant.

Operational analysis is not truly a predictive system. Instead, it provides a rational arrangement of the essential ingredients of any study in an easily accessible format. It can be used for prediction only when a person proposes a study that, even in a different context, can be analyzed into a set of operations that can be seen as equivalent to those about which the outcome is already known. The system would, of course, break down if different outcomes obtained from the same operations that were performed in different settings. For example, one could reasonably consider the domains traditionally labeled perceptual learning and verbal learning as pure stimulus operations. Specifically, the design of a study concerned with retroactive interference (traditionally known as the "A-B, A-C paradigm") is precisely the sequence of Op(5) (S1-S2) followed by Op(6) (S1-S3), in turn followed by a probe trial with Op(1) (S1 alone) under the conditions of incompatibility of the responses associated with S2 and S3. The operational analyst would be surprised if the phenomena of classical conditioning did not obtain in the context of perceptual and verbal learning, and vice versa.[3]

Operant Conditioning: Schedules and Contingencies of Reinforcement

Pure stimulus operations can be imposed in the context of operant behavior and their effects, if any, observed. Specifically, one can put a pigeon in a keypeck chamber and, independently of its behavior, program the delivery of any stimulus event desired (e.g., Skinner, 1948). Autoshaping is the temporal correlation of such events with another stimulus schedule. However, let us temporarily set aside such operations, and consider operant conditioning procedures in which reinforcers are uniquely dependent on the emission of the operant behavior being observed. The keypeck of pigeons is currently the most popular for a number of reasons[4] and we will use it for illustrative purposes.

The defining characteristic of operant conditioning is that operant behavior is freely available, which means simply that the pigeon can peck the key at will. In the simplest case, there are no other stimulus events in the chamber, and the dependent variable is the rate at which this operant behavior is emitted by the organism. The independent variable is the schedule according to which reinforcement for the response is made available. Were there reinforcement for doing so, we could readily fill a small library with a catalogue of the possible schedules that could be designed according to one rule or another. We would need an even larger library if we were to include situations in which other stimuli are introduced into the chamber, correlated in some way with the reinforcement schedule. Needless to say, this prospect is not very attractive to us.

Accordingly, nowhere is it more evident that some kind of logical system is necessary to organize the domain of schedules of reinforcement. Some way must be found to extract from this myriad of possibilities those outcomes that will be interesting in some systematic sense. Although, historically, many people did indeed set about simply to design more and more variations of schedules, run one or two subjects, and file the results in the library, this characterization would be quite inaccurate of contemporary students of operant conditioning. The need for systematization is evident, compartmentalized subareas are defined and analyzed experimentally, and empirical systems are beginning to emerge. For the moment, we are concerned mainly with the nature of several such systems.

Functional Analysis. In our discussion, functional analysis will describe a quite different way to approach the goal of summarizing the empirical knowledge of a domain of interest. In this case, we are not immediately concerned with what the natural environment or an experimenter actually does. A *functional analysis* of operations states a conceptual system in which the outcomes of any particular set of operations can be described. Let us consider a physical example, say, that of determining the time of day. What we need is some natural source of output of energy that is regular with time; any such source would, functionally, be equivalent. We might use the sun, a pendulum, an electric motor, or natural radiation from various radioactive materials. The point of immediate concern is that all of these systems are functionally equivalent, and we really do not care how precisely you go about telling time, provided only that your system is reliable.

In the face of the geometrically expanding plethora of operant schedules of reinforcement, Schoenfeld and his coworkers (e.g., Schoenfeld, Cummings, & Hearst, 1956) set about to develop a functional analysis of such schedules. Their objective was not to describe the operations that experimenters actually perform. What they attempted is a system that will have the functional properties, in the sense of generating the same behavior, of any such actual operations. Because of its elegant simplicity and richness in potential ramifications, we hope to describe it briefly before considering the more familiar approach to systematizing contingencies of reinforcement.

We will describe the system in somewhat different language from the original authors, and we recommend that you study their work for the basic notational system. Let us begin with a physical situation involving the familiar circuit breaker in an electrical wiring system. A circuit breaker has three positions, one of which is "set." In this position, electricity is available, although not necessarily being used at the moment, to the various outlets in your home. The second position is "broken," which means that you have plugged in too many appliances for the wiring system or have somehow shorted the circuit such that you will get only a brief surge of electricity before the circuit is broken. Finally, there is the "reset" position, which is held for some period of time before switching it back into the set position for further use.

Now let us put a circuit breaker into the line running to the food delivery mechanism of an operant chamber, knowing full well that the current required by one firing of that mechanism exceeds the limit of the circuit breaker. Any time the pigeon pecks when the system is set, one reinforcement will be delivered and the circuit broken. Then, we station an assistant near the switch of the circuit breaker and give the following instructions:

"Here is a time schedule. At these points in time after you put the pigeon in the chamber, press the switch over into the reset position, and hold it there for the indicated amount of time, and then switch it back into the set position. Now the pigeon may or may not peck the key and, hence, the circuit may or may not be broken while you are waiting for your next act—but pay no attention to that. Just hold the switch in the reset position at the times indicated in this schedule for the length of time also indicated there. I will worry about what the pigeon does, and meanwhile be working out some new schedules for you to impose later.

Fundamentally, that is all there is to it. According to Schoenfeld, it is true that he cannot duplicate the mechanics of any conventional schedule (except extinction), but what he can do is duplicate the behavior that is generated by such schedules. All he needs to do is to work out a set of instructions for his assistant, and shortly you will observe the pigeon behaving *as if* it were on that other schedule. Since your interest is actually generating that behavior, here is the conceptually simplest way to do it. Furthermore, like doing a trick with your eyes closed, Schoenfeld hopes to accomplish much of this with perfectly regular time intervals. One such instruction would read, "Exactly every minute, hold the circuit breaker in the reset position for exactly ten seconds." Of course, to insure exactness, we can put the assistant to work on more challenging tasks and let electronic timers run the schedule.

We can best understand how this system is going to work, if we pause long enough to consider its rationale. The argument has two features. The first states that the only thing that can actually influence an organism is the probability that at any moment in time a response will be reinforced. The second argument states that when a reinforcement does occur, it increases the likelihood of the emission of that response defined in a micromolecular manner so that it includes all qualitative and quantitative features, such as the immediately preceding interresponse time. There is, of course, the converse assumption that any response that is emitted and not followed by reinforcement decreases in likelihood of recurrence also with respect to its micromolecular features. Thus, an approach to the definition of a response, combined with the empirical principle of reinforcement, gives rise to a functional analysis of schedules of reinforcement.

Recall that Schoenfeld has only two fixed-time intervals with which to work: the time between putting the circuit breaker into the set position and putting it into the reset position, and the time it is held in the reset position before being returned to the set position. He calls these t^D and t^Δ respectively.[5] But lest you think that even so simple a schedule as continuous reinforcement is obvious, because all we have to do is leave the circuit breaker in the set position and dispense with our electronic assistant, it is not quite so simple. Each reinforcement breaks the circuit; we cannot have it reset by a response, because we are constrained to work only with time. The solution is as follows: let t^Δ equal zero (the reset operation is instantaneous) and t^D be some finite period of time shorter than involved in the reinforcement operation. After all, the pigeon has to consume the food, and typically it will eat for the length of time the hopper is available. So we simply go through the motions of resetting the circuit breaker every so often; the operation requires so short a period of time (virtually zero) that no responses could ever get trapped in there. Although the circuit will be broken from time to time, it will be returned to the set position before the pigeon has finished eating.

This is a more complicated method of programming continuous reinforcement than to have a feeding mechanism that does not short out the system and, hence, make it necessary to reset; it is also more complicated than resetting the circuit instantaneously after each response, but this is a small price to pay for a system that can do so much else of what we might want to do with just these two temporal parameters. Practically, the most critical factor is some knowledge of the organism's behavior that will enable us to program reinforcement at times when the organism is likely to be emitting the micromolecular responses desired. This is because the principle of reinforcement does not require a causal dependency of reinforcement on behavior, only that a reinforcer occur after a response is emitted. Conceptually, the most critical factor in the system is the ratio of t^D to $t^D + t^\Delta$, namely, the proportion of the total time during which the system is in either the set (or possibly broken) positions. The other important derivative is $t^D + t^\Delta$ itself, the overall cycle time. If these are plotted on orthogonal coordinates (they can be varied independently or made to covary), the areas corresponding to the various familiar schedules can be mapped. Several examples of such interpretations are given in the abstracts at the end of this chapter. And as might be expected, many different types of schedules are suggested by this system.

Contingencies of Reinforcement. If not revolutionary, Skinner's 1938 book, *The Behavior of Organisms,* clearly deserves a notable place among the most significant publications of that era. It was, indeed, apart from the mainstream of the then current theoretical thinking dominated by such giants as Guthrie, Hull, Pavlov, Thorndike, Tolman, and Watson, and it was destined to drift even further away during the ensuing decade.[6] It is only now, yet another quarter of a century later, that the kind of empirical–theoretical rapprochement reflected in this book could be achieved.

Skinner's influence was simply not to be denied, and partly aided by radical technological advances[7] related to his approach, the empirical domain of operant conditioning grew ever broader and deeper in conceptual analysis. Others were at first hard pressed to assimilate this new knowledge; where were their familiar dependent variables such as latency, speed, amplitude, percent correct, and so on, to say nothing of their accustomed experimental operations? Skinner even quickly abandoned the one point of contact available, namely, his single hypothetical construct—the reflex reserve—and the common measure of response strength—resistance to experimental extinction. Yet lawful relationships continued to emerge between rate of responding in a free-operant situation, and the schedule of reinforcement imposed by an experimenter. Skinner was soon able to proclaim a fait accompli.

This is not to say that the ultimate mission is complete; inevitably in science, much in the areas of both empirical and systematic analysis yet remains to be done. But Skinner's original formulations proved to be a very solid foundation upon which to build. The essence of his approach is so familiar that it hardly bears much repetition here. Skinner found simply that, after depriving an organism of food and giving it shaping instructions about the behavior of interest to the experimenter, the rate of emission of that behavior varied systematically with the schedule of reinforcement. He saw two ways in which the schedule could be designed, one based on counters and the other based on clocks (the ratio and interval schedules, respectively); in either case, the requirement could be constant or variable. Thus arose the four basic schedules, and these gave rise to descriptively different patterns of behavior. More complex schedules could be devised by various kinds of combinations of these basic ones that could be increased in scope by the addition of exteroceptive informative stimuli about the schedule in force. These few statements cover the topics of what would be the introductory chapter of a long book on contingencies of reinforcement.

Unfortunately, that book has not been written, perhaps, because the domain is expanding so rapidly that no one has been willing to attempt a "stop-action" summary of where things stand at present. A great many limited systematic statements have been made, and data are available for even more. But we do not believe that anyone has yet attempted to pull these together in a form reasonably approximating the kind of empirical system that Skinner has in mind. We envisage such a system containing a hierarchy of principles, corollaries, theorems, laws, and facts all interrelated in an empirical mathematico-deductive system from which derivations can be made explicitly and without regard to hypothetical constructs. We have attempted to illustrate this conception of an empirical system in Table 5.2.

Constructing such a system is more than simply putting down the known phenomena in the order in which they come to mind or in which they were discovered. The notion is that these should be hierarchical even within any level designated by a nominal concept. Thus, we have placed the principle of schedules of reinforcement under the principle of positive reinforcement, because we presume the latter to apply more broadly—certainly to include the procedures of instrumental conditioning. We also see the principles of stimulus-differential and response-differential reinforcement under the principle of schedules of reinforcement, because they are particular realizations of schedules of reinforcement correlated with stimuli or responses, respectively; they should probably be placed on the same plane within the level of principles, because there is no logical primacy of one over the other. One might wish to move the principle of concurrent schedules up to the level of the basic principle of schedules, because they differ only in whether one or two manipulanda are concurrently available. And clearly, both stimulus-differential and response-differential schedules could be selectively imposed on each manipulandum.

This last example serves to illustrate how even so incomplete a system as we have presented can lead to novel questions. To the best of our knowledge, no one has studied response-differential and stimulus-differential schedules concurrently in force on different manipulanda. Imagine a differential reinforcement of low rate (DRL) schedule on one key, normally leading to long interresponse times, and a multiple schedule on the other key, which normally would generate two different rates corresponding to the basic schedules in force during the presentation of one or the other of the stimuli on that key. We can suspect that DRL performance, viewed separately, would be improved, because there is another reinforced response available to consume the requisite time; yet, there might be a systematic effect on the rates of responding on the multiple-schedule key. One would be interested in the overall density of reinforcement, especially if the multiple schedules were interval ones. This would further lead to the problem of whether the schedules on each key are interrupted when the pigeon is pecking on the other key, whether they are reset, or whether they are simply allowed to continue their independent timing operations. In the latter case, there might be a greater tendency to change over when the multiple-schedule key is in the less preferred state, but this might in turn depend on the duration of any changeover delay imposed. At this point, the interested empiricist would stop speculating and run some birds in this type of situation to fill in the facts and laws about the procedure.

TABLE 5.2.

Illustrative and Simplified Format of an Empirical System Based on Contingencies of Reinforcement for Free-Operant Behavior.

SYSTEM OF CONTINGENCIES OF REINFORCEMENT

Boundary Conditions		*Setting Operations*	
Steady-state rate of emission of freely available operant behavior		Deprivation Stimulation Shaping	

Principle of Positive Reinforcement

Corollaries	Nonreinforcement	Reinforcement	
Theorems	Operant level Extinction	Rate of response Conditions of reinforcement	

Principle of Schedules of Reinforcement

Corollaries	Fixed ratio	Variable ratio	Fixed interval	Variable interval
Theorems	Rapid rate (running)	Rapid rate (running)	Increasing rate	Moderate steady rate
	Postreinforce- ment pause	Postreinforce- ment pause	Postreinforce- ment pause	Postreinforce- ment pause

Principle of Stimulus-Differential Reinforcement

Corollaries	Stimulus control	Multiple schedules	
Theorems	Differential conditioning Time-out	Discrimination Observing response	

Principle of Response-Differential Reinforcement

Corollaries	Qualitative features	Quantitative features	
Theorems	Differentiation Response topography	Response rate Interresponse time	

Principle of Concurrent Schedules

Corollaries	Schedule preference	Changeover delay	
Theorems	Density of reinforcement Concurrent chains	Density of reinforcement Schedule interruption	

Recognize that although we call this a mathematico-deductive system, it is constructed entirely by induction from empirical facts and laws. That is, you really don't deduce anything you don't already know, at least, if your inductions represent sound generalizations. What you know is found in experimental analysis, not in theoretical premises. What systematization allows is an organization of knowledge into a format from which the implications are more readily apparent and, conceivably, readily available for an adequately programmed computer. In effect, either your deductions are immediately confirmed, or you have erred in constructing your system. If you erred, you begin to search through it for the areas in which your statements were actually overgeneralizations.

Accordingly, one way to use such a system in the design of future research is in the derivation of unexplored combinations of principles and their associated corollaries and theorems, in the expectation of confirming the predictions and increasing confidence in the adequacy of the system. On the other hand, critics are likely to draw implications that they believe to be empirically false; if they can establish these implications, they show that there is a flaw somewhere in the system. Of course, gaps in the system become evident and topics for research. The situation we described above involves schedule interactions that are known, generally, to exist but that are still poorly understood.

It should be apparent that we are not proposing the type of system we have described as the only method of approach, nor even that it is the best method. We might have started with the $t^D - t^\Delta$ system as a more parsimonious way to organize the principles than the familiar schedule approach. Our conclusion is that such systems may not only be useful but are becoming increasingly necessary; this applies to abstract empirical systems and not to theoretical systems.

Instrumental Conditioning: Conditions of Reinforcement

Elsewhere, we have (Logan & Ferraro, 1970) distinguished between operant and instrumental conditioning purely on operational grounds.[8] Our basic proposition was that operant conditioning involves responses that are freely available to the organism, whereas instrumental conditioning involves periodic enabling of the response. The most logical empirical response measure in the former is the rate of emission of the operant behavior; the most logical response measure in the latter is an index of vigor, such as latency, speed, or amplitude. However, our contention is that the principle of reinforcement affects both forms of conditioning and can eventually be integrated into a single empirical or theoretical system. Indeed, the empirical system now to be described also applies to operant conditioning phenomena when properly translated according to the response measures employed.

Let us introduce the principle of stimulus-differential reinforcement in an instrumental context: When two somewhat similar stimuli (S1 and S2) are presented separately and in an irregular sequence, the response being concurrently enabled and the schedules/conditions of reinforcement in the presence of S1 are better to the organism than those that prevail in the presence of S2, the organism will come to respond differentially, more or less, in accord with the appropriate schedules/conditions for each stimulus. For example, we may run rats sometimes in a black runway and reinforce approaching the goal or sometimes run the same rat in a white runway without reinforcement. The principle of stimulus-differential reinforcement says simply that the rat will learn to run rapidly in the black runway and slowly (if at all) in the white runway. The result is called differential instrumental conditioning.

As a part of an empirical system designed to encompass the domain of differential instrumental conditioning, consider the following two laws:

1. After a substantial number of differentially reinforced trials:
(a) R to the more highly reinforced S1 is an increasing concave function of the difference between S1 and S2, but the total effect is small;
(b) R to the less highly rewarded S2 is a decreasing convex function of the difference between S1 and S2, and the total effect is larger than in (a) above;
(c) the curves in (a) and (b) above originate together at substantial R and diverge.
2. After a substantial number of differentially reinforced trials:
(a) R to the more highly rewarded S1 is an increasing concave function of the proportion of trials to S1;
(b) R to the less highly rewarded S2 is an increasing convex function of the proportion of trials to S1;
(c) the extent to which (a) is above (b) depends on the similarity of S1 and S2;
(d) the maximal difference in R obtains when S1 and S2 occur equally often.

These laws summarize a rather large body of literature but their full implications, especially taken jointly, may not be readily apparent in these verbal statements. Accordingly, we present in Figure 5.1 a graphic representation of an empirical system integrating these laws.

Along one axis is the difference between S1 and S2, which is listed as the independent variable in the first law stated above; along a second axis is the percent of trials to S1, which is listed as the independent variable in the second law stated above; the third axis depicts the dependent variable, in this case, some measure of response strength, such as speed of locomotion down each of the two runways. In the figure, R to S1 is shown in heavy solid lines, and R to S2 is shown in dashed lines. What the reader should attempt to see is a canopy with two flaps; the upper one showing R to S1 and the lower one R to S2.

Consider first the line labeled *c* in the upper right portion of the figure. This refers to conditions in which all of the trials are given to the more highly reinforced S1 (S2 being held conceptually in abeyance). Under such circumstances, the difference between S1 and S2 is irrelevant to the behavior in the presence of S1; this line, therefore, depicts the level of responding maintained by continuous reinforcement of a stimulus. In order not to make the graph too complex, the reader will have to imagine raising or lowering this anchoring level of performance according to the amount of reinforcement. Since we know empirically that the speed of locomotion is a negatively accelerated increasing

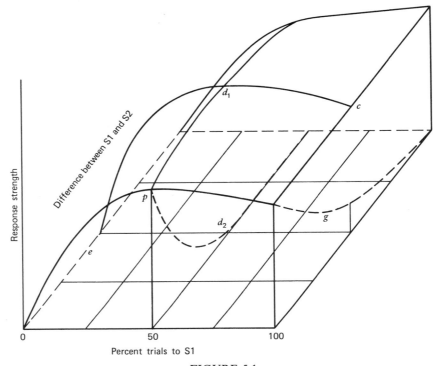

FIGURE 5.1.

Graphic Three-dimensional Representation of the Empirical Laws Concerning the Principle of Differential Reinforcement. The Graph Depicts the Joint Effects on Response Strength of the Percent of Trials to the More Highly Reinforced S1, and the Difference Between It and the Less Highly Reinforced S2.

function of the amount of reinforcement, we can imagine line c being higher with large rewards to S1, lower with small rewards to S1, and collapsing totally to the base of the graph if the larger reward is actually zero.

Next, consider the curve labeled g in the figure. Now we have no measure of response strength to S2, because all of the trials in this plane of the graph are given to S1. But we can imagine a strength to S2 being developed as a result of conditioning to S1. If we subsequently test for it with stimuli at varying degrees of difference from S1, we obtain the dashed curve g. This, on reflection is precisely the empirical gradient of stimulus generalization originating at the point above 100% reinforcement with zero difference.

In all conditions other than the particular plane of the graph that we have just considered, S2 is sometimes presented during acquisition; let us for the moment presume that responding in its presence is not reinforced. We can then go to point p on the graph where half of the trials are given to S1 and half to S2, and where there is no difference between S1 and S2. Again, a little reflection identifies this point as the familiar condition of partial reinforcement. Furthermore, the graph is drawn in such a way as to depict a higher response strength at this point than the corresponding point on line c that, it will be recalled, depicts continuous reinforcement. Accordingly, we have included the partial reinforcement effect on acquisition in our empirical system.

Let us next consider the points d_1 and d_2 together. These apply when half of the trials are given to S1 and half to S2, the stimuli are somewhat different, and reinforcement obtains in S1 and not in S2. These are the defining operations of differential instrumental conditioning. Note that we have shown that responding to S1 (point d_1) is very high, and responding to S2 (point d_2) is very low, which is, of course, the most direct implication of the principle of stimulus-differential reinforcement. Also notice that if the curve of responding to S1 on which point d_1 falls is followed to line c (continuous reinforcement), we have a decrease in response level. This reflects the empirical phenomenon of positive contrast. We also may exhibit other facets; for example, if we follow the upper flap of the canopy back to point p (partial reinforcement), we have depicted an integration of the otherwise conceptually disparate phenomena of positive contrast and the partial reinforcement effect on acquisition.

Continuing on to line e we have a condition in which all of the trials are given to S2, which receives the smaller reward; in our particular illustration, this is zero. Hence, line e is at the baseline level and corresponds to conditions of experimental extinction. Again the reader can invoke perceptual skills and imagine the amount of reinforcement to S2 being greater than zero. This would raise or lower the entire anchoring line e, correspondingly, up to a limit of the height of our original continuous reinforcement line c (reinforcement to S2 cannot, by the statement of the conditions, exceed that to S1 or their labels would thereby be reversed). In doing so, the lower flap would sag in order to depict negative contrast at point d_2. It should be noted that these operations affect point p, and as a matter of historical fact, it was just this analysis that led to the concept of varied reinforcement (Logan, Beier, & Ellis, 1955). Since the partial reinforcement effect on extinction had proven interesting conceptually, it also suggested studying the varied reward effect on extinction (Logan, Beier, & Kincaid, 1956). Both of these represent changing from point p to line e, and it was only a somewhat larger step to envisage changing from points d_1 and d_2 to line e—hence the generalized partial reinforcement effect (Brown & Logan, 1965). Indeed, once we recognize that lines c and e are affected by the conditions of reinforcement to S1 and S2, respectively, and include changes from one set of experimental operations to another, we incorporate a number of interesting phenomena.

As a final explicit illustration from Figure 5.1, return to point p and consider the dashed curve passing through point d_2. This is not quite the postdiscrimination gradient of stimulus generalization, since it depicts only the response strength to a differentially reinforced S2 during acquisition. However, it is very closely related to it, and note that the curve is substantially steeper than our original generalization gradient (curve g). Accordingly, the essence of the effects of differential reinforcement on stimulus generalization are included in this empirical system.

The preceding discussion should suffice to illustrate our major point: empirical systems can be constructed explicitly to include a large number of facts and laws that can be integrated into a convenient system that depicts interrelationships that might not otherwise be found. Furthermore, all of the features of this particular system have yet to be subjected to empirical verification and, hence, the system could be used to generate hypotheses that also might not have occurred. The devoted empiricist would not be content to stop at this juncture. You might ask about differential reinforcement involving different percentages of reinforcement to S1 and S2? Conceptually, at least, this would entail another three-dimensional graph encompassing that domain, but it would have a point of contact with the one depicted here, namely, point p. Fortunately, the mathematics are largely available for working in n-dimensional space, and the empirical systematists of the future are likely to be engaged in this venture.

Empirical Systematic Issues   Pure empiricists do not engage in the same type of controversies that we have discussed with respect to theorists. In the very nature of the case, issues concerning empirical systems can be reduced directly to empirical questions and resolved by experimental analysis. As we have seen, theories are rarely, if ever, overthrown by contradictory evidence, and theorists are quite free to adjust a theory to accommodate somewhat embarrassing facts. But neither a theorist nor a pure empiricist can adjust the facts to suit their systems.

Nevertheless, even though empirical issues are only temporary, they do occur and their substance is worthy of consideration. One way to gain an understanding of such issues is to make an empirical critique of the system presented in Figure 5.1. One may first question the accuracy of the smooth function forms that have been used to interconnect the known points in the conceptual space. For example, we do have evidence suggesting the general accuracy of the points concerning extinction, partial, and continuous reinforcement; yet, we do not have precise information about all of the intermediate conditions. Perhaps the functions should rise to a peak around 50% reinforcement, and look more like a tent than a canopy. And, of course, possibly this contour changes as distinctive cues are provided.

At a somewhat more refined level, an empiricist may object to the coordinates used in the graph. The concept of "difference between S1 and S2" is ambiguous, because the same physical difference can be obtained at various points along the stimulus continuum; we know empirically that these are not equivalent behaviorally. Perhaps, then, that coordinate should be some further transformation, such as the difference between the logarithms of the stimulus values being used. And with respect to "percent of trials to S1," we know that some sequences of presentations lead to different outcomes than other sequences, and this fact is not represented in the system. These are, indeed, empirical systematic issues that are not directly resolved by experimental analysis. They are resolved by conceptual analysis, and we venture the same maxim with respect to empirical systems as applies to theoretical systems: systems are superseded by better systems.

However, in the case of empirical systems, "better" has a much more definitive meaning. If a scientist prefers one empirical system over another because it feels better, appears to involve the really basic behavioral phenomena, or has an intuitive appeal apart from the facts themselves, that scientist has committed the cardinal sin of the pure empiricist. For those with strong empirical convictions, there is one, and only one, criterion of judgment, namely, parsimony. In contrast to the somewhat fuzzy concept of parsimony when applied to theoretical systems, parsimony is logically measureable for empirical systems. If the system is explicit, as it should be, one can simply count the number of assumptions that have been made, the number of data points that need to be estimated empirically, and then count the number of nontrivial implications of the system. (A trivial implication is filling in the gaps after there is already enough information to fit a function mathematically.) The ratio of these defines the parsimony of a system, and other things equal, the more parsimonious system is automatically preferred.

The preceding sentence included a second issue that arises with respect to empirical systems. All laws, and hence all principles and systems, are inherently prefaced by some disclaimer such as "other things equal." It may take the form of "under the conditions of this experiment," "within the limits of the present procedures," or the like. The problem, however, is that the scientist may not be certain about which other things need to be equal or even which of all of the conditions of the experiment were, in fact, important in determining the outcome. An empirical systematist may, accordingly, discount one or another reported observation as some kind of a fluke, unless it can be systematically replicated. This means that at any particular moment in time, an issue may arise about the facts themselves.

This is especially likely to occur when a system implies a phenomenon that has not yet been observed and that fails to appear on early efforts to detect it. This leads us quite naturally into a more general discussion of the boundary conditions of a system. Any system, be it empirical or theoretical, not only should but must have explicit boundary conditions. To give a simile: a system without boundaries is like a sea without a shore; the tides may rise and fall somewhat, in our case atuned to the systematist's momentary feelings of exuberance or caution, but the boundaries need to be well defined. For example, one boundary of the system presented in Figure 5.1 could be: "applies only to conditions in which the sequence of trials is sufficiently irregular to preclude the organism from coming under control of the sequence itself." This boundary is still a bit vague, but we would certainly know to exclude simple alternation sequences (see, e.g., Hulse, 1973), and depending on the presumed capacities of the organism, still higher-order nonrandom transition probabilities. A more abstract system that would parsimoniously encompass both regular and irregular sequences would supersede the one presented.

Any issues about boundaries are ultimately reducible to empirical determination. When an empiricist asserts that this system applies under these circumstances and not under other circumstances, the obvious implication is that a different empirical system will be required to handle the latter. The systematist might well prefer outcomes suggesting that nature designed organisms in such a way that the boundaries of a simple system can be very broad, but when that is not the case, one simply sets about to analyze each experimentally and then systematically as separate domains.

Interestingly, the issue concerning the appropriate breadth of the boundaries of an empirical system equally interest the theorist. This is because all scientists are empiricists first, and theorists themselves strive for elegant empirical systems. If they can then design a theoretical system that implies the premises of an empirical system, all of the implications of the latter are automatically subsumed under the theory. A theoretically minded scientist, looking at the empirical system in Figure 5.1, would delight at the prospect of building a theory around it. Surely some beautiful system of hypothetical constructs involving excitatory potentials, inhibitory potentials, generalization processes, and the like, could be devised as a larger dome over the canopy that the empirist has constructed. The boundaries of a theoretical system are, thus, supposed to be larger than those of the empirical systems that it ostensibly subsumes. If the empiricist delimits a system too narrowly for the theorist, they stand at odds with each other.

Such an issue has indeed occurred during recent history. Since it remains unresolved at this writing, we use it primarily for illustrative purposes. Skinner (1938) clearly asserted a fundamental distinction between respondent (classical) conditioning and operant conditioning. According to him, respondent conditioning involved behaviors he called "respondents," because they are elicited by stimuli of interoceptive or exteroceptive origin. Respondents could come to be elicited by originally neutral stimuli given the procedures of Pavlovian conditioning. He proposed a set of laws concerning this procedure, and distinguished them from the laws of operant conditioning. In the latter case, reference is to behaviors that are emitted by the organism, act upon the environment, modify it in some way, and hence might produce consequences of significance. In particular, the principle of reinforcement applies to operants and not to respondents.

Furthermore, Skinner provided a clear delineation of the boundary conditions of each type of conditioning by means of the relevant nervous system involved. Respondent (classical) laws apply to behaviors mediated by the autonomic system; operant laws apply to behaviors mediated by the somatic nervous system. Hence, his position was clearly stated. Although he considered it an empirical matter, the most straightforward implication is that responses, such as heart rate and other visceral changes, are not subject to the principle of reinforcement.

Shortly thereafter, Hull (1943, 1952) proposed a theory that was to avow: "It seems very unlikely that nature would design one set of behavorial laws for the determination of individual behavior and another set for social-cultural phenomena. . . . " Hull was here asserting that the basic laws would apply to all mammalian behavior of individual organisms and also to their behavior in groups, societies, and cultures. It would indeed be a blow to Hull, if Skinner were correct.

It is true that Skinner was talking about the empirical principle of reinforcement, and Hull was talking about the theoretical postulate of reinforcement, but the latter was presumed to encompass the former. And as it is typically the case when one asserts broader boundaries than claimed by the original systematist, the burden of proof rests upon the one who would extend the boundaries to offer convincing evidence. The resolution of the conceptual issue was, therefore, squarely up to a clear demonstration of modification of visceral responses by means of operant procedures.

But as we have alluded to in previous discussions, such a demonstration has not been accomplished to everyone's satisfaction. Recall that Smith (1954) had contended that apparent classical conditioning in such situations is artifactual, resulting from operant conditioning of skeletal behaviors of which the observed visceral changes are a natural component. And still other problems that we have discussed might be considered. For example, if awareness is indeed important for successful conditioning, perhaps a human subject should be conditioned with the aid of exteroceptive feedback monitoring visceral activity, because these response systems are poorly supplied with afferent sensory nerves (Razran, 1961). The case would be more convincing if the same subject learned a differentiation in order to increase activity in the presence of one distinctive cue and to decrease activity in the presence of another. Perhaps conditions of correlated reinforcement, giving more reward for larger accelerations or decelerations, would bring to bear the laws concerning those techniques. In a case such as this, the proponent is permitted to pull out all the stops; just one convincing demonstration, free of any artifactual interpretation, would be sufficient to make the case.

Since our purpose has been to illustrate the types of issues that can involve empirical systems rather than to try to resolve them in this book, we can rest the case at this point and wait for the evidence to be determined. We can report that DiCara and Miller (e.g., DiCara & Miller, 1968; Miller, 1969) have reported successful operant conditioning of visceral behaviors. However, there have been sufficient difficulties in attempting to replicate these original observations so that the outcome remains clouded. Perhaps the maxim should be invoked that if a phenomenon is of a nature that requires extremely unique preparations to detect it, then it is unlikely to be of very great practical significance. In this instance, however, the conceptual significance is so great that it is likely that attempts will repeatedly be made as technology advances.

Summary   We have described several approaches that one might take toward developing an empirical system, but the reader should not infer that these are in any sense incompatible. The scientist is likely to attempt some form of operational analysis of the domain of interest. This may appear in geometric form to facilitate interconnecting known facts that lead to the extrapolating of unknown hypotheses. These will be subsumed, possibly as subroutines, in an empirical mathematico-deductive system containing principles, corollaries, theorems, laws, and facts. And, of course, there still may be other approaches aimed at the goal of providing a highly abstract, parsimonious organization of empirical knowledge in which all terms are directly reducible to observables.

The reader may have noticed that our discussion of empirical systems has concentrated on procedures falling within the general hypothetical concept of learning. Although learning and motivation are conceptual siblings, the analogy is more like the classic image of an older sister's tolerance of a younger brother. He is there, to be sure, and must be reckoned with, but not as the center of attention. However, we can certainly envisage the nature of an empirical system of motivation. We would proceed in very much the same way, beginning with the patently circular identification of objects or events, whose deprivation would produce a hypothetical state with relatively transitory effects on performance. Similarly, we would identify classes of stimulation that appear to have these same types of effects. These would then be organized around various conditions and parameters of deprivation and stimulation; their effects on the various behavioral indices could be categorized systematically. Although these may be treated as lore by many learning psychologists, there would be neither learning nor performance without motivation, and the importance of such an empirical system is not to be underestimated.

Indeed, the reader should now be ready to anticipate the appearance of the "grand" empirical system. All we really need to do is begin with the awareness that both an experimenter and the natural environment are constrained to do nothing more than present or withhold stimuli. Within such constraints, we first set about in bootstrap, circular fashion, to place stimuli into one or more of the following categories:

1. stimuli that when withheld give rise to motivational states
2. stimuli that when presented give rise to motivational states
3. stimuli that reflexively elicit an observable response
4. stimuli that enable the occurrence of an observable response
5. stimuli that when removed serve as reinforcers
6. stimuli that when presented serve as reinforcers
7. all stimuli not falling into any of the above categories

Whether events are stimuli at all, and if so, into which of the above categories they fall, is determined directly by experimental analysis of their functional relationship to behavior. All events that function as stimuli can be symbolized "S" with superscripts added if they display additional properties. Hence, S^M refers to stimuli of the first two classes, and S^R refers to stimuli of classes 5 and 6. The above classes may not be exhaustive, and finer distinctions may be necessary in order most usefully to develop a terminology of hypothetical concepts. (For example, S^r is used for a secondary reinforcing stimulus.)

We then set about to conceive a grand empirical system of stimulus control. Control over stimuli of the first two classes are pure stimulus operations, serving to set the organism for the task at hand. Stimuli of the third and fourth classes are also pure stimulus operations; the third represents those found in classical conditioning and the fourth those found in instrumental conditioning. Stimuli of the fifth and sixth types are employed in operant and instrumental conditioning, and stimuli of the seventh type can be inserted into any situation and possibly gain appropriate control over behavior.

Such a grand empirical system will thus include everything that can possibly happen to an organism, and it will systematize the behavioral outcome of the various permutations and combinations of the conditions and parameters of controlled stimuli. We grant that such a system is possible in a far distant future, but it would be quite presumptuous to project the exact nature of a grand empirical system. However, we do anticipate that the issues that we have discussed will persist, at least as haunting memories, and that new issues will emerge. After all, this is the nature of an empirical science.

THEORETICAL REINFORCEMENT SYSTEMS

There is no controversy concerning the necessity and usefulness of abstract empirical systems of the type that we have just described. But for whatever reasons, many experimental psychologists are not fully satisfied even by elegant empirical systems. For them, such systems are not sufficient, because an important part of the game of science is the construction of reductive theories that attempt to provide, in the limited sense that we have discussed, some explanation of the empirical phenomena. Why, they ask in the present context, does reinforcement produce these dramatic effects on behavior? With that question, we are off into the realm of theory, hypothetical constructs, postulates, mechanisms, and imaginary designs of pseudo-organisms that might behave the way real organisms do. Just as reinforcement has been a fertile field for systematic empirical analyses, so too, it has nurtured a wide variety of theoretical approaches.

Let us briefly review several of the issues that we have already discussed in some detail. First is the problem of identifying reinforcing states of affairs. We will simply accept the fact that at least some degree of circularity appears to be inherent in this identification problem. It is true that stimuli that give rise to drive states when withheld are also ones that serve as (positive) reinforcers when presented; it is also true that stimuli that give rise to drive states when presented are also ones that serve as (negative) reinforcers when terminated. Hence, there are good reasons to accept the weak form of the drive-reduction hypothesis. But even so, one must yet identify either drive-producing states of affairs *or* reinforcing states of affairs in a circular fashion; after one is identified the other may also follow. Theoretical analyses do not resolve, nor do they amplify or minimize this problem.

For this reason, there is really no new issue involving the necessary and sufficient *conditions* for theoretical accounts of the effects of reinforcement. The issues arise over the *nature* of the processes through which reinforcement works. We have already discussed the first critical issue involved, namely, whether reinforcement affects the hypothetical construct of a basic learning nature, or whether its effects are on some motivational construct. For many reasons in addition to the studies of latent learning, notably the findings that performance changes very rapidly in the appropriate direction when the conditions of reinforcement are changed (e.g., Crespi, 1942, 1944; and Zeaman, 1949), theorists increasingly view the role of reinforcement in motivational terms. We shall place all of these together under the rubric of "incentive theories."

The Nature of Incentive Theory

The defining feature of incentive theories of behavior is that the schedules and conditions of reinforcement affect performance through an acquired motivational factor. Not all theorists call this factor "incentive," and no theorist denies that reinforcement may have other effects on performance than this motivational one. We will be discussing these differences in the remainder of this chapter. But we can make the following statements the basic premises of incentive theories as here defined:

1. Organisms value certain objects or events. Incentive value, however, is not in the object or event itself; instead, it is in the organism having commerce with the object or event.

2. Incentive value is scalable, at least, ordinally. That is, organisms prefer some objects or events over others; such preferences display in a statistical sense some degree of transitivity and consistency.

3. Organisms learn about any contingency relationships that may obtain between behavior and valued objects or events.

4. Other things equal, organisms behave in order to maximize (positive) incentive value; this is accomplished by some kind of selective activation of those behaviors.

These four statements are only a short step away from the empirical principle of (positive) reinforcement. The theorist has introduced the hypothetical construct of "value," but value is anchored to the very same operations used in identifying reinforcers. The empiricist says that the rat pressed the bar because he has been deprived of food and he gets food for doing so; the theorist says that the rat pressed the bar because he is hungry—the rat, therefore, values food, and he presses the bar because there is incentive motivation to do so. The empiricist says that the rat chose the side of the maze containing the larger reward; the theorist says that the rat's choice was a result of the presumption that larger rewards have greater incentive value and, therefore, the rats behave in order to maximize reward. All incentive theories share this feature of interposing the hypothetical construct of value between the antecedent conditions and the consequent behavior. From that point, however, we find no other feature of an incentive theory about which there is unanimity of opinion. Accordingly, we can say that if one chooses to be a theorist, incentive theory is the contemporary method of approach; the details of such a theory, however, are fair game for novel theoretical analyses.

What Is Learned?
A. Referent Behavior
Associations

By "referent behavior" we mean the observable activity of an organism of interest to the theorist, be it a bar press, an alley run, an utterance, or any other response that operates on the environment and is instrumental in obtaining reward. We have already discussed in some detail the theoretical issue concerning the nature of the learning process with respect to the referent behavior, and we have dichotomized the theories into cognitive (S-S) and behavioristic (S-R) camps.[9] Both of these are amenable to incentive theory; value can perfectly well activate cognitions or responses. Accordingly, one issue still dividing incentive theorists is the nature of what is learned vis-à-vis the referent behavior itself. Incentive theory does not significantly alter the case for or against one or the other.

However, one incentive theory has introduced a new alternative answer: there simply is no learning of the referent response itself. According to Mowrer (e.g., 1956, 1960), there is only one learning process, namely, emotional (incentive) learning. Mowrer contends that organisms do not truly learn what to do in any direct sense; instead, they learn the outcome of various courses of action and behave accordingly, not through an association involving the referent response to the situation but through a cybernetic guidance system, which we will shortly discuss. Thus, we have three general classes of incentive theories with respect to the referent behavior: S-S associations, S-R associations, or no associations.

What Is Learned? We have already asserted that all incentive theorists assume that organisms
B. R-S Associations learn that valued objects or events follow the performance of some behavior of interest to the observer. This we will call R-S learning, although a more general expression in the context of the present discussion would be B-S^R learning, which signifies that reinforcing events follow certain behaviors. But the nature of *this* R-S association, as distinct from the association directly involving the referent behavior on the consequent side, is a source of considerable differences.

One issue involves the role of kinesthetic and proprioceptive feedback.[10] It is presumed that all responses produce feedback in this sense, and the association is not really of an R-S nature, but is of an R-s_r-S nature, where capital letters refer to observable events and lowercase letters refer to hypothetical processes. That is, when the feedback from ongoing behavior has historically been followed by reinforcing states of affairs, an $s_r - S$ association is somehow formed. This association may not be direct; we will see that some theorists contend that it is mediated by one or another process. But a necessary feature of incentive theories is to specify how B-S^R, or more specifically R-S, and more completely R-s_r-S learning takes place.

This feature, which is called "valence" by Tolman (1932), "incentive" by Hull (1952) and Spence (1956), "hope" by Mowrer (1960), "excitement" by Sheffield (1966), "go" by Miller (1963), "invigoration" by Cofer and Appley (1964), "amplification" by Estes (1969) and so on, has one potential difficulty most apparent in Mowrer's theory. If the critical associative process is incentive motivation aroused by feedback from behavior, it cannot enter into the determination of that behavior until it is already under way. And, of course, if there is no other type of associative process, behavior would never get under way at all. Nevertheless, this R-s_r-S associative process is an integral aspect of incentive theory, and we will need to consider its interaction with other processes in the determination of behavior. But for the moment, let us continue with the issue concerning the fundamental nature of this process itself.

It is not essential that an incentive theorist assume that the nature of the associative process involved in incentive learning is the same as that involved in the associative process with respect to the referent behavior. This has historically been the case and is certainly desirable in the cause of parsimony. However, Estes (1969) and Logan (1970) have recently proposed the alternative that these associative processes are fundamentally different by assuming that incentive learning is cognitive in nature, whereas operant/instrumental learning reflects S-R associations. This approach is a derivative of the opposing uniprocess theories, and we will concentrate on the latter.

Clearly for Tolman (1932), for whom all associations are cognitive in nature, the postulation of R-s_r-S learning is straightforward. Since an S is on the consequent side of the symbol, an S becomes associated and certainly can be associated with response-produced feedback. It is also associated with the total situation, including all sources of stimulation, but the role of feedback is not especially important in Tolman's theory. His approach, we will call "expectancy of reward," (Tolman used a number of expressions, such as observation-behavior outcome, sign-gestalt expectation, appetite, cathexis, all of which give some added flavor of his style of thinking) and the best symbol for our understanding of it would be S_1-R-s_r-S_2. This is a gestalt or a field expectancy. The situation (S_1), itself, is associated cognitively with the outcome (S_2) but also includes the behavior that is requisite for its attainment. In language that would be characteristic of Tolman, the organism has a cognitive map of the situation; the map includes the possible outcomes and also the appropriate behaviors. The organism knows what leads to what and immediately knows what to do. Excitement may be enhanced when feedback from this behavior comes into play, but the organism has already chosen the path that will maximize reward (and minimize effort). In sum, incentive learning for Tolman is simply a special case of the general approach involving cognitive (S-S) associations.[11]

Life is not so simple for the S-R theorist who adheres rigorously to a uniprocess approach. Such a theorist cannot tolerate an S on the consequent side of an associative process. And although Hull (1952) had introduced the construct of incentive motivation (K), it was Spence (1956) who provided the necessary mediational mechanism required for a pure S-R theory. To set the stage, he first adopted the contiguity assumption with respect to learning, at least, with instrumental reward[12]. He then appealed to a mechanism earlier introduced by Hull (1931) to account for goal-directed behavior: the fractional anticipatory goal response (r_g-s_g).[13]

The logic of the analysis, which is very similar to that employed by others such as Sheffield (1966), is that the strength of r_g-s_g determines K.[14] The strength of r_g-s_g depends on the number of trials, the interstimulus interval (here the delay of reinforcement), and the intensity of the unconditioned stimulus (here the conditions of reinforcement). A goal event itself produces a goal response (R_G) and components that can occur in the absence of the goal object itself and that are compatible with the instrumental response become conditioned through contiguity with all stimuli, including feedback stimuli, antedating the goal. This approach has all the features of Tolman's approach, except that incentive motivation is *mediated* by a hypothetical response mechanism. The organism begins to anticipate the goal immediately upon being introduced into the situation (r_g-s_g is associated with environmental cues), and this anticipation increases as goal-oriented feedback is initiated.[15] To Spence, anticipation is mediated by an anticipatory response; to Tolman, expectancy is directly cognitive in nature. The symbolism of Spence's approach is S_1-r_g-s_g-R-s_r-r_g-s_g-R-S_G-R_G.

In this particular aspect of incentive theory, Mowrer is quite similar to Spence. Mowrer calls the anticipatory response "hope"; although as we have seen, hope cannot be present until feedback is present. Other pure S-R incentive theorists have not been quite so explicit about the nature of the associative process leading to incentive motivation, but they all have similar features. For example, Miller proposes a central "go" mechanism, the activity of which is conditionable by contiguity. Estes proposes an amplifier mechanism that is conditionable by contiguity. Cofer and Appley propose an anticipation-invigoration mechanism that is conditionable. Although all such mechanisms could be conceptualized in cognitive terms, they have appeared more in the character of responses, as hypothetical central activities that become associated with exteroceptive and interoceptive cues. But they are freed from strict dependence on a goal response. Any state of affairs that arouses these mechanisms will lead to acquired incentive motivation; such states of affairs are, of course, reinforcing (positive or negative) ones.

Interaction with Other Constructs: A. Referent Behavior Associations

For convenience, let us refer to associations that directly involve the referent behavior as "expectancy" for cognitive approaches and "habit" for behavioristic approaches. Then continuing to use "incentive" for the R-S association involving reinforcement, we can pose the present issue in the form of a question: How do expectancy/habit and incentive combine? In this terminology, Mowrer has no habit process and, hence, the issue does not arise in his theory. But for all other incentive theorists, this question must be answered.

Hull dealt explicitly with this issue. He postulated that the conditions of reinforcement affect incentive (K) and that incentive directly multiplies habit. Tolman's approach is somewhat less clear because he imbeds expectancy and incentive in a gestalt that is, in principle, an indivisible whole. However, Tolman does identify the classes of independent variables that enter into his theory with expectancy developing as a result of exposure to the situation and incentive developing as a result of reinforcement. Since both features must be present in the gestalt for performance to occur, he is assuming the essence of a multiplicative interaction. Accordingly, both Tolman and Hull basically postulate an incentive construct and combine it with expectancy/habit processes in determining behavior.[16]

Spence, although working within the general framework of Hull's theory, saw the need to specify how incentive (r_g-s_g) comes to have its motivational properties. He entertained several ways in which this might be accomplished. One, which is essentially the same as that adopted by Sheffield, is that the occurrence of r_g leads to conflict, because R_G cannot occur, heightened tension or excitement and, hence, to a higher level of drive. Of course, drive activates habits in a multiplicative manner. An alternative is to accept Hull's construct of stimulus intensity dynamism (V), which assumes that behavior is potentiated in relation to the intensity of prevailing stimuli. Since r_g has its associated response-produced stimulus, s_g, the vigor of the fractional anticipatory goal response will contribute to the overall intensity of the stimulation and, thereby, potentiate responding. In fact, Spence did not fully commit himself to either of these specific interpretations.

The most important point in this discussion arises when we analyze behavior dynamically as a behavioral stream or process taking place more or less continuously over time. Whether we call it hope, or go, or excitement, or invigoration, or amplification, or incentive motivation, what we need to conceptualize is the cybernetic processes taking place. Once behavior is somehow initiated, which for all save Mowrer is by direct associations, the feedback from that behavior begins to contribute motivation to continue along that course of action. Changes in the external environment resulting from the action, and interoceptive sources of feedback, increasingly activate the organism. It becomes a guidance system "homing in" on the optimal behavior. Should the organism stray into actions associated with less optimal reward conditions, the potentiating mechanism diminishes in strength retarding that course of action until the organism gets back on course. Incentive is an attraction toward a goal, not unlike a magnetic field. Indeed, it is just such an analogy that Tolman would find ideal, because he was prone to think in terms of field forces, valences, and vectors. This is the real guts of most incentive theories; but the analogy is perhaps somewhat more fitting for behaviorists. When that gut response says "Right on!" the organism charges ahead.

Although we are primarily interested in discussing the issues that are involved in the design of such a cybernetic system, its broad features deserve further elaboration. Let us begin with an imaginary organism designed as follows. At any moment in time, an organism scans all of the behaviors that are available to it at that time. It makes little difference whether this scanning is done in a purely cognitive fashion, or whether the organism makes hypothetical insipient fractions of the various responses to provide the feedback necessary for that type of incentive theory. What is important is that this scanning operation results in determining the incentive value of each of the various alternatives. Our organism must have three additional features. The first is a rule for scanning; perhaps some version of random sampling without replacement would suffice. Next, the organism needs a special memory in which to store the results of the scan for the appropriate incentive values. Finally, the organism needs a comparator mechanism to rerun through the alternatives, in a priority order, so that it can select the one with the highest momentary value. This would be sufficient to enable a decision about what to do at that moment.

Of course, immediately upon initiating this first movement, our hypothetical organism is at a new choice point that requires this entire process to be repeated in that unique context. And so on progressively. It is at least conceivable that a large electronic computer could be programmed according to these rules and could move a rat from the start of an alley to the goal; perhaps it would be possible to display acceleration in speed as the cues provoking incentive motivation increase with nearness to the goal, but it is unlikely that such a computer could run through our program with the speed at which a real rat runs down an alley.

In spite of the patent inappropriateness of this hypothetical organism as a model of the real organism, it is nevertheless a useful anchoring conceptualization for the fundamental elements of a dynamic incentive theory that uses feedback cues as an integral part of the determination of behavior. But let us compare this description with that of a trained vocalist who is asked to sing a note struck on a piano. We observe first that the singer does not emit just any frequency of sound at random; instead, the very first utterance is reasonably close to the target frequency. Furthermore, any errors detected by the vocalist will rapidly be corrected; once the note both being played and sung are synchronized, it is held in that pose until the signal to stop. What we need, then, is to equip our conceptual organism with the capacity to mimic these observable properties of behavior.

We feel that none of the extant incentive theories has quite accomplished this mission in its totality, but the seeds of such a theory are reasonably well available. To state the analysis in terms of S-R approaches, we would want our hypothetical organism to have an immediate and direct association between the onset of the stimulus and the production of the response. Presumably this association has been formed by our trained vocalist; a novice would be expected to miss the target pitch more substantially at first emission. However, as a result of response generalization, the first emission of even the trained vocalist might be somewhat off target. Our hypothetical organism, therefore, needs an error-detection-correction device similar to the one suggested by Miller (1959). This too is a learnable response in which the organism does not modulate around searching for a match but makes relative responses to relative cues (i.e., the larger the discrepancy, the larger the correction in the correct direction). We believe this type of analysis is valuable to incentive theories.

Accordingly, the notions of both Tolman and Hull are important, because they assumed that both associations involving the referent response and incentive motivation for its performance are immediately available for response initiation. Once initiated, the stimulus complex is automatically changed at least by the introduction of the response-produced cues and, in most cases, by corresponding changes in the external environment or the organism's orientation with respect to it. These, in turn, have their direct associations with the referent behavior and also the presumably enhanced incentive motivation, which leads immediately to the next outflow of behavior. All of the necessary ingredients of a dynamic incentive theory that have reasonable reference to actual behavior are available, but they must be fully formalized and integrated before we can derive unambiguous implications.

Interaction with Other Constructs: B. Drive Motivation

Again taking the lead from both Tolman and Hull, incentive theorists have tended to distinguish between two sources of motivation: drive and incentive. They make this distinction operationally: drive is based on conditions of deprivation and incentive is based on conditions of reinforcement. At least for the duration of any particular behavioral episode, drive is considered to be a state parameter of the organism, whereas incentive displays dynamic properties within the episode. The issue at hand is how these two presumed sources of motivation interact in the ultimate determination of performance.

One route adopted by Tolman and Hull was to keep drive and incentive conceptually separate. Drive to Hull was need-push to Tolman, and incentive to Hull was valence to Tolman. These combined with habit in the case of Hull and expectancy in the case of Tolman to determine performance. Whereas Tolman was rather vague on the details, Hull was explicit with his assumption that all of the factors interact multiplicatively in determining excitatory potential and, hence, the several measures of response strength. The various theorists have approached this issue in different ways.

For example, Cofer and Appley contend that behavior may be energized by either anticipation-arousal or by sensitization-arousal (incentive and drive, respectively); this implies that they combine in an additive fashion. Estes assumes that there is a single generator of amplifier elements for any system; the base rate of firing depends on deprivation (drive) summating with feedback consequences of the response (incentive). Therefore, Estes is also stating a rule in which incentive adds to drive. Miller uses drive as a necessary condition for the increased activity of a go mechanism, resulting from reinforcement, but does not specify whether drive is further required for potentiating this increased activity after conditioning. Mowrer uses drive as a necessary precondition for reinforcement and also makes it clear that this drive must be present for conditioned hope or conditioned relaxation to be invoked. Revusky and Garcia use deprivation in the Guthrian sense of maintaining stimuli and assume that incentive value depends on deprivation (and hence drive) in an associative manner. Sheffield assumes that drive is necessary for the occurrence of the conditioned consummatory response, hence, there is frustration and increased excitement. Spence assumes that drive and incentive are separable and combine additively to determine the total motivation that energizes habits. Let us briefly consider this last formulation and then let the reader reflect on the way in which the resulting issues pertain to the various other theories.

The additive assumption has one very valuable feature: it enables drive motivation to activate habits from the beginning of a trial, and then incentive motivation is contributed through the feedback approach that we have discussed. One price of this gain is that incentive can also activate habits in the absence of drive. Also on the negative side, this assumption appears to restrict incentive motivation to positive values; if, as we shall see, one attempts to treat with punishment in terms of negative incentive, then the possibility would arise that the net-incentive value of an alternative that was both punished and reinforced would be negative—one would hardly want a negative source of motivation amplifying habit. Further, the additive rule has no obvious bounds. In any event, Spence based his assumption on the best available evidence about the results of factorial designs involving variations in both deprivation conditions and reinforcement conditions, and the fact that there was no statistical interaction[17] between these variables suggests a simple additive combination rule. Were one to pursue this argument, however, there is also evidence that drive combines additively rather than multiplicatively with habit; therefore, that component of the equation is also open to question. The general point is simply that it is not enough to postulate an incentive construct; it must be combined in some way with other constructs in the system in order to generate behavioral predictions. There are a number of ways in which this might be accomplished, none of which has gained universal acceptance.

The Specificity of Incentive Motivation

It will be recalled that two extreme positions have been taken with respect to the specificity of drive motivation (cf. Chapter 4). One of these is that drive is a general energizer of learned associations. This approach is epitomized in

Hull's (1943) theory; generalized drive is a state of general arousal and activation that motivates an act of any kind that will reduce or remove the presumed aversiveness of the drive state. In contrast, demand or need-push to Tolman is quite specific; need-push is integrated into a gestalt that includes the expectancy and value of a goal object and the appropriate goal-oriented behavior. There are some reasons to favor one approach over the other, but each must be elaborated somewhat in order to make a reasonable system.

As a particular example, it is known that the addition of an irrelevant source of drive motivation can add potentiation to the relevant drive in mediating performance (e.g., Kendler, 1945). However, its effect is not nearly so great as would obtain with more of the relevant drive. If the irrelevant drive is strong enough, the effect actually reverses. Neither of the extreme positions stated above can accommodate these facts. If one adopts the general drive notion, then it is necessary to bring to bear a further assumption about drive stimuli: although drive as a motivating force is increased by an irrelevant drive, there is also a generalization decrement in learned associations because of the addition of new drive stimuli to which competing responses may well have been attached. Alternatively, one may assert that drive is specific to responses learned and servicing that drive, but then one must appeal to some generalization of this motivating property in somewhat different situations. There appears to be no strong argument favoring one approach over the other with respect to drive, nor is this decision binding on the conceptualization of incentive.

Of course, incentive must somehow be endowed with the capacity selectively to activate those responses that are oriented toward the appropriate goal in the prevailing situation. The most direct way to do this is to posit incentive as a specific source of motivation vis-à-vis the behaviors relevant to the nature of the goal event itself. This is the type of approach indigenous to theories involving drive motivation as specific sources of activation. To Tolman, for example, just as the need-push orients the organism toward behaviors appropriate to the underlying need, the valence of a goal event is correspondingly specific to its functional role in servicing that need.

Hull was also conceptually consistent in not putting subscripts on K, just as he had not on D, and viewed it as a general source of motivation. Either of the approaches proposed by Spence to make r_g-s_g a motivating mechanism would lead to the same result; if the occurrence of r_g in the absence of the goal object is frustrating and hence contributes to D, or if the response-produced s_g contributes dynamism (V) to the total stimulus complex, one simply increases the overall arousal of the organism.

It is instructive to consider Spence's own theory in this regard. He still assumed that D is a general energizer of all habits. But K has somewhat different properties as a general energizer, because it is only brought to bear when goal-oriented behavior is underway. This same image is clear in Sheffield's drive-induction theory: net drive is, at one and the same time, both general and specific. That part of drive resulting from deprivation is general, but the additional drive reflecting incentive motivation is specific (although generalizable) to behaviors in progress.

The reader can now review the various incentive-type theories with these issues in mind and see how they cope with them. It will be seen that Logan assumed D to be a general source of motivation, and sINr to be specific. Estes assumed D (amplifiers) to be specific; therefore, K was also specific by further amplification of the relevant D. As with most theoretical issues all focused on the same hypothetical construct; not only is it impossible to reduce the issue directly to an empirical question, but the logically appropriate resolution depends on other aspects of the theory. We will next consider one aspect that bears on many of the other issues significantly.

What Is Learned? C. The Nature of the Referent Behavior

In our general discussion of the question, "What is learned," we identified four logically possible approaches to response definition: macromolar, macromolecular, micromolar, and micromolecular. The macro-micro distinction concerns quantitative features of the response and the molar-molecular distinction concerns qualitative (topographical) features of the response. Although each of these may be conceived of as a continuum, in practice they tend to be dichotomous. Specifically, a true micromolecular approach to, let us say, a bar press would assert that every miniscule distinction in the topography of the response (stance at the bar, paw or other part of the body used, etc.) and every measureable quantitative difference (force, duration, momentary acceleration and deceleration, etc.) are unique aspects of that particular instance of behavior and are precisely the ones that are learned. There is generalization of these, to be sure, but the focus of the learned association is on the very particular features of the behavior that was emitted at the time of reinforcement. And, necessarily, such an approach with respect to habit associations would automatically apply to incentive learning.

These defining characteristics of a response are, in practice, dichotomous, because as once one leaves the very detailed conception of a micromolecular approach, in either respect, one becomes to some extent either macro, or molar, or both; it becomes a matter of degree. That is, once one begins to aggregate distinguishable behaviors into a single category and treat them as the same response, one is already engaged in macro-type thinking or molar-type thinking. Molar-type thinking aggregates behaviors according to their consequences (an act, in this example, a bar press), and macro-type thinking treats quantitative indices of behavior (strength, in this example, latency or force) as measures of underlying processes.

We believe, also on other grounds, that the most significant systems of the future will approach, insofar as technically possible, a micromolecular response definition, and incentive theories virtually demand it. Simply reconsider the vital role that has been assigned to feedback from ongoing behavior. This feedback, functioning conceptually as stimuli, must have all of the qualitative and quantitative properties well recognized with respect to controlled exteroceptive stimuli. It follows naturally that incentive motivation is focused on the micromolecular features of the response.

This is not to say that what may be called acquired equivalence of responses does not occur. If the programmed conditions of reinforcement do not distinguish among responses within some subset of behaviors that are conceptually distinguishable, incentive will equally accrue to those behaviors that are actually emitted by the organism.[18]

To underscore this point, let us return to our example of the trained vocalist attempting to reproduce the note struck on a piano; add to the instructions a direction to sing loudly or softly. The only way that the vocalist could emit a close approximation at the first sound would be if the habit association involved a micromolecular-response definition—even if the habit association was embedded as a part of a cognitive structure. The only way that the error-detection-correction mechanism can function is with discrepancies of both quantitative and qualitative types in order to bring the behavior literally in tune.

With the exception of Logan (1960), incentive theorists to date have not explicitly recognized this intrinsic property of such theories with its implications to the specificity of incentive motivation. Logan adopted a micromolar assumption about the nature of the response, a contiguity assumption about the conditions of learning, and a specific incentive construct. Habit is simply a function of practice, but because of response generalization and the fact that many less-than-optimal responses will have been practiced extensively, there is a family of habit strengths many of which will be at or near the conceptual limit. He also assumed drive to be a general energizer of habits, so neither of these constructs could serve the necessary directing function. This was accomplished by letting incentive be specific to different micromolar responses (different speeds of running).

According to Logan's analysis of a dynamic incentive theory, the organism is viewed as continuously making choices among alternative micromolar responses. The problem of response initiation is not just to get a rat out of a start box; it occurs at every step along the way. Incentive must, therefore, help select what to do *next*. Although response-produced cues from what the organism has already done so far on that trial and stimuli based on the progress made thus far are present, incentive associated with those must *selectively* energize the next bit of behavior. Logan contents that it is not sufficient to assume that the rat thinks, in effect, "What I'm doing feels pretty good so I guess I'll just keep right on doing it." Suppose he doesn't feel as good then as he could feel, or suppose that the nature of the task is such that it requires changes in behavior in route to the goal? Incentive motivation needs to be ready to guide the next step in the chain.

Accordingly, Logan's view of the important role of feedback is somewhat different, although certainly not inconsistent with the way we have described it thus far. The optimal response in a runway is a straight beeline to the goal; it should have the strongest incentive value already present in the startbox to activate that response immediately upon the opening of the start door. At that juncture, interoceptive and exteroceptive feedback cues, which also have a conditioned expectancy of reward of a certain amount, at a certain time come into play. As long as this progression of cues is all in tune, the rat does appear to keep right on doing what he has been doing. However, should the rat step out of line a bit, the feedback resulting from those cues is associated with a lower incentive than that with which the rat began. This brings about the error-detection mechanism; to *that* set of cues there is another habit family with its related incentive family that can select the response that will get the rat back on the track.

The belief is that a response produces either positive or negative feedback that will guide not what has already transpired but that next behavior that will maximize incentive under current existing circumstances. This is the dynamic essence of incentive theory and remains to be clearly captured in explicit mathematical form. This leads quite naturally to the next issue concerning quantification.

Quantification of
Incentive Motivation

The best way to introduce a discussion of quantification of incentive motivation, and for that matter any hypothetical construct, is to say simply that quantification cannot be done in terms of any empirically defined scale of measurement. Remember that hypothetical constructs are only anchored to empirical referents; they are not defined operationally in empirical language. Accordingly, it is conventional for the quantitatively minded theorist to adopt some arbitrary units (such as between zero and unity, or between minus one and plus one, or whatever) and then provide the anchoring procedure for converting these hypothetical numbers into ones that are operationally meaningful.

Thus no hypothetical construct can be measured directly; this fact consequently affects issues involving interactions. Even probability of response is an abstraction, because at any moment in time a response however defined either occurs or does not occur. If we take seriously (as we believe we must) the micro aspect of response definition, then familiar response measures, such as speed and amplitude, are of little help in quantifying incentive motivation. These indices tell us what the organism did, but very little about the strength of the incentive involved. You may speak slowly and softly, particularly in certain contexts, and have a very, very strong tendency to speak slowly and softly.

This does not imply that speed and amplitude are not interesting data. They remain to be accounted for according to some theoretical system. But if one admits that they cannot be used in the quantification of incentive motivation, then some other measureable aspect of behavior must provide a means of anchoring that construct. The solution appears to lie in our original statements about the essential features of incentive theories: incentive value is scalable, at least ordinally, and organisms prefer objects or events with the greater incentive value to them. Accordingly, indices of preference are the natural empirical referent for scaling incentive value.

What we need, therefore, is an empirical system based on preferences that can be rationalized by an incentive theory. One approach would be the system used by Premack (1971). His interest, of course, was in determining relative reinforcing values of various behaviors in order to use them in an empirical reinforcement system. To an incentive theorist, the interest is not in determining what kinds of activities will increase the likelihood of other kinds of activities, instead, it is in the value that the organism places on those activities (or events).

One approach to this goal of quantification has been explored by Logan

(1965, see also Davenport, 1962) and involves relative quantification. The problem is simply that it is unlikely that we can put any directly meaningful value, in an absolute sense, on one amount of reward as compared with any other amount; yet, ordinally we know that larger amounts are preferred over smaller amounts. But we can introduce the notion of *net incentive* by recognizing that any reinforcement has a number of quantitative aspects and that conditions can be arranged to require subjects to make decisions among alternatives that differ in more than one regard. Specifically in the studies referred to above, Logan pitted amount of reward against delay of reward (larger amount at a longer delay vs. a smaller amount at a shorter delay) and amount of reward against probability of reward (a larger amount at a lower probability vs. a smaller amount at a higher probability). When conceptualizing any conditions of reinforcement in terms of net incentive, based jointly on the amount, delay, and probability, Logan found it possible to provide a reasonable approximation to a quantification of relative incentive value. To put it succinctly: how many more seconds will a rat wait to get another pellet of reward? We do not know in any absolute sense how much an added pellet is worth, but we can find out how many more seconds of delay it is worth.

Whatever the method of quantification, we can best grasp its importance by considering a more detailed analysis of behavior at a choice point. Recognize that a dynamic incentive theory is contending that the organism is continually, moment by moment, deciding what to do next on the basis of the relative incentive value of the available alternatives. Behavior at a choice point is intended to make this hypothetical activity more amenable to direct observation.

Behavior at a Choice Point

We owe it to Tolman for bringing to our attention, prematurely, as history has shown, the importance of observing behavior at a choice point. The reader is encouraged to study Tolman's design of what he called, in his characteristically deceptive manner, a schematic sowbug.[19] This scheme was subsequently developed more extensively by Spence (1960) and still more elegantly by Bower (1959). We will attempt to integrate these ideas as stated in the framework of an S-R theory.

The critical dependent variable is what Tolman called vicarious trial and error (VTE). What he observed is that a rat, coming upon a choice point, stops there and first looks up one alley, then the other, and so on, back and forth until finally running off in one or the other direction. This VTE behavior is not only clearly observable, but it can be counted and shows lawful properties. Specifically, the number of VTE's at first increases and then decreases with training. Indeed, with a purely spatial problem (turn left or right), VTE at the choice point drops out altogether; however, Tolman could envisage the rat making insipient looking-back-and-forth movements while running down the stem of the maze and already oriented to turn in the correct direction. (Interestingly enough, rats do follow their noses. Rats with noses bent slightly to the right prefer, other things equal, right turns, and vice versa.)

Vicarious trial and error is somewhat more interesting in a nonspatial discrimination problem; here the alternatives, let us say, differ in brightness or color, and sometimes an alternative is on one side or the other. Specifically, the rat must choose black over white, regardless of its position. In such situations, VTE behavior is still more evident, never drops completely out, and shows a lawful relation to the difficulty of the discrimination. More difficult tasks produce more looking back and forth, especially at intermediate stages of learning.

Let us give Spence's way of interpreting this VTE behavior using his version of incentive theory. We need to make several dynamic assumptions. The first is that there is presumably an excitatory tendency to approach a stimulus when seen; the strength of this tendency depends importantly on the incentive-motivational component of that tendency, which in turn depends on the history of reinforcement that follows making the approach responses. Second, this excitatory potential is subject to momentary oscillation. Third, there is a threshold value of excitatory potential that must be exceeded before the organism actually makes the approach response. Finally, an organism can only hold an orientation for a brief moment before inherently looking elsewhere. In one of Bowers' models, the organism was allowed to return to "go," so to speak. But his evidence favored his second model, which was the only one considered by Spence; this model stated that if the rat momentarily fatigues of looking in one direction, he automatically looks in the other direction.

Let us see how this theory generates behavior at a choice point. There is no way of predicting which way the rat will look first (except, perhaps, the direction of his nose), because there is nondifferential reinforcement for that response. The black alley is equally likely to be on the right as on the left. Whichever way the rat looks first, he will encounter either a black or a white alley; a momentary value of excitatory approach tendency will be invoked. If that momentary tendency happens to exceed the threshold, the rat is off and running. However, early in training when excitatory tendencies are still weak, it is likely that the tendency will be below threshold, and the rat will reorient in the other direction where he will encounter the other stimulus. Again the momentary tendency may or may not exceed the threshold, leading to immediate approach or further reorientation. You should now be able to visualize Tolman's schematic sowbug in operation. It will look back and forth until it chances to hit upon a superthreshold excitatory potential, and as learning progresses, that will more and more likely be true in the reinforced alley. Eventually the rat will choose errorlessly without any VTE's if it happens to look first into the correct alley, or with exactly one VTE if it happens first to look into the incorrect alley.

If we have succeeded in making this image of choice-point behavior clear, the reader can return to our descriptions of the dynamic analyses of an organism simply approaching a goal. At first, various behaviors will occur that involve various orientations and only by chance will a progression of these ultimately lead the rat to arrive at the goal. Reinforcement there, however, will act most strongly on goal-oriented behaviors, because those were the last ones to occur and, hence, entailed the shortest (within-chain) delay of reinforcement. Thus, they will have somewhat greater incentive value and be more likely to provoke approach, again, culminating in the goal. Progressively, fr m the myriad of behaviors that might occur during the early stages of learning, those that maximize incentive motivation will be selectively potentiated until there is no more dilly dallying around.

Incentive Theory and Effort

Only two of the incentive theorists that we have been discussing have explicitly implicated the notion of effort in their system: Tolman and Logan. It is true that Hull considered the hypothetical construct of reactive inhibition, which is a temporary state of fatigue resulting from making a response and clearly dependent upon the amount of effort involved in the process, but it only arose after the occurrence of the response. What both Tolman and Logan were trying to recognize is that organisms also anticipate the amount of effort that will be required to engage in one behavior or another, and other things equal, will choose the response requiring the least effort.

Since this has the status of a law, it presumably would be included by any other incentive theorist; however, there are undoubtedly many ways in which this might be done. Since so few theorists have addressed themselves to this problem, it would be premature to anticipate the issues that will arise in this connection. Most experiments require relatively effortless responses and anticipated work or effort becomes important only when that aspect of the situation is a significant factor. We do know that the law of least effort does apply (see Logan, 1964); the first issue will almost certainly be whether to incorporate it as an incentive (motivational) type factor or more directly as an associative (learning) type factor.

Summary

Although we have discussed in some detail the various issues that confront incentive theorists, the alternatives are not infinite nor are the problems insurmountable. The issues tend to evolve in a more or less logical progression along the lines of our discussion of them and, depending on the general approach, some issues may not arise or simply take care of themselves. Many of the alternatives are interrelated such that adopting one position on one issue tends to constrain the reasonable alternatives with respect to others. Accordingly, by way of summary, let us attempt to review the issues in abbreviated form.

In constructing an incentive theory, one must first decide on the nature of the two basic associative processes: that involving the referent response and that involving the incentive construct. At this critical point, one might deny the former process, as Mowrer has done (or the latter, if one wishes to reconsider a pure reinforcement theoretical approach). Presently, there appear to be two major alternatives, a cognitive one or a behavioristic one. Historically, most theorists have attempted to follow a uniprocess approach, assuming that both learning processes are either cognitive or behavioristic—but this is not necessary. Of course, a more complex type of approach could be proposed in which one or the other learning process is assumed to have both cognitive and behavioristic features. To some extent at least, these decisions are largely matters of personal style, intuitions, hunches, and reflections of personal experiences somehow related to these processes, and the theorist basically makes a choice and then pursues the further development of the theory.

Assuming that two basic associative processes are involved, the immediate question is how these combine in the determination of performance. It is not unreasonable to assume that this combination rule is some version of a multiplicative one, because the concept of motivation tends to imply activation, energization, and potentiation of associations involving the referent response. But at this juncture, logical alternatives having more the flavor of summation (noninteraction) essentially assume that incentive effects are entirely associative, having no nonassociative properties such as implied by the term "motivation."

The role of deprivation and stimulation in determining response strength must also be considered. As is repeatedly the case with any new hypothetical construct added to a developing theory, not only must the anchoring operations to independent variables be specified, but the interrelationships involving already postulated constructs need to be stated. If we call this added construct "drive," that related to reward schedules and conditions "incentive," and the fundamental process associated with the referent behavior "habit," we now have the three core constructs of an incentive theory; we have anchored them on the antecedent side, described their natures, and postulated their method of combining and/or interacting with each other.

At that juncture, it is important to be more specific about the conceptual nature of the stimulus and the conceptual nature of the response. Recognizing that all experimental operations are the presentation, withdrawal, or withholding of stimuli, the objective is to identify and classify stimuli in some appropriate manner. In this connection, most contemporary incentive theorists have given considerable prominence to proprioceptive and kinesthetic sources of feedback stimuli, as well as to stimuli of exteroceptive origin. On the response side, the issue is how behaviors that differ in microscopic qualitative and quantitative details are to be categorized, unitized, and generally aggregated for the purpose of both explanation and description.

Quantification of the theory, at least in programmatic form, may involve algebra, geometry, the calculus, difference equations, probability theory, finite mathematics, or any other system including pure deductive logic. This is an essential step, because meaningful hypothetical constructs must be anchored to dependent variables; the way in which the purely theoretical constructs, now imbedded in a theoretical system, get translated into observable performance is the final step in the design of a theory. In practice, some theorists prefer to start with this terminal anchoring operation and work back toward the initiating antecedent conditions.

Finally, the boundary conditions of the theory need to be specified, and this leads to consideration of various other important factors that might be included. We only mentioned one of these, namely, the effort involved in the response, but there are certainly others. One may turn to the more biological sources for inherited capacities, dispositions, reflexes, and instincts. Or one may include various developmental processes, perceptual processes, and clinical processes. How broadly the boundaries of the theory are defined again is a matter of choice, although it is in the spirit of theory construction to aspire toward incorporating ever-expanding horizons without too much sacrifice of parsimony.

This summary essentially depicts theory construction as a conceptual maze with many choice points. No one has, or probably ever will, find the end of the maze; nor has anyone yet reached a subgoal that has commanded agreement about the best path through the maze to that point. The theorists we have discussed have taken off in various directions, attempting to cross one hurdle after another in the hopes that it will lead on to a fruitful path rather than to a cul-de-sac. Fortunately, science, including theoretical science, is public knowledge. Contemporary theorists can build upon promising leads from the past and attempt to avoid what proved to be errors in earlier approaches.

As a final comment, it should be clear that theory construction in the sense that we have used the term does not take place in isolation from the laboratory. All theoretical notions derive from and ultimately return to empirical knowledge. The subgoals may be thought of as touchstones, because the theorist is being guided through the conceptual maze by the facts. It is more than just an analogy to characterize theory construction in terms of the kind of dynamic incentive theory that we have described. The only difference is that the existence of a reward at the end of the maze is only an article of faith, because no one has ever savored that reward in more than very fractional form.

GENERAL SUMMARY AND CONCLUSIONS

This chapter has attempted to present several approaches toward dealing with the concept of reinforcement. We found the systems still largely programmatic, but sufficiently advanced to permit a reasonably good preview of what could be done along these lines. At the empirical level, we first reviewed organizations of phenomena around a strict operational analysis, disregarding traditional labels, and observed how doing so reveals interesting relationships. We also saw how graphic systems can be plotted in an interlocking set of multidimensional spaces, the various planes of which correspond to well-established areas of knowledge and concurrently display sources of integration. Finally, we explored the nature of a mathematico-deductive system based on principles, corollaries, and theorems, all directly reducible in operational terms to empirical phenomena, which are either established or served as predictions for future study. We hope the reader is impressed not only with the wealth of empirical knowledge already available but also the means that are also available to organize these data systematically.

In turning to theoretical analyses of the effects of reinforcement, we first recognized that the overwhelming evidence favors attributing these effects to some kind of motivational factor, which we called incentive. We reviewed the essence of a number of incentive theories, focusing attention on the issues involved in constructing an adequate theory of this type. In spite of the variety of approaches adopted by the various theorists, some general communalities emerged. Most pervasive is the role of response-produced feedback in such situations, guiding the organism cybernetically toward the optimal route to a goal. Theorists tend to view incentive as a result of some kind of emotional conditioning that combines directly or indirectly with the motivation resulting from deprivation to potentiate learned habit-type associations. The issue of response initiation was prevalent and, approached in various ways, it was found closely related to the conceptual nature of a response. Through all of these, we can gain a general grasp of the nature of contemporary incentive theories, but none has yet been put forth that deals with all of these issues simultaneously and convincingly.

We stopped our discussion at the very beginning of the topics of concurrent schedules in an operant situation and selective learning in an instrumental situation, because we plan to pick up these analyses in Chapter 9. But we can already anticipate the problem that arises in these more complex situations.[20]

What is needed is a *choice axiom*—a rule by which individual excitatory potentials are converted into choice between several immediately available alternatives. Hull (1943) provided one such axiom. He assumed that each of the competing alternatives has an excitatory potential that varies randomly and independently over time according to a normal probability function. The one that has the highest momentary excitatory potential at the instant of choice is the one the organism chooses. Hull deduced this with the use of Thurstone's law of comparative judgment (1927, or still earlier, student's t test for unrelated means), letting the computed values of excitatory potential be the respective means and assuming some equal values for the sigma of oscillation.

Spence (1956) subsequently attempted to correct Hull's derivation by including the threshold, and he proceeded with the type of dynamic analysis that we have presented in this chapter. This dynamic analysis might not appear to require a new choice axiom but, in fact, it does.

Suppose a rat is given a choice between two alternatives, both containing reinforcement but one larger than the other. Now we know that the rat will eventually come to choose the larger reward consistently. But if we attempt to analyze this situation according to the dynamics of Spence's approach, such an outcome would never be possible. This results because on half of the trials the subject would happen to look first at the alternative containing the lesser reward, and its incentive value would be sufficient to mediate some reasonable probability of approach. Clearly, we need to make the subject stop and look again before proceeding, perhaps with a comparator mechanism to mediate choice of the larger reward.

But the optimist can already begin to anticipate the directions in which this type of thinking will lead. We will want to extend the analysis to the general area of judgment and choice. Among the influential systematists in that area are Bock and Jones (1968), Luce (1959), and Restle (1961). They all postulate a notion of "value" that is very closely akin to what we have called incentive value. Without other ingredients of a dynamic incentive theory, they assume that the probability of choosing one alternative over the other is the ratio of the value of any alternative to the sum of the values of all of the alternatives. If one was to extrapolate the quantitative approach resulting from Logan's work, values would be placed relatively on a unit scale, and choice would depend on the proportion of these values commanded by any alternative raised to some power greater than one. These analyses attempt to show how value can be estimated from various kinds of choice situations and how value may vary from choice to choice.

A more general formulation is decision theory, such as originated in economics (see, e.g., Edwards, 1954). In this theory the analysis begins with concepts of objective utility and objective probability, the latter in uncertain-outcome situations; then there are attempts to transform these concepts into subjective utility and subjective probability. These latter concepts will be recognized as hypothetical constructs akin to incentive motivation. There is also the theory of games (von Neumann & Morgenstern, 1947; see also Rapo-port, 1966) by which maximum-likelihood estimates are made of various possible outcomes. Such theories are normative, computing optimal strategies for behavior rather than descriptive of what organisms actually do. Once we are into the general domain of economics, we will also need to begin to recognize various sociological and anthropological factors.

Hull was just such an optimist,[21] and so is Skinner. Hull attempted to deal with the general concept of value and introduced his last theorem in this way (Hull, 1952, p. 337): "Every voluntary social interaction, in order to be re-peated consistently, must result in a substantial reinforcement to the activity of each party to the transaction." Even the brief abstracts of Skinner's works that we have included here reveal his firm belief that Utopia need not be an idle dream but can already be founded on the basis of sound knowledge of the contingencies of reinforcement that are most appropriate for particular organ-isms in particular situations. True, Hull was a theorist and Skinner is an empiricist, but this difference in their approaches to an understanding of behavior should not conceal their mutual conviction that scientific analysis—be it empirical or theoretical and, especially, the concept of reinforcement—could serve to improve the human lot beyond measure.

We, who are intellectual grandchildren of these two men, share the inspira-tion of their convictions but are more cautious in proclaiming what can already be done. Hull's hope that he had written a general theory of behavior is painfully false, but this is not to imply that his conceptual approach will not eventually lead to an approximation of such a theory. Skinner may be correct that the solutions required for the design of a Utopian environment reside in a thorough understanding of contingencies of reinforcement, but neither he nor anyone else has conveyed that understanding explicitly in print. Further-more, to assert any system as being fully definitive and final would be a religious belief, not a scientific one.

Finally, we do not extole the principle of reinforcement as so ubiquitous that it completely overshadows the other principles of behavior. We may not be able to escape the issues surrounding the concept of reinforcement, but neither can we avoid the other issues described in this book. All of them are inter-twined in the long-range mission of behavior science.

NOTES 1. This is an oversimplification, although in some sense all logical systems can be stated in mathematical terms. But some systematists appear to work more easily with some kinds of formulations than others, some of which are purely verbal and hardly mathematical at all. Other systematists argue that the exist-ing state of knowledge only permits use of the algebra of inequalities (less than, equal to, greater than). To others, a mathematical model that involves differ-ence equations is a happy medium. Still others prefer the continuous processes implied by the calculus that seem more natural. Many also like to visualize their systems geometrically. Quite apart from its role in statistical analyses, mathematics is an increasingly vital prerequisite to a full understanding of conceptual systems in psychology.

2. There are, of course, empirical and theoretical systems designed specifically for the phenomena of classical conditioning (e.g., Prokasy, 1965). Because our focus in this book is on issues, and these are substantially the same, regardless of the learning paradigm employed, we have not singled these out for separate treatment.

3. It is not absolutely essential that the same class of operations yield the same outcome in radically different contexts. Indeed, there are some good reasons to suspect that the same classical conditioning operations have different effects when human cognitive processes are not experimentally controlled (e.g., see Kimble, 1971). Even so, however, the operational analyst would provide for a detailed specification of the subject-selection operations and the setting operations that would thereby allow for instances where the outcome of an operation is importantly affected by such preexperimental operations.

4. Subject selection is not completely arbitrary, being based on such considerations as ease of procurement, docility, ease of maintenance, and where appropriate, location in the phylogenetic scale. Behavioral tasks are then selected on the basis of the capabilities of the selected species, usually involving relatively natural forms of behaviors. A pigeon's keypeck (although not as simple as it might sound) is natural behavior that is discrete and, hence, easy to count. Because the pigeon has excellent vision, illuminated keys readily enable the presentation of discrimination problems directly in the visual field of the subject.

5. Actually there is no limit to the number of fixed-time intervals that could be used in Schoenfeld's functional analysis of reinforcement schedules. Indeed, in later developments of the analysis, Schoenfeld and Cumming (e.g., 1960) added a second pair of set and reset time intervals called τ^D and τ^Δ that parallel the functions of t^D and t^Δ. Although still other time intervals could be added, any further regress of time intervals would seriously compromise the parsimony of this empirical analysis.

6. Although we prefer to think of contemporary theorists and pure empiricists as protagonists, there is no doubt but that vigorous spokesmen, such as Spence and Skinner, were sufficiently critical of each other to be considered antagonists. Skinner was not content simply to say that theories of learning were unnecessary; he not only proceeded to substantiate this claim but further derided the very activity of theory construction. But Spence was prone to pick up the gauntlet and counter in a number of ways. He would begin, "Now see here; you're not so pure an empiricist as you proclaim. You superimpose a stimulus paired with an aversive stimulus on an operant baseline, observe suppression, and refer to a 'conditioned emotional response' that is, after all, not substantially different from my use of the term 'fear'. The difference is one

of degree, of how far away from the empirical data the theorist sets theoretical constructs." And although Skinner would try to interject that his preferred term was "conditioned suppression" in order not to suggest any underlying process, Spence would not be interrupted because his point was already made. He would continue, "And don't you dare lay all of the useless empirical research in the lap of the theorist! People following your example have already begun to clutter up the literature with reams of unsystematic data. Many of those data are based on the behavior of a single subject, but one simply cannot make generalizations without any degrees of freedom. Furthermore, you *do* use statistics, except that yours are 'eyeball statistics' and theorists have long known that the easiest way to camouflage horrendous sources of error variance is to plot the data in cumulative form." Skinner, of course, would reply that Spence was welcome to go into his own laboratory, repeat the experiments and make the observations for himself. Furthermore, fine grain analysis of the cumulative records were fully within the empiricists' range. And given sufficient time, the debate would become polemical. Spence would admit that some theorists were guilty of reifying their hypothetical constructs, but he was not. Some people may infer surplus meaning from his constructs, but he implied nothing more than what was explicit in his equations. And Spence would contend that Skinner did not really get his notions about the design of cultures from an experimental analysis of behavior; those came from his personal philosophy supported by empiricism. In the wake of such arguments, Skinnerians established their own society and published their own journal, amidst the protestations that you dare not to call it *the* experimental analysis of behavior and exclude, by definition, any other approach toward building an empirical foundation of systems of whatever kind. There was sometimes an air of frivolity among students trained by Skinner and those trained by Spence. We end this interlude on the note that neither camp really spent a great deal of time engaging in debates and antics; they were too busy in their respective laboratories doing what they personally thought to be the most fruitful type of empirical research.

7. This point deserves to be underscored. Skinner not only brought with him an empiricist philosophy but also the essential idea of automating experimental control. We earlier discussed the importance of intersubjective reliability, and experimental control could hardly be more impersonal than to have all conditions to which an organism is exposed determined by one kind of automatic device or another. These developments then kept pace with new techniques in the physical sciences, such that mechanical devices gave way to electromechanical devices, then to electronic devices, and the most up-to-date laboratories are now at least working on a mini-computer. Fortunately, scientists are still necessary to design the study, write the program, and interpret the results.

8. The terminology "operant" and "instrumental" developed on somewhat different grounds than that described by Logan and Ferraro. In 1940, Hilgard and Marquis distinguished between instrumental and classical conditioning on the basis of whether or not the occurrence of "reinforcement" was contingent on the performance of the conditioned response. In the former case, the

response was "instrumental" in obtaining reward and applied, regardless of the nature of the response system involved. Previously, however, Skinner (1935) had distinguished between "respondent" (classical) and "operant" conditioning not on the basis of the contingency of reinforcement but instead on the nature of the response system involved. Operants affect (operate upon) the environment, are freely emitted at some operant level, and their rate of emission can be affected by the principle of reinforcement.

9. The distinction between S-R and S-S theories was drawn most clearly in terms of the question, "What is learned?" But, as we noted in Chapter 3, the distinction is really more basic than that; it involves the question, "What is behavior?" Consider first a laboratory rat in a maze. To a cognitive theorist, the rat's behavior is purposive, goal-directed, and insightful, to a behavioristic theorist, the rat is seen as engaging in a sequence of motor acts. Similarly, in the classroom, a student solving an arithmetic problem is seen by the cognitive theorist as organizing the problem in relation to his understanding of mathematics, whereas the behavioristic theorist sees the student executing specific operations, such as addition. The different assumptions about what organisms learn is a result of different ways of looking at what organisms do.

10. The term "feedback" is also often used with respect to the experimental operation of providing knowledge of results or simply giving or not giving the reinforcer. These are, indeed, important forms of feedback, but do not represent the sense of the term as used here. Kinesthetic and proprioceptive feedback have no inherent incentive value; they simply provide information about what the organism is doing at the moment. The contention is that such feedback may acquire incentive value by virtue of being associated with feedback of receiving reinforcers.

11. This description may help the reader better understand why Tolman never really believed that he was guilty of leaving his organisms buried in thought. To him, organisms are not machines grinding out behavior at the mercy of environmental stimuli. Isn't it sufficient to paraphrase the thoughts in a rat's mind as follows: I've been here before; there's usually been food over there and, since I'm hungry, I think I'll just meander over there and see if there's some more available now. What more do you want by way of theoretical explanation? And the perceptive reader will note that although Tolman (1955) ultimately addressed himself to this question, he did so reluctantly; primarily, he tried to expose his notions on the nature of a performance and not to anchor rigorous cognitive processes to behavior.

12. Spence characteristically kept his theorizing very close to the empirical data, whereas Hull was inclined to speculate about much wider horizons than he could substantiate. Spence had obtained somewhat definitive evidence (within his approach) that reinforcement was a necessary condition for classical defense conditioning. He was amused by the possibility of a two-factor theory that was diametrically opposite to that of Mowrer and Skinner; it stated that reinforcement is necessary for classical but not for instrumental conditioning. But he was also aware of an alternative version; reinforcement is necessary

for behaviors motivated by aversive stimulation and not for those motivated by deprivation operations. In either case, his position would run contrary to the prevailing alternative theories of reinforcement.

13. This type of assumption makes the r_g-s_g mechanism do triple duty. As originally introduced by Hull (1931), it served as what he called a "pure stimulus act," in that its only function was to produce stimuli to which adaptive responses have been associated. Subsequently, r_g was viewed as a component of R_G, including some fraction of its reinforcing property; hence, it became a mechanism for secondary reinforcement. Now it is proposed that the s_g has dynamogenic properties.

14. The anchoring of incentive motivation to the fractional anticipatory goal response was nothing short of an inspiration. Place yourself in Spence's position at the time: how might the essence of reinforcement theory as a behavioristic approach to "learning" be salvaged, if reinforcement were a "performance" factor? The answer, once seen, was simple . . . incentive was mediated by an already postulated and not unreasonable hypothetical response. This insight, however, had one major flaw: if incentive is mediated by a response with the properties already ascribed to other S-R associations, then it could behave no differently from other learning processes. Of course, one could appeal to different principles for classical conditioning (of which r_g-s_g is a presumed instance) as opposed to instrumental/operant conditioning, but the burden would be to show how such differences could be rationalized. Specifically, if the Crespi-Zeaman data are taken to imply that amount of reward affects performance more rapidly than could the traditional habit learning, then it is incumbent to show how incentive learning could proceed rapidly enough to account for the findings. This is certainly possible: r_g-s_g is a classically conditioned response, and it could be assumed that associations formed in this paradigm proceed at a faster rate than operant/instrumental responses. But this, in turn, has further implications about possible outcomes of experimental analysis of the classical conditioning situation.

15. One of the problems that arose in connection with this formulation was that r_g is assumed to be a classically conditioned fractional component of the goal response (eating). What was more natural, then, than to use Pavlovian conceptions of salivary conditioning? A rash of experiments were therefore performed, recording both salivation and some food-rewarded response such as bar pressing, in the hopes of finding a perfect correlation between salivation and pressing. Although some interesting data were obtained as a result of these efforts, the overall picture is clearly that salivation does not occur the way r_g was postulated to occur. But r_g is a hypothetical construct and is not dependent on any direct empirical measure; its usefulness is in the functional relationships involving the response it is purported to explain. The r_g-s_g mechanism may not be a good basis for incentive motivation—but *not* because salivation does not perfectly correspond with the occurrence of operant and instrumental responses.

16. The student who truly believes Spence (1956) to the effect that Hull's

theory is entirely in his equations and not in his verbal statements surrounding them, arrives at the curious conclusion that Hull's 1952 theory is identical in this regard with his 1943 theory. In the earlier version, Hull proposed that $H = M(1\text{-}10^{-iN})$, where M is the limit of habit growth over trials dependent on such conditions as the amount of reinforcement; thus $E = H \times D$. In the later version, the amount of reinforcement no longer affects H, which is now equal to $(1\text{-}10^{-iN})$, where N is the number of reinforced trials regardless of amount. Then K becomes a function of amount of reinforcement, and the resulting equation is $E = H \times K \times D$. But K is now the same, mathematically, as the original M! It is only the additional assumptions, particularly the permanence of H and the transitory nature of K, that in any way distinguishes the theories.

17. It should be recognized that no empirical response measure is necessarily a linear measure of the strength of hypothetical constructs. Within limits, one can transform a multiplicative theoretical interaction into an additive empirical interaction, and vice versa.

18. Note that this does *not* mean the class of behaviors defined by an experimenter or the environment is equivalent in the sense that reward would be nondifferential with respect to each of them should they occur. The acquired equivalence of responses results only when distinguishable behaviors are emitted and receive nondifferential reinforcement.

19. This seems an appropriate point to report that most of the systematists that we have been studying were also unusually creative in the design of apparatuses, mechanical devices, and physical models of their theories. The "schematic sowbug" was to mimic the observable behavior of a rat in a maze; it was to show the increases in speed and the reduction in errors characteristic of maze learning, as well as the "looking-back-and-forth." If successful, Tolman could say, "I don't know for sure what's going on inside that real rat, but it does just what this sowbug does and I do know what's going on in there." Hull designed many mechanical devices, including a correlation machine; at the time, his interests were in aptitude testing and he was tired of the countless hours required to compute correlation coefficients on the then existing calculators. Laziness, not used in the perjorative sense, also inspired the design of the Skinner box. Recognize that every time a rat runs down a runway, the experimenter has to traverse that distance twice; once to get the rat, and a second time to bring the rat back to the start. This, combined with a desire for a more controlled environment, led to letting rats press bars, while the experimenter had only to observe the cumulative record of what the rat did. Spence predated the Wisconsin General Test Apparatus designed by Harlow; working with chimpanzees in collaboration with Yerkes, he designed an apparatus for studying choice behavior that was virtually indestructable (even given the strength of a chimp). Spence also reacted to the same problem that bothered Skinner by designing a rotating runway, which was the forerunner of the now familiar shuttle box; the experimenter sat at one end, which was the goal for that trial, rewarded the rat for running to him, and then rotated the runway so that the

rat was at the opposite end. What was the goalbox now became the start box for the next trial. The Hunter decade-interval timer was designed in collaboration with J.S. Brown. We could, of course, proceed with many more examples, but our point is sufficiently made: we are not discussing "armchair" systematists. They were "hands-on" scientists, equally adept in their laboratories as in their studies.

20. The reader of the classic books in this area will observe that authors distinguished between the words "conditioning" and "learning." Indeed, one of the most influential texts of its day (Hilgard & Marquis, 1940) made this distinction in its title. Conditioning was used to refer to situations in which a single response was being observed and some measure of its strength in isolation was estimated. The three basic forms of conditioning satisfy this definition: the dog salivates, the pigeon pecks the key, the rat traverses the alley. Learning was reserved for situations that included an explicit selection from among stimuli or responses, that is, discrimination learning and differentiation learning. Given contemporary theoretical analyses, this distinction may not be as important as it once appeared to be, but it does distinguish when a new behavioral measure is available, namely, percent choice that presumably indicates the relative strengths of the competing alternative behaviors.

21. Hull did not embark upon his theoretical analyses of learning and motivation until after the age of 40. He had previously gained visibility in analyses of aptitude testing and then in hypnosis. Furthermore, he had been inflicted with poliomyelitis and was physically crippled as a result. Nevertheless, he set out on the mission of building a behavior theory based on the fundamental principles of learning and motivation that he envisaged developing into a general theoretical account of all of the behavior sciences. Sympathetic students of Hull are inclined to tread softly on the occasional logical slips in his later writings, attributing them correctly to his haste to get as much done as possible during his few remaining years; unfortunately, he had little time left to wait for the results of all of the empirical analyses necessary for accomplishing his goals.

ABSTRACTS   **Bindra, D. A motivational view of learning, performance, and behavior modification. *Psychological Review,* 1974, *81,* 199–213.**

The theoretical formulation advanced here wholly discards the response-reinforcement principle. It attributes learned behavior modifications to the building of central representations of contingencies between situational stimuli and incentive stimuli; certain situational stimuli are thereby turned into conditioned incentive-discriminative stimuli. It is proposed that central motivational states, generated by the joint influence of organismic-state variables and unconditioned or conditioned incentive stimuli, influence the response-eliciting potency of particular situational stimuli. The specific response form that emerges is a fresh construction created by the momentary motivational state and the spatio-temporal distribution of various distal and contact discriminative-incentive stimuli in the situation. These and related working assumptions are shown to clarify certain long-standing problems of behavior theory and to provide a basis for deriving satisfactory interpretations of several hitherto perplexing phenomena of conditioning, motivational modulation of instrumental behavior, and observational learning.

Bolles, R.C. Reinforcement, expectancy, and learning. *Psychological Review,* 1972, *79,* 394–409.

A variety of recent evidence indicates that contingent reinforcement is neither a necessary nor a sufficient condition for operant learning. This dilemma reopens the old question of What is learned? It is proposed that what laboratory subjects characteristically learn is not a response to a stimulus but rather two kinds of expectancies. One kind of expectancy (S-S*) corresponds rather accurately with environmental stimulus-outcome contingencies, while the second (R-s) is a less faithful representation of response-outcome contingencies. The reinforcement procedure merely permits both kinds to be learned.

Cofer, C.N., & Appley, M.H. *Motivation: Theory and research.* New York: Wiley, 1964. (Pp. 821–825.)

Activity appears following food-deprivation only when the animal may anticipate the occurrence of feeding. Behavior displays an augmentation of vigor over the level that would be present in the same stimulus situation without anticipation. It is as if the anticipation arouses or excites the organism, alerts it, enhances its responsiveness to the available stimuli. Anticipation brings about a state of arousal akin to the arousal of which activation theorists speak. A term which does not imply an intervening arousal state is anticipation-invigoration mechanism (AIM). We conceive the invigoration, coming from anticipation, to be dependent on the stimuli which have regularly antedated or accompanied consummatory behavior.

There is a strong implication in work on sexual, maternal, migratory, and other such phenomena that arousal can occur initially without experience. In accounting for this, Beach suggests, as did Lashley in writing of a variety of instinctive behaviors, that the hormonal state sensitizes the animal selectively with respect to stimuli. When stimuli are introduced, activity increases and the increment is larger in deprived animals than in satiated animals. Arousal is the key factor, so far as motivation is concerned, in behavioral events in which sensitization is critical. We may speak of a sensitization-invigoration mechanism (SIM).

When the behavior energized either by anticipation-arousal or by sensitization-arousal occurs and leads to consummatory behavior, the aroused state must be affected in some way. The feedback from consummatory behavior, sometimes described as reinforcing, evidently permits a given arousal episode to be terminated. Whether this results from satiation, habituation, enjoyment, or some other process is as yet unclear.

Estes, W.K. Outline of a theory of punishment. In B.A. Campbell and R.M. Church (Eds.), *Punishment and aversive behavior.* **New York: Appleton-Century-Crofts, 1969. (Pp. 57–82.)**

The principal addition to earlier stimulus-sampling theory is that of a generator of amplifier elements associated with each of the principal drive systems; e.g., hunger, thirst, pain. Each of these generating sources provides a certain base rate of input of amplifier elements. It is assumed that on any trial the organism draws a sample of the available discriminative cues, some of which may be connected to the reference response as a result of preceding learning, some to competing responses, and perhaps some to neither (neutral). Having drawn a sample, the organism scans these singly until an element is processed which is connected with a permissible response. However, it will evoke a response only if an amplifier element is sampled simultaneously.

It is assumed that the activity of the negative system results in reciprocal inhibition of the activity of generators belonging to positive-drive systems. Conditioning applies to both positive and negative systems. Deprivation provides a relatively steady base rate of amplifier input. Through conditioning by contiguity, changes in drive input is transferred to other stimuli which immediately precede them. The feedback consequence of a response generates an increase in amplifier input which provides a basis for summation and thus facilitates occurrence of the behaviors which follow in the chain. Negative amplifier input, such as resulting from punishment, is also conditionable by contiguity.

Hull, C.L. Goal attraction and directing ideas conceived as habit phenomena. *Psychological Review,* **1931,** *38,* **487–506.**

Let it be assumed that a relatively isolated inorganic world flux takes place in time. In the neighborhood of this world sequence is a sensitive redintegrative organism provided with distance receptors and so constituted as to respond characteristically to the several phases of the world flux with a parallel behavior flux. Phases of the world flux are represented by $S1$, $S2$, etc., and the response flux by $R1$, $R2$, etc., with the final or goal reaction indicated by R_G. Let it be assumed, further, that within the organism there is a source, such as hunger, which produces continually recurring stimulation. Now according to the principle of redintegration, all the components of a stimulus complex which may be impinging on the sensorium at or near the time that a response is evoked tend themselves independently to acquire the capacity to evoke substantially the same response.

There must be added the fact that each act gives rise to a proprioceptive stimulus, s, and these likewise tend to acquire the capacity to evoke the reactions immediately following them. When the behavior sequence is made up entirely of pure-stimulus acts, the goal reaction may occur quite at the outset of the movement, thus dropping out wasteful intervening acts. But in cases where the intervening acts are mainly instrumental in nature, as is obviously the case in maze running, it is physically impossible to drop out any of the acts involved in traversing the true pathway and at the same time reach the goal.

A split-off portion of the goal reaction (r_G) which chances not to be in conflict with the antecedent instrumental series may be displaced backward. Like all other movements, r_G causes characteristic proprioceptive stimulations (s_G). These fractional anticipatory goal reactions are drawn to the beginning of the behavior sequence and maintained throughout it by the action of the drive stimulus (S_D). These two persisting stimuli should have the capacity of forming multiple excitatory tendencies to the evocation of every reaction within the sequence.

Hull, C.L. *A behavior system.* New Haven: Yale University Press, 1952. (Ch. 1.)

Here follow the behavior postulates . . .

   I. Unlearned Stimulus-response Connections ($_sU_R$)
   II. Stimulus Reception (S and s)
   III. Primary Reinforcement (Drive stimulus intensity reduction)
   IV. Habit Formation ($_sH_R = 1 - 10^{-iN}$)
   V. Primary Motivation (D is a function of drive conditions, e.g., deprivation)
   VI. Stimulus-intensity Dynamism ($V = 1 - 10^{-alogS}$)
   VII. Incentive Motivation, the incentive component (K) of reaction potential is a negatively accelerated increasing monotonic function of the weight of food or quantity of other incentive given as reinforcement.
   VIII. Reaction Potential ($_sE_R = D \times V \times K \times {_sH_R}$)
   IX. Inhibitory Potential (I_R, reactive inhibition, and $_sI_R$, conditioned inhibition, combine and subtract from $_sE_R$)
   X. Stimulus Generalization
   XI. Afferent Stimulus Interaction
   XII. Behavorial Oscillation ($_sO_R$)
   XIII. Reaction Threshold ($_sL_R$)
   XIV. Reaction Latency
   XV. Reaction Amplitude
   XVI. Resistance to Experimental Extinction
   XVII. Individual Differences

The fractional antedating goal reaction, together with its proprioceptive stimulus correlate, r_G-s_G is a pure-stimulus act. Each s_G is a stimulus leading to the realization of its particular goal. This mechanism leads in a strictly logical manner to what was formerly regarded as the very heart of the psychic: interest, planning, foresight, foreknowledge, expectancy, purpose, etc.

Irwin, F.W. *Intentional behavior and motivation: A cognitive theory.* New York: Lippincott, 1971.

The theory is of the kind commonly called "cognitive"; it may be called a situation-act-outcome, or SAO, psychology, since its concepts are constructed from these three primitive items. The most elementary constructions of SAO theory are preferences, discriminations, and act-outcome expectancies.

The present system developed from consideration of motivational problems. Learning in the form of acquisition and modification of expectancies plays a central role. Positive or negative preference value of outcomes is not required for this process. It will be supposed that Pavlovian conditioning of certain acts, which then may properly be called responses takes place; this will lead to a two-factor account of special cases of "emotional" motivation. It will also be supposed that a process of automatization of situation-act relations occurs; this means that an act that is intentional at one point in its history becomes at a later point less dependent upon current expectancies and preferences. There is little difference, if any, between such situation-act relations and S-R connections.

Preferences and expectancies are dispositional states of the organism and changes in such states, such as "learning," are processes. In a logical sense they are intervening variables. However, such states and processes are observable, their existence being known by way of behavior.

It is not necessary to introduce the notion of "consciousness" in defining intentional acts, intended outcomes, and the psychological states prior to these. To perceive something and to be conscious that one perceives it, or to desire something and to be conscious that one desires it, are two different things, and the former member of each of these pairs by no means implies the latter.

Logan, F.A. *Incentive: How the conditions of reinforcement affect the performance of rats.* New Haven: Yale University Press, 1960. (Ch. 5.)

I. *Response definition.* The overt R is isomorphic with the hypothetical r of the model; the model is concerned with the probability of r; the r class may be composed of any aggregate for which the determinants of excitatory potential are the same; the several dimensions of r are independent.

II. *Stimulus reception.* The stimulus trace (s) is a function of time.

III. *Primary motivation.* Hunger, thirst, sex, pain, and fear.

IV. *Secondary motivation.* Conditioned fear.

V. *Primary reinforcement.* Occurrence of appropriate goal response (R_G).

VI. *Secondary reinforcement.* Occurrence of fractional part of R_G (r_g).

VII. *Habit strength.* Function of number of reinforced trials.

VIII. *Inhibition.* Increased by nonreinforcement; decreased by reinforcement.

IX. *Effective habit.* sHr - sIr.

X. *Unlearned response tendencies.* Born with or predisposed to acquire (sUr).

XI. *Incentive motivation.* The occurrence of R_G or r_g immediately following a response produces incentive motivation (sINr) for repetition of that response to the coincident stimulus traces. Function of delay, amount, response duration, and changes in reward. sMr is the product of D and sINr.

XII. *Generalization.* Stimulus and response generalization of sHr, sIr, sINr.

XIII. *Excitatory potential.* $sEr = sHr \times sMr$.

XIV. *Effort.* Function of work (sFr) and subtracts from sEr.

XV. *Oscillation.* sEr remains constant for a behavioral unit of time (BUT) and otherwise varies randomly with normal distribution.

XVI. *Temporary inhibition.* Tendency (sTIr) not to repeat same R to same S.

XVII. *Competition of reaction potentials.* Largest sEr will occur.

Mackintosh, N.J. *The psychology of animal learning.* New York: Academic Press, 1974. (Pp. 222–233.)

The presentation of a stimulus established as a classical CS for appetitive reinforcement does not appear to increase the vigour or rate of appetitive instrumental responding. Moreover, the initiation of a chain of instrumental responses cannot be attributed to any antecedent change in a classically conditioned motivational state. In the light of this evidence it seems necessary to reject the idea that instrumental behavior is motivated in any simple way by a classically conditioned system of incentive motivation.

It would seem that activity is appropriate when it is instrumental in leading an animal out of a stimulus situation in which it has learned food does not occur, into a situation in which food has previously been presented. Instrumental responding, therefore, should not be initiated because it is preceded by stimuli signalling food and eliciting salivation, but because performance of the instrumental chain is accompanied or followed by the occurrence of such stimuli and hence by an increase in salivation or anticipation of food.

The motivation for instrumental responding, therefore, is not correlated with the current level of a classically conditioned state of incentive, but with the discrepancy between present and anticipated states (or the "relative valence" of current and future stimulation). Incentives do not motivate instrumental behavior unselectively. Indeed, it is not clear that anything is gained by introducing the concept of motivation at all. The initiation and maintenance of instrumental responses is a consequence of a past history in which such responding has been accompanied by an increase in proximity to reinforcement. Stimuli signalling reinforcement do not instigate responding; as a consequence of past learning they act as goals for responding.

Miller, N.E. Some reflections on the law of effect produce a new alternative to drive reduction. In M.R. Jones (Ed.), *Nebraska Symposium on Motivation.* **Lincoln: University of Nebraska Press, 1963.**

Let us explore the assumption that sudden relief from strong stimulation produces an automatic increase in the activity of any neural circuits that have just been firing. Let us further assume that it is this energization that is responsible for the strong performance which in turn is responsible for learning by contiguity. Let us see where such speculations can lead us:

1. That there are one or more "go" or "activating" mechanisms in the brain which act to intensify ongoing responses to cues and the traces of immediately preceding activities, producing a stronger intensification the more strongly the "go mechanism" is activated.

2. That this "go mechanism" can be activated in a variety of ways, such as by reduction in noxious stimulation, by the taste of food to a hungry animal, by the removal of a discrepancy between an intention and an achievement, etc.

3. That all responses, including the activation of this "go mechanism" are subject to conditioning with contiguity being sufficient.

4. That the strength of the CR is determined to a great degree by the strength of the UCR but also by the number of pairings.

5. That when a chain of cues leads to a UCS for the "go mechanism," it is most strongly conditioned to those nearer to the UCS, but can be conditioned to those farther away with a progressive decline in strength.

6. That every time a CR (including a conditioned "go response") is repeated without reinforcement from the UCS (or perhaps it should be, a CS is presented without a UCS, or the CR is stronger than the UCR), it is subject to a certain amount of weakening, or in other words, experimental extinction.

It can be seen that, after various conditioning trials in its environment, an organism or other device, constructed along these principles, would tend to be guided cybernetically toward the UCS for the "go system," and that it would tend to drop out sequences that doubled back on themselves.

Mowrer, O.H. Two-factor learning theory reconsidered, with special reference to secondary reinforcement and the concept of habit. *Psychological Review,* **1956,** *63,* **114–128.**

We are led to speak of two types of "fear conditioning": conditioned arousal of fear and conditioned relaxation, or relief, thereof. In incremental fear conditioning, the organism is motivated to get rid of an exteroceptive fear stimulus by responding appropriately, and to get rid of an interoceptive fear stimulus by stopping the response producing the stimulus. In decremental fear conditioning, an external stimulus may acquire the capacity to reduce fear or arouse hope (secondary reinforcement in the Pavlov-Hull sense). Internal stimuli may also become conditioned to hope, fear relaxation, or secondary reinforcement.

We are trying to look at the learning involved in so-called habit formation not as the strengthening of a neural connection or pathway between a drive and a particular piece of behavior but rather as the strengthening of the neural pathway between the stimuli produced by a particular response and the phenomenon of secondary reinforcement. All learning is in the nature of sign learning. Thus, habit formation and fear conditioning (incremental type), which were the two factors in the original version of two-factor learning theory, give way to incremental fear conditioning or secondary motivation and decremental fear conditioning or secondary reinforcement.

If on the basis of past experience, the feedback from a given response is positive (hopeful), the response will be facilitated; if the feedback is negative (fearful), the response will be inhibited. Specific actions are determined not by the nature of specific S-R bonds but by the guiding (controlling) action of the reactions which have become conditioned to response-produced stimuli (or their symbolic equivalents).

Mowrer, O.H. *Learning theory and behavior.* New York: Wiley, 1960. (Ch. 7.)

It will be noted that all learning is (by implication) conditioning, so that the theory remains "two-factored" only with respect to the forms of reinforcement involved, i.e., incremental and decremental. Since each of these may involve primary drive or either of two forms of secondary drive, there are thus, in effect, six operationally distinguishable forms of reinforcement; and each of these may be associated with either independent or response-dependent stimulation. Therefore, there are twelve "kinds" of reinforcement:

Active avoidance learning occurs when independent, environmentally produced stimuli are followed by

1. Primary drive increment
2. Secondary drive increment (fear type)
3. Secondary drive increment (disappointment type)

Response inhibition occurs when response-correlated stimulation is followed by 1, 2, or 3 above.

Active approach behavior occurs when independent, environmentally produced stimuli are followed by

7. Primary drive decrement
8. Secondary drive decrement (relief type)
9. Secondary drive decrement (hope type)

Response facilitation occurs when response-correlated stimulation is followed by 7, 8, or 9 above.

Premack, D. Catching up with common sense or two sides of a generalization: Reinforcement and punishment. In R. Glaser (Ed.), *The nature of reinforcement.* New York: Academic Press, 1971. (Pp. 121–150.)

I make the following assumptions in dealing with motivational phenomena:

1. Organisms order the discriminable events of their world on a scale of value.

2. The value that an organism assigns to a stimulus can be measured by the probability that the organism will respond to the stimulus. The probability can be estimated from the duration for which the organism responds. Durations can be compared over all possible stimulus and response dimensions under constraints which reduce to the requirement that either the rate-time functions for the several responses be comparable, or the probabilities compared by momentary rather than average.

3. Value is a unitary dimension.

4. Motivational phenomena—reinforcement, punishment, contrast, arousal—all result from a common state of affairs: a difference is value.

The notion of value will be as helpful as our ability to obtain an untroubled measure of it. The basic test procedure is to provide the subject with a stimulus and to record its contact with it. It should be clear that in talking about response probability I could not have in mind anything comparable to the view that response magnitude or vigor is a predictor variable. Even though it is desirable to take the position that a response is a means of calibrating the value a subject sets on a stimulus, and that the precise contribution which the response factors make to value is a matter for research, we should not swing so far in the other direction as to return to the traditional stimulus error. For example, tradition talks about the reinforcement value of food. But food has no value; we must talk about the value of food when it can be smelled (but not seen), seen (but not smelled), both seen and smelled, eaten, etc. It is part of the advantage of response language to avoid this kind of error automatically.

Rescorla, R.A., & Solomon, R.L. Two-process learning theory: Relationships between Pavlovian conditioning and instrumental learning. *Psychological Review,* 1967, *74,* 151–182.

The history of two-process learning theory is described, and the logical and empirical validity of its major postulates is examined. The assumption of two acquisition processes requires the demonstration of an empirical interaction between types of reinforcement contingencies and (a) response classes, (b) reinforcing stimulus classes, or (c) characteristics of the learned behavior itself. The mediation postulates of two-process theory which argue that CRs are intimately involved in the control of instrumental responding are emphasized, and two major lines of evidence that stem uniquely from these postulates are examined: (a) the concurrent development and maintenance of instrumental responses and conditioned reflexes, and (b) the interaction between separately conducted Pavlovian conditioning contingencies and instrumental training contingencies in the control of instrumental behavior. The evidence from concurrent measurement studies provides, at the very best, only weak support for the mediational hypothesis of two-process theory. In contrast, the evidence from interaction studies shows the strong mediating control of instrumental responses by Pavlovian conditioning procedures, and demonstrates the surprising power of Pavlovian concepts in predicting the outcomes of many kinds of interaction experiments.

Revusky, S., & Garcia, J. Learned associations over long delays. In G.H. Bower (Ed.), *The psychology of learning and motivation* (Vol. 4.) New York: Academic Press, 1970.

Ingestion is a discriminated operant; the relevant discriminative stimuli are produced by deprivation level; and reinforcement involves the nutritive consequences of ingestion. The patterns of internal stimuli (S_d) are assumed to change. The main idea is that different S_d's are correlated with different reward values of the nutritive aftereffects of ingestion, and the animal learns this relationship even though the aftereffects occur throughout a long time interval. S_d's are far more likely to become associated with the physiological aftereffects of ingestion.

Hunger is not a present state of need; hunger occurs when ingestion will be followed by absorption of nutrients at a time when it is beneficial. R_a refers to the reinforcement value of the nutritive aftereffects of ingestion. The role of learning is to insure that eating will anticipate needs. We hope to explain the effects of food deprivation on food rewarded performance in terms of principles that are validated by phenomena other than what is to be explained.

A performance rewarded by food is treated as a response early in a chain, eating is regarded as the terminal response, and R_a is regarded as the reinforcement. Ignoring situational and proprioceptive stimuli, the paradigm is summarized by:

$$S_d \text{ ------ performance ------ } S_d \text{ ------ ingestion ------ } R_a$$

so that S_d enters selectively into the determination of the operant response as well as ingestion. Probabilty of performance is correlated with probability of ingestion. S_d's act as transsituational motives. Food is a secondary reinforcer, its reward value depending on deprivation and hence the ultimate R_a. There are no nonassociative properties of drive.

Schoenfeld, W.N., Cumming, W.W., & Hearst, E. On the classification of reinforcement schedules. *Proceedings of the National Academy of Sciences,* 1956, *42,* 563–570.

We may consider that a schedule of reinforcement acts to maintain behavior through the differential reinforcement of a particular pattern of responses in time (or, equivalently, single responses having certain temporal characteristics with respect to other responses). From this viewpoint the "count" involved in a "ratio" schedule may be only incidental to the generation of a maximal rate of responding, with the crucial factor being the increased probability of reinforcement for responses following each other at short intervals. By implication, then, if external conditions were arranged to favor rapid responding by the organism, we might expect to observe the "bursts" (short period of high response rate) and "breaks" (pauses in responding) so characteristic of "ratio" reinforcement. "Interval" schedules, on the other hand, may differentially reinforce responses preceded by relatively longer intervals of no responding, producing the response rates and temporal distributions characteristic of these schedules. Skinner has noted that "schedules are simply rather inaccurate ways of reinforcing rate of responding."

The projected classification of reinforcement schedules utilizes "time-sampling" contingencies, in the description of which we shall employ the terms t^D and t^Δ. The term t^D represents a period of time during which a specified instrumental response of the organism may be followed by a reinforcing event; t^Δ represents a period of time during which this response will not be followed by a reinforcing event. A fundamental case may be established with these three restrictions: (1) t^D and t^Δ are held constant, (2) t^D and t^Δ are alternated, and (3) only the first response in t^D is reinforced.

Fixed interval schedules are marked by $t^D/t^D + t^\Delta$ approximating or equaling unity (where t^Δ approaches 0 and t^D greater than 0) and comparatively long cycle lengths. Extinction is the case where t^D approaches 0 and t^Δ is greater than 0. Several considerations help to resolve the apparent incompatibility between the two metrics of time and response number. By reducing $t^D/t^D + t^\Delta$ to a sufficiently small value and keeping reasonably long cycle lengths, we favor the adoption by the organism of a high response rate, since on such a schedule reinforcement is more probable or frequent following short interresponse intervals (i.e., high rates). It is an empirical question whether choices of t^D and t^Δ values would result in "ratio" behavior ("breaks" and "bursts," etc.) and whether sudden large decreases in $t^D/t^D + t^\Delta$ would reproduce the known effects of switching an organism to a much higher fixed or mean variable ratio.

Each of the preceding three restrictions might themselves be systematically manipulated. For example, t^D and t^Δ might be varied according to some prearranged program. They could be presented randomly rather than by regular alternations, and any desired probability of reinforcement of other than the first, or more than one, response in t^D. In fact, the entire analysis up to now could be duplicated in any t^D period by including within t^D itself any "interval" or "ratio" schedule so far discussed. Obviously, too, all the usual independent variables of behavioral research, such as drive, could figure as parameters of the present classification.

Seward, J.P. Drive, incentive, and reinforcement. *Psychological Review*, 1956, *63*, 195–203.

Scratch a motivation theory and find the problem of reinforcement. This paper deals with two possible reinforcers: drive reduction and consummatory response. Experiments designed to separate their influence have yielded evidence in support of both. Drive reduction seems to be a sufficient condition for response selection. But rewards apparently do more than reduce drives; as incentives they appear to heighten excitement as well as activate instrumental responses. This poses a problem: How can drive reduction and incentive induction both produce the same result, i.e., strengthen a concurrent response? It is suggested that Guthrie's theory , with the aid of two motivational constructs, drive and goal, offers a solution.

Sheffield, F.D. A drive-induction theory of reinforcement. In R.N. Haber (Ed.), *Current research in motivation.* New York: Holt, 1966. (Pp. 98–122.) (Read at Brown University, November, 1954.)

In this theory the incentive aspects of rewards accounts for their effectiveness. The incentive aspect should be contrasted with the relaxing aspect that is so important to the drive-reduction position. Frustration means a circumstance in which the animal is in a drive state and in which the consummatory response is stimulated but is prevented from occurring for one reason or another. The proposition is that conditioned arousal of a consummatory response is inherently frustrating.

A frustrating situation causes an increase in excitement. We can deduce that the response-produced cues of the correct sequence will become a stimulus sequence of increasing excitement as the instrumental response sequence proceeds toward the final response. Earlier cues in the sequence are conditioned by progressively higher-order conditioning. Excitement can stably work its way back along the cues from the correct response and no other.

Excitement gets channeled into whatever skeletal response happens to be under way at the time the increase in excitement occurs. Any response that, in its incipience, arouses excitement will not be abandoned but rather will be somewhat aggressively executed. Various general and specific cues in the situation will also be conditioned to the consummatory response, making the animal more active. The animal is forced to follow courses of action that maximize conditioned arousal of the consummatory response.

Only a contiguity principle of learning is used. Acquired drive and acquired reward reduce to the same thing. This booster feedback mechanism makes the correct response prepotent even before it becomes habitual and stereotyped.

Skinner, B.F., *Contingenies of reinforcement. A theoretical analysis.* New York: Appleton-Century-Crofts, 1969. (Ch. 4.)

An emphasis on rate of occurrence of repeated instances of an operant distinguished the experimental analysis of behavior from kinds of psychology which observe one or more of the followwng practices:

1. Behavior is taken merely as the sign or symptom of inner activities, mental or physiological, which are regarded as the principal subject matter. These practices have discouraged a careful specification of behavior, and the data obtained with them are seldom helpful in evaluating probability of response as such.

2. Behavior is held to be significant only in meeting certain standards or criteria. The experimenter may not specify what the organism is actually doing.

3. Changes in probability of response are treated as if they were responses or acts. "To discriminate" is not a mode of response.

4. The dimensions studied, though quantifiable, are not related in any simple way to probability of response. Popular measures such as latency and response may not throw much light on probability, and a ratio is of little help in an experimental analysis.

5. The most impeccable statistical techniques and the most cautious operational definitions will not alter the fact that the "tests" for inner entities come from very loosely controlled experimental spaces.

6. The experimenter records and studies a subject's statement of what he would do under a given set of circumstances.

A study of schedules of reinforcement can proceed in a rather Baconian fashion, as a table of the possibilities generated by combination of clocks counters, and speedometers, fixed and variable sequences, and so on is completed. The experimental analysis of behavior dispenses with theories such as probability, decision-making, and games by proceeding to find out.

Spence, K.W. *Behavior theory and conditioning.* New Haven: Yale University Press, 1956. (Ch. 5.)

This theory assumes that stimulus cues in the goal box and from the alley just preceding the goal box become conditioned to the goal response (R_g). Through generalization the stimulus cues at earlier points in the runway are also assumed to acquire the capacity to elicit fractional, noncompetitional components of R_g, (r_g), and the interoceptive stimulus cue (s_g) produced by this response becomes a part of the stimulus complex in the alley and thus should become conditioned to the instrumental locomotor responses. But more important, in addition to this associative function, we have assumed that this r_g-s_g mechanism also has motivational properties.

A number of different conceptions of the manner in which r_g-s_g may operate to affect motivational level have been suggested. One that I mentioned in 1951 was that the occurrence of these responses results in a certain amount of conflict and hence in heightened tension or excitement which might contribute to an increase in general drive level. This conception is very similar to that of Crespi. Another possibility is that s_g provides an internal stimulus dynamism. However, my preference is merely to introduce an intervening variable, K, which represents the motivational property of the conditioned r_g-s_g.

From our assumption that r_g-s_g underlies K, we are necessarily committed to a number of assumptions as to the variables that determine its strength. These are number of conditioning trials, distance from the goal, proprioceptive cues from the running response and any property of the goal object that produces unconditioned consummatory responses of different intensity or vigor.

The theory is that $R = f(E) = H \times (D + K) - I_t$, where H is a function of number of trials, D is a function of time of deprivation, K is a function of number of trials, time of deprivation, and amount of reward, and I_t is a function of number of trials and delay of reward.

This places me in the contiguity camp for instrumental reward conditioning. Incentive is not involved, and reinforcement may be necessary for classical conditioning.

Tolman, E.C. Principles of performance. *Psychological Review,* 1955, *62,* 315–326.

There are four distinctive types of independent variables: (a) present stimulus units; (b) previous presentations of stimulus-unit-response-stimulus-unit sequences; (c) present drive disturbances and currently presented incentive objects; and (d) genetic or early training differences between individual subjects. There are three types of intervening variable systems: (a) discrimination system; (b) belief-expectancy system; and (c) drive and incentive-value system. Need-push is determined by the magnitude of the actual activated drive and also by the goodness of the discrimination of drive stimuli under the given experimental conditions. Valence depends on the incentive value of the reward and the discriminability of the reward in the concrete stimulus context.

The performance vector is a result of (i) the need-push for the reward; (ii) the positive valence of the expected reward; (iii) the need-push against work; and (iv) the negative valence of the expected work. In equation form,
$$Pv = f_x(n_r, \, v_r, \, \exp_r) -$$
$$f_y(n_{-w}, \, v_{-w}, \, \exp_w).$$
This vector specifies the direction and magnitude of the to-be-predicted actual performance. The greater the valence of the expected food, the greater the food need-push, and the greater the expectancy that the food will result, the greater the magnitude of the performance vector. On the other hand, the

greater the magnitude of the need-push against work, the greater the negative valence of the expected work, and the stronger the expectation of this work, the less the performance vector.

A performance is a generalized way of behaving to be discovered and specified only by observing the response in at least two and perhaps more concrete test situations. The motor skill characteristics involved in such a performance are not included in its definition. Performances are all that we ought now, at the present time, try to explain or to predict in detail.

Trowill, J.A., Panksepp, J., & Gandelman, R. An incentive model of rewarding brain stimulation. *Psychological Review,* 1969, *76,* 264–281.

Early data and theories suggested that the properties of rewarding electrical stimulation of the brain (ESB) differ from those of natural rewards such as food or water. It is contended here that such differences are solely due to differences in deprivation and training conditions, rather than to inherent properties in the rewards. Therefore, it is proposed that ESB has the same properties as other rewards and that its motivational properties are inherent in its reinforcement properties in the form of incentive motivation, rather than in the induction of drive energization. Data testing the model are reviewed and are found to support the incentive position. It is further suggested that to the extent that brain stimulation can maintain behavior in the absence of deprivation, the laws for incentive independent of deprivation conditions can be found using brain stimulation.

EXAMINATION ITEMS   Topics for thought and discussion

1.   In what ways might incentive theorists attempt to deal with classical conditioning?

2.   Describe and then discuss what, in the parlance of the text, would be identified as a pure-reinforcement-impure-incentive theory.

3.   Discuss the concept of net incentive. How might the concept be anchored formally within the types of theories we have studied?

4.   Many contemporary learning theorists now believe that learning (as distinct from performance) depends simply on contiguity of stimulus and another stimulus or response. Thus performance results from a motivational factor dependent on reward, and reinforcement is not necessary for learning. Other than latent learning, what kind of data would provide positive evidence for learning by contiguity?

5.   The issue of whether drive motivation and incentive motivation combine additively or multiplicatively is more than a laboratory exercise: there are many practical implications. Explore the difference in the context of self-control.

6.   A fundamental issue in clinical psychology is whether one must attend to the underlying processes generating maladaptive behavior or whether one can properly concentrate directly on the modification of that behavior. What would incentive theory have to say about this issue?

Objective items

1. By its very nature, an incentive construct within a theory is
   a. cognitive
   b. behavioristic
   c. either cognitive or behavioristic
   d. neither cognitive nor behavioristic

2. As the term is used in the text, a dynamic theory is one that views behavior
   a. as purposeful
   b. in relation to awareness
   c. by reference to field forces
   d. continuously over time.

3. Compared with a pure reinforcement theory, an incentive theory has
   a. no difficulty in identifying reinforcers
   b. less difficulty in identifying reinforcers
   c. equal difficulty in identifying reinforcers
   d. more difficulty in identifying reinforcers

4. Which of the following theorists would least likely accept being included under the general category of incentive theorists?
   a. Tolman
   b. Spence
   c. Sheffield
   d. Cofer and Appley

5. Which of the following incentive theorists would appear to be most discordant with the others?
   a. Spence
   b. Mowrer
   c. Miller
   c. Estes

6. A pure reinforcement incentive theory would assume that
   a. both need reduction and drive reduction are necessary
   b. amount of reward affects both learning and motivation
   c. there is more than one kind of learning
   d. there is more than one kind of motivation

7. Imagine yourself in Hull's shoes in 1943 looking at Crespi's data involving shifts in amount of reward. Looking just at those data, the feature you would find most disturbing would be the
   a. fact that speed increased when amount was increased
   b. rate at which speed increased when amount was increased
   c. fact that speed decreased when amount was decreased
   d. rate at which speed decreased when amount was decreased

8. According to incentive theories, the amount of reward
   a. affects the strength of the expectancy and hence its value
   b. does not affect the strength of the expectancy but does affect its value
   c. affects the strength of the expectancy rather than its value
   d. does not affect either the strength of the expectancy of its value

9. To which of the following theorists would the question of how learning and motivation combine not be applicable?
   a. Spence

b. Mowrer
c. Estes
d. Logan

10. If one takes the view that secondary reinforcement and incentive motivation are essentially opposite sides of the same coin, then the information hypothesis of secondary reinforcement would imply that, as an organism approaches a familiar goal, incentive motivation would
    a. increase
    b. decrease
    c. increase then decrease
    d. decrease then increase

11. Which of the following empirical topics with respect to secondary reinforcement is most critical to Mowrer's revised two-factor theory?
    a. efficacy of partial pairing to produce durable secondary reinforcement
    b. secondary reinforcement as related to information value
    c. relation between the discriminative and reinforcing properties or stimuli
    d. secondary reinforcement based on primary negative reinforcement

12. A major problem for incentive theories is how the construct based on reward conditions combines with the construct based on deprivation conditions. In this regard
    a. Estes says additive, Spence says multiplicative
    b. Estes says multiplicative, Spence says additive
    c. Estes and Spence both say additive
    d. Estes and Spence both say multiplicative

13. Sheffield, in proposing a drive-induction theory of reinforcement, assumed that drive induction
    a. is necessary for learning
    b. is both necessary and sufficient for learning
    c. increases performance
    d. decreases performance

14. The sensitization-invigoration mechanism proposed by Cofer and Appley may best be viewed as
    a. equivalent to drive in Hull's theory
    b. a substitute for drive in Hull's theory
    c. a cognitive representation of drive in Hull's theory
    d. unrelated to drive in Hull's theory

15. A major problem for incentive theories, exemplified most clearly in Mowrer's approach, is how feedback can affect
    a. responses antecedent to the feedback
    b. the very response producing the feedback
    c. responses subsequent to the feedback
    d. responses that do not produce feedback

16. As defined in the text, a pure stimulus operation is one that involves
    a. a temporal contingency between two or more stimuli
    b. filtering natural stimuli into fundamental Hertz values
    c. stimulus presentations independent of the organism's behavior
    d. greater learning with more intense stimuli

17. If Schoenfeld's conceptual approach in developing a functional analysis of rein-

forcement schedules had been realized in its idealized form, his basic operation would have been a pure
  a. stimulus operation
  b. response operation
  c. reinforcement operation
  d. drive-reduction operation

18. From an S-R point of view, the advantage of the r_g mechanism for incentive motivation over an expectancy construct is that it
  a. is potentially observable
  b. enables a uniprocess theory
  c. obeys the laws of classical conditioning
  d. has stimulus (s_g) properties

19. Incentive theories based on fractional anticipatory goal responses would predict that two goal events (such as food and sex) would not summate if they involved incompatible overt consummatory responses.
  a. True
  b. False

20. View your own behavior in responding to this question in terms of a Tolman/-Spence type of cybernetic incentive analysis. You should
  a. vacillate among the alternatives until you decide one is right
  b. make systematic paired comparisons between the alternatives
  c. eliminate alternatives until only one is left
  d. take longer answering multiple-choice questions than true-false items because of the larger number of alternatives

ANSWERS TO OBJECTIVE ITEMS

1. (c) One could adopt either approach, although the behavioristic theorist would want to introduce some response mechanism in the process.

2. (d) The word "dynamic" has been used in various ways, but it here refers to systems that are analyzed continuously over time rather than to static analyses that consider only steady-state conditions.

3. (c) The empirical problem of identifying events that have incentive value is precisely the same as identifying reinforcing (and punishing) events.

4. (c) Tolman, Spence, and Cofer and Appley all introduce an explicit incentive-type construct; Sheffield uses excitement to increase a general level of drive, and so the construct is not immediately apparent.

5. (b) Mowrer is unique in not having any associative process involving the referent response itself.

6. (b) It would be logically possible to assume that amount of reward affects both learning and motivation and, indeed, Tolman sometimes admitted that reinforcement might make cognitions clearer and more emphatic.

7. (b) Speed could only increase as a result of additional learning, and that process was assumed to be gradual. The decrease in speed resulting from a decrease in reward could be related to extinction (inhibition) processes that might take place rapidly.

8. (b) The amount of reward is part of what is learned in the R-S association. The strength of that association does not affect the incentive value of various amounts of reward.

9. (b) Since Mowrer has no learning construct with respect to the referent behavior, there is no problem concerning the combination rule.

10. (b) As an organism approaches a familiar goal, the cues are increasingly redundant. This would make them less efficacious according to the information hypothesis.

11. (d) By assuming that reinforcing properties of stimuli are conditionable and apply to both positive and negative reinforcement, and utilizing the same notion for incentive motivation, the difficulty in demonstrating secondary reinforcement based on primary negative reinforcement is embarrassing. The first two alternatives are consistent with his notions, and the third does not bear directly on it.

12. (c) Although approaching the issue from quite different points of view, both Spence and Estes consider incentive as another source of motivation that combines in an essentially additive fashion with drive.

13. (c) Sheffield remained a contiguity theorist with respect to learning. His fundamental conception was that drive reduction was not critical for either learning or performance, but induction of motivation was the important performance factor.

14. (b) The sensitization-invigoration mechanism is certainly related to drive in Hull's system, both being based on deprivation. Cofer and Appley, however, did not view drive as a goading force but viewed it as a disposition to respond or a selective sensitivity to certain events.

15. (b) Of course, feedback can have no further effect on what has already happened and can certainly affect what happens in the future through associations with subsequent behavior. The problem focuses on the here-and-now behavior—the feedback that is going to result from doing something.

16. (c) The operation is called "pure" because it is performed without regard to anything else going on in the environment, most particularly, the behavior of the organism. It does not need to involve two or more stimuli and may or may not involve narrow Hertz bands. Whether greater learning occurs is an empirical question separate from the operation itself.

17. (a) Schoenfeld's goal was to control behavior by delivering reinforcers independently of that behavior, that is, simply drop in pellets according to a temporal schedule. Of course, in practice, he used a reinforcement operation that involved a response operation and possibly a drive-reduction operation.

18. (b) Neither r_g nor expectancy are observable; both obey the laws of classical conditioning, and both have stimulus properties. (Classical conditioning and stimuli are viewed differently by S-R and S-S theorists, but the roles are functionally equivalent.) The advantage is simply that all learning processes can be viewed in terms of S-R associations.

19. (False) Since the mechanism is hypothetical and explicitly involves components that are not incompatible with other responses, there is no need to generalize the incompatibility of the overt consummatory responses to their fractional anticipatory aspects.

20. (a) The analysis does not involve comparisions; you respond when one alternative exceeds your threshold for choosing it. In the process, you may eliminate alternatives, but this means simply that they are below your threshold. Speed depends on excitatory strength and not on the number of alternatives; one alternative in a multiple-choice item may quickly look right to you, whereas a true-false item may puzzle you for a long time.

CHAPTER SIX

AVERSIVE CONTROL

The topic of aversive control is not easy to delineate. This is because most experimental procedures involve some negative feature. When an experimenter deprives an animal of food in order later to control its behavior in a positive manner, the experimenter surely is imposing a state of discomfort. It may be contended that at least some degree of hunger and thirst are inevitable facts of life and, hence, motivating operations based on deprivation are more humane than the application of aversive stimulation. Even so, neither are our natural lives completely devoid of painful experiences and, hence, the systematic analysis of their effects on behavior is an important facet of a complete understanding. In this sense, few control procedures may be viewed as entirely positive.

For our present purposes the domain of aversive control is defined as those situations in which an explicit aversive stimulus is used. In an earlier part of this textbook, we discussed the matter of identifying primary and secondary emotionally negative or aversive stimuli and concluded that this was most satisfactorily accomplished when using a functional approach. Primary aversive stimuli are stimuli the presentation of which leads to a decrease in future response probability and the removal of which leads to an increase in future response probability. Secondary aversive stimuli are stimuli that function as do primary aversive stimuli as a consequence of having been previously paired with primary aversive stimuli.

For various historic reasons, even in the era of grand theories of behavior, none of the major theorists dealt with the domain of aversive control in its entirety.[1] Indeed, the early empirical advances in aversive control were guided more by experimental paradigm than by theory. Two of the generally recognized aversive control paradigms, namely, escape and punishment, derived their impetus from Thorndike's (1913) empirical law of effect and the trial-and-error learning situation. The *escape* paradigm in which a response is shortly followed by the termination of an aversive stimulus and the *punishment* paradigm in which a response is shortly followed by the presentation of an aversive stimulus were used to demonstrate that the probability of an instrumental/operant response is affected by its consequences.

Two other of the fundamental aversive control paradigms, the conditioned emotional response and avoidance paradigms, primarily emanated from the Pavlovian conditioning context. In Pavlovian *defense conditioning* (Bekhterev, 1932), a neutral stimulus is followed by an aversive stimulus, regardless of the occurrence or nonoccurrence of any response. The *conditioned emotional response* (CER) paradigm directly borrows the procedure of defense conditioning and superimposes it upon some instrumental/operant behavioral baseline. Since in defense conditioning the aversive stimulus is presented even if the referent-conditioned response occurs, it would be possible to argue, if one had the systematic bent to do so, that this procedure involves a punishment procedure to the extent that the conditioned response occurs consistently to the conditioned stimulus. (But this is getting a bit ahead of the development that is presented in the sequel.) Now it is sufficient to note that the simple expediency of omitting the aversive stimulus on those occasions when the conditioned response occurs (omission procedure), while presenting it as usual when the conditioned response does not occur, defines the *avoidance* paradigm.

As we shall see, the theoretical treatments of the various aversive control procedures have been importantly influenced by their early paradigmatic contexts. Moreover, there has arisen the issue of theoretical primacy. Which procedure is to be used in functionally identifying aversive events? And not infrequently theorists have asserted that one or another aversive control paradigm is somehow fundamental and can be used to explain the effects produced by the other paradigms. That is, one might attempt to understand the effects of punishment in terms of CER and avoidance or, conversely, one might propose that these latter paradigms produce their effects, because they inadvertently arrange for punishment. It would certainly be parsimonious if all of these paradigms could be reduced conceptually to one but, even so, these claims of primacy are rarely accompanied by a theoretical explanation of how the fundamental paradigm itself produces its effects.

Since both the empirical and theoretical issues in aversive control have mainly developed within the confines of the separate major paradigms, we have organized this chapter around the paradigms of CER, avoidance, and punishment. (There has been little controversy about escape as an instance of negative reinforcement.[2]) The bulk of the discussion will presume the aversive stimulus to be electric shock, since this has been the aversive stimulus most often used empirically and most often discussed theoretically.[3] While other aversive stimuli and experimental procedures will be brought to bear where appropriate, the criterion for their inclusion will be the extent to which they further the systematic analysis of the major paradigms of aversive control as we presently understand them. Accordingly, findings that an organism will respond in order to escape from a stimulus correlated with positive reinforcement (Azrin, 1961) or will respond in order to produce an electric shock in the absence of any immediate positive contingency (e.g., McKearney, 1969) will not be extensively elaborated. To be sure, experiments such as these serve functionally to identify aversive and reinforcing stimuli, and their systematic analyses are related to aversive control. Nevertheless, systematic conceptualizations regarding the fundamental paradigms using shock-aversive stimuli have been both so compartmentalized and so various that we will do well to focus our attention primarily on these.

CONDITIONED EMOTIONAL RESPONSE

Although we do not wish to ascribe primacy to the CER paradigm, we shall begin our discussion of aversive control with it, because it is operationally the simplest of the three that we will consider in some detail. It is what we have previously called a pure stimulus operation: two stimuli, a warning signal, and an aversive stimulus are superimposed on an operant/instrumental baseline, irrespective of the organism's behavior. A still simpler procedure omits the warning signal, in which case the organism is subjected to occasional inescapable, unavoidable, unpredictable aversive stimuli. It is now well established that such "free shocks" have a suppressive effect on appetitive operant/instrumental behavior and even have a deleterious effect on well-learned discriminative responding. What is observed generally in the CER paradigm is the conditioning of this suppressive effect to the warning signal and the discrimination between the environment with and without that signal (Estes & Skinner, 1941). For this reason, conditioned suppression is typically measured by some form of comparison between the baseline level of performance without the signal and the level of responding during the interval between the warning signal and the shock.

The experimental operation in the CER paradigm is that of classical conditioning, and we have previously discussed some of the systematic issues involved. Of concern have been the nature of the associations formed, the conditions for forming these associations, and the possible motivational and/or associational role played by the conditioned stimulus. However, our previous discussions have been focused primarily on appetitive unconditioned stimuli, and we now need to reintroduce these issues in the context of classical defense conditioning where the unconditioned stimulus is aversive. Of principal theoretical concern will be the question of why the stimulus associated with shock suppresses appetitive responding in its presence.

One answer to this question has been formulated in terms of punishment. In the presence of the CER stimulus, bar-press responding for food is adventitiously also punished; that is, the continued occurrence of the response during the interval is shortly followed by shock, although the shock is not dependent on that response. And if the principle of punishment, like the principle of reinforcement, requires only that the punisher occur following a response, its suppressive effect would be understandable. This reliance on the primacy of punishment to account for CER suppression is most plausible when the stimulus-shock pairings are superimposed on an intermittent schedule of food reinforcement, as used in the Estes-Skinner procedure. However, some other mechanism of suppression is suggested by the fact that suppression can be observed to the CER stimulus alone even though the stimulus-shock pairings are conducted off the behavioral baseline or when the opportunity to make the appetitive response is disabled (e.g., Rescorla, 1968). It is possible to retain a punishment hypothesis of CER suppression even in this latter instance by arguing that the CER stimulus has become a secondary punisher by virtue of its having been paired with shock and that presentation of the secondary punisher adventitiously punishes the appetitive response. This possibility is tempered by empirically derived parametric considerations (Kamin, 1965) and, furthermore, it does not readily account for suppression in the presence of the stimuli in the apparatus more generally as it is found in the free-shock procedure.

Instead of explaining CER suppression in terms of adventitious events occurring subsequent to responding, as is the case of the above punishment hypothesis, most systematists have argued that the CER stimulus comes to establish conditions or events that reduce the likelihood of instrumental/operant response occurrence in its presence. That is, the neutral stimulus is considered to become somehow imbued with properties that result in response suppression. The theoretical question then becomes what are these properties; what is learned in the CER?

COGNITIVE ANALYSIS   As may be anticipated from earlier developments of cognitive theory (Tolman, 1932), the cognitive theorist asserts that the CER stimulus becomes a sign for the occurrence of a negatively valued significate and that the resultant expectancy, along with a corresponding demand against the occurrence of the shock, produces response suppression in the presence of the stimulus. In short, the organism comes to expect shock and behaves accordingly. No differences in the development of expectancies are dependent on whether the significate is appetitive or aversive, except that the expectancies are emotionally opposite in direction. However, the demand state established by aversive stimuli may be assumed to be greater than that which usually occurs in the deprivation of appetitive stimuli so that cognitive maps may be more narrow under aversive control. Given two controlling expectancies that are diametrically opposed, such as the expectancy of food and the expectancy of shock, performance will be some difference function of the strengths of the respective expectancies and the corresponding demands and values. The finding by Stein, Sidman, and Brady (1958) that the strength of CER suppression decreases to the extent that positive reinforcement opportunities are available under the baseline reinforcement schedule is consistent with the cognitive position. Given little expectancy of food, an organism should suppress more in the presence of a CER stimulus than if the organism has high expectations of food.[4]

As in the purely appetitive case, it is not clear how expectancies actually eventuate in performance under aversive stimuli other than that organisms respond in accordance with their expectancies. Consider the schema of expectancies needed to account for certain CER data (e.g., Blackman, 1968) that show that performance of the appetitive response in the presence of the CER stimulus depends, in part, on the baseline rate of response.[5] If the baseline response is being performed rapidly prior to presentation of the CER stimulus, suppression to the stimulus typically results. Alternatively, if the baseline response is being performed slowly prior to the presentation of the CER stimulus, an *elevation* in the rate of responding commonly occurs to the CER stimulus. To the extent that cognitive theorists eschew response associations, explanations that rely on micro aspects of the operant response, as must any explanation of the above rate-dependent CER data, are difficult to formulate from cognitive theory. In the instance of the CER aversive control paradigm (and to paraphrase Guthrie), cognitive theorists apparently are content to leave their organisms buried in awful thought.

S-R GENERALIZATION DECREMENT ANALYSIS   The approach of the S-R theorist to the question of "what is learned?" in CER also may be anticipated from the S-R approach to appetitive situations. Succinctly stated, the particular responses that become associated to the stimulus are those responses that occur contiguously with the CER stimulus, which include those responses that are elicited by the shock. As an S-R theorist such as Guthrie (1934) would have it, the presentation of the CER stimulus comes to elicit responses that are characteristic of those elicited by shock. Although the S-R answer to "what is learned?" is comparable for the appetitive and aversive cases, some additional assumptions are necessary before it is possible for the S-R theorist to argue that response suppression is a result of the responses elicited by the CER stimulus.

One assumption that underlies the early thinking of Estes (1941, 1944) is that the responses elicited by the CER stimulus produce characteristic interoceptive cues. When these response-produced cues are added to the appetitive instrumental response situation, they change the prevailing stimulus situation and, thereby, cause a stimulus generalization decrement in appetitive responding. According to this hypothesis, so long as the responses to the CER stimulus are *different* from the appetitive response, such that they produce novel stimuli in the situation, a stimulus generalization decrement will occur and response suppression will result. This hypothesis can account for some CER-like data that are problematic for the cognitive theorist. As one instance, a CER stimulus paired with food should come to elicit responses whose stimulus properties differ from those of bar-pressing. Accordingly, by generalization decrement, a CER stimulus paired with food should suppress appetitive or avoidance bar-press responding, as it apparently sometimes does (Azrin & Hake, 1969; Grossen, Kostansek, & Bolles, 1969).[6] On the other hand, the stimulus generalization decrement hypothesis of CER does not account very well for the data cited above that relate CER suppression to either the rate of reinforcement (Stein et al., 1958) or the rate of response (Blackman, 1968) controlled by the baseline reinforcement schedule. A final bit of data that is difficult to resolve with the stimulus-generalization decrement hypothesis is that a CER stimulus paired with shock will increase rather than decrease bar-pressing behavior maintained by an aversive, shock-avoidance, schedule (Herrnstein & Sidman, 1958; Sidman, Herrnstein, & Conrad, 1957). A CER stimulus paired with shock should cause response mediated disruption of bar-press responding no matter how the bar-press response is maintained.

S-R COMPETING RESPONSE ANALYSIS

The finding that a CER stimulus paired with shock increases responding on an avoidance baseline is also problematic for another S-R hypothesis regarding the mechanism of response suppression under the CER procedure. This second hypothesis may be described under the rubric of the competing-response hypothesis. According to this reasoning, the responses elicited by shock, and that, therefore, become conditioned to the CER stimulus, are not only different from bar-press responses but also are incompatible with bar-pressing. This argument has obvious merit. Shock surely elicits responses of fleeing, freezing, or crouching in the rat, which responses are part of the species-specific defense reaction to shock (Bolles, 1970) and are incompatible with bar-pressing. This eliciting property of shock cannot be reasonably denied. However, it is a considerable step to assume further that all of the behavioral effects produced under a CER procedure are mediated by incompatible responses elicited by the CER stimulus, and apparently it would be wrong to assume so. The competing-response hypothesis can only predict a disruption of bar-pressing in the presence of a CER stimulus. The evidence of an increase in bar-press responding to a CER stimulus under an avoidance schedule is not only problematic to this hypothesis but it is devastatingly so. This is not to suggest that neither stimulus-generalization decrement nor competing responses play a role in CER suppression. But it is clear that some additional mechanism is necessary for S-R theorists to account for the CER behavioral effects that occur across a variety of situations. The competing-response hypothesis has retained what vitality it has, not because competing responses have actually been observed, but because the hypothesis is so theoretically plausible. An alternative, equally plausible S-R hypothesis, and one which is completely unobservable (hypothetical), is the emotional response hypothesis.

S-R EMOTIONAL RESPONSE ANALYSIS

The emotional-response hypothesis has had many theoretical proponents among S-R theorists. These include Thorndike (1931, 1932), Skinner (1938, 1953), Estes (1941, 1944), Miller (1941, 1948), Mowrer (1947), Brown (1951), Solomon (1954), and others. The basic premise is that shock elicits emotional responses and that these emotional responses inhibit bar-press responding when elicited by the CER stimulus to which they have become conditioned. In some instances the nature of the emotional responses has not been specified nor is it stated just how emotional responses inhibit instrumental responding. Presumably they may do so, in part, by causing a stimulus-generalization decrement or by eliciting incompatible responses. At any rate, conditioned emotional responses elicited by the CER stimulus are assumed to inhibit responding maintained by food reinforcement.

In the instance of those S-R theorists who have been directly influenced by the Hullian tradition (e.g., Mowrer, Miller, Brown), the emotional response is explicitly identified as fear. Fear is a response that has stimulus consequences that can be conditioned to other responses and that can elicit responses incompatible with bar-pressing, such as freezing or crouching.

Fear is not only conceptualized as a response and as a stimulus, but it also is conceptualized as a drive that is externally elicited by noxious stimuli. As a drive, fear is expected to possess the properties of energizing behavior when presented and of reinforcing behavior when terminated. The evidence favoring the proposition that fear energizes ongoing behavior is rather sparse (e.g., Brown, Kalish, & Farber, 1951), as it might well be expected that the predominant response to fear is freezing. On the other hand, there exists substantial evidence that is consistent with the proposition that fear reduction is reinforcing (e.g., Brown & Jacobs, 1949; McAllister & McAllister, 1962; Miller, 1941, 1948). Most of this evidence has been obtained in acquired-drive studies where a neutral stimulus is first paired with shock. Subsequently, it is shown that a new response can be learned based on termination of the acquired-drive stimulus.

The emotional-response hypotheses, particularly the fear hypothesis version, have been very successful in accounting for CER behavior and behavior more generally under aversive control. The drive properties of fear make the fear-mediated hypothesis of the CER more flexible than the other response-mediated hypotheses presented so far. This is because the fear hypothesis can account for an increase in behavior in the presence of a CER stimulus in terms of the drive-energizing properties of fear. For example, when avoidance responding is enhanced in the presence of a CER stimulus paired with shock, this is interpreted as showing that the fear elicited by the CER stimulus added to the total drive present and thereby enhanced responding. Alternatively, when the CER stimulus causes a suppression of appetitive responding, an appropriate interpretation is that fear elicited responses incompatible with bar-pressing.

Perhaps in part because of its success, the fear-as-drive hypothesis has attracted both vigorous proponents and opponents. The opponents do not deny that fear is a response to aversive stimuli nor do they deny that emotional responses can be conditioned to stimuli. The questions raised have mostly pertained to the adequacy of the evidence that fear is a drive (Bolles, 1967) and, more forcefully, to the necessity of considering fear as a drive in order to account for aversive control phenomena including the CER (Dinsmoor, 1954; Schoenfeld, 1950). Schoenfeld's (1950) argument is a beautiful exposition of the empirical systematist's approach vis-á-vis the theoretical systematist's, although much of the polemic hinges on semantics. The essence of Schoenfeld's argument is that postulating fear as a drive is neither parsimonious nor necessary and, furthermore, it is circular. The latter criticism revolves around the circular manner of identifying drives in terms of drive-reduction reinforcers and vice versa as was previously discussed in Chapter 4. The other criticisms, regarding parsimony and necessity, Schoenfeld proposes to solve by replacing the drive construct with the concept of secondary aversive stimuli to which no hypothetical construct properties are ascribed.

Although Schoenfeld (1950) gains parsimony by substituting a hypothetical concept for a hypothetical construct, he does not necessarily gain power of explanation regarding the CER. Indeed, some sort of motivational construct seems necessary in order to explain the increment in responding to a CER stimulus under an avoidance baseline. It would seem best for the motivational construct to be general so as to account for the finding that shock avoidance responding can be as well enhanced by a CER stimulus paired with aversive noise as one paired with electric shock (LoLordo, 1967). On the other hand, a drive-motivation approach does not account for the finding that the extent of CER suppression depends on the rate of reinforcement made available under the baseline schedule (Stein et al., 1958). We have already mentioned how a cognitive expectancy type approach does well in handling these latter data but falls short in other instances, because of its inability to predict the occurrence of precise responses.

S-R INCENTIVE MOTIVATION ANALYSIS

As we have seen in Chapter 5, many of the elements apparently needed to explain adequately the varied effects produced on behavior under CER procedures are contained in contemporary versions of incentive theory. At least these theories, in principle, can combine expectancy-like motivational constructs with specific predictions regarding response occurrence (including the prediction of the occurrence of incompatible behaviors to shock). As developed by incentive theorists, such as Miller (1963), Estes (1969), and Logan (1969), the presentation of an aversive stimulus or the presentation of a CER stimulus having a history of association with an aversive stimulus, has effects directly opposite to those produced by the presentation of an appetitive stimulus. Whereas presenting an emotionally positive stimulus will activate a "go" mechanism (Miller, 1963), activate the input of amplifier elements (Estes, 1969), or increment positive incentive (Logan, 1969), the corresponding effects of presenting an emotionally negative stimulus are to activate a "stop" mechanism, to inhibit the input of amplifier elements, or to increment negative incentive.

The behavior predicted by incentive theorists in the CER situation thus depends on the joint influence of the CER stimulus and the positive schedule contingency for responding. For example, in Logan's (1969) incentive theory the probability of a response will depend on the net incentive (the difference between positive incentive and negative incentive) for that response. Similarly for Estes (1969), the probability of a response in the presence of a CER stimulus will depend on the resultant activity of amplifier elements under the reciprocal inhibition of facilitative and inhibitory influences on amplifier input. Whatever the particulars of any one incentive theory, it is important to note again that emotionally negative stimuli are assigned an incentive role that is symmetric but opposite in direction to the one assigned to emotionally positive stimuli. For these incentive theories, what gets learned under the CER paradigm are conflicting or incompatible incentive motivations rather than conflicting cognitions or incompatible habit associations. Once again, however, there does not appear to be any singular theoretical approach that can account for all the reported CER effects. The Achilles' heel for incentive theory is the finding (e.g., Azrin & Hake, 1969) of a positive conditioned suppression, that is, that a CER stimulus associated with an appetitive stimulus will control the suppression of food maintained responding.

SUMMARY
To summarize our discussion thus far, under the basic CER paradigm a stimulus is paired with an aversive stimulus and superimposed upon an instrumental/operant baseline of positive reinforcement or shock avoidance, usually the former. The typical effect is a response suppression under the positive reinforcement baseline and a response elevation under the avoidance baseline. When a CER stimulus paired with an appetitive stimulus is superimposed on either type of baseline, response suppression is the usual result. The theoretical issue is to specify what is learned under the CER paradigm; what is the nature of associations involved in response suppression or response elevation in the presence of stimuli associated with primary emotional events? The theoretical approaches to the issue of CER associations mimic the theoretical approaches to the nature of associations in general. All of the approaches can handle the fundamental CER situation as represented by the referent Estes and Skinner (1941) experiment. They were all generated to do so. However, none of the approaches can handle all of the various CER outcomes.

Both S-S expectancy theory and incentive theory adopt the premise that the presentation of emotionally negative stimuli function in a manner that is symmetric but opposite in direction to that produced by the presentation of emotionally positive stimuli. S-R theory does not distinguish between the nature of associations formed under emotionally positive or negative stimuli. Responses contiguous with the CER stimulus can become associated with that stimulus. What does differ between positive and negative emotional stimuli is the nature of the responses that they elicit and that, therefore, become conditioned to the CER stimulus. It is presumed that species-specific defense reactions and emotional responses, particularly fear, are elicited by aversive stimuli. It is these responses, associated to the CER stimulus, that serve to mediate CER effects. A relevant and related question is what are the conditions necessary for the formation of associations in the CER paradigm? In other contexts this has been identified as the reinforcement-contiguity theoretical issue.

Reinforcement Versus Contiguity: The Conditions of CER Associations

In the CER context the reinforcement-contiguity issue of the conditions of association is of particular interest only to those S-R theorists who hypothesize that CER suppression is somehow mediated by response associations. This is because S-S cognitive theorists uniformly maintain, as in the appetitive case, that expectancies about aversive stimuli are formed exclusively through a contiguity of sign and significate. Furthermore, incentive theorists assign to aversive stimuli a role that is opposite to that of reward and, therefore, must intimately link the occurrence of the aversive stimulus with the incentive value of the CER stimulus. For example, the amount of negative incentive (Logan, 1969), the amount of fear (Mowrer, 1960), or the extent of amplifier-input inhibition (Estes, 1969) is directly determined by the parameters of the aversive stimulus.

Incentive theorists do not exclude or deny that aversive stimuli may have other effects in addition to their incentive motivation effects. Aversive stimuli can serve as discriminative stimuli for responses or as elicitors of responses. To the extent that responses elicited by aversive stimuli are hypothesized by incentive theorists to be associated to antecedent stimuli, the incentive theorist is faced with the same issue as are other S-R theorists. Specifically, what are the necessary and sufficient conditions for S-R association? Generally, incentive theorists have answered this question by asserting that contiguity alone is sufficient for S-R associations to form in aversive control situations. As is to be expected, some other S-R theorists have argued that although contiguity is a necessary condition, it alone is not sufficient: reinforcement is also necessary for associations to form in aversive control paradigms. We will develop this latter theoretical line more fully within the context of the now familiar CER paradigm.

THE DRIVE-REDUCTION HYPOTHESIS

In the defense-conditioning phase of the CER paradigm, wherein a neutral stimulus is paired with an aversive stimulus, drive-reduction reinforcement theorists (e.g., Hull, 1943; Miller, 1951) contend that S-R associations are formed because of the drive-reduction afforded by the termination of the aversive stimulus. Specifically, in the CER case, presentation of the aversive stimulus elicits skeletal and autonomic responses. These elicited responses become associated to the antedating CER stimulus when followed, as they necessarily are, by a reduction in the drive established by the aversive stimulus. Clearly, the mechanism of associative action is the termination of the aversive stimulus and the consequent reduction in drive stimuli.

The drive-reduction version of CER association formation runs afoul of a large amount of empirical data that to some theorists has suggested the conclusion that the termination of aversive stimuli does not create S-R associations. This empirical evidence has been of two general sorts. The first line of evidence pertains to the gradient of delay of reinforcement. The argument is that from a drive-reduction viewpoint, the strength of conditioning to the CER stimulus should be inversely related to the duration of the aversive stimulus. The longer the aversive stimulus, the longer the time to the termination of the aversive stimulus and, consequently, the greater the delay of reinforcement. Several defense conditioning experiments have shown conditioning to be independent of the duration of the aversive stimulus (e.g., Bitterman, Reed, & Krauskopf, 1952; Wegner & Zeaman, 1958; Runquist & Spence, 1959). The prototypic CER experiment on delay of aversive drive-reduction reinforcement was performed by Mowrer and Solomon (1954). These experimenters obtained no differences in bar-press suppresssion to a CER stimulus that had been previously paired either with a short or long duration electric shock. Mowrer and Solomon (1954) argued from their data that shock onset, and not shock termination, was responsible for the suppression mediated by conditioned emotional fear responses to the CER stimulus. This conclusion need not necessarily be accepted by a drive-reduction reinforcement theorist. It is true that delaying shock termination should impair conditioning. But prolonging the presentation of shock should produce a stronger drive so that a stronger reinforcement is produced by the eventual shock termination (e.g., Runquist & Spence, 1959). In short, the decremental effects of delay of reinforcement can be offset to some extent by the incremental effects of magnitude of reinforcement when long- as opposed to short-duration aversive stimuli are used in CER conditioning.

The CER experiment that is most commonly cited as definitively establishing that emotional responses are conditioned to the CER stimulus by the onset rather than by the termination of the aversive stimulus was carried out by Mowrer and Aiken (1954). In this experiment the CER stimulus was initially paired with either the onset or the offset of the aversive stimulus. It was found that appetitive bar-press responding was suppressed more by the CER stimulus paired with the onset of shock than with the CER stimulus paired with the offset of shock. Supporting evidence that shock onset is more effective than shock offset in defense conditioning is available in the literature (e.g., Barlow, 1952; Davitz, 1955).

From these shock onset-shock offset data it would seem that drive-reduction reinforcement need not be invoked in order to account for response suppression in a CER aversive control paradigm. If reinforcement is not necessary, then it could follow that the conditioning of fear and other elicited response components of aversive stimuli to the CER stimulus occurs solely through contiguity. This, of course, is the position maintained by Guthrie (1934, 1935), although this theorist characteristically eschews motivational or emotional considerations, including fear, in favor of learning incompatible responses. Conditioning of fear responses through contiguity is advocated by some two-factor theorists such as Skinner (1938) and Mowrer (1947, 1950). For these latter theorists, some form of reinforcement (functionally identified for Skinner, drive reduction for Mowrer) is necessary for instrumental/operant conditioning of skeletal responses to occur. However, conditioning of those autonomic emotional responses elicited by emotionally negative stimuli proceeds apace through contiguity alone.

Although the evidence pertaining to the effectiveness of shock onset in CER conditioning admittedly makes drive-reduction theorists uncomfortable (e.g., Miller, 1951), it is appropriate here to note again that theoretical approaches are usually not permanently suppressed by empirical evidence. Indeed, two lines of thought tend to salvage the theoretical construct of drive-stimulus reduction in CER conditioning. One argument is that drive reduction can be associated with shock onset as follows. When shock is first presented, it produces a high-drive level. As a result of physiological sensory adaptation, this high drive is immediately followed by a rapid reduction in drive that can reinforce whatever behavior is occurring at the time of shock onset. A second argument is that the onset of shock may elicit actual or incipient escape responses that produce a temporary drive reduction, but one that is sufficient to account for learning.

A different but not unrelated source of reinforcement in CER or defense conditioning is thought by some systematists to be contingent upon responses made prior to the onset of the aversive stimulus. Any response made to the CER stimulus that prepares the organism for the onset of the aversive stimulus, or in some way attenuates the aversive value of the subsequently presented aversive stimulus, will be reinforced (Perkins, 1968; Prokasy, 1965). Essentially this is a response-shaping hypothesis, since the form of the response occurring prior to shock will be differentially affected depending on whether or not it reduces the aversiveness of the onset of shock. The argument is similar to some of those presented above in that it gains whatever acceptance it has primarily through plausibility. It makes good sense that responses preceding shock should be adaptive just as it makes good sense that responses elicited by shock should consist of species-specific defense mechanisms. Nevertheless, such adaptive responses need to be integrated into a systematic framework (either empirical or theoretical), if they are generally to account for aversive control phenomena.

As an aside to the central CER issue of this discussion, it is interesting to note that some contiguity incentive theorists have given as much separate stature to response-mediated emotions associated with the termination of shock as they have to response mediated emotions associated with the onset of shock. Thus, for example, a CER stimulus paired with the offset of shock is assumed to elicit emotional responses of relief (Mowrer, 1960) or relaxation (Denny, 1971; Denny & Weisman, 1964). As with other positive and negative incentive notions, relief and fear logically mediate effects that are symmetric but opposite. Thus, relief should inhibit fear and vice versa. The logical symmetry of this type of incentive approach awaits empirical support. So far, incentive or emotional response hypotheses, such as relief (Mowrer, 1960), have had to bear the burden created by the failure functionally to identify secondary positive reinforcers based on shock termination (cf. Chapter 4).

SUMMARY

To summarize the conditions of S-R associations in CER situations, contiguity and two-factor theorists alike contend that the data that favor the effectiveness of shock onset over shock offset also favor the theoretical position that emotional fear responses are conditioned to antecedent CER stimuli solely through contiguity. The alternative, drive-reduction reinforcement theorist, contends that drive reduction is necessary for such conditioning to take place. As for the data favoring shock onset, the drive-reduction theorist interprets these as demonstrating that shock onset as well as shock offset can be accompanied by drive-reduction.

From either general theoretical approach, it would seem to follow directly that the most advantageous condition for establishing S-R associations would be consistently to follow the CER stimulus with the presentation of an aversive stimulus, lest the association suffer from extinction through the learning of competing responses or through nonreinforcement. Surely associations should be better learned under such a strict defense conditioning procedure than under an omission procedure wherein the occurrence of a referent response (but not its nonoccurrence) leads to the omission of the aversive stimulus. That such is not always the case, and the theoretical speculations as to why it is not always the case, will be discussed next in the context of the avoidance paradigm of aversive control.

AVOIDANCE BEHAVIOR

In the conventional, discrete-trial Pavlovian and instrumental conditioning contexts, an omission or cued-avoidance trial typically begins with the presentation of an originally neutral stimulus. We will designate this stimulus as the conditioned stimulus (CS) for avoidance responding, although the terms CER stimulus or warning stimulus would be equally suitable. The CS is presented some period of time before the impending occurrence of an aversive stimulus and, if the referent response does not occur during this CS period, the aversive stimulus occurs. However, if the referent response does occur during the CS, the presentation of the aversive stimulus is omitted at the end of the trial. It is quite common in the instrumental conditioning situation to arrange response contingencies such that the occurrence of the referent response during a trial also terminates the CS. Often, the referent response also serves to terminate the primary aversive stimulus on nonavoidance trials. This latter contingency is the familiar escape paradigm that is used functionally to identify primary negative reinforcers.

In the free-response operant conditioning context, the commonly studied avoidance procedure is one devised by Sidman (1953); herein it will be referred to as the noncued-avoidance procedure, since it does not entail an explicit, exteroceptive conditioned stimulus for avoidance responding as do the typical Pavlovian and instrumental cued-avoidance procedures. Under the noncued procedure, short-duration aversive stimuli are presented regularly in time.

Assuming that the aversive stimuli are shocks, the time interval between successively presented aversive stimuli is called the shock-shock (S-S) interval. When a referent response occurs, the regular presentation of shocks is suspended for a finite period of time after the response. This response—shock (R-S) interval, that is, the time after a response before the next shock is scheduled to occur, can be manipulated independently of the S-S interval. Since the R-S interval is always timed from the last response (operationally each response resets the R-S interval timer), if the referent response occurs with a frequency of at least $1/(R-S)$, the aversive stimulus can be postponed indefinitely.

If it is assumed that the occurrence of a referent-avoidance response reflects the formation of learned associations, then it is quite appropriate theoretically to ponder about the nature and conditions of such associations. Some potential dilemmas interpose. If the associations are S-S in nature, then it is not immediately apparent what it is that should be considered as the antecedent stimulus (the CS) in noncued avoidance. Furthermore, it is difficult to discern what should be considered as the consequent stimulus of an S-S association for avoidance, since the occurrence of the referent response precludes the occurrence of the aversive stimulus. Are we to assume that antecedent stimuli become associated with the occurrence of nothing?

The antecedent stimulus entering into the association also needs to be identified for an S-R theory of avoidance behavior. And as our preceding discussion of the CER paradigm elaborates, the critical factor determining S-R association formation appears to be the subsequent occurrence of the aversive stimulus. Theoretically then, nonavoidance trials should be classified as conditioning trials, and avoidance trials should be classified as extinction trials. That means, of course, that avoidance responding should not be very stable. Instead, the occurrence of the referent response should wax and wane as it passes through repeated cycles of reconditioning and reextinction. This line of thinking will be followed up more fully in the sequel. For now it will suffice to assert that from a classical S-R position, an avoidance procedure should be less effective in generating a referent-conditioned response than a conventional defense conditioning procedure where the aversive stimulus is presented, irrespective of the referent response.

In the earliest comparisons of defense and avoidance conditioning (Schlosberg, 1934, 1936), the former was indeed found to be superior. However, in subsequent comparisons, contrary evidence was frequently obtained (e.g., Brodgen, Lipman, & Culler, 1938; Hunter, 1935; Sheffield, 1948). A related problem is that avoidance responding is remarkably resistant to extinction in some situations (Miller, 1951; Mowrer, 1960; Solomon, Kamin, & Wynne, 1953; Solomon & Wynne, 1953). This durability has been attributed by some theorists (e.g., Logan, 1951; Sheffield & Temmer, 1950) to the partial reinforcement effect on extinction, but evidence has accumulated in ways that suggest that falling back on conventional conditioning analyses (e.g., partial reinforcement) to explain avoidance behavior cannot adequately handle all of the data. Some other, new or recombined, analyses are necessary.

Before getting too far along into these analyses, it will be well to review the theoretical problem inherent in the avoidance paradigm. Whether cued or noncued avoidance is considered, the nonoccurrence of an aversive stimulus is correlated with an increase in the future probability of a response it shortly follows. Functionally, the nonoccurrence of an aversive stimulus may be said to be identified as a reinforcer. But on other logical, theoretical, and practical grounds, it is difficult to accept or even understand how the nonoccurrence of a stimulus *alone* can constitute a reinforcer (particularly, a drive-stimulus reduction), and therein lies the principal dilemma of the avoidance paradigm. Is it reasonable to consider avoidance as an instance of aversive control when avoidance entails the nonoccurrence of an aversive stimulus? More specifically, avoidance obviously is not determined completely by the aversive stimulus, since organisms often respond better when it is omitted; again, it is not obvious that the nonoccurrence of an aversive stimulus can alone determine behavior. This dilemma has sometimes (e.g., Mowrer, 1947; Schoenfeld, 1950) been phrased as a question, "What reinforces avoidance behavior?" But this particular question is especially pertinent only to reinforcement theorists. The more general question to which the remainder of this section is devoted is "What is the theoretical mechanism of avoidance behavior?"

Punishment by the Primary Aversive Stimulus

One proposed mechanism underlying avoidance responding involves the contention that punishment is the fundamental process in terms of which all aversive control paradigms may be understood. The punishment analyses as propounded by Schoenfeld (1950) and Sidman (1953) essentially states that the occurrence of the aversive stimulus during avoidance conditioning will decrease the future likelihood of any response that it shortly follows. This means, of course, that the avoidance response, being the only response not followed by shock, will simply emerge as the relatively most frequent response, because all other responses have been made less likely by punishment.[7] From this strict viewpoint, the answer to the question "what reinforces avoidance behavior?" is "nothing reinforces avoidance behavior!"

In a functional sense, the avoidance response may be considered to postpone or delay the presentation of the aversive stimulus rather than eliminate it altogether. That is, the avoidance response functionally delays punishment by the duration of the intertrial interval in cued avoidance or by the duration of the R-S interval in noncued avoidance. Nonavoidance responses are punished more immediately. This suggests from a punishment position that avoidance responding should be more reliable, as it is, the longer the delay of punishment; that is, it should be more reliable the longer the intertrial interval (e.g., Brush, 1962) or the longer the R-S interval (e.g., Sidman, 1954).

At the same time, the punishment position seems to demand that avoidance acquisition should be relatively slow, so as to provide adequate opportunities to punish all nonavoidance behaviors, and that avoidance extinction should progress rapidly in the absence of any primary aversive stimulation. This latter prediction follows from the fact that the avoidance response is not directly strengthened but only indirectly made relatively more frequent. As we have stated earlier, and contrary to the present punishment position, avoidance acquisition is sometimes dramatically rapid, and avoidance behavior under extinction is sometimes amazingly durable (e.g., Boren & Sidman, 1966; Solomon & Wynne, 1953). Interestingly, Bolles (1970) has suggested that the punishment hypothesis is suitable for instances of rapid avoidance acquisition, but not for slow avoidance acquisition. This suggestion is predicated on the assumption that the punishment hypothesis is viable only if the referent response is already high in the organism's repertory and that some other mechanism is necessary when the referent response begins as a very low probability response in the situation.

While the punishment hypothesis is clearly limited, it is plausible. It is difficult to deny empirically that punishment of behavior can decrease the future occurrence of that behavior. But it still needs to be explained why punishment decreases the likelihood of behavior occurring. What Schoenfeld (1950) asserts in the avoidance context is that the proprioceptive cues produced by nonavoidance responses, by virtue of their being paired with the aversive stimulus, become secondarily aversive so that it is aversive to make any other than the referent response.

Anger (1963) has offered a slightly different conceptualization that integrates a delay of punishment gradient into his explanation of avoidance. He suggests that temporal discriminations to the time of the next shock are initiated by the avoidance response. Furthermore, it is assumed that there are stimuli that are continuously correlated with postresponse times. Since short postresponse-time stimuli are further removed from punishment than are long postresponse-time stimuli, there is established a delay of punishment gradient to postresponse-time cues that increases in aversiveness from the instant of the avoidance response up to the time of the next scheduled shock delivery. Importantly, the immediate postresponse-time cues of avoidance responding are less aversive than the immediate postresponse-time cues of nonavoidance responding.[8] There remains, of course, the problem of identifying potential postresponse-time cues.

A somewhat different but related manner of treating avoidance learning in terms of punishment by the primary aversive stimulus derives from S-R contiguity theory (Guthrie, 1934; Sheffield, 1948). Briefly, the analysis proceeds as follows. Beginning with a nonavoidance response, an organism will be punished for that response. The punishment will elicit some other response that, through contiguity, is conditioned to the situation and that, therefore, will recur in the situation. If the new S-R association does not involve the referent-avoidance response, the punishment leading to new conditioning process cycles on. If the punishment never elicits a referent response, of course, avoidance learning will never occur. If the referent response is elicited, and consequently conditioned, its occurrence is not punished. But the repeated occurrence of the referent response followed by nothing invites counter conditioning of other responses and extinction. Indeed, the avoidance response should very rapidly extinguish.

The S-R contiguity punishment analysis is straightforward. It suffers, however, from several restrictions: avoidance extinction should always be rapid; defense conditioning should always be superior to avoidance conditioning; and the avoidance response can only be one elicited by shock. Actually, the latter restriction has gained empirical support of relatively recent vintage (cf. Bolles, 1970). At least it has become increasingly clear that response factors are among the most critical, if not the most critical, determinants of avoidance conditioning. When the referent response is one that is naturally or innately elicited by shock (a species-specific defense reaction for Bolles, 1969, 1970), avoidance conditioning proceeds rapidly. Otherwise it does not. Although this is intuitively pleasing, because of its adaptive overtones, there does exist the problem of identifying what responses are natural to the situation. Fighting, fleeing, and freezing have been suggested, but at some point these need to be identified empirically rather than by their presumed adaptive significance. The lesson previously learned from Chapter 4 is that a functional approach promises the best success in identifying psychological concepts. We could, for example, functionally identify natural elicited reactions in terms of the speed of avoidance learning; the quicker the avoidance learning, the more natural the reaction to shock. This is, of course, a circular definition. However, this does not impugn the importance of the response in avoidance learning. Further considerations of the response develop in the context of the escape hypothesis of avoidance.

Escape from the Primary Aversive Stimulus

It is perhaps a pleasant surprise that neither empirical systematists nor theorists have found grounds on which to disagree about the escape paradigm of aversive control. This paradigm is representative of the empirical law of effect; the termination of an aversive stimulus is negatively reinforcing. To be sure, we could here recall issues presented earlier (Chapter 4) regarding the mechanism of primary reinforcement. For example, is it the termination of the shock, itself, the termination of the fear drive established by the shock, or what is it particularly that constitutes the process of reinforcement? But that would only be distracting at this point. Responses that escape from primary aversive stimuli have their future probability of occurrence increased by primary negative reinforcement. The extent to which future response probability is increased depends directly on the amount of reinforcement in terms of the reduction in intensity of the aversive stimulus (e.g., Miller, 1951; Winograd, 1965) and in terms of the length of the period during which the organism is free from aversive stimuli following an escape response (Sidman, 1954). Similarly, escape responding is inversely related to the delay in shock termination following the occurrence of the referent-escape response (e.g., Fowler & Trapold, 1962). With this as a background, we next consider whether or not avoidance behavior can be accounted for in terms of escape from the primary aversive stimulus.

Just such a proposal was made by Hull (1929), and it serves as his example of the acquisition of new S-R connections (1943). The hypothesis is parsimonious. Responses that are elicited by aversive stimuli and that terminate the aversive stimulus, or responses that are arranged to have an explicit escape contingency in the presence of an aversive stimulus, are reinforced by the negative reinforcement corresponding to the termination of the aversive stimulus. As a result of this reinforcement, the escape response becomes conditioned to any antecedent stimuli present at the time of reinforcement. As this learned association gains in strength, the escape response occurs with increasingly shorter latency until a latency sufficiently short to precede the shock occurs. The escape response becomes operationally an avoidance response; the escape response moves forward in time and becomes anticipatory. Solomon and Brush (1956), from a different theoretical perspective than that of Hull, have also suggested that the escape response can emerge as the avoidance response.

In spite of the strong foundation provided by the escape paradigm, and despite the inherent parsimony, it is reasonably well established that avoidance behavior cannot be accounted for solely in terms of escape from the primary aversive stimulus or in terms of primary negative reinforcement. The hypothesis has been criticized on theoretical grounds. For example, Schoenfeld (1950) has proposed that theoretically the escape response cannot move forward of the shock, because it must first occur simultaneously with the shock and would, thereby, be punished.[9] But the escape hypothesis has been damaged more by a number of empirical findings that are directly or indirectly contrary to the notion of an anticipatory escape response. These empirical findings are of this type: avoidance conditioning is sometimes inversely related to the intensity of the aversive stimulus (e.g., D'Amato & Fazzaro, 1966; Moyer & Korn, 1964); avoidance learning can occur even when brief inescapable shocks are used or when no escape response is required or allowed (e.g., Bolles, Stokes, & Younger, 1966; Hurwitz, 1964; Marx & Hellwig, 1964); and an avoidance response can be learned that is different from an explicitly required escape response (Bolles, 1969; Mowrer & Lamoreaux, 1946). The latter Bolles (1969) experiment not only confirms that the escape contingency does not play a consistently significant role in avoidance conditioning, but it also relates the escape contingency to the nature of the avoidance response. If the avoidance response is a natural reaction of the organism to shock, then the avoidance response is learned quickly and independently—whether or not it is the same as the required escape response.

Meyer, Cho, and Weseman (1960) have indirectly argued against the primary escape position by suggesting that a nonescape response, namely freezing, is the most common response to be associated to the CS in avoidance conditioning. Indeed, these researchers argue that any variable (the type of CS, handling, drugs) that will disrupt or inhibit the freezing response to the CS will facilitate avoidance acquisition.[10]

Perhaps it can be successfully argued that the escape from the primary aversive-stimulus factor is an important component of avoidance learning, if the argument is made with respect to reducing the overall density or frequency of aversive stimuli rather than terminating a particular instance of the aversive stimulus (Fantino, 1973). In noncued avoidance, a referent-avoidance response has the effect of escaping from the regular sequence of shocks scheduled according to the S-S interval. In cued avoidance, the avoidance response produces escape from the sequence of shocks scheduled according to the intertrial interval. If reducing the overall density of shocks is functionally a negative reinforcer (Herrnstein, 1969; Herrnstein & Hineline, 1966; Sidman, 1962), then the escape response will be increased in its future probability. Of course, to complete the analysis, it is important to understand that the escape response, in the sense of escaping from an overall density of shocks, is the referent-avoidance response.

Although this latter analysis, involving overall shock-density reduction, may seem to be appropriately discussed under the topic of escape from primary aversive stimuli, it is sometimes the case that empiricists and theorists find the shock-density analysis closely interrelated to the avoidance learning dilemma. This occurs because the shock-density analysis states explicitly that avoidance responses avoid shock (e.g., Herrnstein, 1969), which is the phenomenon that is under theoretical consideration, and that avoidance responses are reinforced by avoidance (Fantino, 1973), which taken by itself seems patently nugatory. Further consideration of this avoidance position is merited.

Avoidance of the Primary Aversive Stimulus

It will be helpful in the subsequent discussion, regarding the role of avoiding primary aversive stimuli in avoidance learning, to have established early on that the dilemma of avoidance learning is more apparent than real for the cognitive theorist. To be sure, the cognitive theorist recognizes that the occurrence of nothing does not *in itself* constitute a meaningful determinant of behavior. But the nonoccurrence of something certainly can be meaningful, if that something were expected; avoidance learning is thereby quickly and readily incorporated by cognitive theory. The organism comes to expect that in the presence of a sign CS, a referent-avoidance response will avoid, in the sense of omit, the presentation of an otherwise to-be-presented aversive significate.

Predictions about the precise form of the avoidance response, or of its relationship to shock elicited or learned escape responses, would simply be inappropriate to the expectancy theorist. Brogden, Lipman, and Culler (1938) in summarizing their classic early work in avoidance take the position that a stimulus, including an avoidance CS, asks a question of the organism and that the avoidance response "which emerges constitutes the organism's reply to that question." This very much represents the essence of any cognitive expectancy position regarding avoidance (e.g., Hilgard & Marquis, 1940; Tolman, 1932). The organism simply responds in accordance with its expectancies. Shock is expected in the situation. It is also expected that the shock will be omitted, given a referent-avoidance response. The response is accordingly made. Confirmation, the nonoccurrence of the shock, occurs. Simply put, for expectancy theorists, the avoidance of the primary aversive stimulus is the mechanism underlying avoidance learning. This position has more widespread appeal than is sometimes supposed (e.g., Solomon & Brush, 1956) and, as we have already noted, it is an integral component of systematic positions that involve the overall density of aversive stimuli (e.g., Herrnstein, 1969; Sidman, 1962).

By way of review of the overall shock-density position, it is asserted that avoidance responses do not produce nothing. Instead, avoidance responses produce a reduction in the overall density of aversive stimuli or in the frequency of occurrence of aversive stimuli per unit period of time. It is important to avoid the primary aversive stimulus because this reduces overall shock density, and a reduction in shock density is reinforcing. What gets reinforced is the referent-avoidance response on which the reduction in overall shock density is contingent. The empirical evidence favoring a shock-frequency reduction position of reinforcement includes findings that organisms will choose long versus short R-S intervals that, of course, are correlated respectively with lower and higher shock frequencies (Sidman, 1954, 1962) as are longer and shorter intertrial intervals (Brush, 1962; Denny & Weisman, 1964). Of particular importance to the hypothesis is an experiment by Herrnstein and Hineline (1966) in which it was demonstrated that organisms will perform avoidance responses simply in order to reduce shock frequency to some nonzero level below that which was prevailing in the absence of avoidance responses.

The argument at hand has some obvious parallels to cognitive S-S expectancy theory, although the proponents of the argument intend to maintain their S-R behaviorist predispositions. The parallel is that in order for a reduction in shock frequency to be reinforcing, the organism has to form some type of an expectancy that a lower level of shock frequency will occur as a consequence of an avoidance response and some type of an expectancy that a higher level of shock will prevail given the nonoccurrence of the response. That is, an absolute, overall, shock density is not by itself reinforcing, not even if it is an absolutely low shock density. A given shock density is reinforcing when it is relatively lower than some other shock density, but this presumes the organism somehow knows the prevailing shock density and anticipates what the ensuing shock density will be, given the occurrence or nonoccurrence of the avoidance response.

Shock-density reduction theorists have not proposed any theoretical mechanism in order to help their organisms accomplish this, other than to suggest that the stimuli associated with the occurrence and nonoccurrence of avoidance responses have the property of a particular statistical relationship to shock frequency. But this suggestion is not so far removed from what we might, in general, expect to be the position of incentive theorists were they to entertain shock density as an incentive condition. Presumably, the statistical relationship between avoidance and nonavoidance responses, and the shock density appropriate to each, would be sufficient to establish differential incentive values for avoidance and nonavoidance categories of response. Actually, incentive theorists have not yet dealt with overall shock density.[11] And perhaps they may not want to inasmuch as there exists evidence that suggests that the momentary consequences of an avoidance response are more important in avoidance conditioning than are changes in overall shock density. For example, two experiments (Bolles & Popp, 1964; Hineline, 1970) have shown that if an avoidance response does not omit the next scheduled shock, but does reduce overall shock density, acquisition of avoidance responses is poor; while if an avoidance response does delay the next scheduled shock, but does not alter overall shock density, avoidance responding is reasonably well acquired. Historically speaking, incentive theories of aversive control are actually less likely to borrow from an avoidance hypothesis of aversive control than they are from a punishment or escape hypothesis. They seem most inclined to build on the foundation provided by still another general approach to aversive control, specifically one that involves stimuli having secondary emotional value.

Escape from the Secondary Aversive Stimulus

The empirical and theoretical analyses that involve escape from secondary aversive stimuli are characterized by being two-stage analyses. Whether the avoidance procedure is a Pavlovian or instrumental discrete-trial procedure involving an explicit cue, or a free-response noncued procedure, the first stage of avoidance acquisition is essentially a defense conditioning or CER stage. That is, until the first avoidance response occurs, avoidance procedures solely involve the pairing of an aversive stimulus with whatever stimuli in the environment antedate the presentation of the aversive stimulus. The duration of this initial CER stage is, of course, not operationally specified by the avoidance procedure but rather is functionally determined by the organism.

The importance of this initial CER stage for our present analyses of avoidance learning is that it is assumed by two-stage theorists of avoidance learning that during this CER stage, any stimuli antedating shock presentation become secondary aversive stimuli. A particular theoretical development or systematic analysis of why and how antedating stimuli become secondarily aversive under the CER procedure depends on the particular theorist or systematist proposing it, as described in the earlier sections of this chapter. No extensive distinctions will be drawn immediately herein between two-stage theorists for whom antedating CER stimuli become aversive because of the conditioning of hypothetical fear responses and their associated fear stimuli either through drive reduction (e.g., Brown, 1949; Miller, 1948) or through contiguity (e.g., Mowrer, 1947, 1960). Neither will essential discriminations be made between two-stage theorists who leave the nature of the emotional response mechanism mediating the aversiveness of the antedating CER stimulus basically unspecified (e.g., Estes, 1941, 1944; Skinner, 1938, 1953; Thorndike, 1931) and two-stage theorists who omit mention of emotional response mechanisms in favor of a strictly functional use of the term secondary aversive stimulus (e.g., Anger, 1963; Dinsmoor, 1954; Schoenfeld, 1950). To reiterate what is essential for our understanding of two-stage theories of avoidance, stimuli antedating the presentation of shock during the first, or CER, stage of avoidance acquisition become secondarily aversive.

Needless to say, the nature of the antedating secondary aversive stimulus will differ both operationally between cued- and noncued-avoidance procedures and theoretically between various systematic approaches. When the functional antedating aversive stimulus is assumed to be a fear-produced stimulus, it is usually presumed that this stimulus is autonomic in nature (e.g., Miller, 1951; Mowrer, 1947).[12] Otherwise, the functional secondary aversive stimulus is taken to be the distal stimulus in the case of exteroceptive cues; proprioceptive stimuli arising from nonavoidance responses in the case of interoceptive cues (e.g., Schoenfeld, 1950); and stimuli, which accompany the passage of time since the last response in the case of postresponse-time cues (Anger, 1963).

All of the above cited two-stage explanations of avoidance learning involve negative reinforcement in the second or escape stage of the explanation. To elaborate, two-stage theories contend that when the avoidance response finally does occur, it does something in addition to omitting or postponing the primary aversive stimulus. This something else that the avoidance response does is, importantly, to reduce or terminate the secondary aversive stimulus. All two-stage theorists consider the secondary negative reinforcement that is a concomitant of escape from the secondary aversive stimulus to be the source of reinforcement for the avoidance response per se. Thus, two-stage approaches to avoidance conditioning uniquely propose an explicit, absolute, source of secondary negative reinforcement for the referent-avoidance response.

The most obvious instance of escape from a secondary aversive stimulus occurs in the conventional instrumental avoidance procedure where the CS for the avoidance response is terminated by the avoidance response. Indeed, this has been the prototype procedure to which all other procedures have been referred and to which all two-stage theories of avoidance learning owe conceptual homage. Escape from secondary aversive proprioceptive stimuli or from secondary aversive postresponse-time cues is somewhat more subtle and, at least for now, terribly more difficult to observe (if, indeed, postresponse-time cues are to be observable at all). The avoidance response escapes from secondary aversive proprioceptive stimuli, because it is incompatible with nonavoidance responses that produce the proprioceptive stimuli that have previously been paired with shock. The avoidance response escapes from secondary aversive postresponse-time cues, because it substitutes short (immediate) postresponse-time cues for longer postresponse-time cues that have been more closely associated with shock. Other sources of secondary negative reinforcement could be discussed, even potentially in terms of reduction in overall shock density. But it might be more instructive at this juncture to review the evidence regarding the escape from secondary aversive stimulus hypothesis of avoidance that has been obtained in the context of the prototype instrumental cued-avoidance procedure.

There are data that clearly suggest that the response contingent termination of a CS for avoidance responding is reinforcing (Mowrer & Lamoreaux, 1942) and that delaying termination of the CS after the avoidance response occurs impairs avoidance responding (Kamin, 1957). The evidence that has been interpreted as being most favorable to two-stage theory and that has been even more strongly interpreted as demonstrating that CS termination may be the only source of reinforcement in instrumental avoidance learning, was first collected in experiments by Kamin (1956, 1957; see also Bolles, Stokes, & Younger, 1966). In these experiments the referent response did one of the following: only terminated the CS, only omitted the shock, or both terminated the CS and omitted the shock. The aspect of these data that supports two-stage theories is that the referent response is maintained in the condition where the response only terminates the CS and does not avoid shock.

However, not all of the evidence supports two-stage avoidance theories. In fact, the most acceptable contemporary summarization of the available evidence is to state that while termination of the avoidance CS is sufficient to reinforce avoidance responding, termination of the CS is not a necessary condition for reinforcement of avoidance responding. Some of the contrary data were obtained in the above described experiments by Kamin (1956, 1957) and Bolles, Stokes, & Younger (1966) in which it was observed that the referent response is also maintained in the group for which the response avoids shock but does not terminate the CS. Other experiments have provided still more troublesome data that show that avoidance responding proceeds quite nicely in the absence of a CS termination, if the referent response instead produces a cue that indicates the primary aversive stimulus is to be omitted (Bolles & Grossen, 1969; Bower, Starr, & Lazarovitz, 1965; D'Amato, Fazzaro, & Etkin, 1968). Since the cue is produced by the avoidance response, it occurs only on avoidance trials and is, therefore, never associated with shock. The cue is literally a safety signal. Mackintosh (1974) in defense of two-stage theory has argued that safety signals, such as those used in the D'Amato, Fazzaro, and Etkin (1968) research, can reinforce avoidance responding in the absence of CS termination, because the safety signal serves as a conditioned inhibitor of the secondary aversive CS stimulus; that is, the safety signal serves to reduce the secondary aversiveness of the CS following the avoidance response. Alternative interpretations to that of Mackintosh (1974) seem to require a still more explicit "incentivelike" approach.

Incentive and Selection of the Avoidance Response

D'Amato, Fazzaro, and Etkin (1968) were, of course, mindful that the safety stimulus used in their experiment was perfectly correlated with the absence of shock when they more generally proposed that any stimulus, including the termination of the avoidance CS, will reinforce avoidance responding only insofar as it serves as a discriminative stimulus for the avoidance of shock. Bolles (1970) also argues that reinforcement of the avoidance response is based on the occurrence of a response-produced safety signal rather than on the termination of a secondarily aversive CS (or for that matter, on the avoidance of shock). But the pointed horns of the avoidance learning dilemma once again seem immiment. If the dilemma arises at all in the first instance, it arises because it is not apparent how avoidance of shock alone can reinforce avoidance responding. How then is it possible to provide a solution to the dilemma by suggesting that a stimulus that serves as a discriminative stimulus for the avoidance of shock can alone reinforce avoidance responding?

Part of the answer to this question has been previously discussed in terms of cognitive expectancy theory. The safety signal initiates an expectancy of the nonoccurrence of shock. That is, expectancy theorists remove the dilemma by imbuing the discriminative stimulus with some hypothetical property. A similar tack is taken by Mackintosh (1974) in proposing that the safety signal is a conditioned inhibitor. Once again the discriminative stimulus is imbued with some hypothetical property (in this case the presumed inhibition of aversiveness) that can then account for the effects produced by the stimulus in the avoidance situation. As we have already discussed in the context of the conditioned emotional response, incentive theorists also quite readily imbue stimuli and/or responses with incentive properties the nature of which are dependent on the conditions of the primary emotional stimuli acting at the time.

Two general incentive approaches to avoidance learning may be taken depending on whether or not the nonoccurrence of a primary aversive stimulus is thought by the theorist to merit a separate incentive construct. Before elaborating on this finer point, however, some more general points should be made. First of all, incentive explanations of avoidance are fundamentally two-stage explanations. The first, CER stage establishes antedating stimuli (be they exteroceptive, autonomic, proprioceptive, or postresponse-time stimuli) with incentive properties appropriate to the occurrence of shock. As was elaborated in an earlier discussion, these incentive properties vary in detail among theorists, but they routinely include the property of producing effects on behavior that are symmetric but opposite in direction to those produced by the presentation of emotionally positive stimuli.

Given a motivated organism in a situation replete with emotionally negative incentive properties, the second-stage task for the incentive theorist of avoidance learning is to account for the fact that the avoidance response is selected for execution over all other possible responses. There are two ways of doing this. One way is to hypothesize that the avoidance response exclusively elicits positive emotions of relief (Mowrer, 1960) or relaxation (Denny, 1971) that potentiate the ongoing avoidance response. This approach is absolute in conception. Although nonavoidance responses elicit negative emotions (e.g., fear), the avoidance response elicits positive emotions.

A more relative approach is to assert that the avoidance response is selected because the net incentive associated with the avoidance situation is more positive (or less negative) in the presence of the avoidance response than it is, given the occurrence of any other (nonavoidance) response. Incentive theorists such as Estes (1969), Logan (1969), and Miller (1963) would subscribe to some version of this relative incentive approach to avoidance learning. Nonavoidance responses are associated with negative incentive, avoidance responses are not. The negative incentive of the total avoidance situation is necessarily less, given the avoidance response than given a nonavoidance response. An organism must be doing something. What the organism selects to do at any moment is that which is associated with the most favorable incentive of the moment.

This relative incentive approach has conceptual similarities to the punishment hypothesis of avoidance, but it has the advantage that not every nonavoidance response needs to be associated with shock in order for the avoidance response to emerge. The incentive approach also aligns itself closely with the overall shock-density reduction analysis, but differs from it in dealing with the momentary properties of events rather than with their longer term distribution through time. Finally, incentive accounts of avoidance are obviously related to two-stage theories involving escape from the secondary aversive stimulus. The critical difference in this latter instance is that the second stage of incentive theory is not tied to the reduction of explicit aversive stimuli. Any operation (terminating a CS, presenting a safety signal, etc.) that changes the net incentive associated with the avoidance response will change the likelihood of the avoidance response occurring. One characteristic that is shared almost equally well among all of the theoretical approaches to avoidance learning, including the incentive approach, is that avoidance responding should reasonably rapidly extinguish in the continued absence of the primary aversive stimulus. The relative durability of avoidance remains somewhat enigmatic for theories of avoidance learning.

Summary   Conventional theoretical analyses have experienced difficulty in accounting for the acquisition and maintenance of avoidance responding. The major stumbling block has been to explain how the omission of the primary aversive stimulus in itself determines avoidance responding. We have concerned ourselves with a variety of proposed explanations. All of the explanations begin by asserting that, in fact, the omission of the aversive stimulus itself does nothing; the nonoccurrence of a stimulus is, by itself, a nonevent. Given this as a premise, some other mechanism of avoidance conditioning is necessary. Three of the approaches directly involve the presentation or removal of the primary aversive stimulus. The punishment hypothesis asserts that the avoidance response passively emerges, because all other responses are suppressed by the presentation of the aversive stimulus. The escape hypothesis asserts that the avoidance response emerges from the escape response that becomes anticipatory, because it is reinforced by the termination of the aversive stimulus. Alternatively, the avoidance hypothesis, in the hands of S-R theorists, asserts that the avoidance response emerges because it is followed by a less dense occurrence of the aversive stimulus than are other responses.

Two-stage theories of avoidance place a heavier reliance on the CER process that purportedly constitutes the first-stage of avoidance learning. Stimuli and nonavoidance responses are imbued with emotional qualities because of their historic association with the aversive stimulus. For S-R theorists the antedating events become secondarily emotion producing or secondarily aversive. For R-S incentive theorists the antedating events become associated with some construct of negative or inhibitory incentive. For both types of theorists, the occurrence of the avoidance response is related to the antedating events. Either the avoidance response occurs because it was previously reinforced by the termination of the secondarily aversive event or, for incentive theorists, the response is selected for occurrence because it is associated with the most favorable incentive conditions of the moment.

None of the theoretical approaches to avoidance learning successfully withstands the challenge of explaining all of the available empirical data on avoidance learning. This is not really surprising inasmuch as the available data are voluminous and often directly contradictory. All told, the analyses based on punishment and escape from primary aversive stimuli seem least capable in this regard. But even these analyses are not completely culpable. Surely responses that are followed by primary negative reinforcement are increased in likelihood. Similarly, the future likelihood of responses that are followed by primary punishment is reduced. There really are no questions regarding the empirical validity of these effects. As we have elsewhere suggested, however, there is controversy over the theoretical mechanisms underlying these effects.

PUNISHMENT   The operation of positive punishment entails presenting an aversive event shortly following the occurrence of a response. Functionally identified, a positive punisher is an aversive event that decreases the future likelihood of a response that it shortly follows. In other words, the functional hallmark of punishment is response suppression. There are no empirical or theoretical restrictions as to the nature of the response that can be punished, whether learned or unlearned, instrumental or consummatory, although the particular parameters of the punishment situation that produce a decrease in the future probability of the response may differ among them. Similarly, there are no restrictions of an empirical or theoretical type that limit the conditioning situation in which punishment can be studied, whether Pavlovian or instrumental/operant, discriminated or nondiscriminated, although again the parameters of the punishment situation that produce response suppression may differ among them.

The empirical literature pertaining to punishment, which is enormous, has been well reviewed by others (e.g., Azrin & Holz, 1966; Church, 1963, 1969; Fantino, 1973; Mackintosh, 1974; Solomon, 1964). The majority of this empirical literature has been generated in instrumental/operant contexts where the punished response has a history of reinforcement; that is, where the punished response is either concurrently being maintained by reinforcement or is undergoing extinction following a previous period of reinforcement. Consequently, many of the reported empirical effects of punishment, and these are sometimes varied, are best understood in terms of interactions between the conditions and schedules of punishment and the conditions and schedules of past or present reinforcement.[13] Further empirical complexities are encountered when the learning situation is made discriminative, or when the response is maintained by an aversive control paradigm, say, an escape or avoidance paradigm.

These operational-empirical nuances are raised here so as to support the making of two preliminary points. The first is that empirical research in the area of punishment leaves no doubt about the functional validity of punishment; under the appropriate set of parameters, punishers reduce the future likelihood of responses they follow. The second point is that empirical research on punishment has outstripped systematic analyses of punishment. Theories of punishment tend to be limited conceptualizations that rarely even make the pretense of being appropriate to all types of punished responses or to all punishment situations. We have witnessed that the boundary conditions surrounding theoretical analyses of other aversive control paradigms are also not very wide.

Our previous discussion of the CER and avoidance learning paradigms fortunately provides a helpful prelude to the study of systematic analyses of punishment. Much of the conceptual thinking regarding aversive control overlaps the several paradigms. This is probably no more apparent than for the S-S expectancy approach to punishment. Whereas CER suppression is viewed simply as the result of an expectancy of shock, and avoidance responding is viewed as an expectancy of the omission of shock that incorporates a response contingency, punishment is viewed as an expectancy of shock that incorporates a response contingency. Organisms have a demand against shock (Tolman, 1932). Accordingly, when organisms come to expect that a given response will be shortly followed by shock, the appropriate performance in the situation is, figuratively, to follow the cognitive map along some other route that will not terminate in the punished response.

There are no essential differences between this S-S punishment analysis and those S-S analyses described earlier for CER and avoidance. Accordingly, it may be reasoned that the S-S expectancy approach is capable of accounting for the fact that the suppressive effects of punishment depend on the distribution of reinforcements programmed by the baseline reinforcement schedule maintaining responding (cf. Azrin & Holz, 1966; Fantino, 1973). After all, performance depends jointly on the totality of expectancies suitable to the situation—both those of reinforcement and those of shock. It might also be reasoned that the S-S expectancy theorist is at odds to explain the changes in micromolar responses that result from differential punishment of micromolor responses (Logan, 1960). Even predictions of general performances under aversive situations are offered sparingly (Tolman, 1955).

Perhaps it might be interesting to speculate further about other similar S-S expectancy, CER, or avoidance analyses and their applicability to the punishment paradigm. For example, it could be proposed that organisms decrease their responding under punishment, because the result of doing so is to reduce the overall density of shock they experience. This is admittedly a strained, and perhaps unfair, extrapolation of the thinking of Sidman (1962) and Herrnstein (1969) regarding avoidance to the punishment situation. But it cannot be denied that response suppression in a punishment paradigm, and response acquisition in an avoidance paradigm, both functionally result in a reduction in the overall density of shocks received over time.

This is not a spurious similarity. It proceeds directly from the avoidance and punishment operations. In avoidance, only the referent response is followed by the omission of shock; all other responses are punished by shock. In punishment, only the referent response is followed by the presentation of shock; all other responses avoid the shock.[14] It should not be surprising that this reciprocity of operations has encouraged some theorists to approach one of the aversive control paradigms in terms of the other paradigm, and still other theorists approach both paradigms with a common analysis. S-S expectancy theory has already been used to exemplify the latter. But despite this opportunity for theorists to strike a harmonious accord among paradigms, the punishment paradigm is still made to stand apart in one important theoretical respect. Punishment has enjoyed a distinct theoretical relationship to the law of effect that is not shared by either the CER or the avoidance paradigms.

The Law of Effect Reconsidered   In our previous consideration of Thorndike's (1911, 1913) law of effect, we stressed the functional empiricism and symmetry of Thorndike's formulation (cf. Chapter 4). Reinforcers are functionally identified in a manner that is symmetric but opposite in direction to that for punishers. Reinforcers increase, and punishers decrease, the future likelihood of responses they shortly follow. Thorndike's own consideration of his law of effect was theoretical as well as empirical (cf. Chapter 3). He was an S-R theorist who believed that the strengthening of associations results from reinforcement and, conversely, but symmetrically, that the weakening of associations results from punishment.

This complementary action of reinforcement and punishment is indeed aptly described in terms of the "stamping in" and "stamping out" of S-R associations. Theoretically, it clearly predicts that response suppression by punishment should be as permanent as response facilitation by reinforcement. When a response is followed by punishment, it should not only have its future likelihood decreased, but it should remain decreased unless and until its associative strength is explicitly increased again through reinforcement. In short, Thorndike's theoretical law of effect asserts that learned S-R associations are reversible through the complementary action of reinforcement and punishment.

Thorndike (1931, 1932) published a series of experiments that led him to reconsider his theoretical law of effect. In some of these, animals were confined for a short period of time if they made an error response. In others, humans were told they were "wrong" when they emitted certain incorrect verbal responses in a paired-associate task. In neither case did the experimental manipulation result in a response suppression when compared with appropriate controls. Indeed, more responses were made in the "wrong" condition than in a condition where responses were not followed by any event. These data, particularly those pertaining to the verbal learning task, caused Thorndike (1932) to reject the punishment half of the theoretical law of effect. That is, punishment was no longer considered by Thorndike to have a direct weakening effect on S-R associations.

Instead of a direct weakening effect on S-R associations, Thorndike proposed that the decrease in response probability produced by punishers is due to an indirect effect of the aversive stimulus. Specifically, Thorndike (1932) proposed that aversive stimuli elicit emotions (e.g., fear, chagrin) and responses (jump back, run away) that compete with the punished response and, thereby, suppress the punished response. Punishment effects are "contingent upon what the annoyer in question makes the animal do." It will be noted that Thorndike has converted to a pure competing response hypothesis of response suppression and, accordingly, does not propose that punishment has any *associative* influence. This is important to note because it leads to the prediction that punishment effects should be temporary; that is, suppressed responses should recover to their prepunishment levels once the aversive stimulus is no longer available to elicit competing responses. Clearly, associative weakening and response-competition theories of punishment lead to diametrically opposed predictions about the fate of suppressed responses once punishment is removed; response suppression will be permanent if it represents weakened S-R associations, and response suppression will be temporary if it is produced by punishment-related competing responses.

Before discussing the permanence or nonpermanence of punishment effects on future response probability any further, it is interesting as an aside to note that Thorndike's theoretical revision regarding punishment has been considered by some to have been based on somewhat weak empirical grounds (e.g., Postman, 1947, 1962). Neither contingent event used by Thorndike (confinement, "wrong") represents a particularly intense event, and there are methodological shortcomings in the paired-associate work. Furthermore, other research was available to Thorndike at the time that showed that electric shock for wrong responses improves discrimination performance (Warden & Aylesworth, 1927). In partial empirical defense of Thorndike, it was subsequently established by Stone (1950; Stone & Walters, 1951) that both "wrong" and a mild electric shock *increase* responses when used in a situation like that of Thorndike's.[15] The critical point of this aside is that, functionally, the use of the word "wrong" following a response is identified as a reinforcer (for both Thorndike, 1932 and Stone, 1950). Thorndike revised his theory on the basis that an event that he thought theoretically should function as a punisher did not so function. This is not the common way for theorists to proceed. Usually, in such a situation theorists will retain their theory and argue that the event at hand is not what it was thought to be, since it did not function as expected. Had Thorndike followed this more common theoretical approach, he would have argued that "wrong" was not functionally a punisher in the situation and, therefore, he would have retained his associative weakening theory of punishment. Some contemporary empirical systematists think Thorndike should have followed this latter course. However, most contemporary theorists agree that associative weakening is not the mechanism by which punishment produces a decrease in behavior. Indeed, as Bolles (1967) has noted, no major theorist has defended the idea that punishment weakens S-R associations, since its abandonment by Thorndike.

To return to the central theme of this section, it is important theoretically whether punishment effects are empirically irreversible and relatively permanent or reversible and temporary. The former empirical outcome supports the theoretical position that punishment reduces associative strength. The latter outcome argues theoretically for the contrary position that punishment does not reduce associative strength. Two series of experiments are very important in this regard: Estes, 1944 and Skinner, 1938. In both of these, previously reinforced responses are subjected to extinction. Punishment is administered to one of two groups of animals at the beginning of extinction and then removed for the remainder of the extinction period. Both of these experimenters observed comparable results. Responding is suppressed by the punisher at the beginning of extinction. However, responding recovers after the removal of punishment, and the total course of extinction is not different between the punished and nonpunished groups by the end of extinction.

The Skinner (1938) and Estes (1944) experiments have been very influential in directing the style of theorizing about punishment. The logic of the experiments is clear. If punishment effectively reduces associative strength, then extinction should proceed more rapidly when responses are punished. But in the words of Estes (1944):

The extinction of a response which has been positively reinforced cannot be accelerated by the application of punishment; the total amount of time necessary for extinction is evidently determined by the conditions of previous positive reinforcement and cannot be reduced by punishment.

Estes (1944) presented another empirical principle emanating from his research, which also has been theoretically influential:

The effects of punishment are contingent upon a close association of the disturbing stimulus with the stimuli which normally provide an occasion for the occurrence of the response (discriminative stimuli). There is no evidence that the correlation of the punishment with the response per se in the role of a "negative reinforcement" is important.

In the above quote, the term "negative reinforcement" should be read to mean "weakener of associative strength." Estes' second empirical principle more simply states that because punishment does not weaken the strength of S-R associations, it is not *important* that the punisher shortly follow the response. Estes (1944) is not here rejecting the empirical principle of punishment, which implies a contingency between response and punisher. He is, however, asserting that such a response contingency is not a necessary condition for response suppression to be produced by aversive stimuli.

By way of summarizing the impact of the Skinner (1938) and Estes (1944) work, we can say that their results give some empirical credibility to Thorndike's (1932) rejection of his original theoretical mechanism of punishment. If punishment effects are temporary, and if a correlation between the response and the punisher is unimportant, then it seems to follow theoretically that punishment does not weaken associative strength. Before considering alternative mechanisms of action by which punishment potentially exerts its effects (theoretically it must do something else, if it does not weaken associations), we will briefly discuss the extent to which the Skinner (1938) and Estes (1944) data empirically compel the rejection of an associative weakening hypothesis.

Empirical Evidence Pertaining to Associative Weakening

One purpose of this section is to lead to the conclusion that despite the influence that the Skinner (1938) and Estes (1944) findings have had, there actually are more convincing data that suggest that response suppression can be relatively permanent and that the response contingency can be an important determinant of punishment suppression.

With respect to the permanence of punishment suppression, permanence appears to be directly related to the intensity of the aversive stimulus used as the punisher. The more intense the stimulus, the greater the suppression that is produced, and the more permanent are the effects (e.g., Appel & Peterson, 1965; Azrin, 1960; Boe & Church, 1967; Camp, Raymond, & Church, 1967; Church, Raymond, & Beauchamp, 1967; Karsh, 1962). For all practical purposes, punishment-produced decreases in the probability of the response appear to be virtually permanent for high-intensity aversive stimuli.

Two lines of evidence suggest that a contingency (in the sense of a temporal correlation) between a response and a subsequent punisher critically determines the extent of response suppression, Estes' (1944) findings notwithstanding. The first line of evidence found that the amount of suppression is inversely related to the length of the delay between the response and the presentation of the aversive stimulus (e.g., Azrin, 1956; Camp, Raymond, & Church, 1967; Kamin, 1959). The second line of evidence involves direct comparisons between contingent shock and noncontingent shock. With only rare exception (e.g., Hunt & Brady, 1955), responses that have a close temporal correlation to shock are reduced substantially more than are responses that do not (e.g.,

Azrin, 1956; Boe & Church, 1967; Church, Wooton, & Matthews, 1970; Rachlin & Herrnstein, 1969; Schuster & Rachlin, 1968).

The reader is reminded of the empirically based conclusion offered at the outset of this section. There can be some degree of permanence to the decrease in behavior produced by punishment, and the temporal relationship between response and punisher is important in determining the extent of the decrease in behavior. It would be pleasing if some empirical resolution of the discrepancies between this conclusion and the earlier Estes and Skinner data were available. It appears that the best that can now be said is that Estes (1944) seems to have grossly underestimated the importance of the response contingency. With respect to the permanence of suppression, it has been suggested (e.g., Azrin & Holz, 1966) that the recovery observed by Estes and Skinner is largely attributable to the discriminative stimulus properties of the aversive stimulus used in their extinction situations.

A discriminative stimulus analysis of the effects of punishment has some plausibility, and it can satisfactorily account for some selected findings regarding punishment. However, it suffers from a lack of generality or general applicability. The basic premise of a discriminative stimulus analysis is beyond criticism. The premise is that the aversive stimuli used as punishers share discriminative properties in common with other stimuli and, thus, function as do other discriminative stimuli. As one example, the introduction of an aversive stimulus into a stimulus situation would be expected to change that stimulus situation because of the discriminative properties of the aversive stimulus. Accordingly, a stimulus-generalization decrement should occur for any response under the control of the stimulus situation that prevails prior to the introduction of the new discriminative (aversive) stimulus. One very major problem with a stimulus-generalization decrement hypothesis of response suppression is that it does not predict differential suppression between a contingent and a noncontingent presentation of the aversive stimulus. (But also note that Estes, 1944, did not find such a difference in his situation.)

Nevertheless, Holz and Azrin (1961) have clearly shown that punishment can serve as a discriminative stimulus for either reinforcement or punishment. There is also reasonable evidence that in at least some situations, the discriminative properties of shock can account for what otherwise may seem to be paradoxical effects of punishment.[16] Among these are the findings that: rats may improve their discriminative performance when shocked for correct responses (Muenzinger, 1934); rats initially shocked with intense shock show greater than expected suppression to weak shock (Karsh, 1963); monkeys with a history of shock avoidance conditioning will respond to response contingent shock punishment (McKearney, 1969); rats with a history of escape from shock will respond longer in extinction if punished with shock than if not (Brown, Martin, & Morrow, 1964).

To return to the Estes (1944) and Skinner (1938) experiments in which punishment was delivered only at the onset of extinction and subsequently removed, the discriminative stimulus analysis of the fact that responding recovered in extinction after the shock was removed is fairly easy to appreciate. The analysis shows that the shock was a discriminative stimulus for nonreinforcement and, thus, the behavior remained suppressed in its presence. When the shock was removed, the stimulus situation was more like the situation that prevailed in the reinforcement condition, which preceded extinction; therefore, responding was increased.

Although it would be erroneous to deny that aversive stimuli have discriminative properties, it is also clear, conceptually, that aversive stimuli have other properties that are unique to aversive stimuli. An important one of these properties is that aversive stimuli elicit behavior that is different from those elicited by other (appetitive) stimuli. Another unique property is that only aversive stimuli can establish secondary aversive stimuli. Still another property is that the termination of an aversive stimulus is negatively reinforcing.

Although the bulk of the empirical literature is consonant with an associative weakening action of punishment, the theoretical arena is hostile toward this point of view, as we have mentioned previously. The alternative theoretical approaches proposed have relied heavily on the nondiscriminative, unique properties of aversive stimuli, taken separately or in combination, in order to account for response suppression.

Theoretical Alternatives to Associative Weakening

By this point in our discussion of aversive control paradigms, the reader has been introduced to a variety of hypothetical concepts and hypothetical constructs. Some of the concepts and constructs first introduced for the CER paradigm reappeared in our discussion of avoidance learning. It will now be the case that some of the concepts and constructs previously discussed for CER and avoidance will reappear as we discuss the S-R associationistic and R-S incentive theoretical alternatives to explaining the effects of punishment. Actually, no new hypothetical concepts or hypothetical constructs will need to be introduced; those already introduced suffice completely for our remaining discussion of punishment. This arises because of the order of presentation chosen for the aversive control paradigms and not because one paradigm is more basic than any other.

S-R Association Alternatives
COMPETING RESPONSE ANALYSIS

Thorndike (1932) turned to a competing response analysis when he rejected his associative weakening hypothesis. The suppressive effects of punishment indirectly result from the elicitation by shock of emotions and responses that are incompatible with the punished response. In other words, the effects of punishment do not result from the weakening of an S-R association but result from the strengthening of S-R associations involving responses that successfully compete with the punished response.

The competing response theory of punishment has been elaborated by S-R contiguity theorists (e.g., Guthrie, 1934; Sheffield, 1948). Punishment elicits responses that are conditioned by contiguity to antecedent stimuli. These S-R associations will compete with (replace) the punished S-R association, if the new associated response is incompatible with the punished response. Alternatively, if the responses elicited by punishment are compatible with the punished response, then a potentiation of the punished response will result. This latter interpretation is usually offered for those seemingly paradoxical situations where punishment produces an increase in the punished response (e.g.,

Brown, Martin, & Morrow, 1964; McKearney, 1969; Melvin & Anson, 1969; Walters & Glazer, 1971).

It is worth noting again that at least for Guthrie, competing response theory is nonmotivational and purely associational: "It is not the feeling caused by punishment, but the specific action caused by punishment that determines what will be learned" (Guthrie, 1934). A nice demonstration of this is to be found in the research of Fowler and Miller (1963) who observed that rats shocked on their forepaws for running slow down, while rats shocked on their hindpaws for running speed up; presumably this is the inevitable outcome when it is considered that shock elicits a backward flinch and a forward lurch, respectively.

It is well established empirically that in each situation where punishment has been shown to increase the punished response (e.g., Fowler & Miller, 1963), increasing the intensity of the aversive stimulus will result in a decrease in the punished response. This is not as problematic for the competing response theorist as might be supposed. All that needs to be assumed is that qualitatively different responses are elicited at different shock intensities and that incompatible responses are uniformly elicited at the highest shock intensities.

Actually, competing response theory is somewhat insensitive to the vagaries suggested by empirical data but seems instead to rely heavily on its plausibility. Competing responses are not usually observed or specified.[17] In the rare instances where competing responses are defined (e.g., Bolles, 1967), there is likely to be an appeal made to the natural or adaptive responses of the organism. However, if competing responses are asserted to be present whenever a punished response is suppressed and to be gone whenever the punished response is recovered, then the theory cannot be discredited and its utility is therefore compromised.

ESCAPE FROM THE PRIMARY AVERSIVE STIMULUS

Another version of the competing response approach arises out of the theoretical framework that drive-reduction reinforcement is necessary for S-R associations to form. The development of this analysis, which was first proposed for punishment by Miller and Dollard (1941), does not differ in any important respects from the Hullian (1929, 1943) analysis of avoidance in terms of escape from the primary aversive stimulus. Very briefly, Miller and Dollard (1941) proposed that shock elicits responses that escape the aversive stimulus and that, thereby, are associated to antecedent stimuli through the drive-reduction reinforcement accompanying the termination of the shock. The termination of punishment thus leads to the learning of new S-R associations that can become anticipatory. If the anticipatory escape responses are incompatible with the punished response, then punishment suppression results. Alternatively, if the anticipatory escape responses are compatible with the punished response, then punishment facilitation results. Fowler and Miller (1963) actually interpreted their forepaw-hindpaw shock experiment in terms of the reinforcement to the shock-elicited behavior by escape from shock.

The escape hypothesis of punishment suffers from the same shortcomings as does the escape hypothesis of avoidance. For one, punishment should not produce an enduring suppression; anticipatory escape responses should extinguish. For another, suppression should not occur when very short-duration shock punishers are used, because the organism would be unable to escape from them. Finally, the punishing efficacy of an aversive stimulus is not reduced when the termination of punishment is delayed (Leitenberg, 1965). Obviously, this is contrary to what should be if drive-reduction reinforcement is necessary for the association of incompatible escape responses to antedating stimuli.

EMOTIONAL RESPONSE ANALYSIS

The essence of the emotional response analysis is that punishment establishes conditioned emotional responses (especially fear) to the situational stimuli present at the time of punishment. It is these conditioned emotional responses that inhibit the referent-punished response. No weakening of the punished S-R association is implied, it latently awaits for the inhibiting emotions to be removed or extinguished. The effects of punishment are always temporary; some recovery will always follow the removal of punishment.

The reader no doubt recognizes this punishment analysis to be the S-R conditioned emotional response analysis presented earlier for the CER paradigm. It was to this analysis that Thorndike (1932), Skinner (1938), and Estes (1944) appealed in order to account for the temporary and nonresponse contingent effects of punishment that they observed—and therein lies the problem. The conditioned emotional response hypothesis of punishment can neither tolerate any permanent effects of punishment nor readily explain the greater suppression sometimes produced by response contingent than produced by noncontingent presentations of aversive stimuli. Actually, the second criticism can be largely negated by hypothesizing that in the response-contingent situation, emotional responses also become conditioned to the proprioceptive stimuli produced by the punished response itself. The idea that response-produced stimuli may be conditioned to emotional responses is not new to our discussion. It is the conceptual backbone of theoretical analyses of avoidance made in terms of escape from a secondary aversive stimulus.

ESCAPE FROM THE SECONDARY AVERSIVE STIMULUS

This analysis follows quite directly from the avoidance analyses of Mowrer (1947) and Schoenfeld (1950) and differs only in that instead of a single referent avoidance response, the punishment situation is conceptualized as consisting exclusively of avoidance responses, with the singular exception of the referent-punished response (Dinsmoor, 1954; Solomon, 1964). Here, it is not important to the analysis whether it is presented in terms of a hypothetical fear drive (Mowrer, 1947; Solomon, 1964) or empirically in terms of secondary aversive stimuli (Dinsmoor, 1954; Schoenfeld, 1950). The analysis follows two stages that are independent of the lexicon by which they are described.

In the first stage, punishment is paired with antedating stimuli, including the proprioceptive stimuli produced by the referent-punished response. Consequently, these stimuli become secondarily aversive and their termination will constitute secondary negative reinforcement. Since only the referent response leads to the presentation of the aversive stimulus, any other response sequence that occurs and that is incompatible with the punished response will be reinforced by the termination of the secondary aversive stimuli associated with performing the punished response. In other words, in the second stage of the analysis, responses that are incompatible with the punished response are negatively reinforced by escape from the secondary aversive stimuli that are associated with the execution of the punished response. The linkage to explanations of avoidance responding is obvious. It is no wonder that some theorists have labeled this analysis of punishment the avoidance hypothesis (e.g., Dinsmoor, 1954). We prefer to think of both the punishment and avoidance explanations as escape hypotheses, since the critical element in each is the negative reinforcement produced by escape from secondary aversive stimuli.

The present theoretical analysis suffers from the shortcomings described for the avoidance situation and from those that characterize other theoretical alternatives we have discussed. From either source, the present theoretical alternative to punishment inherits the problem that it should only permit temporary effects of punishment to occur. The analysis also suffers from a problem that seems to be almost inherent in incentive theories (cf. Chapter 5) but that is unique to S-R association analyses. The problem concerns response initiation. Consider that in order for behavior incompatible with the punished response to be reinforced, it is first necessary that the punished response sequence is initiated. Otherwise, no reinforcement could be derived from the termination of secondary aversive stimuli that accompanies the cessation of the punished response. The problem of response initiation is to explain why the punished response is initiated, if it produces aversive stimuli.

Incentive Motivation Alternatives

It will not be necessary separately to detail the several incentive motivational alternatives that account for the effects of punishment (e.g., Estes, 1969; Logan, 1969; Miller, 1963: Mowrer, 1960; Premack, 1965). The fundamental tenet of incentive theory, as presented before, is that the conditions of aversive stimuli have incentive value that is opposite to that of appetitive stimuli. The occurrence of behavior is a function of the relative net incentive for that behavior. Behavior that is shortly followed by an aversive stimulus will be performed less, not because its associative strength is weakened, but instead because the incentive associated with the selection of that behavior is lessened.

Like the early Thorndike theoretical law of effect, which treated the associative effects of reinforcers and punishers symmetrically, incentive theorists treat the incentive effects of reinforcers and punishers symmetrically (although opposite in direction, of course). There is no need to posit a separate or an indirect mechanism of action to explain why punishment produces its effects according to incentive theory. The behavior that occurs is that which results from the conflict of positive and negative incentive motivations. No asymmetry is implied. Nevertheless, it is not the asymmetry of alternative theoretical approaches that has prevented them from accounting for any permanent effects of punishment. It has been the abandonment of associative weakening as the hypothetical process of punishment together with the failure to propose an alternative, nonassociative mechanism by which the permanent effects of punishment can be explained. Incentive theory, even though symmetric, is no different in this regard.

Summary   The empirical principle of punishment is confirmed beyond doubt. The theoretical task is to explain why it is that punishers lead to a decrease in the future probability of responses they shortly follow. One alternative theoretically entertained by Thorndike early on (1913), but not successfully by anyone else including himself since then, is that punishment weakens S-R associations in a manner symmetric but opposite to the manner in which reinforcement strengthens S-R associations. It is perhaps surprising that theorists have not more readily adopted an associative weakening notion or, alternatively, proposed a nonassociative construct that would theoretically account for long-term effects of punishment. After all, there are data that suggest that punishment has relatively permanent effects. More generally, in the empirical realm, punishment and reinforcement have been repeatedly shown to have similar but opposite effects on a wide variety of behaviors. Empirical systematists rarely miss an opportunity to make this latter observation, nor should they.

Nevertheless, it is a historic curiosity that theorizing about reinforcement and punishment have often proceeded apart. Consequently, punishment has often been quite differently viewed theoretically. The effects of punishment have most often been attributed to the learning (through contiguity or reinforcement) of competing responses or the learning of inhibiting emotions elicited by punishers. Reinforcers also elicit responses and emotions. This fact has largely gone unnoticed theoretically, except by incentive theorists. These latter students of punishment have revived the notion of symmetry between punishment and reinforcement but have done so in terms of the incentive associated with the conditions of reinforcers and punishers.

Learning as a hypothetical construct often has been assigned the property of being relatively permanent. In order to preserve this theoretical nicety, it is necessary to assert that associations can only be strengthened or replaced; associations cannot be weakened. As we have now discussed, punishment does not represent an exception to this theoretical rule.

GENERAL SUMMARY AND CONCLUSIONS

The behaving organism is exposed to a continuous-over-time fluctuation in environmental stimulus events. Stimuli are presented, removed, promised, and canceled. The control exerted over behavior by a stimulus event depends importantly on the nature of the stimulus event. Aversive control of behavior can be direct, as when primary aversive stimuli are presented or removed, or indirect, as when stimuli paired with primary aversive stimuli are presented or removed. But in each and every instance, a behavioral change is the end result of the influence of an aversive stimulus.

It is strange in this context that theorizing about the effects of aversive stimuli has not been pursued with the same vigor as has theorizing about reinforcing stimuli. Surely aversive control is no less important in everyday affairs than is reinforcement control. Perhaps even the contrary may be the usual case. More than one systematist of behavior has lamented the high incidence of aversive control over behavior that occurs in everyday affairs. But this seems to follow quite readily from the abundance of aversive stimuli in the transactions of people and from the efficacy of control that results from their application.

Whatever may be the reason, it seems accurate to state that appetitive stimuli have enjoyed theoretical primacy and that aversive stimuli have had to fit in theoretically as they may. Otherwise, one might expect that there would be far fewer miniaturized and constrained hypotheses regarding the aversive control of behavior. One might also suspect that if theorizing about aversive control were to begin *de novo*, rather than being fit into theoretical constructs already professed to by the theorist, that systematic analyses regarding aversive control would be more integrated and more successful. As we have already pointed out in several places, no one theoretical account seems capable of handling the extant data obtained across the CER, avoidance, and punishment paradigms or, for that matter, obtained within any one of the aversive control paradigms.

There does, however, seem to be a sense of order running through the various systematic approaches to aversive control. In part, this derives from the incentive theorists and cognitive theorists who have seemingly adopted the stratagem of allowing aversive events to act symmetrically with appetitive events, although opposite in direction, no matter what the contingency into which the stimulus event is entered. Order is seemingly imparted as well by systematic attempts to adopt one aversive control paradigm as the basic or fundamental paradigm by which the behavioral effects produced by the other paradigms may be understood. Thus, for example, we have seen proposed a punishment hypothesis of the CER and avoidance paradigms and a conditioned emotional response hypothesis of the punishment and avoidance paradigms. Alternatively, a single conceptual mechanism has been suggested to transcend all of the paradigms; the hypothesis with the most notoriety in this instance is the competing or incompatible response hypothesis.

In spite of the sense of order imparted by the several different approaches to aversive control phenomena, there is no gainsaying that the empirical literature pertaining to aversive control is still in need of systematic and theoretical explanation. No neat parallels to the systematic and theoretical analyses of reinforcement, as revealed in the preceding chapter, are as yet obvious for the domain of aversive control. We will subsequently see that a similar circumstance exists for the domain of transient states of the organism such as result, say, from extinction operations. Quite clearly, the acquisition, initiation, and selection of behavior has been the major concern of systematic analyses of learning and motivation. Perhaps this is as it should be in order, theoretically, to spur the behaving organism into motion. Needless to say, systematic analyses are not complete; they represent an ever evolving attempt to explain the behavior of organisms under every type of stimulus control.

NOTES   1. As an example, neither Tolman (1932) nor Hull (1943) gave theoretical recognition to the effects of punishment, while both Guthrie (1934) and Skinner (1938) dealt with them only briefly.

2. A question regarding negative reinforcement, as exemplified by the escape paradigm, is whether negative reinforcement produces effects that are symmetric to those produced by positive reinforcement in all situations. For the most

part, negative and positive reinforcement produce comparable effects with respect to the quality of the behavior engendered. There are differences, however. For example, organisms tend to acquire behavior more rapidly under an escape than under a positive reinforcement paradigm. Furthermore, organisms tend not to maintain behavior as well under schedules of negative reinforcement, where responding is intermittently reinforced by escape from an aversive stimulus, as they do under schedules of positive reinforcement.

3. It may seem a bit artificial that the bulk of the aversive control research has used electric shock as the aversive stimulus. After all, the occurrence of an electric shock is a relatively infrequent event in everyday affairs and virtually nonexistent in the natural environment of most animals. Nevertheless, it may be argued that any functionally identified aversive stimulus is behaviorally the same as any other in terms of the principles of behavior. And indeed, where other aversive stimuli have been used in research (e.g., heat, cold, wind), the principles of aversive control originally determined with electric shock seem to apply very nicely. Electric shock is so often used because it is easy to specify and to control and, thus, it is convenient for the researcher.

4. An alternative way of stating this relationship is to assert that organisms behaving under a CER paradigm will suppress in the presence of the CER stimulus, but only to an extent that will not lose them reinforcers under the baseline reinforcement schedule. In turn, this implies that the organism will form some sort of expectancy that involves the rate of occurrence or the density of programmed reinforcers in the presence of the CER stimulus.

5. Actually, the dependency of effects produced by experimental operations on the baseline rate of response applies more generally than just in the CER situation. Rate dependency refers to any situation where experimental operations tend to decrease high-rate behavior and to increase low-rate behavior.

6. In the instance where a CER stimulus paired with an appetitive reinforcer has been shown to suppress behavior maintained by positive reinforcement, the term "positive conditioned suppression" has been used. This positive CER seems to occur more reliably when the CER reinforcer and baseline reinforcer are different. When the two reinforcers are the same, a "conditioned facilitation" is more likely to occur.

7. In this and in subsequently presented hypotheses where the presentation of a primary aversive stimulus is asserted to produce suppressive effects, it is instructive to entertain the role played by secondary punishers, that is, by stimuli paired with the primary aversive stimulus. In the case of the punishment hypothesis of avoidance, it is to be expected that the CS in the cued-avoidance case would become a secondary punisher and, therefore, would also suppress any response that it shortly follows.

8. Since postresponse-time cues are supposedly related to events that correlate highly with the passage of time, postresponse-time cues provide a basis for the formation of a temporal discrimination under noncued-avoidance responding. Alternatively, since responding at different postresponse times (but before the

next shock) under noncued-avoidance procedures produces different amounts of reduction in presumed aversiveness, a potential source of differential reinforcement is inherent in the analysis. Organisms under noncued-avoidance schedules do tend to space their responses systematically across time. Whether this spaced responding results from the formation of a temporal discrimination or from differential reinforcement of different interresponse times (or both) is a point for debate among systematists.

9. Actually there is nothing inherent in anticipatory response theorizing that requires the response to move forward continuously so that it must at some time occur simultaneously with the aversive stimulus. Indeed, the response theoretically could become anticipatory in a quite discrete fashion bypassing altogether any simultaneity with the aversive event.

10. As a specific example, it would be predicted from this view that a CS, such as the abrupt dropping of a shuttle-box door, should facilitate avoidance learning, since this CS will elicit a startle response that is incompatible with freezing. The problem in this view is to identify what manipulations will inhibit a freezing response and to determine whether this identification needs to be a functional one made in terms of avoidance learning or whether it can be done independently of the avoidance paradigm.

11. Incentive theorists also have not generally dealt with overall reinforcement density as a parameter of incentive. Incentive constructs have typically been related only to the conditions of reinforcing and aversive stimuli in terms of their magnitude, quality, and delay. The conditions of reinforcing and aversive stimuli across time, that is, their rate or density, are usually given no separate status apart from their absolute number.

12. Although this presumption is in line with much physiological evidence and surely is plausible, the reader is reminded that fear is a hypothetical construct when conceptualized as a drive. Thus presumed, fear-drive stimuli need not be theoretically assigned to a particular locus of occurrence nor could one be established empirically.

13. Obviously it is not necessary always to study the effects of punishment as an interaction with the effects of reinforcement. For example, the unconditioned emission of behavior by organisms can be punished. However, in everyday affairs aversive stimuli do often intrude into ongoing behaviors maintained by reinforcement so that the observed effects of punishers are usually not pure but instead are influenced by the schedules and conditions of ongoing reinforcement as in the laboratory analog.

14. There is nothing inherent in either the avoidance or punishment paradigms that require that there be only one referent response. Several quantitatively and qualitatively different responses might be designated as referent responses under either paradigm. It is important, however, that each referent response enters into an identical operational contingency with the aversive stimulus. Thus, all referent responses are followed by shock in the punishment paradigm

and all referent responses are followed by the omission of shock in the avoidance paradigm.

15. Apparently the effects of an experimenter saying "wrong" following a response by the subject depends, in part, on the nature of the experimental task. Whereas "wrong" tends to increase responses in paired-associate tasks, "wrong" tends to suppress responses in more difficult concept-formation tasks.

16. Since punishment is typically specified functionally in terms of response suppression, any instance in which an aversive stimulus produces an increase in performance necessarily seems paradoxical. Of course, such increases in performance need not be viewed as paradoxical or contrary to a functional specification of punishers. Instead, as we have mentioned in previous discussion, it is possible to look toward setting operations and/or boundary conditions for explanations of the paradoxical effects. Recognition of the discriminative properties of aversive stimuli is only one instance of this.

17. A problem in observing competing responses is the obvious fact that an organism must always be doing something. Thus, if a punished referent response is reduced in frequency of occurrence, some other response(s) must of necessity increase in frequency of occurrence. The task is to discern whether the punished behavior is suppressed because of the occurrence of other behavior or whether other behavior occurs because the punished behavior is suppressed.

ABSTRACTS **Anger, D. The role of temporal discriminations in the reinforcement of Sidman avoidance behavior.** *Journal of the Experimental Analysis of Behavior,* **1963,** *6,* **477–506.**

Animals learn to avoid with the Sidman procedure even though the avoidance response is not followed by the termination of any warning stimulus in the environment. What reinforces this response? The accepted explanation has been that the avoidance response is reinforced when it terminates other behavior that has become aversive by pairing with shock. However, the reinforcement may also be derived from the temporal discriminations that develop with Sidman avoidance. These and other temporal discriminations show that the animal has available some events that vary with the postresponse time. The shock will closely follow the temporal stimuli at long postresponse times and would be expected to make them aversive. The stimuli at short postresponse times would have a relatively low aversiveness due to their more remote relation to shock. Since the avoidance response changes a long postresponse time to a short one, that response would be followed by a decrease in aversiveness which would reinforce it. When sharp temporal discriminations are present, reinforcement from the decrease in aversiveness of temporal stimuli probably plays a dominant role in maintaining the avoidance response.

Azrin, N.H. Some effects of two intermittent schedules of immediate and nonimmediate punishment. *Journal of Psychology,* **1956,** *42,* **3–21.**

The results of this experiment show that immediate punishment was far more effective than nonimmediate punishment in reducing the number of responses regardless of whether the shocks were scheduled after fixed intervals or variable intervals of time. Contrary to Estes' conclusions, these results show that the effectiveness of a punishment depends on the temporal relation between the response and that punishment.

The findings of this investigation are consistent with the view that aversive stimuli act in a direction opposite to that of reinforcers.

Azrin, N.H. Time-out from positive reinforcement. *Science,* **1961,** *133,* **382–383.**

When an organism can itself impose extinction during fixed-ratio food reinforcement, the duration of the extinction period is a function of the number of responses required for reinforcement. Typically, the subject imposes extinction at the start of the usual fixed-ratio run.

Azrin, N.H., & Hake, D.F. Positive conditioned suppression: Conditioned suppression using positive reinforcers as the unconditioned stimuli. *Journal of the Experimental Analysis of Behavior,* **1969,** *12,* **167–173.**

Research has revealed the phenomenon of conditioned suppression in which the rate of responding is reduced during a stimulus that is paired with noncontingent shock. The present study replicated this procedure, but used noncontingent positive reinforcers instead of the aversive shock. The lever-pressing responses of rats were reinforced with food or water. While the rats were responding, a stimulus was occasionally presented and paired with the delivery of a noncontingent positive reinforcer, which was either food, water, or brain stimulation for different rats. The result was a reduction in the rate of responding during the conditioned stimulus. The findings failed to support the interpretation that competing behavior caused the suppression. Another possible interpretation is that the reduction in response rate results from a general emotional state during presentation of a stimulus that is paired with any strong reinforcer, whether the reinforcer is positive or negative.

Blackman, D. Conditioned suppression or facilitation as a function of the behavorial baseline. *Journal of the Experimental Analysis of Behavior,* **1968,** *11,* **53–61.**

Rats were exposed to a multiple schedule of reinforcement. During one component, a barpress was followed by reinforcement only if it occurred between 15 and 20 sec. after the previous response. This differential-reinforcement-of-low-rate (DRL) schedule produced a typical slow rate of responding. During the other component, reinforcement followed the first response to be emitted during limited periods of time which occurred at fixed intervals. These fixed-interval schedules with a limited hold produced higher response rates, described as "interval" or "ratio-like" behavior. Responding during the DRL component increased in frequency during a tone which ended with an unavoidable shock of low intensity, but decreased during the tone when the shock intensity was raised. The "interval" and "ratio-like" responding decreased in frequency during the tone at all shock intensities. Initial acceleration of the DRL responding appeared to be due to adventitious punishment of collateral behavior which was observed between the bar-presses.

Boe, E.E., & Church, R.M. Permanent effects of punishment during extinction. *Journal of Comparative and Physiological Psychology,* 1967, *63,* 486–491.

Observations that a brief period of punishment at the beginning of extinction merely depresses performance temporarily but does not reduce the total number of responses emitted during the course of extinction have provided the strongest empirical basis for rejection of Thorndike's (1913) early view that punishment subtracts strength from a learned connection (the suppression hypothesis).

The lever-pressing response by rats was punished on an intermittent schedule with brief shocks during a 15-min. period at the beginning of extinction. In Experiment 1, total responses during both the punishment period and the entire course of extinction were an exponential decreasing function of punishment intensity. In Experiment 2, punishment (response-contingent shock) suppressed response rate more than noncontingent shocks during a brief punishment period and during subsequent extinction sessions. In both experiments, punishment produced a permanent reduction in the number of responses instead of only temporarily depressing response-rate. Thus a major reason for rejection of the suppression hypothesis is removed.

These results suggest that an adequate theoretical account of punishment must entail at least two factors, one of which requires response contingency and one that does not.

Bolles, R.C. Species-specific defense reactions and avoidance learning. *Psychological Review,* 1970, *77,* 32–48.

Starting with the assumption that animals have innate species-specific defense reactions (SSDRs) such as fleeing, freezing, and fighting, it is proposed that if a particular avoidance response is rapidly acquired, then that response must necessarily be an SSDR. The learning mechanism in this case appears to be suppression of nonavoidance behavior by the avoidance contingency. The traditional approaches to avoidance learning appear to be slightly more valid in the case of responses that are slowly acquired, although in this case, too, the SSDR concept is relevant, and reinforcement appears to be based on the production of a safety signal rather than the termination of an aversive conditioned stimulus.

Bolles, R.C. *Theory of Motivation.* New York: Harper & Row, 1967. (Ch. 14.)

Punishment does not itself change the strength of the response it follows, but provides the opportunity for other learning to occur, either directly or through the mediation of learned fear. *When punishment leads to learning, what is learned are the responses which the punisher elicits, including fear.* Punishment cannot produce the learning of any behavior other than that which it elicits. Fear has a widespread and diffuse effect; it elicits freezing and crouching, and these kinds of behavior compete most effectively with any other kind of behavior we care to punish. There are three distinct sources of stimulation that might be effective in controlling the alternative response. One is the environment, providing stimuli which, prior to punishment, controlled the punished response. The second is the feedback from the fear reaction produced by the punishment which generalizes more or less to the whole situation. And the third is the feedback (proprioceptive stimulus consequences) of the punished act itself.

This response-elicitation or response-competition account of punishment does not commit one to any particular theory of motivation. Different theoretical systems differ not on the question of what effect punishment has, but rather on the question of whether fear is involved. Not since Thorndike abandoned the idea that punishment weakens S-R associations has a major systematist defended it.

Brogden, W.J., Lipman, E.A., & Culler, E. The role of incentive in conditioning and extinctioning. *American Journal of Psychology,* 1938, *51,* 109–117.

How and when an incentive is applied determines the rate and character of resultant conditioning. Every stimulus asks a question or sets a task; and the CR which emerges constitutes the organism's reply to that question. The functional significance of CR is crucial in deciding what form it shall assume; and this significance is itself altered when the incentive is differentially applied.

Brown, J.S., Martin, R.C., & Morrow, M.W. Self-punitive behavior in the rat: Facilitative effects of punishment on resistance to extinction. *Journal of Comparative and Physiological Psychology,* 1964, *57,* 127–133.

In two experiments rats were trained to escape from an electrified start box and runway into a safe goal box. During subsequent "extinction" trials the start box was made safe for all *S*s, but some groups could not reach the safe goal box without enduring shock in part or all of the alley. *S*s shocked in this way in the first study failed to stop running sooner than those given no shock, and in the second study, shocked *S*s resisted extinction significantly longer than nonpunished *S*s. Fewer escape training trials, weaker shock, and more gradual transition from escape training to extinction characterized the second study relative to the first.

D'Amato, M.R., Fazzaro, J., & Etkin, M. Anticipatory responding and avoidance discrimination as factors in avoidance conditioning. *Journal of Experimental Psychology,* 1968, *77,* 41–47.

The hypothesis was advanced that prompt CS termination on CR trials reinforces avoidance acquisition because it serves as an excellent discriminative cue for US avoidance rather than because it leads to fear reduction. It was shown that a cue other than prompt CS termination could serve this function both in delayed and in trace avoidance conditioning paradigms.

Denny, M.R., & Weisman, R.G. Avoidance behavior as a function of length of nonshock confinement. *Journal of Comparative and Physiological Psychology,* 1964, *58,* 252–257.

The results were interpreted as calling drive reduction theorizing into question, while supporting an elicitation theory explanation of reinforcement in terms of response (relaxation-approach). Escape-avoidance behavior is learned as part of an extended behavior chain in which the terminal members are relaxation and approach. The escape component becomes conditioned to the cues associated with shock, while approach is conditioned to the cues associated with shock termination and relaxation. The conditioning follows a contiguity principle. Relaxation is response mediated and takes considerable time to occur. Extinction occurs when the relaxational responses have generalized to the original shock situation and compete with escape-avoidance behavior.

Dinsmoor, J.A. Punishment: I. The avoidance hypothesis. *Psychological Review,* 1954, *61,* 34–46.

The punished response is not an isolated incident, in vacuo, but a member of some sequence or chain of responses which is linked together by a series of discriminative, and thereby secondary reinforcing, stimuli. The stimuli which come immediately before the punished response are paired by the response itself with the ensuing punishment. By virtue of this pairing, they gain an aversive property in their own right. Any form of behavior which is incompatible with some member of the chain and delays the completion of the sequence will be reinforced, and thereby conditioned and maintained, by the corresponding elimination or transformation of these conditioned or secondary aversive stimuli. These responses are functionally equivalent to the responses which are investigated in a formal study of avoidance conditioning.

Estes, W.K. An experimental study of punishment. *Psychological Monographs,* 1944, *57* (3, Whole No. 263).

It appears that the effects of punishment upon the punished response are due to competing reactions aroused by the noxious stimulus. No evidence has been forthcoming to indicate that punishment exerts a direct weakening effect upon a response comparable to the strengthening produced by a reward. A disturbing or traumatic stimulus arouses a changed state of the organism of the sort commonly termed "emotional" and any stimulus present simultaneously with the disturbing stimulus becomes a conditioned stimulus capable of itself arousing the state on subsequent occasions. A great part of the initial effect of punishment is due to this sort of emotional conditioning. In addition to a generalized emotional reaction, a disturbing stimulus usually arouses a withdrawal response which can become conditioned to any stimulus which is contiguous with the disturbing stimulus. Part of the effect of punishment is probably a result of conflict between the competing responses.

The original response is not eliminated from the organism's repertoire, but continues to exist at a state of considerable latent strength. During extinction of withdrawal responses, the original response recovers in strength.

Estes, W.K. Outline of a theory of punishment. In B.A. Campbell & R.M. Church (Eds.), *Punishment and aversive behavior.* New York: Appleton-Century-Crofts, 1969. (Pp. 57–81.)

The primary mechanism of punishment is not a competition of responses but rather a competition of motives. The principal assumptions are (1) that maintenance of any type of nonreflex behavior involves the summation of discriminative or conditioned stimuli with the input of amplifier, or facilitative, elements from drive sources, and (2) that the activation of the negative-drive systems by pain or the anticipation of pain reciprocally inhibits amplifier input from positive-drive sources. Thus, a stimulus which has preceded a traumatic event, e.g., shock, as in the typical CER or punishment paradigm, acquires the capacity of inhibiting the input of amplifier elements from sources associated with hunger, thirst, and the like. If, then, while the animal is performing an instrumental response for, say, food reward, this conditioned stimulus is presented, the facilitative drive input will be reduced and so also the probability or rate of the instrumental response. If, on the other hand, the same stimulus is introduced while the animal is performing a response for escape from shock, there will be no similar reciprocal inhibition between drive sources and thus no suppressive effect.

Estes, W.K., & Skinner, B.F. Some quantitative properties of anxiety. *Journal of Experimental Psychology,* 1941, *29,* 390–400.

Anxiety is here defined as an emotional state arising in response to some current stimulus which in the past has been followed by a disturbing stimulus. The magnitude of the state is measured by its effect upon the strength of hunger-motivated behavior, in this case the rate with which rats pressed a lever under periodic reinforcement with food. Repeated presentations of a tone terminated by an electric shock produced a state of anxiety in response to the tone, the primary index being a reduction in strength of the hunger-motivated behavior during the period of the tone. When the shock was thus preceded by a period of anxiety, it produced a much more extensive disturbance in behavior than an "unanticipated" shock. The depression of the rate of responding during anxiety was characteristically followed by a compensatory increase in rate.

During experimental extinction of the response to the lever the tone produced a decrease in the rate of responding, and the terminating shock was followed by a compensatory increase in rate which probably restored the original projected height of the extinction curve.

Fowler, H., & Miller, N.E. Facilitation and inhibition of runway performance by hind- and forepaw shock of various intensities. *Journal of Comparative and Physiological Psychology,* 1963, *56,* 801–805.

Correlational data from several studies indicate that a punished act may be facilitated or inhibited depending on the nature of the response elicited by punishment. To demonstrate these effects experimentally and to assess alternative interpretations of them, 63 hungry rats were trained to run down an alley to food and different intensities of hind- or forepaw shock (0–75v) at the goal. The hindpaw shock Ss were speeded up and the forepaw Ss slowed down, with these effects being generally greater, the greater the shock intensity. These results fit well with drive-reduction theory in that responses elicited by hind- and forepaw shock and reinforced by escape from pain tend to be compatible and incompatible, respectively, with running. While these relationships are in accord with the reinforcement interpretation offered, the strength of fear and consequent tendency to "freeze" conditioned under more intense shock conditions could easily offset any facilitation of performance in the hindpaw shock condition under higher shock intensities.

Herrnstein, R.J. Method and theory in the study of avoidance. *Psychological Review,* 1969, *76,* 49–69.

Two-factor theories of avoidance were conceived to explain responding in avoidance procedures that closely resemble the Pavlovian paradigm in superficial features, although differing in the fundamental contingency of reinforcement. Both typically involve an arbitrary conditioned stimulus and a trial-by-trial sequence of pairings between the conditioned and unconditioned stimuli. According to two-factor theory, the instrumental reinforcement of avoidance is based on the Pavlovian reinforcement of a drive state in the presence of the conditioned stimulus. It has been shown, however, that the presence of the conditioned stimulus is not necessary for the occurrence of avoidance responding. A procedure in which the sole effect of the avoidance response was a reduction in the average frequency of occurrence of an aversive electric shock proved to be fully adequate to maintain lever pressing in rats, thereby suggesting that not all avoidance requires two factors. The conditioned stimulus may function as a discriminative stimulus for the avoidance response, rather than as a stimulus whose removal is inherently reinforcing, as two-factor theory requires.

Holz, W.C., & Azrin, N.H. Discriminative properties of punishment. *Journal of the Experimental Analysis of Behavior,* **1961,** *4,* **225–232.**

This experiment investigated the discriminative properties of punishment. It was found that when a severe punishment was differentially paired with reinforcement, punishment served to increase responding. Conversely, when an otherwise ineffective punishment was paired with extinction, punishment came to decrease responding.

The fact that punishment does not always suppress responding is often taken as evidence that punishment is an ineffective method of controlling behavior. However, in such cases the discriminative properties the punishment may have acquired should be considered.

Another example of the alleged ineffectiveness of punishment is the finding (Estes, 1944) that punishment does not reduce the number of responses required for extinction. Punishment was initiated at the same time that extinction was begun, so that the punishment is associated with extinction and the termination of punishment reinstated the stimulus situation associated with reinforcement. The discriminative property of this absence of punishment is sufficient to account for the increase of responding that was observed.

Kamin, L.J. The effects of termination of the CS and avoidance of the US on avoidance learning. *Journal of Comparative and Physiological Psychology,* **1956,** *49,* **420–424.**

The empirical facts are clear: both termination of the CS and avoidance of the US contribute to the frequency and latency of CRs. While a combination of CS termination and US avoidance leads to the strongest responding, either of these factors alone adds substantially to response strength. The efficacy of CS termination scarcely seems deducible from a cognitive theory. The efficacy of US avoidance, however, poses problems for any S-R theory.

Kamin, L.J. The delay of punishment gradient. *Journal of Comparative and Physiological Psychology,* **1959,** *52,* **434–437.**

The very well known work of Estes (1944) seems largely to have diverted attention from the temporal factors involved in punishment. Random delivery of punishment, under the conditions of Estes' experiment, inhibited barpressing as much as did punishment immediately following the response. This fact led Estes and others to regard the effects of punishment as relatively nonspecific, and primarily "emotional."

This study reports two experiments concerned with the effects of varying the interval between a learned response and punishment. The Ss were 108 hooded rats given shuttlebox avoidance training to a criterion. The Ss were divided into two groups, and resistance to extinction of the avoidance response was tested with punishment (shock) after no delay, or after 10, 20,

30, or 40 sec. of delay, or without punishment. The inhibitory effect of punishment was in each study a declining monotonic function of delay, suggesting that punishment acts in a manner formally analogous but opposite to reward. The no-punishment groups, however, made significantly more responses than did groups with the longest delays of punishment, supporting Estes' conclusion that punishment has nonspecific, "emotional" effects.

Logan, F.A. The negative incentive value of punishment. In B.A. Camp-bell & R.M. Church (Eds.), *Punishment and aversive behavior.* **New York: Appleton-Century-Crofts, 1969. (Pp. 43–53.)**

The assumption that the effects of punishment are symmetrically opposite to the effects of reward, first stated with respect to learning in the original law of effect, is here proposed with respect to incentive motivation. The assumption is that rewards and punishments do not affect learning directly, their effect on performance being motivational in nature. The net value of an alternative thus depends jointly on the positive incentive associated with the reward and the negative incentive associated with the punishment.

This approach was evaluated experimentally by first training hungry rats in a choice between two alternatives that differed in food reward, and then introducing punishment in the preferred alternative. More specifically, two differences in amount of reward and one difference in delay of reward, all of which had previously been shown to be approximately equivalent in differential positive incentive, were pitted against gradually increasing intensities of shock punishment. In general, the expectation that the same intensity of punishment would be required to reverse the preference based on these differentials in reward was confirmed. Furthermore, partial (50%) punishment was less effective in reversing preference, and it was tentatively estimated that its negative incentive value is less than half that of continuous punishment. Finally, larger reward differentials required stronger shock intensities.

The results of the research are generally consistent with the hypothesis that aversive stimuli given as punishers for selecting one response in preference to another can be understood in terms of a negative incentive construct. Choice is based upon the *net*-incentive motivation associated with each alternative. In short, the parameters of reward determine the value of positive incentive motivation and the parameters of punishment determine the value of negative incentive motivation, and these combine to determine preference for one response over another.

A negative incentive approach toward punishment does not necessarily deny other possible effects of aversive stimuli. The role of aversive stimuli as stimuli and elicitors of responses need to be included in a complete account of punishment. Nevertheless, aversive stimuli given consequent upon a response affect the net-incentive motivation for selecting that response.

LoLordo, V.M. Similarity of conditioned fear responses based upon different aversive events. *Journal of Comparative and Physiological Psychology,* **1967,** *64,* **154–158.**

A new technique was employed to determine whether classically conditioned emotional responses (*CER*s) based upon electric shocks and loud noises were similar. While 8 dogs depressed a panel to avoid electric shock on a Sidman avoidance schedule, they received classical conditioning trials in which CS+ was followed by an unavoidable loud noise US; a second stimulus served as CS−. A classical extinction procedure followed. CS+ acquired the capacity to produce a large increase in rate of avoidance, which disappeared in extinction. These outcomes suggest that CS+ elicited a CER which was similar to the fear response that supports avoidance behavior, and in this way mediated an increase in avoidance rate.

McKearney, J.W. Fixed-interval schedules of electric shock presentation: Extinction and recovery of performance under different shock intensities and fixed-interval durations. *Journal of the Experimental Analysis of Behavior,* **1969,** *12,* **301–313.**

In squirrel monkeys responding under a schedule in which responding postponed the delivery of electric shock, the presentation of *response-dependent shock* under a fixed-interval (FI) schedule increased the rate of responding. When the schedule of shock-postponement was eliminated, so that the only shocks delivered were those produced by responses under the FI schedule, a pattern of positively accelerated responding developed and was maintained over an extended period. When responses did not produce shocks (extinction), responding decreased. When shocks were again presented under the FI schedule, the previous pattern of responding quickly redeveloped. In general, response rates were directly related to the intensity of the shock presented, and inversely related to the duration of the fixed-interval. These results raise fundamental questions about the traditional classification of stimuli as reinforcers or punishers. The basic similarities among FI schedules of food presentation, shock termination, and shock presentation strengthen the conclusion that the schedule under which an event is presented and the characteristics of the behavior at the time the event is presented, are of overriding importance in determining the effect of that event on behavior.

Miller, N.E. Studies of fear as an acquirable drive: I. Fear as motivation and fear-reduction as reinforcement in the learning of new responses. *Journal of Experimental Psychology,* **1948,** *38,* **89–101.**

Albino rats were placed in a simple apparatus consisting of two compartments separated by a door. One was white with a grid as a floor; the other was black without a grid. Before training, the animals showed no marked preference for either compartment. Then they were placed in the white compartment, received an electric shock from the grid, and escaped into the black compartment through the open door. After a number of such trials, the animals would run out of the white compartment even if no shock was on the grid.

To demonstrate that an acquired drive (fear or anxiety) had been established, the animals were taught a *new* habit *without further shocks*. The door (always previously open) was closed. The only way that the door could be opened was by rotating a little wheel, which was above the door, a fraction of a turn. Under these conditions, the animals exhibited trial-and-error behavior and gradually learned to escape from the white compartment by rotating the wheel.

Responses which produce strong stimuli are the basis for acquired drives; such responses may be the basis for certain of the phenomena of learning labeled "expectancy" and neurotic symptoms may be motivated by anxiety and reinforced by anxiety-reduction like the two new responses learned in this experiment.

Mowrer, O.H., & Aiken, E.G. Contiguity vs. drive-reduction in conditioned fear: Temporal variations in conditioned and unconditioned stimulus. *American Journal of Psychology,* 1954, *67,* 26–38.

The results obtained confirm the view that fear-learning occurs more readily (only?) when the initially neutral stimulus is contiguous with the onset of shock than when it is contiguous with the termination of shock. These findings, like those of the preceding study by Mowrer and Solomon, are consistent with the view that there are two basically different forms of learning: sign-learning (conditioning, stimulus-substitution, place-learning) and solution-learning (trial-and-error, response substitution, problem-solving, act-learning). No monistic conception of learning, including Hull's, seems capable of accounting for the presently known facts in a reasonably inclusive and consistent manner.

Mowrer, O.H., & Lamoreaux, R.R. Fear as an intervening variable in avoidance conditioning. *Journal of Comparative and Physiological Psychology,* 1946, *39,* 29–50.

A successful attempt was made to establish conditioned responses which were radically different from the type of response which our rats made to an unconditioned stimulus. Since traditional associationism cannot easily account for our results, we offer an alternative hypothesis.

The electric shock was a primary drive. The conditioned stimulus aroused the secondary drive of fear. If conditions are such that one type of response is necessary to eliminate the primary drive and a different response to eliminate the secondary drive, then the so-called CR and the UnCR will tend to differ appropriately. Thus two distinct sources of reinforcement are detected in avoidance conditioning.

Muenzinger, K.F. Motivation in learning: I. Electric shock for correct response in the visual discrimination habit. *Journal of Comparative Psychology,* **1934,** *17,* **267–277.**

Three groups of rats were taught a black-white discrimination habit with the usual hunger-food tension. The first group was shocked while it traversed the correct alley, the second was shocked in the orthodox fashion while in the wrong alley, and the third was not shocked at all.

The no shock group was definitely inferior to the two shock groups. The distributions of trials to learning criterion and number of errors of the two shock groups were practically coextensive.

On the basis of these facts one may say that the function of moderate electric shock in the visual discrimination habit is general rather than specific, that is, it affects the total performance rather than the part-response it accompanies. Its function is to make the animal respond more readily to the significant cues in the learning situation rather than that of inhibiting or facilitating the response which is shocked.

The results flatly contradict that part of the law of effect which deals with the after-effects of annoyers.

Premack, D. Catching up with common sense or two sides of a generalization. In R. Glaser (Ed.), *The nature of reinforcement.* **New York: Academic Press, 1971. (Pp. 121–150.)**

All motivational phenomena are generated by preference, by the differences in value which normal subjects characteristically assign to the events in their environment. Value can be measured directly by the probability that the subject will respond to the events in question, making it possible to state all motivational functions in terms of response probabilities. The two functions we considered here, reinforcement and punishment, can be stated as follows. If a more probable response is made contingent upon a less probable one, the result will be facilitation—an increase in the base event. If a less probable response is made contingent upon a more probable one, the result will be suppression—a decrement in the base event. Reinforcement and punishment are therefore opposite sides of the same operation; the conditions which make one possible also make the other possible.

Sheffield, F.D. Avoidance training and the contiguity principle. *Journal of Comparative and Physiological Psychology,* **1948,** *41,* **165–177.**

Guinea pigs were trained to run to tone in an activity wheel using unavoidable and avoidable shock situations. It was found that unavoidable shock, administered regardless of the occurrence of a conditioned run, did not consistently evoke running as unconditioned response when shock came during a conditioned run. Rather, the shock under these conditions often evoked behavior incompatible with running. It was further found that the running or non-running character of this unconditioned response determined whether the probability of obtaining conditioned running increased or decreased, respectively, on the following trial. Successive avoidances of shock when a conditioned run prevented shock led to extinction rather than to strengthening of the conditioned response.

The results are interpreted as showing that omission of shock has no strengthening effect and as consistent with the contiguity theory of learning.

Sidman, M. Avoidance conditioning with brief shock and no exteroceptive warning signal. *Science,* 1953, *118,* 157–158.

White rats were the experimental organisms, with lever pressing selected as the avoidance response. Shocks of a fixed 0.2 sec. duration were given to the animal at regular intervals unless the lever was depressed. Each lever depression reset the timer controlling the shock, thus delaying its appearance. The avoidance behavior generated by this procedure can be explained by a model which holds that avoidance responding increases in rate at the expense of other behavior that is depressed by shock. An equivalent statement, in reinforcement terms, is that the avoidance response is strengthened when it terminates incompatible behavior that has been paired with shock. Several lines of evidence indicate that the avoidance rate is not simply some form of temporal conditioning.

Sidman, M. Reduction of shock frequency as reinforcement for avoidance behavior. *Journal of the Experimental Analysis of Behavior,* 1962, *5,* 247–257.

An avoidance technique was used in which rats had two levers available, with independent shock schedules associated with each. Behavioral patterns in initial conditioning and in the maintenance of the responses with various response-shock intervals led to the suggestion that reduction of shock density be considered an important variable in avoidance behavior.

Skinner, B.F. *Science and human behavior.* New York: Macmillan, 1953. (Ch. 12.)

The commonest technique of control in modern life is punishment. The degree to which we use punishment as a technique is limited only by the degree to which we can gain the necessary power. In the long run, punishment works to the disadvantage of all. The aversive stimuli which are needed generate emotions, including dispositions to escape or retaliate, and disabling anxieties.

Punishment produces an immediate effect in reducing a tendency to behave. But the reduction in strength is not permanent.

The first effect of the aversive stimulus used in punishment is confined to the

immediate situation and involves the elicitation of incompatible behavior—
the responses appropriate, for example, to fear or emotional predispositions.
As a second effect of punishment, behavior which has consistently been
punished becomes the source of conditioned stimuli which evoke incompatible behavior. In none of these cases, however, have we supposed that the
punished response is permanently weakened. It is merely temporarily suppressed, more or less effectively, by an emotional reaction.

If a given response is followed by an aversive stimulus, any stimulation which
accompanies the response, whether it arises from the behavior itself or from
concurrent circumstances, will be conditioned. *Any behavior which reduces
this conditioned aversive stimulation will be reinforced.* The most important
effect of punishment, then, is to establish aversive conditions which are
avoided by any behavior of "doing something else." Technically we may say
that further punishment is avoided. If punishment is repeatedly avoided, the
conditioned negative reinforcer undergoes extinction. Incompatible behavior
is less strongly reinforced, and the punished behavior eventually emerges. No
change in the strength of the punished response is implied.

**Stein, L., Sidman, M., & Brady, J.V. Some effects of two temporal varia-
bles on conditioned suppression.** *Journal of the Experimental Analysis of
Behavior,* **1958,** *1,* **151–162.**

The experiment investigated two temporal variables in the Estes-Skinner con-
ditioned-suppression situation namely the stimulus and between-stimulus durations. When stimulus duration was short relative to the duration of the
stimulus-off interval, good suppression was produced and when stimulus
duration was relatively long, poor suppression was produced. The number of
reinforcements obtained under each condition was relatively constant in spite
of wide differences in suppression indicating that the strength of suppression
decreases to the extent that such suppression reduces opportunities for positive reinforcement. After sufficient training, animals will suppress in the stimulus period only to an extent that does not markedly reduce opportunities for
positive reinforcement.

EXAMINATION ITEMS   **Topics for thought and discussion**

1.   Define "avoidable punishment" as a procedure in which the organism can perform a second response to preclude the aversive event otherwise contingent on the
first (reinforced) response. Make a prediction (relative to controls that receive a
matched frequency of unavoidable punishment) about the effects of this procedure
using any theoretical alternative that suits the purpose.

2.   In *Walden Two* (1948), Skinner designed a Utopian community that did not use
punishment in the control of behavior. Discuss Skinner's fundamental idea from both
the empirical and theoretical standpoints.

3.   An eminent psychologist once advocated the following procedure for helping
another person break a bad habit: force him to repeat the act without interruption until

it becomes painful. What is known about punishment that would justify this procedure?

Objective items

1. The punishment hypothesis of avoidance presumes which type of punishment definition?
   a. operational
   b. theoretical
   c. functional
   d. relative

2. "Time out from reinforcement" is an operant procedure under which a reinforced response is disabled for some period of time. This procedure would be best described as involving
   a. primary positive punishment
   b. primary negative punishment
   c. secondary positive punishment
   d. secondary negative punishment

3. Which of the following procedures least involves a contingency with respect to an aversive event?
   a. punishment
   b. conditioned emotional response
   c. escape learning
   d. avoidance learning

4. One of the complexities in studying conditions of punishment is that punishment can only be studied in the context of reinforcement.
   a. True
   b. False

5. Data that indicate that a response-contingent aversive stimulus is more effective than a noncontingent aversive stimulus in producing suppression can be made consistent with Estes' (1944) interpretation of the punishment process.
   a. True
   b. False

6. One of the important functions of the secondary drive of fear is that it
   a. makes the person less sensitive to the environment
   b. interferes with adaptive behavior
   c. reduces the reinforcement of responses
   d. brings with it responses learned in other frightening situations

7. Which of the following statements about punishment is *inconsistent* with Guthrie's theory of contiguous conditioning?
   a. punishment can disrupt ongoing behavior
   b. punishment can enhance ongoing behavior
   c. punishment can produce maintaining stimuli that act like a drive
   d. punishment can fixate or increase stereotopy of behavior

8. Theoretically at least, self-punitive behavior would be most likely to occur if the response was acquired under conditions of
   a. positive control with immediate consequences

b. postive control with delayed consequences
c. aversive control with immediate consequences
d. aversive control with delayed consequences

9. The functional definition of punishment is
a. the occurrence of an event following a response that leads to a decrease in the future likelihood of that response
b. the presentation of an aversive event following a response
c. selective suppression of behavior by stimuli associated with an aversive event
d. negative reinforcement of a response

10. The use of the expression, "passive avoidance" for the operation that defines punishment presumes that the best theoretical account of the effects of this operation is
a. a decrease in drive motivation
b. an increase in drive motivation
c. a decrease in incentive motivation
d. an increase in incentive motivation

11. Which hypothesis regarding the CER would be most troubled by a finding that response suppression occurs to the first presentation of a CER stimulus following stimulus-shock pairings conducted "off the behavioral baseline?"
a. punishment
b. competing response
c. emotional response
d. generalization decrement

12. The finding that a CER stimulus paired with a food US will suppress a bar-press response maintained by appetitive reinforcers follows most readily from which theoretical analysis of the CER?
a. cognitive
b. generalization decrement
c. incentive
d. emotional response

13. Which of the following referent-response contingencies is the *least* efficacious in avoidance learning?
a. termination of the CS and no shock omission
b. termination of the CS and shock omission
c. no termination of the CS and shock omission
d. presentation of a safety signal and shock omission

14. Which of the following empirical characteristics of avoidance learning could be most readily accounted for in terms of escape from the primary aversive stimulus?
a. prolonged acquisition of the avoidance response
b. prolonged extinction of the avoidance response
c. avoidance acquisition when no escape response is required
d. avoidance acquisition using different avoidance and escape responses

15. The finding that complete response suppression by punishment may endure is most easily accounted for by which type of theoretical approach to punishment?
a. cognitive
b. drive reduction
c. emotional response

d. competing response

16. According to the escape from secondary aversive stimulus analysis of punishment, the mechanism which produces response suppression primarily involves
    a. incompatible responses
    b. associative weakening
    c. stimulus-generalization decrement
    d. net incentive

17. The finding that shock onset is more effective than shock offset in producing CER suppression theoretically appears to discredit the usefulness of interpreting CER data theoretically in terms of
    a. drive-reduction reinforcement only
    b. need-reduction reinforcement only
    c. both drive- and need-reduction reinforcement
    d. both drive and need reduction, but actually it does not

18. The shock-density analysis of avoidance learning involves which type of reinforcement definition?
    a. operational
    b. drive reduction
    c. transsituational
    d. relative

19. A strict empiricist would oppose an interpretation of CER data in terms of a fear-drive hypothesis, but the empiricist also would be likely to object to an assertion that the hypothesis is
    a. abstract
    b. insufficient
    c. circular
    d. reductive

20. An associative strength model of punishment would involve the development of
    a. competing responses
    b. inhibitory processes
    c. emotional responses
    d. no new responses or processes

ANSWERS TO OBJECTIVE ITEMS

1. (c) The essence of the punishment hypothesis of avoidance is that the presentation of aversive stimuli will reduce the frequency of all responses, except for the designated avoidance response. Thus, punishment is defined in terms of a behavioral change—the hallmark of a functional definition.

2. (d) Presumably the response is disabled by the removal of a stimulus that enables the response. Since the enabling stimulus is associated with reinforcement, it would be considered secondary reinforcement. Thus, the procedure boils down to the removal of a secondary reinforcer, that is, to secondary negative punishment.

3. (b) The term, "contingency," has been used in several ways which includes simple pairing operations such as in the CER procedure. However, the text has used the term in the sense of a temporal correlation between a response and the occurrence of an emotionally significant event.

4. (False) It is true that punishment is typically studied in the context of reinforcement and is affected by the possible relationship between their schedules and condi-

tions. However, one could perfectly well examine the effects of the punishment of a response with a measurable operant level.

5.   (True) Estes (1944) argued that the response contingency was not important. In light of data to the contrary, Estes could argue that emotional responses become conditioned to proprioceptive stimuli produced by the response and, thereby, could conclude that a response-contingent-aversive stimulus is more effective.

6.   (d) Theoretically, fear is a drive that has stimulus properties and, therefore, can enter into learned associations with responses. These associations can have a variety of effects, but the important factor is that they are specific to the fear drive.

7.   (c) Punishment can elicit incompatible or compatible behavior, and it can serve as a change in the stimulus situation that will protect previously occurring behavior. However, punishment does not produce maintaining stimuli that remain with the organism in the absence of the punisher in the sense that deprivation operations do.

8.   (b) In self-punitive behavioral situations, organisms expose themselves to aversive situations that they later escape. This behavior situation is more likely to occur the more alike the original training condition is to the later test situation.

9.   (a) A functional definition is always stated in terms of changes in behavior and presumes, at least, a temporal contingency with respect to behavior.

10. (c) The "passive avoidance" analysis of punishment states that an organism avoids punishment by not making the punished response. The punished response is inhibited, because it is associated with negative incentive. Thus, incentive is reduced when the response is inhibited.

11. (a) Unlike the other alternatives, the punishment hypothesis does not involve the conditioning of responses to the CER stimulus that can occur in any context. Instead, the punishment hypothesis proposes a suppression effect that is particular to the baseline situation itself.

12.   (b) The generalization decrement is relatively straightforward in that the introduction of any new stimulus, including the CER stimulus, will alter the stimulus situation and, thereby, reduce responding. The other alternatives must predict an increase in responding to the CER stimulus, if they predict any change at all.

13. (c) Only this alternative does not involve some manipulation with respect to the CS, which seems to be the *most* critical factor sustaining avoidance learning.

14. (a) This empirical outcome is the only one not directly in opposition to the conception that the avoidance response is an anticipatory form of the response that escapes shock and that thereby is reinforced by terminating the shock.

15. (a) Actually none of the approaches handle the finding particularly well. The cognitive approach is most appropriate, because it does not postulate S-R associations based on the presence of punishment as do the other three alternatives; the expectancy of punishment can endure in the absence of the punished response.

16. (a) According to this analysis, any response that is incompatible with the punished response is reinforced by the termination of aversive stimuli associated with the punished response and, thus, becomes prepotent with respect to the punished response.

17. (d) These particular findings demonstrate the more general case that theoretical

constructs tend not to be rendered useless by empirical data but rather by other (better) theoretical constructs. Furthermore, the distinction between drive and need reduction is less distinct for aversive than for appetitive situations.

18. (d) Th critical element for the analysis is the density of shock, given a response, relative to the prevailing density of shock, given no response. The absolute density of shock is not relevant nor is it applicable in other situations or procedures.

19. (b) Fear as a drive is a hypothetical construct and, as such, is opposed by empiricists in terms of its circularity, etc. However, the empiricist does not deny that the data can be sufficiently well explained by a hypothetical construct, if one has the inclination to use one.

20. (d) The essence of a strength model is that associative strength is directly altered without the influence of other processes. Thus, reinforcement directly strengthens, and punishment directly weakens associative strength.

CHAPTER SEVEN

SYSTEMATIC ANALYSES OF TRANSITIONAL BEHAVIOR

Transitional behavior refers to any *changes* in behavior that accompany a sustained, operational change in the environment, such as a change in the stimulus situation, the conditions of reward, or the contingencies or requirements of the response. Thus, a large portion of the psychology of learning and motivation, both at the empirical and theoretical levels, is actually devoted to the systematic analysis of transitional behavior. Indeed, much of what has been written in the preceding chapters relates directly to transitional behavior. Consider that learning or the acquisition of associations represents but one specific instance of transitional behavior where the operational change involves causing a reinforcer shortly to follow a response. Similarly, the introduction of a punisher shortly following a response is an operational change that allows for the study of behavioral transitions from the prepunishment to the punishment states.

An operational definition of transitional behavior is sufficient for the purposes of the present chapter. Although transitional behavior can clearly be defined functionally in terms of some specified directional change in behavior, it is not necessary to do so. Furthermore, it is simply inappropriate theoretically to assign specific properties to transitional behavior. Transitional behavior is not necessarily transitory, nor is it necessarily recoverable.

However, transitional behavior may be usefully dichotomized into those behaviors that accompany differentiated operational changes in the environment and those behaviors that accompany nondifferentiated operational changes. The *differential* category is composed of all operational changes that are accompanied by a concomitant change in the exteroceptive antecedent stimulus situation. A ready example of this is conventional discrimination learning where each operational change from reinforcement to nonreinforcement is signaled by a correlated change from an S^+ to an S^- exteroceptive stimulus. *Nondifferential* transitional behaviors are those behaviors that accompany operational changes that are not signalled by concomitant changes in the exteroceptive antecedent stimulus situation. A simple unsignalled change in the magnitude of the reinforcer exemplifies a nondifferential transitional operation.

The present chapter will deal almost exclusively with systematic analyses of nondifferential transitional behaviors. Differential transitional behaviors will be more fully discussed in Chapter 8. This division may be considered arbitrary. Nevertheless, the domain of transitional behavior is simply too broad to be dealt with justly in a single chapter. Although there are communalities between systematic analyses of differential and nondifferential transitional operations, the empirical and theoretical treatments of these historically have been distinct.

Another boundary condition to be discussed in this present chapter needs to be stated at the outset. Specifically, we will primarily discuss those nondifferential transitional behaviors that are related to changes in the conditions and schedules of reinforcers in the discrete-trial context. The reason for this is quite straightforward. With some very notable exceptions (e.g., Weiss, 1970), the majority of systematic analyses of transitional behavior involving changes in the conditions and schedules of reinforcers, which have been made within other conditioning contexts, have involved differential transitional behavior (e.g., Bloomfield, 1969; Nevin & Shettleworth, 1966).

In discussing the conditions and schedules of reinforcers, we will retain the distinction previously made by Logan and Ferraro (1970). The conditions of a reinforcer are its momentary descriptive properties: magnitude, delay, and so on. A schedule refers to a programmed sequence of reinforcers. Thus, in general, conditions describe *what* reinforcers happen, and schedules describe *when* reinforcers happen.

There is one experimental operation where this distinction between conditions and schedules of reinforcers becomes difficult to discern, namely, in the operation of experimental extinction. Operationally, experimental extinction is defined as the nondelivery of a reinforcer that has a nonzero magnitude and a finite delay. Alternatively, extinction can be conceptualized as the delivery of a reinforcer having a zero magnitude and/or an infinite delay. In other words, experimental extinction represents a point of intersection between schedules and conditions of reinforcers inasmuch as experimental extinction represents a mutual endpoint for both the probability of reinforcers (a schedule property) and the magnitude and delay of reinforcers (conditions of reinforcers). This representation assumes that experimental extinction is not orthogonal to all schedules and conditions of reinforcers. Indeed, a zero probability of reinforcement is assumed to be on a continuum with increasing probabilities of reinforcement up to a probability of unity. Similarly, a zero-reinforcer magnitude and an infinte-reinforcer delay are assumed, respectively, to lie on a continuum with decreasing reinforcer magnitudes and increasing reinforcer delays. Since experimental extinction stands in a unique position with respect to the probability and conditions of reinforcers, we will begin our discussion of specific systematic analyses of transitional behaviors by considering the extinction situation.

TRANSITIONAL BEHAVIOR IN EXPERIMENTAL EXTINCTION

The experimental operation of extinction is quite simple; the task of systematically analyzing the transitional behavior that accompanies experimental extinction is not. Operationally, extinction involves a change in reinforcer probability from a nonzero value (we will assume unity in this section) to a value of zero. In other words, extinction involves the consistent nonreinforcement of a previously reinforced response. Transitional behavior in experimental extinction situations has most often been described, functionally, as the eventual reduction in the performance of a previously reinforced response.

Systematic analyses of experimental extinction have been primarily concerned with accounting for the fact that the performance of previously maintained behavior decreases after an operational change from conditioning to extinction. These analyses have met with varying success in attempting to account for the rate, the extent, and the permanence of the observed transitional behavioral changes. Several empirical phenomena are important in this latter regard. Among these are the general findings: first, that rate of extinction is increased when extinction trials are massed as opposed to spaced (e.g., Hill & Spear, 1962; Krane & Ison, 1971). Second, the rate of extinction is inversely related to the magnitude of the reinforcer experienced prior to the transition to extinction (e.g., Hulse, 1958; Wagner, 1961). Still other empirical phenomena of extinction will arise in the context of discussing separate systematic analyses. However, there is one extinction phenomenon that is important to all systematic analyses of simple extinction, namely, the phenomenon of spontaneous recovery. Third, *spontaneous recovery* refers to the empirical fact that following a period of time away from the experimental extinction situation, a reintroduction to the extinction situation is accompanied by an increase in performance of the referent response relative to the performance that prevailed at the end of the previous extinction experience.

Before turning to the discussion of the various theoretical analyses of transitional behavior in experimental extinction, the reader can anticipate that although each of the separate analyses is capable of handling some of the empirical findings on experimental extinction, none of them is capable of handling all of the existing data. In part, this is a result of the process of theory construction. A theorist of extinction must adopt some theoretical assumptions about the origins of the behavior that is to be subjected to the extinction operation. Once the learning assumptions are made, the dictums of theory construction involving parsimony and internal consistency severely limit the hypothetical constructs that may be reasonably adopted by the theorist in order to explain extinction. This is true even though theories of extinction have typically been limited in scope and are not usually of the "big theory" type. Nevertheless, it will become evident that often separate theoretical analyses of extinction are compatible with one another and that a hybrid mixture of two or more theoretical analyses is conceivable and, at times, even desirable.

Cognitive (S-S) Analyses

EXPECTANCY

The fundamental analysis of simple extinction that develops from S-S cognitive expectancy theory (Tolman, 1932) is easy to grasp conceptually, since extinction does not involve any new processes nor is it assigned any new properties. The hypothetical mechanism of extinction is symmetric but opposite in direction to that of reinforcement. Reinforcement serves to confirm S-S expectancies, and the nonoccurrence of reinforcement serves to disconfirm S-S expectancies. Since performance of behavior is related, in part, to the strength of the S-S association, disconfirmation of the expectancy leads directly to a reduction in the performance of the response.

It is not in the spirit of S-S cognitive theory to explain in detail all transitional behavioral changes that accompany an operational change from acquisition to extinction. After all, responses are not required either for an expectancy to be confirmed or for an expectancy to be disconfirmed; confirmations and disconfirmations are cognitive, perceptual matters. It follows from this that referent responses do not need to be executed in order to be extinguished.

Evidence supporting this latter contention can be drawn from several quarters, but it suffices here to note that latent extinction is a reasonably well-established empirical phenomenon (Gonzalez & Shepp, 1965; Moltz, 1957; Seward & Levy, 1949). *Latent extinction* refers to the fact that organisms who are permitted to experience the environment in which reinforcement has been previously received, but without actually receiving reinforcement, will subsequently extinguish responses that lead to that environment more rapidly than will organisms not permitted such experience. In the conventional discrete-trial situation, animals who have repeatedly been placed directly into the distinctive but empty goal box will extinguish responses more rapidly than will animals who have not been placed in the goal box.

There are certain notable parallels between the S-S cognitive theorists' treatments of the latent extinction and latent learning phenomena. Like latent learning, latent extinction is viewed by cognitive theorists as providing a direct challenge to S-R theory. If the referent response does not need to be executed in order for it to be extinguished, perhaps the referent response is not an important constituent of learned associations. As in the case of latent learning, S-R theorists answer the challenge posed by latent extinction in terms of motivational factors rather than in terms of the associative factors being questioned. Instead of waivering in their understanding of the nature of learned associations, S-R theorists typically interpret latent extinction as a procedure under which secondary reinforcement associated with the goal box is extinguished or incentive motivation is reduced. Consequently, more rapid extinction, which follows latent extinction experiences, reflects no weakening of associative strength. The latent extinction phenomenon essentially reflects a decrease in the motivation to perform previously learned associations. Needless to say, the controversy surrounding the latent extinction phenomenon has not been concluded definitively in favor of either S-S or S-R theory.

DISCRIMINATION HYPOTHESIS

There is no gainsaying that the stimulus situation prevailing in extinction is different from that which previously existed in acquisition. Most obviously, extinction does not include the reinforcing stimulus. But extinction also does not include the proprioceptive stimuli that result from interactions with the reinforcer, nor any consequent changes in drive level (Barry, 1958). Furthermore, the nondelivery of reinforcers may occasion changes in the parameters of the extinction situation from those used in acquisition, and these changes may be viewed as giving rise to additional differences in the stimulus situation. Such parameter changes might include changes in the interval of time the subject is retained in the previous reinforcement situation (e.g., the goal box of an alley) or in the intertrial interval (Capaldi, 1966; Hulse, 1958; Sheffield, 1950).

When it relies solely on the disconfirmation of expectancies, S-S cognitive theory is not convincing in accounting for the phenomena of extinction. Its explanatory power is enhanced, however, when the theoretical analysis is expanded to incorporate the differences that exist between the stimulus situations that prevail in acquisition and extinction. Consider that if an expectancy is to be disconfirmed by extinction, the organism first needs to discriminate between the acquisition and extinction situations; that is, the organism must discern that a transition to the extinction operation has been made.

Mowrer and Jones (1945) are generally credited with first proposing what has become known as the discrimination hypothesis of extinction. The hypothesis is that resistance to extinction will be directly related to the difficulty of discriminating the extinction situation from the acquisition situation. In the context of S-S expectancy extinction theory, organisms continue to respond in extinction until they come to discriminate that extinction is in effect and, thus, realize that their expectancy of reinforcement is not any longer valid. Considering the inverse relationship between reinforcer magnitude and resistance to extinction in this context, large magnitude reinforcers yield less responding in extinction, because it is easier to discriminate large reinforcers from extinction than it is to discriminate small reinforcers from extinction.

Although the cognitive-expectancy discrimination hypothesis of extinction can be intuitively pleasing, it is not well anchored theoretically. For example, one cannot always predict the degree of difficulty of the discrimination involved in the transition from a particular acquisition operation to extinction. More often, one is left to infer the difficulty of the discrimination from the extent of response persistence in extinction.

COGNITIVE DISSONANCE

Another distinctly different cognitive concept regarding experimental extinction of previously learned behavior, which is also poorly anchored conceptually, stems from cognitive dissonance theory (Festinger, 1961; Lawrence & Festinger, 1962). As applied to simple extinction situations, cognitive dissonance theory contends that organisms form expectancies about the conditions of reinforcement during acquisition. If an organism then performs a response that is not completely justified by the reinforcer experienced, cognitive dissonance is said to occur. For example, little cognitive dissonance occurs if a rat runs rapidly down an alley way anticipating a large reinforcer and receives it, but considerable dissonance follows rapid running if a very small magnitude reinforcer is received.

When dissonance arises, the organism is assumed to discover extra attractions about the situation that add an amount of value to the situation sufficient to reduce the cognitive dissonance being experienced. In the same example, the rat who runs rapidly and receives only a small reinforcer is expected to discover a sufficient number of extra attractions about the situation in order to compensate for the dissonance caused by the small reinforcer received. ("Added attractions" are hypothetical constructs and, hence, do not need to be identified objectively.) Finally, resistance to extinction is assumed to be a joint function of the strength of the cognitive expectancy formed and the value of the added attractions discovered. As currently formulated, cognitive dissonance theory has difficulty in explaining a number of extinction phenomena.[1]

Behavioristic (S-R) Analyses

ASSOCIATIVE WEAKENING

The hallmark of the S-R associative weakening analysis of simple extinction maintained by Thorndike (1913) and by early Skinner (1938) is its symmetry with a reinforcement position of associative strengthening. Whereas each reinforcer delivered is assumed to increment the strength of the relevant S-R association, each nondelivery of the reinforcer following a response is assumed to decrement S-R associative strength.[2] Indeed, reinforcement and extinction stand in a give-and-take relationship so that only those behaviors reinforced during acquisition are expected to emerge following the transition to extinction. This associative weakening analysis is attractive because of its parsimony. No new processes are proposed to account for extinction, and the extinction construct is not imbued with any distinctive properties of its own.

In spite of its parsimony, this form of the S-R associative weakening analysis is incapable of accounting for many extinction phenomena beyond the obvious functional change in the transitional behavior, that is, the decrease in performance of the previously reinforced response. Consider as one example the empirical generalization that resistance to extinction is greater following training with small rather than with large reinforcers. If extinction directly reflects the strength of the S-R association established during acquisition, then it would be necessary from an S-R associative weakening analysis to assume that small reinforcers produce a stronger S-R association than do large reinforcers—a very untenable assumption for a conventional S-R theory, even if a pure reinforcement position is not adopted. Indeed, as we will see time and again, a number of other extinction phenomena also apparently contradict any assumption that resistance to extinction is a direct reflection of the strength of the learned S-R association established prior to the transition to extinction. In the present theoretical context, either resistance to extinction needs to be abandoned as a direct measure of S-R associative strength, or additional assumptions about the mechanism underlying S-R associative analyses of extinction need to be made.

Essentially, it was this latter approach that was taken by Schoenfeld (1950) who made the assumptions that a number of different S-R associations form during acquisition and that each such association needs separately to be weakened during extinction. Specifically, Schoenfeld (1950) adopted a micromolecular definition of the response and assumed that each occurring quantitatively or qualitatively different variant of the generic referent response enters into a separate association with the stimulus situation prevailing during acquisition. Other systematists have also assumed that a multiplicity of S-R associations is formed during acquisition, but they have either emphasized associations between the stimulus situation and different macromolar responses (D'Amato & D'Amato, 1962) or separate associations between a single generic referent response and different stimuli in the environment (e.g., Estes, 1950; Mackintosh, 1965; Sutherland, 1966).

Actually, the nature of the presumed S-R association is not as critical to the analysis as are the assumptions that the number of different S-R associations formed is inversely related to the strengths of the individual S-R associations and that resistance to extinction is directly related to the number of different S-R associations formed. In other words, greater resistance to extinction results when a larger number of weaker S-R associations need to be extinguished than when a smaller number of stronger S-R associations need to be extinguished.

Schoenfeld's (1950) modification of the fundamental S-R associative weakening analysis instills this approach with additional explanatory power. Witness, for example, that the empirically observed inverse relationship between resistance to extinction and the reinforcer magnitude used in acquisition may be explained by the assumption that smaller reinforcer magnitudes produce weaker S-R associations and, thus, a larger number of different S-R associations during acquisition. Nevertheless, this extension of S-R associative weakening theory is less parsimonious than is its predecessor, and it still cannot account for all demonstrated extinction phenomena. A case in point is the occurrence of an overtraining extinction effect; the phenomenon that reinforced overtraining in acquisition can *reduce* resistance to subsequent extinction (e.g., North & Stimmel, 1960; Theios & Brelsford, 1964). From an S-R associative weakening position, continued reinforcement training should do nothing more than increase the strengths of existing S-R associations (no matter how many in number) up to some asymptotic level; continued reinforcement training surely does not contribute to S-R associative weakening. Obviously, additional factors need to be considered in order to make an S-R associative weakening analysis more generally acceptable.

Before proceeding to alternative theoretical analyses of the transitional behavior that accompanies simple extinction, some mention needs to be made of the S-R associative weakening analysis that can be derived from S-R contiguity theory as represented particularly by Guthrie (1935). According to this theoretical position a specific S-R association is assumed to be formed at full strength through simple contiguity of the stimulus and response. However, this S-R association is readily replaced by another S-R association, unless reinforcement occurs so as to preserve the current (last formed) association. Since experimental extinction entails the withholding of reinforcers following a response, S-R contiguity theory asserts that the particular S-R association manifested by an extinction response is weakened (completely to zero), because it is replaced by some other S-R association. Transitional behavior accompanying a change to extinction decreases gradually in performance not because of a gradual weakening of a single S-R association, but because a large number of different S-R associations are formed to the referent response in acquisition, and each of these associations needs to be separately replaced in extinction.

Guthrie's (1935) theoretical analysis of behavioral changes under extinction has elsewhere been referred to as an interference or as a competing response theory of extinction. This classification of Guthrie's position is understandable inasmuch as the new S-R association, the one which replaces the S-R association to the referent response, *may* involve a response that is incompatible with the referent response. However, it should be understood that Guthrie did not assign any special properties to normal extinction that would serve specifically to elicit incompatible responses, nor did he conceptualize extinction as a fundamental process separate from that of conditioning. S-R associations are formed continuously within a stimulus environment, and they are replaced continuously in the absence of an event that serves to preserve them.

The associative weakening analysis of simple extinction derived from S-R contiguity theory is no more successful in explaining the varied phenomena of extinction than is the early S-R associative weakening analysis derived from pure reinforcement theory. For example, there are simply no justifiable grounds for predicting from the contiguity analysis that resistance to extinction is inversely related to the magnitude of the reinforcer used or to the extent of overtraining given prior to extinction.

Spontaneous recovery is another extinction phenomenon that may seem paradoxical from either a reinforcement or a contiguity S-R associative weakening point of view. How can a response reoccur at increased strength if the association involving the response has previously been weakened or replaced and no opportunity has since been provided to restrengthen the association? The answer provided by both reinforcement and contiguity associative weakening theorists is that a response cannot do this but that this is an incomplete analysis of spontaneous recovery. Granted that during an extinction session there are repeated opportunities for the weakening or replacement of associations previously formed to stimuli present during the session; there is essentially only *one* opportunity for the weakening of associations previously formed to stimuli that occur at the beginning of the session. Thus, while associations to stimuli present during the session may become quite weak or nonexistent during an extended extinction session, associations to the stimuli occurring at the beginning of the session will be relatively well maintained.

Such an analysis correctly predicts that behavior at the beginning of the subsequent extinction session should be performed at a higher level than the behavior that occurred at the end of the preceding extinction session, at least until several extinction sessions have been experienced.[3] This analysis of spontaneous recovery includes a consideration of the stimulus situations present at the time of the operational transition from acquisition to extinction and, consequently, it is compatible with cognitive theories of extinction. Since an S is on the antecedent side of both S-S and S-R constructs, analyses based on changes in the stimulus situation are appropriate for both approaches.

INHIBITION   Certain characteristics are shared by all S-R inhibition theories of extinction. First of all, the association to the referent response reinforced during acquisition is not weakened by the extinction process. Second, the decrease in performance of the referent response that occurs during extinction is attributed to the increase in an inhibitory process that prevents the *performance* of the previously learned association. Third, some aspect of this inhibitory process has the property of being transitory, that is, of decaying with the passage of time or rest.

In the theoretical hands of Pavlov (1927), and of others who adopted similar tenets (e.g., Spence, 1936), inhibition is increased by each nonreinforced trial. Inhibition does not affect response strength directly, but performance of the referent response is a function of the difference between the excitatory response strength acquired during reinforced trials and the inhibition resulting from nonreinforced trials. When the difference between these opposed hypothetical constructs reaches zero, performance of the referent response ceases altogether.

It might be noted as an aside that in the classical conditioning situation studied by Pavlov, extinction is operationally defined as the presentation of the conditioned stimulus not followed by the unconditioned stimulus. Thus, the incrementing of inhibition is not dependent on the occurrence of a response. When the conditioned response no longer occurs to the conditioned stimulus, it is assumed that the difference between excitation and inhibition is zero. However, "extinction below zero" can purportedly be achieved by continuing to present the conditioned stimulus alone. That is, the continuance of extinction trials is expected theoretically to yield an amount of inhibition that exceeds the existing amount of excitation. On the other hand, in the discrete-trial situation studied by Spence (1936), extinction is operationally defined as the nondelivery of a reinforcer following a response and, consequently, "extinction below zero" is not possible conceptually, since inhibition cannot be further increased in the absence of a nonreinforced response. In summary, where the increase in inhibition is postulated to be response dependent, the extent to which inhibition can increase is limited by the amount of excitation currently possessed by the referent-response association.

Pavlov's inhibition construct has the property of being transitory inasmuch as inhibition decays progressively with time. This property of the hypothetical inhibition construct lends itself nicely to interpretations of empirical extinction phenomena that are temporally related. For example, the empirical finding that extinction proceeds more rapidly when the interval between extinction trials is short as opposed to long (e.g., Hill & Spear, 1962; Krane & Ison, 1971) may be attributed to the fact that less inhibition dissipates during short than during long intertrial intervals. Similarly, the dissipation of inhibition across time explains the phenomenon of spontaneous recovery quite directly and, moreover, it predicts correctly that the extent to which the referent response will "spontaneously" recover between a first and second extinction session is a direct function of the amount of time separating the two sessions (e.g., Ellson, 1938).

Inhibition theory is the most facile theory in the context of temporally related extinction effects. As time passes inhibition decays; the underlying excitation is uncovered; and performance emerges. However, if one follows this analysis to an extreme position, it appears that if a long time separates successive extinction exposures, spontaneous recovery should be virtually complete. There is no experimental evidence available in the literature to support this last contention.[4]

Not all hypothetical inhibition constructs used to explain experimental extinction rely solely on the occurrence of a nonreinforced trial for their existence. Indeed, the hypothetical construct of reactive inhibition described by Hull (1943; also Miller & Dollard, 1941) does not. Reactive inhibition is an inhibitory construct that accrues strength *every* time a response is executed, whether the response is reinforced or not. The amount of inhibitory strength resulting from each response occurrence is a direct function of the effortfulness of the response and the rate of executing the response. In brief, reactive inhibition is not a construct peculiar to extinction. Instead, it is a construct analogous to fatigue; reactive inhibition is increased by work and dissipates with rest.

As an inhibitory construct, reactive inhibition subtracts from excitation to determine performance. However, since reactive inhibition accrues at a lesser rate than does excitation, performance continues to increase during reinforced practice, despite the concomitant increase in reactive inhibition that accompanies responding. Performance decreases in extinction because there is no increase in excitation to offset the increase in reactive inhibition.

Fundamentally, reactive inhibition can be invoked theoretically to explain any of the extinction phenomena that can be explained by other transitory inhibition constructs. In addition, it is predicted from the properties of reactive inhibition that rate of extinction will be a direct function of the effort expended to execute the response. The empirical findings regarding this predicted relationship are somewhat conflicting (e.g., Aiken, 1957; Applezweig, 1951; Young, 1966). Needless to say, the construct of reactive inhibition is counterindicated by the phenomenon of latent extinction, unless it is regressively assumed that reactive inhibition is the mechanism by which incentive motivation is extinguished in the empty goalbox and that it is this latter extinction effect that accounts for the latent extinction phenomenon.[5]

Within Hull's (1943) more general theory of reinforcement, reactive inhibition is conceptualized motivationally as a negative drive. As a consequence, the reduction of reactive inhibition constitutes a drive-reduction reinforcement; the reduction of reactive inhibition reinforces whatever response precedes it. The cessation of responding or, more precisely, stopping responding has the consequence of reducing reactive inhibition. Therefore, the response of stopping responding is associatively strengthened to the immediate stimulus situation through drive reduction. Hull (1943) termed this habit of stopping responding—conditioned inhibition. Conditioned inhibition influences performance of the referent response by adding with reactive inhibition to determine the net inhibitory potential that offsets response excitation.

As an associative hypothetical construct, conditioned inhibition has the property of being relatively permanent. This hypothetical construct consequently increases the explanatory capabilities of inhibition extinction theory in several areas. For example, conditioned inhibition may be invoked to account for the facts that spontaneous recovery is never totally complete and that extinction effects can be relatively permanent.

INCOMPATIBLE RESPONSE The decline in the performance of the referent response observed after an operational transition from acquisition to extinction is accompanied by an increase in the performance of other behavior, often by behavior that is incompatible with the referent response. From an S-R associative weakening, inhibition, or S-S cognitive expectancy theoretical viewpoint, the appearance of other behavior in extinction is an inevitable result of the extinction process. The organism behaves continuously over time. If associations or expectancies involving performance of the referent response are weakened, inhibited, or disconfirmed by extinction, some other behavior will necessarily occur. It is not possible to predict precisely from these latter theoretical analyses just what the nature of the alternative behaviors occurring in extinction will be. These nonreferent behaviors emerge only because performance of the referent response is decreased; the behaviors are not directly produced by extinction nor are they assumed to be a property of extinction.

An alternative interpretation of the role of nonreferent responses in extinction is offered by S-R incompatible response theories of extinction. In this theoretical context, incompatible responses are not simply a by-product of extinction. Instead, incompatible responses are the cause of performance decrements in extinction.

The theoretical analysis proceeds as follows. The operation of extinction directly produces responses that are explicitly incompatible with the referent response. The performance of these incompatible responses increasingly competes with or interferes with the performance of the referent response and, as a consequence, progressively prevents the occurrence of the previously reinforced response.

Early forms of incompatible response theories (Wendt, 1936; Zener, 1937) are not very influential primarily because they contain a host of conceptual shortcomings. For example, a specific mechanism or process needs to be hypothesized in order to explain why extinction gives rise to incompatible responses. Alternatively, if incompatible responses are presumed to be an intrinsic property of extinction, it is still necessary to specify how these responses garner and maintain sufficient strength to interfere with the previously predominant referent response.

It should be clear that incompatible response theory does not imply any weakening of the S-R association acquired in acquisition. Incompatible responses interfere with the performance of the referent response, but they do not weaken the learned association to the response. In other words, if after a period of extinction the incompatible responses are somehow themselves interfered with or prevented, a reappearance of the referent response in extinction is expected. As might be anticipated, the phenomenon of spontaneous recovery is interpreted, in this theoretical context, to be a result of a reduction in the influence of incompatible responses that somehow occurs during the time interval when the organism is away from the extinction situation that originally engendered the incompatible responses. The challenge for this interpretation of spontaneous recovery is to explain why the influence of incompatible responses should become less with the passage of time.

Several more recent theorists (e.g., Skinner, 1950) have suggested that the operational transition from acquisition to extinction elicits emotional responses that may be conceptualized as incompatible responses for the purpose of theoretical analysis. A hypothesis concerning the theoretical mechanism underlying the occurrence of extinction-produced emotional responses has been proposed by Amsel (1958) and Spence (1960). In Amsel's subsequent (1962, 1967, 1971) development of what is explicitly an incompatible emotional response theory, the motivational constructs of incentive and generalized drive are relied on in much the same way as they are by Hull (1952) and Spence (1956).

To begin with, organisms are assumed to develop incentive during reinforcement training to an extent determined by the reinforcer conditions. Consequently, the organism comes to expect the occurence of a reinforcer in the experimental situation. When this expectancy is not fulfilled, as it certainly is not after an operational change to extinction, the organism is emotionally frustrated. The amount of frustration experienced is a direct function of the amount of incentive accrued in acquisition. As a hypothetical construct, *frustration* has drive properties that contributes to a generalized drive state and gives rise to hypothetical frustration responses (r_f) and consequent frustration response-produced stimuli (s_f).

Generalized drive energizes whatever S-R associations are appropriate to the situation. Since frustration is assumed to increment generalized drive, it follows that the performance of previously learned behavior is enhanced by extinction-induced frustration. Indeed, it is readily demonstrated empirically (e.g., Amsel & Roussel, 1952) that a transition from acquisition to extinction produces an energizing effect on performance. This empirical effect is labeled the frustration effect, since it is derived so directly from the theoretical notion that nonreinforcement is frustrating. However, the frustration effect is functionally transitory; transitional behavior under extinction eventually shows a reduction in performance.

Within frustration theory, performance decrements during extinction are attributed to the workings of the r_f-s_f mechanism. The hypothetical frustration-produced stimuli elicit responses that are incompatible with the referent response. The vigor of the elicited incompatible responses is determined by the strength of the r_f-s_f mechanism, that is, by the amount of frustration experienced. In summary, performance decrements in extinction are a direct result of frustration-elicited incompatible responses that arise to the extent that an expectancy of a reinforcer is not confirmed.[6]

Frustration theory has gained wide acknowledgement, because it readily handles a large number of the empirical phenomena of extinction, while retaining a reasonable amount of parsimony. For example, since frustration is directly dependent on the previous development of incentive, it is possible to predict that those conditions that increase incentive motivation (say, large as opposed to small reinforcer magnitudes) will increase the rate of extinction. Nevertheless, frustration theory cannot account for a permanent reduction in responding under extinction without making some additional assumptions. Since frustration is conceptualized as a motivational construct, it has the properties of being temporary and reversible. If frustration is temporary, then the incompatible responses elicited by frustration should also disappear, and performance of the referent response should never remain permanently reduced in extinction.

There are two plausible ways to achieve a permanent extinction-produced response reduction within the general domain of frustration theory. The first way is to endow incompatible responses with associative strength to the extinction situation. This can be achieved through the recognition that a reduction in frustration is reinforcing inasmuch as it produces a reduction in generalized drive. Any frustration-induced incompatible responses occurring prior to the time of a reduction in frustration will gain in associative strength and, thus, will be available in the situation even when not elicited by frustration.

A second means of achieving a permanent reduction in extinction responding is to assume that incentive motivation is gradually reduced in extinction. Early in extinction, when incentive motivation is high, response decrements are primarily a result of interference mediated by the $r_f - s_f$ mechanism. Late in extinction, after frustration has dissipated, performance decrements are maintained, because the incentive to perform the referent response is reduced. This later analysis is basically regressive, since some theoretical explanation still needs to be offered to account for the decrease in incentive motivation across extinction.

Most incentive theorists have not proposed any distinctly unique theoretical constructs to account for the extinction of incentive. For example, although Logan has asserted that the rate at which incentive extinguishes is a state parameter of the organism and, therefore, that it is not sensitive to variations in prior acquisition conditions, no special mechanism for the extinction of incentive is proposed (Logan, 1968; Logan, Beier, & Kincaid, 1956). Instead, incentive theorists have usually chosen to account for the extinction of incentive by appealing to one or more of the existing theories developed to account more generally for transitional behavioral changes in extinction.

GENERALIZATION DECREMENT
: All theories of extinction recognize the existence of stimulus differences between acquisition and extinction. However, the various theories differ in the extent to which these stimulus differences are used to explain transitional behavior in experimental extinction. For example, we have already seen that S-R associative weakening theory does not rely extensively on stimulus differences to account for the progressive decrease in performance that extinction produces. However, these stimulus differences are of primary importance to the theory in explaining the fact that reconditioning of a referent response is possible even after S-R associations have been apparently completely weakened by extinction.

The argument made is that S-R associations are formed to the stimuli associated with reinforcers during acquisition. Since these stimuli do not occur in extinction, the corresponding S-R associations are not directly weakened as are all those associations formed to stimuli other than the ones corresponding to reinforcers. As a consequence, in reconditioning when the stimulus situation accompanying a reinforcer is reinstated, some strength still remains in the S-R association to reinforcing stimuli, even though other S-R associations may have been completely weakened in extinction.

Here of particular and immediate concern are those alternative theoretical analyses that have exclusively relied on acquisition-extinction stimulus differences to account for all manners of transitional behavior in extinction. These theories are characteristically S-R in nature, and they revolve around the principle of stimulus-generalization decrement. The heart of the analysis rests with the assumptions that stimulus generalization is a fundamental process of the organism and that response associations are formed to stimuli associated with reinforcers during acquisition. When the stimulus situation is changed in extinction, there is a decrement in performance due to stimulus generalization. The greater the stimulus change in extinction, the less the generalized response strength, and the greater the corresponding decrement in extinction performance.

This fundamental generalization decrement analysis is actually adaptable to any S-R theory of extinction. However, it has had special appeal to those systematists who adhere to a Hullian reinforcement theory of learning. This has occurred because the generalization decrement analysis does *not* involve the weakening of previously reinforced S-R associations in extinction. It will be recalled that Hull (1943) assigns the property of permanence to S-R associations; they can be strengthened asymptotically, but they cannot be directly weakened. According to the generalization decrement analysis, the associations present in extinction are weaker than those present in acquisition. This occurs, however, because the associations present in acquisition gain their strength directly through reinforcement, while those present in extinction benefit solely from generalized response strength.

The first explicit generalization decrement theory of extinction was proposed by Sheffield (1949) and Hull (1952). These theorists assumed that during acquisition, stimulus traces of the occurrence of reinforcement, as well as of the consummatory responses to reinforcement, occur in the organism. Although these stimulus traces decay across time, they persist within the organism so that they constitute part of the stimulus environment present during the subsequent acquisition trial. Consequently, during reinforced practice, responses become associated to the stimulus traces resulting from the prior delivery of reinforcement. Essentially, extinction represents a generalization-test situation in which stimulus traces associated with reinforcers are made progressively more remote.

The primary drawback to this particular generalization decrement theory resides in the transitory nature of the hypothetical stimulus traces. Since these traces decay relatively rapidly across time, the analysis necessarily has difficulty in explaining any extinction phenomena that occur after acquisition training and involve widely spaced trials. Indeed, the basic phenomenon of experimental extinction cannot be easily predicted from the theory, if prior acquisition trials are spaced so far apart that all stimulus traces from a preceding reinforced trial are completely dissipated at the time the next reinforcement occurs.

This shortcoming of stimulus-trace theory is rectified in the modification of generalization decrement theory made by Capaldi (e.g., 1966, 1967). Capaldi assumes that there are unique stimulus characteristics associated with different reinforcer conditions and that organisms form memory traces of these stimulus characteristics. The memory traces are further assumed to be relatively durable and, thus, they are relatively insensitive to degradation with time.

It is important to realize that assigning the property of durability to hypothetical memory traces permits the memory trace of outcomes of several preceding trials, not just of the immediately preceding trial, to enter into associations with the referent response on a succeeding reinforced trial. It is in this way that the progressive decrease in performance of the previously learned response across extinction can be accounted for. At the end of acquisition, the organism has associations that are formed to the memory trace of outcomes of a series of preceding reinforced trials. As extinction progresses, the amount of stimulus change (and, therefore, the magnitude of the generalization decrement) progressively increases as memory traces of nonreinforced trials successively replace memory traces of preceding reinforced trials. A formal treatment of this aspect of Capaldi's (1966) theory has been offered by Koteskey (1972; Koteskey & Hendrix, 1971).

Capaldi's S-R generalization decrement theory of extinction may be further illustrated by reconsidering the inverse empirical relationships that exist between resistance to extinction and reinforcer magnitude and between resistance to extinction and the amount of reinforced overtraining experienced in acquisition. With respect to reinforcer magnitude, larger reinforcers promote greater S-R strength than do smaller reinforcers. However, larger reinforcers are further away from extinction on the continuum of reinforcer magnitude than are smaller reinforcers. This means that a greater stimulus change (generalization decrement) occurs when extinction is instituted after acquisition with large than with small reinforcers. In summary, although large reinforcers produce greater S-R response strength in acquisition, small reinforcers are associated with a greater generalized response strength in extinction and, therefore, a greater resistance to extinction. With respect to the overtraining extinction effect, it is sufficient to argue that overtraining sharpens theoretical generalization gradients so that the extent of generalization from acquisition to extinction is decreased by overtraining, even though overtraining does not affect the actual amount of stimulus change that occurs between acquisition and extinction.

Finally, as might be expected from the emphasis on stimulus conditions, the analyses of spontaneous recovery and reconditioning offered by S-R associative weakening theorists is generally acceptable to S-R generalization decrement theorists of extinction. For example, since the S-R association to a stimulus trace or memory trace is unaffected by extinction, to reinstitute the reinforcer during reconditioning is sufficient to recreate the trace and its corresponding response association.

Summary   Systematic analyses of extinction are impressive in terms of their variety. Indeed, one cannot be faulted for wondering why so many different theories have been constructed in order to handle the intuitively natural observation that performance of a response decreases when the probability of a reinforcer is reduced to zero. It is still further curious that no one of the theories of extinction can handle all of the empirically demonstrable effects on behavior that accompany a transition to the experimental extinction operation. Some theories do better in explaining some effects than others, but no single theory has yet emerged that can explain all the transitional behavior phenomena empirically identified to date.

In all fairness to theories of extinction, transitional behavior in extinction is complex, if one looks beyond the simple decrement in performance that is generally accepted as the functional hallmark of extinction. Moreover, theories of extinction do not have as many degrees of freedom with which to work as do theories of learning. Indeed, at least one degree of freedom must be assigned by extinction theories to whatever theoretical assumptions are made regarding the nature and conditions of associations.

As a case in point, consider the restrictions imposed on the extinction theorist who assumes learned associations are relatively permanent. Such a theorist cannot account for performance decrements in extinction by the convenient device of weakening, replacing, or disconfirming associations. Instead, the theorist needs to argue either that the learned associations are not directly involved in extinction, as in the generalization decrement analysis, or that some other active process exists that can effectively oppose the influence of the learned associations, as in the incompatible response and inhibition analyses.

On the other hand, there is nothing to prevent the future establishment of a general theory of extinction that incorporates the essentials of the several theories already proposed. Many of the existing theoretical constructs are not only compatible, but they also are complementary. For instance, one type of notion may be adopted to account for permanent effects and another notion to account for temporary effects on transitional behavior in extinction. In this context, it seems difficult for us to imagine a future theory of extinction that would not want, in some way, to incorporate the existence of stimulus differences between acquisition and extinction.

Finally, it should be stated that the transitional operation of reducing reinforcer probability from unity to zero, while holding all other experimental conditions constant, is perhaps an infrequent occurrence in everyday affairs. Less artificial situations often entail varied, more subtle, and less extreme changes in the conditions and schedules of reinforcers. Transitional operations more closely approximating such changes will be considered in the remainder of this chapter. However, remembering that extinction represents a conceptual endpoint to all operational changes involving varied and constant probability and conditions of reinforcers will prepare the reader for the discovery that theories of experimental extinction, as discussed thus far, serve as the core for a large number of systematic analyses of transitional behavior.

TRANSITIONAL BEHAVIOR AFTER SHIFTS IN REINFORCEMENT

Up to this point, we have discussed systematic analyses of nondifferential transitional behaviors that accompany an operational change in the reinforcer schedule from a reinforcer probability of unity to a reinforcer probability of zero. Because of the unique status held by the extinction operation with respect to schedules and conditions of reinforcers, it is acceptable to assert conceptually that we have similarly discussed systematic analyses of transitional behavior that accompany an operational change in the reinforcer conditions to a zero reinforcer magnitude or to an infinite reinforcer delay. In this section, we will describe systematic analyses of transitional behaviors that occur under operational changes in the reinforcer conditions that are somewhat less extreme than those that occur in experimental extinction.

The specific concern is with nondifferential discrete-trial situations where reinforcer probability is held constant, usually at unity, but where the conditions of reinforcers are shifted from one nonzero, noninfinite value to another.

Actually, the focus of our discussion will be further restricted to shifts in reinforcer magnitudes, increases and/or decreases, that do not involve a zero reinforcer magnitude. This latter restriction arises from expediency. Reinforcer magnitude shifts have been the most often empirically studied and the most often theoretically analyzed shifts in reinforcer conditions (cf. Black, 1968; Dunham, 1968; Hall, 1966; Mackintosh, 1974).[7]

Herein, our point of reference is the transitional behavior evidenced in the early experiments of Crespi (1942) and of Zeaman (1949). It is significant that these experiments show that when reinforcer conditions are shifted from a small to a large magnitude reinforcer, or from a large to a small magnitude reinforcer, performance of the referent response changes *rapidly* in the expected direction; changes to larger reinforcers occasion increases in performance, and vice versa. This aspect of the Crespi and Zeaman experiments is reminiscent of the earlier Tolman and Honzik (1930) latent learning experiment where changes in the conditions of reinforcers are similarly shown to engender rapid changes in performance of an instrumental response.

The more critical aspect of the Crespi and Zeaman data for our present purposes is not the rate of change in performance but the *extent* of the change in the transitional behavior that accompanies changes in reinforcer magnitude. Essentially, the transitional behavioral phenomena involving the extent of change include: (1) a shift from a small to large reinforcer produces a level of performance *greater* than than expected of an organism who has been trained and maintained with a large reinforcer, and (2) a shift from a large to a small reinforcer produces a level of performance *less* than that expected of an organism who has been trained and maintained with a small reinforcer. Crespi (1942) referred to these effects, respectively, as the "elation" and "depression" effects. We will accept what has become the more common nomenclature in the literature and refer to these effects collectively as successive incentive contrast effects. The respective increases and decreases in transitional behavior, relative to baseline responding under the appropriate reinforcer magnitude, will be referred to as positive incentive contrast and negative incentive contrast effects.[8]

Since the time of Crespi's demonstration, the occurrence of a negative incentive contrast effect has never been doubted empirically. The effect is quite apparently strong and reliable. The positive incentive contrast effect, on the other hand, has had a less impressive empirical history. For well over a decade following Spence's (1956) criticism of the Crespi and Zeaman experiments on methodological grounds,[9] reviewers of the literature on successive contrast effects were led to the conclusion that there were no definitive data to support the existence of a reliable positive contrast effect (e.g., Black, 1968; Dunham, 1968; Mackintosh, 1974).

Several theoretical analyses have been offered to account for asymmetric successive contrast effects (negative contrast but not positive contrast) on transitional behavior that occurs after changes in reinforcer magnitudes. These analyses will be discussed shortly. Other systematists (Bower, 1961; Hulse, 1962) have suggested that the failure to observe reliable positive contrast effects may be, in part, a result of methodological considerations. One cogent argument (Bower, 1961) contends that organisms performing under a large rein-forcer respond as rapidly as possible in the situation. Positive contrast is not observed after a change from small to large reinforcer magnitude, simply because it is not possible to respond any faster than those organisms who have been maintained all along on large reinforcers. For whatever reasons, more recent experiments, which have employed techniques to prevent ceiling effects on responding from coming into play, have demonstrated that under some conditions reliable positive incentive contrast effects do occur (e.g., Lehr, 1974; Mellgren, Seybert, Wrather, & Dyck, 1973; Shanab & Cavallaro, 1975).

Perhaps we have belabored the empirical status of the successive positive incentive contrast effect. But the point must be made—some theories of incen-tive contrast have been developed to handle asymmetric effects, while others have maintained that symmetric effects are theoretically appropriate.[10] Among the asymmetric theories are those that have developed their explana-tions simply based on the empirical data available at the time. Other theories are asymmetric because the postulates of the theory demand that they be. One type of theoretical approach, which has argued consistently for the conceptual existence of symmetric positive and negative incentive contrast effects, is the cognitive analysis to which we turn first.

Cognitive (S-S) Analyses   Before proceeding to S-S cognitive analyses of incentive contrast effects, it might be helpful to review the compatibility of S-S theory with the findings that changes in transitional behavior occur rapidly after operational changes in reinforcer conditions. Briefly, reinforcers are not assigned a direct associa-tive strengthening function but, instead, serve as incentive motivation. Organ-isms perform at whatever level is justified by the incentive amount prevailing at the moment. When incentive amount is abruptly shifted, performance changes accordingly. It will be noted in this context that if performance is solely a function of the absolute amount of incentive, say, as given by the physical characteristics of the reinforcers, then no incentive contrast is an-ticipated. That is, from an absolute incentive point of view, organisms perform as dictated by the current incentive without regard to past reinforcers or to the more general incentive context.

In point of fact, S-S cognitive expectancy theorists have usually endorsed a relative interpretation of incentive amount. Incentive amount is not absolute but, instead, depends on its relationship to expected amounts of incentive or to the preceding and prevailing incentive contexts.[11] Two more specific anal-yses of this type may be derived from Tolmanian expectancy theory and from adaptation level theory.

EXPECTANCY   Tolman (1932) asserted that the occurrence of a reinforcer serves to create an expectancy of the reinforcer, and that the organism performs in accordance with its expectancy for so long as the expectancy is confirmed. Any subsequent occurrence of a zero magnitude reinforcer (extinction) disconfirms the expect-ancy, and the organism ceases to perform. Now in the incentive contrast situation, expectancies for a given reinforcer are neither perfectly confirmed or disconfirmed after the operational change in reinforcer magnitude; expectancies are overconfirmed by changes to a larger reinforcer, and under-confirmed by changes to a lower reinforcer. Incentives are perceived as either greater or less than specified by their absolute amounts, depending on the existing expectancy. In brief, a reinforcer magnitude is perceived as bigger (smaller) if it overconfirms (underconfirms) an expectancy than if it simply confirms an expectancy. Since performance falls in line with the organism's perceived incentive and expectancies, both positive and negative incentive contrast effects are predicted from the analysis.

ADAPTATION LEVEL   Symmetric contrast effects also are predicted from the application of adaptation level theory (Helson, 1964) to conditions of reinforcers (Bevan & Adamson, 1960). This perceptual theory, although stated more formally than the above S-S cognitive analysis, also essentially states that the behavioral effectiveness of a given reinforcer magnitude depends on its perceived magnitude and not on its absolute magnitude. Perceived magnitude is determined by the relationship of the immediate reinforcer magnitude to preceding reinforcer magnitudes. Perceptually, a large reinforcer magnitude is relatively larger when it follows a small than when it follows a large reinforcer, and vice versa for a small reinforcer.

Behavioristic (S-R)   Pure reinforcement S-R theories, such as Hull's (1943), have two problems
Analyses   with the data of the Crespi-Zeaman type. Neither the rate nor the extent of change in the performance of transitional behavior is explicable using pure reinforcement theory. In Chapter 3 we recounted how rapid changes in the performance of a referent response, such as produced by shifts in conditions of reinforcers, stimulated Hull to abandon a pure reinforcement construct in favor of an incentive construct. Thus, armed with incentive motivation, S-R reinforcement theorists attribute the rapid rate of transitional behavior changes in the Crespi-Zeaman experiments to changes in the rapidly modifiable incentive hypothetical construct.

The particulars of incentive-motivation constructs were discussed in Chapter 5. A review of that discussion exhibits that S-R theorists have had a proclivity to adopt absolute incentive constructs. That is, incentive is usually related directly to the conditions of the reinforcer without consideration of the surrounding reinforcer context. No special properties are assigned to incentive that are dependent on other previously received or current reinforcers. Furthermore, the occasional incentive theorist who has been specific on the matter has typically assumed that the rate of change in incentive is also unmodified by prior reinforcer conditions (e.g., Logan, 1968). These observations seem to mean, in the present context, that incentive contrast effects of either the positive or negative type are not readily derived from conventional S-R association theory, even if the explanatory contribution of an incentive-motivation construct is considered.

Obviously, the S-R association theory needs to buttress itself with additional hypothetical constructs or processes in order to account for successive contrast effects. The question that first arises is what successive contrast effects should be accounted for: positive only, negative only, or symmetric effects? One approach to take is to account for symmetric effects and to do so by adopting an S-S cognitive-perceptual position, regarding the relativity of incentive (e.g., Capaldi, 1974), or by applying a number of assumptions, originally derived to explain the selective association of exteroceptive stimuli, to the hypothetical incentive construct (e.g., McHose & Moore, 1976). More often, S-R theorists have focused exclusively on the negative contrast effect and have done so by pointing to the conceptual similarity between shifts from large to small reinforcers and shifts from some reinforcer to none. Three such S-R analyses are presented below.

It should be noted before moving on to these analyses that even if it is assumed that negative contrast operations and extinction operations are conceptually similar, S-R associative weakening analyses of extinction cannot account for negative contrast effects. Although a change from a large to a small reinforcer may be assumed to weaken the existing S-R association, there is no means inherent in an associative weakening extinction analysis by which the association can be made weaker than another S-R association that has been established under the small reinforcer. Some additional property, perhaps that of inhibition, must be assigned to downshifts in reinforcer magnitude in order for an associative weakening analyses to approximate an explanation of the negative incentive contrast effect.

INHIBITION   The most direct extension of an S-R inhibition theory of extinction to negative incentive contrast effects has been made by Black (1968). A somewhat more cognitive, although still S-R inhibition theory approach, has been advocated by Mackintosh (1974). The essentials of the analysis (Black, 1968) are: first, that the excitatory potential for performing the referent response is determined by the absolute magnitude of the reinforcer. Second, like extinction, a reduction in the magnitude of a reinforcer produces an increment in the inhibitory potential; the magnitude of the increment is proportional to the difference between the pre- and postshift reinforcer magnitudes. Continuing this extinction–like analysis, inhibition is assumed to subtract from excitation to determine performance of the transitional behavior.

Since inhibition arises exclusively from a reduction in reinforcer magnitude, no inhibition is established in either a large or small reinforcer magnitude condition prior to a shift in the reinforcer conditions. Nor is inhibition established in an organism shifted from a small to a large reinforcer. Such a shift will engender an increase in behavior up to a level of performance appropriate for a constant large reinforcer, but no positive incentive contrast can occur. Finally, an organism shifted from a large to a small reinforcer will experience an amount of excitation appropriate for a constant small reinforcer. However, performance will be below that anticipated from the amount of excitation alone because of the counteracting effect on performance of the inhibition aroused by the transition to the smaller reinforcer.

INCOMPATIBLE RESPONSE   Crespi's (1942) own analysis of the transitional behavioral effects of shifts in reinforcer magnitude is that these shifts produce a heightened emotionality that somehow produces elevations and depressions in performance. Similarly, the negative incentive contrast effect is attributed by Spence (1956) to disruptive emotional effects produced by a reduction in reinforcer magnitude. However, the most explicit interpretation of negative contrast effects made in terms of emotionality has been derived from Amsel's (e.g., 1958, 1962) frustration theory of extinction (e.g., Bower, 1961; Ison, Glass, & Daly, 1969; Mikulka, Lehr, & Pavlik, 1967).

Two assumptions need to be added to Amsel's incompatible response analysis in order to account for negative incentive contrast. The first is that the incentive established under the preshift reinforcer condition initially generalizes to the postshift reinforcer condition. The second assumption is that, like extinction, a reduction in the reinforcer magnitude relative to that expected will give rise to frustration and the corresponding $r_f - s_f$ mechanism.

To elaborate on the analysis, when there is a downward shift in reinforcer magnitude, frustration is aroused and incompatible responses are elicited by $r_f - s_f$ that interfere with performance of the referent response. At the same time, the expectancy of the preshift reinforcer magnitude gives way to an amount of incentive appropriate to the postshift reinforcer magnitude. Taken together, the initial elicitation of frustration and the eventual decrease in incentive imply that negative incentive contrast effects could be transitory. Transitional behavior should first undershoot the performance level established for constant small reinforcers and then, subsequently, adjust upward to that level.[12]

Although there is evidence that negative contrast effects can be persistent (DiLollo, 1964), there is no evidence to tip the balance finally in favor of transient or permanent contrast effects. It will be noted, however, that if contrast effects do prove to be transient, the systematic analyses discussed up to now will have no difficulty in accounting for the appropriate changes in transitional behavior. S-S cognitive-perceptual theories will assert that with continued exposure to a small reinforcer magnitude, perceived incentive amount becomes consonant with absolute incentive amount. An alternative S-R inhibition analysis will assert that inhibition generated by downward shifts in reinforcer magnitude is temporary and dissipates with time.

GENERALIZATION
DECREMENT

In one sense, the S-R generalization decrement analysis of negative incentive contrast effects is more elegant than are other S-R analyses that are based on theories of extinction. This is so because no new assumptions need to be made in order to accommodate the generalization decrement theory of extinction to negative incentive contrast transitional behavior. Given that during preshift reinforced trials, S-R associations are formed between the referent response and the traces (stimulus or memory) set up by the particular reinforcer magnitude being used, a shift to a lesser reinforcer magnitude (be it small or zero) will effect a change in the relevant stimulus situation and a consequent generalization decrement in the performance of the referent response.

By way of explaining this analysis more fully (Capaldi & Lynch, 1967; Capaldi & Ziff, 1969), it is assumed that organisms establish S-R associations to the stimulus aftereffects of whatever reinforcer magnitude is currently being experienced. In other words, S-R associations are formed to preshift and to postshift reinforcer magnitudes. Performance of the referent response is directly related to the strength of the learned association and to the absolute magnitude of the reinforcer. Consider now the situation involved in a shift from a large to a small magnitude reinforcer. Prior to the shift, an organism has associative strength to large, but not to small reinforcers. Shortly following the shift, the organism still has little associative strength to small reinforcers, but performance occurs because of the generalized response strength from the association to the large reinforcer. This generalized response strength is less than that which exists for direct associations to the memory traces associated with a small reward. Thus, an initial undershooting occurs in the transitional behavior.[13] Transient negative incentive contrast effects may be accounted for by noting that with repeated trials, associative strength to the small reinforcer increases, and generalization from previous S-R associations is no longer of consequence.

The generalization decrement analysis differs from incompatible response and inhibition analyses in not attributing any special property to a downshift in reinforcer magnitude. It is similar to these S-R analyses in that positive incentive contrast is not theoretically derivable. Indeed, in the case of the generalization decrement analysis, some undershooting of performance is expected initially to accompany a change from a small to a large reinforcer. Although transitional behavior increases following an upward shift in reinforcer magnitude solely because of the larger magnitude reinforcer being used, the extent of the increase should be checked somewhat because of generalization decrement from the learned association to the aftereffects of small reinforcer magnitudes. In fact, the literature does contain instances where the performance of a small to large shifted group is less than that of a group maintained on a large magnitude reinforcer (e.g., Mackinnon, 1967).

Summary   Transitional behavior in negative incentive contrast proves to be readily understood from most theoretical analyses of experimental extinction. This is as it should be, considering the conceptual similarities between the operations of extinction and downward incentive shifts. Transitional behavior in positive incentive contrast seems to be far more precarious, both empirically and theoretically. In part, this results because upward incentive shifts are conceptually similar to the acquisition operation. An operational change from a small to a large reinforcer may be related conceptually to an operational change from no reinforcer to some. Thus, theoretical analyses of positive incentive contrast are necessarily constrained directly by the theoretical assumptions made regarding the learning process. This constraint also applies to theories of extinction, although it does so less directly and to a lesser extent. Simply put, if a theorist assumes that performance during acquisition is a joint function of associative strength and absolute incentive magnitude, then the occurrence of a positive incentive contrast enhancement effect is enigmatic. On the other hand, the contrary assumption that incentive magnitude is relative to its context requires that positive contrast be conspicuous.

When during the acquisition of a referent response, the probability or conditions of reinforcement differ from trial to trial, a myriad of acquisition situations is possible. Here we are specifically interested in two out of the vast number of these potential situations. The first is partial reinforcement; the situation where the reinforcer conditions are held constant but where the reinforcer probability is either zero or unity on each trial. During a partial reinforcement session, an organism is reinforced on part of the trials and experiences extinction on the other part. The second situation is the varied reinforcement situation that is conceptually similar to partial reinforcement. In the varied reinforcement situation, reinforcer probability is held constant, usually at unity, while the reinforcer conditions vary between two specified values on each trial. Taking reinforcer delay as an example, an organism is reinforced on every trial; on one part of the trials the reinforcer delay is short, and on the other part the reinforcer delay is long.

A number of fascinating transitional behaviors occur during partial and varied reinforcement situations. Nevertheless, in keeping with the theme established so far for this chapter, we will turn directly to transitional behaviors that occur after an operational change from partial or varied reinforcement to extinction. The principal transitional effect that occurs after varied reinforcement is that resistance to extinction is greater than it is after consistent reinforcement with the preferred reinforcer condition. More specifically, subsequent resistance to extinction is greater when reinforcer amount (delay) is varied between two values than when the reinforcer condition is held constant at the large amount (short delay). This fundamental varied reinforcement effect on extinction is well documented empirically (e.g., Capaldi & Poynor, 1966; Crum, Brown, & Bitterman, 1951; Knouse & Campbell, 1971; Logan, Beier, & Kincaid, 1956).

The principal transitional effect that occurs after partial reinforcement is a resistance to extinction that is greater than it is after an acquisition situation where a reinforcer is delivered on every trial. Assuming that the conditions and number of reinforcers are the same, a situation involving some reinforcement trials and some extinction trials yields greater resistance to extinction than does a situation involving only reinforcement trials. This fundamental partial reinforcement effect on extinction is certainly among the most often studied transitional behavioral effects; this is attested to by the large number of literature reviews devoted to the topic (e.g., Jenkins & Stanley, 1950; Lewis, 1960; Robbins, 1971).

Beyond the fundamental partial reinforcement effect lies a variety of related transitional behavioral effects on extinction that will be of interest in our subsequent discussion of theoretical analyses.[14] Among these are the: (1) *initial nonreinforcement effect*—organisms given nonreinforced trials prior to consistently reinforced trials are more resistant to subsequent extinction than are organisms receiving only reinforced trials (e.g., Spear, Hill, & O'Sullivan, 1964; Robbins, Chart, & Weinstock, 1968; Capaldi & Waters, 1970); (2) *generalized partial reinforcement effect*—organisms given partial reinforcement in one situation are more resistant to extinction following consistent reinforcement in another, related situation than are organisms receiving only consistent reinforcement (e.g., Brown & Logan, 1965; Rashotte & Amsel, 1968); (3) *interpolated partial reinforcement effect*—organisms given a block of partial reinforcement trials interpolated between consistently reinforced trials are more resistant to subsequent extinction that are organisms receiving only reinforced trials (Rashotte & Surridge, 1969; Theios, 1962); and (4) *intertrial reinforcement effect*—under partial reinforcement conditions, organisms receiving intertrial reinforcements after nonreinforced trials are less resistant to extinction than are organisms receiving intertrial reinforcements after reinforced trials (e.g., Black & Spence, 1965; Capaldi & Wilson, 1968; McCain, 1966).

The fundamental varied reinforcement and partial reinforcement effects on extinction have engendered what might seem to be an inordinate amount of theoretical attention. However, these transitional behavioral phenomena stand as touchstones for the utility of basic theoretical constructs and, thus, may well be deserving of the attention given to them. The effects are particularly interesting, because they seem to be counterintuitive. They suggest that a situation that should produce less associative strength, less incentive motivation, or be the less preferred, will yield more transitional behavior after an operational change to extinction than will a situation that should produce greater associative strength, more incentive motivation, or be the more preferred.[15]

Various theoretical analyses have been offered in order to account for these seemingly paradoxical effects. Most of the analyses are derived directly from the theories of experimental extinction already discussed. Of these analyses, some have been successful in explaining a reasonable number (but not all) of the transitional behavioral phenomena. One theoretical approach that has not enjoyed such success is S-R inhibition theory. Given that inhibition is incremented by a nonreinforced response or by an adverse change in the reinforcer conditions, there is no reasonable means of predicting the partial (varied) reinforcement effect on extinction solely from inhibition theory. Those alternative theories that can predict the partial reinforcement effect can also predict the varied reinforcement effect on extinction. This circumstance arises naturally enough from the conceptual similarity of varying the outcomes of acquisition trials between some reinforcer and none and between, say, more reinforcer and less. Accordingly, a comparable analysis applies in each instance for the varied reinforcement effect; however, we will emphasize the partial reinforcement effect.

Cognitive (S-S) Analyses

DISCRIMINATION HYPOTHESIS

The only explanation for the partial reinforcement effect which is derived directly from S-S cognitive theory, incorporates the discrimination hypothesis of extinction. Organisms cease responding in extinction when they realize that the expectancy of reinforcement is not to be confirmed. This realization occurs as a function of the discriminability of extinction from acquisition. When acquisition involves some nonreinforcement, it is harder to discriminate acquisition from extinction and, consequently, responding persists longer in extinction.

We have previously stated that the discrimination hypothesis has wide intuitive appeal. We have also suggested that the analysis generally suffers from its reliance on *post hoc* specifications of the degree of difficulty involved in discriminating a particular acquisition condition from extinction. Furthermore, in accounting for transitional behavior after partial reinforcement, cognitive discrimination analysis is often found wanting. For example, it has been found that a group receiving consistent reinforcement followed by partial reinforcement will be less resistant to extinction than will a group receiving partial reinforcement followed by consistent reinforcement prior to a shift to experimental extinction (Leung & Jensen, 1968; Sutherland, Mackintosh, & Wolfe, 1965). This finding is directly contrary to the cognitive discrimination hypothesis; it would be expected that the group that receives partial, as opposed to consistent, reinforcement just prior to extinction should have the greater difficulty in discriminating that a shift to extinction has occurred.

COGNITIVE DISSONANCE   Cognitive dissonance theory also has been applied to the partial reinforcement effect on transitional behavior (e.g., Lawrence & Festinger, 1962). Once again the analysis follows directly from the type of analysis used to explain experimental extinction after consistent reinforcement. When an organism experiences a nonreinforced trial during partial reinforcement acquisition, cognitive dissonance is aroused, and extra attractions in the nonreinforcement situation are located by the organism in order to reduce cognitive dissonance. To the cognitive dissonance theorist, this implies that when experimental extinction is initiated, organisms previously exposed to partial reinforcement will respond more than the organisms who were exposed to consistent reinforcement, because these latter organisms did not have the opportunity (nor the need) during acquisition to locate added attractions on nonreinforcement trials.

The same type of assumption is made by a conceptually related hypothesis that analysizes the partial reinforcement effect in terms of secondary reinforcement (Denny, 1946). This theoretical position asserts that partial reinforcement creates a stronger response than consistent reinforcement and, thus, a greater resistance to extinction. The underlying mechanism involves the secondary reinforcement that occurs on nonreinforced trials during acquisition. That is, stimuli associated with reinforcement are present on nonreinforced trials (e.g., the goal box), and these secondarily reinforce the referent response made on nonreinforced trials. This analysis has merit when the total number of reinforcements has been equated, but not when the total number of trials has been equated, between a partial and a consistent reinforcement group. In the equated trials situation where the number of reinforcers is necessarily less for the partial reinforcement group, it is necessary to assume that the secondary reinforcers experienced on otherwise nonreinforced trials contribute more to the persistence of the referent response than do the primary reinforcers received on explicitly reinforced trials.

INCENTIVE   Logan, Beier, and Kincaid (1956) have proposed an S-R incentive analysis of the partial and varied reinforcement effects on extinction that has enough in common with the foregoing analyses to be discussed in the general context of cognitive theories. According to the Logan et al (1956) position, performance in extinction persists only for as long as the organism has an expectancy of reinforcement. Reinforcement expectancy is mediated by $r_g - s_g$ that is acquired during acquisition as a direct function of the reinforcer conditions and the number of reinforcements and as an inverse function of the number of nonreinforcements. Thus, the absolute strength of $r_g - s_g$ is greater following consistent reinforcement that it is following partial reinforcement.

One other difference is created during acquisition between the partial and consistent reinforcement groups, and this is the ability for the partially reinforced group to discriminate the occurrence of nonreinforcement trials from reinforcement trials. When the organism in the partial reinforcement group discriminates a nonreinforced trial during acquisition, it stops expecting reinforcement on that trial. In other words, the organism stops emitting $r_g - s_g$ in a situation where they otherwise would be subjected to extinction. Now to proceed from acquisition to experimental extinction, the previous consistently reinforced group initially has a large amount of $r_g - s_g$ strength, but it loses this strength rapidly, since it has not learned to inhibit the emission of $r_g - s_g$ on nonreinforced trials. By way of contrast, the previous partially reinforced group does not begin with as much $r_g - s_g$ strength, but it tends to preserve what strength it has because, during acquisition, it learned to discriminate nonreinforced trials and to inhibit the emission of $r_g - s_g$ on nonreinforced trials.

The Logan et al (1956) analysis differs from the preceding analyses in several ways. Significantly, the discrimination of extinction is not thought to disconfirm an expectancy but, instead, to result in a preservation of the expectancy. Furthermore, the occurrence of nonreinforced trials during acquisition is not thought to be accompanied by events that add to the strength of the partially reinforced referent response (indeed, the opposite is true). The occurrence of nonreinforced trials simply provides the organism with the opportunity to learn to inhibit the performance of the nonreinforced hypothetical $r_g - s_g$ expectancy mechanism.

Behavioristic (S-R) Analyses

ASSOCIATIVE WEAKENING

After partial and varied reinforcement, transitional behavior is quite perplexing to an associative weakening analysis of extinction. This analytical position assumes that resistance to extinction is directly related to the strength of the association at the end of acquisition. The stronger the association, the more the associative weakening that must occur in extinction and, consequently, the greater the resistance to extinction. Of course, the problem is that consistent reinforcement, and not partial or varied reinforcement, should produce the greater associative strength.

S-R associative weakening analyses are considerably more successful in accounting for partial reinforcement effects when the emphasis is placed on the number of S-R associations rather than on the strength of the S-R association formed during acquisition. As was suggested earlier, multiple S-R associations can involve a number of different stimuli associated with the response (Sutherland, 1966; Waller, 1973) or a number of different variants of the response associated with the stimulus situation (D'Amato & D'Amato, 1962; Schoenfeld, 1950). We will follow the latter analysis, particularly that of Schoenfeld

(1950), since this analysis most directly emanates from conventional associative weakening theory.

The critical assumption for the Schoenfeld analysis is that resistance to extinction is a direct function of the number of different S-R associations that need to be weakened by extinction. Acquisition situations that produce strong S-R associations tend to produce fewer S-R associations than do situations that produce lesser amounts of associative strength. This results because when one S-R association is made relatively strong, the likelihood of another S-R association being formed is less than when only relatively weak S-R associations exist.

The partial reinforcement effect occurs, since partial reinforcement generates a larger number of S-R associations than does consistent reinforcement. Consistent reinforcement produces few, stereotyped S-R associations, because it consistently strengthens the strongest existing S-R association. Partial reinforcement produces a greater variability of S-R associations, because the nonreinforcement inherent in partial reinforcement attenuates the strength of the strongest existing S-R association and, thereby, makes it more likely that alternative S-R associations will form.

To further expose the gist of the analysis, consider that large magnitude reinforcers reduce resistance to extinction after consistent reinforcement but increase resistance to extinction after partial reinforcement (e.g., Gonzalez & Bitterman, 1969; Hulse, 1958; Wagner, 1961). Under consistent reinforcement, large magnitude reinforcers produce greater associative strength and, thus, fewer S-R associations than do small magnitude reinforcers. Under partial reinforcement, large magnitude reinforcers also produce greater associative strength than do small magnitude reinforcers. However, this high level of associative strength does not produce the expected stereotypy of S-R associations, because nonreinforcement trials serve to weaken the currently strongest association. As a consequence, the likelihood of other S-R associations occurring and being sizeably strengthened by the large reinforcer is increased. In brief, the nonreinforcement trials during partial reinforcement create a situation where a large number of associations are available, even though a large magnitude reinforcer is used. The partial reinforcement effect follows directly from the assumption that each S-R association must be separately weakened in extinction.

Actually, the multiple S-R associative analysis nicely handles a wide variety of the identified effects on transitional behavior after partial reinforcement. Of the effects identified thus far, only the intertrial reinforcement effect is particularly vexing. From the present theoretical analysis, reinforcements given during intertrial intervals should have little effect on the number or strength of S-R associations formed to the situation, regardless of whether they occur after a reinforced trial or after a nonreinforced trial.

INCOMPATIBLE RESPONSE   The only generally successful analysis of transitional behavior in extinction or incentive contrast situations which has been framed in terms of incompatible responses, has been frustration theory (Amsel, 1958, 1962, 1967). Nevertheless, one other incompatible response analysis that has been forwarded specifically in order to account for the partial reinforcement effect deserves a brief description. The analysis is attributed to Weinstock (1954, 1958). To begin, we find that nonreinforcement elicits incompatible responses. These responses interfere with the performance of the referent response when they are consistently elicited, as in extinction. However, when incompatible responses are inconsistently elicited, as in partial reinforcement, the incompatible responses tend to habituate. Thus, the difference in resistance to extinction that occurs between partially and consistently reinforced groups is a result of the previous habituation of incompatible responses in the former, but not in the latter group.

Actually, this habituation analysis suffers from many of the shortcomings that characterize other incompatible response analyses. A unique aspect of the habituation analysis is the requirement that competing responses be progressively eliminated during partial reinforcement. Attempts to verify habituation of competing responses empirically have been generally unsuccessful (e.g., McCoy & Marx, 1965; Robbins, Chait, & Weinstock, 1968).

To continue the discussion of frustration theory, it is assumed that after an expectation of a reinforcer is formed, nonreinforcement produces frustration, $r_f - s_f$, and accompanying incompatible responses. Just this sequence of events arises in the course of partial reinforcement training. Incentive is formed during early reinforcement trials and subsequent nonreinforcement trials produce frustration. The essence of the frustration analysis of the partial reinforcement effect is as follows. If the organism can be made to perform the referent response while experiencing frustration (which it can, assuming that frustration will condition to the stimulus situation and, thus, become anticipatory) and the referent response is reinforced, then an association is formed between the frustration stimulus (s_f) and the referent response. In other words, during partial reinforcement counterconditioning to the frustration stimulus takes place. Instead of eliciting an incompatible response, frustration becomes associated with the referent response. The organism learns to perform the referent response in the presence of frustration. When the extinction operation is instituted, consistently reinforced organisms experience frustration that elicits incompatible responses, and partially reinforced organisms experience frustration that elicits the referent response.

The frustration analysis of transitional behavior after partial reinforcement is reasonably powerful. However, as discussed above, this analysis suffers from not having specified how incentive changes in extinction and whether the rate of change of incentive in extinction varies as a function of acquisition conditions (Logan, 1968). Moreover, the analysis has some difficulty in accounting for the effects of certain sequential operations during partial reinforcement. The initial nonreinforcement effect is a case in point. Another case is the finding that a partial reinforcement effect occurs even after a small number of acquisition trials (e.g., Capaldi & Deutsch, 1967; McCain & Brown, 1967; Padilla, 1967).

The difficulty in explaining these two latter effects rests with the assumption that frustration occurs on a nonreinforced trial only if the organism has previously established an expectancy of a reinforcer. When nonreinforced trials precede reinforced trials, or when only a very few reinforced trials are given, no partial reinforcement effect is predicted by the frustration analysis because of the assumed lack of incentive in these situations. After all, frustration theory accounts for the fact that there is a direct relationship between resistance to extinction and the total number of partial reinforcement training trials (e.g., Hill & Spear, 1963; Lewis & Cotton, 1959) in terms of the greater incentive acquired and in terms of the increased number of opportunities for counterconditioning to occur to the frustration state that accompany increased numbers of training trials.

GENERALIZATION DECREMENT   In generalization decrement analyses of extinction, the stimulus or memory traces set up during acquisition by the outcomes of preceding trials become associated to the referent response on subsequent reinforced trials. To the extent that these traces resemble extinction, there will be a generalization of associative strength to the extinction situation and a concomitant performance of the referent response in extinction. Alternatively, the more the extinction situation differs from the stimuli that enter into associations during acquisition, the greater the generalization decrement and the less the resistance to extinction.

In applying contemporary generalization decrement theory (e.g., Capaldi, 1966, 1967) specifically to the partial reinforcement effect on extinction, the exact sequences of nonreinforced (N) and reinforced (R) trials experienced by the organism during acquisition are critically important. Three sequential factors can be identified in this regard. The first is the N-length or the number of consecutive nonreinforced trials preceding a reinforced trial. Resistance to extinction is directly related to N-length, because the longer the N-length, the greater the similarity between learned associations to memory traces of preceding trials and the memory traces encountered in extinction. A second factor is the number of times a nonreinforced trial is followed by a reinforced trial, which is referred to as the number of N-R transitions. This factor is directly related to the resistance to extinction, because it is only on a reinforced trial, which immediately follows a nonreinforced trial, that associations are formed between the referent response and the memory trace of the immediately preceding nonreinforcement. The third factor is the number of different N-lengths. This last factor relates somewhat to the associative weakening analyses and is based on the number of different S-R associations (e.g., Schoenfeld, 1950). The larger the number of different N-lengths experienced during partial reinforcement, the larger the number of different associations between the referent response and memory traces of preceding nonreinforcements. Resistance to extinction is a direct function of the number of different N-lengths, since each N-length association adds generalized response strength to extinction.

A very large number of experiments have obtained results that support the credibility of the sequential factors identified by generalization decrement theory. Among the extinction phenomena that are readily explained in sequential terms are the interpolated partial reinforcement effect, the initial nonreinforcement effect, and the intertrial reinforcement effect. Since S-R associations that are formed during partial reinforcement can generalize to extinction, it is of no consequence when, in the course of acquisition, partial reinforcement is experienced, so long as the opportunity for associations to form to nonreinforced memory traces is made available (interpolated partial reinforcement effect). A sequence of nonreinforced trials preceding a reinforced trial increases resistance to extinction, since this sequence of events is optimal for forming associations to a stimulus situation that is similar to the extinction situation, that is, to a stimulus situation that involves memory traces of a series of preceding nonreinforced trials (initial nonreinforcement effect). If an intertrial reinforcement is made to follow a preceding nonreinforced trial, resistance to extinction is decreased after partial reinforcement. This results because the intertrial reinforcement modifies the memory trace of the preceding nonreinforced trial such that on a succeeding reinforced trial, an association is formed to the memory trace of reinforcement instead of to the memory trace of nonreinforcement. Associations formed to memory traces of reinforcement show a large generalization decrement after an operational change to experimental extinction (intertrial reinforcement effect).

One variable that continues to nag the generalization decrement theorist is the length of the intertrial interval. Capaldi essentially shifted generalization decrement analyses away from a reliance on the stimulus trace and toward the adoption of a longer lasting memory trace in order to be better able to account for extinction phenomena, such as the partial reinforcement effect, that occur after highly spaced acquisition trials (e.g., Weinstock, 1954). Nevertheless, there now exist data that suggest that although the sequential variables of N-length and N-R transitions determine resistance to extinction when massed trials are used during partial reinforcement training, these variables are without effect on subsequent extinction performance when spaced trials are used (e.g., Haggbloom & Williams, 1971; Koteskey, 1969; Mackintosh & Little, 1970). Since memory traces are imbued with the property of durability, there is no *a priori* reason why the importance of sequential variables should be at all affected by the length of the intertrial interval used during acquisition. Simply the fact that they seem to be affected, serves again to affirm the fallibility of hypothetical constructs, including those that pertain to transitional behavior after partial reinforcement.[16]

Summary   The separate theoretical analyses of this section can explain the fundamental partial reinforcement effect on extinction. After all, they were designed to do so. The analyses also can account for the varied reinforcement effect on extinction. This may be done in the case of varied reinforcer amounts, by assuming that the small reinforcer amount functions essentially as does extinction under partial reinforcement conditions. That is, it is either assumed that it is more difficult to discriminate small reinforcer amounts than larger reinforcer amounts from extinction, or it is assumed that small reinforcer amounts produce a greater variability of S-R associations than large reinforcer amounts. Yet, still other accounts assume that small reinforcers following large reinforcers produce frustration that can become anticipatory, or that memory traces of small reinforcers enter into associations that generalize more to extinction than do associations involving memory traces of large reinforcers. More succinctly, theoretical analyses of the transitional behavior, which accompanies extinction after varied reinforcement, do not generally propose properties or processes that are uniquely different from those that have been hypothesized to explain the fundamental phenomenon of extinction or the occurrence of incentive contrast.

This latter observation follows readily from those made earlier, regarding the restrictions placed on theoretical analyses of transitional behavior by the theoretical assumptions made regarding the nature and conditions of learning. If analyses regarding shifts in reinforcer conditions are directly fixed by the learning tenets adopted, and if analyses regarding shifts to zero reinforcer probabilities are indirectly restricted by this same choice of doctrine, then it seems reasonable that analyses involving the interplay of both these types of shifts necessarily are similarly constrained. That is, it violates the parsimony and internal consistency criteria of theory construction to apply different sets of assumptions about fundamental processes to different instances of transitional behavior. Consequently, theoretical analyses of different transitional behavior tend to be fabricated from the same theoretical cloth.

GENERAL SUMMARY AND CONCLUSIONS

Transitional behavior is operationally defined as any change in behavior that accompanies a sustained change in the environment. So defined, transitional behavior encompasses a large portion of the domain circumscribed by the psychology of learning and motivation. Indeed, it is interesting to note that the vast majority of the topics discussed so far in this book involve transitional behavior. After all, even where behavior has achieved some degree of constancy under "steady-state" contingencies, the initiation and the termination of these contingencies necessarily entails a change in the environment and, correspondingly, transitional behavior. Thus it arises that the acquisition of associations under reinforcement, the suppression of behavior under punishment, and the reduction of responding under extinction all represent transitional behavior.

It is possibly this very broadness of the domain of transitional behavior that has so far precluded any one systematic analysis from successfully accounting for all of the empirical phenomena that have been identified in this domain. Broad boundary conditions can be the bane of existence for both empirical and theoretical systematists. But consider in fairness to the systematist that the operations of reinforcement, punishment, and extinction are distinctly different and that although these operations all generate transitional behaviors, they may well be expected to do so differently. Furthermore, the empirical phenomena that may be identified under any one of these transitional operations, such as a shift to extinction contingencies, can be exceedingly varied and complex, as we have seen. In summary, the range of possible effects that may obtain on an operational change in an event's schedules or conditions is large, it is so large that it does not seem to be readily contained by any single set of systematic assumptions.

Thus far, in the preceding chapters, we have separately treated the theoretical subjects pertaining to transitional behaviors that result from the onset and offset of reinforcement and punishment. Now in this chapter, we have discussed the theories of transitional behavior that result from the onset of extinction or shifts in reinforcer conditions. However, our separate treatments of the limited conceptualizations of transitional behaviors should not mislead the reader to the conclusion that these separate theoretical approaches are entirely independent of one another. To the contrary, they are not—nor can they be so.

As we have discussed in the main section of this chapter, adopting a theoretical assumption regarding the nature and conditions of association formation directly influences how the theorist can explain changes in behavior that accompany explicit changes in the schedules or conditions of events that determine the behavior. At least these assumptions about learning must be retained as unaltered in all punishment and extinction situations. Actually, the theorist does not have to make assumptions regarding associations first, and then apply them to other transitional behavior situations. Instead, the theorist may make assumptions about reducing behavior first, and then apply these to situations involving the acquisition of behavior. The point is that the dictums of theory construction, specifically those of parsimony and internal consistency, require that limited theories of transitional behavior be interrelated with all others across the various situations. Obviously this requirement may not always be convenient for the theorist. But this requirement is unquestionably necessary if theoretical analyses of transitional behavior are to be useful across the range of situations in which such behavior occurs.

There is another important point to be made, regarding the interdependence of systematic analyses of transitional behavior, that relates to the applicability of these analyses to everyday affairs. First, consider the wide scope of everyday behaviors that are transitional. For example, any attempt to rid oneself of a bad habit implies transitional behavior. Any turn of events, for better or for worse, in one's living or working arrangements sets the scene for transitional behavior, and so on. Further consider that the task of many individuals, the educator or the behavior analyst, is to arrange for the occurrence of transitional behavior in others. In all such cases, the general point must again be made that any realistic attempt to *change* an ongoing behavior must interrelate to a theoretical assumption regarding the origins of that behavior.

Assume that a behavior analyst has as an objective the elimination of a phobia or an addiction in a client. Assume also that the client is willing to accept whatever operation is recommended by the analyst. In this situation the analyst will clearly proceed with a different behavior-change operation that depends on the theoretical approach to transitional behavior adopted. But this adoption depends, in turn, on the theoretical assumption made by the analyst regarding the source of the undesired behaviors.

For example, if these behaviors were assumed to be the manifestation of some cognitive expectancy, the client might be guided by the behavior analyst cognitively to alter this expectancy. Alternatively, if the behaviors were assumed to result from reversible S-R associations, the behavior analyst might require the client to emit the response in the absence of reward. If the behaviors were assumed to be a reflection of permanent S-R associations, the client might be trained to acquire incompatible responses or stimulus control of the undesirable behavior. (Of course, we would hope that the behavioral analyst would want to proceed eventually with whatever procedure that was empirically best suited to the objective of generating the desired transitional behavior.)

In a similar manner, the educator who wishes to affect a behavioral change in a student, either as an increase or a decrease, would be directed by the theoretical approach to transitional behavior that is embraced. Both types of behavior-change agents, the educator and the behavioral analyst, would want to be constantly mindful of the empirical and functional course of the behavior change to be expected as a result of whatever procedures are applied.

However, the totality of possible transitional behavior changes has not yet been completely identified empirically. It would surely aid behavior-change personnel if a final delineation of transitional behaviors was available and was a realistic model of behavior. However, this availability is constrained by the variety of operational changes that so often occur, sometimes spontaneously in everyday occurrences, and by the recognition that not only operational changes but also antecedent environmental stimuli enter into the control of transitional behavior. The applicability of transitional behavior theories to educational and therapeutic situations is by no means restricted to nondifferential transitional behaviors as it may appear to be by the focus of this chapter. For purposes of application, additional consideration must be given to differential transitional behaviors, that is, to transitional behaviors controlled by explicit antecedent stimuli. The next two chapters of this book are devoted to such differential behavior.

NOTES   1. Taken literally, cognitive dissonance theory may be charged with being unable to explain the most fundamental behavioral changes in extinction. An organism should be expected to experience maximum cognitive dissonance after an extinction trial and, thus, the organism should discover added attractions about the extinction situation itself. If responding in extinction is, in part, a function of the presence of added attractions, and if added attractions are engendered by extinction, performance decrements in extinction should not occur. On the other hand, dissonance is only experienced if the organism, in fact, responds in a nonpreferred situation. Therefore, extinction can be accounted for by the assertion that the organism chooses not to respond in this situation.

2. The associative weakening account of extinction is precisely the same as the associative weakening account of punishment. After all, in each case a decrement in the performance of a learned response needs to be accounted for. More generally, for each theory of extinction there is a parallel analysis of punishment. Consider as a further example that in cognitive theory, expectancies are disconfirmed either by extinction or by punishment, and so on for other theoretical analyses.

3. Although the analysis explains the existence of spontaneous recovery, it has difficulty accounting for some of the parameters of the phenomenon. For example, spontaneous recovery increases as a function of the time elapsing

between successive extinction sessions. Since the strength of the association to stimuli occurring at the beginning of the session should not be directly influenced by this temporal variable, the analysis is considered to have some shortcomings.

4. Inhibition theory has difficulty in accounting for permanent extinction effects. If inhibition is temporary, permanent extinction should never be achieved. Thus, there seems to be a trade-off between extinction theories that better explain temporary effects and those that more readily explain permanent effects.

5. Although reactive inhibition may not always play an important role in extinction, the assumption that inhibition is associated with the effort in responding proves to be an important theoretical construct in other contexts. One such context is differential conditioning, which will be discussed in the next chapter.

6. Frustration analysis of extinction is conceptually similar to a fear analysis of punishment; hypothetical fear-produced stimuli elicit responses that are incompatible with the referent response. Indeed, by assuming that fear and frustration generalize, one to the other, it is possible to explain a number of findings that interrelate punishment and extinction. For example, a fear-frustration analysis is quite compatible with the findings that some punishment during acquisition can increase subsequent resistance to extinction and, similarly, that some extinction during acquisition can increase subsequent persistence of responding under punishment.

7. Other shifts in reinforcement have involved shifts in the delay or quality of the reinforcer. The theoretical analyses of these latter operational changes directly parallels the analyses of shifts in reinforcer magnitudes. Combinations of shifts, shifts in both reinforcer magnitude and delay, have not been often studied empirically. However, the theoretical analysis in these cases presumably would involve a direct extension of the analyses made for the simpler cases.

8. More precisely, the present contrast effects may be referred to as nondifferential successive contrast effects, since the shifts in reinforcer magnitude are not accompanied by a concomitant change in the exteroceptive antecedent stimulus situation. Differential successive contrast effects are typically investigated in the free-operant context and involve successive shifts in the schedule of reinforcement that are accompanied by a concomitant change in the exteroceptive antecedent stimulus situation. These latter effects are usually referred to in the literature as behavioral contrast effects. Other differential contrast effects, known as simultaneous contrast effects, can be identified in the discrete-trial discrimination learning context where different, but simultaneously available, reinforcer conditions are associated with separate exteroceptive antecedent stimuli. Furthermore, a punishment positive contrast effect has been identified. This effect is successive and nondifferential and refers to an elevation in responding above prepunishment levels of performance that occurs after a nonsignaled shift from a punishment to a nonpunishment situation.

9. The essence of Spence's criticism is concerned with the lack of appropriate controls in the early experiments. Crespi (1942), for example, compared his small to large shifted group with the large magnitude performance of a second group that had been shifted from large to small magnitude reinforcement. With careful consideration, one can discern that the latter group had not been stabilized on the large reinforcer before the shift but, instead, was still increasing in performance. Thus, it is possible that what appears as positive contrast in the small to large group is actually an artifact of an insufficient amount of training given to the control group. That is, the control group might well have achieved the elevated performance of the small to large shifted group had it simply been maintained for more training on the large reinforcer.

10. Symmetric contrast effects, the occurrence of both positive and negative incentive contrast, do not imply that the magnitude of the contrast effects will be the same in both the positive and negative instances. Empirically, negative contrast effects are often greater than positive contrast effects. Once again, however, ceiling effects on performance and other factors may enter into the determination of specific magnitudes of the separate contrast effects.

11. The assumption that incentive amount is relative is not required by S-S theory, but it is a reasonable assumption and one that seems most consistent with the purpose and essence of cognitve theorizing.

12. Actually, frustration theory can predict that performance in the shifted group may initially be higher than for the control group. This is because the drive properties of frustration may come into play initially to energize performance (frustration effect). This potential elevation in responding should be transient, giving way to the negative contrast effect and the subsequent adjustment to control levels of responding.

13. Generalization decrement theory can also predict that performance in the shifted group may initially be higher than for the control group. The explanation for this occurrence would be that there was an initial, partial failure to discriminate that a shift in the reinforcer conditions (stimulus situation) had occurred. As this discrimination is perfected, the negative contrast effect should emerge.

14. In general, for every extinction effect identified after varied and partial reinforcement, there is a corresponding effect of varied and partial reinforcement on acquisition and punishment. Using the fundamental partial reinforcement effect on extinction (PREE) as a point of reference, there is a partial reinforcement effect on acquisition (PREA) and a partial reinforcement effect on punishment (PREP). The PREA is that organisms under partial reinforcement perform faster during acquisition than do organisms that receive a reinforcer after every trial. The PREP is that organisms are more persistent in responding under punishment, if given partial reinforcement than if given consistent reinforcement. Furthermore, there is a partial reinforcement effect on generalization (PREG). This latter effect refers to the observation that

stimulus generalization is broader after partial than after consistent reinforcement.

15. Not only are there acquisition and punishment effects that correspond to the extinction effects that occur after varied and partial reinforcement, but there are also acquisition, extinction, and punishment effects produced by varied and partial punishment. For example, there is a partial punishment effect on extinction (PPEE) and on punishment (PPEP). The PPEE is that greater resistance to extinction occurs after partial punishment than after consistent punishment during acquisition. The PPEP is that greater persistence to consistent punishment will occur if previously partial punishment, as opposed to none, has been experienced. One implication of the wide variety of effects identified under extinction and punishment is that complete theories of transitional behavior should be capable of dealing with these various effects collectively. To date, no one theoretical analysis is capable of doing this, although many of the analyses of transitional behavior in extinction are readily extended to the punishment situation.

16. It is worth mentioning a theoretical analysis that is designed specifically to account for resistance to extinction following partial reinforcement under a fixed-ratio schedule of reinforcement. The hypothesis is the response-unit hypothesis. According to this position, the partial reinforcement effect occurs following fixed-ratio reinforcement only if each response is counted separately. Instead, if responses are accumulated into units equal to the size of the fixed ratio used in acquisition, then no partial reinforcement effect is obtained. In other words, during fixed-ratio acquisition the ratio becomes the response unit, and it is this response unit that is emitted in extinction to an extent equal to the response unit (of one) emitted after consistent reinforcement. Indeed, the larger response unit might show less persistence because of the greater total effort involved in the response so defined.

ABSTRACTS   **Amsel, A. Frustrative nonreward in partial reinforcement and discrimination learning: Some recent history and a theoretical extension. *Psychological Review*, 1962, *69*, 306–328.**

In a very important area of the analysis of behavior, the explanation of persistence of behavior in the face of nonrewards attributable to partial reinforcement, the role of nonreward as an active process has emerged in both cognitive-expectancy and in S-R conditioning interpretations. The details of the S-R position which I favor in the form of a sequence of hypotheses in terms of stages of practice are as follows:

1. In Stage 1, $r_R - s_R$ (fractional anticipatory reward) is developing with early rewards, and nonreward has no particular effect.
2. After the development of $r_R - s_R$, nonrewards elicit frustration. This is Stage 2.
3. When nonrewards elicit frustration, the cues previously evoking r_R now

also begin to evoke r_F (fractional anticipatory frustration). In Stage 3 these antedating goal response tendencies are temporarily in competition.

4. Since r_R and r_F cannot be elicited separately by differential cues in partial reinforcement and since the temporary conflict in partial reward training is resolved in favor of running to the intermittently rewarding goal, s_F becomes associated with the instrumental approach response in Stage 4 of partial reinforcement training, providing the mechanism for the partial reinforcement effect. When extinction is carried out, partially reinforced subjects have been trained to respond, whereas consistently reinforced subjects have not.

Bevan, W., & Adamson, R. Reinforcers and reinforcement: Their relation to maze performance. *Journal of Experimental Psychology,* 1960, *59,* 226–232.

Adaptation-level theory describes apparent sensory magnitude as a differential between a present stimulus process and an internal norm derived, through a process of pooling, from background and residual (past) stimulation. Extension of the adaptation-level model to reinforcement requires the demonstration that performance efficiency is a function of the apparent rather than the physical intensity of the reinforcing agent. The contrast effects reported in a number of animal experiments with positive reinforcers strongly suggest this to be the case.

Capaldi, E.J. Partial reinforcement: A hypothesis of sequential effects. *Psychological Review,* 1966, *73,* 459–477.

Reinforcement (R) and nonreinforcement (N) or, more precisely, the organism's reactions to these, appear to occasion potent internal stimuli, represented respectively as S^R and S^N, which regulate behavior in a variety of learning situations. According to the present hypothesis, the major determiners of resistance to extinction (Rn) are the three length variables: N-length, number of different N-lengths, and the number of occurrences of each N-length. The number of N trials occurring in succession without interruption by an R trial defines N-length. The basic theoretical assumption here is that S^N is modified by successive N trials and thus is the mechanism underlying the N-length variables.

Stimulus modification continues either until an R trial occurs, in which event S^N is conditioned to the instrumental response and is replaced by S^R, or until the limit of the modification process is reached, a possible event given great numbers of consecutive N trials as in extinction. The important feature is that the higher the value of S^N gaining habit strength for the instrumental response, the greater the amount of generalized habit provided to still higher values of S^N. Since in extinction, the modification process continues without reversal, it follows that Rn will increase with an increase in the value of S^N conditioned to the instrumental response.

Crespi, L.P. Quantitative variation of incentive and performance in the white rat. *American Journal of Psychology,* **1942,** *55,* **467–517.**

Upward shifts in amount of incentive occasion significant "elation" effects. That is to say, the levels of performance of groups shifted from a smaller amount of incentive to a larger become significantly superior to the level of performance manifested by rats receiving the larger amount of incentive who have not had the prior adaptation to a smaller amount. Downward shifts in amount of incentive occasion significant "depression" effects. That is to say, the levels of performance of groups shifted from a larger amount of incentive who have not had the prior adaptation to a larger amount.

The elation-and-depression-effects are taken as an experimental basis for defining a variable within the rat which may be termed on the basis of human analogy an "expectation." The effects associated with quantitative expectations argue for a two-factor theory of incentive value. Incentive value is profitably viewed as proportional to the distance between level of expectation and level of attainment. The attainment of amounts of incentive below the level of expectation is frustrating in proportion to the degree of negative deviation; the attainment of amounts and qualities above the level of expectation is elating in proportion to the degree of positive deviation.

Denny, M.R. The role of secondary reinforcement in a partial reinforcement learning situation. *Journal of Experimental Psychology,* **1946,** *36,* **373–389.**

This study was designed to test the hypothesis that learning under partial reinforcement has been found to proceed in much the same manner as under 100 percent reinforcement because of the operation of secondary reinforcement on ostensibly nonreinforced trials. The following conclusions would appear to be warranted:

1. Learning is more accurately described as a function of the number of reinforcements than the number of practice trials.
2. Secondary reinforcement may operate in a partial reinforcement learning situation, serving to increase the number of effective reinforcements.
3. Resistance to extinction after either equal or unequal practice is not always greater with partial reinforcement than with consistent reinforcement.

Festinger, L. The psychological effects of insufficient rewards. *American Psychologist,* **1961,** *16,* **1–11.**

The absence of reward or the existence of inadequate reward produces certain specific consequences which can account for a variety of phenomena which are difficult to deal with if we use our usual conceptions of the role of reward.

We are here concerned with the dissonance between two possible cognitions. One of these is a cognition the organism has concerning his behavior, namely, I have voluntarily done something which, all other things being equal, I would avoid doing. The other is a cognition about the environment or about the result of his action, namely, the reward that has been obtained is inadequate. This dissonance can be reduced if the organism can persuade himself that he really likes the behavior in which he engaged or if he enhances for himself the value of what he has obtained as a result of his actions. There is, of course, another way to reduce the dissonance, namely, for the organism to change his behavior. That is, having done something which resulted in an inadequate reward the organism can refuse to perform the action again. But as long as the organism is prevented from changing his behavior, the dissonance tends to be reduced by developing some extra preference about something in the situation.

The inclination to engage in behavior after extrinsic rewards are removed is not so much a function of past rewards themselves. Rather, and paradoxically such persistence in behavior is increased by a history of nonrewards or inadequate rewards. I sometimes like to summarize all of this by saying that rats and people come to love things for which they have suffered.

Gleitman, H., Nachmias, J., & Neisser, U. The S-R reinforcement theory of extinction. *Psychological Review,* 1954, *61,* 23–33.

Any theory of learning must deal with the phenomena of extinction as well as those of habit formation. We have tried to show that Hull's treatment of extinction faces a number of serious difficulties. In particular:

1. Recent experiments in the field of "latent extinction" suggest that the actual performance of a response may not be necessary for its extinction.
2. Neither reactive nor conditioned inhibition is clearly or adequately conceptualized. In particular, the "habit of not responding" has never received a satisfactory explanation.
3. Certain paradoxical consequences can be derived from the theory: not only should the learning curve inevitably decline to its starting point with continuous reinforcement, but, in fact, learning should be impossible altogether.
4. Many of these difficulties stem from Hull's assumption that withdrawal of reward introduces nothing essentially new to the situation.

Logan, F.A., Beier, E.M., & Kincaid, W.D. Extinction following partial and varied reinforcement. *Journal of Experimental Psychology,* 1956, *52,* 65–70.

The extinction of an instrumental response is due, at least in part, to the loss of incentive motivation. Incentive motivation is assumed to be dependent upon the fractional anticipatory goal response (r_g). The extinction of an instrumental response is therefore related to the extinction of r_g which is, in turn, a function of the number of unreinforced evocations of r_g. If the conditioned anticipatory r_g on any trial is larger than would be appropriate for the primary reward actually given on that trial, the surplus r_g may occur several times without being reinforced. We propose the hypothesis that the loss of an instrumental response tendency which results from a nonreinforced trial is directly related to the extent to which r_g persists in occurring after the time of reinforcement has passed.

From this assumption, one would expect resistance to extinction to be greatest for Ss who, immediately upon failure to receive an accustomed reward, stop performing the anticipatory goal response, or in subjective terminology, immediately stop anticipating reward. Therefore, to predict relative resistance to extinction, one must determine whether the training conditions allowed S to extinguish r_g to the postreinforcement-time cues, i.e., in everyday terminology, to take "No!" for an answer.

Mowrer, O.H., & Jones, H. Habit strength as a function of the pattern of reinforcement. *Journal of Experimental Psychology*, 1945, *35*, 293–311.

That habitual responses which are rewarded only intermittently are apparently stronger than those which are rewarded after each occurrence does not invalidate the Law of Effect. These experimental results can be explained, either by the "response-unit hypothesis" or by the "discrimination hypothesis," both of which are consistent with the view that reward is the fundamental and crucial determinant of habit strength.

The response-unit hypothesis defines a "response," not as a single, isolated movement, but as the totality of behavior which leads to a given goal. For example, the fact that a rat has to press a bar three times in order to get a pellet of food does not mean that three separate acts, or "responses," have been performed; the sequence of three bar depressions is here conceived as a unitary, integrated, instrumental performance. When "response" is thus redefined in terms of the whole pattern of behavior which proves effective in producing reward during acquisition, it is found that intermittent reinforcement, far from producing greater "habit strength," actually produces reliably less than does continuous reinforcement.

But there is another equally plausible approach to this problem. If, during acquisition, a response (conceived as a more or less isolated movement) occurs repeatedly but is rewarded only now and then, the transition from acquisition to extinction will not be discriminated as sharply as if acquisition has involved reward for each and every response. With "faith" thus established that failure will ultimately be followed by success, "discouragement" is slower to set in (ergo, greater "resistance to extinction") when there is a change in objective conditions from acquisition (occasional reward) to extinction (no reward whatever).

This second interpretation involves the introduction of factors ("faith," discouragement) which disrupt the direct, one-to-one relationship observed in the simplest kinds of situations between reward and behavior. But it should not be supposed that there is any discontinuity between the fundamental laws of learning that can be so easily demonstrated at the lower levels of behavior and the generalizations that seem to hold best at the higher levels.

Seward, J.P., & Levy, N. Sign learning as a factor in extinction. *Journal of Experimental Psychology,* **1949,** *39,* **660–668.**

An experiment was designed to test the sign-learning theory of extinction; the theory, namely, that when reward is removed CS becomes a sign of nonreward and CR drops out through lack of incentive. The deduction tested was that CR could be weakened without itself being elicited, provided that the situation formerly associated with reward was now experienced without it. The results are taken to verify the hypothesis that led to their prediction, with one qualification: the learning that underlies extinction may serve not merely to subtract the incentive but to produce an "emotional" interference with the response.

Sheffield, V.F. Extinction as a function of partial reinforcement and distribution of practice. *Journal of Experimental Psychology,* **1949,** *39,* **511–526.**

The basic hypothesis is that extinction necessarily involves different cues from those used during training. Omission of reinforcement alters the context and produces a certain amount of generalization decrement because of the change in cues. The hypothesis can be applied in explaining the effect of partial reinforcement on extinction as follows.

Occurrence of reinforcement on a given trial produces effects which provide characteristic stimuli at the start of the following trial. When reinforcement is given on every trial, the aftereffects of the reinforcement will be part of the conditioned stimulus pattern on every trial after the first. However, when training with partial reinforcement is given, the subject is exposed, on reinforced training trials that follow nonreinforced trials, to cues which are normally present only during extinction and learns to perform the response in the presence of such nonreinforcement cues.

Thus, the initiation of extinction produces a relatively large change in the conditioning stimulus pattern when it follows training with reinforcement on every trial, but much less change when it follows training with partial reinforcement. Because the response evoked by a generalized stimulus is weaker than that evoked by the reinforced stimulus, the conditioned response during extinction will be weaker in the former case than in the latter.

Weinstock, S. Resistance to extinction of a running response following partial reinforcement under widely spaced trials. *Journal of Comparative and Physiological Psychology,* 1954, *47,* 318–322.

Various studies of partial reinforcement in a runway situation have shown the superior resistance to extinction of partially reinforced as compared with continuously reinforced animals. The following notions, cast in contiguity theory framework, seem to be able to handle these results.

The role of reinforcement is to remove the animal from stimulation. The last response made prior to the termination of the stimulation will then be conditioned. In experimental extinction, reinforcement is withheld. The animal then makes other, or competing, responses which are, in turn, conditioned to the stimulation. The result is a decrement in response strength of the original response class.

The competing responses which the animal makes on a nonreinforced trial habituate during the course of a series of nonreinforced trials. Thus, partially reinforced animals, which have had some number of nonreinforced trials during acquisition, will have their competing responses habituated to some relatively low level. On the other hand, continuously reinforced animals will have had no chance to habituate their competing responses, and they will be at their highest strength during extinction. Thus the continuously reinforced animals will show the greatest decrement in the strength of the running response during extinction.

EXAMINATION ITEMS   **Topics for thought and discussion**

1.   Consider a frustration-theory account of asymptotic speed that compares continuous and partial reinforcement and a fear-theory account of asymptotic speed that compares continuous reinforcement and continuous-reinforcement-and-partial punishment. Assuming some similarity between frustration and fear, what should be the relative resistance to punishment of the groups in the first situation, and the relative resistance to extinction of the groups in the second situation?

2.   How might theories of extinction differ as theories differ between primary reinforcement and secondary reinforcement?

3.   Discuss the implications for S-S cognitive theory if incentive amount is assumed to be absolute rather than relative.

4.   State how inhibition theory might be revised in order to account for the varied reinforcement effect on extinction.

5.   Consider the concept of "extinction below zero" from a cognitive dissonance theoretical framework.

6.   Discuss the relative merits of extant theories of extinction in accounting for the extinction of incentive.

Objective items

1. Tolman's S-S cognitive approach to shifts in reinforcement and to extinction is best classified as a
    a. generalization decrement theory
    b. incompatible response theory
    c. associative strength theory
    d. inhibition theory

2. In ignoring principles of stimulus control, a strict interpretation of Hullian theory would predict that reconditioning following complete extinction should be
    a. quite rapid
    b. equivalent to original conditioning
    c. quite slow
    d. impossible

3. Latent extinction was offered as a challenge to inhibitory theories of extinction. Actually, this empirical phenomenon also severely challenged other theories of extinction, most especially
    a. associative weakening theory
    b. incompatible response theory
    c. incentive theory
    d. cognitive dissonance theory

4. According to Festinger's cognitive dissonance theory, value should be added to the experience of insufficient reward whenever encountered,
    a. including the situations of extinction and punishment
    b. including extinction but excluding punishment
    c. excluding extinction but including punishment
    d. excluding the situations of extinction and punishment

5. In Amsel's frustration theory, frustration is a drive that has properties that are
    a. general and nondirective
    b. general and directive
    c. specific and directive
    d. specific and nondirective

6. Comparing Amsel's frustration theory and Festinger's cognitive dissonance theory, with respect to the rate of extinction following continuous reinforcement,
    a. Amsel would predict a faster rate than Festinger
    b. Festinger would predict a faster rate than Amsel
    c. both would predict the same rate
    d. their relative predictions would depend on the temporal distribution of extinction trials

7. Associative weakening theory of extinction involves the development of
    a. competing response processes
    b. inhibitory processes
    c. discriminatory processes
    d. no new processes

8. In his view of transitional behavior following a shift from a large to a small reward,
    a. Capaldi (aftereffects) would deny frustration and Amsel (frustration) would deny aftereffects
    b. Capaldi would deny frustration and Amsel would not deny aftereffects

    c. Capaldi would not deny frustration and Amsel would deny aftereffects
    d. Capaldi would not deny frustration and Amsel would not deny aftereffects

9. A negative contrast effect would not be predicted by Amsel, if frustration were innately connected to reaction potentials compatible with the reinforced response
    a. True
    b. False

10. The partial reinforcement effect on extinction has attracted special theoretical interest because it
    a. is counterintuitive
    b. is robust, reliable, and replicable
    c. appears to contradict other measures of response strength
    d. appears to counteract the effects of punishment

11. A rat has run some trials down a grey alley to food in a white goal box and some trials down the same grey alley to "no-food" in a black goal box. He will then extinguish more slowly if the black goal box is used during extinction than if the white goal box is used. This result would not be expected if one attended only to the
    a. frustration involved
    b. stimulus-generalization decrement involved
    c. secondary reinforcement involved
    d. response differentiation involved

12. According to Amsel, the amount of frustration engendered by a nonreinforced trial during partial reinforcement acquisition
    a. is constant over trials
    b. increases over trials
    c. decreases over trials
    d. increases then decreases over trials

13. According to the $r_g - s_g$ analysis of extinction put forth by Logan, Beier, and Kincaid, the amount of extinction engendered by a nonreinforced trial during partial reinforcement acquisition
    a. is constant over trials
    b. increases over trials
    c. decreases over trials
    d. increases then decreases over trials

14. According to a Capaldi-type generalization decrement hypothesis of extinction, which sequence of reinforced (R) and nonreinforced (N) responses would be expected to produce the greatest resistance to extinction?
    a. NNRNNR
    b. NRNNNR
    c. NNNNRR
    d. RNNNNR

15. Which of the following daily sequences of reinforced (R) and punished (P) trials would you expect to lead to the greatest resistance to punishment from the viewpoint of a generalization decrement theory?
    a. RRRPPP
    b. PPPRRR
    c. PRPRPR
    d. PRPPRR

16. Given a finite number of trials (say, 100) on a 50% partial reinforcement schedule

involving constant N-lengths (namely, 1, 2, 5, 10, 25, or 50), Capaldi would predict (assuming that learning is reasonably gradual) that subsequent resistance to extinction would be

    a. independent of N-length
    b. an increasing function of N-length
    c. a decreasing function of N-length
    d. an increasing then decreasing function of N-length

17. Suppose a group of rats given 50 partial reinforcement trials followed by 50 regular reinforcement trials is found to be more resistant to subsequent extinction than a second group of rats given 50 regular reinforcement trials followed by 50 partial reinforcement trials. Which theory of extinction could best handle this finding?

    a. multiple S-R association theory
    b. generalization decrement theory
    c. discrimination hypothesis
    d. frustration theory

18. An explanation of the overtraining extinction effect is most readily generated from which theory?

    a. incompatible response theory
    b. generalization decrement theory
    c. incentive theory
    d. inhibition theory

19. Which of the following occurrences is the most difficult to explain from a cognitive analysis of transitional behavior after shifts in reinforcement?

    a. negative contrast but not positive contrast
    b. transient negative and positive contrast
    c. permanent negative and positive contrast
    d. larger negative contrast than positive contrast

20. A multiple S-R association theory analysis of extinction following partial reinforcement would predict that resistance to extinction would be

    a. greater with large rewards than with small rewards
    b. greater with small rewards than with large rewards
    c. the same for both large and small rewards
    d. the same as the relative effect of amount of reward after continuous reinforcement

ANSWERS TO OBJECTIVE ITEMS

1.   (c) Tolman contends that when an expectancy is confirmed it is strengthened, and when it is not confirmed it is weakened. No other processes are involved to determine the strength of expectancies.

2.   (d) Since both habits of responding and of not responding are permanent, complete inhibition should leave no room for further changes in excitatory potential and reconditioning should not be possible.

3.   (a) Only the associative weakening theory argued that a certain number of responses should be executed in extinction because of what was reinforced in acquisition. The other alternatives have provisions to allow extinction to be influenced by factors other than the actual execution of the previously reinforced response.

4.   (a) Insufficient reward should invoke a search for added value, regardless of whether the situation involves extinction or punishment. Indeed, from Festinger's

theoretical vantage point, there should be very little difference in outcome between extinction and punishment situations.

5. (b) Amsel's frustration drive was integrated into Hullian drive-motivation theory. Thus, frustration contributed to generalized drive and energized any ongoing behavior. At the same time, frustration had stimulus properties that permitted it to enter into learned associations with specific responses.

6. (a) There is no reason to presume that conditioned frustration and learned added attractions would change differentially over time. However, anticipatory frustration should immediately begin to elicit incompatible responses, whereas acquired added attractions should prolong extinction somewhat.

7. (d) The essence of an associative strength theory is that extinction results simply from the loss of the tendency acquired during acquisition and, hence, involves no new processes.

8. (d) Capaldi would not deny frustration; indeed, frustrative aftereffects are perfectly compatible with this approach. Nor would Amsel deny that reward and nonreward produce stimuli that could gain control.

9. (True) It is only when the innate responses to frustration are incompatible that a shift from a large to small reward produces a negative contrast effect.

10. (c) Apart from other possible reasons, learning theorists have been especially attracted to the partial reinforcement effect, because partial reinforcement typically produces a weaker response in terms of measures, such as speed, amplitude, or choice; yet, it generates greater persistence.

11. (c) Here we are looking at the behavior antedating the goal box, although aftereffects of the preceding goal-box experience could be included. Hence, no response differentiation is possible until the goal box is encountered. Presumably, there would be less frustration in the black goal box, because the discrimination would be formed before strong anticipation of reward could develop. Stimulus generalization could correctly predict the result. Secondary reinforcement, however, would lead to the opposite prediction, because the white goal box would help to maintain the response.

12. (b) Frustration must increase during early trials, since anticipation of reward must first be developed before nonreinforcement is assumed to be frustrating. It would be possible to assume that frustration subsequently decreases as the organism becomes accustomed to nonreinforcement, but this is not the assumption made by Amsel.

13. (c) The rate of extinction is constant, regardless of the strength of the $r_g - s_g$. However, with increasing trials the organism learns to inhibit the emission of $r_g - s_g$, and so the total amount of extinction decreases across trials.

14. (b) Resistance to extinction for Capaldi depends on generalized response strength to complete extinction that is a function of both N-length and the number of different N-lengths reinforced.

15. (d) Resistance to punishment is operationally similar to resistance to extinction, namely, continuous punishment trials. A generalization decrement theory would assume that rewarded trials following punishment trials would increase persistence, and more so the longer the run of punishment trials during original training.

16. (d) Two factors are important in this prediction. The first is that the larger the

number of transitions, the greater the learning to those unique cues. An N-length of one would maximize this factor, while an N-length of 50 would provide only one transition. The other factor, however, is N-length itself; the longer the run of nonreinforced trials followed by a reinforced trial, the greater the training given to the cues that occur during extinction. Hence, under the stipulated conditions, some intermediate N-length would be optimal for enhancing persistence.

17. (a) Actually, multiple S-R association theory is the only one which can handle such a finding at all. Generalization decrement theory would predict no difference, and discrimination and frustration theories would predict the opposite outcome. According to multiple S-R theory, the initial phase of partial reinforcement would create variability that would be preserved by the subsequent regular reinforcement phase. When regular reinforcement is presented first, response stereotypy results and is only somewhat compromised by the subsequent partial reinforcement phase.

18. (b) All of the theories assume that the relevant hypothetical construct (e.g., incentive, strength) increases with continued training. Generalization decrement theory can make the best predictions in this case by assuming that generalization gradients to nonreinforcement sharpen with continued reinforcement training.

19. (a) Since cognitive analyes have adopted a relative view of incentive magnitude, increases and decreases in reinforcement amounts should, respectively, produce positive and negative contrast effects, although their permanence and magnitude can vary widely.

20. (a) The extinction in partial reinforcement produces an increase in the number of S-R associations that would be differentially reinforced by large as opposed to small rewards. Thus, greater response strength and greater resistance to extinction would occur under the larger reward.

CHAPTER EIGHT

SYSTEMATIC ANALYSES OF THE STIMULUS

Gradually, we have been evolving the view that although the traditional topic heading for this book is learning and motivation, our subject matter could also be described as the stimulus control of behavior. We have observed that the presentation, termination, or withholding of stimuli comprise the fundamental operations involved in controlling motivation, and the repeated recurrence of contingency relationships among stimuli and responses comprise the area of learning. Of course, in a larger sense, all environmental operations that affect the survival of an organism could be viewed as a form of stimulus control, many of which fall outside our admittedly hazy boundary conditions. Take but one example; any form of medication is a stimulus event that affects the organism's well-being and, hence, the potentiality for behavior. Accordingly, we are reviewing selected aspects of the stimulus control of behavior, namely, those environmental operations that appear to affect basic learning and motivational processes.

Given this setting, it seems appropriate to reflect more generally on the nature of a stimulus, particularly the types of stimuli that enter into systematic analyses of learning and motivation. The most important point that we wish to make by way of introduction is that the term "stimulus" can appear at every level of abstractness described in Chapter 2 of this book. There is a tendency to shift gears unobtrusively, but one should be alert to the contextual meaning of the term "stimulus."

Specifically, at the least abstract level of an empirical fact, it is quite sufficient to say that a light of a specified hue at a specified brightness was employed. Those who are familiar with the physics of light energy would object that our description is quite naive, which of course it is, but it would at least suffice to enable anyone else to repeat our operations and presumably generate the same objective stimulus event. And replicability is all we really need in order to state a fact.

However, once we attempt to generate laws at progressively more abstract levels up to fundamental principles, the term stimulus itself becomes more abstract. Surely we do not want to be restricted to that particular light used in that particular situation, but a host of additional factors begin to enter into our expression of "other things equal." First, we will observe that the same objective light stimulus varies depending on the state of adaptation of the organism's eyes and may also be affected by the phase of the day/night cycle at the time of observation. We also note that the same objective light varies with its juxtaposition in the total environment, because much will depend on the orientation of the eyes at the time of stimulus presentation. Furthermore, the same objective light varies not only with its location in this particular environment but with the context more generally, because it is at least somewhat different in different contexts. As we proceed up the scale toward empirical principles, we will certainly not want to be restricted to light energy, but will want to include other sources of stimulation, such as sound energy, to which the organism is also responsive. These illustrate only a few of the inescapable complexities involved in developing abstract empirical systems.

The problem is more complex for the theorist, because even the most detailed and elaborate empirical/operational analysis of the stimulus as controlled by the experimenter or the natural environment will not suffice. Given all these considerations, the theoretical question is: what does the organism "really" see? Now we know that science can never answer *that* question in any ultimate sense, because even though we may use the same word for the same objective stimulus event, there is no way of knowing how it looks to anyone else but ourselves. And yet, the theorist is inclined to turn the argument around and contend that the way we label stimuli affects the way we see them. The proposition is that the way in which a stimulus is perceived by an organism importantly depends on the past experiences of that organism.

The theorist may well make this point at an even more abstract level because one can never see the same stimulus twice. The second presentation is necessarily different from the first presentation, if for no other reason than that it is the second presentation. Similarly, as in more complex environments, there is a saying that one can never step in the same river twice. In short, the theorist will want to get at the fundamental principles governing the way stimuli are perceived by organisms.

Since one's theoretical approach is heavily guided by convictions about the nature of the beast, let us first reflect on the stimulus construct as conceived in cognitive terms. Gestalt psychology is an appropriate general orientation. The essence of this approach is that, just as surely as the environment can do nothing more than control the occurrence or nonoccurrence of stimuli, so too the organism can do nothing more than attempt to organize these stimulus events into some meaningful pattern, whole, or Gestalt. Behavior is viewed as something of an epiphenomenon, something that more or less accurately reflects the organism's view of the world.

Accordingly, one cannot really talk about a light alone as a stimulus, because it is always a part of an indivisible whole. Now it is true that if the light is especially informative about the impending occurrence of events that are significant to the organism, then the perception of the environment may be organized in such a way that the light is the center of attention or at the focal point of the total Gestalt. But all the empiricist's concern about specifying the physical nature of the light stimulus is largely for naught because that does not describe the true nature of the organism's perceptual field. The laboratory exercise demonstrating the tendency of people to see a complete circle when the physical stimulus is an incomplete circle is much more than an exercise to a Gestalt psychologist. It illustrates the important "closure" principle of organization of one's environment. Surely, we have all had those feelings of something missing, something out of place, something keeping our understanding of a personally important facet of our lives from closure. We well know the compelling desire of "getting it all together," of putting everything in its place or right perspective, of seeing clearly why events are happening the way they are.

We have related much of our historical antecedents to Tolman, because he most forcefully brought this style of thinking to behaviorism. If all that the scientist can do is present stimuli to organisms, all the organism can do is present stimuli in return to the scientist. Such stimuli are generated by some form of behavior. In this sense, Tolman may be classified as a cognitive behaviorist, but his interests were not so much in behavior qua behavior. Psychology is the study of the mind, and behavior is interesting primarily as a means of drawing inferences about what is going on in the mind.

More contemporary cognitive behaviorists evince somewhat greater interest in behavior in its own right but still focus on the nature of the stimulus as the primary determinant of the nature of the response. For example, Lawrence (1963) has employed the hypothetical construct of the stimulus-as-coded. According to such a view, an objective light stimulus is not the event that enters into subsequent associative processes. Instead, the organism actively codes the light in some form that is appropriate to the nature of the task. If the stimulus is properly coded, then adaptive behavior follows ipso facto, and nonadaptive behavior reflects an inappropriate coding of the stimulus.

There are many other ways that one could conceptualize the nature of a stimulus in cognitive terms, and perhaps it is the sheer number of these that leads the "behavioristic" behaviorist to minimize the importance of such hypothetical processes in systematic analyses. Obviously, the simplest possible organism would be one to whom the stimulus is nothing more nor less than the energy change that occurs in the environment. Indeed, that has got to be the ultimate empirical anchoring of any hypothetical stimulus construct. Such theorists do not completely deny the possible importance of perceptual principles, but these must be as few and as simple as possible and they must be demanded by the data. So the behavioristic approach begins by assuming that the conceptual sensorium is a more or less accurate representation of the real world, provided only that any necessary receptor orientation is assured. In sum, the most important principles concerning the stimulus to a "behavioristic" behaviorist are those of the sensory processes.

A somewhat common way to envisage the controversy between cognitive and behavioristic conceptualizations of the stimulus is along an imaginary central-peripheral dimension. The hard-core behaviorist would like to rely entirely on the laws of physics, chemistry, and sensory neurophysiology. Some of these laws are concerned in part with the central nervous system, but they are still conceptually peripheral; they are all mechanistic. Stimulus energies may not be transformed linearly by the nervous system and, hence, the field of psychophysics is included by these behaviorists. Furthermore, overt receptor-orienting acts may be necessary to ensure that an environmental stimulus event actually impinges on the sensorium. But while all of these are readily admissible, the behavioristic theorist strongly resists the unleashed admission of central perceptual principles and, at least, demands that they be rigorously anchored on both the antecedent and consequent sides of a theoretical system.

This is the undercurrent that will occupy us through the remainder of this book. Empiricists, of course, forge ahead carefully specifying the objective stimulus event in whatever detail is necessary to generate internally consistent abstract laws and principles of behavior. To them, a systematic relationship between stimulus and response is not only the beginning but also the end of the analysis. In this case, however, many of the empirically interesting questions have, as a matter of historical fact, been generated by theoretical conceptions. Accordingly, we will not attempt to separate the purely empirical approaches in organizing these systematic issues but will continue to try to distinguish between the empirical phenomena and their possible theoretical implications.

THE PRINCIPLE OF STIMULUS GENERALIZATION

Whenever the probability of a response has been changed by any form of reinforcement, nonreinforcement, or punishment, this accrues not only to the stimulus situation involved at the time of these operations, but also to stimulus situations that are similar to it. To some extent at least, this principle of stimulus generalization has the same potential for circularity as the principle of reinforcement. Unless stimulus similarity can be defined in some way that is independent of the generalization process itself, there is no way to predict whether a new test stimulus will provoke a response learned in the context of another stimulus. This problem appears not to have caused as much consternation as the circularity of the empirical law of effect, but it is no less important conceptually.

Probably the reason for this relative lack of concern is a result of the fact that many studies of stimulus generalization have involved variations along a physical dimension of stimulus energy. For example, the amplitude of light or sound energy can be measured according to the laws of physics, and it is not unreasonable to presume that similarity is at least monotonically related to the amount of difference in such energies. But even that approach is not without pitfalls. A tone that is exactly one (or several) octaves away from a training tone leads to greater generalized responding than other test tones that are slightly closer, physically, to the training tone. We are inclined to infer, post hoc, that such tones are more similar, because there is greater generalization between them. Accordingly, we are in pretty much the same bootstrap operation of accepting as a principle that a response will tend to be occasioned by stimuli in systematic relation to their similarity to a training stimulus, and using the amount of generalization as an indication of stimulus similarity.

Hull argued that the principle of stimulus generalization is a logically necessary adjunct to the principle of reinforcement. Since it is conceptually impossible ever to present exactly the identical stimulus twice, there could be no principle of reinforcement without an associated principle of stimulus generalization. This realization gives rise to the concept of a *gradient* of stimulus generalization, and we will begin our discussion of this principle with several issues related to the attempts to describe this gradient mathematically.

Measurement Issues in Generalization

The concept of a gradient implies that coordinates can be set up; on these coordinates response strength can be plotted as a function of stimulus similarity. Basically, there are three important questions. First, is there a gradient at all in the sense that responding is greatest to the original stimulus? One would be disinclined to refer to stimulus control if there were no gradient in this sense. Second, assuming that there is a gradient, what is the function form that best describes the underlying process? Granting the circularity to which we previously have referred, it can be anticipated that the function will be a monotonic one, but there are many mathematical functions that satisfy this requirement. Finally, what is the rate parameter of the equation? This is commonly referred to as the slope of the gradient and is described as being relatively "flat" or relatively "steep."

If one is interested in determining a simple empirical fact, then the requisite research appears obvious enough. First train a response of an organism in the presence of some specified stimulus and then test for responding to somewhat different stimuli. But there is already a problem, because one can properly consider only the very first test trial to be a pure measure of stimulus generalization; all later tests are contaminated by the outcome (reinforcement, non-reinforcement, punishment) of that first test. Specifically, one of the most quoted studies of stimulus generalization (Guttman & Kalish, 1956) involved repeated tests to several stimuli at varying distances from the training stimulus. Now it is true that testing was done under an extinction schedule that followed training under a reinforcement schedule so designed to promote considerable persistence of the response, but even so, the obtained gradients actually developed during the course of testing. The data are no less meaningful empirically, but their interpretation is based on the use of resistance to extinction as the measure of response strength, and this does not always correlate very well with other measures, including response rate in the same general type of experimental situation. The point is that one can never obtain a pure gradient of stimulus generalization from a single subject, even though we may presume there is one conceptually.

Nevertheless, stimulus generalization gradients have been obtained by one means or another in all types of conditioning situations. If one wishes to attempt to integrate these various facts in the form of a law and ultimately a principle, then one cannot avoid searching for some way to equate the units of measurement both within and between situations for both stimuli and responses. From a strictly empirical point of view, this is not absolutely essential; one could have a large number of low-level laws, each unique to particular measures in particular situations. The problem arises at the more abstract, empirical levels and, of course, is a vital aspect of any theoretical system.

MEASURES OF THE STIMULUS

It is said that one cannot add apples and oranges, but such maxims do not apply in the area of stimulus generalization. Indeed, very much on the contrary —the range of generalization and discrimination phenomena is no where better revealed than in a natural language. It is known, for example, (Razran, 1939) that there is greater generalization based on the meaning of words (semantic generalization) than on their sounds (phonetic generalization).[1] Learning a language may be viewed as the acquisition of such similarities and differences (Skinner, 1957).

In many such cases, there is no *a priori* way in which to order the stimulus events. You may ask, for example, whether a circle is more similar to a triangle than to a square, but the physical attributes do not directly order such stimuli with one perceived intrinsically closer to another. Even with physically scalable stimuli, there is no way of knowing in advance whether a change in a qualitative property, such as the pitch of a tone, is greater or less than a change in a quantitative property, such as the loudness of a tone. Generalization occurs along each of these dimensions, but they are largely orthogonal.

In all such cases, one cannot mix apples and oranges in the sense of simply assuming that the units of measurement are the same. Adding one apple increases the size of a fruit basket, but not necessarily as much as adding one orange. In many such cases, we can at least rank order stimulus events according to some property, such as size, and attempt to infer the relative amount of generalization based on that property. But to the quantitatively oriented systematist, such orderings do not provide very powerful mathematical descriptions of the phenomena. Conceptually, at least, stimulus similarity is a continuum and generalization is a correspondingly continuous process.

Accordingly, attempts to describe the stimulus-generalization gradient have typically relied on manipulations of a single stimulus dimension that can be measured along some physical continuum. But even in this restricted context, it quickly becomes apparent that physically equal units of measurement along this continuum are not necessarily equal in any psychological sense. In response to this, some researchers have resorted to the methodology of psychophysics and scaled the stimulus continuum according to the number of just-noticeable–differences separating the stimuli (e.g., Hovland, 1937), or they simply assumed the Weber-Fechner law and transformed the physical continuum into its logarithm (e.g., Razran, 1949). Still others have attempted to cope with this problem by mathematically interrelating operationally different procedures, such as discriminability and generalization (Guttman & Kalish, 1956).

In summary, then, we can make the general point that the *shape* (but not the relative slope) of the generalization gradient will depend on the units by which the stimulus is measured. The abscissa of the graph is an elastic band that can arbitrarily be stretched or contracted at the pleasure of the systematist. There is no "true" shape of the generalization gradient in an empirical sense.[2] A theorist may postulate a particular gradient shape and distort the physical continuum in such a way as to fit the theory, and the implications of the theory may importantly depend on the postulated shape. Generalization, in this sense, is a hypothetical construct to which the pitfall of reification clearly applies.

MEASURES OF THE RESPONSE   Perhaps less obviously, but no less importantly, the units according to which the response is measured affect the stimulus-generalization gradient. At a purely empirical level, one can readily take a dependent measure, such as response latency, and plot gradients of generalization in those terms. At a more abstract level, there is good reason to believe that the same absolute difference in response latency is different in some systematic sense at different points along the continuum. We all know that athletic records may be determined by differences of a fraction of a second, although such differences would be quite inconsequential at lower levels of performance.

So too the ordinate of a graph of stimulus generalization is an elastic band affecting, primarily, the mathematical *slope* of the gradient (and not the relative shape). This problem is most troublesome if one wishes to compare gradients whose origins differ either by design or differ as a result of intrinsic features of the situation. For example, if one wished to study generalization in an operant conditioning context following original training under schedules of reinforcement that generated different basic response rates, then there would almost certainly be a difference in the absolute slopes of the gradients. There are inherent end effects; the physiological limit of response output situated at the upper end, and complete cessation of responding situated at the other end.

For want of a better solution to this problem, it is conventional to speak in terms of *relative* gradients[3] (preferably, in addition to, and not as a substitute for, absolute gradients). A relative gradient sets the point of origin at unity for all conditions to be compared and plots performance in terms of the fraction of the original absolute level. The wary systematist, however, must be cautious about interpreting relative gradients, because they assume that, for example, half as much as you had is the same regardless of how much you had with which to begin. This may not be an unreasonable assumption, but it is by no means universally accepted that psychological measurement properly subscribes to a ratio scale (e.g., Stevens, 1951).

SUMMARY Stimulus generalization is an excellent example of a point that scientists, in practice, often go blithely ahead; nevertheless, in the face of conceptually insurmountable odds, they generate meaningful but hypothetical concepts and constructs. We can never measure a pure generalization gradient of a single subject,[4] any more than a jury can follow a judge's instructions to disregard certain evidence that has already been introduced in a case. The coordinates of a graph of a stimulus-generalization gradient can be pushed and pulled here and there at will. Yet, somehow systematists "know" that there is a gradient in there somewhere, and useful statements can be made about what it must look like, if it could only be seen. But since systematists are apparently doomed to look at the picture through a haze, inevitably somewhat different perceptions arise. The trick in this case is to try to look at the picture through the eyes of each systematist's theory in order to judge the usefulness of each conceptualization.

Theoretical Interpretations of Stimulus Generalization Regardless of the nature of the hypothetical associative process, and regardless of the conditions assumed to be required for its development, it is clear that this process is not restricted to the very particular stimulus involved in acquisition. Since an S is on the antecedent side of both S-S and S-R learning constructs, a theory of stimulus generalization need not be idiosyncratic for one or the other type of theory of learning. Nevertheless, molar views of behavior tend to lead to molar views of the stimulus and a compatible view of stimulus generalization. For example, if learning is held to be an organization of a cognitive field, then a change in some aspect of that field should change, to some extent, the organism's total perception of it. To such a theory, it would be perfectly reasonable to presume that the organism knows well enough that the situation is changed and must now make a separate decision about how best to behave in this different situation. In this instance, there may be no stimulus-generalization decrement, because the change in the stimulus environment is not viewed by the organism as being significant. Indeed, it is only when the difference is significant vis-à-vis the outcome of various behaviors that selective stimulus control obtains. It is just such a view that we will soon describe, but first let us consider several more mechanistic approaches to a theoretical interpretation of stimulus generalization.

THE PHYSIOLOGICAL APPROACH

Pavlov's term for what we now call stimulus generalization was *irradiation,* and this term better describes his physiological interpretation of the phenomenon. His inference was that a particular stimulus projects upon some locus in the sensory nervous system and that the elicited activity in that locus irradiates much in the way that ripples irradiate when a pebble is thrown into a calm body of water. Now the association with a response is actually formed with the sensory locus itself, and this irradiation process is quite coincidental during acquisition.[5]

Suppose, then, that a stimulus is presented whose localized projection is not very distant, physically, from that projection to which a response has become conditioned. As the activity in that different locus irradiates, it will reach into the conditioned locus and excite the associations residing there. The further away the new stimulus locus is from the conditioned locus, the weaker the irradiated activity and, hence, the weaker the excitation of the conditioned association. This approach, therefore, does not assume that there is a gradient of different associative strengths; there is a single associative connection that is differentially tapped by other stimuli in relation to their similarity to the conditioned stimulus.

Pavlov was a physiologist for whom reification was not only permissible but actually the sum and substance of behavioral observations. It is quite possible to provide a reasonable model of this theory. At least according to the place theory of hearing, sound energy transmits wavelike surges of pressure to the fluids in the cochlea that differentially excite receptors strung out spatially. Hence, tones of similar pitch will, indeed, excite nearby receptors, and irradiation in the more central projections of these receptors could readily be conceived of as behaving according to Pavlov's theory. Since these waves of energy have various physical harmonic properties, many of the complexities of auditory generalization could be accommodated. Some other sensory systems, such as spatial location of touch, appear to follow this type of analysis; still others, such as taste and vision, appear to be coded quite differently in the nervous system. Even so, there is clear evidence of overlapping patterns of excitation in the cerebral cortex (Thompson, 1965). This way of thinking may be useful as a *theory* of stimulus generalization, even if we disregard direct physiological implications.

THE FUNCTIONAL APPROACH   The physiological approach would be truly useful, if one could identify the hypothesized loci in the nervous system, somehow measure their irradiation, and predict purely on physiological grounds the degree of generalization between stimuli. Short of this, however, a functional approach becomes the most common among theorists. Stimuli, themselves, are identified functionally in the sense that any describable aspect or property of the environment that can be shown to be able to gain control over behavior is a stimulus,[6] and its similarity to other stimuli is indicated by the amount of generalization of that behavior (e.g., Miller & Dollard, 1941). The functional approach eschews any remotely physiological reduction and has the blatant circularity of an empirical analysis. It is simply postulated that associations formed in the context of one stimulus event somehow generalize in gradient fashion to similar stimulus events, but no mechanism is proposed to account for the process whereby this comes about.

Just as to the physiological approach, stimulus generalization is a premise to the functional approach. But the conceptualization is more that the associative process itself generalizes. That is, similar stimuli are assumed to acquire some associative strength by virtue of conditioning to somewhat different stimuli, and they then stand ready directly to produce the response when the stimuli are presented. This view is most evident in Hull's 1943 formal postulate of stimulus generalization. Some fraction of the habit strength accrued to a training stimulus generalizes to similar stimuli. The reader should note carefully that this is a postulate, not a principle, as we have defined it in this book; generalization of habit strength is embedded in a theory and may have a variety of properties and behavioral manifestations.

THE RANDOM STIMULUS-SAMPLING APPROACH   One way of theorizing about stimulus generalization requires first that we conceptualize a stimulus as an indefinitely large population of potential stimulus elements (Guthrie, 1935). This conceptualization applies even to a very simple stimulus, such as pure tone; of course, it applies as well to complex environmental events. Furthermore, assume that on any trial, the organism effectively samples, at random, from this population of potential elements. If this sample is also somewhat large, then the characteristics of the elements in the sample will closely approximate those of the population. The stimulus-sampling theory of learning assumes that each element is hooked to (associated with) one and only one response in an all-or-none fashion. The probability of any response of interest becomes the proportion of the sampled elements that are associated with that response. Since the trial is terminated by the response of interest, all sampled elements will be returned to the population in a conditioned state and participate in random sampling on later trials (sampling with replacement). Although each elementary association is fully formed on one trial, only gradually will all of the potential elements become associated with the response of interest.

Within such a conceptualization, stimulus generalization can be viewed in terms of the number of potential elements of any new stimulus that are common to the elements of the original conditioned stimulus. Since these elements are purely hypothetical, actual determination of the degree of overlap is functional. The greater the degree of stimulus generalization of a response, the greater the overlap among the elements of the stimuli involved. However, this approach enables one to bring to bear the mathematics of set theory and probability theory in order to make quite elegant derivations about more complex situations involving functionally identified similar stimuli (e.g., Estes, 1959).

Note that although this theory of stimulus generalization was an outgrowth of a particular theory of learning, its fundamental tenets need not be restricted to that theory. All theorists view even a simple stimulus as actually being a stimulus complex. A tone, for example, has at least both pitch and loudness, but presumably also timber, resonance, and other qualitative and quantitative dimensions. Hence, the view of stimulus generalization, resulting at least in part from the number of common elements, is a widely useful approach. However, it does pose another conceptual problem that we can discuss only very briefly.

In its pure form, an elementary view of the stimulus assumes that the hypothetical elements are independent of each other. They have their own associations and are free to go their separate ways. This is, of course, totally antithetical to a Gestalt view of the stimulus that sees these elements as combined into an indivisible whole. Even though Hull adopted an elementary view of the stimulus, he was quick to postulate a process he called "afferent stimulus interaction," whereby each element was to some extent modified by concurrent elements. Consider the impact of such an assumption on a stimulus-sampling theory. Each element would have to be tagged according to the particular constellation of elements sampled on any trial, hence, one could never actually sample the exact element twice. The elegant simplicity of the original theory would be severely tarnished by such a development.[7]

THE SELECTIVE STIMULUS-SAMPLING APPROACH

In order to focus on conceptual relationships among the various approaches and issues, we will describe Lashley's (Lashley & Wade, 1946) account of stimulus generalization in a language somewhat different from that which he espoused. The essence of his theory is that a stimulus is, indeed, composed of a number of potential stimulus elements, but the organism does not sample from these elements at random. Instead, these elements may be conceived of as being arrayed in some hierarchy of generality or abstractness, from the very molecular details of the stimulus to its most global characteristics. The organism starts by sampling the latter type of element, develops associations with it, and behaves accordingly. Now the organism may or may not happen to notice fine grain details of the stimulus during repeated presentations and, to this extent, there is an element of chance with respect to the features that may gain control over behavior. But the one way to ensure that certain features will be selected is to reinforce them differentially. The finer the discrimination required, the more molecular the selected aspects of the stimulus.

To give the reader an understanding of this type analysis, consider how we learn to recognize another person's face. Now the most general characteristic is that it is, in fact, a face. Somewhat more specifically, it is a human face. Then, in addition to having two eyes, a nose, and a mouth, it is framed by two ears and a certain amount of hair. Clearly we can get more and more detailed as we itemize the shade of the skin, the shape and color of the eyes, the size and shape of the nose, the features of the lips, and so on. How far we need to go in this recognition task depends on the similarity of that person's face to others from which we wish to discriminate it. It can become a very subtle task, if we are dealing with identical twins. Lashley's theory proposes that we tend to go only so far as we have to go to make the discrimination, discarding along the way those more global aspects that are of little or no use in determining adaptive behavior. In this context, we may not all make the same discrimination on the basis of the same features.

We hope the reader can envisage from this example the way stimulus generalization occurs. The familiar case of a baby calling all men "Daddy" is an instance of generalization that reflects the fact that discrimination has progressed only so far as to distinguish male human faces from female human faces. In a similar vein, if one conditions a dog to salivate to a tone of a particular pitch and at a particular loudness, none of those details is required by simple conditioning. Its most general feature is that it is a change in stimulus energy. If we have done nothing else to focus on specific energy changes, the organism may respond equally as well to any change we happen to introduce. A light has a common element of a change in energy, and if that is all that is controlling behavior, generalization is complete. Only if we reinforce a tone and a light differentially will the organism necessarily discard this global element of energy change and distinguish sound energy from light energy. Even so, generalization would be complete along all changes in sound energy, unless some further differential reinforcement makes the more abstract features insufficient; if this occurs, the organism is moved to select still finer details of the stimulus as a basis for responding. In sum, complete generalization is inherent between stimuli that are identical in points of detail—detail about which discriminations have been learned.

Because this appoach is frequently misunderstood, we wish to emphasize here that Lashley's view is *not* that generalization is complete in any of the senses that we have previously described. For example, it is not that habit strength accrued to one stimulus generalizes to another stimulus with a flat gradient. Generalization is complete with respect to stimulus elements that are selectively sampled. A gradient with a nonzero slope appears only as a result of *new* learning, that is, associations formed with finer grain details of the stimulus. These associations are necessarily formed only if they are required by conditions of differential reinforcement. The old associations are no longer effective in controlling behavior as they become superseded by these new associations. Except in the larger sense of providing financial support, an older child will not call other men "Daddy."

SUMMARY   By way of summary, we can identify three fundamental issues that have emerged from the various theoretical analyses of stimulus generalization. The first of these is the extent to which, if at all, a stimulus can be conceptualized in terms of separate elements each bearing its own associative connections. The second issue is whether the associative connections at the most molecular level permitted by the theory are of an all-or-none character or whether they can vary in strength. Finally, there is the issue of whether these elements are sampled in their entirety, randomly, or selectively. Each approach, of course, provides a reasonably adequate theoretical account of the empirical principle of stimulus generalization. We wish now to turn to various corollaries of that principle that appear to have some bearing on these theoretical conceptualizations. Since the issues are still very much alive, we can anticipate that the empirical phenomena have not yet led to a generally accepted view.

The Primitive Gradient of Stimulus Generalization

One could develop an interest in the nature of the primitive gradient of stimulus generalization from a purely empirical approach. Once it is known that the slope of the gradient is affected by differential conditioning of two or more stimuli along some continuum, it would naturally be appropriate to seek the limits of this corollary to the basic principle. At the one extreme, one might ask how steep the gradient could become or, effectively, how fine a discrimination the organism can form. At the other extreme, one could ask how flat the gradient would be, if there were no opportunity for differential conditioning. This latter would be the primitive gradient uncontaminated by factors known to affect its slope.

However, the search has some of the aspects of a wild goose chase. This is so because the slope of the generalization gradient becomes steeper during acquisition even with training to a single stimulus. The measurement problems that we have discussed make this latter fact somewhat tenuous, because performance is naturally increasing at the same time. In this case, the problem is conceptually more complex than simply plotting relative gradients, because one does not know what the level of performance would have been to the original stimulus at the time a generalization test is conducted. These difficulties are substantially ameliorated by comparing gradients after the performance has become asymptotic with those obtained after extended training beyond that point. The fact that the gradient becomes steeper with extended training (see, e.g., Hearst & Koresko, 1968) lends credence to the interpretation that the gradient changes throughout acquisition.

It is worth dwelling on this very fundamental empirical phenomenon in order to explore its theoretical implications. Of course, a purely functional theorist can simply make the empirical law a part of the theory and not ask the additional question of why the gradient should get steeper with training to a single stimulus. But if one does ask that question, the answer is likely to reside in some version of stimulus-sampling theory. We can first see that it is contradictory to a completely random sampling approach, because additional training trials bring in, by chance, more and more of the total available potential stimulus elements and, increasingly, associate these with the response. The more elements thus conditioned, presumably, the greater the likelihood that random sampling from similar stimuli would include conditioned elements. Specifically, if half of the elements of the original stimulus overlap with a generalization-test stimulus, and half of the former are conditioned, then only 25% of the latter would be conditioned. When all of the former become conditioned, 50% of the latter would be conditioned. This means that the absolute gradient would have gotten steeper, but the relative gradient would remain invariant. Furthermore, there could be no change in either the absolute or relative gradients with extended training. Accordingly, this simple version of random sampling appears to be inadequate.

Now let us go to the other extreme and assume that the organism samples, selectively, to be sure, only one element and develops an association with it. On this assumption, we would get either complete generalization or no generalization, depending on whether the organism sampled the same element when exposed to a similar stimulus. Clearly, this would not lead to a continuous generalization gradient. Accordingly, assuming one were to follow the general stimulus-sampling approach, the indications are that one would want a non-random sampling mechanism involving some number of the potential elements. Furthermore, the characteristic of this sample must change progressively with training in such a way that would increasingly include only elements that are unique to the training stimulus. But since there is no differential conditioning explicitly involved to provide a basis for selection of such unique elements, a theory built along these lines would have somehow to endow the stimulus and/or the organism with properties that just naturally lead in this direction. Since we are not aware of such a conceptualization, let us return to the quest for the primitive gradient of stimulus generalization.

The real impetus for interest in this question arose from Lashley's theoretical analysis of stimulus generalization. His theory clearly implies a perfectly flat gradient, if all opportunities for differential conditioning are precluded. But although it is easy enough to conceptualize the question, it is extremely difficult to realize the necessary conditions in practice. In classical conditioning, for example, training may be given with a single stimulus; yet, it is still differentiated from the background. Similar arguments can be made in other conditioning contexts, and the issue is made even more complex, if one requires that there be no opportunity for any form of differential reinforcement that involves the stimulus modality under consideration at any time in the organism's past history. Nevertheless, a number of experimenters set out in search of the primitive gradient of stimulus generalization (e.g., Ganz & Riesen, 1962; Mountjoy & Malott, 1968; Peterson, 1961; Riley & Levin, 1971; Rudolph, 1969).

We cannot review these studies in detail, but the complexities should be readily apparent. To use one example, the eye requires some amount of light for normal development of the retina and that makes rearing under conditions of total darkness somewhat suspect. This physical deficit can be eliminated by rearing in a monochromatic environment, but it is technically difficult to avoid some gradations in brightness around which some conceivable discrimination may have been learned, and perceived color varies with brightness.[8] Conditions that completely preclude differential conditioning in the learning environment, itself, are also technically difficult to achieve. Recall that we can only get a single pure measure from each subject!

The generally, but by no means universally, accepted conclusion from the various efforts made along these lines is that there probably is some primitive gradient of stimulus generalization with a slight, yet nonzero, slope. Those who favor Lashley's point of view contend that there were methodological flaws in those studies that obtained a gradient. However, that ultimate question is not critical, because clearly the primitive gradient does not display an amount of differential responding that would have a very powerful impact on typical studies of stimulus generalization. Accordingly, the important theoretical issue is how best to account for the fact that differential conditioning results in a relatively steep gradient. Lashley would still contend that such procedures bring behavior under the control of new distinguishing features of the stimuli. The alternative is to bring one's theory of extinction to the differential conditioning paradigm, and assume that these procedures represent the interaction of the processes of acquisition and extinction.

Differential Conditioning[9]

Perkins (1953) and Logan (1954) have underscored the point that many procedures, such as simple classical conditioning, involve a form of discrimination learning. Once stated, the point is obvious: the organism must discriminate between the presence and the absence of the conditioned stimulus. The most immediate implication of this realization is that conditioning should be better the more distinctive the conditioned stimulus. As a particular case in point, more intense stimuli provide a greater change and, hence, an easier discrimination. There are other important implications. First is the recognition that a stimulus can be a decrease as well as an increase in the level of stimulation. It is not necessarily the case that these changes are identical in their ability to gain control over behavior, but a stimulus is nevertheless a change in energy in either direction.

Another implication is that stimulus control is properly inferred only from differential responding in the presence and absence of a stimulus or, more generally, between two levels of stimulation. That is, behavior must change in relation to the change in stimulation to enable the inference that stimulus control is being exerted. Indeed, this line of reasoning could lead to the proposition that discrimination learning is the most fundamental behavioral process. It is when stimuli provide information about the impending occurrence (or potential occurrence) of events of emotional significance to the organism that they gain control over adaptive behavior. The first process that must come into play is the discrimination of antecedent stimulus events.

If we were to attempt to develop that theme, however, it would be necessary to analyze our use of the term "discrimination" in greater detail. There are two sources of potential ambiguity with this term: its status as a hypothetical concept or hypothetical construct, and its operational delineation. Furthermore, these sources of ambiguity are often confounded with each other.

First, consider the use of the term as a hypothetical concept. In this sense, discrimination simply summarizes the many facets of differential stimulus control of behavior.[10] It subsumes the laws resulting from experimental analysis of those situations in which stimulus-differential responding can be observed. This meaning of the term does not imply any underlying psychological process, but it implies process when used as a hypothetical construct in a theory. Our natural language predisposes us to think of such internal processes when we use the word, and the theorist explicitly intends this implication. A pure empiricist would say that an organism does not learn to discriminate between stimuli, because discrimination is not a behavior. What organisms learn is to respond differently, and there is no need to invoke imaginary powers or processes in describing differential performance. The theorist, of course, contends that discrimination is indeed a hypothetical internal process, that organisms learn to "tell the difference" between the stimuli, and that discrimination is just as fundamental a construct as generalization.

Furthermore, to some theorists, there are two operationally different ways to tap this underlying process. One involves *differential conditioning* in which two or more stimuli are presented separately on one occasion or another, and the conditions of reinforcement/punishment are different depending on which stimulus is present. This is a go-no-go discrimination, but it differs from simple conditioning in that the organism must distinguish more than simply the presence or absence of a stimulus. Adaptive behavior requires the organism to respond in the presence of one explicit stimulus when presented and to behave differently in the presence of a second explicit stimulus when presented. The second procedure is called *discrimination learning*. It involves the simultaneous presentation of two stimuli that enables the organism to make a choice between them. The pure empiricist who eschews the view of an underlying discriminative process is inclined to distinguish between these two procedures on operational grounds and, accordingly, treat with them separately. Some theorists are equally disposed to this distinction, because they contend that discrimination learning involves a quite different hypothetical process from differential conditioning. Since we will be discussing this latter contention extensively in the next chapter, we will attempt to concentrate here on differential conditioning and its effects on gradients of stimulus generalization.

THE POSTDIFFERENTIAL REINFORCEMENT-GENERALIZATION GRADIENT

The general corollary is clear: differential reinforcement of two or more stimuli along some stimulus dimension steepens the slope of the gradient of stimulus generalization. This steepening effect is greater the larger the differential in reinforcement or punishment and also is greater the more similar the stimuli, up to some point, where the difference between the stimuli is very small or nonexistent. In the latter case, the procedure functionally reduces to varied reinforcement of the same stimulus and results in a flat generalization gradient.

These phenomena typically are tested by following differential conditioning with test presentations of stimuli not only intermediate, between the original training stimuli, but also stimuli outside that range. The finding of special interest is that the level of responding is not maximal precisely at the point of the originally positive stimulus. Instead, the maximal level of responding occurs in the presence of stimuli that are displaced somewhat in the direction away from the originally negative stimulus. This phenomenon is called the *peak shift* [11] and gives a more complete picture of the postdifferential reinforcement-generalization gradient. The gradient is steeper in the range of stimuli between the originally positive and negative stimuli but continues to rise beyond the originally positive stimulus, reaching a peak and then decreasing to stimuli still further removed from the training stimuli. (Sometimes the peak is not actually shifted, but more of the area under the gradient is displaced away from the negative stimulus.)

We have already described Lashley's approach to a theoretical understanding of the postdifferential reinforcement-generalization gradient. His understanding was that the organism searches for and increasingly focuses on some distinguishing features of the stimuli. The more such features are found, the less the empirical degree of generalization between them. The peak shift was not a well-known phenomenon at the time of Lashley's writings, but we can probably project from his more general approach how he would account for it. The most distinguishing features of the stimuli would be the difference between them along the dimension involved in their differential reinforcement,

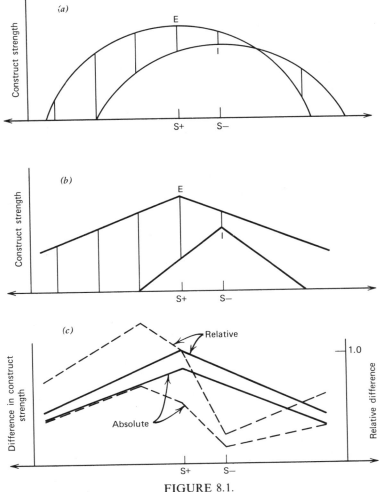

FIGURE 8.1.

Derivation of the Postdifferential Conditioning-Generalization Gradient from Hypothetical Gradients of Excitation and Inhibition. (See text for explanation.)

and some degree of extrapolation along that dimension would be a quite reasonable outcome. For example, if in a visual intensity problem one is trying to make a judgment of whether this is the bright stimulus or the dim stimulus during the original learning, then a somewhat brighter stimulus would be still more distinctively bright.

Lashley's account is therefore based on new learning, that is, new excitatory processes developed with respect to new-to-the-organism stimulus features. An alternative is to bring to bear one's theory of extinction. Of those theories discussed in Chapter 7, the most effective one in the present context is some version of the Pavlov-Hull-Spence construct of inhibition. According to such a theory, nonreinforcement to S— is tantamount to extinction, and it is reasonable to assume that the resulting inhibitory process generalizes around S— in the same theoretical sense that the excitatory process generalizes around S+. The theorist needs only to postulate certain features of these gradients such that their combination will rationalize the observed phenomena.

There are at least two ways in which this can be done. One derivation is depicted in Figure 8.1a in which it is assumed that the generalization gradients of both excitation and inhibition are positively accelerated around S+ and S—, respectively, and have equal absolute slopes. Given the further assumption that performance is simply the subtraction of the strength of the inhibitory process from that of the excitatory process at each stimulus value, the resulting net strength is shown by the vertical lines between the two generalization gradients. It can be seen that not only is there greater net strength at S+ than at S— but that this net strength is still larger at stimuli displaced from S+ in the direction away from S—. Thus, this graph provides one account of the peak-shift phenomenon.

Figure 8.1b gives an alternative conceptualization that uses linear generalization gradients. (These same general statements would equally apply to negatively accelerated gradients.) In order to rationalize the empirical gradient in terms of the difference between excitatory and inhibitory processes, given this shape of the gradients, it is necessary further to assume that the absolute slope of the inhibitory gradient is steeper than that of the excitatory gradient. Again a steeper slope and a peak shift can be seen, but to emphasize the point, we have displayed the net (excitation minus inhibition) gradients in both absolute and relative form in Figure 8.1c.

In that graph, the solid lines depict the absolute and relative excitatory gradients as obtained from Figure 8.1b and assumes simple conditioning to S+. As would be expected, these gradients are both quite flat without any differential conditioning procedure. The dashed lines depict the net gradients after differential conditioning, the absolute gradient obtained by subtraction of the inhibitory gradient from the excitatory gradient, and the relative gradient obtained by setting the net value equal to unity at S+ and depicting the remaining points in relation to that value. This last function brings into bold relief two of the features of the postdifferential conditioning-generalization gradient. It is distinctly steeper in the range between S+ and S— and shows a clear peak shift. However, this analysis implies that the absolute gradient should everywhere be lowered by differential conditioning, and this implication is not supported by the facts.

There is one additional set of facts that have a very interesting bearing on this excitatory-inhibitory approach. Terrace (1968) has shown that if differential responding is established by the use of essentially errorless procedures and then tests for generalization, the gradient between S+ and S− is steepened but the complete gradient does not show a peak shift. This, at least, permits the interpretation that errors of commission (i.e., responding to S−) are necessary for this feature to appear in the gradient, and those are precisely the experiences that most clearly implicate some inhibitory process in differential conditioning. We were able to derive the peak shift only by arranging gradients such that there was a greater loss of inhibition than of excitation as the test stimuli were moved away from the training stimuli. If the training procedure does not involve the accretion of an inhibitory process, then there would be no competing gradients from which to infer a peak shift.

GENERALIZATION OF INHIBITION

We have already employed the concept of an inhibitory generalization gradient in the preceding derivation of the postdifferential conditioning-generalization gradient but, for the empiricist, there are two problems with this analysis. First, of course, the gradients of excitation and inhibition involve hypothetical constructs. Second, the empirical gradient is presumed to involve the joint action of these two processes. What better illustration of theoretical folderol could there be than blithely arranging the heights, shapes, and slopes of hypothetical gradients in both absolute and relative terms and in such a way as to obtain differences with a rough correspondence with the empirical gradient? Given enough degrees of freedom, one could fit anything after the fact and, accordingly, predict nothing. The theorist might counter that these postulates have wider implications than just these data, and indeed they do, but even the theorist would prefer to operate with more empirical evidence concerning hypothetical constructs.

Let us begin, then, with a straightforward empirical phenomenon. A *conditioned inhibitor* is a stimulus that, as a result of prior experiences, tends to reduce the level of responding normally maintained by other stimuli. As background, let us consider the phenomenon of *external inhibition*. This term refers to the fact that the likelihood of the occurrence of a conditioned response in the presence of a conditioned stimulus may be reduced by the simultaneous occurrence of some extraneous stimulus event. In the context of external inhibition, this additional source of stimulation has had no particular prior experimental history. As an obvious example, if one unexpectedly shocks a dog before ringing a food bell, there is likely to be a substantial reduction in conditioned salivation. This phenomenon is typically understood on the basis of a stimulus-generalization decrement. The added stimulus changes the total stimulus complex and, correspondingly, reduces the conditioned response tendency. It is also frequently the case that the added stimulus is naturally associated with responses that are incompatible with the conditioned response and leads to a decrement as a result of these competing response tendencies. But regardless of such theoretical interpretations inhibition, in at least this sense, is a meaningful hypothetical concept. One stimulus may decrease the likelihood that another stimulus will provoke its customary response.

A conditioned inhibitor is just such a stimulus, but it is one that has acquired inhibitory properties as a result of explicit training. An illustration of the referent procedure might look like this; reinforce a response in the presence of a light alone, and nonreinforce that response in the presence of that same light when a tone is also present. Organisms learn this discrimination and respond appropriately. The evidence that the tone has acquired inhibitory properties results from the addition of the tone to other conditioned stimuli with which it has never before been paired. If a response has separately been conditioned to a tactile stimulus, for example, that response will be weakened if the tone is presented along with the tactile stimulus.

Conditioned inhibition, in this sense, is a form of external inhibition. Pavlov distinguished both of these sources of inhibition from what he called *internal inhibition,* which is the type of hypothetical process that we have heretofore referred to simply as inhibition. Internal inhibition was presumed to accrue to the negative stimulus as a result of differential conditioning. Although many recent systematists (e.g., Wagner, 1969) do not subscribe to Pavlov's distinction between conditioned inhibition and internal inhibition, and their reasons are quite solidly based on empirical evidence, it is worth pausing long enough to try to understand the conceptual basis for the distinction as viewed by Pavlov.

For Pavlov, the referent procedure for establishing a conditioned inhibitor involved a discrimination that could not be based on the light stimulus, because it was present on all trials. This means that its excitatory tendency has to be the same both with and without the tone, and differential responding of necessity requires an inhibitory process of some kind. Furthermore, the tone is not simply orthogonal to the light; it involves a different sense modality and the kind of generalization gradients that we have heretofore described would not appear to apply. It is for this reason, so Pavlov reasoned, that a conditioned inhibitor has its widespread potential for inhibiting other conditioned responses, such as those involved with tactile stimuli. In contrast, internal inhibition involves a process occurring along some continuum within the same modality and, hence, could not be viewed as a form of external inhibition.[12]

Apart for empirical evidence, many contemporary theorists do not maintain Pavlov's distinction, because one can conceptualize a light alone and a light-plus-tone as being placed on a continuum, at least with respect to tone intensity. Furthermore, if we conceptualize any stimulus, such as a light, as being composed of many stimulus elements, differential conditioning along an intramodality continuum still involves distinguishing the relevant features. This means that the inhibitory process involved in simple differential conditioning is of the same kind as that involved in the establishment of a conditioned inhibitor. Thus, the important questions concern the range of generalization in this process. Specifically, a nonreinforced low-intensity light might acquire inhibitory properties as a result of differential conditioning with a reinforced high-intensity light, but not be as effective a conditioned inhibitor as the tone in our reference procedure, because inhibition became focused on light-intensity features and included generalized excitatory tendencies from the high-intensity light. The tone is purer in these regards and might, therefore, show greater generalization of its inhibitory properties to a tactile stimulus.

With this background, it is clear that some more direct, empirical approach is desirable with respect to inhibitory processes. However, this does not imply that the theoretical analyses are uninteresting but only that they are operating to this point with too few constraints. Here, the problem is to devise a technique for studying stimulus-generalization gradients of inhibition, at least in the sense of demonstrating that a stimulus can come to control the behavior of not-responding. The technique must avoid any concomitant changes in the excitatory process, while the conditioned inhibitory stimulus is varied systematically.

Jenkins (e.g., 1962) and his colleagues devised such a technique and variations of it have subsequently been employed by others (e.g., Honig, Boneau, Burstein, & Pennypacker, 1963). To illustrate this procedure, we could train a pigeon to peck at a blank key on a reinforcement schedule while, at other times, a vertical line is superimposed on the key and an extincton schedule is in force. Thus, the pigeon learns a discrimination between the presence and absence of the vertical line, and subsequent testing for inhibitory control can be done by varying the tilt of the line superimposed on the key. The general result is that there is more responding with a tilted line than with the original vertical line, even though line tilt was not varied during original differential conditioning and line tilt is presumably orthogonal to the positive blank key. That is, there is no reason to believe that the tilted line is either closer or further away from the blank key than the vertical line and, hence, the increase in responding reflects differential control of not-responding along the line-tilt dimension.

Another approach could be first to reinforce nondifferentially a number of stimulus values along the continuum of interest and, thus, presumably establish high and equal excitatory tendencies. Extinction can then be imposed on a single stimulus value followed by testing to other values. The suppressive effects of extinction are maximal at the selected value and decrease in gradient fashion (i.e., performance increases with stimulus values more different from the extinguished value). These results provide empirical evidence supporting the introduction of conditioned inhibition as a hypothetical concept (although this latter procedure invokes internal inhibition in Pavlov's conceptualization). Of greater theoretical import is the fact that if one obtains inhibitory gradients and excitatory gradients separately, then one should be able to combine the two gradients to predict the postdifferential reinforcement-generalization gradient, which presumably involves the joint action of both processes. Reasonable success has been achieved by this systematic approach (Hearst, 1969). However, it would be premature to draw any strong conclusions as yet because of the various types of measurement problems that we have described.

Contrast in Differential Conditioning

Thus far, we have concentrated on differential conditioning situations in which one of two discriminable stimuli is the occasion of reinforcement and the other is the occasion of nonreinforcement. This is the most common procedure in experimental analyses of the principles involved in differential conditioning and is not an uncommon occurrence in the everyday world. However, more commonly in the latter context, there are situations in which the schedules/

conditions of reinforcement/punishment are different for discriminable stimuli. Such situations have been studied experimentally and have led to the introduction of another concept that affects not only the slope of the postdifferential conditioning-generalization gradient but also its height.

Our focus on reinforcement versus nonreinforcement led us to a discussion of excitatory tendencies and inhibitory tendencies, both of which are used as hypothetical concepts or hypothetical constructs. This type of analysis would not appear to be quite so readily applied to differential conditioning in which the "negative" stimulus is actually reinforced, but to a lesser degree. In differential classical conditioning, the stimuli may be associated with different intensities of the unconditioned stimulus or with different interstimulus intervals; in differential instrumental conditioning, the amount, delay, or probability of reward may differ; in differential operant conditioning, the prevailing schedules of reinforcement may differ. In the latter two procedures, punishment may also be involved, differentially, with respect to the prevailing stimulus. Although these latter conditions might quite reasonably involve inhibitory tendencies, they are commonly thought of as avoidance tendencies because their effects appear to be more than simply a passive "no-go."

The horizons of differential conditioning are vastly expanded by such considerations. In relation to this enormous domain, the range of conditions that has been studied experimentally is somewhat small, but one phenomenon has emerged in a sufficiently wide variety of situations and merits the status of an abstract empirical law and invites theoretical analysis. This phenomenon is currently called *differential contrast,*[13] although other terms have been used from time to time. The basic experimental evidence exhibits that performance to the more highly reinforced stimulus tends ultimately to be superior to that which obtains without its being embedded in a situation, including other occasions with a different stimulus and a lesser reward (positive contrast). Conversely, performance to the lesser reinforced stimulus tends ultimately to be inferior to that which obtains without its being embedded in a situation, including other occasions with a different stimulus and a better reward (negative contrast). Quite obviously, the empirical description of these differential contrast effects is closely aligned to the empirical description presented for nondifferential contrast effects in the preceding chapter.

Note that differential contrast is directly contradictory to the implications of the excitation-inhibition analysis on which we have leaned so heavily heretofore. Responding to the positive stimulus should be weakened by generalized inhibitory tendencies from the negative stimulus, and responding to the negative stimulus should be strengthened by generalized excitatory tendencies from the positive stimulus. This inference is not unique to this approach. To state the same conclusion in terms of incentive theory, for example, the relative incentive values should generalize from one stimulus to the other, thus, weakening the stronger and strenthening the weaker. As a final complication, we can no longer think of differential conditioning in this context as a go-no-go discrimination, because the organism should (and does, albeit at a lower-than-predicted level) continue to respond to the "negative" stimulus.

Accordingly, the postdifferential conditioning-generalization gradient is steeper than implied by an excitatory-inhibitory analysis. This does not deny the utility of such an approach but it does, from the point of view of an empirical systematist, require that the net-response tendency be raised with respect to the positive stimulus and lowered with respect to the negative stimulus from those which the combined gradients alone would predict. With differential contrast effects thus established empirically, the theorist attempts to account for them in terms of hypothetical processes. There are undoubtedly many ways in which this might be done, but the most successful approaches have involved directly transferring theoretical explanations of nondifferential contrast effects (cf. Chapter 7) to the differential conditioning situation and its corresponding differential contrast effects.

Transfer Phenomena   Although it is not always easy to make the distinction, the term "transfer" is generally used in reference to the effects of one kind of training upon learning or performance in a somewhat different situation. It is typically presumed that transfer involves processes that are in some sense more complex than simple generalization of excitatory and inhibitoy tendencies of a go-no-go nature, although such tendencies may provide a mechanism for understanding transfer effects. For example, we speak of the transfer from playing softball to playing baseball partly in terms of the generalization of similar responses to similar stimuli. But there is no sharp line of demarcation involved, and we have used the term "transfer" to set apart several generalization-type phenomena that appear to involve somewhat different processes than those that we have thus far considered.

SET TO DISCRIMINATE   A good illustration of this distinction has been proposed by Thomas (e.g., Thomas, Freeman, Svinicki, Burr, & Lyons, 1970). His contention is that differential conditioning not only sharpens the generalization gradient with respect to the stimulus dimension involved in that discrimination, but also has a similar effect on other stimulus dimensions and, indeed, other stimuli in the same general environmental context. For example, differential conditioning with respect to the pitch of a tone will sharpen the generalization gradient with respect to the loudness of the tone. Furthermore, differential conditioning of tones will facilitate differential conditioning of lights. To state the hypothesis in terms of the Lashley type of approach, the organism is presumed to adopt a general set to attend to finer grain details of the stimuli that are encountered and, hence, shows less generalization and a steeper gradient as a result. Thomas has obtained several types of evidence supporting this hypothesis and has applied it to various problematic phenomena, such as selective attention (Thomas, Burr, & Eck, 1970).

TRANSFER ALONG A   The phenomena placed under this rubric involve the rate of differential condi-
CONTINUUM   tioning as affected by prior differential conditioning of stimuli along the same continuum. They derive directly from observations by Pavlov to the effect that difficult discriminations are more readily formed, if preceded by training on an easier discrimination involving the same stimulus dimension; hence, it is sometimes called the easy-to-hard effect. It is important to note that this effect

obtains with respect to all of the training given. That is, the total number of trials required to reach some arbitrary criterion of differential conditioning, involving two very similar stimuli, is smaller if some of those trials are given with stimuli that differ more widely along that continuum.

This phenomenon was studied systematically by Lawrence (1952, 1955), who also noted that the basic phenomenon could, with proper selection of excitatory and inhibitory gradients, be derived from such an analysis. This requires gradients such as previously presented in the context of the peak shift (Figure 8.1) and also requires that the location of the initial conditions and the ultimate conditions are properly located along the stimulus continuum. Logan (1966) extended this line of reasoning and demonstrated that the location of the initial conditions does indeed affect the transfer effect. Specifically, the effect is greatest if the ultimate negative stimulus is also negative in the initial easy condition, with the positive stimulus moved progressively toward it. He has also shown (Logan, 1971) that the optimal conditions do not involve extensive training on the easy problem. All of these results can be derived from generalization gradients of excitation and inhibition and the effects of both the amount of training and differential conditioning on the slopes of these gradients.

However, as noted both by Logan and Mackintosh (Mackintosh & Little, 1969), there is one further finding that cannot be accommodated by any yet conceived (and, perhaps, conceivable) form of generalization gradients. This enigmatic finding is that learning a difficult discrimination is facilitated by training on an easier problem along that continuum, even if the easy problem is reversed in direction from the difficult problem. If a louder tone is reinforced during initial easy differential conditioning, there is a positive transfer to subsequent conditions that involves a difficult discrimination with the softer tone reinforced. We will defer further discussion of this finding until the next chapter when reversal learning will be discussed at some length, but the reader should also bear this enigma in mind when reading the upcoming discussion on attention.

ACQUIRED DISTINCTIVENESS OF CUES

Another phenomenon that will influence our thinking on the subject of attention but that conceptually involves the generalization process has been identified by Lawrence (1949). The essential procedure can be summarized in this way. First train a subject to choose between two similar stimuli. Although this is a choice situation, it presumably also produces a steepening of generalization gradients of excitation and inhibition with respect to the two stimuli. Next, train the subject to make different responses (say, turning right or turning left) to the same two stimuli involved in the first stage. It is found that learning the second problem is facilitated as a result of having learned the first.

This is called acquired distinctiveness of cues, because it appears that the stimuli have become functionally more different as a result of the prior discrimination training and, hence, there is less generalization between them when new problems are encountered. Therefore, the steepened generalization gradients are not restricted to the particular response involved in learning the initial discrimination, but become properties of the stimuli, viewed relative to each other.

This phenomenon is readily extrapolated to the effects of language on stimulus generalization by humans. Learning different words for somewhat different stimuli involves a form of differential conditioning that enhances the distinctiveness of those stimuli. Conversely, of course, learning the same word for somewhat different stimuli should enhance their similarity. This approach has given rise to the notion of *mediated generalization*. The response learned during the initial conditioning is presumed to occur, at least in surrogate form, during subsequent learning tasks. If that response is the same, its feedback will mediate greater generalization. If those responses are different, their feedback will mediate less generalization. Compelling as this analysis is, Grice (1965) has raised serious questions about the viability of response-mediated generalization.

Summary of Stimulus Generalization

Stimulus control is inferred when an organism's behavior in the presence of a stimulus is different from the behavior in the absence of the stimulus. A stimulus may lead to an increased rate of occurrence of a response, in which case we speak of excitatory tendencies, or it may lead to a decreased rate of occurrence, in which case we speak of inhibitory tendencies. In either case, it is the difference in behavior that indicates that some degree of control is being exercised by a stimulus.

We are interested in stimulus control in a more finely tuned sense. That is, we would like for both excitatory and inhibitory tendencies to be at least somewhat specific to the particular stimulus involved in a learning experience. At the same time, we recognize the principle of stimulus generalization to the effect that somewhat similar stimuli are also likely to lead to a learned response and, accordingly, we infer selective stimulus control from a generalization gradient with a nonzero slope. The greater the slope of the gradient, the finer the degree of stimulus control involved.

Thus far, we have discussed some of the major factors that are known to affect the extent of generalization of learned response tendencies. We first noted that although generalization may be extremely broad under highly specialized conditions of rearing and training, the typical result of all conditioning procedures with typical organisms displays a generalization gradient with an appreciable slope. We also noted that this slope increases progressively with continued training. This signifies that even though performance may have reached some asymptotic level as customarily recorded, learning is still continuing with respect to the degree of precise stimulus control being acquired.

This evidence of selective stimulus control is adequate for the purposes of empirical systematists and also for theorists who adopt a functional approach when including stimulus generalization within their theories. Other theorists, however, have speculated about the possible underlying basis for the generalization process from which to derive the effects of various factors that further affect the range of generalization. Some physiologically oriented theorists have proposed overlapping neural systems that tend to excite each other. The more prevalent view involves a conceptualization of even a simple stimulus as being composed of a large number of potential stimulus elements of which only a sample is operative on any particular occasion. Thus, generalization becomes viewed in terms of the number of elements of an originally conditioned stimulus that is shared by similar stimuli. The greater the similarity, the greater the overlap and, hence, the greater the generalization. But the degree of conceptual overlap is estimated from the amount of generalization; thus, the concept of similarity is functionally circular.

We have reviewed a number of procedures known to sharpen stimulus control, the most effective of which is differential reinforcement of two (or more) stimuli differing along the very dimension used for subsequent generalization tests. This procedure not only steepens the generalization gradient, but shifts the point of peak performance further away from the negative stimulus than the positive stimulus itself. This steepening of the gradient may be conceptualized theoretically as resulting from two opposing tendencies, excitatory and inhibitory, established respectively at the positive and negative stimuli. There is some empirical evidence supporting this conceptualization.

But we also found that there are contrast effcts and transfer effects that are not readily reduced to simple gradients of excitation and inhibition. These phenomena reflect back upon the theoretical analysis of the stimulus as a potential source of stimulus elements, and the issue becomes one of determining the rules according to which samples are drawn from the population of elements. Since one possible rule involves selective attention, we will review the evidence with respect to it in some detail before discussing more general issues of selective stimulus control.

SELECTIVE ATTENTION

Although the issue is sometimes phrased in such a way as to permit the interpretation, there really is no fundamental controversy concerning the existence of an attention process. We are all much too familiar with this process in our everyday behavior to require explicit examples. It is evident that the myriad of energies bombarding our sensoriums is too complex and too large to comprehend in an instant. Furthermore, since most systematists are prone to base some of their principles and/or postulates on the behavior of animals other than humans, it would be antithetical to deny the universality of at least some rudimentary form of this process. Although it might be interesting to explore the implications of a system that assumed that attention is not a significant factor in the determination of learned behavior, relegating it to the status of a mentalistic epiphenomenon, such a view has not gained favor. The reasons for this are probably largely philosophical and therefore not within the scope of this book.

Interestingly enough, what has heretofore been the most fundamental issue with respect to other processes has not preoccupied systematists concerned with attention. This issue would concern the *nature* of attention. With what kind of a process are we dealing? But instead of attempting to answer this question, systematists have enjoyed a *carte blanche* in using the term loosely. They freely refer to "salience," "perspicuity," "vividness," and similar ideas that seem to be little more than after-the-fact accounts of factors that appear to have been controlling the organism's attention. In sum, we currently tend to take the existence of and the nature of attention for granted.

One other disclaimer is appropriate. Issues concerning attention processes have not been greatly concerned with selective control by interoceptive stimuli. For obvious practical reasons, experimental analysis has focused on manipulatable exteroceptive stimuli, but conceptual analysis should acknowledge all sources of stimulation. This would appear to be especially important in the context of fine response differentiations where attention might well be concentrated on feedback stimuli.

Given this premise, the issue can then be phrased in the form of a question: What are the circumstances under which attention *must* be introduced in developing a systematic analysis of behavior? One may contend that attention is always operative (even though it may lapse from time to time), but it would indeed be an epiphenomenon if it did not enter differentially into the system. So we find the specific issues oriented toward the identification of phenomena that either belie the utility of any simple-minded (i.e., intuitively obvious) notions about the attention process or those that appear to demand its introduction.

The term "attention" is widely used both in the sense of a hypothetical concept and in the sense of a hypothetical construct. It tends to imply a reductive process and this implication is quite intentional on the part of a theorist. The empiricist prefers a less prejudicial term, such as "differential stimulus control." It is really this latter concept that is inferred from the various phenomena to be discussed and that then leads to the induction of a hypothetical internal process. In this spirit, we have organized this section around the various empirical outcomes that suggest whether differential stimulus control either did or did not occur. Quite naturally, these phenomena are of the transposition type in order to determine what aspects of a complex stimulus actually gained some degree of control over behavior.

OVERSHADOWING Pavlov first reported a phenomenon that subsequently was observed repeatedly in all types of conditioning situations. If the conditioned stimulus is an explicit compound of, say, a light and a tone, and these elements are subsequently tested separately, only one of them may provoke a conditioned response, while the other is largely ineffective. This phenomenon of *overshadowing* appears to be especially likely to occur after a relatively small amount of training and when one stimulus element is distinctly more perspicuous to the organism than the other. Overshadowing lends itself quite readily to attentional interpretations. Whatever stimulus element gains the organism's attention is the one that will gain control over behavior.

However, this phenomenon is not decisively critical of nonattentional approaches. Although such theories assume that all elements of a stimulus complex gain some control over behavior, it is not at all necessary that the rate at which such control is gained and their conceptual limits be equal. It would be necessary to make explicit assumptions about the variables that control the rate and limit parameters (e.g., stimulus intensity), but such assumptions would be perfectly compatible with the fundamental logic of nonattentional theory. Furthermore, the fact that some control is typically exercised by the lesser stimulus element is not only consistent with this view but requires an attention theory to posit that attention can, at least to some extent, be divided between the elements.

Even though the phenomenon of overshadowing is not generally considered to be definitive with respect to the issue, it is nevertheless important for two reasons. The first is simply pragmatic: in any other tests of selective control gained by elements of a compound stimulus, it is necessary to rule out overshadowing as a possible interpretation. The second reason for discussing overshadowing is that it should force the theorist to think carefully about the conceptual status of attention as a hypothetical construct.

If we ask the nonattentional theorist *why* perspicuous stimuli gain greater control over the response, the answer is likely to be that such stimuli attract the organism's attention! Suspecting the trap, the theorist may properly refuse to answer the question and say no more than that the theory postulates that associative strength is a function of stimulus intensity (and other features, such as size, distinctiveness, novelty, and so on). Interestingly enough, the attention theorist would accept such a statement without much controversy, because that is only part of what is meant by attention as a hypothetical construct. The nonattentional account still places the determination of behavioral control in some inherent feature of the stimulus. Such theorists want the organism to be active in selecting those aspects of the stimulus complex to which associations are formed.

This point is itself often overshadowed and therefore bears repeating. There simply is no question that differential stimulus control occurs in the empirical sense and that some elements of a compound stimulus may come to exercise greater control than others. But the nonattentional theorist claims that such selection is done, in a sense, by the stimuli; perspicuous stimuli have a power not shared by relatively inconspicuous stimuli. It is only when these straightforward deterministic rules are violated that the attention construct is demanded.

Such phenomena can indeed be found, but the burden of theory construction still rests upon the attentional theorist's shoulders. Recall that meaningful hypothetical constructs must be securely anchored to both antecedent and consequent variables. It is certainly not sufficient to posit some homunculus in the organism's head and further assert that it scans the sensory input and arbitrarily selects this or that aspect on which to focus attention. To avoid *reductio ad absurdum*, the theorist clearly must postulate an attention process that makes explicit contact with the empirical world. Presumably, the other types of phenomena that we will be discussing may help to delineate types of conditions that give rise to this construct and some may indicate the way this construct affects subsequent performance.

Redintegration and Compounding

There are two phenomena that appear to stand at odds with the phenomenon of overshadowing. One, *redintegration,*[14] refers to the fact that both elements of a compound stimulus may alone be sufficient to evoke the response acquired in the context of the compound. But there is also the opposite phenomenon of *compounding,* which refers to the fact that the response may be occasioned only by the compound and not by the elements separately. To the best of our knowledge, no one has attempted to integrate all three phenomena within a single minisystem, although there are several conceptualizations that might serve this purpose.

Both redintegration and compounding are most likely to occur when the stimuli involved in the compound are relatively equal in perspicuity. Such conditions apparently prevent overshadowing and enable the separate elements to acquire some control over behavior. Redintegration appears to be most likely to occur after a reasonably small amount of training, at which stage each element is able separately to provoke some level of responding. Compounding clearly requires extensive training; the response-evocation potential of the elements apparently is lost during extended exposure to compound conditioning.

It should be understood that the behavioral outcome described by both redintegration and compounding could be established by appropriate conditions of differential reinforcement. If one separately reinforced the elements, in addition to reinforcing the compound, the elements would naturally gain control over behavior. If one separately nonreinforced the elements, while reinforcing the compound, the elements would naturally lose control over behavior. The important point is that these outcomes may occur without such explicit training to the elements in isolation.

These phenomena place some constraints on theories of attention. Redintegration clearly indicates that attention can be divided between the elements of a compound; the organism does not have to select one or the other element as a basis for developing associations. It would then have to be assumed, *post hoc,* that attention eventually focuses on the uniqueness of the compound; however, it is not readily apparent why the elements should lose associations that were earlier in evidence. But whatever approach one adopts, compounding appears to require that the compound be viewed functionally as *a* stimulus.

One way to conceptualize these phenomena in this light is to contend that testing with the elements separately is effectively a test for stimulus generalization from the compound to the elements. It is not unreasonable to assume that there is some degree of similarity between the compound and its elements and, hence, one can readily derive the phenomenon of redintegration. To derive compounding requires the assumption that extended training sharpens the generalization gradient, now in an absolute sense. Continued exposure to compound conditioning progressively narrows the range of stimulus generalization and ultimately even excludes the elements presented separately. (But note that we have shifted the theoretical issue to the conditions that lead a compound stimulus to be treated by the organism as a single stimulus rather than as a compound of separate elements.)

If a theorist attempts to cope with the question of why the gradient should be sharpened by extended training without differential reinforcement, appeal would probably be to some attention–like process. However, such an attention process would be quite the antithesis of Lashley's view, because it would contend that the organism is progressively bringing in more and more of the fine-grain detailed stimulus features, namely, those reflecting patterning or stimulus interaction. As these gain increasing control, those based on the elements associated with the uniqueness of the stimuli in the compound lose correspondingly. Such an approach would assume that the conditions of reinforcement can only support a certain total amount of associative strength to be distributed among all of the potential (conceptual) elements of a stimulus. This would be tantamount to a zero-sum probability theory such that associations to the compound-specific elements are gained at the expense of associations to the unique-stimulus elements. Such a theory could embody some form of a selective attention process, although one could alternatively argue that the compound-specific elements occur on every trial and eventually hoard the potential associative strength.

Incidental Cue (Blocking)   Presumably in the general context of attempting to determine whether stimulus control could be shifted from one cue to another, Pavlov introduced a second cue compounded with a previously conditioned stimulus. The result that draws our immediate interest is the fact that the added stimulus acquired little or no control over behavior. Since it was known independently that both elements of the compound in these studies would gain some degree of associative strength, the evidence indicates that a previously conditioned stimulus can overshadow an added stimulus, although they are equally perspicuous. In this context, the phenomenon is referred to as *blocking*.

Blocking appears to follow quite readily from attention theories. It is reasonable to assume that the original conditioning focuses attention on the cue present during such training; hence, the organism, for all intents and purposes, would not even notice the addition of a second cue. In contrast, nonattentional theories are hard pressed to account for blocking, because the added cue occupies an appropriate position relative to reinforcement and therefore associations should be formed.

However, Kamin (e.g., 1969) has reported a series of studies that at least question this simple conclusion. Using the CER paradigm, he observed that if at the same time that a new cue is added to the stimulus complex, there is a concomitant increase in the intensity of the unconditioned stimulus, then the added cue does gain some degree of control over behavior. His contention is that the organism does indeed notice the added cue in the typical blocking procedure but associations are formed only if the conditions are changed in such a way as to surprise the organism. So long as the familiar cue correctly predicts the environmental events, the added cue is functionally ignored. But if the conditions are changed, the organism tends to associate the change with the added cue.

This approach has a certain amount of homey appeal, even though the fundamental notion of surprise is not readily anchored. For example, we may eat again at a restaurant advertised as being under new management, but if the food is not any better, we do not change our associations with the restaurant. A functionally similar idea has been stated more formally by Wagner (e.g., 1969) and Rescorla (e.g., 1969). This approach, which is referred to as a modified continuity theory, assumes that an unconditioned stimulus can support a certain total amount of associative strength that would normally be divided between equally salient cues when used in a compound during original acquisition. However, if one of the cues is first trained separately, it will preempt all of the available associative strength such that, when a new cue is added, there is nothing left for it to share. Since a stronger unconditioned stimulus can support a greater amount of total associative strength, an added cue can participate in gaining some portion of this additional strength available for acquisition. Whereas the classic nonattentional approach assumes that a stimulus will gain control simply by virtue of being appropriately situated in time with respect to an unconditioned stimulus, the modified version of this theory assumes that all stimulus elements of a compound will gain control only insofar as the combined associative strengths of the elements is still below the total available strength.

Thus, modified continuity theory has the virtue of being able to explain not only the original blocking phenomenon but also the unblocking effect resulting from a concurrent increase in the intensity of an unconditioned stimulus. The challenge is now shifted back to attention theorists. If the explanation of the blocking phenomenon is that the organism's attention has become centered on the original cue, then there is no obvious reason for attention to be diverted to the added incidental cue as a result of increasing unconditioned stimulus intensity. And if only those cues commanding attention acquire associative strength, then any possible additional strength should accrue to the original stimulus. In this connection, it is important to note that Kamin has shown that unblocking can be detected after only one trial with the increased intensity of the unconditioned stimulus. On that very first trial the organism's attention could not possibly have been diverted by the new value of the unconditioned stimulus, because it has not yet occurred. Kamin has suggested that the changed conditions apparently cause the organism to reflect back upon recent stimulus events that might have foretold of the impending change.

Among the additional predictions made by modified continuity theory is the effect of decreasing, rather than increasing, the intensity of the unconditioned stimulus at the time an incidental cue is added to the stimulus complex. The theory assumes that the added cue will participate in any change in associative strength that results from a change in the conditions. Since a weaker unconditioned stimulus can support less total associative strength, the added cue must begin to develop negative values. This prediction has been confirmed when the changed conditions are those of extinction; the added cue becomes a conditioned inhibitor. However, if the unconditioned stimulus is only decreased in intensity rather than completely eliminated, the added cue comes to elicit the response rather than to inhibit it (Feldman, 1972).

The overall pattern of results is therefore not particularly satisfying even from a purely empirical point of view. We know that if there are no concomitant changes in the conditions, an added cue does not gain any control over behavior, but it does gain positive control if the conditions are either increased or decreased short of extinction. In this last procedure, the added stimulus acquires inhibitory properties. Therefore, we do not have a simple empirical function, and none of the theoretical analyses has yet resolved the apparent complexities.

Cue Value: Reliability and Validity

A conditioned stimulus is an event that occurs more or less contiguously in time with another event of emotional significance to the organism. The reason we say "more or less" is that although we may conceptualize perfect temporal contiguity by means of hypothetical processes, such as a stimulus trace or a memory, operationally the objective events rarely occur at precisely the same time. The conditioned stimulus in classical conditioning may precede the unconditioned stimulus by some interval of time, and conditioned stimuli in operant/instrumental conditioning are temporally removed from the ultimate reinforcer by at least the length of time required to execute the requisite behavior chain. Actually, we know that effective conditioned stimuli must precede the occurrence of an emotionally significant event by at least some minimal period of time, which is possibly related to the neural transmission time. For this reason, conditioned stimuli are better thought of as antecedent stimuli and, for the theorist, they are the events that occur on the input side of any hypothetical associative connection.

Because conditioned stimuli convey information, they are frequently referred to as cues, signals, or signs that introduce to the organism the impending occurrence of emotionally significant events or their potential occurrence that is contingent upon the emission of a response instrumental in their attainment. We wish now to define three hypothetical concepts related to what may generally be thought of as the information value of conditioned stimuli. From among the essentially equivalent terms that might be used, we will refer to cue reliability, cue validity, and cue value. (Instead of the latter term, for example, we might have used conditioned stimulus value, sign value, signal value, or information value.) These concepts are not always carefully distinguished in the literature.

By cue *validity* we will mean the extent to which the emotionally significant event consistently follows the cue. A perfectly valid cue is one for which this is always the case; in logical terms, if A then B. A perfectly valid cue may not predict every occurrence of the emotionally significant event, but every time the cue occurs, so does the other. It is this fact that leads us also to introduce the concept of *cue reliability;* this term refers to the extent to which the emotionally significant event is consistently preceded by the cue. Let us rehearse these concepts in the context of a concrete example.

Assume that an emotionally significant event, say, an unconditioned stimulus (US) in classical conditioning, is programmed by the environment to occur aperiodically over time. This is a stimulus schedule (Logan & Ferraro, 1970) onto which we can superimpose another stimulus (cue) schedule, in various degrees of correlation with the US schedule. We have three logically possible events, the US alone, the cue alone, and the cue and US together. Let us first take just two of these, the US alone and the cue + US. In this case, the cue is a perfectly valid predictor of the US and its reliability will depend on the percentage of trials of the US alone. Next, let us take the combination of events that includes the cue alone and the cue + US with the US never occurring alone. In this case, the cue is a perfectly reliable predictor of the US and its validity will depend on the percentage of trials with the cue alone. Finally, let us consider the combination of cue alone and US alone. Since the events are never paired in this combination, the cue becomes a perfectly valid and reliable predictor of the *non*occurrence of the US.

When all three events are included within the same experimental paradigm, we have a combination of cue reliability and cue validity that gives rise to the net-*cue value*. A cue will have value to the extent that it conveys information about the impending occurrence or nonoccurrence of the US greater than that already contained in the overall US schedule itself. (If the US usually comes along about every minute, you already know that without a cue.) It is this line of reasoning that led Rescorla (1967) to propose a truly random-control procedure for classical conditioning. In this procedure, the cue schedule and the US schedule are totally uncorrelated such that the US is just as likely to occur in the absence of the cue as in its presence.[15] Such a cue would be of no value to the organism.

Although these concepts are most readily defined in the context of classical conditioning, they apply also to operant/instrumental conditioning. In an instrumental context, for example, if we run a rat sometimes in a white alley and never reinforce that response, and sometimes run the rat in a black alley and reward that response 50% of the time, black becomes a perfectly valid but not perfectly reliable predictor of reinforcement. (White is a perfectly valid and reliable predictor of nonreinforcement.) Although most studies utilize cues that are perfectly valid and reliable cues to reinforcement and nonreinforcement, it should now be clear that there is an underlying continuum of cue value that can be experimentally manipulated.

We have called cue value a hypothetical concept, because it is a property that cannot be measured with respect to a cue in isolation. It cannot be pointed at, thus it is hypothetical. However, it is a concept because it can be reduced to point-at-able operations. It should be emphasized that we are not using "value" as a hypothetical construct in the sense that we have previously used the term incentive value. We are not saying anything about how much the information is worth to the organism, only its predictive value vis-à-vis an emotionally significant event. It is the incentive value of the latter that should affect the theoretical value of the information.

It is thus an empirical question whether cue value is systematically related to stimulus control. Although we might reasonably anticipate that a stimulus will gain control in direct relation to its cue value, and although this is probably a good generalization with respect to cues presented separately, it has proven not to be true when several cues are sometimes presented in a simultaneous compound. We are unable even to assert that control is greatest by cues with the higher cue value; those with lower cue value gain less control than their independently computed value would appear to justify. Accordingly, we are concerned with the effects of *relative* cue value on stimulus control.

A single experimental design can be used to illustrate the general phenomenon (Wagner, Logan, Haberland, & Price, 1968). A US is always preceded by a light, which is half the time compounded with a high tone and half the time with a low tone. However, the US occurs on only half of the total trials. Hence, the light is a perfectly valid but not perfectly reliable predictor of the US. Interest centers on the behavior of two groups that differ in the correlation of the US with the tones. In the uncorrelated condition, the US occurs half of the time with respect to each compound. In this case, the pitch of the tone is also a perfectly valid but not perfectly reliable predictor of the US. When the elements are subsequently tested separately, it is found that the light alone, the high tone alone, and the low tone alone all more or less equally evoke the conditioned response. But in the correlated condition, the US occurs on that half of the trials containing the high tone and, hence, does not occur on that half of the trials containing the low tone. In this situation, the pitch of the tone is made a perfectly reliable (and valid) cue and subjects correspondingly learn this discrimination. They respond in the presence of the high tone and not in the presence of the low tone.

Of particular interest is the behavior observed when the light is presented separately. In recalling the experimental paradigm, note that the light has the same degree of validity and reliability in the correlated condition as it has in the uncorrelated condition. The US occurs half of the time that it occurs. But the observation is that the light has gained little or no control over behavior and therefore much less than that produced by the uncorrelated condition. The subjects simply do not respond to the light when it has been compounded with a more reliable cue.

It would certainly appear that this finding strongly implicates an attentional process. It is as if the subjects paid no attention at all to the light as their concentration became focused on the tones, as the reliable cue to the occurrence of the US. This is not only a reasonable interpretation but it also accounts for another important phenomenon. If the subjects are first trained with the light alone on a 50% schedule of reinforcement and then the tones are superimposed as in the correlated condition of the preceding study, not only do the tones gain differential control over behavior, but the light loses whatever degree of control it had enjoyed as a result of the prior training (Feldman, 1972). Apparently, attention becomes shifted to the tones as the more reliable stimulus feature. This finding is especially important to approaches, such as Kamin's (1969) "surprise" account of unblocking. In this case, we have an added cue that does gain control, even though there is no overall change in the frequency of reinforcement that might surprise the organism. Its greater reliability is sufficient.

Before leaning too strongly toward attentional interpretations of the phenomena involving cue value, we should consider modified continuity theory in this context. Recall the fundamental assumptions: reinforced trials increase the associative strength of all cues in a compound only to the extent that the total associative strength of those cues is below the level that can be supported by the US. Nonreinforcement correspondingly leads to a decrease in the associative strength of all cues present on such trials. Considering first the comparison of the correlated and uncorrelated conditions, both should begin with trial-by-trial increments and decrements of associative strengths to all cues—the light, the high tone, and the low tone. But the high tone will always enjoy increments, while the low tone always suffers decrements; the light will experience both increments and decrements, depending on which tone it happened to be paired with on each trial. Since the light will repeatedly be gaining some strength when it is compounded with the high tone, that strength will lead to responding in the compound of light and low tone, and both will be decremented. The low tone will functionally become negative (a conditioned inhibitor), while the light loses some of the strength it has. This process will continue until the strength of the high tone, combined with a small amount of residual strength associated with the light, equals the total associative strength that the US can support. Thereafter, there will be no further increments to either. At the same time, the low tone will become sufficiently negative to offset the residual positive strength of the light, so that their combination is zero as is appropriate to the omission of the US. Modified continuity theory can, therefore, account for the relatively little residual control ultimately based on the light, although it could not accommodate to a complete lack of control by the light.

This same trial-by-trial analysis can be applied to the situation in which the light is first trained on a 50% schedule before the tones are superimposed as in the correlated condition. In this case, the light will begin the second phase with a substantial amount of associative strength; as some of this is lost in compound with the low tone, some of that loss will be picked up by the high tone when it occurs and is reinforced. The analysis leads in the same direction even though, in the limiting state, the low tone should be somewhat more negative, and the light somewhat more positive than would obtain without prior separate conditioning to the light.

Accordingly, at least the direction of these and various other results involving relative cue value can be handled by modified continuity theory without the introduction of any selective attention process. All presented stimulus elements participate equally in any changes in associative strength that are warranted by the subsequent reinforcement or nonreinforcement. This approach does not disprove attention theories. It simply suggests that it may not be necessary to introduce such processes in accounting for the empirical phenomena in this area.

**Summary of Selective
Attention**

Let us attempt to summarize the various phenomena that we have discussed by adopting the opposite strategy. We followed the somewhat common approach of basically assuming that organisms do not engage in selective attention as a rule; we then identified instances in which such a process appeared to be required. The opposite approach would be to assume that organisms always engage in selective attention and then to develop our understanding of this process by negative instances. That is, we can identify instances in which the organism appeared *not* to be attending to the stimuli that the experimenter had in mind.

In developing such an approach, the simplest assumption would be that the organism can attend to one and only one stimulus at a time, but we have seen that this pure noncontinuity assumption needs to be modified. The phenomenon of redintegration, in which several elements of a compound stimulus may be shown independently to gain at least some degree of control over behavior, is sufficient to rule out this extremely simplistic assumption. But at this juncture, there are several options available. One is to follow the lead of modified noncontinuity theory and assume that the organism can (does?) attend to several features of the environment simultaneously. The only sure thing about such a theory is that the organism does not attend to everything and, hence, it is somewhat selective.

Another alternative is suggested by Logan's (1971) construct of a perceptor orienting response. This idea formulates that the organism can, indeed, only attend to one thing at a time in the sense of the focus of attention. The reason that it is called a perceptor rather than a receptor orienting response is that it is intended to apply not just to vision, but to the entire perceptual field that includes all sense modalities concurrently. But vision is the model of this hypothetical response: the awake organism is constantly scanning the array of energies emanating from the interoceptive and exteroceptive environment, focusing on first one and then another and, of course, then returning to some more frequently than others. If such an organism is endowed with a short-term memory, then even though only one stimulus element is at the very center of attention, other elements will be in the process of fading but will still be present with some degree of clarity.

Because this latter approach has not yet been systematically developed, we mention it primarily to illustrate that there still remain various ways in which a selective attention process could be conceptualized. Recall that this section began by noting that issues involving the *nature* of selective attention have not been the target of much controversy. If we adopt this inverted position and accept selective attention as a kind of given, much in the way that we accept learning as a given, then we would be oriented to discuss alternative approaches to an understanding of its nature.

In this regard, attention must not only impose limits on the range of stimuli that can be attended to simultaneously, it also must allow for the other-than-chance individual differences presumably on the basis of some kind of associative process. Attention theories are frequently characterized as two-stage theories, because they assume that the organism first engages in some form of information-processing activity with respect to the input stimuli and then develops associations with respect to that processed information. This way of describing the process suggests a cognitive view of its nature instead of a view that refers to attentional responses or perceptor-orienting acts.

Even at the relatively informal level of our understanding of an attention process, we can easily comprehend most of the phenomena from such a point of view. Clearly the overshadowing effect shows that not all stimulus elements of a compound gain equally in the control of behavior, and this is consistent with the conceptualization of a system with a limited channel capacity. Not everything can be processed at the same time, and there is nothing antithetical to such a system in allowing certain stimulus features, such as perspicuity, to help determine the information on which attention is focused. These are quite natural, frequently adaptive tendencies, but trained organisms can learn to overcome them when the conditions of reinforcement require other foci of attention for optimal adjustment. We know from transposition-type tests that not all organisms, even of the same species, attend to precisely the same features of a complex stimulus. Clearly there must be more to the subject of attention than could be understood purely by stimulus features, such as perspicuity, salience, intensity, and the like.

Redintegration phenomena pose no serious problems for attention theory, at least if we have granted that several features may be attended to simultaneously. Actually even that is not necessary in a dynamic attention theory. We can readily imagine an organism introduced to a very novel situation to which few learned attentional mechanisms transfer—a situation where the organism is exposed to stimuli with no distinctive properties selectively to attract attention, attending to one aspect on some trials and another aspect on other trials. Each would therefore be gaining associative strength and this would happen until and unless some feature became dominant over repeated exposures. The idea of compound elements is as compatible with attention approaches as with nonattentional theories; indeed, it is more compatible because the phenomenon of compounding suggests that the compound features of a stimulus, although less perspicuous by nature, increasingly become integrated into a gestalt. As attention focuses on this integrated whole, the elements themselves lose their identity.

It is true that the more recent evidence concerning the blocking phenomena places some burden on attention theories. It is clear enough that added cues do not typically garner attention that is already dominated as a result of prior experiences, and we can anticipate a related need for a more dynamic (trial-by-trial in this case, as well as within-trial) analysis of attention learning. One of the beauties of modified continuity theory is that it offers just such an analysis. We cannot, in conscience, endow our organism with a limited channel capacity whose limits can be expanded and contracted according to the conditions of reinforcement. But we can say that the organism has many other things to which it must attend other than the events occurring in the experimental environment of interest to the researcher. It is certainly not unreasonable to presume that the extent to which some portion of this limited capacity is devoted to the experimental task is dependent on the emotional significance of the events occurring there.

It is quite possible that the trends of both modified continuity theory and modified noncontinuity theory are converging on some such form of rapprochment. Wagner (1971) refers to "signal value" rather than "associative strength," and this term lends itself more readily to an interpretation of the significance that the organism attaches to various stimulus events in the environment. Mackintosh (1975) has incorporated many features of the mathematical analysis of differential rates of association formation that are related to both stimulus and organismic properties, and particularly the conditions of reinforcement, as developed by modified continuity theory. If these developments are indicative of future trends, then what was once a controversy may be reduced to relatively fine details of alternative theories, and these may be more readily resolved by systematic experimental analysis.

However, before we allow the context of this chapter to lead us precipitously toward the approach of accepting attention as a ubiquitous process, present in all situations involving learned associations, we should reflect on the larger implications of such a position. An intuitively compelling understanding of attention would identify it as a conscious process; at least one reasonable interpretation of the meaning of conscious processes in humans is that they can be verbalized. In effect, this means that the person is aware of the stimulus elements occupying attention at any moment, and it may be recalled in our discussions in Chapter 3 that some theorists have contended that awareness should be included among the necessary conditions of associations. Although this remains a legitimate proposition on logical grounds, no such position has yet been stated rigorously with sufficient generality to account for the many instances in which associations apparently are formed without awareness. To use one of a multitude of possible examples, we have all learned to make many subtle discriminations that we would be very hard pressed to attempt to explain verbally.

Furthermore, all of our discussion in the contexts of awareness and attention have been concerned with the formation of associations and have not extended those potential constructs to the maintenance of the performances reflecting such associations.[16] Viewed in a sufficiently micromolecular fashion and encompassing all ongoing response systems, there are potentially as many output elements as there are input elements. Are we to presume that we are consciously attentive to everything that we are doing all of the time? Were that the case, attention would have a virtually unlimited channel capacity! Small wonder, then, that many theorists are reluctant to open this Pandora's Box.

GENERAL SUMMARY AND CONCLUSIONS

We have organized this chapter around the areas of stimulus generalization and selective attention because some experimental operations appear more closely related to one or the other, but it should be clear that they are not truly independent processes. At least to the extent that attentional processes are invoked, they inevitably pertain to generalization. That is, our analysis of generalization importantly is based on our conception of the stimulus events that are actually controlling behavior. Insofar as these are selective with respect to the environment, then generalization applies to those selected aspects of the total stimulus. Indeed, this type of reasoning leads many systematists, such as Brown (1965), to conceptualize generalization in terms of some form of overlapping stimulus-element approach. Thus, the question becomes one of the extent to which the selection is more or less random, determined by properties of the environment, or affected by the perceiving organism.

In fact, many analysts have followed the lead of Klüver (1933) that there really is no generalization process at all. The only behavioral process is that of discrimination, and what we see as (and call) stimulus generalization is nothing more nor less than the result of a failure to discriminate between stimuli. Instead of looking at the number of common elements shared by stimuli, we can turn the picture upside down and look at the number of different elements not shared by those stimuli. The generalization-discrimination issue is the extent to which behavior is being controlled by common elements or distinctive elements. It is not unreasonable to assume an indefinitely large number of potential stimulus elements, a limited channel capacity of the organism, and a finite-scanning time. Accordingly, not all elements can be processed on any single occasion of stimulus occurrence. Attention becomes an abstract term for whatever perceptual processes are involved in the determination of which elements will be available, and generalization and discrimination are simply opposite sides of the very same coin.

The image of the big picture that emerges from this vantage point is that distinctions among familiar terms, such as perception, attention, generalization, and discrimination, are linguistic symbols artificially imposed on a basically integrated set of phenomena. It is really no more meaningful to talk about one or the other, or for that matter, about one independently of the others. The type of organization that we have followed in this chapter must, therefore, be viewed in terms of a limited output channel capacity. We simply cannot yet transmit this big picture all at once, in no small measure, because it still remains to be beautifully integrated. Therefore, we are constrained to transmit bits and pieces of the picture as seen by both classic and contemporary systematists and hope that the reader can put these together in some meaningful perspective.

In focusing this chapter on the nature of the stimulus in conditioning, we conspicuously have left out a corresponding chapter on the nature of the response. This omission should not be interpreted as an implication that response factors are of any less conceptual significance than stimulus factors. Instead, it is a reflection of the fact that attempts to study response factors are inherently less direct and, therefore, substantially more complex empirically.

Consider for example the principle of response generalization. It is easy enough to state this principle in terms of the organism's tendency to emit responses that are similar to that which was actually reinforced, again in systematic relation to the degree of similarity. But it is impossible to study this process directly, because one must inevitably change the stimulus concurrently. A classic study by Wickens (1938) is a case in point. He first trained humans to avoid an electric shock to the finger by withdrawing with an upward motion away from the shock source. He then placed the finger below the shock source such that a downward motion would be required to avoid the shock and observed a substantial generalization of adaptive behavior to this new situation. Although the subject could, in principle, press harder with an upward force against the shock source, actual movement in that direction was precluded by the change in the stimulus situation.

Another noteworthy attempt to study response generalization was devised by Brown (1951, 1958). He first trained human subjects to move a lever from a central starting position to particular locations around a semicircular target, scoring performance in terms of accuracy. He then trained subjects to aim the movement of the lever to two different locations depending on which of two stimuli was presented; subsequently, he tested for generalization by presenting stimuli intermediate between the training stimuli. Clearly this is a study of stimulus and response generalization concurrently.

There are still other contexts in which the process of response generalization appears to be implicated. The most obvious context is implied in the fact that behavior varies from occasion to occasion. There is some variability in even the most virtuoso performance. Although some of this may be attributed to variation in the stimulus situation, it is reasonable to presume that there is output variability as well as input variability. It is this very fact that makes the study of response generalization uniquely difficult, because whereas we can present stimuli at the discretion of the experimenter, the emission of responses is largely determined by the subject. Efforts to disable one or another response inevitably involve changing the stimulus environment.

Accordingly, it is simply and usually assumed that response generalization follows the same fundamental principles that apply to stimulus generalization. An argument can be made for this assumption: response differentiation is presumably based on proprioceptive and kinesthetic feedback stimuli and hence becomes a special case of stimulus discrimination although based on response-produced stimuli. If one accepts this reasoning, then the two processes reduce to the same process at a sufficiently abstract level of conceptual analysis.[17] But this may prove to be little more than an easy way out, and theorists are naturally free to posit any differences between these processes that appear to generate useful predictions.

To return then to the systematic analyses of stimulus generalization, the evidence that we have reviewed leads us to the conclusion that a simple, direct, physiologically based conceptualization of a "pure" gradient with a unique shape and an inherent slope is almost certain to be inadequate. This means that we are working in a space devoid of fixed coordinates; systematic analyses are therefore especially tenuous. Let us illustrate the potential difficulties in the area of conflict resolution where some stimulus (or response) has been associated with both reward and punishment. This area has led to creative applications of generalization gradients; we will focus on the approach proposed by Miller (e.g., 1944, 1964), although quite similar reasoning was also described by Lewin (1935).

The fundamental assumptions of this analysis are: that reward at a goal establishes an approach tendency based on the conditions of reinforcement at that goal; that punishment at a goal establishes an avoidance tendency based on the conditions of punishment at that goal; and that the latter gradient is steeper than the former. Our stated conclusion at least forces one to question this last assumption as a universal principle. If the slopes of the gradients can be modified, more or less, at will, then surely conditions could be arranged to make the approach gradient steeper than the avoidance gradient. Indeed, Hearst (1965) has proposed just such an analysis as a result of his research. However, in some situations, the assumptions may be quite reasonable.

Consider a spatial conflict, that is, moving toward or away from some goal location in space or, more generally, any behavior chain leading on to some goal response. Now as one gets closer and closer to the goal, one's positive incentive based on the reward increases as does one's negative incentive based on the punishment. Since both of these factors are related to the changing pattern of stimulation at different distances from the goal, and since these changes are the same for both factors, there is no basis for assuming that their slopes would be different. However, Miller has suggested that we must also attend to the drive motivation underlying the *net*-approach tendency (approach minus avoidance). *If* one assumes that the drives applicable to these two tendencies are different, being some appetitive drive such as hunger in the case of approach and fear in the case of avoidance, and *if* one further assumes that drive motivation combines multiplicatively with incentive motivation, *then* the resulting gradients would be steeper for avoidance than for approach. This is because both sources of motivation are increasing in the case of avoidance, while only incentive motivation is increasing in the case of approach. Thus, regardless of how we locate the gradients in our poorly defined coordinate system, these slopes will differ in the postulated manner.

Miller has described a number of implications of this analysis, of which we can mention only a few. The most immediate result is that the net-approach tendency should get progressively weaker as a conflict goal is approached. This is because the avoidance tendency is increasing more rapidly than the approach tendency. If these gradients intersect, such that the avoidance tendency exceeds the approach tendency at the goal, the organism will stop short of the goal. This leads to what is the most important practical application of this analysis: if the amount of reinforcement and the intensity of punishment are such that the resulting gradients of generalization intersect, the organism will vacillate at some distance from the goal, being unable to move completely away, because at some far distance the approach is stronger than the avoidance, but also being unable to move completely to the goal, because at some close distance the avoidance is now stronger than the approach.

There are many profound clinical applications of Miller's analysis (see especially, Dollard & Miller, 1950). Since many behavior disorders can be traced to underlying personal conflicts, this analysis has important implications for treatment. Clearly conflicts can be resolved only by changing the heights of the approach and/or avoidance gradients, and among the many detailed implications of the analysis is the common negative therapeutic effect that results from simply attempting to increase the approach tendency. Such efforts do successfully move the person closer to the goal but, at that point, the conflicting tendencies are *both* stronger leading to still greater misery than experienced at a farther distance from the goal.

Accordingly, we do not wish to give the impression that the complexities inherent in systematic analyses that involve generalization processes are insurmountable. We have raised the caution flag because it is all too easy to presume that generalization gradients are more or less fixed parameters in the stimulus control of behavior. Instead, meaningful systematic analyses involving such gradients need to be made at a more molecular level, including consideration of those factors known to affect such gradients. It is safe to assume that such generalization will occur, but the extent of generalization is not predetermined.

NOTES   1. In this connection, it might also be noted that Grant (e.g., 1972) has reported that the word "red" presented in blue letters serves as a functionally less effective conditioned stimulus than when there are no such incongruities involved. This type of finding further supports the idea that some kind of processing takes place with respect to the stimuli involved in associations.

2. Spence was inclined to defend this particular gradient shape by arguing that generalization must be complete at least insofar as the just-noticeable difference; hence, the gradient must start out flat and develop with positive acceleration. At a more sophisticated level, however, the just-noticeable difference is itself a statistical concept related to an underlying continuous process.

3. There is a general point with respect to any dependent measure that is derived from several response measures. A ratio can obviously be arrived at from any number of possible values of the response measures, and it is often important to know whether a larger ratio was obtained by increasing the numerator or decreasing the denominator. This is not to say that there is anything of intrinsic fundamental meaning in any response measure; transformations are not only legitimate but often necessary to reveal an underlying systematic order for the purposes of abstract principles and theories. However, when two response measures are involved, transformations may sometimes be misleading particularly when the response measures involved have inherent limits.

4. The solution implied by the fact that only one pure measure can be obtained from one subject is not so simple as running a few more subjects. We must be aware that there are undoubtedly considerable individual differences both with respect to absolute response measures and relative response measures. One subject may show more responding to a generalization-test stimulus because that subject is generally more responsive and also because of a wider range of generalization. This implies that a somewhat substantial number of subjects would be required at each point to obtain a "true" generalization gradient and, even then, it would not represent the true gradient for any individual subject.

5. This is not the way that Pavlov is usually interpreted, and being unable to read Russian ourselves, we are not in a position to argue the case. Our purpose in giving this orientation is to encourage the reader to be sensitive to the way in which one's thinking can be affected, if the intention is for a theory to describe the way the system really works, that is, true physiological reduction. One could contend that irradiation during original conditioning leads to associations that are formed with the lesser degree of excitation taking place at nearby stimulus locations. This is the typical interpretation of Pavlov, and leads to the further question of how, in reality, a strong stimulation of these different stimuli during generalization tests leads to a weaker response. The association itself should be just as strong, although it was made to a weak version of the test stimulus. Clearly, we are dealing with the macro-micro distinction that we have made earlier with respect to responses, but now with respect to stimuli. In attempting to deal with that issue, we need to consider empirical evidence concerning generalization along stimulus-intensity dimensions. Specifically, if the association is formed with a very particular level of neural activity in the original stimulus location, then there would be a generalization decrement if the intensity were changed there. Concurrently, if the

original conditioning was to the particular level of neural activity in adjacent locations, a similar decrement would arise. But if we follow this micro line of reasoning, we now have no physiological explanation of the stimulus-generalization process itself. That is, why should different intensities of stimulation, either weaker or stronger, lead to a generalization decrement? It was precisely this kind of problem that led what were once known as "neo-Pavlovian" theorists to take a purely functional approach.

6. Although any purely functional identification of stimuli is logically circular, it is also a very powerful approach that deserves to be underscored. The argument is that, since there is no way to know whether an event is a stimulus other than by trying it out, so too any properties of events that function as stimuli may be called stimuli. For example, we may functionally identify a person's "style," "manner," "bearing," "sex appeal," and other such traits and treat them as stimulus properties of that person without necessarily contending with the fine-grain features and their complex interactions that give rise to these abstracts traits.

7. The solution to this problem of stimulus interactions is not so simple as postulating "compound elements," at least if these elements are going to be conceptualized as unique and carrying their own associations. Each sample would be to some extent, at least, unique and each element would be colored by the particular combination of other elements in the sample. Another sample might be similar because it has many overlapping elements but, nevertheless, any particular element would have to be different. One could say that the patterning effect only changes the element slightly, but that approach leads inevitably to a strength analysis of generalization.

8. Although we are focusing on differential conditioning as the basis of steepening the slope of the gradient of generalization, there is some evidence that simple exposure to stimuli that differ in one way or another enhances their distinctiveness. This is sometimes thought of as pure perceptual learning, although one may wish to contend that some kind of adventitious differential reinforcement must have been involved during such exposures.

9. Here, although we are dealing with differential conditioning with respect to stimuli, differential conditioning can also take place with respect to responses. That is, reinforcement may be made contingent upon the occurrence of one particular response as distinguished from somewhat similar responses. We call this "differentiation" and generally presume that the underlying principles are comparable. However, this is quite gratuitous, because the types of distinctions we are making for stimulus conditions cannot be made for response operations. We inevitably give an organism a choice among responses and hence are observing response selection controlled by the organism; we simply can not realize the concept of a go-no-go response differentiation. Accordingly, differentiation learning is comparable to discrimination learning as we are using the term. Nevertheless, the basic operation that involves differential reinforcement may be programmed with respect to responses as well as to stimuli.

10. There is some degree of both conceptual and terminological confusion in this area, and we have chosen to use the least ambiguous terms. Operationally, stimuli may be presented separately or simultaneously. At a conceptual level, we may presume that either operation involves the same underlying process and call that "discrimination," but doing so gives it something of the status of a hypothetical construct. We prefer to label operations by terms that do not have this theoretical flavor in order to keep the nature of any systematic analysis clear. For example, we may refer to a "go-no-go discrimination" but that is really better conceptualized as a "discriminated differentiation," because the organism learns the appropriate response in the presence of the prevailing stimulus. What we have called "differential conditioning" is sometimes called "successive discrimination" and this is quite descriptive if one interprets it strictly in operational terms. After all, an organism may successively expose itself to stimuli that are operationally presented simultaneously (VTE behavior), and a theorist may contend that a single stimulus presentation still involves a comparison with some memory of that in relation to other stimuli that have been encountered. "Successive discrimination" has also been used for discriminated differentiation in which one response is reinforced in the presence of one stimulus, and another response is equally reinforced in the presence of another stimulus, In contrast, the *operations* of differential conditioning are unambiguous in classical, operant, and instrumental contexts and involve differential reinforcement of the same molar response depending on the prevailing stimulus. The other terms are perfectly legitimate provided only that they are interpreted in operational terms and clearly identified by the context. In similar fashion, here "discrimination learning" and "differentiation learning" are intended in the operational sense of giving the organism a choice among stimuli *or* among responses, and differentially reinforcing that choice. Very few experiments involve their conceptual combination where the organism may both choose a stimulus to which to respond and, then, a response to make in the presence of the chosen stimulus. A "discriminated differentiation" occurs when the experimenter controls the stimulus from occasion to occasion and, differentially reinforces the response chosen depending on the prevailing stimulus.

11. The peak-shift phenomenon is quite pervasive and by no means restricted to the very particular context in which we have presented it. The more abstract principle is that whenever the schedules/conditions of reinforcement/punishment differ as they do between the separate presentation of stimuli that differ along some identifiable continuum, then maximal responding will be shifted along that continuum in the direction away from the less preferred schedule/condition and, quite probably, the minimal performance will correspondingly be shifted along the continuum in the direction away from the more preferred schedule/condition. We have presented only the very particular situation involving reinforcement versus nonreinforcement; this situation enables a conceptual analysis based on excitation and inhibition. Clearly, the more abstract statement of the law would require a more abstract theoretical analysis that might involve associative, motivational, or perceptual processes. There are also

important considerations involving the difference between the stimuli and reinforcers/punishments involved.

12. This is a good point in our discussion to reemphasize the importance of trying to think in the way theorists think by using the mechanics and language of their theory, if you indeed wish to understand their theory. Pavlov did not use the expression "internal inhibition" in the sense of distinguishing it as a process postulated to take place inside the organism. All of his postulates were internal in this sense, including external inhibition. "Internal" referred to the dimensional properties of stimulus control. He thought that differential conditioning led to excitatory and inhibitory processes that were, more or less, confined to the stimulus continuum, generalized along that continuum, and were conceptually "internal" to it. External inhibition, in contrast, was not thought of as being dimensionally specific; it was conceived of as a property of the stimuli that could serve to reduce the likelihood of various conditioned responses involving various types of stimuli. Thus, an external inhibitor or a conditioned inhibitor could act on the internal inhibition involved in differential conditioning and lead to disinhibition (inhibition of inhibition). It was important to Pavlov to keep these processes conceptually separate; he would consider it to be quite inappropriate to refer to internal inhibition as conditioned inhibition in the same sense as a conditioned inhibitor.

13. A similar disclaimer with respect to our restricted illustrations that we made in the context of the peak shift also must be made for differential contrast effects. Recognizing the wide range of potential situations involving differential conditions/schedules of reinforcement/punishment, we should realize that differential contrast effects are extremely pervasive. Perhaps the most general formulation would be that insofar as the conditions/schedules are able to generate any difference in behavior when they prevail separately, those differences will be enhanced by their being interspersed. If the conditions/schedules would sustain some level of performance in each situation separately, then contrast can be observed in both directions. However, interspersing extinction in the presence of one stimulus, while reinforcing a response in the presence of another stimulus, leads to positive contrast; this is also the case with suppressing behavior by punishment in one component of the interspersed schedule. Accordingly, it should no more be assumed that contrast requires two levels of reinforcement, any more than it should be assumed that the peak shift only occurs in the context of reinforcement-nonreinforcement.

14. Scholars to some extent may object to our use of the term "redintegration" in this context, because it is historically employed to describe the presumed perceptual tendency to reconstruct an entire complex image from observing only a portion of that total picture. Specifically, for example, you may "see" a person's face, but you actually see it from many different perspectives and tend to redintegrate a single image, regardless of orientation. Behaviorally, however, the evidence for redintegration exhibits that a person will tend to respond the same way to this or that feature of the face, presented separately. Many mistaken identities have been based on a glimpse of a unique feature.

We have used this term for want of a better one to refer to this phenomenon of behavioral control by separate elements of a compound (complex) stimulus event.

15. One may object to the truly random control procedure, at least when it is generalized to operant/instrumental situations, because it explicitly entails occasional adventitious contingencies between a response and a reinforcer. Since we know that only very infrequent reinforcement is sufficient to sustain a substantial amount of behavior, the few permitted by the truly random procedure could be sufficient. This argument should be reviewed in the context of superstitions and autoshaping.

16. Miller and Dollard (1941) have proposed to reconcile this problem by the use of Hull's concept of "short-circuiting" of initially long behavior sequences. This concept describes that a person may begin to learn a response with the use of verbal instructions, often self-produced. In effect, you say to yourself, first do this, then do that, and now is the time to do whatever is supposed to come next. Having memorized the instructions, you repeat them to yourself and they guide your initial fumbling steps. However, concomitant with those verbal stimuli (pure stimulus acts to Hull, cue-producing responses to Miller and Dollard) are the ongoing exteroceptive stimulus events, and these are progressively gaining control over behavior. In due time, the requisite behavior runs off automatically, short-circuiting through the principle of the anticipatory response; the self-instructions are no longer necessary. However, this is a denial of attentional mechanisms with respect to highly practiced skills.

17. Still there is an unresolved conceptual difficulty with this position. Stimuli are discriminated by virtue of being present at the time of discrimination. If responses are differentiated on the basis of differences in feedback stimuli, those stimuli are not available until the responses have been emitted. This poses the same type of problem as we encountered in a cybernetically controlled incentive-motivation theory. It is clear that different responses will produce different feedback, and that the difficulty of differentiation is somehow related to the similarity of such feedback. But it is not clear how that feedback can enter into the differentiation process itself.

ABSTRACTS   **Kamin, L.J. Selective association and conditioning. In N.J. Mackintosh and W.K. Honig (Eds.).** *Fundamental issues in associative learning.* **Halifax: Dalhousie University Press, 1969.**

The most recent conception at which we have arrived seems capable of integrating all the data already presented. The notion is this: perhaps for an increment in an associative connection to occur, it is necessary that the US instigate some "mental work" on the part of the animal. This mental work will occur only if the US is unpredicted—if it in some sense "surprises" the animal. Thus, in the early trials of a normal conditioning experiment, the US is an unpredicted, surprising event of motivational significance, and the CS-US association is formed. Within the blocking experiment, the occurrence of the US on the first compound trial is to some degree surprising and some little learning can be demonstrated to have occurred on the transitional trial but on no other compound trial. Finally, if in the blocking experiment US intensity is radically increased when compound training is begun, the new US is obviously surprising, and no block is observed.

Precisely what mental work is instigated by a surprising US? Suppose that, for an increment in an associative connection to occur, it is necessary that the US provoke the animal into a "backward scanning" of its memory store of recent stimulus input; only as a result of such of a scan can an association between CS and US be formed, and the scan is prompted only by an unpredicted US, the occurrence of which is "surprising." This sort of speculation, it can be noted, leaves perception of the superimposed CS-element intact. The CS-element fails to become conditioned not because its input has been impeded but because the US fails to function as a reinforcing stimulus. We have clearly moved some distance from the notion of attention to the CS —perhaps to enter the realm of "retrospective contemplation" of the CS.

Kramer, T.J., & Rilling, M. Differential reinforcement of low rates: A selective critique. *Psychological Bulletin,* 1970, *14,* 225–254.

The literature relevant to the differential reinforcement of low rates of responding (DRL) is reviewed with respect to measurement of the behavior, bursts of responding, sequential dependencies, extinction and reconditioning, comparative aspects, punishment, reinforcement of two interresponse times, amount of deprivation and reinforcement, behavioral contrast, stimulus generalization. This review suggests that (a) bursts of responding could be due to a lack of stimulus feedback, (b) similar interresponse times tend to follow each other, (c) the development of mediating behavior is correlated with responding which is more appropriate to the schedule contingencies, and (d) subjects "preferred" short interresponse times. The shape of the stimulus generalization gradients after training on a DRL schedule is either peaked, flat, or inverted depending on the schedule value and prior training. Studies loosely concerned with response generalization suggest that responding under this schedule may be qualitatively different from responding under a variable-interval schedule. Experimental approaches for investigating the possible inhibitory and/or aversive properties of differential reinforcement are indicated.

Lashley, K.S., & Wade, M. The Pavlovian theory of generalization. *Psychological Review,* 1946, *53,* 72–87.

The conditioned reaction is initially undifferentiated. When a single stimulus is presented, reaction is associated only with the most conspicuous characters that differentiate it from the otherwise uniform environment. After a discriminative reaction has been established, systematic variation of the stimuli always reveals that, of the many variables which differentiate the stimuli for the human observer, relatively few, often not more than one, are effective for the discriminative reaction of the animal. The fundamental assumption of neo-Pavlovian theory, that in conditioning all aspects of the stimulus are associated with the reaction, is demonstrably false.

With continued training the subject may or may not develop reaction to a greater variety of aspects of the stimulus, may or may not show narrowing of the effective range on a stimulus dimension. Apparently such changes are a matter of chance noting of differences, generally with little regularity. Stimulus generalization is generalization only in the sense of failure to note distinguishing characteristics of the stimulus. What is associated in any given case can be discovered only by systematic variation of the stimulus and such analysis reveals great individual differences depending upon innate tendencies to perceptual organization, the past experience of the organism, and emphasis on one or another attribute given by the experimental situation.

This definition for the animal of stimulus dimensions is a fundamental problem of generalization. It does not occur in conditioning to a single stimulus but is somehow a function of differential training with two or more stimuli on the same dimension. The dimension itself is created by or is a function of the organism and only secondarily, if at all, a property of the physically definable character of the stimuli.

To develop a gradient of similarity, comparison of two or more objects is necessary, either a direct comparison of sensory impressions or comparison of sensory impressions with traces of previous ones. Such a comparison establishes relational attributes which are just as fundamental as are any of the attributes derived from a single stimulus. It is, in fact, difficult to cite any stimulus attribute which is not dependent upon the integration of ratios of stimulus action. In discrimination the direction of a difference is far more readily detected than are any absolute properties of the stimuli compared. The association of response is to relations between stimuli, which is the essential character of generalization.

Lawrence, D.H. Acquired distinctiveness of cues: I. Transfer between discriminations on the basis of familiarity with the stimulus. *Journal of Experimental Psychology*, 1949, *39*, 770–784.

The present experiment was based on the hypothesis that previous experience of a subject with various cues, irrespective of the instrumental behavior originally associated with them, is an important determinant of the rapidity of learning in a new situation involving the same cues. In order to test for this transfer effect and at the same time separate out the influence of previous experience with a cue from the influence of the instrumental behavior, the animals were first trained on a simultaneous discrimination and then tested on a successive discrimination. The assumption was that the instrumental responses learned in one situation would neither facilitate nor hinder the learning of new instrumental responses in the second; any transfer obtained would have to be attributed to previous familiarity with the stimuli employed.

It was found that the positive transfer animals, who were familiar with the relevant cue, learned the successive discrimination significantly more rapidly than did either the negative transfer or the control animals. The explanation offered of this transfer on the basis of familiarity with a cue was in terms of the acquired distinctiveness of cues. It was assumed that a mediating process was established during the simultaneous discrimination training that tended to enhance the distinctiveness of the relevant cue. This mediating process transferred to the successive discrimination. As a result of this enhanced distinctiveness of the relevant cue in the test situation, new instrumental responses were associated with this familiar cue more rapidly than with the unfamiliar one.

Mackintosh, N.J. Selective attention in animal discrimination learning. *Psychological Bulletin,* 1965, *64,* 124–150.

Two classes of experiment on the role of attention in discrimination learning are reviewed: (a) Investigations of the effect of attention on the amount learned about different cues have been interpreted as disproving noncontinuity theory (according to which animals attend to only one cue at a time). The fact that animals learn something about a second cue, however, does not prove that attention has no effect on learning, and more recent evidence shows that it does. This position which we may call a modified noncontinuity theory, states simply this: that animals do not classify their stimulus input with equal effectiveness in all possible ways at once, and it should, therefore, be possible to influence what an animal attends to by appropriate training procedures.

Accordingly, (b) if animals do not automatically attend to all cues, part of what they must learn in order to solve a discrimination problem is to attend to the relevant cue. Experiments on the acquired distinctiveness of cues, transfer along a continuum, and reversal learning provide evidence for the importance of such classificatory learning.

Mackintosh, N.J. A theory of attention: Variations in the associability of stimuli with reinforcement. *Psychological Review,* 1975, *82,* 276–298.

According to theories of selective attention, learning about a stimulus depends on attending to that stimulus; this is represented in two-stage models by saying that subjects switch in analyzers as well as learning stimulus-response associations. This assumption, however, is equally well represented in a formal model by the incorporation of a stimulus-specific learning-rate parameter into the equations describing changes in the associative strength of stimuli. Theories of selective attention have also assumed (a) that subjects learn to attend to and ignore relevant and irrelevant stimuli (i.e., that the learning rate parameter may increase or decrease depending on the correlation of a stimulus with reinforcement) and (b) that there is an inverse relationship between the probabilities of attending to different stimuli (i.e., that an increase in the learning rate parameter to one stimulus is accompanied by a decrease in that rate to others). The first assumption is used to explain the phenomena of acquired distinctiveness and dimensional transfer, the second those of overshadowing and blocking. Although the first assumption is justified by the data, the second is not: overshadowing and blocking are better explained by the choice of an appropriate rule for changing the learning rate parameter, such that it decreases to stimuli that signal no change from the probability of reinforcement predicted by other stimuli.

Miller, N.E. Some implications of modern behavior theory for personality change and psychotherapy. In D. Byrne and P. Worchel, (Eds.), *Personality change*. New York: Wiley, 1964.

Conflict seems to play a central role in many forms of mental disturbance. The following assumptions of a simple theoretical model have been studied one at a time in separate simple experiments and verified: (a) the tendency to approach a goal is stronger the nearer the subject is to it (gradient of approach); (b) the tendency to avoid a fear stimulus is stronger the nearer the subject is to it (gradient of avoidance); (c) the strength of avoidance increases more rapidly with nearness then that of approach (greater steepness of avoidance gradient); (d) the strength of the tendencies to approach and avoid vary directly as the strength of drive upon which they are based (increased drive raises height of entire gradient).

In the case of a relatively weak conflict based on unrealistic fears, it presumably is relatively easy to produce therapeutic changes by moderate increases in the strength of the drive to approach, so that the subject reaches the goal, extinguishing and counterconditioning his fears. Presumably most subjects whose avoidance is weak enough so that they can be induced to change in this way do not reach a psychotherapist.

This situation is contrasted with one in which strong avoidance is motivated by strong fear, so that the subject with moderate motivation to approach remains far from the goal. In this case it will take very strong approach motivation to bring him to the goal and inducing such motivation will produce a great increase in fear. Trying to force severe neurotics nearer to the goal is not an effective way of producing a favorable change. When the same amount of advance to the goal is produced by lowering the gradient of avoidance, we would expect a paradoxical increase in the strength of fear actually elicited but the increase produced in this way is much less than results from increasing the strength of motivation to approach.

Rescorla, R.A. Pavlovian conditioned inhibition. *Psychological Bulletin*, 1969, *72*, 77–94.

The notion of conditioned inhibition is examined and a definition is suggested in terms of the learned ability of a stimulus to control a response tendency opposed to excitation. Two techniques of measuring inhibition are outlined: (a) the summation procedure in which an inhibitor reduces the response that would normally be elicited by another stimulus and (b) the retardation-of-acquisition procedure in which an inhibitor is retarded in the acquisition of an excitatory conditioned response (CR). Examples of the use of these procedures are given for a variety of unconditioned stimulus (US) modalities. Several possible operations for generating conditioned inhibitors are reviewed: extinction following excitatory conditioning, discriminative conditioning, arrangement of a negative correlation between a conditioned stimulus (CS) and a US, use of an extended CS-US interval, and presentation of a stimulus in conjunction with US termination. A review of the literature on these operations suggests that conditioned inhibitors are not generated either by simple extinction procedures or by pairing a stimulus with US termination. By contrast, for both salivary and fear conditioning the other procedures do appear to generate inhibitors. Most of the procedures generating conditioned inhibitors can be described as arranging a negatively correlated CS and US.

Thomas, D.R. The use of operant conditioning techniques to investigate perceptual processes in animals. In R.M. Gilbert and N.S. Sutherland (Eds.), *Animal discrimination learning.* New York: Academic Press, 1969.

Discrimination training (of all types) steepens generalization along the dimension of the positive stimulus. We have inferred from the steepened gradient a heightened attention to the dimension in question. On the basis of all of the studies presented it cannot be doubted that extra-dimensional discrimination training steepens gradients of generalization along irrelevant dimensions including those from other modalities than that involved in such training. On the other hand, extra-dimensional pseudodiscrimination training seems to have absolutely no effect. This is in contrast to the flattening effect of inter-dimensional nondifferential training. This discrepancy may indicate a difference in the range of situations to which attention and "non-attention" generalize.

We have thought of attention more generally as a tendency to attribute significance to stimulus differences, which transfers positively to new situations and to new stimulus dimensions. Both narrow and broad views of attention would lead to the expectation that intra-dimensional discrimination training would steepen gradients of generalization. A narrow view has difficulty with the results of inter-dimensional training studies. In the face of the evidence, it seems clear that attention can be either specific or general, and that rather than arguing about which condition is typical, it would be more fruitful to attempt to determine the circumstances under which the two types or levels of attention attain.

Wagner, A.R. Stimulus validity and stimulus selection in associative learning. In N.J. Mackintosh and W.K. Honig (Eds.), *Fundamental issues in associative learning.* Halifax: Dalhousie University Press, 1969.

To summarize a pattern of recent findings, it appears that the signal value accruing to an E_1 depends upon its history of relative informativeness as compared to that of other concomitant cues, in announcing the occurrence of E_2. When B is experienced only in compound with A, the compound announcing reinforcement, B may be viewed as competing with A for any signal value which results from such experience. A useful empirical generalization is that the outcome of this competition will depend upon the relative validities of A and B, which may be manipulated in part by the experience the subject receives with A alone.

A general statement of this position would be of the following form: when a configuration of stimuli is followed by an E_2, there will be an increment in the signal value of a component (the component will be more reacted to as a signal for E_2) the amount of which will be a direct function of the degree to which the combination of components is not already maximally behaved toward as a signal for E_2. Consistency would argue for an assumption symmetrical to this acquisition assumption. For example: when a configuration of stimuli is not followed by E_2, there will be a decrement in the signal value of a component (the component will be less reacted to as a signal for E_2) the amount of which will be a direct function of the degree to which the combination of components is behaved toward as a signal for E_2.

It is obvious that this theoretical approach needs to be fleeced out before we can properly evaluate it. Still, it is attractive in its conceptual simplicity, and in comparison to the small step which it asks us to make from simple conditioning-extinction theory, it may take us a considerable distance. Is it not consoling then to find that, although the continuity-noncontinuity controversy is dead, we may still have with us a "modified-continuity vs. modified-noncontinuity controversy"?

EXAMINATION ITEMS

Topics for thought and discussion

1. Hull stated that the principle of stimulus generalization is a necessary adjunct to the principle of reinforcement. Relate this statement to the view that there is no fundamental principle of generalization and that the empirical phenomena all derive from the fundamental principles of discrimination learning.

2. Reflect on the observation that you may perfectly well engage in some well-practiced skill, such as walking, but feel quite awkward if you consciously attend to how you are walking or performing this skill.

3. The contention is that response generalization is a special case of stimulus generalization based on proprioceptive cues. Responses are different to the extent to which they feel different; hence, differentiation is related to the distinctiveness of such feedback cues. Relate this conceptual approach to the problem of response initiation that we encountered in the context of incentive theories.

Objective Items

1. From a systematic point of view, the *least* important feature of a gradient of stimulus generalization is
   a. the stimulus dimension involved
   b. whether there is a gradient at all

    c. its shape
    d. its slope

2.   According to the physiological (Pavlovian) theory of stimulus generalization (irradiation), the shape of the gradient is
    a. initially positively accelerated (bowed down)
    b. linear
    c. initially negatively accelerated (bowed up)
    d. indeterminate

3.   In comparing the random and selective stimulus-sampling approaches to generalization, the elements that are sampled are
    a. specified by both approaches, and differ in which elements are sampled
    b. specified by the random approach but not by the selective approach
    c. specified by the selective approach but not by the random approach
    d. not specified by either approach

4.   The most troublesome feature of the phenomena of overshadowing, redintegration, and compounding, taken collectively, for an attention theory is that
    a. more than one element may control behavior
    b. intense stimuli typically dominate over weaker ones
    c. control may change during the course of compound conditioning
    d. it is impossible to predict which phenomenon will appear

5.   As a cue to being financially rewarded for investing money in rare books, offers to sell you rare books are
    a. perfectly reliable and perfectly valid
    b. perfectly reliable but not perfectly valid
    c. not perfectly reliable but perfectly valid
    d. neither perfectly reliable nor perfectly valid

6.   Which of the following systematic analyses is *least* suggested by the studies of "inhibitory gradients?"
    a. conditioned inhibition as a hypothetical concept
    b. conditioned inhibition as a hypothetical construct
    c. differential excitation of responding
    d. differential excitation of not-responding

7.   Among the constraints on the excitation-inhibition derivation of the slope of the postdifferential reinforcement-generalization gradient is the slope of the primitive gradient.
    a. True
    b. False

8.   According to Miller's analysis of conflict, a negative therapeutic effect (increased conflict and misery) would result from either just lowering the avoidance gradient or just raising the approach gradient (short of eliminating the conflict entirely).
    a. True
    b. False

9.   The term "generalization" is *correctly* used as a
    a. hypothetical concept only
    b. hypothetical construct only
    c. hypothetical concept and construct at the same time
    d. hypothetical concept or construct at different times

10. A stimulus-sampling theory of stimulus generalization is *least* compatible with
    a. an S-S theory
    b. a gestalt theory
    c. an S-R reinforcement theory
    d. an S-R contiguity theory

11. Half the time white is on the left with black on the right, and half the time the positions are reversed. The subject is rewarded regardless of the response chosen in the former case and not in the latter. This is an instance of
    a. differential conditioning of molecular responses
    b. differential conditioning of molar responses
    c. discrimination learning of molecular responses
    d. discrimination learning of molar responses

12. Which of the approaches to response definition would be most favored by an interpretation of response generalization in terms of stimulus generalization?
    a. macromolar
    b. macromolecular
    c. micromolar
    d. micromolecular

13. To which of the hypotheses with respect to secondary reinforcement is the blocking phenomenon most similar?
    a. discriminative-stimulus hypothesis
    b. stimulus-change hypothesis
    c. information hypothesis
    d. elicitation hypothesis

14. The effects of differential reinforcement/punishment on the generalization gradient favors an incentive theory as opposed to alternative theories provided punishment is viewed as negative incentive.
    a. True
    b. False

15. In computing stimulus validity, one uses the percentage of times
    a. the stimulus is preceded by reinforcement
    b. the stimulus is followed by reinforcement
    c. reinforcement is preceded by the stimulus
    d. reinforcement is followed by the stimulus

16. This is an oddity problem. To an absolute/continuous/nonattentional theorist, which of the following phenomena would appear most different?
    a. transfer along a continuum
    b. differential conditioning
    c. peak shift
    d. compounding

17. The summation hypothesis assumes that the response tendencies associated with each cue combine additively in determining the response tendency to their simultaneous presentation. Which of the following theorists most warmly embraces the summation hypothesis?
    a. Kamin (surprise theory)
    b. Mackintosh (modified noncontinuity theory)
    c. Wagner (modified continuity theory)

d. Thomas (general attention theory)

18. The procedure of first conditioning to a range of stimuli along a continuum, then extinguishing to one of them, and finally testing for generalization would not imply an inhibitory gradient according to a strength theory of extinction.
    a. True
    b. False

19. We say that overshadowing is most likely to occur when one stimulus is more perspicuous than the other, because the one stimulus
    a. is more intense than the other
    b. is more distinctive than the other
    c. attracts the organism's attention
    d. overshadows the other

20. From the point of view of an empirical systematist, the phenomena concerning generalization and attention are conceptually
    a. essentially independent
    b. related at a low level of abstractness
    c. related at a high level of abstractness
    d. essentially mutually interdependent

ANSWERS TO OBJECTIVE ITEMS

1. (a) The systematically important questions are whether there is a gradient and, if so, what are its shape and slope? The presumption is that the principle applies to any stimulus dimension.

2. (d) There is nothing inherent in the physiological approach to specify, in advance, the way neural activity spreads over the distances between the loci of different stimuli. Hence, on just those grounds, it could be any shape.

3. (d) Both approaches give rules for sampling, but neither is sufficiently determined to specify the elements actually sampled. Interestingly enough, the random approach comes the closest because the sample at least has the characterstics of the population, whatever that may be. The selective approach is completely indeterminate in these regards.

4. (c) All of the phenomena imply important aspects of an attention construct, but the most troublesome would be to account for changes in control without changes in conditions.

5. (c) They are certainly valid; you cannot be rewarded without such a cue (offer). However, they are not reliable because you might not make money on the purchase.

6. (c) Alternatives (a) and (d) are substantially the same and are reasonable empirical systematic analyses of the phenomena. Alternative (b) is the corresponding theoretical interpretation. Alternative (c) might be developed from a strength theory of extinction, although it is not clear how this would generate inhibitory gradients.

7. (True) Although the impetus for the search for the primitive gradient was Lashley's theory, were it true, the excitation-inhibition account of the postdifferential reinforcement gradient would necessarily be inadequate, because it is based on primitive gradients.

8. (True) Changing either gradient in the indicated direction will move the person closer to the goal and induce greater conflict and hence misery. The negative thera-

peutic effect would be greater as a result of increasing approach than decreasing avoidance because of the relative slopes of the gradients.

9.   (d) Generalization processes are used in both empirical and theoretical systems. However, the word cannot correctly have both meanings in the same breath, so to speak.

10.   (b) Although a gestalt theory is, in some sense, cognitive, it is more in the nature of a perceptual theory in which stimulus elements have no independent identity. The stimulus-sampling theory is derived from S-R contiguity notions but is compatible with any associationistic approach to learning.

11.   (b) Although the subject can choose the response, reward is not differential with respect to choice. Hence, the requisite response is the molar aggregate of responding in either direction, and is a case of differential conditioning of whether or not to respond.

12.   (d) Although the conditions of reinforcement might lead to the formation of response concepts along qualitative and/or quantitative dimensions, much as occurs with respect to stimuli, the fundamental approach must distinguish among all responses that produce feedback stimuli differing in any way.

13.   (c) One could contend that the added cue in the blocking paradigm conveys no new information and gains no control, because it is redundant with the initial cue.

14.   (False) If one were an incentive theorist, the effects could most readily be accommodated by a notion of negative incentive and its resulting generalization. However, the effects do not demand an incentive interpretation of the fundamental effects of reward and punishment.

15.   (c) Alternatives (a) and (d) are irrelevant, because the term does not apply to events after reinforcement. Alternative (b) refers to stimulus reliability; even if reinforcement never occurred without the stimulus, the stimulus could still occur without reinforcement and hence not be perfectly reliable. If the stimulus never occurred without reinforcement, reinforcement could still occur without the stimulus and hence not be perfectly valid.

16.   (d) The first three alternatives can be reasonably accommodated by generalization of excitation and inhibition along some continuum. But compounding does not involve any explicitly established inhibitory process.

17.   (c) This is a crucial assumption of modified continuity theory; each element has some strength, and their combined strength is limited by the conditions of reinforcement. The other approaches do not invoke an explicit summation hypothesis and are more concerned with separate control by the elements.

18.   (True) If "inhibition" is used as a hypothetical concept, then the results of the procedure can be called "inhibitory gradients." But if one invokes hypothetical constructs, then there is no inhibition in a strength theory of extinction.

19.   (d) This is a totally circular description. The concepts of "psychological intensity," "distinctiveness," and "attention-attracting" are all after-the-fact, commonsensical explanations of why one stimulus may overshadow another.

20.   (c) Generalization and attention are not related at a low level of abstractness, because the procedures involved in each case can be clearly distinguished at an

operational level. However, from a systematic point of view, they are not independent because, at a higher level of abstractness, they are both related to selective stimulus control—in the first case by a particular value along a continuum and in the second case by an element of a stimulus complex. Even so, they are not mutually interdependent empirically; this arises only at the theoretical level of analysis.

CHAPTER NINE

SYSTEMATIC ANALYSES OF CHOICE BEHAVIOR

In a very real sense, all behavior can be viewed as a choice by the organism of what to do next. We have repeatedly encountered this type of conceptualization throughout our discussions of the various systematic analyses thus far considered. These may be viewed, in general, as "go-no-go" decisions involving whether and when to respond. We now wish to consider situations that involve a choice among stimuli (discrimination learning) and/or among responses (differentiation learning).

The distinction we are making can be seen most readily in the very basic behavioral process of reaction time. In *simple reaction time,* a subject is instructed to press a key as quickly as possible after a signal is given. Under these instructions, the subject must detect the presence of the signal from the background noise level. According to present models of this situation (e.g., Grice, 1968), the subject is assumed to adopt some criterion based on the signal-to-noise ratio and to respond when the sensory input exceeds that criterion.[1] This involves a go-no-go decision.

In *choice reaction time,* the situation is changed in order to enable two responses, such as pressing either a left key or a right key. The instructions are to press the left key when one stimulus is presented and the right key when another stimulus is presented. Accordingly, the subject must do more than simply detect the presence of a stimulus; the decision of which key to press (a differentiation) depends on which stimulus occurs (a discrimination). Choice reaction times are longer than simple reaction times, presumably because these additional psychological processes are required. Our concern in this chapter is with the systematic analyses of these processes in more complex situations involving learning and motivation.

THE CLASSIC ISSUE OF EMERGENTISM

Before discussing the more specific issues involved in systematic analyses of discrimination and differentiation learning, let us set the stage with a much more fundamental issue. This issue occurs at a number of points in the conceptual hierarchy of behavioral science and concerns the notion of *emergentism.* The emergent thesis states that, at certain critical levels of abstractness, something new appears that could never be understood by analysis of the more molecular components. Indeed, in its strong and true form, emergentism contends that the components do not have an independent meaning when they are part of an emergent compound.

A simple, physical example is water. We may decompose water into a compound of hydrogen and oxygen, but we could never fully understand the properties of water from a study of those elements separately. Even saying that these elements have an affinity for each other would not be enough, because hydrogen no longer acts like hydrogen when combined with oxygen. It is no longer a gas and neither is oxygen, because they combine into a liquid at normal temperatures. The components have lost their identity and something totally different has emerged.

In the larger scheme of things, one point of emergence is the appearance of life. Another is the presumed evolution of organisms. It is also contended by many that something new emerged with the mutation of humans, specifically, the mind with freedom of the will. There are other less dramatic examples that could be given, but we hope these illustrations are sufficient in describing the fundamental concept of emergentism. Among the clear implications of this thesis is that no amount of study of the more molecular component processes will lead to a systematic analysis of the more molar phenomena and, furthermore, those principles will no longer apply.

Quite naturally, the antithesis of emergentism is that a complete understanding of the simpler processes would enable one to derive the results of their combination. A weaker form of nonemergentism asserts that the principles governing the simpler processes will still apply, but new principles may be required to describe the more complex processes. It seems appropriate that the final content chapter of this book be concerned with the first point in a purely behavioral hierarchy at which the issue of emergentism becomes paramount. To be sure that the reader grasps this extremely important point, let us briefly review the logic of the ordering of the preceding chapters of this book. (If one accepts emergentism here, it will be easier to accept emergentism at still higher levels of abstractness; rejecting the emergent thesis here may make one more resistant to its acceptance later.)

The first two chapters were conceived of as a prelude. We wished to set the stage for a study of systematic analyses by discussing the nature of learning and motivation and then the conceptual difference between the use of these terms as hypothetical concepts or hypothetical constructs. The goal of these chapters was to create the groundwork for our primary mission. Then we were ready to embark on the basic, pervasive, and overriding issues of the nature and conditions of learning as observed in relatively simple situations presumed to involve the learning process.

We left that discussion with four logically possible alternatives, still fundamentally unresolved. Learning is either cognitive (S-S) or behavioristic (S-R) in nature, and in either case either does or does not require reinforcement in addition to contiguity for its development. But whatever one's preference in these regards, the empirical law of effect endures like the Rock of Gibraltar. It may be somewhat battered and worn with age, but if you don't pay it due respect, your system is doomed to wreck upon its base. So we set about the description of the ways in which reinforcing and punishing events might be identified and then discussed the various approaches to systematizing the effects of such events on behavior. Through all of this, we attended primarily to very simple responses that either did not occur or occurred with some probability, at some rate or speed, with some amplitude, and with particular topographical features.

This discussion led naturally to the issues related to the effects of changing from one set of conditions to another, and then to a discussion of the effect of differential applications of these principles to different stimuli. According to those with a strong bent toward emergentism, this is the end of the line. Just put an organism, particularly a human organism, in a complex environment containing a number of stimuli and enabling a number of responses, and even the most elegant little systems will be lost. It is much more than just a new ball game, more even than moving into the big leagues; it is now a different game altogether—different facts, different laws, different principles, different theories. With this argument, this should really be the first chapter of another book on systematic analyses of behavior—the take-off point for systems that can deal with real-life situations.

We agree that the topic of choice behavior is indeed such a take-off point for more complex phenomena and, hence, the issue of emergentism is not only the most important feature of this chapter but is probably also the most critical one for the entire book. For if we cannot see this simply as the next logical step up the ladder of conceptual abstractness, with probably the addition of new principles but certainly with the old principles clearly relevant, then we have set impenetrable boundary conditions on the systems that we have been discussing. Or perhaps only some class of these systems can cross this barrier successfully. Those that can might well gain in stature with respect to the simpler situations, because they offer more promise of leading on to larger domains. As with all other issues of this nature, this one is by no means resolved.

Direct Empirical Extrapolation

Let us first focus the issue of emergentism on a very particular context. In the differential conditioning of, let us say, a rat running from a start box to a goal box, we arrange the conditions such that on half of the trials the runway is black and reward is in the goal box, while on the other half of the trials the runway is white and there is no reward in the goal box. On each trial, therefore, the rat must make a go-no-go decision as to whether or not to run and must make this decision on the basis of the brightness of the runway because the food is not detectable from the start box. We know, of course, that this is a relatively simple problem for a rat; soon we observe fast running down the black runway and either no running or very slow locomotion down the white runway.

Now let us simply put the two runways side by side and give the rat a choice between them. The simplest possible form of our question is whether the rat will choose the black alley. Regardless of one's theoretical approach to what the rats learned during the differential conditioning phase of this study, the obvious prediction from a nonemergent point of view is that the rat will indeed choose the black alley. The evidence from this particular approach to the issue is overwhelmingly positive for the nonemergent thesis. But this does not imply that the rat behaves in this new choice situation with the same speed and decisiveness of a rat previously trained on the simultaneous presentation-discrimination problem. Although the gross evidence with respect to the runway that is ultimately chosen is clear, it is equally clear that the rat does not make this transition without, so to speak, breaking stride.

The evidence with respect to the issue under consideration is less clear if the study involves the opposite sequence of problems. In this case, the rats are first trained on the simultaneous presentation-discrimination problem and learn consistently and rapidly to choose the black alternative in preference to the white alternative. When subsequently tested in the two runways separately, they tend to run much more readily down the white one than do animals that have been trained with the runways only presented on separate trials.

There are other lines of direct empirical evidence that the choice decision is not identical with the go-no-go decision. For example, in many studies the two procedures are mixed; the rats sometimes are forced to run down one runway, sometimes to run down the other runway, and sometimes given a choice between them. It is routinely found that there is considerable correlation between their differential speeds of running and their choice behavior but the correlation is by no means perfect (e.g., Logan, 1952). In most of these situations, differences in speeds appear well before consistent preference is observed, and in some cases it is tempting to say anthropomorphically that the rat "knows" perfectly well that this is the wrong way to go, but nevertheless continues to go that way.

As we have seen all too frequently heretofore, this apparently straightforward, direct, empirical resolution of a conceptual issue is not conclusive. One cannot contend that the choice situation is totally different, but neither can one assert that it is simply more of the same. The issue becomes a question of whether it is more appropriate to believe that the principles of differential conditioning still apply but require some additional postulates unique to choice behavior, or whether the conceptual analysis of choice behavior is fundamentally different but permits some transposition–like inferences about the separate presentation of the stimuli.

We must, therefore, move the emergentism issue into the theoretical arena where it originated. For our purposes, it will be profitable first to outline in some detail one influential nonemergent point of view—that of Spence. It should be emphasized that here we are considering his early theory of discrimination learning (i.e., before he became an incentive theorist), but most of the conceptual issues are epitomized by this early theory. We will then develop these issues in relation to it.

Spence's Early Theory of Discrimination Learning

Beginning in 1936 and continuing until the Second World War, Spence developed a theory of discrimination learning that, on the one hand, would appear to be most vulnerable to attack by the proponents of emergent processes and yet, on the other hand, that accepted that challenge. It was vulnerable because it derived directly from the behavioristic (S-R) theories of Pavlov, Watson, Thorndike, and Hull and made the simplest possible assumption that the choice between alternatives would be determined by which of the competing excitatory potentials happened to be greatest. We will now quote from the first of several articles by Spence (1936, 1937, 1938, 1939, 1940, 1941, 1942).

Krechevsky termed systematic pre-solution responses 'hypotheses' and, like Lashley, interpreted them as attempts at solution of the problem by the rat, with the implication that they represented a kind of behavior superior in some manner to that usually described as 'trial-and-error.' Furthermore, he concluded that these experimental facts offer conclusive evidence of the inadequacy of 'trial-and-error' theories of learning, because, as he claimed, they contradict the assumption made by the latter that the learning process is, in its early stages, random and haphazard in nature. But a sophisticated 'trial-and-error' theory of learning would not hold that the order of sequence of trial acts is a haphazard affair, but rather would conceive it as proceeding according to definite principles or laws.

Discrimination learning involves the relative strengthening of the excitatory tendency of a certain component of the stimulus complex as compared with that of certain other elements until it attains sufficient strength to determine the response. By the conditions of the experiment the relevant stimulus component is always reinforced and never frustrated, whereas, irrelevant components receive both reinforcement and frustration. The principle of reinforcement assumes that if a reaction is followed by reward, which may be defined in terms of the occurrence of a final or consummatory response, the excitatory tendencies of the immediate stimulus components are reinforced or strengthened by a certain increment, I. The principle of inhibition or frustration states that when a reaction is not rewarded i.e., when the final or consummatory response is prevented from taking place, the excitatory tendences of the active stimulus components are weakened by a certain decrement, D. It assumes that this weakening is due to an active, negative process, inhibition, which, adding itself in algebraic fashion to the positive excitatory tendencies, results in lowered strength values.

Certain further assumptions have also been made as to the relative amount of strengthening and weakening the excitatory tendencies of S-R connections undergo with reinforcement and non-reinforcement, particularly as to variations in amount in different stages of the learning process (see Table 1).

The various stimulus aspects in the discrimination situation are undoubtedly considerable in number. The essential ones in producing the selective response, however, are the visual appearances of the two stimuli containing the incentive and the two stimuli to be differentiated, e.g., circular and triangular forms. It may be assumed that the organism has acquired, in its past experience, reaction tendencies of orienting towards and approaching each of these stimuli so that we have the following four S-R connections: S_{LB} (left box) — R_A (approach response), S_{RB} (right box) — R_A (approach response), S_c (circular form) — R_A (approach response), and S_t (triangular form) — R_A (approach response). That is to say, it may be assumed that at the beginning of the discrimination experiment the organism already has these S-R connections established in some degree and that, depending upon the amount and kinds of previous experience, they will each have certain, finite strengths between 0 and 100.

Examination of this stimulus response scheme will show that the four stimulus components are so arranged or paired that there are only two opposed or competing sets of excitatory tendencies. Now which of these opposing sets of stimulus components the animal will respond to on any particular trial by approaching, will depend upon which has the greater aggregate of excitatory tendencies eliciting such a response.

In Table 2 is presented a complete account of the learning process in this hypothetical case. The first two columns of this table show the number of the trial and the position of the positive stimulus. The third column gives the combined strengths of the excitatory tendencies leading to the response of approaching the stimuli at the left box, which on one trial may be S_c and S_{LB} and on another S_t and S_{LB}, as shown in the

TABLE 1

Showing the Strengthening and Weakening Effects of Reinforcement and Nonreinforcement for Various Strengths of Excitatory Tendencies or S-R Connections

STRENGTH OF EXCITATORY TENDENCY (s)	STRENGTHENING EFFECT OF A SINGLE REINFORCEMENT $I = \dfrac{3.99}{555} e\,(s - 50)^2$	WEAKENING EFFECT OF A SINGLE FAILURE OF REWARD $D = .05\,s - .5$
1	.05	.00*
5	.10	.00*
10	.22	.00
15	.44	.25
20	.79	.50
25	1.30	.75
30	1.94	1.00
35	2.66	1.25
40	3.33	1.50
45	3.81	1.75
50	3.99	2.00
55	3.81	2.25
60	3.33	2.50
65	2.66	2.75
70	1.94	3.00
75	1.30	3.25
80	.79	3.50
85	.44	3.75
90	.22	4.00
95	.10	4.25
99	.05	4.45

*"*D*" is assumed to be zero for all values of "*s*" less than 10.

following three columns. The same data for the response of approaching the stimuli at the right box are given in the next four columns. The final columns indicate to which set of stimuli the approaching response is made and whether this response is correct or not, an incorrect choice being bracketed. The consequences of the responses upon the strengths of the various excitatory tendencies always appear in the next row beneath, which represents their status for the ensuing trial. With the successive reinforcements of the excitatory tendencies of S_c and the failure of reinforcement of those of S_t, the difference between their strengths becomes gradually larger until sufficiently great to offset consistently, any other differences that exist between the two competing sets of stimulus components. Learning is completed only when this stage is reached.

In summary, the behavioral phenomena characteristic of discrimination learning,

Table 2
Showing a Hypothetical Case of Learning in Which the Initial Excitatory Tendencies Are Assumed to be as Follows:
$$S_{lb} = 80.20, \; S_{rb} = 80.00,$$
$$S_c = 10.00, \text{ and } S_t = 10.00$$

STRENGTH OF COMPONENT EXCITATORY TENDENCIES

Trial	Pos. (+) S	Left	S_C	S_t	S_{LB}	S_C	S_t	S_{RB}	Right	Response
			R_A				R_A			
1	L	90.20	10.00		80.20		10.00	80.00	90.00	L
2	R	90.97		10.00	80.97	10.22		80.00	90.22	(L)
3	R	87.42		10.00	77.42	10.22		80.00	90.22	R
4	L	87.87	10.45		77.42		10.00	80.80	90.80	(R)
5	L	87.87	10.45		77.42		10.00	77.25	87.25	L
6	R	88.45		10.00	78.45	10.67		77.25	87.92	(L)
7	L	85.69	10.67		75.02		10.00	77.25	87.25	(R)
8	R	85.02		10.00	75.02	10.67		73.90	84.57	(L)
9	R	81.77		10.00	71.77	10.67		73.90	84.57	R
10	L	82.71	10.94		71.77		10.00	75.35	85.35	(R)
										4
11	L	82.71	10.94		71.77		10.00	72.10	82.10	L
12	R	83.50		10.00	73.50	11.20		72.10	83.30	(L)
13	R	80.37		10.00	70.37	11.20		72.10	83.30	R
14	L	81.84	11.47		70.37		10.00	73.75	83.75	(R)
15	L	81.84	11.47		70.37		10.00	70.60	80.60	L
16	L	84.00	11.75		72.25		10.00	70.60	80.60	L
17	R	83.90		10.00	73.90	12.04		70.60	82.64	(L)
18	R	80.70		10.00	70.70	12.04		70.60	82.64	R
19	L	83.04	12.34		70.70		10.00	72.45	82.45	L
20	R	82.55		10.00	72.55	12.65		72.45	85.10	R
										7
21	R	82.55		10.00	72.55	12.99		74.05	87.04	R
22	L	85.88	13.33		72.55		10.00	75.47	85.47	L
23	L	87.84	13.69		74.15		10.00	75.47	85.47	L
24	R	85.55		10.00	75.55	14.06		75.47	89.53	R
25	R	85.55		10.00	75.55	14.45		76.72	91.17	R
26	L	90.41	14.86		75.55		10.00	77.82	87.82	L
27	R	86.80		10.00	76.80	15.28		77.82	93.10	R
28	L	92.54	15.74		76.80		10.00	78.82	88.82	L
29	L	94.12	16.22		77.90		10.00	78.82	88.82	L
30	R	88.90		10.00	78.90	16.73		78.82	95.55	R
										10

such as the non-random, systematic nature of the pre-solution responses, have been shown to be entirely consistent with a 'trial-and-error' type of learning theory. Employing clearly defined principles of reinforcement and non-reinforcement (inhibition), a hypothetical picture or logically possible account of the nature of discrimination has been developed. This theoretical structure provides a rational account of such phenomena as, for example, position responses and the habit of perseveration-with-success-and-alternation-with-failure, and, unlike the so-called insight-hypothesis, which states that the organism, itself, initiates various responses (termed hypotheses) as attempts at solution of the problem until the correct one is hit upon, permits of an account of the conditions determining the appearance and succession of these various modes of response.

While no attempt has been made in the present article to work out in detail the experimental implications of these theoretical principles the following deductions have been made.

1. Naive, untrained animals will tend to show a more pronounced tendency towards position habits than experienced animals in the solution of discrimination problems.

2. The response pattern of perseverating on the side which is correct and of shifting to the other on failure will tend to predominate in the experienced animal.

3. In naive animals that show a long, perfectly consistent position response in the learning period the solution of the problem will occur simultaneously with the abolishment of the position habit.

4. If the positive and negative relation of the cue stimuli are reversed before the animal is responding to the correct stimulus more often than chance a greater number of trials will be required to learn the reversed problem than would have been necessary for the original problem. A corollary of this deduction is that this difference will be proportional to the time between the beginning of the training and the reversal of the positive and negative stimuli.

5. Animals will manifest sytematic modes of response in an insoluble problem, in which no stimulus is regularly the corect one.

Presolution Behavior and Hypotheses

Krechevsky reflected the predominant presumption of the era, namely, that the approaches deriving from Pavlov, Thorndike, and Hull necessarily imply that behavior occurrs, more or less, by chance during the presolution period (i.e., during the time when the ostensible learning curve hovers around 50% correct with respect to the relevant discriminanda). This seems implicit in the expression "trial-and-error" learning, because the organism has no knowledge about the situation and could best engage in essentially random activity until appropriate response tendencies begin to develop. In contrast, Krechevsky (1932) proposed that organisms in general, and rats in particular, do not engage in any such haphazard approach to a discrimination problem.

Krechevsky contended that organisms adopt hypotheses about the correct solution to the problem and systematically test these out one by one. Discrimination learning is a simple problem-solving task and behavior only appears to be random. The organism is presumed to be testing some hypothesis, and during that time the behavior is actually systematic with respect to the wrong hypothesis and is, necessarily, at a chance level with respect to the correct hypothesis.

There are several conceptual difficulties with this approach. Most important, one cannot always be sure what hypothesis the organism is testing, during any series of trials, during the presolution period. There are frequently response sequences consistent with some hypothesis that the experimenter could construct, such as going to the left, but Krechevsky never rigidly tied down how long a hypothesis might be retained for testing. Thus it is simply assumed that the organism must be testing some hypothesis or other, while performance appears random with respect to the relevant discriminanda. A second problem is that the general approach permits the possibility that an organism might be testing more than one hypothesis on any particular trial. This multiple-hypothesis approach, which we will subsequently encounter as the modified noncontinuity theory, suffers from being unable to specify, in advance, how many hypotheses the organism might be entertaining.

Spence quickly disposed of the misinterpretation that "random" means "unsystematic." He did not propose cognitive hypotheses, but he did propose that an organism may have various differential response tendencies generalized to the new situation from past experiences and would behave systematically with respect to those tendencies so long as they dominated the net-response tendency. Thus, he derived the observed facts that behavior is not truly random during the presolution period, that systematic behavior appears and reappears, all the while learning is taking place with respect to the relevant discriminanda. So it was this feature of continuous learning that became the focal point of the controversy.

In its strong form, Krechevsky's theory asserted that the organism is learning nothing at all about the relevant cues so long as incorrect hypotheses are being tested. On the contrary, Spence asserted that the organism is gradually learning about the relevant cues, even while behaving systematically on other bases. Thus emerged what is known as the *continuity-noncontinuity* controversy, because the further implication of Krechevsky's theory is that learning should occur suddenly. Once the organism hits on the correct hypothesis, it will be confirmed by the testing and thenceforth immediately be retained.

Typical learning curves show a gradual improvement, but these are based on averaging the performance of a group of subjects; the apparent gradualness of the curve could readily result from averaging a number of essentially discontinuous performances of individual subjects. Analysis of individual records is not conclusive. Some subjects indeed show an almost discontinuous change from near chance (vis-à-vis the relevant discriminanda) to near perfect performance—but not all do. The noncontinuity theorist can attempt to dismiss the failure of sudden solution to measurement artifacts; the subject might show an intermediate level of performance by occasional chance correlations of the relevant cue with the hypothesis that the subject is testing. Furthermore, Spence was able to derive sudden improvement in performance from his theory that the underlying learning processes develop continuously.

At this juncture, the argument is a standoff. Continuity theory appears to imply random behavior gradually developing into discriminative performance but can also accommodate systematic presolution behavior and sudden improvement. Noncontinuity theory appears to imply systematic presolution behavior and sudden improvement but can also accommodate random behavior and gradual solution. Since both kinds of behavior can be observed in the typical discrimination learning study, neither theory holds the weight of evidence in its favor. Accordingly, Spence proposed a more analytic experimental approach. If Krechevsky was correct that, even if not always detectable in the data, the subjects are testing and rejecting hypotheses during the presolution period, then it should be possible to reinforce the ultimate incorrect stimulus during this time with no deleterious effects on subsequent discrimination learning. Specifically, if in a black-positive versus white-negative discrimination learning situation, a rat initially tests a variety of position hypotheses, then reinforcing the white stimulus during that stage should have no effect on learning when the rat finally gets around to the black-white hypothesis.

Spence's theory clearly makes the contrary prediction, since nonreinforcing the to-be-positive stimulus and reinforcing the to-be-negative stimulus should begin to build up contrary differentials in excitatory tendencies that would have to be overcome after reversal. Of course, to be fair to Spence, one would have to give enough prereversal trials to permit this differential to be appreciable. Also, in fairness to Krechevsky, one could not give so many prereversal trials that at least some subjects might have begun to test the relevant hypothesis, even though it was not clearly evident in performance.

In the early studies, there was the complication of whether or not to count only trials after reversal for comparison with a control group for whom the discrimination was not reversed and for which one naturally counts trials from the very beginning of training. In one sense, counting only postreversal trials is legitimate, because Spence's theory implies that the relevant discriminanda at that point would have a contrary difference in excitatory tendencies. However, in another sense it is incorrect, because Spence's theory also implies that the prereversal trials would have begun to neutralize differential control by position cues. Furthermore, Spence correctly contended that Krechevsky's theory would predict no difference in total trials, since the reversal group should be learning neither more nor less about the relevant discriminanda during the presolution period.[2]

To make a long story shorter, Spence "won" this controversy. Spence could predict that reversal would retard discrimination learning, if the relevant discriminanda were situated so as not to require overt receptor-orienting acts to obtain effective differential stimulation. Accordingly, evidence (e.g., Ehrenfreund, 1948) that reversal during the presolution period impairs discrimination learning when the stimuli are readily perspicuous, but does not when they are inconspicuous, appeared to settle the continuity-noncontinuity controversy as waged between Spence and Krechevsky. (Lashley was to contend that, if the rat had to be looking at the relevant discriminanda, then it must be attending to them and testing some hypotheses about them. And the general continuity-noncontinuity issue remains evident in even the most recent conceptual systems.)

Spence did not win the controversy in the sense of clearly disproving the notion that organisms test hypotheses when confronted with a new discrimination problem. To accommodate the data, one would have to permit the testing of several hypotheses concurrently (modified noncontinuity theory, Mackintosh, 1965). However, Spence did win a very critical point for at least the weak form of the nonemergent thesis, because he demonstrated that one could correctly predict discrimination learning from a theory based on conditioning situations with the addition of the simplest choice axiom; that is, the alternative with the strongest net excitatory tendency will prevail.

THE STIMULUS IN
DISCRIMINATION
LEARNING

Confronted with the principle of discrimination learning, the theorist sets about to account for it in terms of hypothetical constructs and hypotheses that discuss the underlying nature of the processes involved. Differences of opinion in these regards will almost inevitably arise leading to controversies and attempted empirical resolutions. Perhaps the most fundamental of these issues concerns the conceptual nature of the stimulus in discrimination learning. According to the nonemergent view of Spence, the stimulus in discrimination learning is substantially the same as in differential conditioning. There are alternative emergent views, but let us first specify Spence's approach symbolically.

The Absolute View

Spence assumed that each stimulus has some excitatory tendency (E, which he initially symbolized "s") to elicit an approach response. Whenever a response to one stimulus is followed by reinforcement, E gains in strength and, whenever a stimulus is not followed by reinforcement, E loses in strength. This latter effect was assumed to result from some kind of inhibitory (I) process[3] but the essential ingredient for the present descriptive purposes is that E is incremented and decremented on a trial-by-trial basis according to the occurrence of reinforcement and nonreinforcement.

Symbolically, then, Spence viewed discrimination learning as resulting from the competition of the following alternatives:

$$^S\text{black}^{E_R}\text{Approach} = f \text{ (reinforcement)}$$
$$^S\text{white}^{E_R}\text{Approach} = f \text{ (nonreinforcement)}$$

where the black and white stimuli have separate excitatory potentials to elicit approach, based on their histories of reinforcement and nonreinforcement. This is called the absolute view of the stimulus, because each stimulus is assumed to have its own excitatory potential based on its unique associations with consequences, and while these tendencies are assumed to generalize to other stimuli according to their degree of similarity, the essence of the theory is absolute stimulus control. The associative processes are the same as in differential conditioning but, when the organism is given a choice, the one with the larger value of E will occur. We will use an analogous symbol system for the alternative views, although their verbal descriptions are different.

The Relational View

Lashley (1942) proposed that something did emerge when two stimuli are presented simultaneously and the organism is given a choice between them. Their absolute properties no longer control behavior. Instead, it is a relationship between the stimuli that determines choice behavior, and relationships are not inherent in any single stimulus viewed in isolation. Whiteness and blackness are no longer important, except in giving rise to the relational concepts of lighter and darker. Hence, choice is based on the following competing tendencies:

$$^S darker^{E_R} Approach = f \text{ (reinforcement)}$$
$$^S lighter^{E_R} Approach = f \text{ (nonreinforcement)}$$

According to this view, the organism is presumed to compare the stimuli, detect the difference between them, and respond on the basis of the resulting relationship. There is also generalization based on such relationships.

The Configurational View   A third point of view is derived from Gestalt theory and is stated formally by Gulliksen and Wolfle (1938). This view assumes that a stimulus complex is inherently indivisible; one cannot properly talk about absolute stimulus elements nor even the relationships among them. What emerges is a "whole," a configuration within which the organism learns the adaptive response. Symbolically,

$$^S black\text{-}white^{E_R} left = f \text{ (reinforcement)}$$
$$^S black\text{-}white^{E_R} right = f \text{ (nonreinforcement)}$$
$$^S white\text{-}black^{E_R} right = f \text{ (reinforcement)}$$
$$^S white\text{-}black^{E_R} left = f \text{ (nonreinforcement)}$$

where the first two are in competition (the stronger one being chosen) on half of the trials, and the last two apply to the other half of the trials. Accordingly, the organism has to solve each configuration separately, although generalization may also occur between configurations.

Summary   It should be apparent that the basic principle of discrimination learning could equally be described in absolute, relational, or configurational terms. That is, these terms all have a basis for predicting choice of the reinforced stimulus, as they must, because that is the fundamental principle for which they were designed. They also would agree that the more similar the stimuli, the more difficult the discrimination—in each case on the basis of the degree of generalization between the competing alternatives. But note we are reintroducing the what-is-learned issue, only now with respect to the stimulus. Not surprisingly, behavioristic (S-R) theories are prone toward an absolute view of the stimulus, and cognitive (S-S) theories are prone toward relational or configurational views. A molecular view of the response begets a molecular view of the stimulus, and a molar view of the response begets a molar view of the stimulus. But as we have repeatedly emphasized, these affinities are not inviolate.

TRANSPOSITION OF DISCRIMINATION   Proponents of the relational view of the stimulus in discrimination learning found in the *transposition*[4] phenomenon a basis for challenging the absolute view. Let us imagine a stimulus continuum numbered 1 through 7 from darker to lighter. Subjects are first trained in a simultaneous discrimination paradigm to choose S4$^+$ in preference to S5$^-$. Lashley viewed the subject as having learned to choose the darker of the stimuli, whereas Spence viewed the subject as having a stronger excitatory potential for S4 in an absolute sense. What, then, should happen if the subject is presented on a probe-test trial with S3 versus S4? If the subject had learned to choose the darker stimulus, it would now choose S3; although it would appear that if the animal had learned to approach S4, it would continue to do so in the test trial.

Lashley found that rats consistently chose S3 on such a probe test, a stimulus they had never before encountered, in preference to the one with which reward had previously been consistently associated. Spence replicated the study in somewhat different contexts and found the same result: in a "near" test (i.e., one in which the test stimuli are close to the training stimuli, in this case, including the original S+), subjects respond in a manner directly derivable from a relational view of the stimulus.

In this case, Spence was able to derive the phenomenon of transposition from his absolute view by taking into account the principle of stimulus generalization. This derivation was shown graphically in Figure 8.1a, although the derivation was originally made for transposition rather than for the peak-shift phenomenon. This derivation not only accounts for the original findings but has further implications about other probe tests. Specifically, transposition–like behavior should decrease as the distance from the original training stimuli is increased (i.e., 3 vs 4, 2 vs 3, 1 vs 2) and actually reach a point at which the opposite of transposition should occur. The subject should choose the brighter stimulus in a "far" test. When Ehrenfreund (1952) confirmed that prediction, the tide shifted. Relational theory could reasonably handle the decrease in transposition behavior, as distance from the original stimuli increased, by assuming that a generalization decrement resulted from using stimuli quite different from those involved in training, but the reversal of preference was embarrassing. The reversal is small and the relational theorist may thus attempt simply to dismiss it as experimental error, but it has subsequently been observed with sufficient frequency to merit consideration.

Although his absolute approach appeared victorious in this limited area, Spence was aware that relational properties can gain control over behavior. If a subject is presented with various combinations of stimuli, that is, S1 versus S2, S2 versus S3, S3 versus S4, and so on, and is consistently rewarded for choosing the darker stimulus, regardless of the pairing, most subjects will learn to behave adaptively. Accordingly, Spence (1952) subsequently elaborated his theoretical position to add that any stimulus is a compound of stimulus elements, some of which may be relational ones. His assumption remained that elements based on the absolute properties of the stimulus are the more conspicuous ones, and these gain predominant control over behavior when they are adequate for solution. However, there are also relational elements in the stimulus compound. This special assumption also has additional implications, specifically, that learning to respond on a purely relational basis should be more difficult than learning to respond when absolute properties are adequate, although even this prediction depends on the similarity of the stimuli.

We cannot review all of the research that has been done in the context of this particular controversy. It is worth noting, however, that developmental psychologists (e.g., Kuenne, 1946) have studied this phenomenon with the interesting result that young children respond to transposition tests in a manner very much like the early results with rats (i.e., decreasing incidence of transposition–like choice accompanied by reversal of choice in far tests). However, older children and adults tend to show more or less complete transposition even in far tests. Learning the concept "darker-than" involves precisely the kind of training necessary to bring behavior under control of relational elements, and it would appear that once humans have acquired such a concept, the perspicuity of such elements is enhanced.

DISCRIMINATED DIFFERENTIATION

As indicated previously, the configurational approach is an outgrowth of Gestalt conceptions that a stimulus complex is a "whole" that cannot meaningfully be decomposed into elements—be they absolute or relational. The stimulus configuration, black-white, comprises a unitary event that is to be distinguished from white-black. Note that this approach can handle not only the simple fact of discrimination learning but also the phenomenon of transposition. It would be assumed that the response to any test situation would be on the basis of generalization from the training configuration. Specifically, training with S4-S5-left and S5-S4-right should generalize to S3-S4-left and S4-S3-right and mediate apparent transposition behavior. Accordingly, some new, different test is necessary to compare the absolute with the configurational approaches.

Bitterman (e.g., 1953) and his colleagues devised such a test. Their reasoning was as follows: the conventional discrimination situation should be relatively difficult, because the animal must distinguish between black-white and white-black, configurations that are quite similar and differ only in the position of the relevant stimuli. It should be easier to distinguish black-black from white-white, because there is less similarity between these two configurations. They deduced that the learning of a discriminative differentiation,[5] namely, black-black-right versus white-white-left, should be easier than the familiar discrimination between black-white-left versus white-black-right.

Furthermore, they correctly derived the opposite prediction from an absolute approach. The discriminative differentiation procedure requires not only distinguishing the discriminanda entirely on the basis of absolute properties presented separately, but also requires the further differentiation of which response is associated with which stimulus. Accordingly, the simultaneous discrimination task that permits relational elements to contribute whatever they might and involves only learning to approach the positive stimulus should be easier than a discriminative differentiation. When Bitterman reported his original results, they fit the prediction of the configurational approach and contradicted the prediction of the absolute approach.

In this case, the controversy was not resolved by a theoretical coup followed by confirmed predictions embarrassing to the alternative view, but instead by the fact that the original findings simply did not stand up to the ultimate test of systematic replication. The majority of studies that have made the same comparison in a variety of contexts have found that simultaneous discrimination learning proceeds considerably faster than discriminative differentiation. There may, of course, be particular procedures and particular parameters in which the results vary. The difference between the discriminanda, their spatial separation, the intertrial interval, the amount of reward, or a host of other factors might be combined in such a way as to make discriminative differentiation a simpler process (see, e.g. Bitterman & Wodinsky, 1953). But the general conclusion is that it is more difficult than simple discrimination learning.

However, it must be recognized that a discriminative differentiation can be learned; this suggests that configurational cues can indeed gain control over behavior. Even though such learning may be more difficult, just as relational learning is more difficult, a complete understanding of the stimulus cannot exclude these findings. Accordingly, it is reasonable to conclude that absolute properties of the stimulus can and frequently do gain control over behavior, and any theoretical interpretation must assume that these properties give rise to distinctive representations. At the same time, there are at least relational and configurational representations of stimuli, and possibly others yet to be identified. Learning may be involved with any or all of these, and may generalize along the variety of dimensions thus implied. In effect, this is a functional empirical identification of effective discriminative stimuli, and we are still far from an adequate theoretical analysis of the stimulus, even in the context of simple discrimination learning.

RESPONSE DIFFERENTIATION

The systematic analysis of response differentiation has received nowhere near the attention given to stimulus discrimination. As we have suggested previously, this is probably because the topic is intrinsically more complex for two almost inescapable reasons. First, the basis for response differentiation is presumably some form of feedback, and these cues are not readily available for operational determination or experimental control. Second, the behaviors in question must be emitted by the organism, thereby largely restricting the study of response differentiation to free-choice analyses. Also in this latter context, the number of potential behaviors is inevitably extremely large and can only be arbitrarily dichotomized into two classes of responses in a manner analogous to the analysis of a black-white discrimination problem.

Nevertheless, response learning is no less important conceptually than stimulus learning, since differentiations among responses constitute the essence of skilled behavior. At least insofar as differentiation is a form of discrimination based on feedback stimuli, most if not all of the issues related to stimulus leaning inevitably arise equally in response learning. Indeed, we have already explored one such issue with the question of what is learned. Two facets of that question concern the nature of the stimuli to which organisms learn to respond, and the nature of the responses that organisms learn to make to those stimuli. In that context, the issue involved the macro-micro and the molar-molecular distinctions among quantitatively and qualitatively different behaviors, respectively.

Regardless of the approach that one takes with respect to this issue, any systematic analysis must take into account the fact that organisms both can and do learn to differentiate among quantitatively and qualitatively different responses. Therefore, the question that arises can be posed in the same form that we have been using with respect to stimuli. Recall that Lashley contended that organisms do not learn to discriminate among stimuli (generalization is complete), unless they are exposed to differential reinforcement with respect to those stimuli. A similar contention would be that organisms do not learn

to differentiate among responses, unless they are exposed to differential reinforcement with respect to those responses. This is what we have called the
molar view of behavior; organisms learn "acts" that are equivalent by virtue
of having the same effects upon the environment. This view was subscribed to
by all classic systematists save Guthrie, who contended that organisms actually learn "movements," by which he meant the qualitatively molecular features of the response. It is interesting then that theorists, such as Hull and
Spence, would adopt an absolute (molecular, elementary) view of the stimulus
and a molar view of the response.

This discrepancy is even clearer when discerning the quantitative variations
in stimuli and responses. Although additional dynamogenic properties were
frequently ascribed to stimulus intensity (cf. Miller & Dollar, 1940; Hull,
1952), differences in intensity were assumed to have absolute cue value. In
contrast, quantitative variations in behavior were treated not only as part of
the same macromolar response, but as indices of the strength of that response.
No one has provided a mechanism comparable to Lashley's that would enable
response differentiation on the basis of differential reinforcement. Such an
analysis might contend that organisms increasingly focus attention on progressively finer grain details of behavior only if required to do so by the conditions
of reinforcement. But even without such a mechanism, some assumption along
these lines is at least implicit in all macromolar approaches to response definition.

Accordingly, most of the conceptual issues that should arise in the context
of response differentiation have failed to receive their legitimate share of experimental and systematic analysis. Indeed, the ones that have been addressed
have been treated with scantily and viewed as somewhat tangential to the
mainstream of the analysis of stimulus control. Although we personally consider this to be a case of sad neglect, our treatment of these issues unfortunately
has much of this same flavor.

The First Response   Let us grant that reinforcement increases the likelihood of the repetition of a
response in the future; that punishment decreases that likelihood; and that the
differential application of reinforcement and punishment, vis-à-vis exteroceptive stimuli, bring that response under stimulus control. Any such analysis
simply assumes that the behavior of interest will somehow be emitted by the
organism; the behavior is already there. To give one obvious example from this
chapter, Spence started his subjects out with appreciable approach tendencies
to all elements of the stimulus configuration, although a rat might never have
seen anything the likes of a triangle or a circle in its life. Anyone who has
attempted to train another organism is intimately familiar with the frustration
of being ready and eager with abundant praise and rewards, if only some
desired behavior would occur. A theory that cannot produce the first response
is obviously incomplete.

This problem is not resolved by the procedure of shaping. Valuable as this
technique is from a practical viewpoint, the organism must be assumed already
to be emitting some behaviors that overlap in some regards with the behavior
of interest. One approach is to postulate an activity drive (Campbell &

Sheffield, 1953), exploratory tendency (Myers & Miller, 1954), or simply an innate predisposition to emit behaviors of a generic class, such as vocalizing. These do not help very much in determining what the organism will do, but at least they get the organism doing something.

One way to get the first response is through classical conditioning. The occurrence of a response in a particular situation can be occasioned *de novo* provided that there is some unconditioned stimulus that will elicit that response. Lashley, it may be recalled, sometimes caused his rats to jump by cracking them on the rump with a whip! More commonly, however, he used a shaping procedure in which the gap over which the rat must jump was progressively lengthened, relying on the innate tendency to approach the smell of food to get the action started.

Another way of getting the behavior of interest to begin was used extensively by Konorski (e.g., 1967) and involves what is aptly translated as "putting through." He taught dogs to press bars by manually raising the dog's paw from the floor, placing it on the bar, and pressing down. The results of this procedure led to his particular version of incentive theory, which is one that is becoming increasingly popular in the contemporary scene. Konorski assumed that the proprioceptive feedback stimuli resulting from the paw being lifted to the bar become associated with reward and, hence, acquire incentive motivational value. All that is needed in such a theory is to get these expectations to cause the organism to make the response on its own initiative. Doing so appears to require a cognitive type of analysis.

If one presumes that thinking about a response more–or–less automatically causes that response to occur, then it would be sufficient to say that Konorski's dogs come to think about pressing the bar because such thoughts have been reinforced, and just thinking about doing it leads to its occurrence. In this connection, it is interesting to reflect back upon Watson's contention that organisms think peripherally; when you think of moving your finger, the muscles in your finger make at least incipient movements. Of course, Watson considered these movements to be the sum and substance of thinking, whereas Konorski turned the causal chain around. First you think about doing something and, then, the muscles tag along automatically.

This kind of reasoning is presumably the one that Mowrer (1976) would adopt in attempting to resolve his dilemma of getting behavior started. That is, a rat leaves a start box, because he is thinking about running to the goal. It is also quite similar to the position taken by Estes (1969). In his terminology, the organism remembers the responses that previously occasioned reward and emits them in accord with these memories. There are, however, two monumental problems with this appealing approach. Returning to Mowrer, one still needs to get the *thoughts* started. If thoughts are also controlled by incentive factors (e.g., it makes you "feel" good just to think about pleasant experiences), you have to start such thoughts in order to get the feedback from them in order to know how you feel about them. With respect to Estes, more is the pity that we simply cannot do all of the things that we can think about doing! A golfer may conjure up all kinds of illusions while lining up a putt without ultimately seeing the ball go into the cup.

Although such problems appear monumental, they will most probably succumb to further conceptual analysis and help deal with yet another method of inducing the first response—this is *imitation*. Observational learning has been documented experimentally, since early in the history of behaviorism (e.g., Crawford & Spence, 1939), and a quite elegant systematic analysis of imitation was undertaken by Miller and Dollard (1940). Among the issues that arise in this context are (1) whether there is an innate tendency, at least in some organisms, to imitate; (2) whether imitation is in some way related to the similarity of the model to the imitator (i.e., same size, sex, species, and so on); and (3) whether imitation involves some form of incipient responding during observation accompanied by vicarious reinforcement. Dollard and Miller took the position that imitation was a learnable response acquired as a result of reinforcement for matching one's behavior with that of a model. An important aspect of their analysis is responding relative to the cues of a discrepancy between one's own feedback and that from a model. Recently, Gewirtz has elaborated extensively on the idea of vicarious reinforcement (e.g., Gewirtz & Stingle, 1968).

Accordingly, there are various ways to approach the problem of producing the first response, not the least of which with humans is giving verbal instructions. This inevitably leads to the issues concerning the nature of voluntary responses (see, e.g., Kimble & Perlmuter, 1970), but we will arbitrarily declare that extremely important area beyond the scope of this section.[6]

Correlated Reinforcement[7]

Given now that behavior, at least of the generic class of interest, is being emitted, we can reasonably discuss some of the issues related to the differential reinforcement of particular instances of that behavior. Skinner (1938) formally introduced the concept of differential reinforcement of response rate in an operant conditioning situation, and he also demonstrated that other quantitative features of the response, such as its duration, can be selectively learned. Because the expression "differential reinforcement" has a tendency historically to be associated with all-or-none schedules and conditions of reinforcement, Notterman (e.g., 1959) introduced the expression "proportional reinforcement" to suggest more easily the conditions in which reward is progressively related to some quantitative property of an operant, such as the force of a bar press. We have chosen to use Logan's (1960) expression "correlated reinforcement" because it would appear to be even more general and indicative of the extremely large range of possible conditions in which some feature of the reward can be given in relation to some feature of behavior. In this context, the term is most appropriate for some quantifiable property of the reward, such as its amount, delay, or probability, as it may be correlated with some quantifiable property of a response, such as its latency, speed, rate, force, or duration. Differential reinforcement may be and often is also given with respect to qualitative features of behavior, primarily topographical aspects that can be objectively identified, such as which paw a rat uses in pressing a bar but also including more subjective evaluations of "style."

One of the issues that must yet be resolved is whether the distinction between variations in qualitative and quantitative properties of behavior can be maintained in a truly micromolecular analysis of a response. All of the experimenters who have studied correlated reinforcement with respect to quantitative dimensions of the response have observed that the subjects learn one or another ritual in satisfying the imposed criterion. For example, Logan (1960) noted that his rats often ran very rapidly up and down the runway in order to consume time before completing the response, and Amsel (Amsel & Rashotte, 1969) has shown that the idiosyncratic features of such behavior reappear during extinction after an interpolated phase of uncorrelated reinforcement during which they gave way to consistently fast running. In a similar manner, pigeons have been observed to strut around the cage several times between responses on a DRL schedule. The question is whether the conditions of correlated reinforcement are actually selectively increasing the likelihood of topographical features of the response that, coincidentally, happen to consume an appropriate amount of time. This issue is an extremely difficult one to address experimentally.

Because one of us (Logan, 1960) has previously attempted to outline the range of possible conditions of correlated reinforcement, we will not repeat those here. Suffice it to say that reinforcement can be correlated with a response positively (more for more) or negatively (more for less), discontinuously (all-or-none) or continuously (incremental), monotonically or nonmonotonically, and the correlation may have any function form conceivable. Furthermore, different dimensions of the reward can be correlated differently with different dimensions of the response, as when faster responses receive a larger average reward but with lower probability. In view of the staggering size of this domain, we can provide little more in the way of systematic analysis than Logan's conclusion that, not only *can* organisms learn to respond in accord with the way reinforcement is correlated with various quantitative and qualitative properties of that behavior, they inevitably *do* learn such properties. This is the antithesis of the molar view of behavior, and extends Guthrie's insistence on the learning of movements (topographical properties) to include quantitative properties. We have called this the micromolecular level of analysis and it contends that organisms learn acts as a result of *non*differential reinforcement rather than learning movements as a result of differential reinforcement. Furthermore, if one assumes that organisms "naturally" do whatever they are thinking about doing, then the micromolecular approach to response definition can be adopted by uniprocess cognitive theories.

SPATIAL LEARNING

To the experimental psychologist concerned primarily with animal learning and motivation during the period following the advent of behaviorism, the apparatus of choice was clearly the maze. This was a quite natural development, because the white rat was also the organism of choice and spatial learning intuitively appears to be a "natural" for a rat. Mazes could readily be constructed to vary in length and presumed difficulty; errors could be arbitrarily defined and objectively counted; and organismic factors, such as drive motivation and cortical damage, could be studied in that context. In retrospect, however, the maze was actually too complicated a situation for the neophyte science of behavior.

Nevertheless, it is important to reserve a place for spatial learning in a complete systematic analysis in part because that is the context in which many of the issues that we have discussed arose. The what-is-learned question initially involved maze learning, and the hypothetical construct of a cognitive map is most conducive to thinking in terms of spatial orientation. The studies of latent learning were also developed in the context of multiple-unit T-mazes. We do not wish to imply that spatial learning totally dominated the experimental analysis of learning during the 1920s and 1930s; notable among the other devices was the Lashley jumping stand for the study of nonspatial discrimination learning. But the maze was quite ubiquitous.

Some of the issues that arose in the study of maze learning are somewhat specific to that situation. One of these, for example, involves centrifugal swing (e.g., Ballachey & Buel, 1934). Especially if the choice points are relatively close together, the rat naturally comes out of one turn with physical rather than psychological forces favoring the other turn at the next choice point. However, even in this context, it proved to be useful to reduce the problem to the study of alternation in a simple T-maze. Let us begin with that issue and then briefly mention a variety of additional issues whose antecedents, at least, were in the maze.

Alternation Behavior

As just mentioned, a high incidence of alternation in maze running by rats could be attributed to the physical dynamics of the maze. However, Tolman (1938) was more inclined to think of alternation as a reflection of a basic curiosity or exploratory drive, and research (e.g., Montgomery, 1952) lent credence to this interpretation. The alternative approach was sometimes called the "inhibition of reinforcement," and Hull formally postulated a reactive inhibition construct. This seemed consistent with the fact that, when rats are run in a T-maze, there is a tendency to alternate the direction of turns from trial to trial, regardless of whether or not the preceding trial was reinforced (see Dember & Fowler, 1958). Since this alternation tendency decreases with the time between trials (e.g., Walker, 1956), there would appear to be a temporary response inhibition process. However, Glanzer (1953) posed the "What is alternated?" question in a + maze much like the one used in the "What is learned?" controversy, except that the arms of the maze differed in brightness. Glanzer found that when the rats were started from the opposite side, they tended to alternate the stimulus and hence repeat the response. This finding suggests that alternation is also based on exteroceptive stimuli in the T-maze, although this could hardly account for alternation in the multiple-unit maze. But it does place this issue in the context of the larger issue of the cues involved in spatial learning.

Cues in Spatial Learning

We have previously discussed the controversy involving the control of maze behavior by proprioceptive and intramaze cues as opposed to extramaze cues (cf. Chapter 3). Many of the difficulties in the early studies arose from the indiscriminate use of elevated mazes (simply boards along which the rat crept for fear of falling) that provided abundant extramaze cues, and enclosed mazes that tended to confine the sources of stimulation to proprioceptive and intramaze cues. Within the terminological system that we have employed, this places spatial learning in an ambiguous position. Insofar as maze learning is based on approaching distinctive exteroceptive stimuli, it would be viewed as a form of discrimination learning. Insofar as maze learning is based on differences in proprioceptive feedback, it would be viewed as a form of differentiation learning. This implies that the distinction between discrimination and differentiation is somewhat artificial and is actually useful only where the experimental conditions explicitly restrict learning to exteroceptive or interoceptive stimuli. Otherwise, organisms utilize all cues available for the solution of a problem and the basis of their solution may be shown to change over training. For example, Mackintosh (1965) has shown that rats are more likely to be place learners after a relatively small amount of training but become response learners after extended training. It is largely for this reason that the systematic experimental analysis of the selective control of behavior has shifted from the complex environment of a maze to compound stimuli whose elements can to a greater extent be controlled by the experimenter in operant and instrumental contexts.

Insight
Although the most quoted example of insight in animals is Sultan—Köhler's chimpanzee who joined two sticks together in order to make one that was long enough to reach a distant banana—insightful behavior was more systematically observed in spatial learning situations (e.g., Maier, 1937). A rat could first be trained to climb one ladder to reach the top of a table containing a reward. The rat was next trained to climb a different ladder to reach a reward in a different location on the top of the same table, but with a barrier restricting the rat to that side of the table now containing the reward. After a number of such experiences, the rat was placed directly on the side of the table opposite from the reward and the question was whether the rat could put the prior experiences together, thereby climbing down the one ladder and back up the other ladder to obtain the reward. Albeit with some difficulty, some rats display insightful solutions to this form of the Umweg problem.[8]

The phenomenon of insight touches on a number of the basic issues that we have heretofore discussed. Can an organism integrate responses insightfully or must one invoke a cognitive learning construct? Can reinforcement be necessary if the organism has never before emitted the behavior in question? Can learning really be gradual and continuous when the phenomenon is partly identified by sudden solution? Indeed, almost all of the major issues could be posed in this context. To use but one example, would an insightful solution to Maier's problem be more or less likely if the first stage of training had been conducted with partial reinforcement? Unfortunately, such systematic questions about insight have not yet been analyzed experimentally, and we are left with phenomenon in search of a theory.

Correction
The multiple-unit maze inherently involves a correction procedure. The rat may enter a cul-de-sac but can then retrace to correct the error and proceed

on toward the goal. From the point of view of theorists such as Hull and Spence (1938), this procedure poses a problem because it can not be analyzed simply in terms of reinforcement/nonreinforcement conceptualizations.

It is worth dwelling for a moment on the complexities involved in spatial learning from such a conceptual approach. There are no special problems at choice points where the subject makes the correct turn initially; that response is reinforced and an increment in associative strength should result. However, an entry into a cul-de-sac is not nonreinforced but receives delayed reinforcement. And which is more, the time of that delay is not under experimental control, depending instead on how far the subject pursues the incorrect route, and how long it takes to retrace to the choice point. Finally, the cues then encountered are not the same, because the choice point is approached from the incorrect arm of the maze rather than from the correct path. Although it is clear that there should be some relatively greater strengthening of the correct response on error trials, the correction inherent in the procedure means that the differential increment should be less than had the subject chosen correctly initially.

Spence and Hull (1938) showed that these conjectures were reasonable ones. They compared the correction and noncorrection procedures in a T-maze, but even so, a further complication arose. In the noncorrection procedure, the subject is simply removed from the end box without reward and although this should lead to an increment in inhibitory potential, there is no obvious way to equate the groups on the number of reinforced trials that was, at that time, the principal variable affecting habit in Hull's theory. In an effort to surmount this difficulty, Spence and Hull chose to compare the procedures during reversal, that is, after the subjects had initially learned to turn in one or the other direction and now reward was placed in the opposite arm of the maze. This ensured that all rats would begin reversal learning with a dominant error tendency and their prediction was that the correction subjects would learn more rapidly, because even though the incorrect turn received delayed reinforcement, there would be a more than offsetting increment in the approach tendency vis-à-vis the correct alternative. This and various other implications concerning the time required to complete each trial were generally confirmed.

The Goal-Gradient Hypothesis

Following this same general line of reasoning based on differential delay of reinforcement, Hull (1932) deduced that errors in a multiple-unit maze should be eliminated in backward fashion. Hull referred to this situation as "heterogeneous trial-and-error learning with terminal reinforcement" because the responses required in the behavior chain differ (right and left turns) and reward is not received until the rat ultimately arrives at the goalbox. According to his view, therefore, each turn is learned on the basis of delayed reinforcement, the actual time of delay depending on the number of subsequent errors made on each trial. Clearly, the last link of the chain should be learned most readily, because it is most immediately followed by the reward. At this point in the analysis a new complication arises because the learned turning response should now tend to become anticipatory and aid or hinder earlier choices depending on whether the same turn is appropriate at those choice points. That such anticipatory tendencies do indeed exist was demonstrated in a study by Spragg (1933). By using a maze requiring a RRRRRRRL sequence of turns, Spragg was able to show that the terminal left turn response tended to interfere with learning at earlier choice points progressively as the rat came closer and closer to the last critical turn. (In elevated mazes, there were comparable anticipatory errors of going prematurely toward the location of the reward.)

Accordingly, the conceptual analysis involved in the goal-gradient hypothesis involves two fundamental points—that of delayed reward and that of the anticipatory response. The latter, of course, is not confined to the very last turn because, as each choice is learned, that tendency will also tend to become anticipatory. Overcoming these tendencies should also work backward from the goal on the basis of delayed reinforcement, although the early choice points occupy the relatively most distinctive positions and should, therefore, suffer less from erroneous anticipatory tendencies than intermediate choice points.[9]

It was at this juncture in the conceptual analysis of spatial learning that Tolman came closest to becoming a reinforcement theorist. He never veered from his belief that rats develop cognitive maps on the basis of simple exposure to the cues in the maze, but he did contend that reward may make certain regions of the map especially clear. He referred to this as the law of emphasis (Tolman, 1932) and contrasted it with the law of effect, because an electric shock in the correct arm of the maze could also emphasize regions of the cognitive map and thereby facilitate learning. That is, a cognitive map is, to some extent at least, oriented around emotionally significnt events in the environment and the psychological clarity of the map fades with distance from such areas. This provides, in a sense, a cognitive interpretation of the goal-gradient hypothesis because the evidence is substantial (e.g., Spence, 1932) that errors in heterogeneous response chains tend to be eliminated in backward fashion.

Genetic Factors

Among the issues of persisting interest is the hereditability of certain traits and abilities, and the role of the maze in experimental psychology naturally led to efforts to study this problem in that context. Both Tryon (1929) at the University of California and Heron (1935) at the University of Minnesota successfully bred strains of rats that were "maze-bright" or "maze-dull." The ultimate biological basis of this difference is not yet established, and the difference between the strains is to some extent confined to very particular mazes rather than being a general trait that might be called "intelligence." In general, the dull rats take longer running through the maze, even if one equates for the greater number of errors involved. Accordingly, the selective breeding could equally involve various motivational factors as well as learning ability.

Summary of Spatial Learning

A great many conceptual issues were raised and a number of systematic analyses undertaken during the era of the maze in experimental psychology. We have considered several of these in previous chapters and have touched on a number of additional ones here. Even these should be considered as only illustrative and we might mention a few more. Rats learn mazes somewhat more rapidly after a period of wakefulness (Bunch, Frericka, & Licklider, 1938); intramaze delay of various kinds has a deleterious effect on performance anterior to the delay but not posterior to it (e.g., Brown & Dalrymple, 1951); the spatial orientation of the maze can be arranged such that rats take the longer path to food (Snygg, 1936). Of more comparative interest were attempts to study the relative maze-learning abilities of rats and humans, and it was found that adult humans tend to learn mazes in an all-or-none fashion on the basis of verbal mediating responses (e.g., McGeoch & Peters, 1933), whereas rats are more oriented toward proprioceptive and exteroceptive cues directly related to each choice point of a maze.

Probably the most challenging phenomena in the maze were experimental demonstrations of insightful solutions to spatial problems. From a systematic point of view, however, these studies suffer from the fallacy of hypostatization, that is, mistaking the naming of a phenomenon for an explanation of it. Although we may be inclined to think of insight as a totally new discovery, instead of simply the novel combination of previously learned behaviors (ideas), even that limited sense of the term remains as little more than a conceptual pigeonhole to be yet explained.

Hull tried. The goal-gradient hypothesis dominated experimental analyses of spatial learning, and Hull (1935) expanded it in terms of the fractional anticipatory goal response as a mechanism for the assembly of behavior segments into novel combinations. The essence of that analysis is easier to describe in the context of the advantage of working backward from a goal in many problem-solving situations (Miller & Dollard, 1940). If you are at point A and desire to get to a goal (point G), then an adaptive problem-solving approach is to determine that you can get to point G from point F, to point F from point E, and so on, backwards to point A. The number of potential errors that must be eliminated may be considerably fewer taking this approach rather than exploring all of the avenues available initially from point A. Hull's analysis describes how r_g-s_g working backward from the goal can lead to the combination of several separately learned segments. But many of the instances of insightful behavior severely strain such an analysis. In the example previously given, the rat placed at what was the goal of the initial training task must now reverse the anticipatory response mechanism in order to anticipate the start of that segment that has become the subgoal starting point of the second segment. Although it is clear enough how a rat at a customary start might anticipate the goal, it is by no means clear how a rat now at a customary goal anticipates the customary start. Yet that is what Maier's rats apparently did.

In any event, one of us has in Hull's handwriting his concurrence with the following statement by Tolman (1938): "I believe that everything important in psychology (except perhaps such matters as the building up of a super-ego, that is everything save such matters as involve society and words) can be investigated in essence through the continued experimental and theoretical analysis of the determiners of rat behavior at a choice-point in a maze." To that Tolman added the following quote: "To my ratiocinations I hope you will be kind, as you follow up the wanderings of my amazed mind."

**TRANSITIONAL
BEHAVIOR IN CHOICE**

In addition to the various changes in the conditions and schedules of reinforcement/punishment that were discussed in Chapter 7, such conditions can also be changed with respect to their correlation with exteroceptive stimuli and/or with response requirements. Of this myriad of possible transitional behavior phenomena, the one that has received by far the greatest amount of systematic analysis is the reversal of a nonspatial discrimination. Specifically, reinforcement is now associated with the previously nonreinforced stimulus and vice versa. The fact that all organisms typically can and do adjust to such changes is not only very well established empirically but is also of obvious adaptive significance.

Even more forcefully than one's analysis of extinction is constrained by one's analysis of acquisition in the context of simple conditioning, one's analysis of discrimination reversal is almost entirely determined by one's approach to discrimination learning itself. Simply on the grounds of parsimony, discrimination-reversal learning should involve the same processes with the exception that the point of origin is the hypothetical state of the organism resulting from the preceding training. Although this extrapolation from original learning to reversal learning is true in general, it is most obvious in the case of an absolute, continuous discrimination-learning theory, such as that of Spence.

According to Spence's theory, original-discrimination learning will have generated, by virtue of producing some criterion level of discriminative behavior, a difference in approach tendencies with respect to the relevant discriminanda sufficient to mediate consistent choice of the correct stimulus. Reversal of the contingencies of reinforcement simply reverse the incremental and decremental processes resulting from reinforcement and nonreinforcement, ultimately leading to an appropriate change in their respective tendencies. Accordingly, under most circumstances, this aspect of the reversal of a discrimination should require more trials than the original acquisition of the discrimination. An exception to this deduction would arise only in the case where there were very strong preexisting differentials in approach tendencies. (For example, rats typically have a basic preference for black as opposed to white exteroceptive stimuli.)

Indeed, it is generally found that discrimination reversal proceeds more slowly than the original-discrimination learning (see, e.g., Sperling, 1965). However, this outcome is not rigidly required by Spence's theory because of the concurrent neutralization of initial position tendencies. Recall that in the context of reversal during the presolution period, it was necessary to count all trials in order legitimately to address the continuity-noncontinuity controversy in that setting. This is because nondifferential reinforcement with respect to position is also taking place, and if initial tendencies vis-à-vis irrelevant cues are presumed to be reasonably different, there will be a corresponding facilitation of reversal learning resulting from their prior neutralization. Accordingly, one cannot derive from Spence's theory a universal prediction as regards the number of trials required to reach some criterion of original-discrimination learning and the number of trials required, counting now only from that point, to learn a discrimination reversal. However, in general, the more difficult the

original problem as reflected in the persistence of systematic incorrect responding, the relatively greater will be the facilitating effect of neutralizing control
by irrelevant cues to offset the inevitably deleterious effect of starting reversal
learning with the relevant cues having tendencies opposite in direction to those
now required.

Interestingly enough, this same indeterminacy applies to all theoretical
analyses of discrimination-reversal learning. All must have a source of negative
transfer from acquisition to reversal, simply because the requisite process is in
the opposite direction. But all also have some source of positive transfer. For
example, Lashley would contend that the subjects will have learned to discriminate between the stimuli and to detect their relative properties. If one did
focus on just the first of these sources of positive transfer, one could presume
that the stimuli are now more discriminable or that the gradients of generalization have been steepened (Denny, 1970). Focusing on the second source of
positive transfer, one could presume that having learned to attend to the
relevant stimulus dimension facilitates reversal along that same dimension
(Sutherland & Mackintosh, 1971). Accordingly, the mere fact of discrimination-reversal learning and its comparison with original-discrimination learning
are of systematic interest but are not of particular value in favoring one
approach or the other.

Of greater systematic consternation is another fact that is frequently observed but infrequently reported and that is more or less equally embarrassing
to most approaches. It is the fact that during reversal subjects frequently revert
to responding systematically on the basis of position before control by the new
positive cue becomes dominant (e.g., Mackintosh, 1963; Logan, 1968). Clearly,
if the basis for a positive transfer effect is the neutralization of position tendencies as in Spence's theory, the adaptation of irrelevant cues as in Restle's theory
(1955), or attention to the relevant cues (Sutherland & Mackintosh, 1971),
there is no obvious reason for these erroneous tendencies to reappear during
reversal. Apparently, such tendencies are merely suppressed and reassert
themselves when the basis for the original discrimination is made ineffective.
This fact should be borne in mind in considering overtraining, because it is also
applicable in that context.

Overtraining and Reversal

A very extensive literature has developed around a phenomenon reported by
Reid (1953). The observation of immediate interest was that subjects given
extended training beyond a reasonable criterion of acquisition of the original
discrimination problem learned the reversal of that discrimination more rapidly than subjects for whom reversal was instituted immediately on reaching
criterion. This phenomenon has been sufficiently well documented so that it
is referred to as the "overtraining reversal effect" and it has entered importantly in contemporary analyses of discrimination learning. This is because it
can be viewed as a transposition-type analysis of what is learned during original discrimination learning.

The overtraining reversal effect does not, itself, necessarily favor one or
another theory of discrimination learning. Since all theories have some source
of positive transfer from acquisition to reversal, and no theory is explicit about

at what stage of original training this component of what is being learned is complete, the expected outcome of overtraining hinges importantly on one's criterion for deciding when *over*training begins. It is undoubtedly, at least, partly for this reason that the phenomenon itself, although certainly robust, must be treated somewhat gingerly. Moderately difficult nonspatial discriminations involving a large reward quite consistently result in an overtraining reversal effect. In contrast, it is unlikely to be observed in an easy spatial learning task with a small reward (see Paul, 1965). In the latter circumstance, there may actually be no way to establish a criterion of performance on the original task without inevitably giving some overtraining. Accordingly, the boundaries of the phenomenon remain somewhat obscure.

Nevertheless, the general effects of extended training appear to favor some kind of stimulus learning process that is not associative with respect to the referent response. This is not to deny the importance of position tendencies, such as emphasized by Spence; the fact that they not only appear but also reappear attests to their role at least in animal discrimination learning. However, contemporary theorists do not attempt to rely on just those tendencies to account for the wide range of results obtained in the context of the overtraining reversal effect. Since the only other associative process directly involving the referent response (that associated with the relevant cues) should be further solidified by extended training, some other feature of discrimination learning appears to be implicated.

Among the many approaches that might be proposed, one of the more formal is that of Lovejoy (1966, 1968). This elegant mathematical model embodies two processes, one determining the tendency to select, observe, or attend to the relevant stimuli and the other determining the tendency to respond to such stimuli. Both of these are presumed to increment and decrement as a result of reinforcement and nonreinforcement, but the rates of such changes are not constrained to be equal. According to such a two-stage model, reversal learning is facilitated by extended training, because the stimulus-selection process is presumed to be strengthened further by such training. In addition, Lovejoy's model correctly implies that overtraining actually leads to a greater initial persistence of the original choice, followed by systematic behavior with respect to irrelevant cues, and then followed by achieving a criterion of reversal more rapidly than obtains without extended training. But as Mackintosh (1974) has clearly pointed out, it is not at all apparent how the difficulty of the original discrimination could substantially alter these conclusions, whereas this is an important factor in determining the detectability of an overtraining reversal effect. As Lashley would contend, subjects learn more about the relevant stimulus dimension, if required to learn a relatively fine discrimination.

Nonreversal Shifts   Although reversal learning has been the most extensively studied of the possible changes in the contingencies of reinforcement after discrimination learning, a number of others have also been employed particularly in comparison with the ease of simple reversal learning. The terminology for such changes is not entirely consistent in the literature and, moreover, neither are the data. Nevertheless, it is important to consider several of these changes and the overall pattern of results.

The conceptually simplest comparison is between reversal learning and a nonreversal shift. Consider a situation in which, during original discrimination learning, one relevant stimulus dimension, say, the brightness of the exteroceptive stimuli, is compounded with one irrelevant stimulus dimension, say, the shape of the visual display. In simple reversal learning, shape continues to be irrelevant and the correlation of reinforcement with brightness is reversed. In a *nonreversal shift,* brightness is now made irrelevant and reinforcement is correlated with shape. It is easy to see that an absolute, continuous theory, such as Spence's, must predict that the latter would be the more readily acquired.

According to that theory, original discrimination learning must lead to the development of differential approach tendencies with respect to the relevant cues which exceeds that which obtains with respect to any irrelevant cue. Nondifferential reinforcement of the latter will have tended toward the neutralization of any preexisting differences with respect to irrelevant cues. Hence, even though neutralization may not be complete, the difference must be less for irrelevant cues than the relevant cues, and the subsequent increments and decrements in approach tendencies should lead to appropriate differences more rapidly for the former. Results consistent with these expectations have been obtained (e.g., Kendler & Kendler, 1969), although the evidence is by no means universal (see Wolff, 1967).

Alternatively, postdiscrimination shifts may involve changes in the particular stimulus values along either the relevant or irrelevant dimension. *Intradimensional shifts* require a new discrimination between stimuli differing in the same stimulus dimension as was initially relevant; *extradimensional shifts* also require a new discrimination but between stimuli differing in a previously irrelevant dimension. The evidence comparing these two types of shifts is pleasantly consistent: intradimensional shifts are acquired more readily than extradimensional shifts. Furthermore, if the contingencies involved in the shifted conditions are such as to enable a solution on the basis of either the previously relevant or a previously irrelevant dimension (*optional shifts*), subsequent tests indicate that stimulus control is focused on the former.

The same general conclusion that holds with respect to the overtraining reversal effect appears even more strongly to be suggested by the general pattern of results involving nonreversal shifts. Some process, such as selective attention, that favors control by a stimulus dimension that was initially relevant would appear to be mandated. Of course, this could involve learning not to attend to irrelevant stimulus dimensions (e.g., Kemler & Shepp, 1971) or their adaptation (Restle, 1955). It is also possible that the results can be understood in terms of mediational processes (Kendler, Kendler, & Ward, 1972). However, the systematic experimental analysis of the domain is still insufficient to give clear direction toward the most useful conceptual analysis.

**DISCRIMINATION
LEARNING SET
(LEARNING TO
LEARN)**

We are most indebted to Harlow and his associates (e.g., Harlow, 1949) for a systematic experimental analysis of a form of learning that appears to transcend simple discrimination learning. A *discrimination learning set* is inferred from the fact that an organism, when exposed to a series of discrimination learning problems of the same general class but differing in the specific stimuli involved, learns to solve such problems with fewer and fewer errors. In the limiting case, the organism will make at most one error, perseverating if the first choice happened to be correct, and switching if that choice happened to be incorrect. Harlow's contention is that the typical superiority of humans over other animals can be traced largely to the fact that we have been exposed to a graduated series of discrimination learning problems and have learned, in effect, algorithms for their solution.

Learning sets are not restricted to object-discrimination problems of the type most commonly studied by Harlow. For example, a reversal learning set is acquired as a result of repeated reversals where the organism ultimately learns to switch after a single error on the now reversed problem. Matching-to-sample, oddity, and similar paradigms require the organism to develop a set to solve problems of a particular generic class. Such learning sets may involve spatial cues as well as nonspatial cues.

Harlow's analysis of learning-set formation bears some resemblance to the theories of both Spence (1936) and Restle (1955). The latter theorists assume that potential but irrelevant cues become neutralized as a result of nondifferential reinforcement. Specifically, a second nonspatial discrimination problem could be solved more readily because spatial cues have been neutralized (brought to the same level of associative strength) during the first discrimination learning problem. But error-factor theory goes beyond such conceptualizations.

In essence, error-factor theory assumes that an organism begins even the first learning problem with maximal associative strengths already established to all of the potential stimulus factors (elements, cues). This is a result of the organism's past history and, most especially, the pretraining conditions in which the organism is taught the simple mechanics of the situation. In Harlow's work, for example, the monkey is taught that there is sometimes food in one of the wells embedded in the tray of the Wisconsin General Test Apparatus. And from that point, the monkey has no preconceptions about what the experimenter is going to make relevant in order to obtain food in the future. Error-factor theory does not require the assumption that the organism explicitly selects hypotheses about the available cues in the situation, although the organism will display systematic behavior based on natural tendencies to alternate, to perseverate, and even inadvertently to develop differential strengths to irrelevant cues (errors). But gradually, over a series of problems, these potential sources of error are eliminated; natural tendencies are inhibited in favor of the appropriate aspects of the problem.

In relation to the earlier controversies, error-factor theory is not quite fish or fowl. It is based on an extremely important set of phenomena for which other theories are not fully prepared. It does contain many features of a nonemergent theory, such as that of Spence, combining elementary associations in the determination of behavior and modifying these associations in a continuous manner. But it also suggests that the emergent process of hypothesis testing actually emerges gradually during the learning experiences of the organism. Simple trial-and-error behavior gives way to insightful solutions as the organism develops a learning set. It is possible, then, that the nonemergent approach contains the seeds of its own destruction, or at least the principles according to which it is superseded by new, more abstract principles.

GENERAL SUMMARY AND CONCLUSIONS

We have cast this chapter in the context of emergentism, because no other issue is quite so fundamental to behavior science. We could actually have started this theme sooner. Pavlov and Watson both asserted that all behavior, including the most elegant of human accomplishments, is reducible to complex combinations of unlearned and learned reflexes. No one could deny the facts of classical conditioning, but few could accept the thesis that all behavior was to be understood in those terms. Thorndike, and more systematically, Skinner, adopted a segregated position—operant/instrumental conditioning is still rigorously deterministic but involves different principles and, if one is so inclined, different theories. The eminence of Tolman and Hull can be traced in no small measure to their efforts to conceptualize all forms of conditioning within one theoretical system.

In doing so, they looked at classical conditioning through the eyes of operant/instrumental principles. To Tolman, classical conditioning is a cognitive affair; the organism learns about the contingency relationship between the conditioned and unconditioned stimuli and behaves adaptively on the basis of that knowledge. To Hull, reinforcement is necessary to strengthen all mechanistic S-R associations, the US in classical conditioning is obviously a reinforcer, and the only issue is to identify the fundamental nature of reinforcement (drive reduction).

Thus, no one forcefully and effectively asserted a strong emergentism point of view with respect to the various conditioning situations, although it could be contended that classical conditioning is merely an incidental phenomenon that has no bearing on the really interesting features of *purposive* behavior controlled by contingencies of reward and punishment. But when we study learning, that is, choice behavior, which presumably if extrapolated goes on to decision making, concept formation, problem solving, and the so-called higher mental processes, the emergent thesis clearly reveals itself. Those with crystal balls anticipated that if the dam preserving the uniqueness of the mind and individual freedom of choice breaks at the point of even simple discrimination leaning in animals, then so many of the things we cherish about our own personal behavior will appear to be in jeopardy. We do not profess to have a crystal ball and something, indeed, may emerge that violates all of the basic principles and operates at a totally different level.

However, we are impressed with the way in which Spence was able to accept the challenge by people, such as Lashley and Krechevsky, and as one by one they asserted that phenomena, such as presolution reversal and transposition, simply could not be handled by any extension of conditioning principles, he derived from his theory that these phenomena are affected by identifiable independent variables. The presumed uniqueness of the phenomena vanished as they were subsumed within the same comprehensive theory. The reason that we contend that those who prefer to study behaviors far removed from the situations with which we have been concerned in this book nevertheless should understand those principles clearly is because the presumption that such topics require new conceptualizations with new language systems may prove to be in error. The best safeguard against finding oneself in such a position is to know not only the weaknesses but also the strengths of alternative approaches.

We have repeatedly contended that many of the issues that are a half-century (or more) old keep reappearing in some form or other. The most fundamental issue is no exception. One way to state the Tolman-Hull controversy, the issue of cognitive (S-S) versus behavioristic (S-R) approaches, is to pose the question: "Does the organism contribute anything to the determination of behavior?" It is easy to set up "straw men" for the behavioristic approach and saddle it with the image that organisms are merely passive creatures who respond like puppets to the stimuli that are imposed on them. But this was never intended by such approaches. Pavlov proposed a "second signal system" and Hull proposed "pure stimulus acts" both of which were intended to endow the organism with the ability to produce stimuli to which historically adaptive behavior had been associated. These were largely programmatic ideas but clearly attest to the possibility of some degree of self-control.

It is equally easy to set up "straw men" for cognitive approaches by saddling them with indeterminacy. Since one can never see the cognitive processes of another organism in action, at least not in the same sense as one can see an operant response charting out a cumulative record, one can never know what is really going on in that organism's mind. The freedom allowed by self-determination precludes rigorous predictions about behavior, except perhaps its fundamental unpredictability. But cognitive theorists, indeed, have been successful in making predictions about behavior, some of which have proven quite embarrassing to behavioristic theories of the period; so the cognitive approach, although also largely programmatic, is certainly not sterile.

Thus the now familiar issue appears in contemporary style as the question of how best to conceptualize the role the organism plays in the S-O-R paradigm. Is that role, itself, determined by the same basic principles as those induced from observation of overt responses or are these covert activities of a different nature to which we ascribe the generic label "cognitive?" Using older jargon, we have a refined version of the mind-body problem, and with it—the issue of emergentism.

Stated in that way, the issue becomes more philosophical than scientific, which is to say that it cannot be ultimately answered. It is largely for this reason that many experimental psychologists treat science as a kind of game. But this game with nature is not a frivolous one; indeed, the stakes with respect to the behavior sciences are extremely high. It is a game in the sense of adopting the empiricist's ground rules of science as a working hypothesis, because there is no way to determine the potential value of the nonemergent thesis without exploring the limits of that thesis. However, we submit that just as surely as empiricist scientists inevitably strive for ever higher levels of abstractness in their systematic approaches toward an understanding of behavior, others will steadfastly contend that they have still failed to capture the true essence and the real meaning of behavior.

Although it cannot be resolved, this issue is of vital importance because it bears importantly on many persisting controversies. Specifically, the two areas to which there appear to be the most immediate applicability of systematic analyses of learning and motivation are fraught with this underlying issue. First, there is the controversy between the practical teaching of specific subject matters in schools and "education" in its richest and fullest sense. Second is the distinction between "mental health" and the "behavior disorders." It is contended that learning the various tables and the rules for addition, subtraction, multiplicaton, and division are not the same as understanding arithmetic. It is contended that relieving a patient of compulsive symptoms is not the same as treating schizophrenia. Similarly, simply ensuring equal opportunities regardless of sex, age, race, or creed does not remove prejudicial feelings. In all of these examples, and many more that could be cited, the contention is that "understanding," "mental health," and "prejudice" are not just more than the sum of their component behaviors; they have emergent existences at a different level from them. Let us try to bring this fundamental idea into focus with a discussion of attempts used to deal with the notion of self-control.

One position is that some humans (presumably, the mature and mentally healthy human) have a mind, the mind has a will, and the will has both freedom and power. Such a view is antithetical to empirical science. Yet people do, at times, at least appear to control their own behavior. The scientific goal of predicting and controlling behavior would be doomed to failure, except for animals, if people possess a whimsical freewill. But perhaps the outlook is not quite so predetermined.

We can attempt to treat some aspects of self-control from a basically empirical approach. In Chapter 1, we noted that Logan (1966) had studied conditions of negatively correlated reinforcement with rats, specifically, a condition in which the rats were rewarded with an amount of reward that was equal to the time required to traverse a short runway. In those studies, the longer the rat took, the bigger the reward. Logan attempted to predict the equilibrium speeds in terms of his earlier (Logan, 1965) research on decision-making in rats (see Chapter 5). The important finding was that, given a choice between two runways one of which contained a larger reward, the rats would choose the large-reward runway even if a considerable delay was imposed on receipt of the reward; yet, the rats would not wait that long for the larger reward in the situation involving negatively correlated reinforcement in a single runway. Instead, their behavior could be understood only in terms of a dynamic analysis in which the rats were continuously making the decision as to whether waiting another second in order correspondingly to increase the amount of ultimate reward was worth it. In sum, the rats would prefer to wait for the larger reward, if they had to make a binding decision at the very start of the runway; they could not restrain themselves, if they were given the "freedom" to choose to take the available reward *now* rather than wait for a larger reward.

These results can be understood in terms of empirical gradients of delay of reinforcement, because the same absolute difference in delays has less relative effect the longer the delays involved. The difference between an hour and an hour and a half does not seem to be as long as the difference between now and a half hour from now. Rachlin (Rachlin & Green, 1962) has shown similar results in pigeons and has also applied the reasoning to humans in the context of making contracts with respect to their behavior. For example, the morning after a late night spent before the television set, the student may firmly resolve to study for certain that night. At that point, the delay of gratification in watching television does not seem so much shorter than the delay of the anticipated greater gratification from studying. Probably, every reader has experienced such resolutions that fade into one or another rationalization for their being broken. In this example, the resolution is easily broken, because after dinner the television is here and now, whereas the tangible rewards for studying are still delayed.

Rachlin contends that this is the reason that knowledgeable people make contracts involving other people so that they are binding. You may have money automatically transferred into a saving account, because you know that you may need it in the future but that if you have it in your pocket, you are likely to spend it. According to this empirical analysis, it is not a question of "will power" in keeping one's resolutions about cutting down on television, or alcohol, or coffee, or cigarettes, or fattening foods, or daydreaming, or the movies, or even preoccupation with sex. There is no need to speculate whether the rats regretted their impatience after having eaten the small amount of food. The principles involving delayed gratification are quite well established, and self-control requires their recognition and behavior appropriate to them. For example, hand a friend one of your favorite records with a signed note saying, "If I so much as turn on the television tonight, this is yours!" At this point, the potential punishment and the potential gratification are both delayed, but both will become immediate at the same time. Furthermore, the learning of such self-control responses is assured because of the immediate reward of getting your record back.

There are also theoretically oriented approaches to self-control. For example, Bandura (Bandura & Walters, 1963) contends that self-control is acquired through modeling on parental behavior and receiving at least vicarious reinforcement as a result. Alternatively, Logan (1973) has proposed that people typically acquire a secondary self-control drive that is based on aversive experiences associated with the lack of such control; they also learn self-control habits that are intrinsically reinforced by successful self-control. This position is somewhat similar to that of Premack (Premack & Anglin, 1973), except that self-control responses are assumed to be extrinsically reinforced by parents. All of these analyses are related to Miller's proposal that people learn verbal cue-producing responses that mediate voluntary control over overt behavior.

Accordingly, contemporary behaviorists are far from denying that people play a very important role in the determination of their behavior. Their contention is only that such control is itself a reflection of the same fundamental principles of behavior. To be sure, this is a denial of the freedom of the will as an emergent process with properties that defy deterministic laws. There is no question that people can be taught successful techniques of self-control— the question is whether that is all there is to it.

NOTES   1. Although we have presented reaction time as a simple behavioral process, it should not be inferred that an understanding of the relevant phenomena is therefore simple. Among the complexities in simple reaction time is the differential effect of stimulus intensity when studied within-subject and between-subject, the effect being more pronounced in the former design. Among the complexities in choice reaction time is the effect of insructions emphasizing accuracy or speed. Furthermore, there are learning (associative) processes involved in any study of reaction time, and there are also motivational effects associated with any pay-off provisions in the study. Accordingly, reaction time is simple only in a relative sense.

2. It is of historical interest that many of the apparent contradictions in early studies of discrimination learning resulted from a lack of standardization of apparatus, procedure, and terminology. Specifically in the context of the Krechevsky-Spence controversy, Krechevsky employed a procedure devised by Lashley in which the spatial locations of the stimuli were not changed after an error, but remained the same until the subject made a correct choice, all of which constituted one "trial." This approach was a quite reasonable extrapolation of the correction procedure inherent in maze learning where the subject may make any number of errors in route to the goal during a single trial. However, according to Spence's type of analysis, each choice was a "trial." Lashley's procedure can be seen as neutralizing position tendencies repeatedly within a single trial and, hence, favoring the appearance of one-trial learning. Furthermore, to complicate the picture, an error in the Lashley jumping stand resulted in a bumped nose and fall into a net, which were obviously aversive (some rats refused to jump) and, hence, added punishment rather than simple nonreinforcement. However, Lashley's procedure was intended to mimic a subject arriving at the blind end of a cul-de-sac, although rats do not actually run head on into a dead-end wall.

3. Note that Spence's assertion that the decrement in excitatory potential, occasioned by nonreinforcement, reflects an active inhibitory process was quite gratuitous. The mathematics would only be manageable for original learning, if one proposed to stay within the bounds of zero and one hundred. Furthermore, even such an approach would be assuming, according to Spence's formulae, that inhibition resulting from nonreinforcement accrues at a different rate from excitation resulting from reinforcement.

4. In the progressive distillation of the controversy over transposition by subsequent analysts, the complication that related to the units of measurement along the stimulus dimension is frequently overlooked. It is conventional to plot the stimuli as being equally spaced along the stimulus continuum, usually

on the presumption of an underlying logarithmic psychophysical scale. In principle, the transposition controversy is not restricted to such combinations of stimuli, although they do comprise an absolute relationship, such as "twice as dark" rather than simply "darker." On the one hand, it would be interesting to compare the theories for other combinations of stimuli. On the other hand, the reversal of transposition might be attributed to the breakdown of the logarithmic scale in far tests. This would certainly arise if one conceptualized the psychological dimension as being circular, as in the case of color vision, such that far tests in one direction actually began to approach the original discrimination from the other side.

5. We have avoided the use of the expression "successive discrimination" because it is frequently used in the literature for two operationally distinct procedures. Both discriminative differentiation and differential conditioning involve the separate (successive) presentation of the stimuli; the former involves an explicit response selection feature with the procedural potential for correction, and the latter involves a go-no-go difference in responding. Clearly, there is still a lack of terminological standardization and we can only caution the reader that attempts to shortcut a detailed operational analysis of an experiment by relying on the author's title and summary may lead to inappropriate bedfellows and rather peculiar progeny.

6. Voluntary behavior, per se, is not beyond the scope of this book; indeed, our discussion of self-control directly addresses that topic. What is beyond the scope of this book concerns characteristically human behaviors, such as adopting a "set" vis-à-vis being a subject in a psychological experiment. Most human subjects are not volunteers (although neither are animals) but are enticed to participate in conjunction with a course requirement. Our neglect of these types of issues is not intended to deny their fundamental importance.

7. In a very real sense, reinforcement is always correlated with the response in operant and instrumental conditioning. For example, a rat must, at least, make contact with a bar in an operant situation or, at least, traverse a runway in an instrumental situation. It is important to recognize this fact, particularly, if one is measuring the force with which the rat presses the bar or the speed at which the rat runs. However, these criteria are typically set at a very minimal level sufficient only to determine in an objective fashion that the behavior did, in fact, occur. The expression "correlated reinforcement" is usefully employed when there is explicit differential reinforcement among responses falling within the same general class of behaviors.

8. It is well worth the reader's time to dwell for a moment on the problem of identifying the occurrence of insight in an animal. Kohler knew Sultan very well and felt that he could tell from a "cock of the head," a "gleam in the eye," or an "Aha! expression on the face" that an inspirational idea had occurred. In contrast, Maier's rats might well have retreated from the frustrating barrier to an extent that they happened to find themselves back at the common start point. Viewing the concept introspectively, not all "insights" turn out to be

brilliant adaptive solutions to a problem, which we discover only after many hours of following what turned out to be a blind alley.

9. Although we cannot go into the details here, the reader should recognize the relationship between this analysis of the goal gradient and the serial position effect in human learning. The primacy effect is presumably related to the distinctiveness of the beginning, and the recency effect is presumably related to the immediacy of reinforcement. Of course, the analysis is considerably more complex than this, but the details were worked out systematically in *Mathematico-deductive theory of rote learning* (Hull et al, 1939).

ABSTRACTS   **Harlow, H.F. Learning set and error factor theory. In S. Koch (Ed.), *Psychology: A study of a science* (Vol. 2). New York: McGraw-Hill, 1959. (pp. 492–537.)**

The operation of the stimulus-perseveration error factor is deduced from errors involving repetitive choice of the incorrect stimulus object. A more persisting error factor is that of differential cue, which results from interacting response tendencies when there is ambiguity between the object rewarded and the position rewarded. Perhaps the most persistent error factor is response shift, which may be described as a strong tendency to respond to both stimuli in the object-discrimination learning situation. Position-habit errors, which are consistent responses to either the right or left regardless of the position of the correct object appear to represent an essentially unimportant error source for primates. There are also unique patterns of responses made to irrelevant aspects of the stimulus situation, i.e., responses to those stimuli which are not correlated with the reward to the same degree as the correct object or cue. Irrelevant stimuli act as error-factor producers.

In 1959 the author demonstrated that rhesus monkeys learn successive non-spatial discrimination problems with progressively greater facility and referred to this phenomenon as the result of the formation of a learning set. One of the most striking phenomena associated with learning set formation is the change in problem difficulty following multiple-problem practice. The initial problems of a class are learned slowly in a trial-and-error fashion. After learning set formation the same kind of problem is solved immediately in an insightful fashion. Analysis of error factor elimination led us to a uniprocess position based on inhibition, for we could find no evidence that learning evolves from the formation of new associations.

Hull, C.L. The goal gradient hypothesis and maze learning. *Psychological Review,* 1932, *39,* 25–43.

From the hypothesis that there exists an excitatory gradient extending with positive acceleration approximately according to the logarithmic law in an upward direction from the beginning of a maze to the reward box, there may be deduced the following principles of behavior:

1. That the animal will tend to choose the shorter of two alternative paths to a goal.

2. That the greater the difference between the length of the paths (the standard path remaining constant), the more readily will the shorter path be chosen.

3. That the readiness of choosing the shorter path will not be affected by the absolute difference between the alternatives, provided the paths to be discriminated maintain a constant ratio to each other. (Weber's law.)

4. That animals will come to choose the direct path to a goal rather than enter blind alleys.

5. The long blinds will be more readily eliminated than short ones.

6. That the order of elimination of blind alleys will tend to be in the backward direction.

7. That long mazes will be learned with greater difficulty than short ones.

8. That animals in traversing a maze will move at a progressively more rapid pace as the goal is approached.

9. That of two alternative paths to a common goal the animal will traverse the early section of the shorter path at a faster rate than that of the parallel section of the longer one.

10. That the final parallel sections of two alternate paths each of different length leading to a common goal will be traversed at approximately equal speed.

11. That animals after having eliminated a blind will tend to pause at its entrance while pursuing the shorter path.

12. That under certain circumstances segments of pure-stimulus-act sequences will drop out, producing what is known as "short-circuiting."

13. That fragments of goal reactions will tend to intrude into instrumental act sequences, producing the phenomenon of ideo-motor action and directive or guiding ideas.

Krechevsky, I. "Hypotheses" in rats. *Psychological Review,* 1932, *39,* 516–532.

It is rapidly being recognized by many writers on the theory of learning that our older concepts are inadequate and have outlived their usefulness as even fruitful working hypotheses. Very few serious experimenters would now wish to defend the concept that a learned response consists of a number of independent S-R connections. Gradually, the concept that a learned response is an integrated unity, a systematic whole, has gained the acceptance of most animal psychologists.

Krechevsky presents three lines of evidence based on analysis of individual learning curves showing (1) systematic responding with respect to position during the pre-solution period greater than could be attributed statistically to chance, (2) reversion to systematic position responding during reversal of a brightness discrimination, and (3) systematic responding with an insoluble problem.

The term "hypothesis" has merely been chosen as a convenient tag for such behavior, convenient because it carries with it the following behavior characteristics: (1) behavior which is systematic; (2) behavior which is purposive (displaying an "if-then" character); (3) behavior which involves some degree of abstraction; and finally (4) behavior which does not depend entirely upon the immediate environment for its initiation and performance. Neither the "laws" of frequency nor of effect could possibly play any role in setting up any definite form of response, and yet the animal did show such behavior. These "hypotheses" then must be initiated in part by the animal himself. They are the animal's interpretations of the data.

Summarizing, we may point out that in the face of all recent experimental evidence, helter-skelter, trial-and-error learning must go by the board as a valid description of the learning process. Learning consists of changing from one systematic, generalized, purposive way of behaving to another and another until the problem is solved.

Lashley, K.S. An examination of the "continuity theory" as applied to discrimination learning. *Journal of General Psychology,* 1942, *26,* 241–265.

The position opposed to the theory of Spence has recently been rechristened the "Lashley theory." Since Spence's treatment of the foundling seems less than just, I am willing to accept the responsibilities of paternity, though from a certain purposive cast in the infant's features, I suspect that I am cockold. The assumptions of the opposed theory are:

1. The mechanism of nervous integration is such that when any complex of stimuli arouses nervous activity, that activity is immediately organized and certain elements or components become dominant for reaction while others become ineffective. This constitutes a "set" to react to certain elements. Such an organization is in part described by Gestalt principles of perception, in part by principles of attention.

2. In any trial of a training series, only those components of the stimulating situation which are dominant in the organization are associated. Other stimuli which excite the receptors are not associated because the animal is not set to react to them.

The question whether all stimuli acting at the time of response become associated with the response or whether the set of the animal determines a selective association can be tested by very simple experiments. If the animal is given a preliminary organization or set to respond to one component of a stimulus and is then trained in a situation where this component is combined with another, conditioned-reflex theory requires that both components be associated. The alternate theory predicts that no new association will be formed, provided that the new component does not arouse a perceptual organization dominant over the first.

Perhaps the basic difference in point of view which has given rise to this discussion is with respect to the origin of perceptual organization. Pavlov and his followers have assumed that all elements of a stimulus which excite the receptor are, primitively, equally effective for behavior, and have sought to account for perceptual organization in terms of stimulus contiguity and repetition. Opposed to this is the view that perceptual organization is a function of inherent characteristics (nervous structure) of the organism and always antedates association. Such a conception should, in turn, be distinguished from that expressed in field theories, which seem to hold that the process of organization (closure) is identical with fixation in memory.

Levine, M. Human discrimination learning: The subset-sampling assumption. *Psychological Bulletin,* 1970, *74,* 397–404.

It has been commonly assumed in hypothesis models of discrimination learning that a subject samples a single hypothesis and that this hypothesis dictates his response. An alternative assumption, termed subset-sampling, is that a subject samples several hypotheses at a time. He may then either take one, a working hypothesis, as the basis for his response, or he may make the response consistent with the majority of the hypotheses in his subset. Data that favor the subset-sampling assumptions are: (a) Methods for measuring the size of the hypothesis universe show that the subject is evaluating and correctly rejecting several hypotheses per trial. (b) During the criterion run of correct responses, latencies decrease until the subject holds only the correct hypothesis. After this point the latencies are constant. (c) In experiments with two relevant and redundant cues, subjects occasionally learn both solutions. (d) Some stimulus sequences produce a preponderance of response to one side in excess of that predicted by the single-hypothesis assumption.

Lovejoy, E. Analysis of the overlearning reversal effect. *Psychological Review,* 1966, *73,* 87–103.

For the first model it was assumed that "attending to the relevant dimension" was a response, which was strengthened by reward and weakened by nonreward. "Choosing white after attending" was also assumed to be a response and was assumed to change in a similar fashion. The second model assumed that the subject made only one response on any trial, which might be "attend and choose white," "attend and choose black," or "do not attend to the relevant stimuli."

A crucial assumption in the first model is that when the subject fails to attend, no change occurs in this chance of correct choice on attending trials. This means that the attending response and the choice response are dissociated, which is reminiscent of Krechevsky's notion of "hypothesis behavior." It has strong experimental implications but the mathematical analysis is very difficult.

The second model is closer to the "continuity" view of learning. All trials affect all probabilities. The crucial difference between the two models is the effect of nonrewarded nonattention trials. Both models assume that this event makes attending more likely, but the second model predicts that the animal "forgets" what he had previously learned about the relevant stimuli. There is evidence that the dissociation assumption of the first model may be necessary.

Medin, D.L. Role of reinforcement in discrimination-learning set in monkeys. *Psychological Bulletin,* 1972, *88,* 305–318.

Following a review of empirical research on the role of reinforcement in learning-set formation, the major theoretical explanations of learning-set formation in monkeys are analyzed. Studies showing that a reward can function to decrease as well as increase the probability of choosing an object cast doubt upon theories based on an automatic strengthening function of reward. Hypothesis or strategy selection theories avoid this problem by assuming hypotheses, rather than responses, are subject to reinforcement principles, but hypothesis theories are at best incomplete in their treatment of retention. A theory which assumes that learning-set formation results from between-problem stimulus generalization of feedback from expected rewards is consistent both with the retention studies and with experiments on the function of reward in learning set, suggesting that learning-set formation need not be considered a complex abstractive process.

Mowrer, O.H. "How does the mind work?" *American Psychologist,* 1976, *31,* 843–857.

In my 1960 books, I had already anticipated a difficulty in explaining the entire process of habit formation and inhibition by means of the conditioning of hope or fear, respectively, to response-produced stimuli. The theory presented no special problems as far as punishment and the resulting inhibition of a response were concerned. A previously punished response starts to occur, this set up a flow of sensory impulses which have been associated with punishment and, as a result, are now conditioned stimuli for fear, and the subject finds that the quickest and best way to eliminate the fear thus generated is to inhibit the previously punished response.

But before a habit can provide sensory feedback that arouses hope or positive secondary reinforcement, it must be in some way selected from innumerable other possible responses and then initiated. Once chosen and initiated, the sensory feedback from the response in question can provide both hopes and fears to guide it to its proper culmination or to inhibit it.

In order to deal with this problem adequately, I had to have recourse to the concept of image, which was operationalized as a conditioned sensation. In classical conditioning, we conjecture that the first thing that occurs when the CS is presented is an anticipation or image of the impending UCS and that in instrumental conditioning, an image of the correct response precedes, selects, and initiates the response itself. Not only do we mentally "plan our day," but each and every action, before it occurs, is visualized, considered, and decided upon or rejected, unless these actions have, by long usage, become more or less automatic, that is, subject to the control of lower centers of the brain—a point of view not significantly different from or an advance beyond William James's "ideo-motor" concept.

Restle, F. A theory of discrimination learning. *Psychological Review,* 1955, *62,* 11–19.

In solving a two-choice discrimination problem the subject learns to relate his responses correctly to the relevant cues. At the same time his responses become independent of the irrelevant cues. These two aspects of discrimination learning are represented by two hypothesized processes, "conditioning" and "adaptation."

Intuitively, a conditioned cue is one which the subject knows how to use in getting reward. On each trial of a given problem a constant proportion of unconditioned relevant cues becomes conditioned. To the extent that a conditioned cue affects performance, it contributes to a correct response only, whereas an unconditioned relevant cue contributes equally to a correct and to an incorrect response.

Intuitively, an adapted cue is one which the subject does not consider in deciding upon his choice response. If a cue is thought of as a "possible solution" to the problem, an adapted cue is a possible solution which the subject rejects or ignores. On each trial of a given problem a constant proportion of unadapted irrelevant cues becomes adapted. An adapted cue is nonfunctional in the sense that it contributes neither to a correct nor to an incorrect response.

The fundamental simplifying assumption of this theory is that the rates at which relevant cues become conditioned and irrelevant cues become adapted are the same and equal to the proportion of relevant cues in the problem. This proportion is the same as the fraction of unconditioned cues conditioned on each trial, and the fraction of unadapted cues adapted on each trial.

EXAMINATION ITEMS **Topics for thought and discussion**

1. Let us redesign the Lashley jumping stand such that, rather than having the two stimuli closely adjacent, they are somewhat widely separated. How might this modification affect discrimination learning according to the three approaches to identifying the nature of the stimulus for discrimination learning?

2. Discuss the conceptual relationship between the problem of getting the very first response in a learning situation and the problem of getting behavior initiated in a cybernetic, feedback controlled behavior theory.

3. Draw upon your own experiences in an effort to develop a definition of insight

that is objective and might be generally accepted. Then attempt to develop insight as a hypothetical construct rigorously anchored to both antecedent and consequent events. At least describe what a theory of insightful behavior would look like.

Objective items

1. To a cognitive behaviorist, the mind is to behavior most like
    a. love is to marriage
    b. fire is to water
    c. hope is to fear
    d. light is to heat

2. The best way to describe the emergent thesis is the contention that the whole
    a. is more than the sum of its parts
    b. is different from the sum of its parts
    c. depends on the molecular arrangement of its parts
    d. depends on the addition of some new process which changes its parts

3. According to the mathematics used by Spence in his early theory of discrimination learning, inhibition as an "active, negative process" is not employed. This is because the equations used would require inhibition to be
    a. functionally passive
    b. functionally incremented
    c. sometimes passive
    d. sometimes decremented

4. Which of the following (true) empirical observations in rats is most consistent with hypothesis-testing by an intelligent organism?
    a. frequent initial choice of position as the hypothesis
    b. perseveration of a wrong position hypothesis
    c. infrequency of wrong hypothesis along the relevant continuum
    d. occasional lack of perseveration of correct hypothesis

5. The fact that rats previously reinforced for responding to only one of two stimuli presented separately tend to choose that one stimulus when the two stimuli are presented together is
    a. interpretable by both the relational and the configurational views
    b. interpretable by the relational view but not the configurational view
    c. not interpretable by the relational view but interpretable by the configurational view
    d. not interpretable by either the relational or the configurational view

6. Monkeys develop discrimination learning sets even if the number of trials per problem is arbitrarily restricted such that they do not really solve the early problems. This fact is consistent with error factor theory and
    a. consistent with both Krechevsky and Spence
    b. consistent with Krechevsky but not with Spence
    c. inconsistent with Krechevsky but consistent with Spence
    d. inconsistent with both Krechevsky and Spence

7. The classic use of the transposition procedure to address the question "What is learned?" that involved the Lashley and Spence theories of discrimination learning, indicated that
    a. the procedure is fundamentally sound

    b. the procedure is fundamentally unsound

    c. the question itself is a blind alley

    d. more than one test may be necessary

8. Dissonance theory would be classed as an emergent position.

    a. True

    b. False

9. Endowing humans with a "second signal system" (language) or organisms more generally with "pure stimulus acts" (cue-producing responses) bestows a meaningful freedom of choice.

    a. True

    b. False

10. A philosopher of science might properly criticize the construct of "hypothesis" in Krechevsky's theory, because it is not anchored to

    a. antecedent conditions

    b. consequent responses

    c. either antecedent conditions or consequent responses

    d. antecedent conditions in some situations and consequent responses in other situations.

11. The most serious defect in Restle's stimulus-sampling theory of discrimination learning is the absence of a procedure for

    a. increasing the tendency to the positive stimulus

    b. decreasing the tendency to the negative stimulus

    c. the subject to determine which dimensions are irrelevant

    d. the subject to determine which response to make

12. In his explanation of discrimination learning, Spence assumes that the amount of increment of excitatory potential added by each reinforced trial is

    a. equal

    b. a negative growth function of the number of training trials

    c. a function of the number of training trials that first goes up with positive acceleration, then becomes negatively accelerated and goes down so that the curve looks like a normal distribution

    d. dependent on something else other than the number of training trials

13. Which of the following phenomena concerning the reversal of a discrimination most favors a nonattentional as compared with an attentional theory?

    a. reversal during the presolution period

    b. reversal learning set

    c. overtraining reversal effect

    d. reversal versus nonreversal shifts

14. One inescapable problem with "putting through" as a procedure to produce the first response entails

    a. a stimulus-generalization decrement

    b. reinforcement as an effect of the response

    c. transposition

    d. insight

15. According to the goal-gradient analysis, errors in a *homo*geneous response chain with terminal reinforcement should be eliminated

    a. in a backward order

   b. equally at various distances from the goal
   c. most rapidly at intermediate choice points
   d. in a forward order

16. As a procedure for producing the first response, autoshaping is most like
   a. shaping
   b. exploratory behavior
   c. classical conditioning
   d. generalization from past experience

17. In a + maze with black and white arms, the rat turns right into white and is reinforced. Then starting from the opposite side, the rat turns right into black. Which of the following propositions would *not* be supported? The rat
   a. either learns stimuli and does not alternate or learns responses and does not alternate
   b. either learns stimuli and does not alternate or learns responses and alternates
   c. either learns stimuli and alternates or learns responses and does not alternate
   d. either learns stimuli and alternates or learns responses and alternates

18. If an organism has learned a simultaneous discrimination and is then presented with one of the stimuli separately, the relational theorist would logically expect reasonably adaptive behavior.
   a. True
   b. False

19. Tolman's law of emphasis is most similar to the
   a. strong law of effect
   b. weak law of effect
   c. strong drive-reduction hypothesis
   d. weak drive-reduction hypothesis

20. If one considered nonreinforcement to be aversive, error-factor theory could be likened to the
   a. incompatible response analysis of punishment
   b. avoidance analysis of punishment
   d. punishment analysis of avoidance
   d. escape analysis of avoidance

ANSWERS TO   1.   (a) The really important events to a cognitive behaviorist are the processes of the
OBJECTIVE ITEMS   mind. Behavior is interesting to the extent that it leads to correct inferences about cognitive processes. For example, what is important is whether two people love each other; marriage may or may not follow from love or correctly be inferred from it. The other possible analogies are more strained.

2.   (b) To some extent at least, the notion of emergentism could be described in all of these ways, although the last one would have to contend that the added process has no meaning independent of this whole. But the best characterization is that the whole is not just more than the sum of its parts but is uniquely different from their simple summation.

3.   (d) The mathematics would have been much more complex had Spence actually used an equation, such as excitation minus inhibition, and computed these separately. The same net value could then be obtained in a number of different ways and the changes in each resulting from reinforcement and nonreinforcement would have to

be specified. If he kept in his bounds of zero to 100, inhibition would sometimes have to be decremented.

4.   (a) It is perhaps not unreasonable for position to be a likely hypothesis for an intelligent organsm. But interestingly enough, the other observations were already embarrassing. It is not obvious why even a rat would take so long to disconfirm a hypothesis, why they invariably start out in the right direction with the relevant continuum, or how any subject could have a relapse after once getting well started on the solution.

5.   (b) Although it would be possible to assume that organisms make some kind of comparison with memory in the separate-presentation procedure and, hence, could adjust to the simultaneous presentation, it is difficult to imagine an organism learning about a configuration never before encountered.

6.   (a) Krechevsky would not care if the stimuli were changed during the presolution period; solutions would be quite rapid once the correct hypothesis (stimulus shape) was hit upon. Spence would contend that, although particular excitatory strengths could not be developed, preexisting differentials in position tendencies would become neutralized until a single reinforcement or nonreinforcement of the new stimuli would be sufficient to tip the scales. (Error-factor theory is more like the latter, except that there are more sources of initial differential tendencies than just position.)

7.   (d) It would be an overgeneralization to draw conclusions about the fundamental soundness of the procedure. In this case and for this version of the question, using several tests revealed the reversal in far tests that favors the absolute law. In a similar vein, Tolman contended that it might take several transposition–like tests to determine the act that the organism was really performing.

8.   (True) The basic contention that all aspects of a complex situation must be consonant with each other (or else the organism is motivated to remove the dissonance) implies that the value of an event is determined by the entire situation and could not be determined independently of it.

9.   (False) The emission of these responses is completely determined. According to these approaches, you may learn self-control techniques and be motivated to exercise them, but you are actually deceived into believing that *you* are making decisions. ("You" and "I" are emergent constructs.) Choices are a result of unique genetic endowment and environmental history.

10. (c) Hypotheses are not anchored to antecedent conditions; they are generated by the organism with no rules for their generation. They are also not anchored on the consequent side, because the behavior does not necessarily reveal the hypothesis being considered on any trial.

11. (c) In this theory, relevant and irrelevant are defined by the experimenter, and the appropriate incremental and decremental processes are simply applied. On the first trial, for example, all cues should be equally incremented or decremented depending on the outcome, since all are equally present and nondifferentially reinforced.

12. (d) The increments and decrements are assumed to depend on the preexisting level of excitatory potential, regardless of how many trials were involved in arriving at that particular state.

13. (a) The fact that reversal during the presolution period did impair discrimination learning clearly is inconsistent with Krechevsky's version of attention theory. Various

aspects of the data in the other contexts may pose some problems for attentional as compared with nonattentional theories, but the problems appear to be fewer for the attentional approach.

14. (a) The cues provided by the experimenter or the apparatus to achieve "putting through" are part of the original learning context, and a subject-initiated response must be made in their absence.

15. (a) The reasoning involving delayed reinforcement is equally the same. A homogeneous chain should be learned more rapidly than a heterogeneous chain, because anticipatory response tendencies are adaptive.

16. (c) Both autoshaping and classical conditioning involve the presentation of an unconditioned stimulus independent of the organism's behavior. This is not to say that autoshaping must be conceptualized as an instance of classical conditioning, but the other alternate answers all involve some form of response-dependant reinforcement.

17. (c) Given the possibility of including an alternation tendency (inhibition of reinforcement), one could say that the rat learned to approach white and alternates rather than learning to turn right. Conversely, had the rat gone the other way, one could say that the rat learned to turn right and alternates rather than learning to approach white.

18. (True) The relationship involved would have to be a memorial representation of the previous stimuli, an assumption that is equally necessary to account for differential conditioning or even simultaneous presentation-discrimination learning, where the organism must look back and forth.

19. (b) His notion is that reinforcement emphasizes regions of the map, but emphasis may arise from other kinds of events.

20. (c) According to the punishment analysis of avoidance, avoidance responses emerge because other responses are punished; according to error-factor theory, correct behavior results because errors are eliminated.

CHAPTER TEN

EPILOGUE

Our goal in this textbook has been to present our best understanding of some of the persisting systematic issues in the areas of learning and motivation, illuminated by their recent historical developments. We did not attempt to trace them back into antiquity, that is, to the early philosophers who could be seen as anticipating many of them. The advent of behaviorism seemed a logical starting point, because it led to the generally accepted definition of our science and importantly affected the way in which these issues were conceptualized. We would underscore the fundamental thesis of behaviorism: In the last analysis and after all the words are said and done, it is the behavior of organisms in the presence of stimuli that provides the empirical foundation for all of psychology. We must first accept that proposition and agree upon objective, reliable, and ideally nonprejudicial measures of that behavior. From that point we may begin to engage in systematic analyses and debate the issues that we have encountered and others that will almost certainly appear in the future.

Let us begin here with the issue of pure empiricism versus theory. We believe that the fuel for this fire has largely been consumed. Most important, all scientists are empiricists and being a theorist in no way detracts from one's role as an empiricist. We have agreed that behaviorists do not *have* to be theorists, but we have also stated that theories in the reductive sense, as we have used this term, may prove to be useful for some empirical scientists at least some of the time. Of course, insofar as one's objectives go beyond the prediction and control of behavior and aspire to an explanation of that behavior in some "true" sense, then reductive theory is an integral, indeed, dominant part of the enterprise. This is not only the case for physiological psychologists whose interests are in the workings of the brain but also for cognitive psychologists whose interests are in the workings of the mind.

Regardless of one's bent in these theoretical endeavors, scientists are always anticipating moving on to ever more abstract levels of analysis. Even the pure empiricist, who is true to the spirit of operational objectivity, is working with some ideas of the way a system is going to emerge from experimental analysis. We called this conceptual analysis, because the scientist qua empiricist is attempting to visualize some subgoal of organizing knowledge. We are prone to take somewhat large steps toward such subgoals, returning to do the painstaking experimental analysis only when we find that we have stumbled along the way. We are inclined to camouflage under "other things equal" those things that we know will need to be done someday, but we tend to temporarily bypass these stumbling blocks in order to be the first to reach a subgoal as we conceptualize it.

We would like to destroy, once and for all, the impression that the pure empiricist is a methodical plodder who carefully takes extremely small steps in order to be certain of a sound footing. One does not need to introduce hypothetical constructs in order to let one's fancy fly. We would equally like to destroy the impression that theorists navigate in some abstract level of discourse that is free of empirical constraints. Indeed, we believe that the competition between the empiricist and the theorist is healthy for our science, provided the issue is not viewed as an either-or controversy.

Once we have agreed upon this rapprochement, the important issue is to decide what particular lines of experimental work are likely to prove to be the most useful at any particular point in our research. Our basic approach to this issue is unequivocal: research should be guided by some developing systematic analysis, flexible enough either to test the system from time to time along the way or to help choose among several alternative ways of systematizing the available knowledge. We see little merit in the I-wonder-what-would-happen-if approach to research, at least as a steady diet. What is of greater import for an understanding of the role of conceptual systems in science are the important and meaningful lines of research evidence that may be shelved and largely ignored if they do not fit into some larger system.

Among the dramatic illustrations of this last point is research that was done in the 1930s by Brunswik (1939). He made the quite reasonable argument that the natural environment is frequently arranged in such a way that reward is sometimes here and sometimes there. For example, lower prices may be found more frequently in one grocery store than another, but there are times when the opposite is true. So he raised the obvious question of how organisms adapt to maze situations in which, rather than reward always being in one location and never in the other, reward is in one or the other location with some probability. He observed that rats can adapt to such inconsistent conditions of reinforcement, generally choosing the more frequently rewarded location, the greater the probability that reward is there, and roughly matching their probability of choice to the probability of rewards.

These results evinced little more than a passing nod of recognition at the time of their initial discovery. But this domain of probability learning was to take on a drastically different image of significance with the appearance of statistical learning theory (e.g., Estes, 1950). Here finally was a theory in which probability of reinforcement had an important bearing on learning and behavior in a choice situation. It implied the counterintuitive result that organisms would still sometimes choose the less frequently rewarded alternative and, indeed, at about the probability with which it was reinforced. There then ensued, over a decade after Brunswik's pioneering work, a flurry of probability matching studies, because they were seen as contradictory to alternative theories, based on maximization of reward. Given the impetus of a systematic analysis, the identical line of research was quickly replicated and extended to touch upon fundamental issues, such as the nature and conditions of learning, hypothesis testing, the role of motivation, incentive theories, and even the tendency to believe that there should be about half true and half false items in a true-false examination. It may be personally satisfying to formulate a truly creative idea, and diligent scholars may someday faintly recall that research along those lines was done some time ago, but little more will be said of these ideas without a system.

In that spirit, it would be tempting to study the old psychological literature for phenomena that have simply been gathering dust on library shelves, and ask whether they should be resurrected in the contemporary scene. For example, the early demonstrations of insightful behavior by animals remain as incontrovertible empirical demonstrations that have never been fully integrated into a systematic analysis of behavior. It is even more tempting to review the recent literature for phenomena that clearly deserve to have their day in court but that are already cooling off on the back burner. However, it would be quite inappropriate for us either to make such judgments or to draw any conclusions about which of the various contemporary approaches is the most promising. From a historical point of view, it does appear that efforts to resolve controversies between widely divergent points of view are not likely to succeed. They may help sharpen one or the other system and, to that extent, have value over and above their direct contribution to empirical knowledge; however, they are not likely to resolve the underlying issues.

Accordingly, although we do believe that meaningful research should be guided by some evolving system, be it empirical or theoretical, it is probably best to pit two closely related systems against each other—and in this way exhibit an outcome that can prove to be more definitive. In the third chapter of this book, we reviewed two of the most basic theoretical issues, namely, the nature and conditions of associations. But it is not totally apparent from that basically historical analysis that the same experiment can be interpreted quite differently by different theorists. An example of such a conclusion would be: If learning is fundamentally of an S-R nature, then reinforcement is necessary *or* if reinforcement is not necessary, then learning is fundamentally cognitive in nature. The experiment calls for one assumption that determines which other follows, but it does not tell you which initial assumption to make.

Nevertheless, we believe that many of these fundamental issues will persist and be progressively refined by analysis. For example, one of the festering controversies that we have only skirted in this book concerns the extent to which principles derived from experimental analysis of animal learning and motivation have a bearing on an understanding of human behavior. Almost without exception, behaviorists have explicitly accepted—as an implication of the doctrine of evolution—that humans occupy their niche in the phylogenetic scale but are governed by the same fundamental principles as apply to other organisms. The tendency has been to ignore or, at least, to minimize the importance of obvious biological differences among the various species in the search for commonalities vis-à-vis the determinants of behavior.

Salutary as this goal may be, there are increasingly insistent reasons to believe that proclamations about its attainment have been premature. Indeed, the issue can now be reformulated not simply by setting *homo sapiens* apart from other animals, but rather as setting each species somewhat apart from each other species. Ethologists (e.g., Hinde, 1970) in the biological tradition have long contended that each species has developed unique capabilities for adapting to its natural environment, and they have carefully described the stimuli that release quite complex chains of behavior, such as those involved in reproduction. Bolles (1970) has clearly documented the evidence indicative of predetermined species-specific reactions to aversive stimuli that serve to constrain the principles that we discussed in Chapter 6. Seligman (1970) has collated the evidence from a variety of sources to support the thesis that organisms are selectively prepared for the formation of certain kinds of associations and may well be predisposed *not* to form certain other kinds of associations. When all of these arguments are assembled, it becomes clear that the early behaviorists glossed over the inescapable biological determinants of behavior. In further pursuit of this thesis, not only are there interspecies differences, there are also intraspecies differences and, moreover, both long-term maturational and short-term motivational variations within a single organism. Of course, if this thesis were developed to the extreme, then each organism would be conceived of as being uniquely different at each moment in time—a proposition that we must always recognize as being fundamentally correct. However, it is in the abstract nature of science to suppress as many such differences as possible in the search for uniformities and regularities.

Accordingly, the issue about the generality of the laws of learning as formulated from studies of conditioning becomes an empirical question. That is, any generalization extended to include new species, new behaviors, new environments, where "new" defines any context in which a particular generalization has not heretofore been evaluated, remains a hypothesis as equally subject to disconfirmation as confirmation. Faced with disconfirmations, the systematist must clearly redefine the boundary conditions of the system; although in all probability, the systematist also will likely search for a more abstract formulation that will encompass all of the disparate findings. Science is, itself, an ever-changing process.

Indeed, it is precisely for this reason that we have attempted to focus on the abstract issues that appear to transcend the unique contexts in which they appear. There is, for example, the recurrent issue of the level of molarity at which to cast a behavorial analysis. Now for the purposes of a narrowly-defined system, this issue is also an empirical one. Any level of description at which lawful relationships can be determined is, by that very fact, a meaningful level. The rationale that has led many systematists in the direction of a dynamic, micromolecular analysis of behavior does not deny the usefulness of more molar conceptualizations. The thesis is simply that behavorial acts are made out of movements and that an analysis focusing first on the movements will generate a better understanding of behavior.

The antithesis proposition that no amount of molecular analysis will capture the true essence of molar behavior must be viewed as a prophecy that deserves critical analysis. Consider the contention that the "whole is more than the sum of its parts." Surely one interpretation of this statement should encounter little dispute. The arguments that we have made for conceptual systems are testimony enough: An *integrated* set of principles or postulates comprising an empirical or theoretical system generate more implications than merely the sum of the implications of each premise separately. In quite similar fashion, the integrated utterance of the string of phonemes involved in saying the word "psychology" is more than the sum of the phonemes taken separately or in any other sequence. We would be hard-pressed to extol the virtues of conceptual systems in science and, at the same time, deny that micromolecular bits of behavior can become integrated into a dynamic, meaningful act. We take this to be the sense of Hull's (1943) belief that, "An ideally adequate theory even of so-called purposive behavior ought, therefore, to begin with colorless movement and mere receptor impulses as such, and from these build up step by step both adaptive behavior and maladaptive behavior."

Hull's belief is in sharp contrast to that of Bower (1975): "The upshot, I think, is that the behaviorist's insistence upon colorless, purposeless movements as the 'units' of behavior is best viewed as a mistake. Actions are simply not reducible to, or equivalent to, a set of movements." As we understand this position, we must accept, for example, that the phonemes in the word "psychology" have *no* meaning and, hence, even the integrated sum of them would be meaningless. The contention is that the molar unit is not just *more* than the sum of its molecular parts, but is *different from* any conceivable amplification of properties inherent in the parts themselves. The inference that Bower would have us draw from this argument is that the smallest unit that can form the basis for an understanding of meaningful and purposive behavior is a unit that, itself, has meaning and purpose.

As profound and irreconcilable as this issue may appear to be, we venture that it may prove to be largely semantic, resting largely on the definition or connotation of "meaning." It is true that a micromolecular movement appears to be meaningless when isolated from the context in which it occurs, but it is really meaningless only if its deletion in no way alters the consequences of the act. The full meaning of a movement cannot be determined outside of the contexts in which it appears, and ostensibly the same movement may have quite different meanings in different contexts. It should be clear that these statements apply not simply to the verbal behavior of humans, but to all behavior of all organisms. Meaning and purpose do not reside in behavior itself; they are descriptive abstractions of a process nature, inferred from the dynamic interaction of organism and environment. They have no real existence.

Indeed, there is the heart of the issue dividing behavioristic behaviorists from cognitive behaviorists. It is largely semantic; witness the following contention of Estes (1975): "It begins to appear that there may be real profit in complementing the almost exclusively behavioral orientation of earlier theories of conditioning and animal learning with one which treats with the *same* phenomena in terms of the processing and transformation of information" (italics added). It is not so much in search of new explanations and fruitful, new channels of research, as it is in the language used to describe behavior. But the real issue is not semantic in the denotative sense; it is in the connotation of surplus meaning associated with cognitive terminology, as contrasted with the colorless language of neobehaviorism, that separates the poles of this controversy. Since, in the final analysis, understanding is a subjective experience, the resolution of the issue may well reside merely in its recognition. Whether one chooses to deprecate a system as being teleological on the one side, or mechanistic on the other, would appear to be more a matter of taste and style than of right or wrong.

But whatever one's predilection in such regards, our prognosis is that future efforts to integrate the field of learning and motivation are inevitable. The aspiration for a systematic analysis of behavior at a sufficiently abstract level to encompass all behaviors of all organisms is inherent in the scientific enterprise.

GLOSSARY

Abstraction. A verbal summary of events that omits some of the details of the events. The number of details omitted determines the degree of abstractness of the summary.

Act. Any behavior that physically alters the environment or changes the organism's relationship to the environment.

Act, pure stimulus. Any behavior, especially verbal behavior, that has no apparent function other than to produce stimuli to mediate adaptive behavior.

Act, receptor-orienting. The behavior of orienting one's sensory receptors toward a source of stimulation.

Alternation. The observed tendency not to repeat the emission of a response nor to reexpose oneself to a stimulus.

Analysis, conceptual. This subsumes all types of explanation that are more abstract than that given by the basic experimental data.

Analysis, empirical. An abstract conceptual analysis in which all terms are defined operationally.

Analysis, experimental. A convergence of research designs directed to the answers of empirical questions.

Analysis, functional. An organization of procedures around their results rather than their specific mechanics.

Analysis, operational. A detailed specification of the procedures involved in all aspects of an experiment.

Analysis, systematic. A highly abstract conceptual analysis of either the empirical or theoretical type.

Analysis, theoretical. An abstract conceptual analysis that involves the introduction of hypothetical constructs.

Association. A theoretical construct that represents the outcome of the hypothesized internal process of learning.

Associative weakening. The theoretical position that nonreinforcement of a response weakens the S-R association to that response.

Attention. A hypothetical concept referring to differential stimulus control by an element of a stimulus compound or feature of a complex stimulus environment.

Attention, selective. A hypothetical construct referring to the organism's assumed role in selecting elements of a stimulus compound or of a complex stimulus environment that gain control over behavior.

Avoidance conditioning, cued. An instrumental or operant conditioning procedure in which responding delays or precludes the occurrence of an aversive stimulus that is preceded by a warning stimulus.

Avoidance conditioning, noncued. An instrumental or operant conditioning procedure in which responding delays or precludes the occurrence of an aversive stimulus that is not preceded by a warning stimulus but that usually occurs regularly across time.

Awareness. A hypothetical construct that represents the outcome of an organism's cognitions and that humans can report verbally.

Behavior. A term that encompasses all actions of an organism, regardless of whether or not they are objectively identified.

Behavior chain. A sequence of actions that serve to achieve some terminal event.

Behaviorism. The position that the science of psychology is concerned only with the actions of organisms and not with their cognitive processes as ends in themselves.

Blocking. Empirically, the failure of a stimulus to gain control over behavior, even though it is appropriately situated to do so, as a result of being combined with another previously conditioned stimulus.

Centrifugal swing. Physical forces that favor going in an opposite direction after making a turn in a maze.

Cognition. Hypothesized internal processes that refer to symbolic or mental events, such as expecting, thinking, noticing, and confirming.

Cognitive approach. The position that the science of psychology is importantly concerned with the cognitions of organisms and not just with their actions.

Cognitive dissonance. A hypothetical construct that arises when there is a discrepancy between an organism's behavior and the outcome received for that behavior, or between an organism's belief and behavior.

Cognitive map. A hypothetical construct representing the organization of cognitions into a schema that can serve to direct responding.

Compounding. The observed tendency to respond only to the combination of the elements of a compound stimulus and not to the elements separately.

Concept. A descriptive term that subsumes several positive instances, or a number of operations that display similar functional relationships, and excludes all negative instances or disparate functional relationships.

Concept, hypothetical. A concept is hypothetical, as opposed to empirical, when it cannot be observed directly but instead must be inferred from observations.

Conditioned emotional response procedure. A procedure in which a classical conditioning operation is superimposed on an instrumental or operant conditioning response baseline.

Conditioning, classical. A procedure in which an unconditioned stimulus is correlated with the prior occurrence of a conditioned stimulus without regard to response occurrence.

Conditioning, classical defense. A classical excitatory conditioning procedure in which the unconditioned stimulus is an aversive stimulus that is positively correlated with the prior occurrence of a conditioned stimulus.

Conditioning, classical differential. A classical conditioning procedure in which an unconditioned stimulus is positively correlated with one conditioned stimulus and less positively or negatively correlated with a second conditioned stimulus. This procedure combines aspects of classical excitatory conditioning and classical inhibitory conditioning.

Conditioning, classical excitatory. A classical conditioning procedure in which an unconditioned stimulus is positively correlated with the prior occurrence of a conditioned stimulus so that the unconditioned stimulus regularly follows the conditioned stimulus.

Conditioning, classical higher-order. A procedure in which a conditioned stimulus is positively correlated with the prior occurrence of a conditoned stimulus that had previously been involved in classical excitatory conditioning.

Conditioning, classical inhibitory. A classical conditioning procedure in which an unconditioned stimulus is negatively correlated with the prior occurrence of a conditioned stimulus so that the unconditioned stimulus explicitly does not follow the conditioned stimulus.

Conditioning, classical omission. A classical conditioning procedure in which the unconditioned stimulus is not presented if a conditioned response occurs in the presence of the conditioned stimulus.

Conditioning, classical temporal. A procedure in which an unconditioned stimulus occurs at regular intervals of time without regard to response occurrence and in the absence of any identified exteroceptive conditioned stimulus.

Conditioning, differential instrumental/operant. An instrumental/operant conditioning procedure in which an emotional stimulus is positively correlated with the response in the presence of one discriminative stimulus and less positively or negatively correlated with the response in the presence of a second discriminative stimulus.

Conditioning, instrumental. A procedure in which an emotional stimulus is correlated with the prior occurrence of a periodically enabled response.

Conditioning, operant. A procedure in which an emotional stimulus is correlated with the prior occurrence of a freely available response.

Conditions. A descriptive account of the quantitative and qualitative circumstances that prevail in any situation.

Conditions, association. The momentary quantitative and qualitative properties of a learned association, such as its strength and its stimulus and/or response end terms.

Conditions, boundary. The range of situations to which a system is applicable.

Conditions, punisher. The momentary quantitative and qualitative properties of a punisher, such as its intensity, duration, and quality.

Conditions, reinforcer. The momentary quantitative and qualitative descriptive properties of a reinforcer, such as its amount, delay, and quality.

Conditions, response. The momentary quantitative and qualitative descriptive properties of a response, such as its speed, force, and topography.

Construct, hypothetical. An imaginary process, invented by a theorist, to which various properties may be ascribed and that must be anchored to independent and dependent variables. If more than one hypothetical construct is involved in a theory, their interrelationships must be specified.

Context. The general environment in which behavioral processes occur.

Contiguity. A situation in which two or more events occur together, in space and/or time. Events that do so are said to be contiguous.

Contingency. A specification of a temporal correlation of events such that one event shortly follows the occurrence of some other event (positive contingency) or does not follow the other event (negative contingency).

Contrast, behavioral. A situation where the rate of an operant response differs from that appropriate to the prevailing schedule of reinforcement/punishment as a result of experience with other schedules.

Contrast, incentive. A situation where the speed of an instrumental response differs from that appropriate to the prevailing conditions of reinforcement/punishment as a result of experience with other conditions of instrumental conditioning.

Contrast, negative. Incentive contrast and behavorial contrast are negative when performance of the response is below the level that is appropriate to the prevailing conditions/schedules.

Contrast, positive. Incentive contrast and behavioral contrast are positive when performance of the response is above the level that is appropriate to the prevailing conditions/schedules.

Contrast, simultaneous. A situation where positive or negative contrast effects are observed during exposure to different conditions/schedules of reinforcement/punishment in differential conditioning situations.

Contrast, successive. A situation where positive or negative contrast effects are observed following a sequence change in the conditions/schedules of reinforcement/punishment.

Corollary. A major elaboration of an abstract principle or postulate.

Correction procedure. An instrumental conditioning procedure that enables the organism to retrace from an error and pursue the correct response on every trial.

Counterconditioning. Any conditioning procedure in which a new, incompatible response is learned in order to supplant a previously learned response.

Cue. Any stimulus event bearing some informative relationship to some other stimulus event of emotional significance to the organism.

Cue reliability. The consistency with which a cue is followed by an emotionally significant event.

Cue validity. The consistency with which an emotionally significant event is preceded by a cue.

Cue value. The conceptual combination of cue reliability and validity.

Data. The record of observations made by the scientist. Data are sometimes referred to as the protocol.

Deduction. The process of drawing conclusions from stated premises according to the rules of logic.

Definition, functional. A definition that states the changes in behavior that must occur for a term to be used.

Definition, operational. A definition that states the conditions and the procedures that must be satisfied for a term to be used.

Definition, relational. A definition that states the empirical relationships between events that must pertain for a term to be used.

Definition, theoretical. A definition that states the nature of the hypothetical constructs that must be assumed for a term to be used.

Definition, transprocedural. A definition that states that an operationally defined term can only be used if it applies as well to a more general set of procedures.

Definition, transsituational. A definition that states that a functionally defined term can only be used if it applies across all situations.

Demand. A cognitive hypothetical construct that derives from drive motivation and that gives value to a goal object.

Description. A narrative summary of the conditions of which behavior is a function. All empirical statements are descriptive and state at some level of abstractness the operations performed and the observations made.

Determinism. A philosophical position that all observations displaying intersubjective reliability are the result of natural laws that can be discovered by the methods of science and used to predict future observations.

Differentiation. A procedure in instrumental or operant conditioning in which two responses are simultaneously available and a different consequent event results from making one or the other response.

Discrimination. A procedure in instrumental or operant conditioning in which two discriminative stimuli are simultaneously available and a different consequent event results from the choice of one or the other stimulus.

Discrimination hypothesis. The theoretical position that resistance to extinction is directly related to the difficulty of discriminating the extinction situation from the acquisition situation.

Discriminative differentiation. A procedure in instrumental or operant conditioning in which different responses are correlated with emotional stimuli and dependent on the prevailing discriminative stimulus.

Disinhibition. Empirically, this term refers to the reappearance of an extinguished response in the presence of a novel, often intense, stimulus.

Drive. A theoretical construct that represents a type of motivation that is often based on biological needs.

Drive, activity. A specific instance of drive that is postulated to be based on the need to be active.

Drive, exploratory. A specific instance of drive that is postulated to be based on the need to explore novel environments.

Drive, extrinsic. Any instance of drive activation that is produced by exteroceptive stimulus conditions.

Drive, generalized. A nonspecific drive that is produced by any primary or secondary source of drive. Given the existence of a generalized drive, there is only one drive to which all sources of drive contribute.

Drive, irrelevant. Any instance of a drive that is inappropriate to the nature of the reinforcer used during the learning of a response.

Drive, primary. Conditions or sources of drive that arise without training. These conditions often involve biological needs that result from deprivation or stimulation operations.

Drive, secondary. Conditions or sources of drive that arise because of their prior association with a punisher.

Drive, specific. A nongeneralized drive that is produced by a particular primary or secondary source of drive. Given the existence of specific drives, there is a different drive associated with each separate source of drive.

Dual-process (multi-). The position that an experimental or theoretical phenomenon occurs as a result of two (several) processes.

Emergentism. The thesis that the result of combining several molecular elements is conceptually different from any simple summation of the properties of those elements considered separately.

Emphasis, law of. The proposition that regions of a cognitive map containing emotionally significant events will have special clarity.

Empiricism. An approach that avoids reductive theory and restricts itself instead to the use of empirical relationships at various levels of abstractness.

Escape conditioning. An instrumental or operant conditioning procedure in which responding terminates a primary or secondary aversive stimulus.

Expectancy. A cognitive hypothetical construct that represents a learned association between an antecedent stimulus and a subsequent stimulus or between a sign and a significate.

Extinction. A procedure that entails the consistent nonreinforcement of a previously reinforced response. Extinction is manifested functionally by a gradual decrease in performance of the response.

Extinction below zero. Theoretically, a situation in which inhibition is greater than excitation so that the difference of excitation minus inhibition is less than zero (negative).

Extinction, latent. Empirically, a reduction in the resistance to extinction of a referent response that occurs in the absence of any prior nonreinforced execution of the response.

Extinction, resisance to. A measure of the persistence of a response after all reinforcement of the response has been discontinued. Resistance to extinction may be specified in terms of the number of responses emitted, or in terms of the amount of time that elapses, prior to the complete cessation of responding.

Fact. A summary of data usually accompanied by some type of statistical analysis concerning its reliability.

Feedback. Stimuli that are produced by responses or follow responses that can infuence the future probability of response occurrence.

Feedback, informative. Any stimulus following a response that distinguishes the class of behaviors into which the response falls.

Feedback, negative. Any stimulus produced by a response that tends to decrease the future probability of occurrence of this very response.

Feedback, positive. Any stimulus produced by a response that tends to increase the future probability of occurrence of this very response.

Fixation. An observed increase in the persistence of a punished response.

Frustration. A hypothetical construct that describes the postulated condition that develops when an expectancy of a reinforcer is not fulfilled; that is, frustration results when a previously reinforced response is no longer reinforced.

Frustration effect. Empirically, a transient energizing effect on an organism's performance that accompanies an operational change from reinforcement to nonreinforcement.

Function, concave. The shape of a curve in which the upper edge is bowed upward.

Function, convex. The shape of a curve in which the upper edge is bowed downward.

Function, monotonic. A function in which the process is ever increasing or ever decreasing.

Function, negatively accelerated. A function in which the changes get progressively smaller.

Function, nonmonotonic. A function in which the process first increases and then decreases, or vice versa.

Function, ogival. A function in which the changes first get progressively smaller and then progressively larger, or vice versa.

Function, positively accelerated. A function in which the changes get progressively larger.

Generalization decrement. The extent to which there is a decreased level of performance as a result of a change in the stimulus situation from that present during acquisition of the response.

Generalization, phonetic. The observed tendency to emit a learned response in the presence of a word that sounds somewhat similar to the word present during acquisition of the response.

Generalization, response. The observed tendency to emit responses that are somewhat similar to the response learned during acquisition.

Generalization, semantic. The observed tendency to emit a learned response in the presence of a word that sounds different but that is somewhat similar in meaning to the word present during acquisition of the response.

Generalization, stimulus. The observed tendency to emit a learned response in the presence of a stimulus that is somewhat similar to the stimulus present during acquisition of the response.

Gestalt. Theoretically, the integration of a complex stimulus situation into an indivisible whole.

Goal gradient. The proposition that the links of a behavior chain are differentially strengthened by the terminal reinforcement as a result of the relationship between delay of reinforcement and distance from the goal.

Gradient, generalization. The decreasing tendency to emit responses as a function of the difference between stimuli or responses.

Gradient, inhibitory. The decreasing generalization of the effects of extinction on responding to a particular stimulus that is a function of the difference between stimuli.

Gradient, postdifferential-conditioning. The stimulus-generalization gradient following differential reinforcement of two or more stimuli along the relevant continuum.

Gradient, primitive. The stimulus-generalization gradient that would be found in the complete absence of prior differential reinforcement of stimuli along the relevant continuum.

Gradient, relative. The stimulus-generalization gradient transformed mathematically in order to set performance to the original stimulus at unity and to express performance to other stimuli relative to that value.

Habit. A hypothetical construct that represents a learned association between a stimulus and a response.

Hypostatization. The presumed logical fallacy of accepting the naming of a phenomenon for an explanation of it.

Hypothesis. A statement of the expected outcome of some set of experimental operations, usually based on some systematic analysis.

Imitation. Behavior emitted in response to stimuli that are provided by the overt behavior of another organism.

Incentive. A theoretical construct that represents a type of motivation that is based on the expectation of the consequences of making a particular response.

Incentive magnitude. The hypothetical strength of incentive motivation. Incentive magnitude can be conceptualized as absolute or relative.

Incentive magnitude, absolute. The conceptual position that incentive magnitude may be directly related to the conditions of events without regard to the preceding or prevailing incentive context.

Incentive magnitude, relative. The conceptual position that incentive magnitude is related to the preceding and/or prevailing incentive context and cannot be directly related to the conditions of events.

Incentive, negative. Incentive motivation that results from the expectation that an aversive event will occur following a response.

Incentive, net. Incentive motivation that results from the combination of positive incentive and negative incentive.

Incentive, positive. Incentive motivation that results from the expectation that a reinforcing event will occur following a response.

Induction. Induction is the logical process of going from a set of particular statements to a more general statement that subsumes the former.

Inhibition. A hypothetical concept referring to a decrease in performance of a response that results from the presentation of a stimulus. (See *disinhibition*.)

Inhibition, conditioned. Empirically, this refers to a decrease in performance that results from the presentation of a previously nonreinforced stimulus. Alternatively, this refers to a theoretical inhibition that develops as a result of habit formation to the response of stopping responding.

Inhibition, external. Empirically, a decrease in performance resulting from the addition of a stimulus to a conditioned stimulus.

Inhibition, internal. A performance decrease resulting from nonreinforcement of a stimulus along the same continuum as a reinforced stimulus.

Inhibition, reactive. A theoretical inhibition that occurs as a result of responding, regardless of whether or not responding is reinforced.

Inhibition, theoretical. A hypothetical construct that describes the hypothesized internal process that opposes habit.

Initial nonreinforcement effect on extinction. The empirical generalization that organisms given nonreinforced trials, prior to consistently reinforced trials, are more resistant to subsequent extinction than are organisms receiving only consistently reinforced trials.

Insight. The sudden appearance of adaptive behavior that frequently involves the combination of previously learned responses into novel combinations.

Intertrial reinforcement effect on extinction. The empirical generalization that under partial reinforcement conditions, organisms receiving intertrial reinforcement after nonreinforced trials are less resistant to subsequent extinction than are organisms receiving intertrial reinforcement after reinforced trials.

Intervening variable. A term that efficiently summarizes an interrelated set of empirical functions.

Irradiation. A hypothetical neural process in which stimuli excite nearby sensory foci.

Law. A statement usually in the form—if A then B—that summarizes a number of observations of a relationship between two variables.

Law of effect, empirical. A law that defines reinforcers and punishers functionally, that is, in terms of behavior changes.

Law of effect, strong theoretical. The theoretical position that all reinforcers consist of drive-stimulus reductions.

Law of effect, weak theoretical. The theoretical position that all drive-stimulus reductions constitute reinforcers but that all reinforcers do not necessarily consist of drive-stimulus reductions.

Learning. A hypothetical construct that refers to a relatively permanent process that results from practice and is reflected in a change in performance.

Learning, differentiation. The behavior of choosing from among somewhat similar responses on the basis of differential reinforcement.

Learning, discrimination. The behavior of choosing from among somewhat similar stimuli on the basis of differential reinforcement.

Learning, latent. Learning that results from practice without obvious reinforcement but not evident in performance until a reinforcer is provided.

Learning, observational. Empirically, the emission of adaptive behavior after watching another organism emit the correct response or choose the correct stimulus.

Learning, place. Learning inferred from the emission of behavior that is consistently oriented with respect to a particular location, although particular responses or response sequences may vary.

Learning, response. Learning inferred from the consistent performance of particular responses or response sequences without regard to the resulting location of the behavior.

Learning, reversal. The readjustment of behavior when response contingencies are changed in order to reverse the reinforcement/nonreinforcement relationships.

Learning, selective. A generic term subsuming both differentiation learning and discrimination learning.

Learning set. The rapid solution of a problem by an organism who has had prior experience with a number of problems of the same type.

Macro response definition. In response definition, a macro approach treats quantitative differences among responses as an index of response strength.

Massed-trials extinction effect. The empirical generalization that the rate of extinction is increased when extinction trials are massed as opposed to spaced.

Mechanism. A hypothetical process that is employed by a theory to enable modification of objectively presented stimuli by the organism.

Micro response definition. In response definition, a micro approach treats responses that differ quantitatively as different responses, although different responses may be aggregated in order to produce lawful empirical relationships.

Model. A model is a system borrowed from some domain other than that one under consideration; with a model, the scientist attempts to describe the workings of the undefined system using the laws of the model.

Molar response definition. In response definition, a molar approach aggregates all qualitatively different responses that result in the same consequence.

Molecular response definition. In response definition, a molecular approach treats responses that differ qualitatively as different responses, although different responses may be aggregated in order to produce lawful empirical relationships.

Movement. Any behavior that has no direct effect on the physical environment and does not change the organism's relationship to the environment.

N-length. The number of consecutive nonreinforced trials that precede a reinforced trial.

N-R transitions. The number of times a nonreinforced trial is followed by a reinforced trial.

Need. A biologal state of the organism that results from deprivation of a substance necessary for survival or from injurious stimulation.

Noncorrection procedure. A selective learning procedure in which a trial is terminated by nonreinforcement after an error.

Operant level. The rate at which an operant response occurs in the absence of prior conditioning.

Operation, deprivation. The conditions and procedures used by an experimenter to establish a need in the organism.

Operation, experimental. The conditions and procedures established by an experimenter during a period of observing behavior.

Operation, measurement. Techniques used for the recording and analysis of behavior during an observation episode.

Operation, probe. Techniques used to change the observation situation for the purpose of determining the effects of an experimental operation.

Operation, pure response. Procedures that apply when observations of the occurrence of behavior are made without the intervention of stimuli.

Operation, pure stimulus. Techniques that involve the presentation or withdrawal of stimuli that are carried out without consideration of the organism's behavior.

Operation, response-selection. Techniques that consist of the determination of the behaviors to be observed and the categorization of responses for identification purposes.

Operation, setting. The conditions and procedures established by an experimenter prior to a period of observing behavior.

Operation, stimulus-selection. Techniques used for choosing class and parameter values of stimulus events in an experiment.

Operation, subject-selection. Techniques used for choosing species of subject, subclasses within that species, and assignment to the experimental conditions.

Overshadowing. Empirically, the selective control of behavior by only one element of a compound stimulus with little or no control by other equally valid elements.

Overtraining extinction effect. The empirical generalization that rate of extinction is inversely related to the amount of overtraining under consistent reinforcement, and directly related to the amount of overtraining under partial reinforcement.

Overtraining reversal effect. The empirical generalization that reversal learning is more rapid as a result of training that has been extended beyond criterion performance.

Paradigm. A specification of the operations to which an organism is exposed before or during a period of observing the organism's behavior.

Parameter. Particular quantitative values along some dimensions of an event that are used in an experiment.

Parsimony. An inexact estimate of the ratio of the number of phenomena subsumed by a system relative to the number of assumptions or parameters required by the system.

Partial punishment effect on extinction. The empirical generalization that resistance to extinction is greater after partial punishment than after consistent punishment.

Partial punishment effect on punishment. The empirical generalization that response persistence under consistent punishment is greater after exposure to partial punishment than after no prior exposure to punishment.

Partial reinforcement effect on acquisition. The empirical generalization that a response is performed more rapidly during acquisition with partial reinforcement than with consistent reinforcement.

Partial reinforcement effect on extinction. The empirical generalization that resistance to extinction is greater after partial reinforcement than after consistent reinforcement.

Partial reinforcement effect on extinction, generalized. The empirical observation that organisms given partial reinforcement in one situation are more resistant to extinction following consistent reinforcement in another, related situation than are organisms receiving only consistent reinforcement.

Partial reinforcement effect on extinction, interpolated. The empirical observation that organisms given a block of partial reinforcement trials interpolated between consistently reinforced trials are more resistant to subsequent extinction than are organisms receiving only reinforced trials.

Partial reinforcement effect on generalization. The empirical observation that stimulus generalization is broader after partial reinforcement than after consistent reinforcement.

Partial reinforcement effect on punishment. The empirical generalization that response persistence to punishment is greater after partial reinforcement than after consistent reinforcement.

Peak shift. The empirical observation that following differential instrumental/operant conditioning, the highest level of performance occurs to a stimulus displaced from a positive stimulus in the direction away from a negative stimulus.

Principle. A highly abstract empirical law that has attained wide generality and broad-based supporting evidence.

Process. A change that occurs as a result of time or operations performed during an experimental episode. (See dual-process and uniprocess.)

Psychophysics. The area of psychology in which psychological stimulus scales are related to physical stimulus scales.

Punisher. Any event that decreases the future probability of the occurrence of a response it shortly follows.

Punisher, negative. An event that functions as a punisher when removed.

Punisher, positive. An event that functions as a punisher when presented.

Punisher, primary. An event that functions as a punisher without training.

Punisher, secondary. An event that functions as a punisher because of its prior association with a punisher.

Punishment. A procedure in which a response is followed by a punisher.

Punishment, consistent. A procedure that involves following a response with a punisher after every response occurrence.

Punishment, correlated. A procedure in which some dimension of the punisher is varied systematically in relation to some dimension of the response.

Punishment, differential. A procedure that involves selectively punishing the emission of a particular class of responses or punishing the selection of particular stimuli.

Punishment, nondifferential. A procedure that entails giving the same punisher for the emission of different responses or the same punisher for selecting different stimuli.

Punishment, partial. A procedure that involves following a response with a punisher on only a portion of response occurrences.

Punishment, principle of. Whenever a response is closely followed in time by a punisher, the tendency for that response to reoccur in the future is decreased.

Punishment, schedule of. A specified program for punisher availability that is based on the passage of time or on the number of responses emitted.

Putting through. The procedure of physically guiding an organism through the desired behavior.

Reaction time. A measure of the latency of a response following the onset of a stimulus.

Reaction time, choice. A measure of the latency of one of two responses that follows the onset of one of two stimuli.

Redintegration. The tendency to respond to only one aspect or element of a complex stimulus in the way that was learned in relation to the entire stimulus complex.

Reduction sentences. The hierarchical chain of steps that is required to reduce an empirical or hypothetical concept to its operations or empirical referents.

Reification. The giving of a semblance of reality to hypothetical constructs as if they exist, in some sense, in other than their role in a theory.

Reinforcement. A procedure in which a response is followed by a reinforcer.

Reinforcement, consistent. A procedure that involves following a response with a reinforcer after every response occurrence.

Reinforcement, differential. A procedure that involves selectively reinforcing the emission of a particular class of responses, while nonreinforcing similar responses, or the process of reinforcing the selection of particular stimuli, while nonreinforcing selection of similar stimuli.

Reinforcement, nondifferential. A procedure that gives the same reinforcer for the emission of different responses or for selecting different stimuli.

Reinforcement, partial. A procedure that entails following a response with a reinforcer on only a portion of response occurrences.

Reinforcement, principle of. Whenever a response is closely followed in time by a reinforcer, the tendency for that response to reoccur in the future is increased.

Reinforcement, proportional. A procedure in which the amount of reinforcement varies directly with the amplitude of the response.

Reinforcement, schedule of. A specified program for reinforcer availability that is based on the passage of time or on the number of responses emitted.

Reinforcement, terminal. A procedure in which a reinforcer is given only after the correct completion of a series of responses in a behavior chain.

Reinforcement, theory of. The theoretical position that reinforcement is necessary for learning to occur. A *pure* reinforcement theory asserts that the extent of learning is determined, in part, by the conditions of reinforcement.

Reinforcement, vicarious. A hypothetical condition of reinforcement that is derived from observing another organism receive a reinforcer for engaging in some behavior.

Reinforcer. Any event that increases the future probability of occurrence of a response it shortly follows.

Reinforcer, generalized. An event that functions as a reinforcer because of its prior association with a large number of different reinforcers.

Reinforcer-magnitude-extinction effect. The empirical generalization that the rate of subsequent extinction is inversely related to reinforcer magnitude under consistent reinforcement, and directly related to reinforcer magnitude under partial reinforcement.

Reinforcer, negative. An event that functions as a reinforcer when removed.

Reinforcer, positive. An event that functions as a reinforcer when presented.

Reinforcer, primary. An event that functions as a reinforcer without training.

Reinforcer, secondary. An event that functions as a reinforcer because of its association with a reinforcer.

Relationship, functional. A stated or implied mathematical statement of the way in which one factor correlates with another.

Respondent. A response that belongs to a class of behaviors that are directly elicited by identifiable stimuli.

Response, anticipatory. A response that antedates its original time of occurrence as a result of stimuli that precede it.

Response, avoidance. A response that delays or precludes the occurrence of an aversive stimulus.

Response, conditioned. A response that is elicited by a conditioned stimulus as a result of its contingency with an unconditioned stimulus.

Response, consummatory. A response that reduces a need established through deprivation.

Response definition. See *micro, macro, molar,* and *molecular* response definitions.

Response, disposition. The hypothetical tendency to perform a particular response in a given stimulus situation.

Response, emotional. A response that is elicited by an emotional stimulus that can have motivational properties.

Response, escape. A response that terminates a primary or secondary aversive stimulus.

Response, fear. An emotional response that is elicited by an aversive stimulus.

Response, fractional goal. The hypothetical components of an overt goal response that can become anticipatory.

Response, incompatible (competing). A response that physically cannot be performed at the same time as another response.

Response, instrumental. A response that is periodically enabled by the environment and that belongs to a class of behaviors that act on the environment to produce the same consequent.

Response, operant. A freely available response that belongs to a class of behaviors that act on the environment to produce the same consequent.

Response, referent. A response that has been designated as the response on which experimental operations or contingencies are based.

Response, relaxation. A hypothetical response that accompanies drive-stimulus reduction reinforcement and that can become anticipatory.

Response, relief (relaxation). An emotional response that is elicited by the termination or the omission of an aversive stimulus.

Response, unconditioned. A response that is elicited by an unconditioned stimulus without training.

Satiation, need. The observed reduction in the tendency to emit a consummatory response that results from a reduction in need.

Satiation, response. The observed reduction in the tendency to emit a response that results from repeated performance of the response.

Satiation, stimulus. The observed reduction in the tendency to respond to the same stimulus immediately.

Schedule. A schedule refers to a programmed sequence of events that specifies when events happen.

Schedule, chain. A complex schedule in which the component schedules are presented sequentially and are accompanied by a concomitant exteroceptive antecedent stimulus.

Schedule, complex. Any schedule that combines two or more component schedules either at random or sequentially.

Schedule, fixed-interval. A schedule in which the time between events is constant, although one response must be made at the end of each interval in order to obtain the event.

Schedule, fixed-ratio. A schedule in which a constant number of responses is required in order to obtain the event.

Schedule, fixed-time. A schedule in which the time between events is constant, and no response is required in order to obtain the event.

Schedule, mixed. A complex schedule in which the component schedules are presented randomly without any concomitant change in the exteroceptive antecedent stimulus.

Schedule, multiple. A complex schedule in which the component schedules are presented randomly and are accompanied by a concomitant exteroceptive antecedent stimulus.

Schedule, tandem. A complex schedule in which the component schedules are presented sequentially without any concomitant change in the exteroceptive antecedent stimulus.

Schedule, variable (random) interval. A schedule in which the time between events is variable (random), although one response must be made at the end of each interval in order to obtain the event.

Schedule, variable (random) ratio. A schedule in which the number of responses required in order to obtain the event is variable (random).

Schedule, variable (random) time. A schedule in which the time between events is variable (random), and no response is required in order to obtain the event.

Shift, extradimensional. A change in the contingencies of reinforcement after discrimination learning such that a previously irrelevant stimulus dimension is differentially reinforced while the previously relevant stimulus dimension is made irrelevant.

Shift, intradimensional. A change in the contingencies of reinforcement after discrimination learning such that differential reinforcement holds with new values along the previously relevant stimulus dimension.

Shift, nonreversal. A change in the contingencies of reinforcement after discrimination learning such that a previously irrelevant stimulus modality is differentially reinforced, while the previously relevant stimulus modality is made irrelevant.

Shift, optional. A change in the contingencies of reinforcement after discrimination learning such that reinforcement is differential between stimuli differing along both the previously relevant and a previously irrelevant dimension.

Sign. A cognitive hypothetical construct that refers to the meaning assigned to a stimulus because of its relationship to a subsequent stimulus.

Significate. A cognitive hypothetical construct that represents the value assigned to a stimulus that is contingent upon a preceding stimulus.

Spontaneous recovery. Empirically, the reappearance of an extinguished response that occurs after a lapse of time.

State. The conditions of a system at any point of time.

Stimulus. Any objectively identifiable event that functions as such in the principles of behavior.

Stimulus, absolute. A definition of the stimulus in terms of the specific qualitative and quantitative properties of the event, as measured independently of other events.

Stimulus-as-coded. A hypothetical construct referring to the stimulus as transformed by the organism prior to association formation.

Stimulus, aversive. A stimulus whose termination leads to an increase in the future probability of responses that preceded the termination.

Stimulus, compound. A stimulus that consists of two or more stimuli presented simultaneously or in succession.

Stimulus, conditioned. A stimulus that elicits a conditioned response because of its contingency with an unconditioned stimulus.

Stimulus, configurational. A definition of the stimulus in terms of the indivisible aggregation of stimulus elements into a whole.

Stimulus, discriminative. A stimulus that sets the occasion for some response to occur as a result of differential instrumental/operant conditioning.

Stimulus, drive. A hypothetical distinctive stimulus that arises in conjunction with a specific drive.

Stimulus, eliciting. A stimulus that reliably evokes a response either with or without training.

Stimulus, emotional. A stimulus that functions as a punisher or reinforcer either with or without training.

Stimulus, exteroceptive. A stimulus that originates from outside the organism.

Stimulus, informative. A stimulus that reduces uncertainty by reliably predicting the occurrence of an event.

Stimulus, interoceptive. A stimulus that originates within the organism.

Stimulus, maintaining. A stimulus that is associated with a state of the organism and, therefore, is not situation-specific or response-specific.

Stimulus, neutral. A stimulus that has no emotional significance to an organism.

Stimulus, postresponse-time. Theoretically, a stimulus that is correlated with events that change as a function of the passage of time since the last response.

Stimulus, proprioceptive. A stimulus that is produced by the response and that produces information regarding response occurrence in terms of proprioception.

Stimulus, redundant. A stimulus that conveys no new information or only information already known to the organism.

Stimulus, reinforcing. A stimulus whose presentation leads to an increase in the future probability of responses that preceded the presentation.

Stimulus, relational. A definition of the stimulus in terms of the qualitative and quantitatiave properties of an event relative to those of other events in the situation.

Stimulus, response-produced (feedback). A stimulus that is produced by the response and that produces information regarding response occurrence in terms of proprioception and kinesthetics and in terms of response-dependent changes in the exteroceptive environment.

Stimulus, safety. A stimulus that signifies that an impending aversive event has been delayed or omitted.

Stimulus, time-dependent. Theoretically, a stimulus that is correlated with events that change as a function of the passage of time since the last stimulus or response.

Stimulus trace. A hypothetical construct referring to events occurring in the organism when stimulated and that persist for a finite time after the stimulus is removed.

Stimulus, unconditioned. A stimulus that elicits an unconditioned response without training.

Stimulus, warning. A stimulus that signifies that an aversive event is imminent.

System, empirical. An integrated set of laws and principles that, collectively, lead to implications about the domain of interest.

System, hypothetico-deductive. A theoretical system that uses hypothetical constructs and is stated in a form suitable for derivations by the use of formal logic.

System, mathematico-deductive. An empirical system that uses hypothetical concepts and is stated in a mathematical form suitable for deductions by the use of formal logic.

System, second signal. A term that refers to the use of words as a source of stimulation to guide adaptive behavior.

System, theoretical. An integrated set of postulates, involving hypothetical constructs, that leads to implications about the domain of interest.

Theorem. An inference from the principles in a system that is used in drawing further implications from the system.

Theory, reductive. A reductive theory postulates hypothetical constructs that involve molecular determinants of empirical observations.

Transfer. The general effect of learning in one situation that influences learning and performance in another situation.

Transitional behavior. Any changes in behavior that accompany a sustained explicit operational change in the environment.

Transitional behavior, differential. Any changes in behavior that accompany a sustained, explicit operational change in the environment that is accompanied by a concomitant change in the exteroceptive antecedent-stimulus situation.

Transitional behavior, nondifferential. Any changes in behavior that accompany a sustained, explicit operational change in the environment that is not accompanied by a concomitant change in the exteroceptive antecedent-stimulus situation.

Transposition. Responding to a new set of stimuli on the basis of the relationships among them that have been acquired from experience with other similar sets of stimuli.

Two-stage theory. Any theoretical approach that proceeds by stages where the second stage is dependent on the occurrence of the first stage. Two-stage theory may or may not involve dual-process theory.

Uniprocess. The position that an experimental or theoretical phenomenon occurs as a result of a single process.

Varied reinforcement effect on extinction. The empirical generalization that subsequent resistance to extinction is greater when reinforcer conditions are varied than when the reinforcer condition is held constant at the preferred condition.

NOTE ON THE BIBLIOGRAPHY

In order not to interrupt the text too extensively, we have not attempted to list in the separate chapters all of the relevant references that pertain to the various topics. Instead, we have indicated illustrative references as an aid to the reader who is interested in reading selected originals. However, we have included in the bibliography a considerably more extensive listing in the hope that doing so would increase the value of the bibliography for systematic analyses. To accomplish this goal, we have used a simple reference system. The first number in each of the following listings indicates the chapter in this book to which the reference can apply most directly. (Since many of the references are relevant to several chapters, we have indicated only the first of these.) Following the chapter number is a page number when explicit reference was made in the text (again, the first where there are more than one), and a plus sign indicates that an abstract is given at the end of that chapter.

In order to list an extensive bibliography in a reasonable space, we have adopted an unorthodox format, which is also very convenient to use for locating references. First, we list the last name of the first author, and his or her initials without spaces. If there is one coauthor, that person's last name is listed; if there are several coauthors, we have simply listed an "etal". These rules enable authorship to be given in the limited space provided so that the goal of listing the entire reference on a single line of type is accomplished.

We have similarly been constrained to use abbreviations and various shortenings of the complete titles of articles, but the critical terms are included so that the substance of the title is captured within the available space. In the case of chapters that are contained in an edited volume, the last name of the first editor is given in parentheses, and the book itself can then be found under the name of the editor. This arrangement permits all of the titles to begin in the same column and, with this format, it is easy to scan for titles of interest.

We have adopted abbreviations for the professional journals and a listing of these is provided before the bibliography proper. Most of these will be familiar to the reader, since they are commonly employed informally. The year of publication (with the "19" omitted) appears in the same columns for all references and, in the case of books, an abbreviated indication of the publisher follows. A list of these abbreviations is also provided before the bibliography proper. For journal articles, we have provided the volume number preceding a shilling (slash mark) with the number of the first page of the article following.

Although this format will require a bit of "getting used to," we have found it an exceptionally convenient one for most practical purposes. To be sure, a certain amount of information is lost in the contractions required, but everything that is necessary in a bibliography for identifying and locating relevant references is retained.

JOURNAL ABBREVIATIONS

ABEX	ACTA BIOLOGICA EXPERIMENTALIS
AJPH	AMERICAN JOURNAL OF PHYSICS
AL+B	ANIMAL LEARNING AND BEHAVIOR
AMJP	AMERICAN JOURNAL OF PSYCHOLOGY
AMP	AMERICAN PSYCHOLOGIST
AMSC	AMERICAN SCIENTIST
ANB	ANIMAL BEHAVIOR
ARPH	ANNUAL REVIEW OF PHILOSOPHY
ARVP	ANNUAL REVIEW OF PSYCHOLOGY
AUJP	AUSTRALIAN JOURNAL OF PSYCHOLOGY
BEH	BEHAVIOUR
BLPS	BULLETIN OF THE PSYCHONOMIC SOCIETY
BJP	BRITISH JOURNAL OF PSYCHOLOGY
BSC	BEHAVIOR SCIENCE
CD	CHILD DEVELOPMENT
CEAB	CONFERENCE ON THE EXPERIMENTAL ANALYSIS OF BEHAVIOR
CJP	CANADIAN JOURNAL OF PSYCHOLOGY
CPMG	COMPARATIVE PSYCHOLOGY MONOGRAPHS
HEDR	HARVARD EDUCATIONAL REVIEW
H+B	HORMONES AND BEHAVIOR
QJEP	QUARTERLY JOURNAL OF EXPERIMENTAL PSYCHOLOGY
JABP	JOURNAL OF ABNORMAL PSYCHOLOGY
JASP	JOURNAL OF ABNORMAL AND SOCIAL PSYCHOLOGY
JEAB	JOURNAL OF THE EXPERIMENTAL ANALYSIS OF BEHAVIOR
JEXP	JOURNAL OF EXPERIMENTAL PSYCHOLOGY
JCP	JOURNAL OF COMPARATIVE PSYCHOLOGY
JCPP	JOURNAL OF COMPARATIVE AND PHYSIOLOGICAL PSYCHOLOGY
JGNP	JOURNAL OF GENERAL PSYCHOLOGY
JGTP	JOURNAL OF GENETIC PSYCHOLOGY
JP	JOURNAL OF PSYCHOLOGY
JPER	JOURNAL OF PERSONALITY
JPH	JOURNAL OF PHILOSOPHY
JPSP	JOURNAL OF PERSONALITY AND SOCIAL PSYCHOLOGY
JSP	JOURNAL OF SOCIAL PSYCHOLOGY
L+M	LEARNING AND MOTIVATION
NYAS	NEW YORK ACADEMY OF SCIENCES
PHB	PHYSIOLOGY AND BEHAVIOR
PHRV	PHILOSOPHICAL REVIEW
PHSC	PHILOSOPHY OF SCIENCE
PBL	PSYCHOLOGICAL BULLETIN
PL+M	PSYCHOLOGY OF LEARNING AND MOTIVATION
PMG	PSYCHOLOGICAL MONOGRAPHS
P+MS	PERCEPTUAL AND MOTOR SKILLS
PMTK	PSYCHOMETRIKA
PNAS	PROCEEDINGS OF NATIONAL ACADEMY OF SCIENCE
PNMG	PSYCHONOMIC MONOGRAPHS
P+P	PERCEPTION AND PSYCHOPHYSICS
PRC	PSYCHOLOGICAL RECORD
PRP	PSYCHOLOGICAL REPORTS
PRV	PSYCHOLOGICAL REVIEW
PSC	PSYCHONOMIC SCIENCE
SC	SCIENCE
SCAM	SCIENTIFIC AMERICAN
SCM	SCIENTIFIC MONTHLY
UCPP	UNIVERSITY OF CALIFORNIA PUBLICATIONS IN PSYCHOLOGY
VLVB	JOURNAL OF VERBAL LEARNING AND VERBAL BEHAVIOR

PUBLISHER ABBREVIATIONS

A+B	BOSTON--ALLYN AND BACON
ACAD P	NEW YORK--ACADEMIC PRESS
ALDINE	CHICAGO--ALDINE
A-C	NEW YORK--APPLETON-CENTURY
A-C-C	NEW YORK--APPLETON-CENTURY-CROFTS
BASIC	NEW YORK--BASIC BOOKS
B-COLE	BELMONT--BROOKS-COLE
CENTRY	NEW YORK--CENTURY
CHANDL	SCRANTON--CHANDLER
COLMBA	NEW YORK--COLUMBIA UNIVERSITY PRESS
CROFTS	NEW YORK--CROFTS
DALHSE	DALHOUSIE--DALHOUSIE UNIVERSITY PRESS
DUKE	DURHAM--DUKE UNIVERSITY PRESS
LERLBA	HILLSDALE--LARRY ERLBAUM ASSOCIATES
FREEMN	SAN FRANCISCO--FREEMAN
G/S	NEW YORK--GRUNE AND STRATTON
H-B	NEW YORK--HARCOURT-BRACE
H-M	BOSTON--HOUGHTON MIFFLIN
HARPER	NEW YORK--HARPER
HARVRD	CAMBRIDGE--HARVARD UNIVERSITY PRESS
HOLDEN	SAN FRANCISCO--HOLDEN
H-DAY	SAN FRANCISCO--HOLDEN-DAY
HOLT	NEW YORK--HOLT
H+ROW	NEW YORK--HARPER AND ROW
H-R-W	NEW YORK--HOLT, RINEHART, AND WINSTON
KNOPF	NEW YORK--KNOPF
LIPPIN	PHILADELPHIA--LIPPINCOT
LIVERT	NEW YORK--LIVERIGHT
MACMIL	NEW YORK--MACMILLAN
MARKHM	CHICAGO--MARKHAM
MCG-H	NEW YORK--MCGRAW-HILL
METHUN	LONDON--METHUEN AND COMPANY
MIAMI	MIAMI--MIAMI UNIVERSITY PRESS
PENGN	BALTIMORE--PENGUIN PRESS
P-HALL	ENGLEWOOD CLIFFS--PRENTICE-HALL
RONALD	NEW YORK--RONALD
S-F	GLENVIEW--SCOTT-FORESMAN
STANFD	STANFORD--STANFORD UNIVERSITY PRESS
U CHI	CHICAGO--UNIVERSITY OF CHICAGO PRESS
U MICH	ANN ARBOR--UNIVERSITY OF MICHIGAN PRESS
U NEBR	LINCOLN--UNIVERSITY OF NEBRASKA PRESS
U SCAL	LOS ANGELES--UNIVERSITY OF SOUTHERN CALIFORNIA PRESS
U WISC	MADISON--UNIVERSITY OF WISCONSIN PRESS
WILEY	NEW YORK--WILEY
W.C.B.	DUBUQUE--WILLIAM C. BROWN
YALE	NEW HAVEN--YALE UNIVERSITY PRESS

BIBLIOGRAPHY

```
4-      ABEND,R.                      SEC REINF VS EXPLOR DRIVE          PSC  67  7/163
9-      ABORDO,E.J.RUMBAUGH           R-CONTINGENT LEARNING SET          PRP  65 16/797
8-      ADAMS,D.L.ALLEN               COMPOUND STIM CONTROL AND R RATE   JEAB 71 16/201
7-277   AIKEN,E.G.                    EFFORT VARIABLE IN INSTRU RESPONSE JEXP 57 53/ 47
9-      ALBERTS,E.EHRENFREUND         AGE OF CHILDREN AND TRANSPOSITION  JEXP 51 41/ 30
7-      ALLISON,J.                    TIME SPENT IN THE GOAL BOX         PSC  67  7/165
6-      ALLISON,J.ETAL                BRIGHTNESS PREFER/SHUTTLE PERFORM  PSC  67  8/269
8-      AMES,L.L.YARCZOWER            WAVELENGTH DISCRIM ON STIM GEN     PSC  65  3/311
5-      AMSEL,A.                      ANXIETY AND CONSUMMATORY RESPONSE  JEXP 50 40/709
7-      AMSEL,A.                      THREE-FACTOR THEORY OF INHIBITION  AMP  51  6/487
8-      AMSEL,A.                      DURATION OF DISCRIMINANDA          JCPP 52 45/341
7-278   AMSEL,A.                      ROLE OF FRUSTRATIVE NONREWARD      PBL  58 55/102
7+278   AMSEL,A.                      FRUSTRATION IN PARTIAL REINF       PRV  62 69/306
7-278   AMSEL,A.                      PARTIAL REINFORCEMENT ON VIGOR     PL+M 67  1/  2
7-278   AMSEL,A.                      FRUSTRATION + REGRESSION (KIMMEL)       71 ACAD P
8-      AMSEL,A.                      INHIBITION IN DISCRIM (KENDLER)         71 A-C-C
9-389   AMSEL,A.ROSHOTTE             SLOW RESP PATTERNS IN EXTINCTION   JCPP 69 69/185
7-279   AMSEL,A.ROUSSEL               MOTIV PROPERTIES OF FRUSTRATION    JEXP 52 43/363
9-      AMSEL,A.WARD                  EXPERIENCE WITH DISCRIMINANDUM     PMG  65 79/  4
7-      AMSEL,A.ETAL                  PARTIAL REINF WITHIN/BETWEEN SUBJ  PMG  66 80/628
7-      AMSEL,A.ETAL                  PARTIAL REINF AFTER MINIMAL ACQ    JEXP 68 77/530
8-      AMSEL,A.ETAL                  TRIAL SEQUENCE AT 24-HR ITI        PSC  69 15/119
7-      AMSEL,A.ETAL                  PARTIAL REINF AFTER EXTENDED REINF JEXP 69 82/578
9-      ANDERSON,A.C.                 TIME DISCRIMINATION IN THE RAT     JCP  32 13/ 27
6-      ANDERSON,D.C.ETAL             PRESHOCK EFFECTS ON PUNISHMENT     PMG  68 65/  3
7-      ANDERSON,N.H.                 RESIST EXTINCTION AND TRANSFER     PRV  63 70/162
7-      ANDERSON,N.H.GRANT            CHOICE WITH DOUBLE STIM ELEMENTS   JEXP 57 54/305
4-132   ANDERSSON,B.LARSSON           HYPOTHALAMIC POLYDIPSIA COND       ABEX 56 36/377
4-      ANDRONICO,M.P.FORGAYS         SENSORY STIM AND SECONDARY REINF   JP   52 54/209
2-      ANGELL,J.R.                   STRUCTURAL AND FUNCTIONAL PSYCH    PHRV 03 12/243
2-      ANGELL,J.R.                   BEHAVIOR AS A CATEGORY OF PSYCH    PRV  13 20/255
6+225   ANGER,D.                      TEMPORAL DISCRIM IN SIDMAN AVOID   JEAB 63  6/477
9-      ANGERMEIER,W.F.ETAL           REARING ON DISCRIM LRNG IN MONKEYS PSC  67  8/379
7-      APPEL,J.B.                    AVERSIVE CONTROL OF OPERANT DISC   JEAB 60  3/ 35
6-239   APPEL,J.B.PETERSON            EFFECT OF SHOCK INTENSITY          PRP  65 16/721
7-277   APPLEZWEIG,M.H.               FUNCTION OF EFFORT ON RESPONDING   JCPP 51 44/225
9-      ARMUS,H.L.                    DRIVE LEVEL AND HABIT REVERSAL     PRP  58  4/ 31
4-      ARMUS,H.L.GARLICH             SEC REINF AND SCHED PRIMARY REINF  JCPP 61 54/ 56
4-      ARMUS,H.L.SNIADOWSKI          STARTLE DECR AND SEC REINF STIM    PSC  66  4/175
4-      ARMUS,H.L.ETAL                PRIMARY REINF ON SECONDARY REINF   PRP  62 11/203
4-      ARMUS,H.L.ETAL                SEC REINF AND PRIMARY REINF SCHED  JCPP 64 57/313
4-      ARMUS,H.L.ETAL                SEC REINF STIM ON AUDITORY STARTLE PRP  64 14/535
2-      ARNOLD,W.J. (ED)              NEBRASKA SYMPOSIUM ON MOTIVATION        69 U NEBR
7-      ASHIDA,S.BIRCH                TRAINING ON INCENTIVE SHIFT        PSC  64  1/201
8-      ATKINSON,R.C.ESTES            STIMULUS SAMPLING THEORY (LUCE)         63 WILEY
4-126   AYRES,J.J.B.                  CONDITIONED SUPPRESSION AND INFORM JCPP 66 62/ 21
6+239   AZRIN,N.H.                    IMMED AND NONIMMEDIATE PUNISHMENT  JP   56 42/  3
6-239   AZRIN,N.H.                    PUNISHMENT INTENSITY AND VI REINF  JEAB 60  3/123
6+212   AZRIN,N.H.                    TIME-OUT FROM REINFORCEMENT        SC   61 33/382
6+215   AZRIN,N.H.HAKE                POSITIVE CONDITIONED SUPPRESSION   JEAB 69 12/167
6-100   AZRIN,N.H.HOLZ                PUNISHMENT (HONIG)                      66 A-C-C
8-      BABB,H.                       PROPORTIONAL REINF OF IRRELEVANT S JCPP 56 49/586
8-      BABB,H.                       STIMULUS COMPLEX TO COMPONENTS     JCPP 57 50/288
9-      BACON,H.R.ETAL                NON-SPATIAL REVERSAL IN CHICKENS   ANB  62 10/239
7-      BACON,W.E.                    PARTIAL REINF/AMOUNT OF TRAINING   JCPP 62 55/998
7-      BACON,W.E.                    RESIST EXTINCTION AFTER BLOCKING   JEXP 65 69/515
4-      BADDELEY,A.D.                 SEC REINF FOR WRONG RESPONSE       AMJP 60 73/454
7-      BADIA,P.                      EFFECTS OF CHANGE OF SCHEDULE      JEXP 65 70/559
8-      BAILEY,C.J.                   EFFECTIVENESS OF DRIVES AS CUES    JCPP 55 48/183
```

9-	BAIRD,J.C.BECKNELL	EARLY FORM EXPOSURE ON DISCRIM	PRC	62	12/309
9-	BAKER,R.A.LAWRENCE	SIMULT/SUCCESSIVE TRANSPOSITION	JCPP	51	44/378
8-	BAKER,T.W.	COMPONENTS OF COMPOUND CS	PBL	68	70/611
8-	BAKER,T.W.	COMPONENT STRENGTH AND NO. TRIALS	JEXP	69	79/347
9-390	BALLACHEY,E.L.BUEL	CENTRIFUGAL SWING IN A MAZE	JCP	34	17/201
9-403	BANDURA,A.WALTERS	SOCIAL LRNG, PERSONALITY DEVEL		63	H-R-W
9-	BARGE,E.M.DOAN	CONDITIONAL DISCRIMINATION LRNG	PSC	69	15/161
6-220	BARLOW,J.A.	SECONDARY MOTIVATION	AMP	52	7/273
4-	BARLOW,J.A.	SEC MOTIVATION THRU CLASSICAL COND	PRV	56	63/406
1-	BARLOW,J.A.	STIMULUS AND RESPONSE		68	H-R
4-	BARNES,G.W.BARON	EFFECT SENSORY REINF ON EXTINCTION	JCPP	61	54/461
6-	BARON,A.ETAL	DELAY OF PUNISHMENT OF AVOIDANCE	JEAB	69	12/029
8-	BARON,M.R.	STIM CONTROL/GENERALIZ (MOSTOFSKY)		65	STANFD
7-	BARRET,R.J.ETAL	COMPLETE/INCOMPLETE REWARD REDUCT	PSC	65	3/277
4-107	BARRY,H.III	STRENGTH OF DRIVE ON LEARNING	JEXP	58	55/473
8-	BARRY,H.III.ETAL	DISCRIM ALCOHOL AND NONDRUG COND	PRP	65	16/072
9-	BAUER,F.J.LAWRENCE	CHOICE POINT/GOAL CUES ON DISCRIM	JCPP	53	46/241
6-	BAUM,M.	R PREVENTION/AVOIDANCE EXTINCTION	PRP	66	18/ 59
6-	BAUM,M.	AVOIDANCE EXTINCTION/R PREVENTION	PBL	70	74/276
4-	BAUM,W.M.	CORRELATION-BASED LAW OF EFFECT	JEAB	73	20/137
9-	BAUM,W.M.RACHLIN	CHOICE AS TIME ALLOCATION	JEAB	69	12/861
1+ 11	BEACH,F.A.	DESCENT OF INSTINCT	PRV	55	63/401
1+ 11	BEACH,F.A.	SEXUAL ATTRACTIVITY IN FEMALES	H+B	76	7/105
9-	BEALE,I.L.	AMOUNT OF TRAINING PER REVERSAL	JEAB	70	14/345
9-	BECK,C.H.ETAL	OVERTRAINING AND REVERSAL	JCPP	66	62/332
4-116	BECK,R.C.	SEC REINF AND SHOCK TERMINATION	PBL	61	58/ 28
9-	BECKER,G.M.	SUBJECTIVE PROBABILITY AND UTILITY	PRV	62	69/136
8-	BEECROFT,R.S.	GSR EXTINCTION AFTER DIFF REINF	PSC	65	3/ 61
8-	BEER,B.VALENSTEIN	TONE DISCRIM WITH REINF BRAIN STIM	SC	60	32/297
8-	BEERY,R.G.	NEG CONTRAST AND DELAY OF REWARD	JEXP	68	77/429
9-	BEHAR,I.	OBJECT ALTERNATION LEARNING	JCPP	61	54/539
9-	BEHAR,I.	CUES IN LEARNING SET FORMATION	PRP	62	11/479
9-	BEHAR,I.	POS/NEG CUES IN DISCRIM LEARNING	JCPP	62	55/502
9-	BEHREND,E.R.BITTERMAN	PROBABILITY MATCHING IN THE FISH	AMJP	61	64/542
9-	BEHREND,E.R.ETAL	HABIT REVERSAL IN THE FISH	JCPP	65	60/407
6-208	BEKHTEREV,V.M.	HUMAN REFLEXOLOGY		32	INTN P
7-	BENEFIELD,R.ETAL	FRUSTRATION AND POSITIVE CONTRAST	JCPP	74	86/648
8-	BENINGER,R.J.	POS CONTRAST OF REWARD QUALITY	PSC	62	29/307
9-	BERCH,D.B.	NOTE CONTINUITY THEORY REVISITED	PRV	71	78/260
7-	BERG,R.F.ETAL	INTERTRIAL REINFORCEMENT	PSC	69	15/ 37
2-	BERGMANN,G.	EMPIRICIST PHILOSOPHY OF PHYSICS	AJPH	43	11/248
2-	BERGMANN,G.	EMPIRICIST PHILOSOPHY OF PHYSICS	AJPH	43	11/335
2- 56	BERGMANN,G.	EMPIRICIST SYSTEM OF SCIENCES	SCM	44	/240
1-	BERGMANN,G.	THEORETICAL PSYCHOLOGY	ARPH	53	4/435
2-	BERGMANN,G.	CONTRIBUTIONS OF JOHN B. WATSON	PRV	56	63/265
2-	BERGMANN,G.	PHILOSOPHY OF SCIENCE		57	U WISC
2-	BERGMANN,G.SPENCE	OPERATIONISM AND THEORY IN PSYCH	PRV	41	48/ 1
4-	BERGUM,B.O.	GENERALIZATION IN SEC REINF	JEXP	60	59/ 47
1+ 10	BERKSON,G.	DELAYED RESP IN GIBBONS	JCPP	62	55/040
4-111	BERLYNE,D.E.	CONFLICT, AROUSAL, CURIOSITY		60	MCG-H
9-	BERNSTEIN,I.S.	VISUAL CUES IN ABSTRACT ODDITY	JCPP	61	54/243
8-	BERNHEIN,J.W.WILLIAMS	CONTRAST IN MULTIPLE SCHEDULE	JEAB	67	10/243
9-	BERRY,R.N.ETAL	REVERSAL DISCRIM IN SIMPLE RUNNING	JEXP	43	32/325
9-	BERRYMAN,R.ETAL	TRANSFER OF SIMULTANEOUS ODDITY	PRP	65	17/767
4-	BERSH,P.J.	SEC REINF FOR OPERANT RESPONSE	JEXP	51	41/ 62
8-	BESCH,N.F.ETAL	NONCORRECTION METHOD IN DRIVE DISC	PRP	62	11/246
8-	BESCH,N.F.ETAL	CORRECT/NONCORRECT AND DRIVE DISCR	JEXP	63	65/414
9-	BESSEMER,D.W.STOLLNITZ	RETENTION OF DISCRIM (SCHRIER)		71	ACAD P
7-	BEVAN,W.	MOTIV AND SOCIAL INTERACT (HARVEY)		63	RONALD
7+286	BEVAN,W.ADAMSON	REINFORCERS AND REINFORCEMENT	JEXP	60	59/226
9-	BIEDERMAN,G.B.	ORE AND NONMONOTONICITY OF S-	PSC	67	7/385
9-	BIEDERMAN,G.B.	REINF AND ITI ON DISCRIMINATION	PSC	67	8/215
8-	BIEDERMAN,G.B.	STIMULUS FUNCTION IN DISCRIM	JEAB	68	11/459

9-	BIEDERMAN,G.B.	CONTINUITY THEORY REVISITED	PRV	70 77/255
9-	BIEDERMAN,G.B.	CONTINUITY THEORY REVISITED	PRV	72 79/178
6-	BIEDERMAN,G.B.ETAL	FACIL AVOID BY DISSOCIATION OF CS	PSC	64 1/229
8-	BINDER,A.	COMPONENT AND PATTERN LEARNING	PSC	66 4/415
4-	BINDRA,D.	MECHANISMS OF REINF AND MOTIV		69 U NEBR
1-	BINDRA,D.	CLASSICAL/OPERANT COND (BLACK)		72 A-C-C
5+191	BINDRA,D.	MOTIVATIONAL VIEW OF LEARNING	PRV	74 81/199
8-	BINDRA,D.MOSCOVITCH	ATTENTION AND OBSERVING RESPONSE	PSC	65 3/223
8-	BIRCH,D.	REINF/NONREINF RATIO ON DISCRIM	JCPP	55 48/371
9-	BIRCH,D.	MOTIV SHIFT IN COMPLEX LEARNING	JEXP	58 56/507
7-	BIRCH,D.	MOTIV INTERP OF EXTINCTION (JONES)		61 U NEBR
9-	BIRCH,D.ETAL	REVERSAL OF SINGLE S PRESENTATION	JEXP	60 60/ 36
8-	BIRCH,D.ETAL	EXTINCTION FOLLOWING DISCRIM TRNG	JEXP	63 65/148
3-	BIRCH,H.G.BITTERMAN	REINF AND LRNG/SENSORY INTEGRATION	PRV	49 56/292
3-	BIRCH,H.G.BITTERMAN	SENSORY INTEGRATION/COGNITIVE TH	PRV	51 58/355
8-	BIRKIMER,J.C.	ELEMENTS OF COMPOUND DISCRIM STIM	JEAB	69 12/431
9-384	BITTERMAN,M.E.	SPENCE ON PATTERNING	PRV	53 60/123
9-	BITTERMAN,M.E.COATE	NATURE OF DISCIMINATION LEARNING	JCPP	50 43/198
8-	BITTERMAN,M.E.ELAM	DISCRIM AFTER NONDIFF REINF	AMJP	54 67/133
8-	BITTERMAN,M.E.MCCONNELL	SET IN SUCCESSIVE DISCRIMINATION	AMJP	54 67/129
9-385	BITTERMAN,M.E.WODINSKY	SIMULT/SUCCESSIVE DISCRIM	PRV	53 60/371
6-220	BITTERMAN,M.E.ETAL	EFFECTS OF US DURATION	AMJP	52 65/256
8-	BITTERMAN,M.E.ETAL	PERCEPTUAL DIFF AND NONDIFF REINF	JCPP	53 46/393
8-	BITTERMAN,M.E.ETAL	PERCEPT DIFF AND NONDIFF REINF/PUN	JCPP	53 46/475
4+120	BITTERMAN,M.E.ETAL	SEC REINF AND DISCRIM HYPOTHESIS	AMJP	53 66/456
9-	BITTERMAN,M.E.ETAL	SIMULTANEOUS/SUCCESSIVE DISCRIM	AMJP	55 68/237
6-	BLACK,A.H.	AUTONOMIC AVERSIVE COND. (BRUSH)		71 ACAD P
6-	BLACK,A.H.MORSE	AVOIDANCE WITHOUT A WARNING STIM	JEAB	61 4/ 17
5-	BLACK,A.H.PROKASY (EDS)	CLASSICAL COND II. RESEARCH/THEORY		72 A-C-C
5-	BLACK,A.H.ETAL	OPERANT COND OF AUTONOMIC (DAVIS)		77 LERLBA
5-	BLACK,R.W.	COMBINATION OF DRIVE AND INCENTIVE	PRV	65 72/310
7-284	BLACK,R.W.	SHIFTS IN REWARD MAGNITUDE	PRV	68 75/114
5-	BLACK,R.W.	INCENTIVE MOTIVATION (ARNOLD)		69 U NEBR
5-	BLACK,R.W.	REWARD IN INSTRUMENTAL COND	PL+M	76 10/199
7-291	BLACK,R.W.SPENCE	EFFECTS OF INTERTRIAL REINF	JEXP	65 70/ 59
6+214	BLACKMAN,D.	CONDITIONED SUPPRESSION BASELINE	JEAB	68 11/ 53
8-	BLAKESLEE,P.GUNTER	CROSS-MODAL TRANSFER OF DISCRIM	BEH	66 26/ 76
9-	BLANCHARD,E.B.YOUNG	SELF-CONTROL OF CARDIAC FUNCTION	PBL	73 79/145
9-	BLEHERT,S.R.	PATTERN DISC LRNG IN MONKEYS	PRP	66 19/311
3-	BLODGETT,H.C.MCCUTCHAN	PLACE VS RESPONSE LEARNING	JEXP	47 37/412
3-	BLODGETT,H.C.MCCUTCHAN	PLACE VS RESPONSE LEARNING	JCPP	48 41/ 17
1-	BLOOM,B.S.	TIME AND LEARNING	AMP	74 29/682
7-	BLOOM,J.M.CAPALDI	COMPLEX PATTERNS OF PARTIAL REINF	JCPP	51 54/261
7-	BLOOM,J.M.MALONE	SINGLE ALTERNATION PATTERNING	PSC	68 11/335
8-	BLOOMBERG,R.WEBB	DEGREE OF SINGLE DRIVE AND SPAT R	JEXP	49 39/628
8-	BLOOMFIELD,T.M.	TWO TYPES OF BEHAVIORAL CONTRAST	JEAB	66 9/155
8-	BLOOMFIELD,T.M.	CONTRAST AND REL REINF FREQUENCY	JEAB	67 10/151
8-	BLOOMFIELD,T.M.	PEAK SHIFT ON LINE TILT	JEAB	67 10/361
7-269	BLOOMFIELD,T.M.	BEH CONTRAST/PEAK SHIFT (GILBERT)		69 ACAD P
9-	BLOUGH,D.S.	DELAYED MATCHING IN PIGEON	JEAB	59 2/151
8-	BLOUGH,D.S.	DEF/MSMT IN STIM GEN (MOSTOFSKY)		65 STANFD
8-	BLOUGH,D.S.	ANIMAL SENSORY PROCESSES (HONIG)		66 A-C-C
8-	BLOUGH,D.S.	GENERALIZATION AS SIGNAL DETECTION	SC	67 58/940
8-	BLOUGH,D.S.	GRADIENT SHAPE AND SUMMATION	JEAB	69 12/ 91
8-	BLOUGH,D.S.	ATTENTION SHIFTS IN DISCRIMINATION	SC	69 66/125
8-	BLOUGH,D.S.	OPERANT GENERALIZATION/DISCRIM	ABP	75 04/ 3
9-	BLUM,R.A.BLUM	FACTUAL ISSUES IN CONTINUITY	PRV	69 56/ 33
8-	BOAKES,R.A.HALLIDAY (ED)	INHIBITION AND LEARNING		72 ACAD P
5-184	BOCK,R.D.JONES	JUDGMENT AND CHOICE		68 HOLDEN
6+239	BOE,E.E.CHURCH	PERMANENT EFFECTS OF PUNISHMENT	JCPP	67 63/486
6-	BOE,E.E.CHURCH	PUNISHMENT		68 A-C-C
9-	BOLLES,R.C.	REVERSAL IN HUNGRY/THIRSTY RATS	JCPP	58 51/349
4-	BOLLES,R.C.	IS THE CLICK A TOKEN REWARD	PRC	61 11/163

6+217	BOLLES,R.C.	THEORY OF MOTIVATION		67	H-ROW
6-226	BOLLES,R.C.	AVOIDANCE AND ESCAPE LEARNING	JCPP	69	68/355
6+215	BOLLES,R.C.	DEFENSE REACTIONS AND AVOID LEARN	PRV	70	77/ 32
6-	BOLLES,R.C.	SPECIES-SPECIFIC DEFENSE R (BRUSH)		71	ACAD P
5+192	BOLLES,R.C.	REINF, EXPECTANCY, + LEARNING	PRV	72	79/374
6-	BOLLES,R.C.	AVOIDANCE LEARNING PROBLEM	PL+M	72	6/ 97
1-	BOLLES,R.C.	LEARNING THEORY		75	H-R-W
9-	BOLLES,R.C.	LRNG/MOTIVATION/COGNITION (ESTES)		75	LERLBA
6-232	BOLLES,R.C.GROSSEN	INFORMATIONAL S ON AVOIDANCE LRNG	JCPP	69	68/ 90
6-	BOLLES,R.C.GROSSEN	CS IN SHUTTLE-BOX AVOIDANCE LRNG	JCPP	70	70/165
6-229	BOLLES,R.C.POPP	PARAMETERS OF SIDMAN AVOIDANCE	JEAB	64	7/315
6-227	BOLLES,R.C.ETAL	CS TERMINATION AND AVOIDANCE	JCPP	66	62/201
6-	BOLLES,R.C.ETAL	EXTINCTION OF SHUTTLEBOX AVOIDANCE	L+M	71	2/324
9-	BONEAU,C.A.COLE	DECISION THEORY AND PSYCHOPHYSICS	PRV	67	74/123
8-	BONEAU,C.A.HONIG	CONDITIONAL DISCRIMINATION TRAIN	JEXP	64	66/ 89
9-	BOOTH,J.H.HAMMOND	CONFIGURAL COND THRU OVERTRAINING	JEXP	71	87/255
7-	BOREN,J.J.	RESIST/EXTINCTION AND FR	JEXP	61	61/304
6-225	BOREN,J.J.SIDMAN	REPEATED COND/EXTINCT OF AVOIDANCE	JCPP	66	61/475
2-	BORING,E.G.	HISTORY OF EXPERIMENTAL PSYCHOLOGY		29	A-C
2-	BORING,E.G.	HISTORY OF EXPERIMENTAL PSYCHOLOGY		50	A-C-C
2-	BORING,E.G.	HISTORY OF INTROSPECTION	PBL	53	50/169
2-	BORING,E.G.	ROLE OF THEORY IN EXPER PSYCHOLOGY	AMJP	53	66/169
2-	BORING,E.G.LINDZEY	HISTORY OF PSYCH IN AUTOBIOGRAPHY		67	A-C-C
8-	BORN,D.G.ETAL	CONDITIONAL DISCRIMINATION LRNG	JEAB	69	12/119
8-	BORN,D.F.PETERSON	COMPONENTS OF COLOR-FORM COMPOUND	JEAB	69	12/437
8-	BORNSTEIN,M.H.	NOTE ON PEAK SHIFT	PBL	74	81/804
8-	BOWEN,J.STRICKERT	DISCRIM LRNG AND INTERNAL STIMULI	PSC	66	5/297
5-179	BOWER,G.H.	CHOICE POINT BEHAVIOR (BUSH)		59	STANFD
9-	BOWER,G.H.	SERIAL DISCRIM LEARNING (BUSH)		59	STANFD
7-284	BOWER,G.H.	A CONTRAST EFFECT IN DIFF COND	JEXP	61	62/196
9-	BOWER,G.H.	RESP STRENGTH AND CHOICE (NAGEL)		62	STANFD
4-	BOWER,G.H.	SEC REINF AND FRUSTRATION	PRP	63	12/359
4-114	BOWER,G.H.	COGNITIVE PSYCHOLOGY (ESTES)		75	LERLBA
8-	BOWER,G.H.GRUSEC	PAVLOV DISCRIM ON OPERANT DISCRIM	JEAB	64	7/401
8-	BOWER,G.H.KAUFMAN	TRANSFER ACROSS DRIVES OF DISCRIM	JEAB	63	6/445
8-	BOWER,G.H.TRABASSO	ATTENTION AND LEARNING		68	WILEY
8-	BOWER,G.H.TRAPOLD	REWARD MAG IN DIFF INSTR COND	JCPP	59	52/727
6-232	BOWER,G.ETAL	RESPONSE-PRODUCED CHANGE IN CS	JCPP	65	59/ 13
4-126	BOWER,G.ETAL	VALUE OF KNOWING REINF IS DUE	JCPP	66	62/184
9-	BOWMAN,R.E.	DISCRIM LRNG SET AND SEC REINF	JCPP	63	56/429
9-	BOYD,B.O.WARREN	SOLUTION OF ODDITY PROBLEM BY CATS	JCPP	57	50/258
9-	BOYER,W.N.CROSS	NUMBER OF TRIALS ON REVERSAL	PSC	65	2/139
9-	BOYER,W.N.ETAL	AMBIGUOUS CUE PROBLEMS IN MONKEYS	PMS	66	22/883
4-	BOYLE,R.E.	SECONDARY REINF AND PRE	JCPP	61	54/566
9-	BRACKBILL,Y.O-HARA	REWARD AND PUN ON DISCRIM IN CHILD	JCPP	58	51/747
7-	BRADLEY,H.W.WONG	EXTINCTION AND COMPETING RESPONSES	PSC	69	17/189
9-	BRADLEY,J.I.	PRESOLUTION TRIALS IN DISCRIM LRNG	PRP	61	8/155
2-	BRAITHWAITE,R.B.	SCIENTIFIC EXPLANATION		55	COLMBA
9-	BRAMEL,D.WARREN	RETENTION OF DISCRIM BY CATS	JGTP	60	96/241
4-106	BRANDAUER,C.M.	ACTION OF IRRELEVANT DRIVES	JEXP	53	45/150
6-	BRETHOWER,D.M.REYNOLDS	PUNISHMENT ON UNPUNISHED BEHAVIOR	JEAB	62	5/191
7-	BRETHOWER,D.M.REYNOLDS	FACILITATIVE EFFECT OF PUNISHMENT	JEAB	62	5/191
2- 40	BRIDGMAN,R.W.	LOGIC OF MODERN PHYSICS		56	MACMIL
4-	BROGDEN,W.J.	NON-ALIMENTARY ASPECTS OF FOOD RF	JEXP	42	3/326
6+223	BROGDEN,W.J.ETAL	INCENTIVE IN COND AND EXTINCTION	AMJP	38	51/109
9-	BRONSTEIN,P.SPEAR	SPATIAL DISCRIMINATION AND AGE	JCPP	72	78/208
7-	BROOKS,C.I.	FRUSTRATION AFTER LIMITED REINF	JEXP	69	81/403
7-	BROOKS,C.I.DUFORT	EXTINCTION AND AMOUNT OF REWARD	PSC	67	9/165
9-	BROOKSHIRE,K.H.ETAL	OVERTRAINING REVERSAL, RAT + CHILD	JCPP	61	54/ 98
8-	BROWN,B.L.	STIM GEN AND SALIVARY CONDITIONING	JCPP	70	71/467
9-	BROWN,H.ETAL	COMPLEX SPATIAL ARRANGEMENTS DISCR	P+MS	65	21/395
4-118	BROWN,J.L.	DRIVE ON LEARNING WITH SEC REINF	JCPP	56	49/254
6-	BROWN,J.S.	GRADIENTS OF APPROACH/AVOIDANCE	JCPP	48	41/450

4-	BROWN,J.S.	PLEASURE-SEEKING BEHAVIOR + DRIVE	PRV	55	62/169
4-	BROWN,J.S.	MOTIVATION OF BEHAVIOR		61	MCG-H
8-351	BROWN,J.S.	STIM GEN AND DISCRIM (MOSTOFSKY)		65	STANFD
6-	BROWN,J.S.	SELF-PUNITIVE LOCOMOTN (CAMPBELL)		69	A-C-C
6-216	BROWN,J.S.JACOBS	FEAR IN MOTIVATION AND ACQUISITION	JEXP	49	39/747
6-216	BROWN,J.S.ETAL	CONDITIONED FEAR AND STARTLE RESP	JEXP	51	41/317
5-352	BROWN,J.S.ETAL	BIDIRECTIONAL GRADIENTS OF R GEN	JEXP	51	41/ 52
8-352	BROWN,J.S.ETAL	SPATIAL GEN OF VOLUNTARY RESPONSE	JEXP	58	55/354
6+240	BROWN,J.S.ETAL	SELF-PUNITIVE BEHAVIOR	JCPP	64	57/127
7-	BROWN,P.L.JENKINS	CONDITIONED INHIB AND EXCITATION	JEXP	67	74/255
4-	BROWN,P.L.JENKINS	AUTOSHAPING PIGEONS KEYPECK	JEAB	68	11/ 1
5-161	BROWN,R.T.LOGAN	GENERALIZED PARTIAL REINF EFFECT	JCPP	65	60/ 64
7-	BROWN,R.T.WAGNER	RESISTANCE TO PUNISHMENT/EXTINCTN	JEXP	64	68/503
9-394	BROWN,W.L.DALRYMPLE	EFFECTS OF INTRA-MAZE DELAY	JCPP	51	44/604
4-	BROWN,W.L.HALAS	TERMINAL EXTINCTION IN MULT-T-MAZE	JGTP	57	90/ 89
9-	BROWN,W.L.MCDOWELL	RESPONSE SHIFT LRNG SET IN MONKEYS	JCPP	63	56/335
9-	BROWN,W.L.ETAL	NOVELTY LEARNING SETS	JCPP	59	52/330
9-	BROWN,W.L.ETAL	ABSOLUTE/RELATIVE INTERMED SIZE	AMJP	59	72/593
9-	BROWN,W.L.ETAL	TWO-TRIAL LEARNING SET FORMATION	JCPP	65	60/288
9-	BROWNSTEIN,A.	INSTR PERF/RATE OF RESP IN CHOICE	JEXP	62	63/ 29
5-418	BRUNSWICK,E.	BEHAVIOR DETERMINED BY PROBABILITY	JEXP	39	25/175
6-	BRUSH,F.R.	SHOCK INTENSITY AND AVOIDANCE	JCPP	57	50/547
6-224	BRUSH,F.R.	INTERTRIAL INTERVAL AND AVOIDANCE	JCPP	62	55/888
6-	BRUSH,F.R. (ED)	AVERSIVE CONDITIONING AND LEARNING		71	ACAD P
8-	BRUTKOWSKI,S.DABROWSKA	TEMPORAL FACTORS IN DIFF INST COND	ABEX	64	25/359
4-	BUCHANAN,G.N.	PUNISHMENT-ESCAPE EVENTS ON CHOICE	JCPP	58	51/355
4+120	BUGELSKI,B.R.	EXT WITH AND WITHOUT SUBGOAL REINF	JCP	38	26/121
4-120	BUGELSKI,B.R.	PSYCHOLOGY OF LEARNING		56	HOLT
9-	BULLOCK,D.H.BITTERMAN	HABIT REVERSAL IN THE PIGEON	JCPP	62	55/958
9-	BUNCH,M.E.	TRANSFER OF RATIONAL LRNG AND TIME	JCP	36	22/325
9-394	BUNCH,M.E.ETAL	MAZE LEARNING AND WAKEFULNESS	JCP	38	26/499
7-	BURT,D.H.WIKE	ALTERNATE PARTIAL/ALTERNATE DELAY	PRP	63	13/439
5-	BUSH,R.R.ESTES (EDS)	MATHEMATICAL LEARNING THEORY		59	STANFD
8-	BUSH,R.R.MOSTELLER	MODEL OF STIM GEN AND DISCRIM	PRV	51	58/413
2-	BUSH,R.R.MOSTELLER	STOCHASTIC MODELS FOR LEARNING		55	WILEY
9-	BUSS,A.H.	RIGIDITY IN REVERSAL/NONREVERSAL	JEXP	53	45/ 75
9-	BUSS,A.H.	STIM GENERALIZATION AND MATCHING	PRV	67	74/ 40
4+111	BUTLER,R.A.	VISUAL EXPLORATION MOTIVATION	JCPP	53	46/ 95
8-	BUTTER,C.M.	STIM GEN ALONG 1 AND 2 DIMENSIONS	JEXP	63	65/339
8-	BUTTER,C.M.	EFFECTIVE STIM FOR PATTERN DISCRIM	PSC	65	2/325
4-	BUTTER,C.M.THOMAS	SEC REINF AND AMOUNT PRIMARY REINF	JCPP	58	51/346
8-	BYRD,L.D.JACKSON	SECOND ORDER PATTERNS OF RESPONSE	JEAB	69	12/713
8-	BYRNE,D.WORCHEL (EDS)	PERSONALITY CHANGE		64	WILEY
9-	CAKMAK,M.B.SPEAK	DISCRIMINATION BETWEEN REWARDS	PSC	67	7/ 97
8-	CALVIN,A.D.	LRNG DURING NONDIFFERENTIAL REINF	JEXP	53	46/248
4-118	CALVIN,J.S.ETAL	SEC REINF AND CONSUMMATORY BEHAV	JCPP	53	46/176
6-239	CAMP,D.S.ETAL	TEMPORAL RELATION OF RESP AND PUN	JEXP	67	74/114
6-	CAMPBELL,B.A.CHURCH (ED)	PUNISHMENT AND AVERSIVE BEHAVIOR		69	A-C-C
5-	CAMPBELL,B.A.KRAELING	DRIVE LEVEL AND AMOUNT OF REWARD	JEXP	53	45/ 97
9-386	CAMPBELL,B.A.SHEFFIELD	RANDOM ACTIVITY AND DEPRIVATION	JCPP	53	46/320
3+ 69	CAMPBELL,D.T.	WHAT IS LEARNED VIA TRANSPOSITION	PRV	54	61/167
9-	CAMPBELL,D.T.	ADAPTIVE BEHAVIOR FROM RANDOM RESP	BSC	56	1/105
9-	CAMPBELL,D.T.KRAL	TRANSPOSITION, SHIFT IN BACKGROUND	JCPP	58	51/592
7-	CAMPBELL,P.E.ETAL	REGULAR AND IRREG PARTIAL REWARD	JCPP	70	72/210
7-	CAMPBELL,P.E.ETAL	SPACED-TRIALS REWARD EFFECTS	JCPP	72	81/360
9-	CAPALDI,E.J.	OVERLEARNING REVERSAL IN SPATIAL	P+MS	63	16/335
7-	CAPALDI,E.J.	N-LENGTH ON RESISTANCE TO EXTINCT	JEXP	64	68/230
7+271	CAPALDI,E.J.	HYPOTHESIS OF SEQUENTIAL EFFECTS	PRV	66	73/459
7-281	CAPALDI,E.J.	STIMULUS SPECIFICITY--NONREWARD	JEXP	66	72/410
7-296	CAPALDI,E.J.	SEQUENTIAL VARIABLES/PARTIAL REINF	JEXP	67	74/161
7-281	CAPALDI,E.J.	SEQUENTIAL HYPOTHESIS (SPENCE)		67	ACAD P
7-	CAPALDI,E.J.	ROLE OF REWARD MAG (REYNIERSE)		70	U NEBR
7-	CAPALDI,E.J.	SUCCESSIVE NEGATIVE CONTRAST	JEXP	72	96/433

7-287	CAPALDI,E.J.	PARTIAL/CONSISTANT REWARD ORDER	JEXP	74 02/954
7-	CAPALDI,E.J.CAPALDI	MAGNITUDE OF PARTIAL REWARD	JCPP	70 72/203
7-295	CAPALDI,E.J.DEUTSCH	PRE/LIMITED ACQUISITION TRAINING	PSC	67 9/171
7-	CAPALDI,E.J.HAGGBLOOM	RESP EVENTS AND ANIMAL MEMORY	AL+B	75 3/ 1
7-	CAPALDI,E.J.HART	PRE/SMALL AMOUNT OF TRAINING	JEXP	62 64/166
7-	CAPALDI,E.J.KASSOVER	SEQUENCE AND ITI IN EXTINCTION	JEXP	70 84/470
7-	CAPALDI,E.J.LYNCH	PATTERNING AT 24-HOUR ITI	PSC	66 6/229
7-288	CAPALDI,E.J.LYNCH	REPEATED SHIFTS IN REWARD MAG	JCPP	67 75/226
7-	CAPALDI,E.J.LYNCH	POST-REWARD MAGNITUDE AND EXTINCTN	JCPP	68 65/179
7-	CAPALDI,E.J.MINKOFF	SCHEDULE EFFECTS AT A LONG ITI	PSC	67 9/169
7-	CAPALDI,E.J.MINKOFF	ORDER OF LARGE AND SMALL REWARDS	JEXP	69 81/156
7-290	CAPALDI,E.J.POYNOR	AFTEREFFECTS AND DELAY OF REWARD	JEXP	66 71/ 80
9-	CAPALDI,E.J.SENKI	TRIALS/PROBLEM ON REVERSAL	PRP	61 8/227
7-	CAPALDI,E.J.SPIVEY	INTERTRIAL REINF AT 24-HR INTERVAL	PSC	64 1/181
7-	CAPALDI,E.J.SPIVEY	STIM CONSEQUENCES OF REINF	PSC	64 1/403
9-	CAPALDI,E.J.STEVENSON	REVERSAL AND AMOUNT OF TRAINING	JCPP	57 50/195
7-	CAPALDI,E.J.WARGO	N-R TRANSITIONS/SPACED TRIALS	JEXP	63 65/318
7-290	CAPALDI,E.J.WATERS	INTERPRETATION OF SMALL-TRIAL PHEN	JEXP	70 84/518
7-291	CAPALDI,E.J.WILSON	INTERTRIAL REINFORCEMENT	PSC	68 13/169
7-288	CAPALDI,E.J.ZIFF	SCHEDULE AND NEG CONTRAST EFFECT	JCPP	69 68/593
7-	CAPALDI,E.J.ETAL	SCHEDULE EFFECTS AFTER LIMITED ACQ	JEXP	68 78/521
7-	CAPALDI,E.J.ETAL	SUCCESSIVE ACQUISITION/EXTINCTION	JCPP	68 66/128
7-	CAPALDI,E.J.ETAL	ANTIC REWARD ON NONREWARD TRIALS	PSC	70 18/ 61
9-	CARLTON,P.L.	DISCRIMINATION LEARNING	SC	59 30/341
2-	CARNAP,R.	TESTABILITY AND MEANING	PHSC	36 3/419
5-	CARR,H.A.	DISCUSSION OF LAW OF EFFECT	PRV	38 45/191
8-	CARR,R.M.BROWN	ASSOCIATION ALONG SPATIAL GRADIENT	JGTP	60 97/131
8-	CARTER,D.E.ETAL	CONTROL AUDITORY DISC BY VISUAL S	P+P	66 1/242
8-	CATANIA,A.C.	CONTRAST IN MULT/CONCURRENT SCHED	JEAB	61 4/335
8-	CATANIA,A.C.	INTEROCULAR TRANSFER OF DISCRIM	JEAB	65 8/147
9-	CATANIA,A.C.	CONCURRENT OPERANTS (HONIG)		66 A-C-C
8-	CATANIA,A.C.	REINF AND STIM CONTROL (GLASER)		71 ACAD P
4-	CATANIA,A.C.	SELF-INHIBITING EFFECTS OF REINF	JEAB	73 19/517
1-	CERMAK,L.S.	PSYCHOLOGY OF LEARNING		75 RONALD
6-	CHAMPION,R.A.	APPROACH-AVOIDANCE CONFLICT	PRV	61 68/354
8-	CHAMPION,R.A.SMITH	INCENTIVE MOTIVATION AND DIFF COND	AUJP	62 14/ 24
9-	CHAMPION,R.A.SMITH	AMOUNT OF REINF ON DISCRIM LRNG	JEXP	66 71/529
4-	CHAPMAN,R.F.CARLSON	GB CUES AND LATENT EXTINCTION	PRP	63 13/855
8-	CHASE,S.	MULTIDIMENSIONAL STIMULUS CONTROL	JCPP	68 66/787
9-	CHASE,S.HEINEMANN	CHOICES BASED ON REDUNDANT INFORM	JEXP	72 92/161
9-	CHISAR,D.A.SPEAR	PROACTIVE INTERFERENCE IN T-MAZE	PSC	68 11/107
8-	CHISUM,G.T.	TRANSPOSITION AND NUMBER TRIALS	JCPP	65 59/419
9-	CHORAZYNA,H.KONORSKI	ABSOLUTE VS RELATIVE CUES	ANB	62 22/ 11
8-	CHRISTIE,R.	DRIVE DISCRIM AND IRRELEVANT MOTIV	JEXP	51 42/ 13
9-	CHUNG,S.H.HERRNSTEIN	CHOICE AND DELAY OF REINFORCEMENT	JEAB	67 10/ 67
6-235	CHURCH,R.M.	VARIED EFFECTS OF PUNISHMENT	PRV	63 70/369
6-235	CHURCH,R.M.	RESPONSE SUPPRESSION (CAMPBELL)		69 A-C-C
9-	CHURCH,R.M.CARNATHAN	DIFF REINF OF SHORT LATENCY RESP	JCPP	63 56/120
6-239	CHURCH,R.M.ETAL	INTENSITY/DURATION OF PUNISHMENT	JCPP	67 63/ 39
6-240	CHURCH,R.M.ETAL	DISCRIM PUNISH AND THE CER	L+M	70 1/ 1
4-	CLAYTON,F.L.	SEC REINF AND REINF SCHEDULING	PRP	56 2/377
4-	CLAYTON,F.L.	CUE STRENGTH AND COND REINF VALUE	PRP	62 10/231
4-	CLAYTON,F.L.SAVIN	SEC REINF AFTER CRF AND VR REINF	PRP	60 6/ 99
9-	CLAYTON,K.N.	FORCED TRIALS ON DISCRIM REVERSAL	JCPP	62 55/992
9-	CLAYTON,K.N.	SPATIAL OVERLEARNING AND REVERSAL	P+MS	63 17/ 83
9-	CLAYTON,K.N.	REWARD IN SELECTIVE LRNG (TAPP)		69 ACAD P
9-	CLAYTON,K.N.KOPLIN	REWARD PROBABILITY AND MAGNITUDE	PSC	64 1/381
9-	COATE,W.B.GARDNER	SOURCES OF TRANSFER IN REVERSAL	JEXP	65 70/ 94
5+169	COFER,C.N.APPLEY	MOTIVATION--THEORY AND RESEARCH		64 WILEY
2-	COHEN,M.R.NAGEL	LOGIC AND SCIENTIFIC METHOD		34 H-B
6-	COHEN,P.S.	DELAY AND INTENSITY OF PUNISHMENT	JEAB	68 11/789
9-	COLE,J.	DISCRIM REVERSALS IN MONKEYS	JCPP	51 44/467
9-	COLE,J.	IMPORT OF COLOR AND FORM IN DISCR	JCPP	53 46/ 16

2-	COLE,J.K. (ED)	NEBRASKA SYMPOSIUM ON MOTIVATION		72	U NEBR
8-	COLE,L.E.ETAL	S ORDER AND RATE ON COND DISCRIM	JGNP	42	26/ 35
9-	COLE,M.HOPKINS	PROACTIVE INTERFERENCE IN MAZE	PSC	68	10/365
8-	COLEMAN,S.T.ETAL	FADING IN CS- IN DIFF EYELID COND	PSC	65	3/467
7-	COLLIER,G.MARX	SHIFTS IN MAGNITUDE OF REINF	JEXP	59	57/305
7-	COLLIER,G.ETAL	RELATION OF CONSUM RESP AND REINF	JEXP	61	62/484
4-	COLLIER,G.H.ETAL	ECOLOGICAL DETERMINANTS OF REINF	PHB	72	9/705
2- 80	CONANT,J.B.	ON UNDERSTANDING SCIENCE		47	YALE
2-	COOMBS,C.H.	A THEORY OF DATA		64	WILEY
6-	COONS,E.E.ETAL	DISAPPEARANCE OF AVOIDANCE RESP	JCPP	60	53/290
4-	COPPOCK,H.W.	S PRECEDING SHOCK + POS SEC REINF	JCPP	54	47/109
4-	COPPOCK,H.W.CHAMBERS	INTRAVENOUS INJECTIONS OF GLUCOSE	JCPP	54	47/355
2-	COTTON,J.W.	ON MAKING PREDICTIONS FROM HULL	PRV	55	62/303
7-	COTTON,J.W.ETAL	VARYING NUMBER OF NONREWARD TRIALS	PSC	67	9/489
7-	COUGHLIN,R.C.	FRUSTRATION EFFECT AND EXTINCTION	JEXP	70	84/113
9-	COUTANT,L.W.WARREN	REVERSAL/NONREVERSAL CATS + RHESUS	JCPP	66	61/484
4-118	COWLES,J.T.	FOOD TOKENS FOR LEARNING BY CHIMP	CPMG	37	14/ 96
8-	COWLES,J.T.	PRE-DELAY REINF IN DELAYED RESP	PRV	41	48/225
9-	COWLES,J.T.FINAN	TEMPORAL DISCRIM IN RATS	JP	41	11/335
5-	COWLES,J.T.NISSEN	REWARD EXPECTANCY IN DELAYED RESP	JCP	37	24/345
8-	CRANFORD,J.L.CLAYTON	EXPOSURE ON COMPOUND DISCR LRNG	JCPP	70	71/497
9-	CRANNELL,C.W.	DISTRIBUTION OF RUNS ON INSIGHT	JP	40	9/311
4-131	CRAVENS,R.W.RENNER	CONDITIONED APPETITIVE DRIVE STATE	PBL	70	73/212
9-	CRAWFORD,F.T.	SPATIAL REVERSAL LRNG BY MONKEYS	JCPP	62	55/869
9-388	CRAWFORD,M.P.SPENCE	OBSERVATIONAL LEARNING OF DISCRIM	JCP	39	27/133
5+167	CRESPI,L.P.	QUANTITATIVE VARIATION/INCENTIVE	AMJP	42	55/457
5-167	CRESPI,L.P.	AMOUNT OF REINF AND PERFORMANCE	PRV	44	51/341
9-	CROSS,H.A.BOYER	OVERLEARNING ON HABIT REVERSAL	PSC	66	4/245
9-	CROSS,H.A.BROWN	TRIALS/EXPERIENCE ON REVERSAL	JCPP	65	59/429
9-	CROSS,H.A.TYER	ORE AND AGE OF PRESCHOOL CHILDREN	PSC	66	6/175
4-122	CROWDER,W.F.ETAL	SEC REINF/RESP FACIL ON EXTINCTION	JP	59	48/299
4-122	CROWDER,W.F.ETAL	SEC REINF/RESP FACIL ON ACQUISITN	JP	59	48/303
4-122	CROWDER,W.F.ETAL	SEC REINF/RESP FACIL ON RECOND	JP	59	48/307
4-122	CROWDER,W.F.ETAL	SEC REINF/RESP FACIL ON RETENTION	JP	59	48/311
7-290	CRUM,J.ETAL	DELAYED REINF ON RESISTANCE TO EXT	AMJP	51	64/228
8-	CUMMING,W.W.BERRYMAN	COMPLEX DISC OPERANT (MOSTOFSKY)		65	STANFD
8-	CUMMING,W.W.ECKERMAN	S CONTROL OF DIFFERENTIATED RESP	PSC	76	3/313
9-	DABROWSKA,J.	REVERSAL LEARNING AND COMPLEXITY	ABEX	62	22/139
2-	DALLENBACH,K.M.	PLACE OF THEORY IN SCIENCE	PRV	53	60/ 33
9-	DALRYMPLE,S.D.STRETCH	DISRUPTION OF REVERSAL LRNG SET	QJEP	66	18/250
6-	DALY,H.B.	ESCAPE FROM FRUSTRATION	PL+M	74	8/187
4-	D-AMATO,M.R.	DRIVE SHIFT AND SEC REINF	AMP	53	8/338
4-	D-AMATO,M.R.	SEC REINF AND MAG PRIMARY REINF	JCPP	55	48/378
4-118	D-AMATO,M.R.	TRANSFER SEC REINF HUNGER-THIRST	JCPP	55	49/352
9-	D-AMATO,M.R.	DISTRIBUTION VARIABLES IN DISCRIM	CJP	60	14/216
9-	D-AMATO,M.R.	TRANSFER BRIGHTNESS, BAR TO MAZE	JCPP	61	54/548
9-	D-AMATO,M.R.	SALIENT IRRELEVANT CUE ON ORE	PSC	65	3/ 21
9-	D-AMATO,M.R.	DELAYED MATCHING/SHORT TERM MEMORY	PL+M	73	7/227
7-273	D-AMATO,M.R.D-AMATO	PRE FOLLOWING PLACED TRIALS	JGNP	62	66/ 17
6-227	D-AMATO,M.R.FAZZARO	AVOIDANCE AND INTENSITY OF SHOCK	JCPP	66	61/313
8-	D-AMATO,M.R.FAZZARO	ATTENTION AND CUE-PRODUCING RESP	JEAB	66	9/469
8-	D-AMATO,M.R.JAGODA	EXTINCTION TRIALS ON DISC REVERSAL	JEXP	60	59/254
9-	D-AMATO,M.R.JAGODA	OVERLEARNING IN DISCRIM REVERSAL	JEXP	61	61/ 45
9-	D-AMATO,M.R.JAGODA	OVERLEARNING AND POSITION REVERSAL	JEXP	62	64/117
4-	D-AMATO,M.R.LACHMAN	SEC REINF, REWARD SCHED, TEST SIT	JCPP	58	51/737
9-	D-AMATO,M.R.SCHIFF	OVERLEARN ON BRIGHTNESS REVERSAL	JEXP	65	69/375
8-	D-AMATO,M.R.ETAL	EXTINCTION AFTER DISCRIM TRAINING	JEXP	62	64/526
6-	D-AMATO,M.R.ETAL	TYPE/INTENSITY OF SHOCK IN AVOID	JCPP	66	61/313
6+232	D-AMATO,M.R.ETAL	ANTICIPATORY R AND AVOID DISCRIM	JEXP	68	77/ 41
4-106	DANZIGER,K.	INTERACTION OF HUNGER AND THIRST	QJEP	53	5/ 10
9-	DARBY,C.L.RIOPELLE	OBSERVATIONAL LEARNING IN MONKEY	JCPP	59	52/ 94
4-	DAVENPORT,D.G.SARDELLO	INTERMITTENT REWARD AND SEC REINF	PSC	66	6/417
9-	DAVENPORT,J.W.	CHOICE AND SPEED IN DISCR REVERSAL	JCPP	59	52/349

5-179	DAVENPORT,J.W.	INTERACTION OF AMOUNT AND DELAY	JCPP	62	55/267
9-	DAVENPORT,J.W.	MAG OF REINF ON DISCRIM REVERSAL	PRP	63	12/655
9-	DAVENPORT,J.W.	PERCENT REINF ON DISCRIM REVERSAL	JCPP	63	56/038
6-	DAVIS,H.	RESPONSE DURING ESCAPE (DAVIS)		77	LERLBA
5-	DAVIS,H.HURWITZ (EDS)	OPERANT-PAVLOVIAN INTERACTIONS		77	LERLBA
6-	DAVIS,H.ETAL	SIGNALS BEFORE AND AFTER SHOCK	JEAB	72	17/277
9-	DAVIS,R.H.	SIMULTANEOUS/SUCCESSIVE DISCRIM	JCPP	57	50/207
9-	DAVIS,R.T.	POSITION PREFERENCES IN MONKEYS	JGTP	57	91/233
6-220	DAVITZ,J.R.	FEAR AT SHOCK BEGINNING AND END	JCPP	55	48/152
8-	DEARMOND,D.	MULTIPLE PUNISHMENT SCHEDULE	JEAB	66	9/327
1-	DEESE,J.	PSYCHOLOGY OF LEARNING (2ND ED)		58	MCG-H
1-	DEESE,J.HULSE	PSYCHOLOGY OF LEARNING (3RD ED)		67	MCG-H
4-	DELORGE,J.	FI BEHAVIOR MAINTAIN BY COND REINF	JEAB	67	10/271
1-	DEMBER,W.N.	MOTIVATION AND COGNITIVE REVOLUTN	AMP	64	29/161
1-	DEMBER,W.N.	THE NEW LOOK IN MOTIVATION	AMSC	64	53/409
9-390	DEMBER,W.N.FOWLER	SPONTANEOUS ALTERNATION BEHAVIOR	PBL	58	55/412
1+ 11	DEMENT,W.	EFFECT OF DREAM DEPRIVATION	SC	60	31/705
2-	DENNIS,W. (ED)	READINGS IN HISTORY OF PSYCHOLOGY		48	A-C-C
7+292	DENNY,M.R.	SEC REINF IN PARTIAL REINF SIT	JEXP	46	36/373
4-	DENNY,M.R.	DIFF END BOXES IN T-MAZE LRNG	JEXP	48	38/245
9-396	DENNY,M.R.	ELICITATION TH AND ORE (REYNEIRSE)		70	U NEBR
6-221	DENNY,M.R.	RELAXATION THEORY (BRUSH)		71	ACAD P
7-	DENNY,M.R.	THEORY OF EXTINCTION (KENDLER)		71	A-C-C
6+221	DENNY,M.R.WEISMAN	NON-SHOCK CONFINEMENT AND AVOID	JCPP	64	58/252
9-	DETERLINE,W.A.	OPERANT DISCRIMINATION REVERSAL	JEAB	60	3/247
8-	DEUTSCH,J.A.	DOUBLE DRIVE LEARNING IN RATS	QJEP	58	10/207
8-	DEUTSCH,J.A.	HULL-LEEPER DRIVE DISCRIMINATION	QJEP	59	11/155
1-	DEUTSCH,J.A.	STRUCTURAL BASIS OF BEHAVIOR		60	U CHI
9-	DEUTSCH,J.A.	DISCRIMINATION AND INHIBITION	SC	67	56/988
8-	DEUTSCH,J.A.BIEDERMAN	MONOTONICITY OF NEGATIVE STIMULUS	PSC	65	3/391
9-	DEUTSCH,J.A.CLARKSON	REASONING IN THE RAT	JEXP	59	61/150
8-	DEUTSCH,J.A.DEUTSCH	ATTENTION	PRV	63	70/ 80
1-	DEVILLIERS,P.HERRNSTEIN	LAW OF RESPONSE STRENGTH	PBL	76	83/131
2-	DEWEY,J.	REFLEX ARC CONCEPT IN PSYCHOLOGY	PRV	96	3/357
5-165	DICARA,L.V.MILLER	INSTRUMENTAL LRNG OF VASOMOTOR R	SC	68	59/485
4-	DICKSON,A.PEARCE	APPETITIVE/AVERSIVE INTERACTIONS	PBL	77	84/690
8-	DICKSON,J.F.THOMAS	OPERANT DISCRIM AND REINFORCEMENT	JCPP	63	56/829
7-288	DILOLLO,V.	INCENTIVE CHANGES AND PERFORMANCE	JCPP	64	58/327
7-	DILOLLO,V.BEIR	NEGATIVE CONTRAST EFFECT	PSC	66	5/ 99
4-125	DINSMOOR,J.A.	DISCRIM AND REINF FUNCTIONS OF S	JEXP	50	40/458
4-	DINSMOOR,J.A.	PR WITH DISCRIM STIM ON RESIST EXT	JCPP	52	45/ 31
8-	DINSMOOR,J.A.	HUNGER ON DISCRIMINATED RESPONDING	JASP	52	47/ 67
6+217	DINSMOOR,J.A.	PUNISHMENT--AVOIDANCE HYPOTHESIS	PRV	54	61/ 34
6-	DINSMOOR,J.A.	PUNISHMENT--EMPIRICAL FINDINGS	PRV	55	62/ 96
4-	DINSMOOR,J.A.CLAYTON	CHAINING/SEC REINF BASED ON SHOCK	JEAB	63	6/ 75
4-117	DINSMOOR,J.A.CLAYTON	COND REINF AND SHOCK TERMINATION	JEAB	66	9/547
4-	DINSMOOR,J.A.ETAL	REGULAR AND PERIODIC SEC REINF	JGTP	53	48/ 57
9-	DOBRZECKA,C.ETAL	QUAL VS DIRECTIONAL CUES IN DISCR	SC	66	53/ 87
3-	DODWELL,P.C.BESSANT	LEARNING W/OUT SWIMMING IN MAZE	JCPP	60	53/422
8-354	DOLLARD,J.MILLER	PERSONALITY AND PSYCHOTHERAPY		50	MCG-H
4-	DOLLARD,J.ETAL	FRUSTRATION AND AGGRESSION		39	YALE
8-.	DONOVICK,P.J.ROSS	REINF S- IN DIFF CONDITIONING	PRP	64	14/107
8-	DUFORT,R.H.ETAL	ONE-TRIAL DISCRIM REVERSAL	JCPP	54	47/248
6-	DULANY,E.JR	AVOID LRNG OF PERCEPTUAL DEFENSE	JASP	57	55/333
7-	DUNHAM,P.J.	INCENTIVE CONTRAST AND DEPRIVATION	JCPP	67	64/485
7-284	DUNHAM,P.J.	CONTRASTED CONDITIONS IN REINF	PBL	68	69/295
6-	DUNHAM,P.J.	PUNISHMENT--METHOD AND THEORY	PRV	71	78/ 58
7-	DUNHAM,P.J.MARX	FRUSTRATION--SUPPRESSION EFFECT	JCPP	67	63/ 45
8-	ECK,K.O.THOMAS	PRIOR DISCRIM AND NONDIFF REINF	JEXP	70	83/511
8-	ECKERMAN,C.O.	PROBABILITY OF REINF AND S CONTROL	JEAB	69	12/551
8-	ECKERMAN,D.A.	S CONTROL BY PART OF COMPLEX STIM	PSC	67	7/299
8-	EDWARDS,D.C.	PRIOR EXPERIENCE ON DIFF COND	PRP	66	18/343
5-185	EDWARDS,W.	THEORY OF DECISION-MAKING	PBL	54	51/380

9-	EDWARDS,W.	SUBJECTIVE PROBABILITY FROM CHOICE	PRV	62	69/109
8-	EGETH,H.	SELECTIVE ATTENTION	PBL	67	67/ 41
4+126	EGGER,M.D.MILLER	SEC REINF AND INFORMATION VALUE	JEXP	62	64/ 97
4-126	EGGER,M.D.MILLER	EXPER STUDY/INFORMATION HYPOTHESIS	JCPP	63	57/132
4-	EHRENFREUND,D.	PARTIAL REINF + SEC REINF STRENGTH	JP	48	37/241
9-380	EHRENFREUND,D.	CONTINUITY WITH PATTERN VISION	JCPP	48	41/408
4-	EHRENFREUND,D.	SEC REINF IN BLACK-WHITE DISCRIM	JCPP	49	42/ 1
9-383	EHRENFREUND,D.	THE TRANSPOSITION GRADIENT	JEXP	52	43/ 81
4-	EHRENFREUND,D.	GENERALIZATION OF SEC REINF	JCPP	54	47/311
7-	EHRENFREUND,D.	DRIVE/SUCCESSIVE MAGNITUDE SHIFTS	JCPP	71	76/418
7-	EHRENFREUND,D.BADIA	DRIVE AND INCENTIVE ON RESPONSE	JEXP	62	52/ 85
4-	EISENBERGER,R.	REWARDS THAT DO NOT REDUCE NEEDS	PBL	72	77/319
4-	EISENBERGER,R.ETAL	NEC AND SUFF CONDITIONS FOR REINF	JEXP	57	74/342
4-	ELAM,C.B.TYLER	SEC REINF IN NEW LEARNING SIT	AMJP	60	73/440
4-	ELAM,C.B.ETAL	SEC REINF AND DISCRIM HYPOTHESIS	JCPP	54	47/381
7-	ELLIS,D.J.	INHIBITION THEORY AND EFFECT	PRV	53	60/383
8-	ELLISON,G.D.	DIFF SALIVARY COND TO TRACES	JCPP	64	57/373
4-	ELLSON,D.G.	TOKEN REWARD HABIT IN DOGS	JCP	37	24/504
7-276	ELLSON,D.G.	RECOVERY FROM EXTINCTION	JEXP	38	23/339
9-	ENINGER,M.U.	HABIT SUMMATION IN SELECTIVE LRNG	JCPP	51	45/604
9-	ENINGER,M.U.	DURATION OF STIM AT TIME OF CHOICE	JEXP	51	41/440
9-	ENINGER,M.U.	GENERALIZED APPROACH/AVOID ON DISC	JCPP	53	46/398
8-	ERICKSON,C.K.	FACIL R IN DISCRIM AVOIDANCE SIT	PSC	67	8/ 37
9-	ERIKSEN,C.W.	CORRECTION PRACTICE ON DISCR LRNG	AMJP	58	71/350
9-	ERIKSEN,C.W.	DISCRIM LRNG WITHOUT AWARENESS	PRV	60	67/279
2-	ERIKSEN,C.W. (ED)	BEHAVIOR AND AWARENESS		62	DUKE
9-	ERLEBACHER,A.	REVERSAL AND PERCENT REINF	JEXP	63	66/ 84
1+ 10	ERON,L.D.ETAL	T.V. VIOLENCE AND AGGRESSION	AMP	72	27/253
8-	ESPOSITO,N.J.	DISCRIM SHIFT LRNG IN YOUNG CHILD	PBL	75	82/432
8-	ESTES,W.K.	CONDITIONED ANTICIPATION AS DISCR	JEXP	43	32/150
6+265	ESTES,W.K.	EXPERIMENTAL STUDY OF PUNISHMENT	PMG	44	57/263
8-	ESTES,W.K.	PAVLOVIAN CS ON OPERANT	JEXP	48	38/173
4+118	ESTES,W.K.	MOTIV COND NECESSARY FOR SEC REINF	JEXP	49	39/306
4-	ESTES,W.K.	GENERALIZ SEC REINF FROM PRIMARY D	JCPP	49	42/286
7-273	ESTES,W.K.	STATISTICAL THEORY OF LEARNING	PRV	50	57/ 94
2-	ESTES,W.K. (ED)	MODERN LEARNING THEORY		54	A-C-C
7-	ESTES,W.K.	STAT THEORY, SPONTANEOUS RECOVERY	PRV	55	62/145
2-	ESTES,W.K.	OF MODELS AND MEN	AMP	57	12/609
4-	ESTES,W.K.	S-R THEORY OF DRIVE (JONES)		58	U NEBR
8-324	ESTES,W.K.	STATISTICAL APPROACH (KOCH)		59	MCG-H
2-	ESTES,W.K.	LRNG THEORY/NEW MENTAL CHEMISTRY	PRV	60	67/207
9-	ESTES,W.K.	ALL-OR-NONE PROCESSES IN LEARNING	AMP	64	19/ 16
5+193	ESTES,W.K.	THEORY OF PUNISHMENT (CAMPBELL)		69	A-C-C
5-169	ESTES,W.K.	ISSUES IN ASSOC TH (MACKINTOSH)		69	DALHSE
1-	ESTES,W.K. (ED)	HANDBOOK/LEARNING + COG. PROC.		75	LERLBA
9-421	ESTES,W.K.	STATE OF FIELD OF LEARNING (ESTES)		75	LERLBA
8-	ESTES,W.K.BURKE	THEORY OF STIMULUS VARIABILITY	PRV	53	60/276
9-	ESTES,W.K.HOPKINS	PATTERN VS COMPONENT DISCRIM LRNG	JEXP	61	61/322
6+213	ESTES,W.K.SKINNER	QUANT PROPERTIES OF ANXIETY	JEXP	41	29/390
1-	ESTES,W.K.ETAL	MODERN LEARNING THEORY		54	A-C-C
9-	ESTES,W.K.ETAL	PROBABILISTIC DISCRIMINATION LRNG	JEXP	57	54/233
9-	ESTES,W.K.ETAL	ALL-OR-NONE EFFECTS OF LEARNING	JEXP	60	60/329
9-	ETTLINGER,G.	CROSS-MODAL TRANSFER IN MONKEYS	BEH	60	16/ 56
8-	EVANS,S.	FLEXIBILITY OF ESTABLISHED HABITS	JGNP	36	14/177
4-	EVANS,W.O.	POS/NEG TEND TO S ASSOC WITH SHOCK	JEAB	62	5/335
6-227	FANTINO,E.	AVERSIVE CONTROL (NEVIN)		73	S-F
9-	FANTINO,E.NAVARICK	RECENT DEVELOPMENTS IN CHOICE	PL+M	74	8/147
8-	FARTHING,G.W.	SIGNAL FOR FREE FOOD ON OPERANT	PSC	61	23/343
8-	FARTHING,G.W.	OVERSHADOW IN SUCCESSIVE COMPOUND	PSC	62	28/ 29
8-	FARTHING,G.W.HEARST	TRAINING ON GRADIENT OF INHIBITION	JEAB	68	11/743
8-	FARTHING,G.W.HEARST	ATTENTION TO COMPOUNDS OR ELEMENTS	L+M	70	1/ 65
5-	FEATHER,N.T.	MOWRER-S REVISED TWO-FACTOR THEORY	PRV	63	70/500
7-	FEHRER,E.	EFFECTS OF AMOUNT OF REINF	JEXP	56	52/167

2-	FEIGL,H.	OPERATIONISM AND SCIENTIFIC METHOD	PRV	45	52/243
8-344	FELDMAN,J.M.	ADDED CUE CONTROL, PREDICTABILITY	JEXP	72	91/318
8-	FELSINGER,J.M.	GENERALIZATION OF EXTINCTION	JEXP	44	34/477
8-	FERRARO,D.P.ETAL	TRANSFER OF A DIFFERENTIATION	JCPP	68	66/793
4-125	FERSTER,C.B.	STIM PRESENT IN ACQ ON EXTINCTION	JEXP	51	42/442
4-117	FERSTER,C.B.	TIME-OUT FROM POSITIVE REINF	PMG	58	72/ 1
5-	FERSTER,C.B.SKINNER	SCHEDULES OF REINFORCEMENT		57	A-C-C
7+272	FESTINGER,L.	EFFECTS OF INSUFFICIENT REWARDS	AMP	61	16/ 1
9-	FIDELL,S.BIRCH	OVERTRAINING ON REVERSAL LEARNING	PSC	67	8/ 27
9-	FIELDS,P.E.	SERIAL MULTIPLE VISUAL DISCRIM	JCPP	53	46/ 69
9-	FIELDS,P.E.	MULTIPLE DISCRIMINATION LEARNING	JCPP	54	47/473
4-107	FINAN,J.L.	CONDITIONING UNDER VARYING HUNGER	JCP	40	29/119
4-	FINGER,F.W.MOOK	BASIC DRIVES	ARVP	71	22/ 38
9-	FITZWATER,M.E.	REINF AND NONREINF IN DISCRIM	JCPP	52	45/476
7-	FLAHERTY,C.F.KELLEY	DEPRIVATN/SUCCESSIVE NEG CONTRAST	BLPS	73	1/365
8-	FLEMING,R.A.ETAL	ARITH CORRECTNESS AS DISCRIM IN CR	JEXP	68	77/286
8-	FLEMING,R.A.ETAL	DIFF COND TO RIGHT/WRONG ARITH CS	JEXP	68	77/295
8-	FLEMING,R.A.ETAL	TRUTH AND FALSITY AS CS	JEXP	68	78/178
6-	FOREE,D.D.LOLORDO	SIGNALLED AND UNSIGNALLED AVOID	JEAB	70	13/283
8-	FOREE,D.D.LOLORDO	ATTENTION IN PIGEON--FOOD + SHOCK	JCPP	73	85/551
9-	FORGAYS,D.G.LEVIN	CHANGE OF STIM ON REVERSAL	JCPP	59	52/191
9-	FORGUS,R.H.	FORM PRE-EXPOSURE ON FORM DISCRIM	JCPP	58	51/ 75
4-	FORT,J.G.	SEC REINF WITH PRESCHOOL CHILDREN	CD	61	32/755
1-	FOSS,B.M. (ED)	INFANT BEHAVIOUR		59	METHUN
8-	FOTH,D.L.RUNQUIST	VERBAL SIMILARITY IN DIFF COND	JEXP	69	80/ 9
7-	FOWLER,H.	SUPPRESSION/FACILITATION (BRUSH)		71	ACAD P
6+242	FOWLER,H.MILLER	HIND- AND FORE-PAW SHOCK	JCPP	63	56/801
6-226	FOWLER,H.TRAPOLD	ESCAPE AND DELAY OF REINFORCEMENT	JEXP	62	63/464
9-	FOWLER,H.WISCHNER	DIFFICULTY AND SHOCK ON DISCRIM	JEXP	65	69/413
6-	FOWLER,H.WISCHNER	PUNISHMENT IN DISC LRNG (CAMPBELL)		69	A-C-C
9-	FOWLER,H.ETAL	SIGNALLING/AFFECTIVE FUNCTION OF S	AL+B	73	1/ 81
4-	FOX,R.E.KING	REINF SCHEDULE ON SEC REINF	JCPP	62	54/266
8-	FRANKEN,R.E.	STIMULUS CHANGE AND ATTENTION	JCPP	67	64/499
9-	FREEBURNE,C.M.TAYLOR	SHOCK RIGHT/WRONG IN SAME SUBJECT	JCPP	52	45/264
4-	FREIDES,D.	GOALBOX CUES AND PATTERN OF REINF	JEXP	57	53/361
8-	FRICK,F.C.	ANALYSIS OF OPERANT DISCRIMINATION	JP	48	26/ 93
8-	FUHRER,M.J.	DIFF VERBAL COND OF HEART RATE	JCPP	64	58/283
3-	GALANTER,E.SHAW	CUE VS REACTIVE INHIBITION	JCPP	54	47/395
7-	GALBRAITH,K.ETAL	WITHIN-SUBJECTS PRE	JEXP	68	77/547
7-	GALLUP,G.G.HARE	RESIDUAL FRUSTRATION EFFECT	PSC	69	16/ 41
4-	GAMZU,E.SCHWARTZ	S-CONTINGENT/R-INDEPENDENT FOOD	JEAB	73	19/ 65
4-	GAMZU,E.WILLIAMS	ASSOCIATIVE FACTOR IN AUTO-SHAPING	JEAB	73	19/225
8-	GANZ,L.	EFFECT ANCHOR S ON GEN GRADIENT	JEXP	63	65/270
8-	GANZ,L.	GENERALIZATION/DISCRIM (MOSTOFSKY)		65	STANFD
8-327	GANZ,L.RIESEN	DARK-REARING ON ST GENERALIZATION	JCPP	62	55/ 92
8-	GANZ,L.WILSON	INNATE GENERALIZATION OF FORM	JCPP	67	63/258
8-	GARCIA,J.ETAL	BIOL CONSTRAINTS ON COND (BLACK)		72	A-C-C
9-	GARDNER,R.A.	THREE REVIEWS OF ORE	PBL	66	66/416
9-	GARDNER,R.A.COATE	REWARD VS NONREWARD IN DISCRIM	JEXP	65	69/579
1-	GARRY,R.KINGSLEY	NATURE AND CONDITIONS OF LEARNING		70	P-HALL
9-	GATLING,F.P.	STUDY CONTINUITY VIA HABIT REVERSE	JCPP	51	44/ 78
9-	GATLING,F.	REPEATED STIMULUS REVERSALS	JCPP	52	45/347
9-	GEIER,F.M.ETAL	EMOTIONALITY,HYPOTHESES, AND VTE	CPMG	41	17/ 3
2-	GELDARD,F.A.	EXPLANATORY PRINCIPLES IN PSYCH	PRV	38	46/411
9-	GENGERELLI,J.A.MOWRER	BRAIN STIM ON BLACK/WHITE DISCRIM	JCPP	56	49/513
9-	GENTRY,G.V.ETAL	TRANSPOSITION OF INTERMEDIATE SIZE	AMJP	59	72/453
8-	GERRY,J.E.	EXTINCTION/PUNISH ON PEAK SHIFT	PSC	71	23/ 33
9-388	GEWIRTZ,J.L.STINGLE	LEARNING GENERALIZED IMITATION	PRV	68	75/374
9-	GHISELLI,E.E.HENRY	SENSORY ACUITY ON DISCRIMINATION	JGTP	36	49/498
9-	GIBSON,A.R.TIGHE	REVERSAL OF CUES AFTER CHOICE	JCPP	67	64/158
9-	GIBSON,E.J.ETAL	PROLONGED EXPOSURE TO PATTERNS	JCPP	58	51/584
9-	GIBSON,E.J.ETAL	VISUAL STIMULATION DURING REARING	JCPP	59	52/ 74
4-	GILBERT,R.M.MILLENSON	REINFORCEMENT--BEHAVIORAL ANALYSES		72	ACAD P

9-	GILBERT,R.M.SUTHERLAND	ANIMAL DISCRIMINATION LEARNING		69	ACAD P
4-118	GILBERT,T.F.STURDIVANT	FOOD-ASSOCIATED S ON LOCOMOTION	JCPP	58	51/255
2-	GINSBERG,A.	HYPOTHETICAL CONSTRUCTS/INTERV VAR	PRV	54	61/119
8-	GLADIN,L.L.DENNY	SEQUENTIAL CUE AND FIXATION	JCPP	55	48/ 94
9-390	GLANZER,M.	STIMULUS SATIATION IN ALTERNATION	JEXP	53	45/387
6-	GLASER,R. (ED)	NATURE OF REINFORCEMENT		71	ACAD P
7+306	GLEITMAN,H.ETAL	S-R REINF THEORY OF EXTINCTION	PRV	54	61/ 23
4-	GLICKMAN,S.E.	RESPONSE AND REINFORCEMENT (HINDE)		73	ACAD P
4-	GLICKMAN,S.E.SCHIFF	BIOLOGICAL THEORY OF REINFORCEMENT	PRV	67	74/ 81
7-	GODBOUT,R.C.ETAL	SMALL TRIAL PRE	PSC	68	13/153
9-	GOER,M.H.	POSITION PREFERENCE AND DISCRIM	JEXP	58	55/492
9-	GOLDBERT,S.E.CLARK	RELATIONAL VS STIM LRNG IN DISCRIM	JGNP	55	86/187
8-	GOLDSTEIN,H.SPENCE	DIFF COND AND MAGNITUDE OF REINF	JEXP	63	65/ 86
1-	GOLDSTEIN,H.ETAL (EDS)	CONTROVERSIAL ISSUES IN LEARNING		76	A-C-C
9-	GOLLIN,E.S.	CONDITIONAL DISCRIM IN CHILDREN	JCPP	65	60/422
9-	GOLLIN,E.S.	CONDITIONAL DISCRIM IN CHILDREN	JCPP	66	62/454
7-294	GONZALEZ,R.C.BITTERMAN	SPACED-TRIALS PRE	JCPP	69	67/ 94
5-	GONZALEZ,R.C.DIAMOND	TEST SPENCE-S THEORY OF INCENTIVE	AMJP	60	73/396
9-	GONZALEZ,R.C.SHEPP	SIMULT/SUCCESSIVE DISCR REVERSAL	AMJP	61	74/584
7-271	GONZALEZ,R.C.SHEPP	EFFECT OF ENDBOX PLACEMENT	AMJP	65	78/441
9-	GONZALEZ,R.C.ETAL	RELATIONAL DISC INTERMEDIATE SIZE	JCPP	54	47/385
7-	GONZALEZ,R.C.ETAL	OBSERVATIONS ON DEPRESSION EFFECT	JCPP	62	55/578
9-	GOODRICH,K.P.ETAL	CONTINUITY/NONCONTINUITY POSITIONS	PRC	61	11/105
5-	GOSS,A.E.WISCHNER	VTE AND RELATED BEHAVIOR	PBL	56	63/ 35
9-	GOSSETTE,R.L.COHEN	SPATIAL SUCCESSIVE REVERSAL	PRP	66	18/367
9-	GOSSETTE,R.L.HOOD	DRIVE AND INCENTIVE ON REVERSAL	PSC	67	8/217
7-	GRAGG,L.BLACK	SHIFTS IN DRIVE AND REWARD MAG	PSC	67	8/177
8-	GRAHAM,D.T.	EXPER TRANSFER OF CONDITIONING	JEXP	44	34/486
8-	GRAHAM,F.K.	INHIBITION/EXCITATION IN TRANSFER	JEXP	43	33/351
8-	GRANDINE,L.HARLOW	GENERALIZATION OF SINGLE LEARNED S	JCPP	48	41/327
8-	GRANT,D.A.	DISCRIM SEQUENCES OF STIM EVENTS	AMP	54	9/ 62
1-	GRANT,D.A.	CLASSICAL/OPERANT COND (KIMBLE)		64	ACAD P
1-	GRANT,D.A.	CLASSICAL/OPERANT COND (MELTON)		64	ACAD P
8-354	GRANT,D.A.	INFO-PROC OF VERBAL CS (BLACK)		72	A-C-C
7-	GRAY,J.A.	SODIUM AMOBARBITAL AND FRUSTRATION	JCPP	69	69/ 55
8-	GRAY,V.A.MACKINTOSH	CONTROL BY IRRELEVANT STIMULUS	BLPS	73	1/193
9-	GREEN,E.J.MEINIG	RESP PROBABILITY IN DISCRIM LRNG	SC	57	26/339
8-	GREEN,E.J.ETAL	SCHEDULES OF REINF AND DISCR LRNG	JEAB	69	2/293
3- 71	GREENSPOON,J.	REINFORCING EFFECT OF SOUNDS	AMJP	55	68/409
5-	GRICE,G.R.	GRADIENT OF REINF IN MAZE LEARNING	JEXP	42	30/475
4-	GRICE,G.R.	SEC REINF AND DELAYED REWARD	JEXP	48	38/ 1
8-	GRICE,G.R.	VISUAL DISCRIM OF R TO SINGLE STIM	JCPP	48	38/633
8-	GRICE,G.R.	VISUAL DISCRIM AFTER EXTINCTION	JCPP	51	44/149
9-	GRICE,G.R.	HUNTER-S TEST OF TRANSPOSITION TH	BJP	53	44/257
8-	GRICE,G.R.	RESP-MEDIATED GEN (MOSTOFSKY)		65	STANFD
9-371	GRICE,G.R.	S INTENSITY AND R EVOCATION	PRV	68	75/359
4-118	GRICE,G.R.DAVIS	IRREL THIRST ON LEARNING WITH FOOD	JEXP	57	53/347
8-	GRICE,G.R.DAVIS	MEDIATED S EQUIVALENCE/DISTINCTIVE	JEXP	58	55/565
4-	GRICE,G.R.GOLDMAN	GENERALIZED EXTINCTION + SEC REINF	JEXP	55	50/197
8-	GRICE,G.R.SALTZ	GENERALIZATION IN SIZE DIMENSION	JEXP	50	40/702
5-	GRINDLEY,G.C.	AMOUNT OF REWARD ON LEARNING	BJP	29	20/173
8-	GRINGS,W.W.	COMPOUND STIM TRANSFER (PROKASY)		62	A-C-C
8-	GROSSEN,N.E.	AVERSIVE DISCRIM S ON APPETITIVE R	JEXP	71	88/ 90
6-215	GROSSEN,N.E.ETAL	APPETITIVE STIM ON AVOIDANCE	JEXP	69	81/340
7-	GROSSLIGHT,J.H.RADLOW	PATTERNING EFFECT OF N-R SEQUENCE	JCPP	56	49/542
7-	GROSSLIGHT,J.H.RADLOW	PATTERNING EFFECT OF N-R SEQUENCE	JCPP	57	50/ 23
9-	GROSSLIGHT,J.H.ETAL	REINF SCHED IN HABIT REVERSAL	JEXP	54	48/173
8-	GRUSEC,T.	ERRORS AND SHOCK ON PEAK SHIFT	JEAB	68	11/239
9-	GULLIKSEN,H.	RELATIVE VS ABSOLUTE SIZE DISCRIM	JGTP	32	40/ 37
9-382	GULLIKSEN,H.WOLFLE	THEORY OF LEARNING AND TRANSFER	PMTK	38	3/127
8-	GUTH,G.L.	PATTERNING WITH COMPOUND STIMULI	JCPP	67	63/480
2-	GUTHRIE,E.R.	PSYCHOLOGICAL EXPLANATION	PRV	33	40/124
3+ 75	GUTHRIE,E.R.	REWARD AND PUNISHMENT	PRV	34	41/450

1- 44	GUTHRIE,E.R.	PSYCHOLOGY OF LEARNING		35	HARPER
4-109	GUTHRIE,E.R.	ASSOCIATION AND THE LAW OF EFFECT	PRV	40	47/127
1-	GUTHRIE,E.R.	PSYCHOLOGY OF LEARNING (REV)		52	HARPER
5-	GUTTMAN,N.	OPERANT R/CONCENTRATION OF SUCROSE	JEXP	53	46/213
8-	GUTTMAN,N.	GEN GRADIENTS AROUND DIFF REINF S	JEXP	59	58/335
8-	GUTTMAN,N.	DISC ON GENERALIZATION (MOSTOFSKY)		65	STANFD
8-319	GUTTMAN,N.KALISH	DISCRIMINABILITY AND STIM GEN	JEXP	56	51/ 79
8-	GYNTHER,M.D.	DIFF EYELID COND AND SIMILARITY	JEXP	57	53/438
7-	HAAS,R.B.ETAL	SATIATION AFTER PARTIAL REINF	PSC	70	18/296
8-	HABER,A.KALISH	DISCRIMINATION FROM GENERALIZATION	SC	63	42/412
5-	HABER,R.N. (ED)	CURRENT RESEARCH IN MOTIVATION		66	HOLT
8-	HABERLANDT,K.R.	TRANSFER ALONG CONTINUUM/CLASSICAL	L+M	71	2/164
8-	HADLEY,R.FRENCH	IRRELEVANT S IN S-R DISCONTIGUITY	PSC	67	7/ 35
7-	HAGGARD,D.F.	ACQUISITION AND REINF SCHEDULES	PRC	59	9/ 1
7-297	HAGGBLOOM,S.J.WILLIAMS	RESIST EXTINCTION/PARTIAL REINF	PSC	71	24/ 16
8-	HAILMAN,J.P.	SPECTRAL PECKING PREFERENCE	JCPP	69	67/465
9-	HAIRE,M.	CONCERNING MCCULLOCH-S DISCUSSION	PRV	39	46/298
9-	HAIRE,M.	REPETITIVE ERRORS IN DISCRIM LRNG	JCP	39	27/ 79
6-	HAKE,D.F.AZRIN	CONDITIONED PUNISHMENT	JEAB	65	8/279
4-	HALL,J.F.	FREQ PRIMARY REINF ON SEC REINF	JCPP	51	44/246
4-	HALL,J.F.	SEC REINF/DRIVE AND PRIMARY REINF	JCPP	51	44/462
1-	HALL,J.F.	CLASSICAL COND/INSTRUMENTAL LRNG		65	LIPPIN
7-284	HALL,J.F.	PSYCHOLOGY OF LEARNING		66	LIPPIN
8-	HALL,J.F.PROKASY	ABSOLUTELY DISCRIMINABLE TONES	P+MS	61	12/175
9-	HAMMES,J.A.	FEAR AND DIFFICULTY ON VISUAL DISC	JCPP	56	49/481
8-	HAMMOND,L.J.	DIFFERENTIAL CER AND S- RESPONDING	PSC	66	5/337
8-	HANSON,H.M.	DISCRIM ON S GEN FOR SPECTRUM STIM	SC	57	25/888
8-	HANSON,H.M.	DISCRIMINATION ON GENERALIZATION	JEXP	59	58/321
8-	HANSON,H.M.	S GEN AFTER 3-STIM DISCRIM LRNG	JCPP	61	54/181
9-	HARLOW,H.F.	DISCRIMIN SERIES AND REVERSAL	JGNP	44	30/ 3
9-	HARLOW,H.F.	DISCRIM PROBLEMS BY RHESUS MONKEYS	JGNP	45	32/213
9-	HARLOW,H.F.	OBJECT AND PATTERN DISCRIMINATIONS	JGNP	45	32/317
9-	HARLOW,H.F.	NAIVE MONKEYS ON OBJ/PATTERN DISCR	JGNP	45	33/225
9-399	HARLOW,H.F.	THE FORMATION OF LEARNING SETS	PRV	49	56/ 51
9-	HARLOW,H.F.	DISCRIM LEARNING BY MONKEYS	JEXP	50	40/ 26
9+406	HARLOW,H.F.	ERROR FACTOR + LEARNING SET (KOCH)		59	MCG-H
1+ 11	HARLOW,H.F.	AFFECTIONAL PATTERNS (FOSS)		59	METHUN
9-	HARLOW,H.F.POCH	MULTIDIMENSIONAL STIMULUS DISCRIM	JCP	45	38/353
9-	HARLOW,H.F.WARREN	TRANSFER OF DISCRIM LEARNING SET	JCPP	52	45/482
4+105	HARLOW,H.F.ETAL	LEARNING BY A MANIPULATION DRIVE	JEXP	50	40/228
9-	HARLOW,H.F.ETAL	INFANT RHESUS ON DISCRIM LRNG SET	JCPP	60	53/113
9-	HARRIS,J.H.THOMAS	RUNWAY ALTERNATION W/OUT HANDLING	PSC	66	6/329
7-	HARRIS,S.J.ETAL	NONREINF EFFECTS ON BEHAVIOR	JEXP	62	64/388
8-	HARTMAN,T.F.	TRANSFER WORD TO OBJECT IN DIFF CR	JEXP	65	69/194
8-	HARTMAN,T.F.GRANT	CS-US INTERVAL ON DIFF EYELID COND	JEXP	62	64/131
9-	HARTMANN,G.W.	SPATIAL SEPARATN OF DISCRIMINANDA	JGTP	36	49/249
2-	HARVEY,A.J. (ED)	MOTIVATION + SOCIAL INTERACTION		63	RONALD
9-	HAYES,K.J.ETAL	DISCRIM LEARNING SET IN CHIMPS	JCPP	53	46/ 99
9-	HAYES,K.J.ETAL	CONCURRENT DISCRIMINATION LEARNING	JCPP	53	46/105
8-	HEARST,E.	MULT SCHED TIME-CORRELATED REINF	JEAB	60	3/ 49
8-353	HEARST,E.	APPROACH-AVOID AND GEN (MOSTOFSKY)		65	STANFD
8-	HEARST,E.	BREAKDOWN OF DISCRIM BY STRESS	JEAB	65	8/135
8-	HEARST,E.	SUMMATION OF EXCITATION/INHIBITION	SC	68	62/303
8-334	HEARST,E.	EXCITATION AND INHIB (MACKINTOSH)		69	DALHSE
8-	HEARST,E.	CONTRAST AND STIM GENERALIZATION	JEAB	71	15/355
8-	HEARST,E.	ANALYSIS OF COND INHIB (BOAKES)		72	ACAD P
5-	HEARST,E.	PAVLOV COND AND DIRECTED MOVEMENTS	PL+M	75	9/216
1-	HEARST,E.	CATEGORIES OF ASSOC LRNG (ESTES)		75	LERLBA
8-326	HEARST,E.KORESCO	AMT/TRNG ON STIM GENERALIZATION	JCPP	68	66/133
8-	HEARST,E.PETERSON	TRANSFER BETWEEN OPERANT RESPONSES	JEXP	73	99/360
9-	HEATHCOTE,M.J.CHAMPION	RELATIVE VALENCE THEORY	AMJP	63	76/679
1-	HEBB,D.O.	ORGANIZATION OF BEHAVIOR		49	WILEY
2+ 45	HEBB,D.O.	NEUROLOGICAL IDEAS IN PSYCHOLOGY	JPER	51	20/ 39

9-	HEBERT,J.A.KRANTZ	TRANSPOSITION--A RE-EVALUATION	PBL	65	63/244
2-	HEIDBREDER,E.	SEVEN PSYCHOLOGIES		33	A-C-C
8-	HEINEMANN,E.G.CHASE	CONDITIONAL STIMULUS CONTROL	JEXP	70	84/187
8-	HEINEMANN,E.G.CHASE	STIM GENERALIZATION (ESTES)		75	LERLBA
8-	HEINEMANN,E.G.RUDOLPH	DISCRIM ON STIM GENERALIZATION	AMJP	63	76/653
8-	HEINEMANN,E.G.ETAL	DISCRIM CONTROL OF ATTENTION	SC	68	60/553
3-	HELSON,H.	PROPOSITIONS OF GESTALT PSYCHOLOGY	PRV	33	40/ 12
7-	HELSON,H.	ADAPTATION LEVEL	PRV	48	55/297
7-286	HELSON,H.	ADAPTATION-LEVEL THEORY		64	H-ROW
8-	HENDERSON,K.	WITHIN-S PREA AND LATER DISCR LRNG	JEXP	66	72/704
4-	HENDERSON,R.L.	STIM INTEN DYNAMISM AND SEC REINF	JCPP	57	50/339
4-	HENDRY,D.P.COULBOURN	INFORMATIVE S NOT POS DISCRIM S	PSC	67	7/241
8-	HENDRY,D.P.ETAL	GENERALIZATION OF COND SUPPRESSION	JEAB	69	12/799
4-	HERMAN,R.L.AZRIN	PUNISHMENT BY NOISE	JEAB	64	7/185
9-393	HERON,W.T.	INHERITANCE OF MAZE LRNG ABILITY	JCP	35	19/ 77
4-	HERON,W.T.SKINNER	HUNGER DURING STARVATION	PRC	37	1/ 51
9-	HERON,W.T.SKINNER	EXTINCTION IN MAZE BRIGHT/DULL	PRC	40	4/ 11
9-	HERRICK,R.M.	LEVER DISPLACEMENT DIFFERENTIATION	JCPP	64	57/139
8-	HERRICK,R.M.ETAL	S+/S- RATES DURING OPERANT DISCRIM	JCPP	59	52/359
4-	HERRNSTEIN,R.J.	RATE OF PRIMARY REINF ON SEC REINF	JEAB	64	7/ 27
6+227	HERRNSTEIN,R.J.	METHOD AND THEORY IN AVOIDANCE	PRV	69	76/ 49
4-	HERRNSTEIN,R.J.	ON THE LAW OF EFFECT	JEAB	70	13/243
2-	HERRNSTEIN,R.J.BORING	SOURCE BOOK IN HISTORY OF PSYCH		65	HARVD
8-	HERRNSTEIN,R.J.BRADY	COMPONENT INTERACT IN MULT SCHED	JEAB	58	1/293
6-227	HERRNSTEIN,R.J.HINELINE	NEG REINF/SHOCK FREQ REDUCTION	JEAB	66	9/421
6-215	HERRNSTEIN,R.J.SIDMAN	UNAVOID SHOCKS ON REINF BEHAVIOR	JCPP	58	51/380
1+ 10	HESS,E.H.	IMPRINTING	SC	59	30/130
8-	HICKOK,C.W.ETAL	REVERSAL DIFF EYELID CONDITIONING	JGNP	67	76/125
9-	HICKS,L.H.	OVERTRAIN ON PLACE/RESP REVERSAL	PRP	64	15/459
1-	HILGARD,E.R.	THEORIES OF LEARNING		48	A-C-C
1-	HILGARD,E.R.	THEORIES OF LEARNING (2ND ED)		56	A-C-C
2-	HILGARD,E.R.	LEARNING THEORY AND INSTRUCTION		64	U CHI
1-	HILGARD,E.R.BOWER	THEORIES OF LEARNING (3RD ED)		66	A-C-C
1-	HILGARD,E.R.BOWER	THEORIES OF LEARNING (4TH ED)		75	P-HALL
1-187	HILGARD,E.R.MARQUIS	CONDITIONING AND LEARNING		40	A-C
8-	HILGARD,E.R.ETAL	COND DISCRIM WITH/WITHOUT VERBAL R	AMJP	37	49/564
8-	HILGARD,E.R.ETAL	KNOWLEDGE OF S-RELATIONS ON DISCR	AMJP	38	51/498
8-	HILGARD,E.R.ETAL	COND DISCRIM RELATED TO ANXIETY	JEXP	51	42/ 94
9-	HILL,C.W.	CONCURRENT CONDITIONAL DISC REVERS	ANB	67	15/ 67
3-	HILL,C.W.THUNE	PLACE AND RESPONSE LEARNING	JEXP	52	32/289
1-	HILL,W.F.	LEARNING--PSYCH INTERPRETATIONS		63	CHANDL
1-	HILL,W.F.	LEARNING--PSYCH INTERPRETATIONS		71	CHANDL
7-270	HILL,W.F.SPEAR	RESIST EXTINCT AND TRIAL SPACING	JEXP	62	64/636
9-	HILL,W.F.SPEAR	CHOICE BETWEEN MAGNITUDES OF REINF	JCPP	63	56/723
9-	HILL,W.F.SPEAR	OVERLEARNING AND REVERSAL	JEXP	63	65/317
7-296	HILL,W.F.SPEAR	PERCENT REINF, ACQ LEVEL, EXTINCTN	JEXP	63	65/495
7-	HILL,W.F.WALLACE	PERCENT AND MAGNITUDE OF REWARD	JEXP	67	73/544
9-	HILL,W.F.ETAL	OVERTRAINING PROCEDURE ON REVERSAL	JEXP	62	64/533
9-419	HINDE,R.A.	ANIMAL BEHAVIOUR		70	MCG-H
2-	HINDE,R.STEVENSON (EDS)	CONSTRAINTS ON LEARNING		73	ACAD P
6-229	HINELINE,P.N.	NEG REINF WITHOUT SHOCK REDUCTION	JEAB	70	14/259
6-	HINELINE,P.N.HERRNSTEIN	TIMING IN AVOIDANCE	JEAB	70	13/113
4-	HODGE,C.C.CROWDER	SEC REINF AND INTERPAIR INTERVAL	PRP	60	6/ 71
6-	HOFFMAN,H.S.	STIM ASPECTS OF AVERSIVE CONTROL	JEAB	65	8/ 89
6-	HOFFMAN,H.S.	DISCRIMINATED AVOIDANCE (HONIG)		66	A-C-C
8-	HOFFMAN,H.S.	STIM FACTORS IN SUPRESS (CAMPBELL)		69	A-C-C
8-	HOFFMAN,H.S.FLESHLER	STIM GEN OF SUPPRESS AFTER DISCRIM	JEAB	64	7/233
8-	HOFFMANN,F.K.ETAL	PROBLEM DIFF ON DISCRIM REVERSAL	JCPP	56	49/547
1-	HOLLAND,J.G.SKINNER	ANALYSIS OF BEHAVIOR		61	MCG-H
9-	HOLMAN,E.W.	TESTS FOR SPONTANEOUS ALTERNATION	PRV	66	73/427
6+	HOLZ,W.C.AZRIN	DISCRIM PROPERTIES OF PUNISHMENT	JEAB	61	4/225
6-	HOLZ,W.C.AZRIN	DISCRIM/AVERSIVE PROPERTIES OF PUN	JEAB	62	5/229
9-	HOMME,L.E.	COVERANTS--OPERANTS OF MIND	PRC	65	15/501

9-	HONIG,W.K.	TRANSPOSITION FROM GEN GRADIENT	JEXP	62	64/239
8-	HONIG,W.K.	DISCRIM TRNG ON GEN OF PUNISHMENT	JEAB	66	9/377
1-	HONIG,W.K. (ED)	OPERANT BEHAVIOR		66	A-C-C
8-	HONIG,W.K.	ATTENTION/GENERALIZATION (GILBERT)		69	ACAD P
8-	HONIG,W.K.DAY	DISCRIM/GEN ON DIMENSION OF S DIFF	SC	62	38/ 29
1-	HONIG,W.K.JAMES (EDS)	ANIMAL LEARNING		71	ACAD P
8-	HONIG,W.K.ETAL	EXTINCTION AND DISCRIM ON S GEN	JEXP	59	58/145
8-334	HONIG,W.K.ETAL	POSITIVE AND NEGATIVE GEN GRADIENT	JCPP	63	56/111
9-	HONZIK,C.H.TOLMAN	PUNISHMENT ON LEARNING	JCP	38	26/187
9-	HOOPER,R.	OVERLEARNING REVERSAL EFFECT	JEXP	67	73/612
4-	HOPKINS,C.O.	QUANT/QUAL OF FOOD ON SEC REINF	JEXP	55	50/339
9-	HOREL,J.A.ETAL	SPATIAL ARRANGEMENT ON DISCR LRNG	JCPP	61	54/546
8-	HOVING,K.L.	TYPE OF DISCR TRNG ON GENERALIZATN	JEXP	63	66/514
8-320	HOVLAND,C.I.	TONE FREQUENCY GENERALIZATION	JGNP	37	17/125
8-	HOVLAND,C.I.	TONE INTENSITY GENERALIZATION	JGTP	37	51/279
9-	HSIAO,H.H.	RATS- INSIGHT IN SPATIAL COMPLEX	UCPP	29	4/ 57
7-	HUANG,I.HUANG	EFFECT OF INITIAL REWARD	PSC	70	18/ 39
8-	HUDE,T.S.TRAPOLD	CS FOR WATER ON FOOD RESPONSE	PSC	67	9/513
8-	HUGHES,C.R.NORTH	PARTIAL CORRELATION BETWEEN CUES	JCPP	59	52/126
4-	HUGHES,H.ADAMS	TERMINATION SHOCK AS SEC REINF	PSC	67	8/179
4-	HULICKA,I.M.CAPEHART	IS THE CLICK A SEC REINFORCER	PRC	60	10/ 29
6-226	HULL,C.L.	FUNCTIONAL INTERP OF COND REFLEX	PRV	29	36/495
3+ 67	HULL,C.L.	SIMPLE TRIAL-AND-ERROR LEARNING	PRV	30	37/241
5-	HULL,C.L.	KNOWLEDGE AND PURPOSE AS HABIT	PRV	30	37/511
5+170	HULL,C.L.	GOAL ATTRACTION, DIRECTING IDEAS	PRV	31	38/487
9+392	HULL,C.L.	THE GOAL GRADIENT HYPOTHESIS	PRV	32	39/ 25
8-	HULL,C.L.	HABITUATION TO INTERNAL STIMULI	JCP	33	16/255
5-	HULL,C.L.	SPEED OF LOCOMOTION GRADIENT	JCPP	34	17/393
9-	HULL,C.L.	CONCEPT OF HABIT-FAMILY HIERARCHY	PRV	34	41/ 33
9-	HULL,C.L.	CONCEPT OF HABIT-FAMILY HIERARCHY	PRV	34	41/134
9-394	HULL,C.L.	MECHANISM OF PROBLEM SOLUTION	PRV	35	42/219
9-	HULL,C.L.	CONFLICTING PRYCHOLOGIES OF LRNG	PRV	35	42/491
9-	HULL,C.L.	MIND, MECHANISM, ADAPTIVE BEHAVIOR	PRV	37	44/ 1
9-	HULL,C.L.	FIELD-FORCE PROBLEMS IN CHILDREN	PRV	38	45/271
9-	HULL,C.L.	SIMPLE TRIAL-AND-ERROR LEARNING	JCP	39	27/233
9-	HULL,C.L.	BEHAVIORISM AND PSYCHOANALYSIS	NYAS	39	1/ 78
8-	HULL,C.L.	PROBLEM OF STIMULUS EQUIVALENCE	PRV	39	46/ 9
8-	HULL,C.L.	PATTERNING OF COND STIMULI	JEXP	40	27/ 95
2-	HULL,C.L.	INTERVENING VAR IN BEHAVIOR THEORY	ARVP	43	50/273
9-	HULL,C.L.	VALUE, VALUATION, NATURAL-SCIENCE	PHSC	43	11/125
2+ 44	HULL,C.L.	PRINCIPLES OF BEHAVIOR		43	A-C-C
9-	HULL,C.L.	INDIVIDUAL DIFFERENCES IN THEORY	PRV	45	52/ 55
9-	HULL,C.L.	MORAL VALUES AND BEHAVIORISM	NYAS	45	7/ 90
8-	HULL,C.L.	AFFERENT NEURAL INTERACTION	PRV	45	52/133
8-	HULL,C.L.	PRIMARY STIMULUS GENERALIZATION	PRV	47	54/120
9-	HULL,C.L.	TERMINAL REINF ON TRIAL-AND-ERROR	JEXP	48	37/118
9-	HULL,C.L.	SERIAL REINF ON TRIAL-AND-ERROR	JEXP	48	38/ 17
8-	HULL,C.L.	STIMULUS INTENSITY DYNAMISM	PRV	49	56/ 67
9-	HULL,C.L.	A PRIMARY SOCIAL SCIENCE LAW	SCM	50	71/221
9-	HULL,C.L.	QUALITATIVE DISCRIM LEARNING	PRV	50	57/303
5-	HULL,C.L.	BEHAVIOR POSTULATES + COROLLARIES	PRV	50	57/173
4-109	HULL,C.L.	ESSENTIALS OF BEHAVIOR		51	YALE
3+ 78	HULL,C.L.	A BEHAVIOR SYSTEM		52	YALE
8-	HULL,C.L.BASS	IRRADIATION OF TACTILE CR	JCP	34	17/ 47
2-	HULL,C.L.ETAL	LATENCY AND NUMBER OF REINF	JEXP	47	37/214
2-	HULL,C.L.ETAL	QUANTIFICATION OF HABIT	PRV	47	54/237
2-	HULL,C.L.ETAL	MOMENTARY REACTION POTENTIAL	JEXP	47	37/510
2-	HULL,C.L.ETAL	POOLED REACTION POTENTIALS	PRV	48	55/216
7-	HULL,C.L.ETAL	REACTION POTENTIAL IN EXTINCTION	JEXP	51	40/194
4-	HULL,C.L.ETAL	TRUE/SHAM FEEDING AS REINF	JCPP	51	44/236
7-270	HULSE,S.H.	AMOUNT AND PERCENTAGE OF REINF	JEXP	58	56/ 48
7-	HULSE,S.H.	DISCRIMINATION OF THE REWARD	JEXP	62	64/227
7-284	HULSE,S.H.	REINFORCEMENT SHIFT EFFECTS	JEXP	62	64/451

5-163	HULSE,S.H.	PATTERNED REINFORCEMENT	PL+M	73	7/313
4-	HULSE,S.H.STANLEY	EXTINCT AND PARTIAL AND SEC REINF	JEXP	56	52/221
7-	HUMPHREYS,L.G.	RANDOM ALTERNATION OF REINFORCEMT	JEXP	39	25/141
6-239	HUNT,H.F.BRADY	EFFECTS OF PUNISH AND -ANXIETY-	JCPP	55	48/305
2-	HUNT,J.M. (ED)	PERSONALITY + BEHAVIOR DISORDERS		44	RONALD
9-	HUNTER,I.M.L.	TRANSPOSITION BEHAVIOR IN CHILDREN	BJP	52	43/113
9-	HUNTER,I.M.L.	THEORIES OF TRANSPOSITION	JCPP	53	46/493
6-223	HUNTER,W.S.	CONDITIONING AND EXTINCTION IN RAT	BJP	35	26/135
8-	HURWITZ,H.M.B.CUTTS	DISCRIM AND OPERANT EXTINCTION	BJP	57	48/ 90
6-227	HURWITZ,H.M.B.	DISCRIM AVOIDANCE TRAINING	SC	64	45/070
8-	HURWITZ,H.M.B.ROBERTS	SUPPRESS AVOID BY PRE-AVERSIVE S	PSC	69	17/305
8-	HUSTED,J.R.MCKENNA	RATS AS DISCRIMINATIVE STIMULI	JEAB	66	9/677
5+195	IRWIN,F.W.	INTENTIONAL BEH AND MOTIV		71	LIPPIN
9-	ISON,J.R.	SPATIAL REVERSAL AND SUCROSE CONC	JEXP	64	67/495
8-	ISON,J.R.ADINOLF	EXT AFTER DIFF INSTRUMENTAL COND	JEXP	68	77/350
9-	ISON,J.R.BIRCH	ENDBOX PLACEMENT ON T-MAZE REVERSE	JEXP	61	62/200
8-	ISON,J.R.CLAIBORN	SEC REINF ON DIFF INSTR COND	PSC	67	7/161
8-	ISON,J.R.GLASS	LONG TERM EFFECT OF DIFF REINF MAG	JCPP	68	65/524
8-	ISON,J.R.KRANE	INDUCTION IN DIFF INSTRU COND	JEXP	69	80/183
7-	ISON,J.R.PINCKNEY	INITIAL PARTIAL REINF TRIALS	PSC	68	12/ 37
7-288	ISON,J.R.ETAL	REWARD MAGNITUDE CHANGES	JEXP	69	81/ 81
9-	JACKSON,T.A.DOMINGUEZ	TRANSPOSITION BY CHILDREN	JEXP	39	24/620
9-	JACKSON,T.A.ETAL	TRAINING ON RELATIVE/ABSOLUTE RESP	JEXP	38	23/578
9-	JAMES,H.	ADAPTATION LEVEL AND TRANSPOSITION	PRV	53	60/345
2-	JAMES,W.	PRINCIPLES OF PSYCHOLOGY		90	H-R-W
4-	JAMES,W.T.	SEC REINF IN OPERANT SITUATION	JGTP	54	85/129
9-	JARVIK,M.E.	CONTIGUITY OF CUE AND INCENTIVE	JCPP	56	59/492
9-	JARVIK,M.E.ETAL	INTERFERENCE ON DELAYED MATCHING	JEXP	69	81/ 1
7-	JENKINS,H.M.	DISCR TRAINING AND EXTINCTION	JEXP	61	61/111
8-	JENKINS,H.M.	STIM CONTROL IN OPERANT DISCRIM	PBL	65	62/365
8-	JENKINS,H.M.	GENERALIZATION/INHIB (MOSTOFSKY)		65	STANFD
8-125	JENKINS,H.M.HARRISON	DISCR ON AUDITORY GENERALIZATION	JEXP	60	59/246
8-334	JENKINS,H.M.HARRISON	GRADIENTS OF INHIBITION AFTER DISC	JEAB	62	5/435
8-	JENKINS,J.J.HANRATTY	DRIVE INTENSITY DISCRIMINATION	JCPP	49	42/228
4-	JENKINS,W.O.	TEMPORAL GRADIENT OF DERIVED REINF	AMJP	50	63/237
7-290	JENKINS,W.O.STANLEY	PARTIAL REINF--REVIEW + CRITIQUE	PBL	50	47/193
7-	JENSEN,A.C.G.D.COTTON	SUCCESSIVE ACQ AND EXTINCTIONS	JEXP	60	60/ 41
9-	JEROME,E.A.ETAL	DRIVE ON MULTIPLE-DOOR LEARNING	JCPP	57	50/588
9-	JOHN,E.R.ETAL	OBSERVATIONAL LEARNING IN CATS	SC	68	59/489
8-	JOHNSON,D.F.	SELECTIVE STIM CONTROL IN PIGEON	JCPP	70	70/298
8-	JOHNSON,D.F.CUMMING	SOME DETERMINERS OF ATTENTION	JEAB	68	11/157
2-	JOHNSON,H.M.	VERIFY HYPOTHESES/IMPLICATIVES	AMJP	54	67/723
9-	JOHNSON,R.C.ZARA	RELATIONAL LRNG IN YOUNG CHILDREN	JCPP	60	53/594
9-	JOHNSON,R.N.	BRAIN S REINF AND LEARNING SET	PSC	66	6/315
6-	JOHNSTON,J.M.	PUNISHMENT OF HUMAN BEHAVIOR	AMP	72	27/103
7-	JONES,E.C.BRIDGES	COMPETING RESPONSES AND PRE	PSC	66	6/483
8-	JONES,L.V.	DISTINCTIVENESS OF CUES IN PIGEON	JCPP	54	47/253
4-	JONES,M.R. (ED)	SYMPOSIUM ON MOTIVATION		55	U NEBR
2-	JONES,M.R. (ED)	SYMPOSIUM ON MOTIVATION		56	U NEBR
2-	JONES,M.R. (ED)	SYMPOSIUM ON MOTIVATION		57	U NEBR
2-	JONES,M.R. (ED)	SYMPOSIUM ON MOTIVATION		58	U NEBR
2-	JONES,M.R. (ED)	SYMPOSIUM ON MOTIVATION		59	U NEBR
2-	JONES,M.R. (ED)	SYMPOSIUM ON MOTIVATION		61	U NEBR
5-	JONES,M.R. (ED)	SYMPOSIUM ON MOTIVATION		63	U NEBR
1-	JONES,M.R. (ED)	SYMPOSIUM ON MOTIVATION		64	U NEBR
4-	JONES,M.R. (ED)	SYMPOSIUM ON MOTIVATION		69	U NEBR
8-	KALISH,H.I.HABER	DEPRIVATION ON DISC/GENERALIZATION	JCPP	65	60/125
6-	KAMIN,L.J.	TRAUMATIC AVOIDANCE LEARNING	JCPP	54	47/ 65
6+231	KAMIN,L.J.	CS TERMINATION AND US AVOIDANCE	JCPP	56	49/420
6-231	KAMIN,L.J.	DELAY OF SEC REWARD IN AVOIDANCE	JCPP	57	50/445
6-	KAMIN,L.J.	TERMINATION OF CS/AVOIDANCE OF US	CJP	57	11/ 48
6+239	KAMIN,L.J.	DELAY OF PUNISHMENT GRADIENT	JCPP	59	52/434
8-	KAMIN,L.J.	ATTENTION LIKE PROCESSES (JONES)		60	MIAMI

6-213	KAMIN,L.J.	CS TEMP AND INTENSITY (PROKASY)		65	A-C-C
8+343	KAMIN,L.J.	SELECTIVE ASSOCIATION (MACKINTOSH)		69	DALHSE
8-347	KAMIN,L.J.	PREDICTABILITY/SURPRISE (CAMPBELL)		69	A-C-C
6-	KAMIN,L.J.ETAL	FEAR OF CS IN AVOIDANCE	JCPP	63	56/497
4-	KANFER,F.H.	INCENTIVE VALUE, GENERALIZED REINF	PRP	60	7/531
4-119	KANFER,F.H.MATARAZZO	SEC AND GENERALIZED REINF IN HUMAN	JEXP	59	58/400
6-239	KARSH,E.B.	REWARDED TRIALS/PUNISH INTENSITY	JCPP	62	55/ 44
6-240	KARSH,E.B.	CHANGES IN PUNISHMENT INTENSITY	SC	63	40/084
4-	KASS,N.ETAL	TRAINING SCHEDULE AND COND REINF	PSC	66	6/183
7-	KATZEV,R.	EXTINCTION AVOID/DELAYED WARNING	JEXP	67	75/339
6-	KEEHN,J.D.	WARNING S ON UNRESTRICTED AVOID	BJP	59	50/125
4-	KEEHN,J.D.	POSTSTIM CONDITIONS ON SEC REINF	JCPP	62	55/ 22
9-	KELLEHER,R.T.	REVERSAL AND NONREVERSAL SHIFTS	JEXP	56	51/379
4-	KELLEHER,R.T.	INTERMITTENT COND REINF IN CHIMP	SC	56	24/679
4-	KELLEHER,R.T.	MULT SCHED COND REINF WITH CHIMP	PRP	57	3/485
4-	KELLEHER,R.T.	COND REINF IN CHIMP	JCPP	57	50/571
4-	KELLEHER,R.T.	FR SCHED OF COND REINF WITH CHIMP	JEAB	58	1/281
8-	KELLEHER,R.T.	CONCEPT FORMATION IN CHIMPANZEES	SC	58	28/777
4+121	KELLEHER,R.T.	SCHED OF COND REINF DURING EXTINCT	JEAB	61	4/ 1
4-	KELLEHER,R.T.	CHAINING/COND REINF (HONIG)		66	A-C-C
4-	KELLEHER,R.T.	COND REINF IN SECOND-ORDER SCHED	JEAB	66	9/475
4+123	KELLEHER,R.T.FRY	STIM FUNCTIONS IN CHAINED FI SCHED	JEAB	62	5/167
4-121	KELLEHER,R.T.GOLLUB	REVIEW POSITIVE COND REINFORCEMENT	JEAB	62	5/543
8-	KELLEHER,R.T.ETAL	OBSERVING RESPONSE IN PIGEON	JEAB	62	5/ 3
6-	KELLEHER,R.T.ETAL	MAINTAIN BEH BY UNAVOIDABLE SHOCK	JEAB	63	6/507
4-101	KELLER,F.S.SCHOENFELD	PRINCIPLES OF PSYCHOLOGY		50	A-C-C
8-	KELLICUTT,M.H.	RESP DURATION DURING OPERANT DISCR	JEXP	67	73/ 56
9-	KELLOGG,W.N.WOLF	HYPOTHESES AND RANDOM ACTIVITY	JEXP	40	26/588
9-398	KEMLER,D.G.SHEPP	TRANSFER OF DIMENSIONAL RELEVANCE	JEXP	71	90/120
8-	KENDALL,S.B.	MIXED AND MULT FI SCHED BEHAVIOR	PSC	64	1/165
8-	KENDALL,S.B.	COMPETING BEHAVIOR AND OBSERVING R	PSC	65	3/279
8-	KENDALL,S.B.	OBSERVING R IN MIXED FI-FR SCHED	JEAB	65	8/305
8-	KENDALL,S.B.GIBSON	DISCRIM S REMOVAL ON OBSERVING R	PRP	65	15/545
4-	KENDLER,H.H.	INFLUENCE OF SUB-GOAL ON MAZE LRNG	JCP	43	36/ 67
4-106	KENDLER,H.H.	DRIVE INTERACTION I	JEXP	45	35/ 96
4-107	KENDLER,H.H.	DRIVE INTERACTION II	JEXP	45	35/188
9-	KENDLER,H.H.	HUNGER AND THIRST ON SPATIAL LRNG	JEXP	46	36/212
9-	KENDLER,H.H.	MOTIVATED/SATIATED COND ON LRNG	JEXP	47	37/545
3+ 77	KENDLER,H.H.	LATENT LEARNING IN A T-MAZE	JCPP	47	40/265
3-	KENDLER,H.H.	COMMENTS ON THISTLETHWAITE	PBL	52	47/ 47
3+ 70	KENDLER,H.H.	WHAT IS LEARNED-- A BLIND ALLEY	PRV	52	59/269
9-398	KENDLER,H.H.KENDLER	REVERSAL-SHIFT BEHAVIOR	PBL	69	72/229
9-	KENDLER,H.H.KENDLER	DISCRIM + COGNITIVE DEVEL (ESTES)		75	LERLBA
9-	KENDLER,H.H.KIMM	REINF AND CUE FACTORS IN REVERSAL	PSC	64	1/309
9-	KENDLER,H.H.KIMM	SIZE OF REWARD ON REVERSAL LRNG	JEXP	67	73/ 66
9-	KENDLER,H.H.LACHMAN	REINF SCHED AND DRIVE ON REVERSAL	JEXP	58	55/584
9-	KENDLER,H.H.LACHMAN	FORCED REINF/NONREINF ON REVERSAL	PRP	61	8/329
8-	KENDLER,H.H.LAW	SELECTIVE ASSN OF DRIVE STIMULI	JEXP	50	40/299
9-	KENDLER,H.H.SPENCE (EDS)	ESSAYS IN NEOBEHAVIORISM		71	A-C-C
9-	KENDLER,H.H.ETAL	HUNGER TO THIRST IN A T-MAZE	JEXP	52	44/ 1
9-398	KENDLER,H.H.ETAL	OPTIONAL INTRA/EXTRA DIMENS SHIFTS	JEXP	72	95/102
9-	KENDLER,T.S.	STIM DIFFERENCE ON TRANSPOSITION	JEXP	50	40/552
8-	KENDLER,T.S.	CONTINUITY/CUE DOMINANCE (KENDLER)		71	A-C-C
9-	KENDLER,T.S.KENDLER	REVERSAL/NONREVERSAL SHIFTS	JEXP	59	58/ 56
9-	KENDLER,T.S.ETAL	DIMENSIONAL DOMINANCE	JEXP	70	83/309
7-	KERNSTEDT,G.C.	REINF PATTERN, AMOUNT, ITI	JCPP	71	75/421
4-	KIEFFER,J.D.	DIFF RESP RATES AND NEUTRAL STIM	JEAB	65	8/227
2-	KIMBLE,D.P. (ED)	LEARNING, REMEMBERING, FORGETTING		64	ACAD P
7-	KIMBLE,G.A.	TWO-FACTOR THEORY OF INHIBITION	JEXP	49	39/ 15
1-	KIMBLE,G.A.	HILGARD/MARQUIS COND AND LRNG		61	A-C-C
1-	KIMBLE,G.A.	FOUNDATIONS OF COND AND LEARNING		67	A-C-C
5-186	KIMBLE,G.A.	COGNITIVE INHIBITION (KENDLER)		71	A-C-C
9-388	KIMBLE,G.A.PERLMUTER	THE PROBLEM OF VOLITION	PRV	70	77/361

6-	KIMMEL,H.D. (ED)	EXPERIMENTAL PSYCHOPATHOLOGY		71	ACAD P
5-	KIMMEL,H.D.	INSTR COND OF AUTONOMIC RESP	AMP	74	29/325
8-	KIMMEL,H.D.PENNYPACKER	DIFF GSR COND AND CS-US INTERVAL	JEXP	63	65/559
9-	KINTSCH,W.WIKE	PARTIAL DELAY OF REINF ON REVERSAL	PRP	57	3/ 11
7-	KIRKPATRICK,D.RIETAL	SIZE OF GOAL BOX AND PRE	JEXP	64	68/515
6+105	KISH,G.B.	LRNG WITH ONSET OF ILLUMINATION	JCPP	55	48/261
4-	KLEIN,R.M.	INTERMIT PRIMARY REINF + SEC REINF	JEXP	59	58/423
4-	KLINGER,E.	DISENGAGEMENT FROM INCENTIVES	PRV	75	82/ 1
8-351	KLUVER,H.	BEHAVIOR MECHANISMS IN MONKEYS		33	U CHI
6-	KNAPP,R.K.	ACQ AND EXTINCTION OF AVOIDANCE	JCPP	65	60/272
4+125	KNOTT,P.D.CLAYTON	DURABLE SEC REINF USING BRAIN STIM	JCPP	66	61/151
7-290	KNOUSE,S.B.CAMPBELL	PARTIALLY DELAYED REWARD	JCPP	71	75/116
2- 44	KOCH,S.	CLARK L. HULL (ESTES)		54	A-C-C
1-	KOCH,S. (ED)	PSYCH--STUDY OF A SCIENCE (V 2)		59	MCG-H
)-	KOCH,S. (ED)	PSYCH--STUDY OF A SCIENCE (V 5)		63	MCG-H
5-	KOCH,S.DANIEL	SATIATION ON HABIT OF MAX STRENGTH	JEXP	45	35/167
1-	KOFFKA,K.	PRINCIPLES OF GESTALT PSYCHOLOGY		35	H-R-W
1-	KOHLER,W.	GESTALT PSYCHOLOGY		29	LIVERT
1-	KOHLER,W.	GESTALT PSYCHOLOGY TODAY	AMP	58	14/727
8-	KOMMERS,D.	SUCCESSIVE VISUAL DISCR IN RATS	JCPP	59	52/217
9-387	KONORSKI,J.	INTEGRATIVE ACTIVITY OF THE BRAIN		67	U CHI
9-	KORONAKOS,C.ARNOLD	FORMATION OF LRNG SETS IN RATS	JCPP	57	50/ 11
7-297	KOTESKEY,R.L.	UNREINF-REINF SEQUENCES	PSC	69	14/ 34
7-282	KOTESKEY,R.L.	STIMULUS SAMPLING MODEL OF PRE	PRV	72	79/161
7-282	KOTESKEY,R.L.HENDRIX	DOUBLE AND SINGLE ALTERNATION	JEXP	71	88/423
7-	KOTESKEY,R.L.STETTNER	N-R SEQUENCES IN PRE	JEXP	68	76/198
9-	KOVACH,J.K.	INNATE/ACQUIRED COLOR PREFERENCES	JCPP	71	75/386
7-	KRAELING,D.	AMOUNT OF REWARD AND LEARNING	JCPP	61	54/560
8+360	KRAMER,T.J.RILLING	SELECTIVE CRITIQUE OF DRL	PBL	70	74/225
7-270	KRANE,R.V.ISON	EFFECT OF INTER-STIMULUS INTERVAL	JCPP	71	75/129
9+378	KRECHEVSKY,I.	HYPOTHESES IN RATS	PRV	32	38/516
9-	KRECHEVSKY,I.	HYPOTHESES IN PRE-SOLUTION PERIOD	UCPP	32	6/ 27
9-	KRECHEVSKY,I.	GENESIS OF HYPOTHESES IN RATS	UCPP	32	6/ 45
9-	KRECHEVSKY,I.	DOCILE NATURE OF HYPOTHESES	JCP	33	15/429
9-	KRECHEVSKY,I.	HEREDITARY NATURE OF HYPOTHESES	JCP	33	16/ 99
9-	KRECHEVSKY,I.	BRAIN MECHANISMS AND HYPOTHESES	JCP	35	19/425
9-	KRECHEVSKY,I.	CONTINUITY OF PROBLEM SOLVING	PRV	38	45/107
9-383	KUENNE,M.R.	LANGUAGE AND TRANSPOSITION	JEXP	46	36/471
2-	KUHN,T.S.	STRUCTURE OF SCIENTIFIC REVOLUTION		52	U CHI
8-	KWATERSKI,S.E.MOORE	DIFF COND AND OPPOSING INSTRU R	JEXP	69	79/547
9-	LABERGE,D.	GENERALIZATION GRADIENTS IN DISCR	JEXP	61	62/ 88
9-	LABERGE,D.SMITH	SELECTIVE SAMPLING IN DISCRIM LRNG	JEXP	57	54/423
2-	LACHMAN,R.	MODEL IN THEORY CONSTRUCTION	PRV	60	67/113
8-	LACHMAN,R.	RATIO SCHED ON BRIGHTNESS DISCRIM	JEXP	61	62/ 80
9-	LACHMAN,S.J.	SIMULT/SUCCESSIVE DISCR AND PUNISH	PRP	63	13/127
4-	LAMBERT,W.W.ETAL	ACQ AND EXT IN TOKEN-REWARD SIT	JEXP	53	45/321
4-	LANDAUER,T.K.	DELAY OF AN ACQUIRED REINFORCER	JCPP	64	58/374
5-	LANDAUER,T.K.	REINFORCEMENT AS CONSOLIDATION	PRV	69	76/ 82
2-	LANIER,L.H.	DESCRIPTIVE CATEGORIES OF PSYCH	PMG	38	50/211
2-	LASHLEY,K.S.	BEHAVIORISTIC INTERP/CONSCIOUSNESS	PRV	23	30/329
1-	LASHLEY,K.S.	BRAIN MECHANISMS AND INTELLIGENCE		29	U CHI
9+381	LASHLEY,K.S.	CONTINUITY THEORY AND DISCRIM LRNG	JGNP	42	26/241
8+324	LASHLEY,K.S.WADE	THEORY OF GENERALIZATION	PRV	46	53/ 72
4-117	LAWLER,E.E.	SEC REINF STIM AND SHOCK REDUCTION	QJEP	65	17/ 57
8+337	LAWRENCE,D.H.	FAMILIARITY ON ACQUIRED DISTINCT	JEXP	49	39/770
8-	LAWRENCE,D.H.	SELECTIVE ASSN IN CONSTANT S SIT	JEXP	50	40/175
8-337	LAWRENCE,D.H.	TRANSFER OF DISCR ALONG CONTINUUM	JCPP	52	45/511
8-337	LAWRENCE,D.H.	TRANSFER OF DISC AND GENERALIZATN	JGNP	55	52/ 37
8-317	LAWRENCE,D.H.	NATURE OF A STIMULUS (KOCH)		63	MCG-H
7-272	LAWRENCE,D.H.FESTINGER	DETERRENTS AND REINFORCEMENT		62	STANFD
9-	LAWRENCE,D.H.HOMMEL	DIFF GOAL BOXES ON DISC WITH DELAY	JCPP	61	54/552
4-	LAWSON,R.	AMT PRIMARY REWARD AND SEC REINF	JEXP	53	46/183
4-	LAWSON,R.	DISCRIMINATION AND SEC REINF	JCPP	57	50/ 35

1-	LAWSON,R.	LEARNING AND BEHAVIOR		60	MACMIL
4-	LAWSON,R.MARX	FRUSTRATION AND SEC REINFORCEMENT	JCPP	58	51/742
9-	LEARY,R.W.	AMBIGUOUS CUE PROBLEMS BY MONKEYS	AMJP	58	71/718
9-	LEARY,R.W.	SERIAL DISCRIM LRNG BY MONKEYS	JCPP	58	51/ 82
9-	LEARY,R.W.	SPONTANEOUS REVERSALS IN DISCRIM	CJP	62	16/228
8-	LECHART,B.T.GISHOP	DISCRIM BASED ON R-PRODUCED STIM	P+P	67	2/301
7-285	LEHR,R.	PARTIAL REINF AND POS CONTRAST	AL+B	74	2/221
4-	LEIMAN,A.H.ETAL	SEC REINF IN DISCRIM WITH CHILDREN	CD	61	32/349
4-117	LEITENBERG,H.	TIME-OUT AS AN AVERSIVE EVENT	PBL	65	64/428
6-243	LEITENBERG,H.	R INITIATION AND R TERMINATION	PRP	65	16/569
4-	LENZER,I.I.	CONVENTIONAL AND BRAIN REINF	PBL	72	78/103
7-	LEONARD,D.W.	AMOUNT AND SEQUENCE OF REINF	JCPP	69	67/204
7-292	LEUNG,C.M.JENSEN	SHIFTS IN PERCENTAGE OF REINF	JEXP	68	76/291
4-	LEVIN,S.M.STERNER	POSITIVE SEC REINF IN HUMANS	PSC	66	6/ 47
2-	LEVINE,D. (ED)	NEBRASKA SYMPOSIUM ON MOTIVATION		65	U NEBR
2- 43	LEVINE,G.BURKE	MATHEMATICAL MODEL TECHNIQUES		72	ACAD P
9-	LEVINE,M.	NON-CONTINUITY THEORY	PL+M	69	3/101
9+409	LEVINE,M.	HUMAN DISCRIM LEARNING	PBL	70	74/397
9-	LEVINE,M.HARLOW	LRNG SETS AND ODDITY PROBLEMS	AMJP	59	72/253
9-	LEVINE,M.ETAL	TRIALS/PROBLEM ON DISC LRNG SET	JCPP	59	52/396
4-106	LEVINE,S.	IRRELEVANT DRIVE AND LEARNING	PRP	56	2/ 29
6-	LEVINE,S.	UCS INTENSITY AND AVOIDANCE	JEXP	66	71/163
4-	LEVY,G.W.BEVAN	RESP UNDER FI AND CONT SEC REINF	JGTP	57	91/ 83
4-	LEVY,N.	SECONDARY INHIBITION AND SEC REINF	JCPP	57	50/ 29
8-353	LEWIN,K.	DYNAMIC THEORY OF PERSONALITY		35	MCG-H
7-290	LEWIS,D.J.	PARTIAL REINFORCEMENT LITERATURE	PBL	60	57/ 1
7-296	LEWIS,D.J.COTTON	PARTIAL REINF--ITI + NUMBER TRIALS	JCPP	59	52/598
4-	LEWIS,G.W.MICHELS	QUALITY OF FOOD REINF ON SEC REINF	JGTP	61	98/ 49
4-	LEWIS,M.	EFFORT ON SEC REINF CHOICE-VALUE	PRP	65	16/557
7-	LOBB,H.RUNCIE	INTERTRIAL REINFORCEMENT	PSC	67	9/ 25
6-223	LOGAN,F.A.	AVOIDANCE AND NONAVOIDANCE COND	JEXP	51	42/390
5-	LOGAN,F.A.	ROLE OF DELAY OF REINFORCEMENT	JEXP	52	43/393
9-374	LOGAN,F.A.	ESTIMATES OF DIFF EXCITATORY POT	PRV	52	59/300
8-328	LOGAN,F.A.	STIMULUS INTENSITY DYNAMISM	PRV	54	61/ 77
3+ 68	LOGAN,F.A.	MICROMOLAR APPROACH TO BEHAVIOR	PRV	56	63/ 63
2+ 58	LOGAN,F.A.	THE HULL-SPENCE APPROACH (KOCH)		59	MCG-H
3+ 14	LOGAN,F.A.	INCENTIVE		60	YALE
9-	LOGAN,F.A.	SPECIFICITY OF DISCRIM TO CONTEXT	SC	61	33/355
9-	LOGAN,F.A.	DISCRETE-TRIALS DRL	JEAB	61	4/277
9-	LOGAN,F.A.	CONDITIONAL-OUTCOME CHOICE BEHAV	PRV	62	69/467
5-	LOGAN,F.A.	PERFORMANCE SPEED IN EDUCATION	HEDR	63	33/178
1- 14	LOGAN,F.A.	FREE BEHAVIOR SITUATION (JONES)		64	U NEBR
5-179	LOGAN,F.A.	DECISION-MAKING BY RATS I	JCPP	65	59/ 1
5-179	LOGAN,F.A.	DECISION-MAKING BY RATS II	JCPP	65	59/246
8-337	LOGAN,F.A.	TRANSFER OF DISCRIMINATION	JEXP	66	71/616
1+ 13	LOGAN,F.A.	NEG CORRELATED AMT/REINF	JCPP	66	62/ 31
9-	LOGAN,F.A.	VARIABLE DRL	PSC	67	9/393
7-280	LOGAN,F.A.	INCENTIVE THEORY/CHANGES IN REINF	PL+M	68	2/ 1
7-	LOGAN,F.A.	FRUSTRATION + CORRELATED NONREINF	JEXP	68	78/396
6+257	LOGAN,F.A.	NEG INCENTIVE/PUNISH (CAMPBELL)		69	A-C-C
1-169	LOGAN,F.A.	FUNDAMENTALS OF LRNG AND MOTIV		70	W.C.B.
9-	LOGAN,F.A.	THE SMOKING HABIT (HUNT)		70	ALDINE
8-337	LOGAN,F.A.	THEORY OF DISCRIM LRNG (KENDLER)		71	A-C-C
6-	LOGAN,F.A.	DOMINANCE AND AGGRESSION (KIMMEL)		71	ACAD P
9-	LOGAN,F.A.	REINF AND EDUCATION (GLASER)		71	ACAD P
9-	LOGAN,F.A.	ANIMAL LEARNING AND NOW	AMP	72	27/055
9-403	LOGAN,F.A.	SELF-CONTROL--HABIT/DRIVE/INCENTIV	JASP	73	81/127
1-	LOGAN,F.A.	FUND OF LRNG AND MOTIV (2ND ED)		76	W.C.B.
6-	LOGAN,F.A.BOICE	AVOIDANCE OF A WARNING SIGNAL	PSC	68	13/ 53
6-	LOGAN,F.A.BOICE	AGGRESSIVE BEHAVIOR IN AVOIDANCE	BEH	69	34/161
4-158	LOGAN,F.A.FERRARO	DISCRETE TRIAL/FREE R (SCHOENFELD)		70	A-C-C
4-	LOGAN,F.A.SPANIER	CHAINING AND NONCHAINING DELAY	JCPP	70	72/ 98
4-	LOGAN,F.A.SPANIER	DELAY OF FOOD AND WATER REWARD	JCPP	70	72/102

8-	LOGAN,F.A.WAGNER	DIRECTION OF CHANGE IN CS	JEXP	62	64/325
1-	LOGAN,F.A.WAGNER	REWARD AND PUNISHMENT		65	A+B
1-	LOGAN,F.A.ETAL	BEHAVIOR THEORY AND SOCIAL SCIENCE		55	YALE
5-161	LOGAN,F.A.ETAL	VARIED REINFORCEMENT ON SPEED	JEXP	55	49/260
7+280	LOGAN,F.A.ETAL	VARIED REINFORCEMENT ON EXTINCTION	JEXP	56	52/ 65
6+217	LOLORDO,V.M.	COND FEAR AND DIFF AVERSIVE STIM	JCPP	67	64/154
4-116	LOLORDO,V.M.	COND REINF FROM AVERSIVE SITUATION	PBL	69	72/193
7-	LONGSTRETH,L.E.	PRE--FRUSTRATION AND INCOMPAT RESP	JEXP	64	67/581
4-	LONGSTRETH,L.E.	FRUSTRATION RATHER THAN SEC REINF	PSC	66	4/425
4-	LONGSTRETH,L.E.	COGNITIVE INTERP/SEC REINF (COLE)		72	U NEBR
9-	LOPATTO,D.WILLIAMS	SELF CONTROL	PRC	76	26/ 3
4-	LOTT,D.F.	SEC REINF AND FRUSTRATION	PBL	67	67/197
3+ 77	LOUCKS,R.B.GANTT	CONDITIONING OF STRIPED MUSCLES	JCP	38	25/415
9+397	LOVEJOY,E.	OVERLEARNING REVERSAL EFFECT	PRV	66	73/ 87
9-397	LOVEJOY,E.	ATTENTION IN DISCRIM LEARNING		68	H-DAY
6-	LOW,L.A.LOW	CS-US INTERVAL AND AVOIDANCE	JCPP	62	55/059
7-	LUBOW,R.E.	LATENT INHIBITION	PBL	73	79/398
5-184	LUCE,R.D.	INDIVIDUAL CHOICE BEHAVIOR		59	WILEY
2-	LUCE,R.D.GALANTER (EDS)	HANDBOOK OF MATH PSYCHOLOGY		63	WILEY
2-	LUCHINS,A.S.LUCHINS	VARIABLES AND FUNCTIONS	PRV	54	61/111
7-	LUDVIGSON,H.W.GAY	CONTRAST EFFECTS IN DIFF COND	JEXP	67	75/ 37
7-	MAATSCH,J.L.	REINF AND EXTINCTION PHENOMENA	PRV	54	61/111
4-	MABRY,J.	COND REINF IN ANIMAL INTERACTION	JEAB	60	3/288
8-	MACCASLIN,E.F.	PRIOR TRAINING ON GENERALIZATION	AMJP	52	65/ 1
9-	MACCASLIN,E.F.	SIMULT/SUCCESSIVE DISC AND S SIM	AMJP	54	67/308
4-	MACCASLIN,E.F.ETAL	SEC REINF AND PARTIAL REINF	AMP	52	7/274
2+ 41	MACCORQUODALE,K.MEEHL	HYPOTHETICAL CONSTRUCTS/INTERV VAR	PRV	48	55/ 95
4-	MACCORQUODALE,K.MEEHL	COGNITIVE LRNG WITHOUT COMPETITION	JCPP	49	42/383
9-	MACGILLIVARY,M.E.STONE	EXPLANATION OF SYSTEMATIC ERRORS	JGTP	30	38/484
7-289	MACKINNON,J.R.	DIFFERENTIAL MAGNITUDE OF REINF	JEXP	67	75/329
8-	MACKINTOSH,N.J.	IRREGULAR LRNG COND AND HULLIAN TH	JGTP	57	46/233
9-	MACKINTOSH,N.J.	REVERSAL LRNG IN OCTOPUS	QJEP	62	14/ 15
9-	MACKINTOSH,N.J.	OVERTRAIN ON REVERSAL/NONREVERSAL	JCPP	62	55/555
9-	MACKINTOSH,N.J.	VISUAL DISCRIM IN GOLDFISH	ANB	63	11/135
9-	MACKINTOSH,N.J.	TRANSFER ANGLE TO BRIGHTNESS	QJEP	63	15/212
9-396	MACKINTOSH,N.J.	IRRELEVANT CUES ON REVERSAL	BJP	63	53/127
9-	MACKINTOSH,N.J.	OVERTRAINING ON EXTINCTION OF DISC	JCPP	63	56/842
9-	MACKINTOSH,N.J.	OVERTRAINING ON DIMENSIONAL TRANSF	QJEP	64	16/250
9-	MACKINTOSH,N.J.	OVERTRAINING ON POSITION REVERSAL	QJEP	65	17/127
8-	MACKINTOSH,N.J.	ATTENTION ON GENERALIZATION GRAD	BJP	65	56/ 87
8-	MACKINTOSH,N.J.	INCIDENTAL CUE LEARNING IN RATS	QJEP	65	17/293
9-391	MACKINTOSH,N.J.	OVERTRAINING, REVERSAL, EXTINCTION	JCPP	65	59/ 31
8+362	MACKINTOSH,N.J.	SELECTIVE ATTENTION IN DISC LRNG	PBL	65	64/124
7-273	MACKINTOSH,N.J.	SINGLE-STIMULUS PRETRAINING	AMJP	65	78/116
9-	MACKINTOSH,N.J.	PRETRAINING ON PROBABILITY LEARN	P+MS	67	25/629
8-	MACKINTOSH,N.J.	OVERTRAINING REVERSAL EFFECT	PMG	69	67/ 2
2-	MACKINTOSH,N.J. (ED)	ISSUES IN ASSOCIATIVE LEARNING		69	DALHSE
8-	MACKINTOSH,N.J.	BLOCKING AND ATTENTION ENHANCEMENT	JCPP	70	73/ 78
8-	MACKINTOSH,N.J.	OVERSHADOWING AND BLOCKING	QJEP	71	23/118
5+196	MACKINTOSH,N.J.	PSYCHOLOGY OF ANIMAL LEARNING		74	ACAD P
8+350	MACKINTOSH,N.J.	THEORY OF ATTENTION	PRV	75	72/276
9-	MACKINTOSH,N.J.	CLASSICAL TO DISCRIM LRNG (ESTES)		75	LERLBA
9-	MACKINTOSH,N.J.HOLGATE	OVERTRAINING ON EXTINCTION OF DISC	JCPP	65	60/260
8-	MACKINTOSH,N.HONIG (EDS)	ISSUES IN ASSOC LEARNING		69	DALHSE
8-337	MACKINTOSH,N.J.LITTLE	INTRA/EXTRADIMENSIONAL SHIFTS	PSC	69	14/ 5
7-297	MACKINTOSH,N.J.LITTLE	PATTERNS OF REINF UNDER EXTINCTION	PSC	70	20/ 1
8-	MACKINTOSH,N.J.LITTLE	TRANSFER ALONG A CONTINUUM	CJP	70	24/362
9-	MACKINTOSH,N.MACKINTOSH	IRRELEVANT CUES ON REVERSAL	QJEP	63	15/236
9-	MACKINTOSH,N.J.MACKINTOSH	OVERTRAINING ON NONREVERSAL SHIFT	JGNP	64	05/373
8-	MACKINTOSH,N.J.TURNER	BLOCKING AND NOVELTY OF CS	QJEP	71	23/359
9-	MAHAN,J.L.RUMBAUGH	OBSERVATIONAL LRNG IN MONKEYS	P+MS	63	17/686
9-391	MAIER,N.R.	QUAL DIFF IN DISCRIM LRNG OF RATS	JCP	39	27/289
6-	MAIER,N.R.F.	FRUSTRATION		49	MCG-H

1-	MAIER,N.R.F.SCHNEIRLA	MECHANISMS IN CONDITIONING	PRV	42 49/117
6-	MAIER,S.F.ETAL	LEARNED HELPLESSNESS (CAMPBELL)		69 A-C-C
4-	MALAGODI,E.F.	TOKEN REWARD HABIT IN THE RAT	PRP	67 20/335
4-	MALAGODI,E.F.	FR SCHEDULES OF TOKEN REINF	PSC	67 8/469
8-	MALOTT,M.K.	S DEPRIVATION ON STIM CONTROL	JCPP	68 66/276
8-	MALOTT,R.W.CUMMING	MULT SCHED OF IRT REINF	PSC	65 2/259
3-	MALTZMAN,I.M.	REPLY TO THISTLETHWAITE	PBL	52 49/ 52
2-	MANDLER,G.KESSEN	LANGUAGE OF PSYCHOLOGY		59 WILEY
9+	MANDLER,J.M.	S+ AND S- IN REVERSAL + TRANSFER	JCPP	68 66/110
8-	MANNING,A.A.ETAL	ISI ON CLASSICAL DISCRIM COND	JEXP	69 80/225
8-	MARINER,R.W.	REINF DURATION ON PEAK SHIFT	JEAB	69 12/769
8-	MARSH,G.	EXPLANATIONS OF TRANSFER OF DISCR	JCPP	69 68/268
8-	MARSH,G.D.	NUMBER OF TEST STIM ON DISCRIM	JCPP	67 64/284
6-	MARTIN,B.	REWARD AND PUN OF SAME GOAL RESP	PBL	63 60/441
6-	MARTIN,R.C.MELVIN	VICIOUS CIRCLE BEHAVIOR	PSC	64 1/415
2-	MARX,M.H.	HYPOTHETICAL CONSTRUCTS/INTERV VAR	PRV	51 58/235
2-	MARX,M.H.	PSYCHOLOGICAL THEORY		51 MACMIL
7-	MARX,M.H.	COMPETING RESP INTERP OF EXTINCTN	PRP	63 12/729
1-	MARX,M.H. (ED)	THEORIES IN CONTEMPORARY PSYCH		63 MACMIL
1-	MARX,M.H. (ED)	LEARNING-- PROCESSES		69 MACMIL
6-227	MARX,M.H.HELLWIG	AVOIDANCE COND WITHOUT ESCAPE	JCPP	64 58/451
4-	MARX,M.H.MURPHY	EXTINCTION WITHOUT MOTIVATING CUE	JCPP	61 54/207
7-	MARX,M.H.PIEPER	INCENTIVE CONTRAST ON ACQUISITION	PRP	62 10/635
4-	MASON,D.J.	SECONDARY REINF AND PARTIAL REINF	JCPP	57 50/264
8-	MASSARO,D.W.MOORE	DIFF CLASSICAL AND AVOIDANCE COND	JEXP	67 75/151
6-	MASTERSON,F.A.	TERMINATION OF A WARNING SIGNAL	JCPP	70 72/471
8-	MATSUMOTO,R.T.	RELATIVE REINF EFFECT IN DIFF COND	JCPP	69 68/589
9-	MATTHEWS,W.A.	SUTHERLAND-S THEORY OF DISCRIM	BJP	66 57/ 25
6-	MAURER,A.	CORPORAL PUNISHMENT	AMP	74 29/614
2-	MAZE,J.R.	DO INTERVENING VARIABLES INTERVENE	PRV	54 61/226
9-	MCALLISTER,W.R.	SPATIAL RELATIONS OF GOAL OBJECTS	JCPP	52 45/531
6-216	MCALLISTER,W.MCALLISTER	CS AND APPARATUS CUES IN ACQ FEAR	PRP	62 11/749
6-	MCALLISTER,W.MCALLISTER	MSMT OF CONDITIONED FEAR (BRUSH)		71 ACAD P
6-	MCALLISTER,W.R.ETAL	US INTENSITY IN AVOIDANCE	JCPP	71 74/426
7-291	MCCAIN,G.	PRE AND SMALL NUMBER OF TRIALS	PNMG	66 1/251
8-	MCCAIN,G.	PRE AFTER MINIMAL ACQUISITION	PSC	68 13/151
7-	MCCAIN,G.	PRE AFTER MINIMAL ACQUISITION	PSC	69 15/146
7-	MCCAIN,G.	REWARD MAGNITUDE AND INSTRU RESP	PSC	70 19/139
7-	MCCAIN,G.	PREE AFTER MINIMAL ACQUISITION	PSC	70 18/313
7-295	MCCAIN,G.BROWN	PARTIAL REINF/SMALL NUMBER TRIALS	PSC	67 7/265
7-	MCCAIN,G.ETAL	REWARD MAGNITUDE ON INSTRU RESP	PNMG	71 3/249
9-	MCCLEARN,G.E.	DIFFERENTIATION LRNG BY MONKEYS	JCPP	57 50/436
9-	MCCLEARY,R.A.LONGFELLOW	INTEROCULAR TRANSFER OF PATTERN	SC	61 34/418
4-	MCCLELLAND,D.C.MCGOWN	VAR FOOD REINF ON SEC REINF	JCPP	53 46/ 80
7-295	MCCOY,D.F.MARX	COMPETING RESPONSES AND PRE	JEXP	65 70/352
4-	MCCRYSTAL,R.J.CLARK	EXTINCTION AND SCHED OF SEC REINF	PRP	61 8/325
9-	MCCULLOCH,T.L.	FORMATION OF DISCRIMINATION HABITS	PRV	39 46/ 75
9-	MCCULLOCH,T.L.BRUNER	ELECTRIC SHOCK ON SUBSEQUENT LRNG	JP	39 7/333
9-	MCCULLOCH,T.L.PRATT	PRESOLUTION PERIOD IN WEIGHT DISC	JCP	34 18/271
9-	MCCUTCHAN,K.ETAL	ALTERNATING HUNGER/THIRST ON LRNG	JCPP	51 44/269
9-	MCDOWELL,A.A.BROWN	RESPONSE PERSEVERATION LRNG SETS	JCPP	63 56/032
9-	MCDOWELL,A.A.BROWN	RESPONSE SHIFT LEARNING SET	JCPP	63 56/572
9-	MCDOWELL,A.A.ETAL	LEARNING SETS IN NAIVE RHESUS	JGTP	64 06/253
4-106	MCFARLAND,D.J.	INTERACTION OF HUNGER AND THIRST	JCPP	64 58/174
9-394	MCGEOCH,J.A.PETERS	ALL-OR-NONE ELIMINATION OF ERRORS	JEXP	33 16/504
2-	MCGUIGAN,F.J.	CONFIRMATION OF THEORIES IN PSYCH	PRV	56 63/ 98
1-	MCGUIGAN,F.J.	APPROACHES TO COND AND LEARNING		73 WILEY
4-	MCGUIGAN,F.J.CROCKETT	SEC REINF S MUST BE DISCRIMINATED	JEXP	58 55/184
7-	MCHOSE,J.H.	TRIAL SEQUENCE AND PATTERNED RESP	PSC	67 9/281
8-	MCHOSE,J.H.	FRUSTRATION IN S-DISCRIM CONTRAST	JEXP	69 81/256
5-	MCHOSE,J.H.	RELATIVE REINFORCEMENT EFFECTS	PRV	70 77/135
7-	MCHOSE,J.H.LUDVIGSON	INCOMPLETE REDUCTION OF REWARD	JEXP	65 70/490
8-	MCHOSE,J.H.LUDVIGSON	DIFF COND WITH NONDIFF REINF	PSC	66 6/485

7-287	MCHOSE,J.H.MOORE	EXPECTANCY, SALIENCE AND HABIT	PRV	76 83/292
7-	MCHOSE,J.H.PETERS	NEG CONTRAST/INCENTIVE AVERAGING	AL+B	75 3/239
7-	MCHOSE,J.H.TAUBER	CHANGES IN DELAY OF REINF	PSC	72 27/291
4-	MCKEARNEY,J.W.	SCHEDULES OF ELECTRIC SHOCK	JEAB	69 12/301
6+212	MCKEARNEY,J.W.	FI SCHEDULES OF SHOCK	JEAB	69 12/301
4-	MCKEEVER,B.FORRIN	SEC REINF AND INFORMATION VALUE	PSC	66 4/115
4-	MCNAMARA,H.J.	DRIVE AND DISC ON R WITHOUT REINF	PRP	63 12/683
4-	MCNAMARA,H.J.PAIGE	ELABORATION OF DURABLE SEC REINF	PRP	62 11/801
5-149	MECHNER,F.	NOTATION SYSTEM FOR BEHAVIOR	JEAB	59 1/133
9+410	MEDIN,D.L.	REINF IN DISCRIM LEARNING SET	PBL	72 77/305
9-	MEDIN,D.L.	CONTEXT IN DISCRIMINATION LRNG	PL+M	75 9/263
9-	MEDIN,D.COLE	COMPAR PSYCH AND COGNITION (ESTES)		75 LERLBA
8-	MEDNICK,S.A.FREEDMAN	STIMULUS GENERALIZATION	PBL	60 57/169
1-	MEDNICK,S.A.ETAL	LEARNING		73 P-HALL
6-101	MEEHL,P.E.	CIRCULARITY OF LAW OF EFFECT	PBL	50 47/ 52
3-	MEEHL,P.E.MACCORQUODALE	LATENT LEARNING IN THE T-MAZE	JCPP	48 41/372
9-	MEEHL,P.E.MACCORQUODALE	FAILURE TO FIND BLODGETT EFFECT	JCPP	51 44/178
2-	MEISSNER,W.W.	INTERVENING CONSTRUCT CONTROVERSY	PRV	60 67/ 51
4-	MELCHING,W.H.	INTERMITTENTLY PRESENTED NEUTRAL S	JCPP	54 47/370
7-	MELLGREN,R.L.	NUMBER OF TRIALS ON POS CONTRAST	JCPP	71 77/329
7-	MELLGREN,R.L.	CONTRAST USING DELAYED REINF	L+M	72 3/185
8-	MELLGREN,R.L.OST	TRANSFER OF PAVLOVIAN TO OPERANT	JCPP	69 67/390
7-285	MELLGREN,R.L.ETAL	PRESHIFT REINF MAG ON POS CONTRAST	AMJP	73 86/383
8-	MELLO,N.K.	INTEROCULAR GENERALIZATION	JEAB	66 9/ 11
2-	MELTON,A.W. (ED)	PSYCH OF HUMAN LEARNING		64 ACAD P
6-	MELVIN,K.B.	VICIOUS CIRCLE BEHAVIOR (KIMMEL)		71 ACAD P
6-242	MELVIN,K.B.ANSON	FACILITATIVE EFFECT OF PUNISHMENT	PSC	69 14/ 89
4-	MELVIN,K.B.BROWN	NEUTRALIZE AVERSIVE S BY PAIR FOOD	JCPP	64 58/350
6-	MELVIN,K.B.MARTIN	PUNISHMENT ON RESIST EXTINCTION	JCPP	66 62/491
9-	MEYER,D.R.	FOOD DEPRIVATION ON REVERSAL	JEXP	41 41/ 10
9-	MEYER,D.R.	DIFFERENTIAL REINF ON REVERSAL	JEXP	51 41/268
9-	MEYER,D.R.	INTER/INTRAPROBLEM RELATIONSHIPS	JCPP	51 44/162
9-	MEYER,D.R.	PROBABILITY OF REINF ON DISC LRNG	JCPP	60 53/173
9-	MEYER,D.R.HARLOW	DEVELOPMENT OF TRANSFER TO PATTERN	JCPP	49 42/454
6-227	MEYER,D.R.ETAL	PROBLEMS OF CONDITIONING AVOIDANCE	PRV	60 67/224
9-	MEYER,D.R.ETAL	DISCRIMINATIVE PERF BY MONKEYS	JCPP	61 54/175
9-	MEYER,D.R.ETAL	INCENTIVE ON LRNG AND TRANSFER	JEXP	66 72/289
9-	MEYER,M.E.	COMBINATIONS OF DISCRIMINANDA	JCPP	64 58/146
9-	MEYERS,B.MCCLEARY	INTEROCULAR TRANSFER OF PATTERN	JCPP	64 57/ 16
9-	MEYERS,J.L.	SEQUENTIAL CHOICE BEHAVIOR	PL+M	70 4/109
7-	MIKULKA,P.J.PAVLIK	DEPRIVATION, COMPETING R ON PREE	PRP	66 18/ 95
7-288	MIKULKA,P.J.ETAL	REINF SCHEDULE AND REWARD SHIFTS	JEXP	67 74/ 57
8-	MILES,C.G.	OVERSHADOWING IN OPERANT COND	PSC	69 16/107
8-	MILES,C.G.JENKINS	OVERSHADOWING IN OPERANT COND	L+M	73 4/ 11
8-	MILES,C.G.ETAL	REDISTRIBUTING S CONTROL	QJEP	70 22/478
4-120	MILES,R.C.	SEC REINF/DEPRIVATION AND HABIT	JCPP	56 49/126
4-	MILES,R.C.	SEC REINF THRU SPON RECOVERY	JCPP	56 49/496
4+118	MILES,R.C.WICKENS	SEC REINF ON PRIMARY HUNGER DRIVE	JCPP	53 46/ 77
4-113	MILLER,G.ETAL	PLANS AND STRUCTURE OF BEHAVIOR		60 H-R-W
8-	MILLER,L.	STIM COMPOUNDING IN INSTRU COND	PSC	69 16/ 46
8-353	MILLER,N.E.	STUDIES OF CONFLICT (HUNT)		44 RONALD
6+216	MILLER,N.E.	FEAR AS AN ACQUIRABLE DRIVE	JEXP	48 38/ 89
4-124	MILLER,N.E.	LEARNABLE DRIVE/REWARD (STEVENS)		51 WILEY
3+	MILLER,N.E.	THE LAW OF EFFECT (JONES)		59 U NEBR
2- 47	MILLER,N.E.	LIBERALIZATION S-R CONCEPTS (KOCH)		59 MCG-H
6-	MILLER,N.E.	RESISTANCE TO PAIN AND FEAR	JEXP	60 60/137
4-	MILLER,N.E.	ANALYTIC STUDIES OF DRIVE/REWARD	AMP	61 16/739
5+169	MILLER,N.E.	ALTERNATIVE TO D REDUCTION (JONES)		63 U NEBR
8+353	MILLER,N.E.	BEH THEORY AND PERSONALITY (BYRNE)		64 WILEY
5-165	MILLER,N.E.	LEARNING OF VISCERAL RESPONSES	SC	69 63/434
2- 72	MILLER,N.E.DOLLARD	SOCIAL LEARNING AND IMITATION		41 YALE
4+105	MILLER,N.E.KESSEN	FOOD VIA STOMACH AND VIA MOUTH	JCPP	52 45/555
9-	MILLER,R.E.MURPHY	DISC LRNG WITH STIM RELATIONSHIPS	JCPP	56 49/ 80

9-	MILLER,R.E.MURPHY	CUE, RESP, REWARD LOCATION IN DISC	JEXP	64	67/120
9-	MILLER,R.E.ETAL	OBJECT QUALITY DISCRIM TASK	JCPP	55	48/ 29
9-	MISCHEL,W.GILLIGAN	DELAY OF GRATIFICATION	JASP	64	69/411
4-	MOGENSON,G.J.	SEC REINF AND REWARDING BRAIN STIM	PRP	65	16/163
4-	MOLTZ,H.	LATENT EXTINCTION AND SEC REINF	JEXP	53	49/395
7-271	MOLTZ,H.	LATENT EXTINCTION, FRACTIONAL RESP	PRV	57	64/229
9-390	MONTGOMERY,K.C.	EXPLORATORY BEHAV AND ALTERNATION	JCPP	52	45/ 50
4-111	MONTGOMERY,K.C.	EXPLORATORY DRIVE IN LEARNING	JCPP	54	47/ 60
4-	MONTGOMERY,K.C.SEGALL	LRNG BASED ON EXPLORATORY DRIVE	JCPP	53	46/ 96
9-	MONTGOMERY,K.C.SEGALL	EXPLORATORY DRIVE AND DISCRIM LRNG	JCPP	55	48/225
4-	MOOK,D.G.	SACCHARIN PREFERENCE IN THE RAT	PRV	74	81/475
9-	MOON,L.E.HARLOW	ANALYSIS OF ODDITY LEARNING	JCPP	55	48/188
7-	MOORE,J.N.MCHOSE	REWARD DELAY ON NEG CONTRAST	BLPS	75	6/497
8-	MOORE,J.W.	FREQ/INTENSITY OF CS ON DIFF COND	JEXP	64	68/250
4-	MORNINGSTAR,M.ETAL	STIMULUS DURATION ON SEC REINF	PSC	66	4/357
7-	MORRISHON,J.H.PORTER	MAGNITUDE OF REWARD	PSC	65	3/531
4-	MORROW,J.E.ETAL	REINF/DISCRIM FUNCTIONS OF STIM	PSC	65	2/ 61
3-	MORSE,W.H.SKINNER	SECOND TYPE OF SUPERSTITION	AMJP	57	70/308
8-	MORSE,W.H.SKINNER	STIM CONTROL OF OPERANT BEHAVIOR	JEAB	58	1/103
6-	MORSE,W.H.ETAL	FI SCHEDULE OF SHOCK PRESENTATION	SC	67	57/215
9-	MOSS,E.M.HARLOW	ROLE OF REWARD IN DISCRIM LEARNING	JCPP	47	40/333
1-	MOSS,F.A. (ED)	COMPARATIVE PSYCHOLOGY		34	P-HALL
8-	MOSTOFSKY,D.I. (ED)	STIMULUS GENERALIZATION		65	STANFD
8-	MOSTOFSKY,D.I. (ED)	ATTENTION THEORY AND ANALYSIS		70	A-C-C
4-	MOTE,F.A.FINGER	EXPLORATORY DRIVE AND SEC REINF	JEXP	42	31/ 57
8-327	MOUNTJOY,P.T.MALOTT	RESTRICTED REARING ON GENERALIZATN	PRC	68	18/575
4-102	MOWRER,O.H.	S-R ANALYSIS OF ANXIETY	PRV	39	46/553
3+ 76	MOWRER,O.H.	ON THE DUAL NATURE OF LEARNING	HEDR	47	17/102
6-221	MOWRER,O.H.	LEARNING THEORY AND PERSONALITY		50	RONALD
5+168	MOWRER,O.H.	2-FACTOR LRNG THEORY RECONSIDERED	PRV	56	63/114
5+168	MOWRER,O.H.	LEARNING THEORY AND BEHAVIOR		60	WILEY
9+387	MOWRER,O.H.	HOW DOES THE MIND WORK	AMP	76	31/843
6+220	MOWRER,O.H.AIKEN	TEMPORAL VARIATIONS IN CS AND US	AMJP	54	67/ 26
7+272	MOWRER,O.H.JONES	HABIT STRENGTH/PATTERN OF REINF	JEXP	45	35/293
6-	MOWRER,O.H.KEEHN	INTERTRIAL AVOIDANCE RESPONSES	PRV	58	65/209
6-231	MOWRER,O.H.LAMOREAUX	AVOIDANCE AND SIGNAL DURATION	PMG	42	54/247
6+227	MOWRER,O.H.LAMOREAUX	FEAR AS AN INTERVENING VARIABLE	JCP	46	39/ 29
6-220	MOWRER,O.H.SOLOMON	CONTIGUITY VS DRIVE REDUCTION	AMJP	54	67/ 15
6-227	MOYER,K.E.KORN	US INTENSITY AND AVOIDANCE	JEXP	64	67/352
8-	MOYER,M.J.ROSS	S COMPLEXITY AND ISI IN DIFF COND	JEXP	69	81/469
6+240	MUENZINGER,K.F.	SHOCK FOR CORRECT RESPONSES	JCP	34	17/267
9-	MUENZINGER,K.F.	EFFECT OF SHOCK-RIGHT IN DISC LRNG	JEXP	48	38/201
9-	MUENZINGER,K.F.BAXTER	SHOCK PRETRAINING ON DISCR LRNG	JCPP	57	50/252
9-	MUENZINGER,K.F.EVANS	BLACK PREFERENCE OR ARTIFACT	PRP	57	3/493
9-	MUENZINGER,K.F.FLETCHER	SHOCK ESCAPE VS FOOD IN DISCR LRNG	JCP	36	22/ 79
9-	MUENZINGER,K.F.NEWCOMB	JUMPING A GAP AND SHOCK ON DISCRIM	JCP	36	21/ 95
9-	MUENZINGER,K.F.POWLOSKI	SHOCK/RIGHT ON CORRECTION/NONCORR	JEXP	51	42/118
9-	MUENZINGER,K.F.ETAL	SHOCK RIGHT/WRONG ON DISCRIM LRNG	JCP	38	26/177
9-	MUENZINGER,K.F.ETAL	AVOID/ACCELERATION IN SHOCK/RIGHT	JEXP	52	43/115
8-	MUNN,N.L.COLLINS	DISCRIM OF RED BY WHITE RATS	JGTP	36	48/ 72
8-	MURDOCK,B.B.	THE DISTINCTIVENESS OF STIMULI	PRV	60	67/ 16
2-	MURPHY,G.	HISTORICAL INTRO TO MODERN PSYCH		29	H-R-W
9-	MURPHY,J.V.MILLER	CONTIGUITY OF CUE AND REWARD	JCPP	55	48/221
9-	MURPHY,J.V.MILLER	CUE, REWARD, RESP LOCATION IN DISC	JEXP	58	56/ 26
9-	MURPHY,J.V.ETAL	INTER-ANIMAL CONDITIONING, MONKEY	JCPP	55	48/211
6-117	MURRAY,A.K.STRANDBERG	COND REINF/REMOVAL OF AVERSIVE S	JCPP	65	60/281
6-	MYER,J.S.	NONCONTINGENT AVERSIVE S (BRUSH)		71	ACAD P
9-387	MYERS,A.K.MILLER	EXPLORATION BUT NO LEARNED DRIVE	JCPP	54	47/428
4-	MYERS,J.L.	SEC REINF/REVIEW RECENT EXPER	PBL	58	55/284
8-	MYERS,J.L.	DELAY OF REINF ON OPERANT DISCRIM	JEXP	58	55/363
9-	MYERS,J.L.	SEQUENTIAL CHOICE BEHAVIOR	PL+M	70	4/109
4-	MYERS,J.L.MYERS	SECONDARY REINF IN CHILDREN	JEXP	66	72/627
4-	MYERS,N.A.	PARTIAL/CONT SEC REINF ON EXTINCT	JEXP	60	60/172

4-	MYERS,N.A.MYERS	SEC REINF SCHEDULES IN EXTINCTION	JEXP	62	64/586
4-	MYERS,N.A.MYERS	DISCRIM HYPOTHESIS OF SEC REINF	JEXP	65	70/ 98
4-	MYERS,N.A.ETAL	SEC REINF/NUMBER OF REINF TRIALS	CD	61	32/765
4-	MYERS,W.A.TRAPOLD	STRENGTH OF GENERALIZED SEC REINF	PSC	66	5/321
2-	NAGEL,E.ETAL (EDS)	CONGRESS FOR PHILOSOPHY OF SCIENCE		62	STANFD
8-	NAHINSKY,I.D.	TRANSFER OF DRIVE INTENSITY DISC	JCPP	60	53/598
9-	NASH,S.J.MICHELS	FIGURAL INTERACTIONS IN SHAPES	JEXP	66	72/132
8-	NATHAN,M.A.SMITH	DIFF COND EMOTIONAL RESPONSE	JEAB	68	11/ 77
9-	NAVARICK,D.J.FANTINO	TRANSITIVITY OF CHOICE	JEAB	62	18/389
8-	NAVARICK,D.J.FANTINO	STOCHASTIC TRANSITIVITY	PRV	74	81/427
4-	NEGZGER,M.D.	S ASSOCIATED WITH SHOCK REDUCTION	JEXP	57	53/184
3-	NEISSER,U.	COGNITIVE PSYCHOLOGY		67	A-C-C
4-	NEVIN,J.A.	COND REINF IN CHAINING SITUATION	JCPP	64	58/367
8-	NEVIN,J.A.	DECISION THEORY IN DISCRIMINATION	SC	65	50/105
4-119	NEVIN,J.A.	GENERAL COND REINF IN SATIATED RAT	PSC	66	5/191
9-	NEVIN,J.A.	REINF SCHED ON SIMULTANEOUS DISCR	JEAB	67	10/251
8-	NEVIN,J.A.	STIM CONTROL OF NOT-RESPONDING	JEAB	68	11/715
1-	NEVIN,J.A. (ED)	STUDY OF BEHAVIOR		73	S-F
9-	NEVIN,J.A.BERRYMAN	CHAINING AND TEMPORAL DISCRIM	JEAB	63	6/109
7-269	NEVIN,J.A.SHETTLEWORTH	CONTRAST EFFECTS IN MULT SCHED	JEAB	66	9/305
8-	NEWMAN,F.L.BARON	GENERALIZATION ALONG ANGULARITY	JCPP	65	60/ 59
8-	NEWMAN,F.L.BENISFIELD	TRAINING ON STIM CONTROL, ATTENTN	JCPP	68	66/101
9-	NISSEN,H.W.	POSITIONAL SEQUENCES IN DISCRIM	JP	39	8/ 57
9-	NISSEN,H.W.	COMPLEX COND REACTIONS IN CHIMPS	JCPP	51	44/ 9
5-	NISSEN,H.W.ELDER	AMOUNT OF INCENTIVE ON DELAYED R	JGTP	35	47/ 49
9-	NISSEN,H.W.ETAL	REINF AND HYPOTHESIS IN DISCRIM	JEXP	53	45/334
9-	NOER,M.C.HARLOW	DISCRIM OF AMBIVALENT CUE STIM	JGNP	46	34/168
8-	NORTH,A.J.	SUCCESSIVE DISCRIM REVERSALS	JCPP	50	43/442
9-	NORTH,A.J.	EXTENDED SERIES OF DISC REVERSALS	JCPP	50	43/461
9-	NORTH,A.J.	SUCCESSIVE/SIMULTANEOUS DISCRIM	JEXP	56	51/ 54
8-	NORTH,A.J.	ACQUIRED DISTINCTIVENESS OF FORM	JCPP	59	52/339
9-	NORTH,A.J.	REVERSALS WITH SPACED TRIALS	JCPP	59	52/426
8-	NORTH,A.J.	CONDITIONAL DISCRIM IN RUNWAY	JCPP	59	52/345
9-	NORTH,A.J.	DEGREE OF LEARNING ON REVERSAL	PRP	59	5/405
8-	NORTH,A.J.LANG	CONDITIONAL DISCRIM IN RATS	JGTP	61	98/113
8-	NORTH,A.J.MCDONALD	PROBABILITY OF REINF ON DISC LRNG	JCPP	59	52/342
8-	NORTH,A.J.MCDONALD	PATTERNING IN STIM COMPOUNDS	JCPP	59	52/430
7-	NORTH,A.J.MORTON	SUCCESSIVE ACQUISITION/EXTINCTION	JCPP	62	55/974
7-274	NORTH,A.J.STIMMEL	EXTINCTION AFTER MANY REINF	PRP	60	6/227
8-	NORTH,A.J.ETAL	CONDITIONAL DISCRIM AND PATTERNING	JCPP	58	51/711
4-	NOTTERMAN,J.M.	REINF, DISCRIM, AND SEC REINF	JEXP	51	41/161
9-388	NOTTERMAN,J.M.	FORCE DURING BAR PRESSING	JEXP	59	58/341
9-	NOTTERMAN,J.M.BLOCK	RESP DIFF DURING DISCRIM LRNG	JEAB	60	3/289
3-	NOTTERMAN,J.M.MINTZ	DYNAMICS OF RESPONSES		65	WILEY
9-	O-CONNELL,R.H.	ALTERNATION + RESP TO STIM CHANGE	JCPP	64	57/362
4-	OLDS,J.	PRACTICE ON SEC APPROACH DRIVE	JEXP	53	46/232
4+105	OLDS,J.MILNER	REINF BY ELECTRICAL STIMULATION	JCPP	54	47/419
6-	OLTON,D.S.	SHOCK-MOTIVATED AVOIDANCE BEHAVIOR	PBL	73	79/243
6-	OSGOOD,C.E.	TOLMAN-S THEORY OF AVOID TRAINING	PRV	50	57/133
1-	OSGOOD,C.E.	METHOD/THEORY IN EXPER PSYCHOLOGY		53	OXFORD
7-	OVERSTREET,L.CAMPBELL	ITR AND REWARD DELAY	PSC	69	17/303
7-295	PADILLA,A.M.	A FEW ACQUISITION TRIALS	PSC	67	9/241
5-	PADILLA,A.M.	INCENTIVE AND BEHAVIORAL CONTRAST	JCPP	71	75/464
4-	PAIGE,A.B.MCNAMARA	SEC REINF AND DISCRIM HYPOTHESIS	PRP	63	13/679
9-397	PAUL,C.	OVERLEARNING ON HABIT REVERSAL	PBL	65	63/ 65
7-	PAUL,L.	PERFORMANCE WITH NO REWARD	PSC	69	14/224
9-	PAVLIK,W.B.BORN	PARTIAL REINF ON SELECTIVE LRNG	PRP	62	11/575
7-	PAVLIK,W.B.COTTON	A REVERSED PRE	JEXP	65	70/417
1- 44	PAVLOV,I.P.(ANREP,TR)	CONDITIONED REFLEXES		27	OXFORD
8-	PECKHAM,R.AMSEL	FRUSTRATION IN DIFF COND	JEXP	67	73/187
9-	PENNES,E.S.ISON	DISCRIM AND REVERSAL/EXTINCTION	JEXP	67	74/219
8-	PENNINGTON,D.F.THOMSON	DISCRIM WITH HIGHLY DISTRIB TRIALS	JEXP	58	56/ 95
4-107	PERIN,C.T.	BEHAVIOR-- TRAINING AND HUNGER	JEXP	42	30/ 93

5-	PERIN,C.T.	DELAY OF REINFORCEMENT GRADIENT	JEXP	43	32/ 37
4-	PERKINS,C.C.	SEC REWARD AND GRADIENTS OF REINF	JEXP	47	37/377
8-218	PERKINS,C.C.	CS INTENSITY AND RESP STRENGTH	JEXP	53	46/225
6-221	PERKINS,C.C.	CONCEPT OF REINFORCEMENT	PRV	68	75/155
8-	PERKINS,C.C.ETAL	DIFFICULTY OF DISC ON GENERALIZATN	JEXP	59	57/181
7-	PETERS,D.P.MCHOSE	PRESHIFT REWARD ON NEG CONTRAST	JCPP	74	86/ 85
9-	PETERSON,M.E.RUMBAUGH	OBJECT-CONTRACT CUES IN LRNG SET	P+MS	63	16/ 3
8-327	PETERSON,N.	MONOCHROMATIC REARING ON S CONTROL	SC	61	36/774
7-	PIEPER,W.A.MARX	WITHIN-SESSION INCENTIVE CONTRAST	PRP	63	65/568
8-	PIERREL,R.SHERMAN	GENERALIZATION AFTER DISCRIM LRNG	JEAB	60	3/313
8-	PIERREL,R.SHERMAN	INTENSITY DIFF ON DISCRIM/GENERAL	JEAB	62	5/ 67
8-	PIERREL,R.ETAL	DISCRIM LRNG ON GENERALIZATION	JEAB	63	6/545
4-	PILLEY,J.W.LEEMING	ALTERED GOAL BOX CUES ON PRE	PRP	66	19/259
7-	PILLEY,J.W.LEMMING	PRE/ALTERED GOAL BOX CUES	PRP	66	19/259
2-	PLATT,J.R.	EXCITEMENT OF SCIENCE		62	H-M
8-	PLATT,J.R.GAY	REINF MAG ON DIFF COND	JEXP	68	77/393
4-118	PLATT,J.R.WIKE	INACCESSIBLE FOOD AS SEC REINF	PRP	62	11/837
4-	PLATT,J.R.WIKE	REINF FOR NONHUNGRY-NONTHIRSTY RAT	PRC	64	14/311
8-	PLATT,J.R.ETAL	DISCRIM CONTRAST AND CHAINING	JEXP	69	83/ 38
8-	PLISKOFF,S.S.GOLDIAMOND	DISCRIM PROPERTIES OF FR PERF	JEAB	66	9/ 1
4-	PLISKOFF,S.S.TOLLIVER	SIGN REVERSAL OF COND REINF	JEAB	60	3/323
4-	PLISKOFF,S.S.ETAL	DISCR HYPOTHESIS AND REWARDING ESB	PRC	64	14/179
8-	PLISKOFF,S.S.ETAL	RESP/REINF RATES IN MULT SCHED	JEAB	68	11/271
9-	POLIDORA,V.J.FLETCHER	S-R SPATIAL CONTIGUITY ON DISCRIM	JCPP	64	47/224
9-	POLIDORA,V.J.THOMPSON	PATTERN COMPLEXITY ON DISCRIM	P+MS	64	21/ 71
9-	PORTER,J.J.	FREE/FORCED TRIALS ON DISCRIM	PRP	64	15/279
4- 99	POSTMAN,L.	STATUS OF THE LAW OF EFFECT	PBL	47	44/489
6-237	POSTMAN,L.	REWARD AND PUNISHMENT (POSTMAN)		62	KNOPF
4-	POWELL,D.R.PERKINS	SEC REINF AND DURATION OF GOAL R	JEXP	57	53/106
2-	PRATT,C.C.	LOGIC OF MODERN PHYSICS		39	MACMIL
9-	PRATT,J.G.	WEIGHT DISCR PROBLEM IN RATS	JCP	38	25/291
7-	PRATT,P.A.HALPERN	ITR AND EXTENDED ACQUISITION	PSC	69	14/203
4+103	PREMACK,D.	POSITIVE REINFORCEMENT	PRV	59	66/219
6-244	PREMACK,D.	REINFORCEMENT THEORY (LEVINE)		65	U NEBR
5-178	PREMACK,D.	REINF AND PUNISHMENT (KIMMEL)		71	ACAD P
5+199	PREMACK,D.	REINFORCEMENT/PUNISHMENT (GLASER)		71	ACAD P
9-403	PREMACK,D.ANGLIN	SELF-CONTROL IN MAN AND ANIMALS	JASP	73	81/137
8-	PREMACK,D.COLLIER	DURATION OF LOOKING AS DEP VAR	PSC	66	4/ 81
7-	PREMACK,D.HILLIX	SHIFT EFFECTS IN CONSUMMATORY RESP	JEXP	62	63/284
9-	PRENTICE,W.H.	CONTINUITY IN HUMAN LEARNING	JEXP	49	39/182
9-	PRINCE,A.I.JR	PUNISHMENT ON VISUAL DISCRIM LRNG	JEXP	56	52/381
5-186	PROKASY,W.F. (ED)	CLASSICAL CONDITIONING		65	A-C-C
6-221	PROKASY,W.F.	CLASSICAL EYELID COND (PROKASY)		65	A-C-C
8-	PROKASY,W.F.ETAL	SEQUENTIAL EFFECTS IN DIFF COND	PSC	68	12/ 58
9-	PUBOLS,B.H.	OVERLEARN ON VISUAL/SPATIAL DISCR	JCPP	56	49/243
9-	PUBOLS,B.H.	SUCCESSIVE DISCRIM REVERSAL LRNG	JCPP	57	50/319
9-	PUBOLS,B.H.	DELAY OF REINF ON DISCRIM REVERSAL	JCPP	58	56/ 32
9-	PUBOLS,B.H.	HYPOTHESIS BEHAVIOR IN REVERSAL	PRV	62	69/241
8-	PURTLE,R.B.	PEAK SHIFT-- A REVIEW	PBL	73	80/408
9-	RABINOWITZ,F.M.	SEQUENTIAL DEPENDENCIES IN CHOICE	PBL	70	74/141
8-	RACHLIN,H.	CONTRAST AND MATCHING	PRV	73	80/217
1-	RACHLIN,H.	BEHAVIOR AND LEARNING		76	FREEMN
9-403	RACHLIN,H.GREEN	COMMITMENT AND SELF CONTROL	JEAB	62	17/ 15
6-240	RACHLIN,H.HERRNSTEIN	NEGATIVE LAW OF EFFECT (CAMPBELL)		69	A-C-C
5-	RAMOND,C.K.	DELAY OF REINF AND DEPRIVATION	JEXP	54	47/248
4-107	RAMOND,C.K.	PERFORMANCE AND HUNGER	JEXP	54	48/265
2-	RAMSPERGER,A.G.	PHILOSOPHY OF SCIENCE		42	CROFTS
5-185	RAPOPORT,A.	TWO-PERSON GAME THEORY		66	U MICH
7-291	RASHOTTE,M.E.AMSEL	THE GENERALIZED PRE	PSC	68	11/315
7-291	RASHOTTE,M.E.SURRIDGE	PRE/INTERPOLATED CONTINUOUS REINF	QJEP	69	21/156
7-	RASHOTTE,M.E.ETAL	GENERALIZATION OF THE PRE	PSC	68	11/173
4+122	RATNER,S.G.	REINF/DISCRIM PROPERTY OF CLICK	PRP	56	2/332
8-319	RAZRAN,G.	SEMANTIC CONDITIONING	SC	39	90/ 69

8-320	RAZRAN,G.	STIMULUS GENERALIZATION OF COND	PBL	49	46/337
4-	RAZRAN,G.	SECOND-ORDER COND AND SEC REINF	PRV	55	62/327
5-165	RAZRAN,G.	OBSERVE UNCONSC/INFER CONSCIOUS	PRV	61	68/ 81
9-	REESE,H.W.	DISCRIMINATION LEARNING SET	PBL	64	61/321
9-	REESE,H.W.	INTERMEDIATE SIZE TRANSPOSITION	JCPP	65	59/413
9-	REESE,R.SCHRIER	DISCRIM LRNG WITH OPTION TO SWITCH	JEAB	67	10/367
9-396	REID,L.S.	NONCONTINUITY THRU CONTINUITY	JEXP	53	46/107
4-	REID,L.S.SLIVINSKA	GENERALIZED SEC REINF IN EXTINCT	JCPP	54	47/306
8-	REINHOLD,D.B.PERKINS	METHOD OF TRAINING ON GENERALIZATN	JEXP	55	49/423
4-	RENNER,K.E.	GOALBOX CUES ON GRADIENT OF REINF	JCPP	63	56/101
8-346	RESCORLA,R.A.	PROPER CONTROL PROCEDURE FOR COND	PRV	67	74/ 71
6-213	RESCORLA,R.A.	SHOCK IN PRESENCE/ABSENCE OF CS	JCPP	68	66/ 1
8-343	RESCORLA,R.A.	COND INHIB OF FEAR (MACKINTOSH)		69	DALHSE
8+363	RESCORLA,R.A.	PAVLOVIAN CONDITIONED INHIBITION	PBL	69	72/ 77
6-	RESCORLA,R.A.HETH	REINSTATEMENT OF FEAR	ABP	75	04/ 88
6-	RESCORLA,R.A.LOLORDO	INHIBITION OF AVOIDANCE BEHAVIOR	JCPP	65	59/406
5+199	RESCORLA,R.A.SOLOMON	PAVLOVIAN COND AND INSTRU LEARNING	PRV	67	74/151
9+396	RESTLE,F.	THEORY OF DISCRIM LEARNING	PRV	55	62/ 11
3+ 69	RESTLE,F.	DISCRIMINATION OF CUES IN MAZES	PRV	57	64/217
5-184	RESTLE,F.	JUDGMENT AND CHOICE		61	WILEY
8-	RESTLE,F.	INTENSITY EFFECT IN GENERALIZATION	PRV	64	71/514
9-	RESTLE,F.	SIGNIFICANCE OF ALL-OR-NONE LRNG	PBL	65	64/313
1-	RESTLE,F.	MATHEMATICAL MODELS IN PSYCHOLOGY		71	PENGN
9-	RETHLINGSHAFER,D.	MOTIVATION ON VISUAL DISCRIM	JCP	41	32/583
1+ 10	REVUSKY,S.GARCIA	LRND ASSN OVER LONG DELAYS	PL+M	70	4/ 1
2-	REYNEIRSE,J. (ED)	NEBRASKA SYMPOSIUM ON MOTIVATION		70	U NEBR
9-	REYNOLDS,B.	REINF MAG ON BLACK-WHITE DISCRIM	JEXP	49	39/760
7-	REYNOLDS,G.S.	BEHAVIORAL CONTRAST	JEAB	61	4/ 57
8-	REYNOLDS,G.S.	INTERACTIONS IN MULT SCHEDULE	JEAB	61	4/107
7-	REYNOLDS,G.S.	RELATIVITY OF RESP AND REINF	JEAB	61	4/179
8-	REYNOLDS,G.S.	ATTENTION IN THE PIGEON	JEAB	61	4/203
8-	REYNOLDS,G.S.	PROCESS OF DISCRIMINATION	JEAB	61	4/289
4-	REYNOLDS,G.S.	ON SOME DETERMINANTS OF CHOICE	JEXP	63	66/ 53
5-	REYNOLDS,G.S.	PRIMER OF OPERANT CONDITIONING		68	S-F
8-	REYNOLDS,G.S.	INDUCTION, CONTRAST, EXTINCTION	JEAB	68	11/453
7-	REYNOLDS,G.S.CATANIA	BEHAVIORAL CONTRAST/REINF RATE	JEAB	61	4/387
8-	REYNOLDS,G.S.LIMPO	SOME CAUSES OF BEHAVIORAL CONTRAST	JEAB	68	11/543
8-	REYNOLDS,G.S.LIMPO	ATTENTION/GENERALIZATION IN DISCR	JEAB	69	12/911
1-	REYNOLDS,G.S.ETAL (EDS)	CONTEMPORARY EXPERIMENTAL PSYCH		73	S-F
4-	REYNOLDS,W.F.ETAL	SEC REINF AFTER DIRECT PLACEMENT	PRP	61	8/345
4-	REYNOLDS,W.F.ETAL	SEC REINF AND METHOD OF TESTING	JEXP	63	66/ 53
4-	REYNOLDS,W.F.ETAL	MAZE LEARNING BY SEC REINFORCEMENT	PRP	63	12/775
4-	REYNOLDS,W.F.ETAL	SEC REINF AND REWARD MAGNITUDE	PRP	64	15/ 7
9-	RICKERT,E.J.	FEEDBACK IN DISCRIM AND DIFF	JEXP	69	82/148
9-	RIESEN,A.H.	DELAYED REWARD IN DISCRIM LEARNING	CPMG	40	15/ 54
9-	RILEY,D.A.	EFFECTIVE STIM IN DISCRIM LRNG	PRV	58	65/ 1
9-	RILEY,D.A.	DISCRIMINATION LEARNING		68	A + B
8-327	RILEY,D.A.LEVIN	MONOCHROMATIC REARING ON GEN	JCPP	71	75/399
9-	RILEY,D.A.ETAL	STIM COMPARISON ON TRANSPOSITION	JCPP	60	53/415
9-	RILEY,D.A.ETAL	TRAINING LEVEL ON TRANSPOSITION	JCPP	63	56/104
9-	RILEY,D.A.ETAL	ADAPTATION LEVEL/INTERMEDIATE SIZE	PRV	66	73/252
8-	RILLING,M.	TIME-OUT ON MULT FR SCHED	JEAB	68	11/129
9-	RIOPELLE,A.J.	SUPPRESSION IN LEARNING SETS	JCPP	53	46/108
9-	RIOPELLE,A.J.	LEARNING SETS FROM MINIMUM STIM	JEXP	55	49/ 28
9-	RIOPELLE,A.J.	OBSERVATIONAL LRNG OF POSITION	JCPP	60	53/426
9-	RIOPELLE,A.J.ADDISON	TEMPORAL FACTORS IN PATTERN DISCR	JCPP	62	55/926
9-	RIOPELLE,A.J.CHINN	POSITION HABITS AND DISCRIM LRNG	JCPP	61	54/178
9-	RIOPELLE,A.J.SHELL	TEMPORAL CONTIGUITY OF S AND R	JCPP	60	53/590
6-	RITCHIE,B.F.	REINFORCEMENT THEORY OF AVOIDANCE	PRV	51	58/383
8-	RITCHIE,B.F.	CUES IN DOUBLE-DRIVE DISCRIM	JCPP	59	52/602
9-	RITCHIE,B.F.ETAL	CONTINUITY IN DISC OF PATTERNS	JCPP	50	43/168
7-290	ROBBINS,D.	REVIEW-- PARTIAL REINF IN ALLEYWAY	PBL	71	76/415
7-290	ROBBINS,D.ETAL	EFFECTS OF NONREINF ON BEHAVIOR	JCPP	68	66/659

4-	ROBERTS,C.L.ETAL	SEC REINF BASED ON STIMULUS-CHANGE	JEXP	61	61/339
7-	ROBERTS,W.A.	SHIFTS IN REWARD MAGNITUDE	PSC	66	5/ 37
7-	ROBERTS,W.A.	PRE/VARYING MAGNITUDE OF REWARD	JCPP	69	67/395
9-	ROGERS,C.R.SKINNER	CONTROL OF HUMAN BEHAVIOR	SC	56	24/057
9-	ROGERS,R.C.BAYROFF	RESP ERRORS IN COND DISCRIM	JCPP	43	35/317
9-	ROSS,L.E.	EQUAL REINF OF DISCRIMINANDA	JCPP	62	55/260
9-	ROSS,L.E.	R TO PREVIOUS CUE IN A NEW PROBLEM	JCPP	62	55/944
9-	ROSS,L.E.ETAL	DIFF EYELID COND WITH MASKING	PSC	67	9/333
7-	ROSS,R.R.	POSITIVE AND NEGATIVE PRE	JEXP	64	68/492
9-	ROTHBLAT,L.C.WILSON	INTRA/EXTRADIMENSIONAL SHIFTS	JCPP	68	66/549
9-	ROWLEY,J.B.BOLLES	FORM DISCRIM IN WHITE MICE	JCPP	35	20/205
3-	ROZEBOOM,W.W.	WHAT IS LEARNED/EMPIRICAL ENIGMA	PRV	58	65/ 22
9-	RUDD,R.G.	INTERMEDIATE SIZE TRANSPOSITION	JCPP	57	50/292
8-327	RUDOLPH,R.L.	MONOCHROMATIC REARING ON S CONTROL	JCPP	69	67/ 50
8-	RUDOLPH,R.L.	MONOCHROMATIC REARING ON DISCRIM	JEAB	72	17/107
8-	RUDY,J.W.WAGNER	STIM SELECTION (ESTES)		75	LERLBA
7-	RUDY,J.W.ETAL	WITHIN SUBJECTS PRE	JCPP	70	72/105
8-	RUNQUIST,W.N.	DIFF AVOIDANCE EYELID COND	PRP	62	11/ 43
6-220	RUNQUIST,W.N.SPENCE	PERFORMANCE AND US DURATION	JEXP	59	57/249
8-	RUNQUIST,W.N.ETAL	DIFF COND AND INTENSITY OF US	JEXP	58	55/ 51
1-	SAHAKIAN,W.S.	PSYCHOLOGY OF LEARNING		70	MARKHM
9-	SALDANHA,E.L.BITTERMAN	RELATIONAL LEARNING IN THE RAT	AMJP	51	64/ 37
4+122	SALTZMAN,I.J.	LEARNING WITHOUT PRIMARY REINF	JCPP	49	42/161
4-	SALTZMAN,I.J.	GENERALIZATION OF SEC REINF	JEXP	50	40/189
5-	SALTZMAN,I.KOCH	LOW HUNGER ON MAXIMUM HABIT	JEXP	48	38/347
9-	SANDERS,B.	REVERSAL/NONREVERSAL SHIFTS	JCPP	71	74/292
9-	SARASON,I.G.ETAL	INTERTRIAL INTERVAL IN DISCRIM	JCPP	56	49/ 77
8-	SAUNDERS,J.C.	DISCRIM OF CLICK INTENSITY	JEAB	69	12/951
9-	SCHADE,A.F.BITTERMAN	OVERLEARN ON DIMENSIONAL SHIFT	PSC	65	3/283
9-	SCHADE,A.F.BITTERMAN	DIMENSIONAL SET ON REVERSAL	JCPP	66	62/ 43
9-	SCHAEFER,H.H.	COUNTING BEHAVIOR IN MONKEYS	PRP	63	13/791
6-223	SCHLOSBERG,H.	CONDITIONED RESPONSES IN WHITE RAT	JGNP	34	45/303
6-223	SCHLOSBERG,H.	CONDITIONED RESP BASED ON SHOCK	JGNP	36	49/107
4-	SCHLOSBERG,H.	SUCCESS AND LAWS OF CONDITIONING	PRV	37	44/279
4-	SCHLOSBERG,H.PRATT	SEC REWARD AND INACCESSIBLE FOOD	JCPP	56	49/149
8-	SCHMITT,D.R.MAXWELL	STIM CONTROL IN COOPERATION	JEAB	68	11/571
8-	SCHOEFFLER,M.S.	RESPONSE TO COMPOUNDS OF DISCRIM S	JEXP	54	48/323
6-217	SCHOENFELD,W.N.	ANXIETY, ESCAPE, AND AVOIDANCE		50	G/S
7-273	SCHOENFELD,W.N.	REG/PERIODIC REINF ON EXTINCTION	CEAB	50	20/ 1
5-	SCHOENFELD,W.N. (ED)	THEORY OF REINFORCEMENT SCHEDULES		70	A-C-C
5-186	SCHOENFELD,W.N.CUMMING	TEMPORAL CLASS OF REINF SCHEDULES	PNAS	60	46/750
4-125	SCHOENFELD,W.N.ETAL	CONDITION NECESSARY FOR SEC REINF	JEXP	50	40/ 40
5+153	SCHOENFELD,W.N.ETAL	CLASSIFICATION OF REINF SCHEDULES	PNAS	56	42/563
9-	SCHRIER,A.M.HARLOW	AMOUNT OF INCENTIVE ON DISCRIM	JCPP	56	49/117
2-	SCHRIER,A.M.ETAL (EDS)	BEHAVIOR OF NONHUMAN PRIMATES		71	ACAD P
4-	SCHRODER,H.M.	DEVEL/MAINT OF PREFERENCE VALUE	JEXP	56	51/139
2-	SCHULTZ,D.P.	HISTORY OF MODERN PSYCHOLOGY		69	ACAD P
9-	SCHULZ,R.W.LAWRENCE	SATIATION/DEPRIVATION ON DISC LRNG	AMJP	58	71/563
8-	SCHUR,P.	PREEXPOSE ELEMENTS OF COMPOUND S	JCPP	76	76/123
6-240	SCHUSTER,R.RACHLIN	NEGATIVE LAW OF EFFECT	JEAB	68	11/777
9-	SCHUSTERMAN,R.J.	SUCCESSIVE REVERSAL, ONE-TRIAL LRN	JCPP	64	58/153
9-	SCHWARTZ,R.M.ETAL	OPTIONAL INTRA/EXTRADIMENS SHIFTS	JCPP	71	77/470
9-	SCOTT,T.C.	EFFECT OF DIFFICULTY ON THE MAZE	JP	37	1/261
6-	SCULL,J.W.	INTERP OF FRUSTRATION EFFECT	PBL	73	79/352
9-	SEEMAN,W.WILLIAMS	HULL-LEEPER DIFFERENCE	JEXP	52	44/ 40
4-	SEGAL,B.CHAMPION	STIM ASSOCIATED WITH FOOD DEP	AUJP	66	18/ 57
4-	SEGAL,E.F.	COND REINF IN MULT-CHAIN SCHEDULE	PSC	64	1/175
4-	SEGAL,E.F.	CONDITIONED REINFORCEMENT	PSC	65	2/135
4-	SEGAL,E.F.	COND REINF WITH FOOD AND SHOCK	PSC	65	2/137
2+ 60	SELIGMAN,M.E.P.	GENERALITY OF LAWS OF LEARNING	PRV	70	77/406
6-	SELIGMAN,M.E.P.CAMPBELL	PUNISHMENT ON EXTINCTION OF AVOID	JCPP	65	59/295
6-	SELIGMAN,M.E.P.ETAL	UNPREDICT/UNCONTROL SHOCK (BRUSH)		71	ACAD P
8-	SENF,G.M.MILLER	POS INDUCTION IN DISCRIM LRNG	JCPP	67	64/121

3-	SEWARD,J.P.	EXPER ANALYSIS OF LATENT LEARNING	JEXP	49	39/177
4-	SEWARD,J.P.	SEC REINF AS TERTIARY MOTIVATION	PRV	50	57/362
5-	SEWARD,J.P.	MOTIVATING FUNCTION OF REWARD	PBL	51	48/130
5-	SEWARD,J.P.	THEORY OF MOTIVATION IN LEARNING	PRV	52	59/405
5-	SEWARD,J.P.	HOW ARE MOTIVES LEARNED	PRV	53	60/ 99
2-	SEWARD,J.P.	CRITIQUE OF INTERVENING VARIABLES	PRV	55	52/155
3-	SEWARD,J.P.	REINFORCEMENT AND EXPECTANCY	PRV	56	63/105
5+202	SEWARD,J.P.	DRIVE, INCENTIVE, AND REINF	PRV	56	63/195
7+271	SEWARD,J.P.LEVY	LATENT EXTINCTION	JEXP	49	39/660
4-118	SEWARD,J.P.LEVY	CHOICE-POINT BEHAVIOR/SEC REINF	JCPP	53	46/334
7-	SHANAB,M.E.BILLER	DELAY AND REWARD MAG SHIFT	L+M	72	3/179
7-285	SHANAB,M.E.CAVALLARO	POS CONTRAST AFTER REWARD SHIFT	BLPS	75	5/109
7-	SHANAB,M.E.MCCUISTION	DELAY AND REWARD MAG SHIFTS	PSC	70	21/264
7-	SHANAB,M.E.ETAL	EFFECT OF SHIFT IN REWARD DELAY	JGNP	73	89/ 59
6+223	SHEFFIELD,F.D.	AVOIDANCE AND CONTIGUITY PRINCIPLE	JCPP	48	41/165
7-	SHEFFIELD,F.D.	CONTIGUITY PRINCIPLE IN LRNG TH	PRV	51	48/362
5+169	SHEFFIELD,F.D.	DRIVE-INDUCTION THEORY (HABER)		66	HOLT
4+102	SHEFFIELD,F.D.ROBY	REWARD-- NONNUTRITIVE SWEET TASTE	JCPP	50	43/471
6-223	SHEFFIELD,F.D.TEMMER	RESIST EXTINCTION OF ESCAPE/AVOID	JEXP	50	40/287
4-110	SHEFFIELD,F.D.ETAL	REWARD VALUE OF COPULATION	JCPP	51	44/ 3
4-	SHEFFIELD,F.D.ETAL	CONSUMMATORY BEHAVIOR REINF	JCPP	54	47/349
7+281	SHEFFIELD,V.F.	PARTIAL REINF/DISTRIB OF PRACTICE	JEXP	49	39/511
7-271	SHEFFIELD,V.F.	RESIST EXTINCTION/DISTRIB TRIALS	JEXP	50	40/305
9-	SHEPP,B.E.EIMAS	INTRA/EXTRADIMENSIONAL SHIFTS	JCPP	64	57/357
9-	SHEPP,B.E.SCHRIER	INTRA/EXTRADIMENSIONAL SHIFTS	JCPP	69	67/199
9-	SHERMAN,J.A.THOMAS	PREFERENCE BETWEEN FR AND VR SCHED	JEAB	68	11/689
8-	SHERMAN,J.G.PIERREL	DISCRIM ON INTENSITY GENERALIZATN	JEAB	61	4/237
9-	SHERMAN,M.STRUNK	SINGLE/DOUBLE DISCR ON TRANSPOSITN	JCPP	64	58/449
8-	SHETTLEWORTH,S.NEVIN	RELATIVE R RATE AND RELATIVE REINF	JEAB	65	8/199
8-	SHIMP,C.P.	CONCURRENT REINF OF 2 IRTS	JEAB	69	12/403
9-	SHIMP,C.P.	THE BEHAVIORAL UNIT (ESTES)		75	LERLBA
8-	SHINKMAN,P.G.	VISUAL DEPTH DISCRIM IN ANIMALS	PBL	62	59/489
6+222	SIDMAN,M.	AVOIDANCE WITH NO WARNING STIMULUS	SC	53	18/157
6-224	SIDMAN,M.	TEMPORAL PARAMETERS OF AVOIDANCE	JCPP	53	46/253
6-224	SIDMAN,M.	DELAYED-PUNISHMENT EFFECTS	JCPP	54	47/145
8-	SIDMAN,M.	TIME DISCRIM IN FREE OPERANT SIT	JCPP	56	49/469
2-	SIDMAN,M.	TACTICS OF SCIENTIFIC RESEARCH		60	BASIC
6+227	SIDMAN,M.	REDUCTION OF SHOCK FREQ AS REINF	JEAB	62	5/247
6-	SIDMAN,M.	AVOIDANCE BEHAVIOR (HONIG)		66	A-C-C
6-215	SIDMAN,M.ETAL	MAINTENANCE OF AVOIDANCE	JCPP	57	50/553
4-116	SIEGEL,P.S.MILBY	SEC REINF AND SHOCK TERMINATION	PBL	69	72/146
9-	SIEGEL,S.	OVERTRAINING AND TRANSFER	JCPP	67	64/471
4-	SIMON,G.W.ETAL	SEC REINF ON PRIMARY THIRST DRIVE	JCPP	51	44/ 67
8-	SINGER,G.ETAL	GENERALIZATION AND EASY-TO-HARD	JCPP	69	69/ 528
9-	SINHA,M.M.	REINF SINGLE S ON DISCRIM LRNG	JCPP	58	51/ 87
9-	SKINNER,B.F.	INHERITANCE OF MAZE BEHAVIOR	JGNP	30	4/342
4-	SKINNER,B.F.	ELICITATION OF EATING REFLEXES	PNAS	30	16/433
1-	SKINNER,B.F.	THE CONCEPT OF THE REFLEX	JGNP	31	5/427
1-	SKINNER,B.F.	DRIVE AND REFLEX STRENGTH	JGNP	32	6/ 22
1-	SKINNER,B.F.	DRIVE AND REFLEX STRENGTH II	JGNP	32	6/ 38
2-	SKINNER,B.F.	RATE OF FORMATION OF COND REFLEX	JGNP	32	7/274
2-	SKINNER,B.F.	RATE OF EXTINCTION OF COND REFLEX	JGNP	33	8/114
8-	SKINNER,B.F.	RATE OF ESTABLISHMENT OF DISCRIM	JGNP	33	9/302
9-	SKINNER,B.F.	MSMT OF SPONTANEOUS ACTIVITY	JGNP	33	9/ 3
7-	SKINNER,B.F.	RESISTANCE TO EXTINCTION IN COND	JGNP	33	9/420
8-	SKINNER,B.F.	ABOLISHMENT OF A DISCRIMINATION	PNAS	33	19/825
7-	SKINNER,B.F.	EXTINCTION OF CHAINED REFLEXES	PNAS	34	20/234
8-	SKINNER,B.F.	DISCRIM WITHOUT PREVIOUS COND	PNAS	34	20/532
2-	SKINNER,B.F.	GENERIC NATURE OF CONCEPTS OF S+R	JGNP	35	12/ 40
3+	SKINNER,B.F.	TWO TYPES OF CONDITIONED REFLEX	JGNP	35	12/ 66
8-	SKINNER,B.F.	DISCRIM ON CHANGE IN PROPERTY OF S	JGNP	35	12/313
8-	SKINNER,B.F.	FAILURE TO OBTAIN DISINHIBITION	JGNP	36	14/127
4-	SKINNER,B.F.	REINF EFFECT OF DIFFERENTIAT STIM	JGNP	36	14/263

5-		SKINNER,B.F.	COND WITH INTERVAL OF TIME/REINF	JGNP	36 14/279
4-		SKINNER,B.F.	COND/EXTINCTION AND DRIVE	JGNP	36 14/296
4-		SKINNER,B.F.	THIRST AS AN ARBITRARY DRIVE	JGNP	36 15/205
3-	70	SKINNER,B.F.	TWO TYPES OF CONDITIONED REFLEX	JGNP	37 16/272
1+	41	SKINNER,B.F.	BEHAVIOR OF ORGANISMS		38 A-C
4-		SKINNER,B.F.	MAINTAINING A DEGREE OF HUNGER	JCP	40 30/139
2-		SKINNER,B.F.	OPERATIONAL ANALYSIS /PSYCH TERMS	PRV	45 52/270
5-		SKINNER,B.F.	OPERATIONAL ANALYSIS OF TERMS	PRV	45 52/291
2-		SKINNER,B.F.	WALDEN TWO		48 MACMIL
5-152		SKINNER,B.F.	-SUPERSTITION- IN THE PIGEON	JEXP	48 38/168
2-	45	SKINNER,B.F.	ARE THEORIES OF LEARNING NECESSARY	PRV	50 57/193
1-		SKINNER,B.F.	HOW TO TEACH ANIMALS	SCAM	51 85/ 26
3+	99	SKINNER,B.F.	SCIENCE AND HUMAN BEHAVIOR		53 MACMIL
2-		SKINNER,B.F.	CONTRIB OF EXPER ANAL BEH TO PSYCH	AMP	53 8/ 69
2-	54	SKINNER,B.F.	SCIENCE AND THE ART OF TEACHING	HEDR	54 24/ 86
2-		SKINNER,B.F.	CASE HISTORY OF SCIENTIFIC METHOD	AMP	56 11/221
8-320		SKINNER,B.F.	EXPERIMENTAL ANALYSIS OF BEHAVIOR	AMSC	57 45/343
5-149		SKINNER,B.F.	DIAGRAMMING REINF SCEDULES	JEAB	58 1/ 67
9-		SKINNER,B.F.	REINFORCEMENT TODAY	AMP	58 13/ 94
2-		SKINNER,B.F.	TEACHING MACHINES	SC	58 28/969
8-		SKINNER,B.F.	PIGEONS IN A PELICAN	AMP	60 15/ 28
9-		SKINNER,B.F.	WHY WE NEED TEACHING MACHINES	HEDR	61 31/377
2-		SKINNER,B.F.	TEACHING MACHINES	SCAM	61 05/ 90
2-		SKINNER,B.F.	OPERANDUM	JEAB	62 5/224
9-		SKINNER,B.F.	TWO -SYNTHETIC SOCIAL RELATIONS-	JEAB	62 5/531
9-		SKINNER,B.F.	BEHAVIORISM AT FIFTY	SC	63 40/951
5-		SKINNER,B.F.	OPERANT BEHAVIOR	AMP	63 18/503
8-		SKINNER,B.F.	STIM GENERALIZATION (MOSTOFSKY)		65 STANFD
2-		SKINNER,B.F.	PHYLOGENY/ONTOGENY OF BEHAVIOR	SC	66 53/205
2-		SKINNER,B.F.	WHAT IS EXPER ANAL OF BEHAVIOR	JEAB	66 9/213
2-		SKINNER,B.F.	THE TECHNOLOGY OF TEACHING		68 A-C-C
2+	52	SKINNER,B.F.	CONTINGENCIES OF REINFORCEMENT		69 A-C-C
9-		SKINNER,B.F.	AUTOSHAPING	SC	71 73/752
9-		SKINNER,B.F.	BEYOND FREEDOM AND DIGNITY		71 KNOPF
9-		SKINNER,B.F.	ABOUT BEHAVIORISM		74 KNOPF
9-		SKINNER,B.F.	STEEP/THORNY WAY TO BEH SCIENCE	AMP	75 30/ 42
5-		SKINNER,B.F.MORSE	CONCURRENT ACTIVITY UNDER FI REINF	JCPP	57 50/279
5-		SKINNER,B.F.MORSE	VERY LONG EXPERIMENTAL SESSIONS	JEAB	58 1/235
5-		SKINNER,B.F.MORSE	FI REINF OF RUNNING IN A WHEEL	JEAB	58 1/371
8-		SLUCKI,H.ETAL	OPERANT DISCRIM OF INTERCEPTIVE S	JEAB	65 8/405
3-		SMEDSLUND,J.	PROBLEM OF WHAT IS LEARNED	PRV	53 60/157
3+	76	SMITH,K.	CONDITIONING AS ARTIFACT	PRV	54 61/217
9-		SMITH,K.U.	PAIRED/UNPAIRED STIM DISCRIM	JGTP	36 48/ 29
4-		SMITH,M.F.	TOKEN REWARD HABIT IN THE CAT	JGNP	39 20/475
8-		SMITH,M.P.	S TRACE GRADIENT IN VISUAL DISCRIM	JCPP	51 44/154
4-		SMITH,M.P.BUCHANAN	SEC REINF BY CUES ASSOC WITH SHOCK	JEXP	54 48/123
2-		SMYTH,H.D.	FROM X-RAYS TO NUCLEAR FISSION	AMSC	47 35/485
5-149		SNAPPER,A.G.ETAL	REINF SCHEDULES (SCHOENFELD)		70 A-C-C
9-394		SNYGG,D.	TAKE THE LONGER MAZE PATH TO FOOD	JP	36 1/153
6-235		SOLOMON,R.L.	PUNISHMENT	AMP	64 19/239
6-227		SOLOMON,R.L.BRUSH	ANXIETY AND AVERSION (JONES)		56 U NEBR
4-		SOLOMON,R.L.CORBIT	OPPONENT PROCESS-- CIGARET ADDICT	JABP	73 81/158
4-		SOLOMON,R.L.CORBIT	OPPONENT PROCESS THEORY OF MOTIV	PRV	74 81/119
6-223		SOLOMON,R.L.WYNNE	TRAUMATIC AVOIDANCE LEARNING	PMG	53 67/354
6-216		SOLOMON,R.L.WYNNE	TRAUMATIC AVOIDANCE LEARNING	PRV	54 61/353
4-122		SOLOMON,R.L.ETAL	TRAUMATIC AVOIDANCE LEARNING	JASP	53 48/291
9-		SPAET,T.HARLOW	MULT SIGN PROBLEM WITH ODDITY	JCP	43 35/119
7-		SPEAR,N.E.	CHOICE/REWARD MAG AND PERCENT	JEXP	64 68/ 44
7-		SPEAR,N.E.	ABSENCE OF SUCCESSIVE CONTRAST	PRP	65 16/393
7-		SPEAR,N.E.	RETENTION OF REINFORCER MAGNITUDE	PRV	67 74/216
8-		SPEAR,N.E.HILL	SIMULT/SUCCESSIVE CONTRAST	JEXP	65 70/510
7-		SPEAR,N.E.PAVLIK	SIMULT/SUCCESSIVE CONTRAST EFFECTS	PMG	66 80/618
7-		SPEAR,N.E.SPITZNER	EFFECT OF INITIAL NONREWARDED TR	JEXP	67 74/525

8-	SPEAR,N.E.SPITZNER	MAG OF REINF ON CONTRAST AND EXT	JCPP	69	68/427
7-290	SPEAR,N.E.ETAL	PERF AFTER INITIAL NONREWARDED TR	JEXP	64	69/ 25
9-	SPENCE,K.W.	RELIABILITY OF THE MAZE	CPMG	32	8/ 1
9-	SPENCE,K.W.	ORDER OF ELIMINATING BLIND ALLEYS	JCP	32	14/ 9
9-	SPENCE,K.W.	VISUAL ACUITY IN CHIMPANZEE	JCP	34	18/333
9-374	SPENCE,K.W.	NATURE OF DISCRIMINATION LEARNING	PRV	36	43/427
3- 72	SPENCE,K.W.	ANALYSIS OF VISUAL DISCRIM HABIT	JCP	37	23/ 77
9-374	SPENCE,K.W.	STIMULI WITHIN SINGLE DIMENSION	PRV	37	44/430
9-	SPENCE,K.W.	HIGHER MENTAL PROCESSES IN ANIMALS	PBL	37	34/806
9-374	SPENCE,K.W.	GRADUAL VS SUDDEN SOLUTION	JCP	38	25/213
9-374	SPENCE,K.W.	TRANSPOSITION IN DISCRIMINATION	PRV	39	46/ 88
9-	SPENCE,K.W.	MULTIPLE CHOICE PROBLEMS BY CHIMPS	CPMG	39	15/ 55
9-374	SPENCE,K.W.	CONTINUOUS VS NONCONTINUOUS INTERP	PRV	40	47/271
9-	SPENCE,K.W.	FAILURE OF TRANSPOSITION IN SIZE	AMJP	41	54/223
9-	SPENCE,K.W.	INTERMEDIATE SIZE PROBLEM BY CHIMP	JEXP	42	36/257
2-	SPENCE,K.W.	THEORETICAL INTERP LRNG (MOSS)		42	P-HALL
2-	SPENCE,K.W.	NATURE OF THEORY IN PSYCHOLOGY	PRV	44	51/ 47
9-	SPENCE,K.W.	TEST OF CONTINUITY/NONCONTINUITY	JEXP	45	35/253
4-	SPENCE,K.W.	SEC REINF IN DELAYED REWARD LRNG	PRV	47	54/ 1
2-	SPENCE,K.W.	POSTULATES/METHODS OF BEHAVIORISM	PRV	48	55/ 67
8-	SPENCE,K.W.	EYELID CONDITIONING AND ITI	JEXP	50	40/716
3+ 67	SPENCE,K.W.	COGNITIVE VS S-R THEORIES OF LRNG	PRV	50	57/159
3- 66	SPENCE,K.W.	THEORETICAL INTERP/LRNG (STEVENS)		51	WILEY
5-	SPENCE,K.W.	THEORETICAL INTERP/LRNG (STONE)		51	P-HALL
8-383	SPENCE,K.W.	NATURE OF R IN DISCRIMINATION LRNG	PRV	52	59/ 89
2-	SPENCE,K.W.	MATHEMATICAL FORMULATIONS/LEARNING	PRV	52	59/152
2-	SPENCE,K.W.	MATHEMATICAL THEORIES OF LEARNING	JGNP	53	49/283
8-	SPENCE,K.W.	EYELID COND AND INTENSITY OF US	JEXP	53	45/ 57
2-	SPENCE,K.W.	LATENCY AND SPEED IN S-R THEORY	PRV	54	61/209
9- 54	SPENCE,K.W.	LEARNING THEORY/TECHNOLOGY OF EDUC	HEDR	54	29/ 84
2+169	SPENCE,K.W.	BEHAVIOR THEORY AND CONDITIONING		56	YALE
2-	SPENCE,K.W.	EMPIRICAL/THEORETICAL STRUCTURE	PHSC	57	24/ 97
9-	SPENCE,K.W.	BEHAVIOR THEORY AND SELECTIVE LRNG		58	U NEBR
6-	SPENCE,K.W.	EMOTIONALLY BASED DRIVE IN LRNG	AMJP	58	71/131
5-179	SPENCE,K.W.	BEHAVIOR THEORY AND LEARNING		60	P-HALL
4-	SPENCE,K.W.	COGNITIVE FACTORS IN EXTINCTION	SC	63	40/224
4-	SPENCE,K.W.	ANXIETY IN EYELID CONDITIONING	PBL	64	61/129
7-	SPENCE,K.W.	PRESENCE OF US DURING EXTINCTION	JEXP	66	70/642
8-	SPENCE,K.W.BEECROFT	DIFFERENTIAL COND AND ANXIETY	JEXP	54	48/399
4-	SPENCE,K.W.FARBER	COND/EXTINCTION AND ANXIETY	JEXP	53	45/116
8-	SPENCE,K.W.FARBER	ANXIETY IN DIFF EYELID COND	JEXP	54	47/127
6-	SPENCE,K.W.GOLDSTEIN	EMOTION-PRODUCING INSTRUCTIONS	JEXP	61	62/291
9-	SPENCE,K.W.GRICE	FINAL AND SUBGOALS IN DISTANCE	JCP	42	37/179
9-392	SPENCE,K.W.HULL	CORRECTION VS NONCORRECTION	JCP	38	25/127
3-	SPENCE,K.W.KENDLER	TESTS OF SIGN-GESTALT THEORY	JEXP	48	38/106
3+ 77	SPENCE,K.W.LIPPITT	TEST OF SIGN-GESTALT THEORY	JEXP	46	36/491
8-	SPENCE,K.W.PLATT	US INTENSITY IN EYELID COND	PBL	66	65/ 1
1-	SPENCE,K.W.ROSS	FORM AND LATENCY OF EYELID RESP	JEXP	59	58/376
6-	SPENCE,K.W.RUNQUIST	CONDITIONED FEAR ON EYELID REFLEX	JEXP	58	55/613
7-	SPENCE,K.W.RUTLEDGE	OVERLEARNING ON EXTINCTION--EYELID	PSC	64	1/315
9-	SPENCE,K.W.SHIPLEY	DIFFICULTY OF BLIND ALLEYS	JCP	34	17/423
6-	SPENCE,K.W.SPENCE	SEX AND ANXIETY IN EYELID COND	PBL	66	63/137
3-	SPENCE,K.W.TANDLER	REINFORCING US WITH EQUATED DRIVE	JEXP	63	65/ 35
6-	SPENCE,K.W.TAYLOR	ANXIETY AND UCS IN EYELID COND	JEXP	51	42/183
4-	SPENCE,K.W.TRAPOLD	REINF SCHEDULES IN EYELID COND	PNAS	62	47/860
6-	SPENCE,K.W.WEYANT	ANXIETY ON COND WITHOUT WARNING S	JEXP	60	60/146
6-	SPENCE,K.W.ETAL	IRRELEVANT MOTIVATION-REWARD	JEXP	50	40/539
6-	SPENCE,K.W.ETAL	SHOCK AND ANXIETY IN EYELID COND	JEXP	54	48/404
9-	SPENCE,K.W.ETAL	ANXIETY IN COMPETITIONAL PA LRNG	JEXP	56	52/296
8-	SPENCE,K.W.ETAL	DIFF COND AND US INTENSITY	JEXP	58	55/ 51
8-	SPENCE,K.W.ETAL	US INTENSITY AND HABIT STRENGTH	JEXP	58	55/404
8-	SPENCE,K.W.ETAL	US INTENSITY WITHIN SUBJECT	SC	58	28/774
8-	SPENCE,K.W.ETAL	DIFFERENTIAL COND AND HUNGER	JEXP	59	58/ 8

7-	SPENCE,K.W.ETAL	US ON EXTINCTION OF EYELID RESP	JEXP	63 66/286
7-	SPENCE,K.W.ETAL	EXTINCTION AND DISCRIMINABILITY	JEXP	64 67/545
7-	SPENCE,K.W.ETAL	INTERTRIAL REINFORCEMENT AND PRE	PSC	65 3/205
9-395	SPERLING,S.E.	REVERSAL AND RESISTANCE TO EXTICT	PBL	65 63/281
9-	SPERLING,S.E.	SUPPLEMENT--REVERSAL + EXTINCTION	PBL	65 64/310
6-	SPERLING,S.E.VALLE	HANDLING-GENTLING AS POS SEC REINF	JEXP	64 67/573
3+ 71	SPIELBERGER,C.D.	AWARENESS IN VERBAL COND (ERIKSEN)		62 DUKE
9-	SPIKER,C.C.	STIM SIMILARITY ON DISCRIM LRNG	JEXP	56 51/393
?-	SPIVEY,J.E.	N-R TRANSITIONS ON RESIST EXTINCT	JEXP	67 75/ 43
7-	SPIVEY,J.E.HESS	PARTIAL REINF TRIAL SEQUENCES	PSC	68 10/375
7-	SPIVEY,J.E.ETAL	REINF AFTEREFFECTS AND TRAINING	PRP	68 22/ 35
7-	SPIVEY,J.E.ETAL	PRE/PATTERN AND INTERTRIAL REINF	PSC	68 10/377
7-	SPIVEY,J.E.ETAL	N-R TRANSITIONS/INTERTRIAL REINF	PRP	68 22/765
7-	SPIVEY,J.E.ETAL	R DECREMENT/SHIFT REINF SCHEDULE	PSC	69 13/143
9-393	SPRAGG,S.D.S.	ANTICIPATION IN MAZE ERRORS	JCP	33 15/313
8-	STADDON,J.E.R.	MULTIPLE FI SCHEDULES	JEAB	69 12/583
1-	STADDON,J.E.R.	THEORY/REINF SCHEDULES (GILBERT)		72 ACAD P
8-	STADDON,J.E.R.	TEMP CONTROL, ATTENTION, MEMORY	PRV	74 81/375
8-	STADDON,J.E.R.	COMPETITION IN COND (DAVIS)		77 LERLBA
7-	STANLEY,W.C.CLAYTON	TEST OF WEINSTOCK-S HYPOTHESIS	PRP	55 1/421
9-	STAUB,E.ETAL	SELF-CONTROL AND PREDICTABILITY	JPSP	71 18/157
4-	STEBBINS,W.C.	AMOUNT REINF ON DISCRIM/SEC REINF	JCPP	59 52/721
4-125	STEIN,L.	SEC REINF ESTABLISHED WITH ESB	SC	58 27/466
4-	STEIN,L.	CHEMISTRY OF PURPOSIVE BEH (TAFT)		69 ACAD P
6+214	STEIN,L.ETAL	TEMPORAL VARIABLES/COND SUPPRESS	JEAB	58 1/151
4-	STEINMAN,W.M.	GENERALIZED CONDITIONED REINF	PRC	66 16/457
9-	STETTNER,L.J.	PERSISTENCE OF DISC, EQUAL REINF	JCPP	65 60/262
2-	STEVENS,S.S.	OPERATIONAL DEFINITIONS/CONCEPTS	PRV	35 42/517
2-	STEVENS,S.S.	PSYCHOLOGY AND SCIENCE OF SCIENCE	PBL	38 36/221
8-321	STEVENS,S.S. (ED)	HANDBOOK OF EXPERIMENTAL PSYCHOL		51 WILEY
9-	STEVENSON,H.W.BITTERMAN	INTERMEDIATE SIZE TRANSPOSITION	AMJP	55 68/274
9-	STEVENSON,H.W.ISCOE	OVERTRAINING AND TRANSPOSITION	AMJP	54 47/251
8-	STEVENSON,J.G.	ORDER OF TEST S ON GENERALIZATION	JEAB	66 9/457
4-	STEVENSON,J.G.REESE	TWO SCHED OF PRIMARY/COND REINF	JEAB	62 5/505
9-	STEWART,C.N.WARREN	CATS ON DOUBLE ALTERNATION PROB	JCPP	57 50/ 26
9-	STOLLNITZ,F.SCHRIER	SPATIAL SEPARATION OF CUE AND RESP	JCPP	62 55/876
5-	STOLZ,S.B.LOTT	NET LOSS OF REINFORCEMENT	JCPP	64 57/147
2-	STONE,C.P. (ED)	COMPARATIVE PSYCHOLOGY		51 P-HALL
6-238	STONE,G.R.	EFFECT OF NEGATIVE INCENTIVE	JGNP	50 42/179
6-238	STONE,G.R.WALTERS	NEGATIVE INCENTIVES IN SERIAL LRNG	JEXP	51 41/411
9-	STRETCH,R.G.ETAL	TRAINING CRITERIA ON REVERSAL	JCPP	63 56/719
9-	STRETCH,R.G.ETAL	TRIALS/PROBLEM + ITI ON REVERSAL	JCPP	64 57/461
4-	STUBBS,A.	COMPETITIVE COND REINF AND DRL	PSC	67 8/299
8-	STUBBS,A.	DISCRIM OF STIMULUS DURATION	JEAB	68 11/223
7-	SURRIDGE,C.T.	PERF AT 12-MIN/20-SEC ITI	PSC	67 9/501
7-	SURRIDGE,C.T.AMSEL	A -PATTERNING- EFFECT	PSC	65 31/373
7-	SURRIDGE,C.T.AMSEL	SINGLE ALTERNATION REINF SCHEDULE	PSC	65 3/131
?-	SURRIDGE,C.T.AMSEL	SINGLE ALTERN/RANDOM PARTIAL REINF	JEXP	66 72/361
7-	SURRIDGE,C.T.AMSEL	CONFINEMENT DURATION AND PATTERN	PSC	68 10/107
7-	SURRIDGE,C.T.ETAL	INTERPOLATED EXTINCTION ON REACQ	JEXP	66 72/564
7-	SURRIDGE,C.T.ETAL	RESIST EXTINCT/SMALL TRIAL NUMBER	PSC	67 7/ 31
8-	SUTHERLAND,N.S.	VISUAL DISC OF SHAPE IN OCTOPUS	QJEP	58 10/ 40
8-	SUTHERLAND,N.S.	DISC OF STIM ORIENTATION, OCTOPUS	JCPP	58 51/452
8-	SUTHERLAND,N.S.	THEORY OF SHAPE DISCRIMINATION	JCPP	59 52/135
8-	SUTHERLAND,N.S.	DISC OF SQUARE AND RECTANGLE	JCPP	60 53/ 95
8-	SUTHERLAND,N.S.	DISC OF OPEN AND CLOSED FORMS	JCPP	60 53/104
8-	SUTHERLAND,N.S.	DISC OF HORIZONTAL/VERTICAL EXTENT	JCPP	61 54/ 43
8-	SUTHERLAND,N.S.	DISC OF SQUARES AND CROSSES	JCPP	62 55/939
8-	SUTHERLAND,N.S.	DISC OF OPEN/CLOSED SHAPES BY RATS	QJEP	64 16/268
9-	SUTHERLAND,N.S.	SUCCESSIVE REVERSALS WITH 2 CUES	QJEP	66 18/ 97
7-273	SUTHERLAND,N.S.	PARTIAL REINF/BREADTH OF LEARNING	QJEP	66 18/289
9-	SUTHERLAND,N.S.	COMPARATIVE STUDY OF SHAPE DISCRIM	JCPP	69 67/160
9-	SUTHERLAND,N.S.ANDELMAN	LRNG WITH 1 OR 2 CUES	PSC	67 7/107

9-	SUTHERLAND,N.S.CARR	TRANSFER OF OPEN/CLOSED DISCRIM	QJEP	62	14/140
9-	SUTHERLAND,N.S.CARR	SIZE OF SHAPE DISCRIM	QJEP	63	15/225
9-	SUTHERLAND,N.S.HOLGATE	TWO-CUE DISC LRNG IN RATS	JCPP	66	61/198
9-	SUTHERLAND,N.MACKINTOSH	OPTIONAL EXTRADIMENSIONAL REVERSAL	PSC	66	5/343
9-396	SUTHERLAND,N.MACKINTOSH	MECHANISMS OF ANIMAL DISCRIM LRNG		71	ACAD P
7-	SUTHERLAND,N.S.ETAL	TRANSFER SIMULT DISC ON CONTINUUM	JCPP	63	56/150
7-292	SUTHERLAND,N.S.ETAL	EXTINCTION AND ORDER OF REINF	JEXP	65	69/ 56
7-	TACKER,R.S.WOY	MOTIV PROPERTIES OF NONREWARD	PSC	68	10/103
2-	TAPP,J.T. (ED)	REINFORCEMENT AND BEHAVIOR		69	ACAD P
5-	TARPY,R.M.SAWABINI	REVIEW OF REINF DELAY	PBL	74	81/984
8-	TEAS,D.C.BITTERMAN	PERCEPTUAL ORGANIZATION IN RATS	PRV	52	59/130
8-	TERMAN,M.KLING	DISCRIM OF BRIGHTNESS DIFFERENCES	JEAB	68	11/ 29
8- 57	TERRACE,H.S.	DISC LRNG WITH AND WITHOUT ERRORS	JEAB	63	6/ 1
8-	TERRACE,H.S.	ERRORLESS TRANSFER OF A DISCRIM	JEAB	63	6/223
8-	TERRACE,H.S.	EXTENDED TRNG ON CONTRAST/PEAK SFT	JEAB	66	9/613
8-	TERRACE,H.S.	STIMULUS CONTROL (HONIG)		66	A-C-C
8-	TERRACE,H.S.	DISCRIM LEARNING AND INHIBITION	SC	66	54/167
8-332	TERRACE,H.S.	DISC LRNG, PEAK SHIFT, CONTRAST	JEAB	68	11/727
8-	TERRACE,H.S.	ERRORS ON EXTINCTION AFTER DISCRIM	JEAB	69	12/571
8-	TERRACE,H.S.	BY-PRODUCTS OF DISCRIM LEARNING	PL+M	72	5/195
8-	TERRY,W.S.WAGNER	SHORT-TERM MEMORY IN PAVLOV COND	ABP	75	04/122
6-	TESTA,T.J.	CAUSAL RELATIONSHIPS IN AVOIDANCE	PRV	74	81/491
7-291	THEIOS,J.	PRE THROUGH BLOCKS OF CRF	JEXP	62	64/ 1
6-	THEIOS,J.	TWO-STAGE ALL-OR-NONE LEARNING	PRV	63	70/403
4-107	THEIOS,J.	DRIVE STIMULUS GENERALIZATION	JCPP	63	56/691
6-	THEIOS,J.	MATH MODELS/AVERSIVE COND (BRUSH)		71	ACAD P
7-274	THEIOS,J.BRELSFORD	OVERLEARNING-EXTINCTION EFFECT	JEXP	64	67/463
7-	THEIOS,J.MCGINNIS	ORDER OF PARTIAL/CONTINUOUS REINF	JEXP	67	73/479
7-	THEIOS,J.POLSON	NONRESPONSIVE PARTIAL REINF	JCPP	62	55/987
3-	THISTLETHWAITE,D.	CRITICAL REVIEW OF LATENT LEARNING	PBL	51	48/ 97
3-	THISTLETHWAITE,D.	REPLY TO KENDLER AND MALTZMAN	PBL	52	59/ 51
8+364	THOMAS,D.R.	ANIMAL PERCEPTUAL PROC (GILBERT)		69	ACAD P
8-	THOMAS,D.R.	STIMULUS SELECTION (REYNEIRSE)		70	U NEBR
8-	THOMAS,D.R.	ADAPTATION LEVEL IN STIM GENERALIZ	PL+M	74	8/ 91
4-125	THOMAS,D.R.CARONITE	DISCRIM ON STIM GEN OF COND REINF	JEXP	64	68/402
4-	THOMAS,D.R.DEROSA	GEN OF REINF AND DISCRIM STIM	JEXP	66	72/260
8-	THOMAS,D.R.KONICK	R MEASURE IN STIM GENERALIZATION	JEAB	66	9/239
4-	THOMAS,D.R.WILLIAMS	STIM GEN OF POSITIVE COND REINF	SC	63	41/172
8-	THOMAS,D.R.WILLIAMS	3-STIM DISCRIM ON GENERALIZATION	JEAB	63	6/171
8-	THOMAS,D.R.ETAL	MIRROR-IMAGE TRANSFER EFFECTS	JEAB	66	9/567
4-126	THOMAS,D.R.ETAL	INFORMATION VALUE AND COND REINF	JEXP	68	76/181
8-	THOMAS,D.R.ETAL	DELAY BEFORE TESTING GENERALIZATN	JEAB	69	12/105
8-	THOMAS,D.R.ETAL	STIM CONTROL AFTER PRE-EXPOSURE	JEXP	69	79/375
8-336	THOMAS,D.R.ETAL	EXTRADIMENSIONAL TRNG ON GENERALIZ	JEXP	70	83/ 1
8-336	THOMAS,D.R.ETAL	STIM SELECTION IN DISCRIM LRNG	JEXP	70	86/ 53
8-	THOMAS,D.R.ETAL	NONSPECIFIC TRANSFER OF DISCRIM	JCPP	71	74/ 96
8-	THOMPSON,C.P.VANHOESEN	COMPONENT INTENSITY ON COMPOUND	JCPP	67	64/128
8-	THOMPSON,R.	APPROACH-AVOIDANCE IN DISCRIM	JEXP	53	45/341
8-	THOMPSON,R.	APPROACH-AVOIDANCE IN DISCRIM	JCPP	54	47/133
9-	THOMPSON,R.	STIM COMPARISON ON TRANSPOSITION	JEXP	55	50/185
9-	THOMPSON,R.	STIM COMPARISON ON TRANSPOSITION	JEXP	55	50/501
8-322	THOMPSON,R.F.	NEURAL BASIS OF GEN (MOSTOFSKY)		65	STANFD
9-	THORESON,E.MAHONEY	BEHAVIORAL SELF-CONTROL		74	H-R-W
2- 44	THORNDIKE,E.L.	ANIMAL INTELLIGENCE		11	MACMIL
4- 98	THORNDIKE,E.L.	EDUCATIONAL PSYCHOLOGY		13	COLMBA
3-216	THORNDIKE,E.L.	HUMAN LEARNING		31	A-C-C
1- 98	THORNDIKE,E.L.	PSYCHOLOGY OF LEARNING		31	COLMBA
4-	THORNDIKE,E.L.	FUNDAMENTALS OF LEARNING		32	COLMBA
2-	THORNDIKE,E.L.	CONNECTIONIST PSYCHOLOGY		49	A-C-C
5-	THURSTONE,L.L.	PSYCHOPHYSICAL ANALYSIS	AMJP	27	38/368
5-184	THURSTONE,L.L.	LAW OF COMPARATIVE JUDGMENT	PRV	27	34/273
5-	THURSTONE,L.L.	MEASUREMENT OF VALUES		59	U CHI
9-	TIGHE,L.S.	PERCEPTUAL PRETRAINING ON REVERSAL	JEXP	65	70/379

9-	TIGHE,T.J.	REVERSAL/NONREVERSAL SHIFTS	JCPP	64 58/324
9-	TIGHE,T.J.	OVERTRAIN ON REVERSAL/EXTRADIMEN	JEXP	65 70/ 13
9-	TIGHE,T.J.	SUBPROBLEM ANALYSIS OF DISCR LRNG	PL+M	73 7/183
9-	TIGHE,T.J.LEATON	ESCAPE FROM CONFLICT	PSC	66 6/129
9-	TIGHE,T.J.TIGHE	OVERTRAINING AND OPTIONAL SHIFT	JCPP	66 62/ 49
9-	TIGHE,T.J.ETAL	SUCCESSIVE CLASSICAL REVERSALS	JEAB	68 11/199
4-	TIMBERLAKE,W.ALLISON	RESPONSE DEPRIVATION + PERFORMANCE	PRV	74 81/146
2-	TITCHENER,E.B.	POSTULATES OF STRUCTURAL PSYCHOL	PHRV	98 7/449
2-	TOLMAN,E.C.	NERVE PROCESS AND COGNITION	PRV	18 25/423
2-	TOLMAN,E.C.	INSTINCT AND PURPOSE	PRV	20 27/217
2-	TOLMAN,E.C.	NEW FORMULA FOR BEHAVIORISM	PRV	22 29/ 44
8-	TOLMAN,E.C.	NEW ACCOUNT OF SENSATION QUALITY	PRV	22 29/140
2-	TOLMAN,E.C.	CAN INSTINCTS BE GIVEN UP IN PSYCH	JABP	22 17/139
2-	TOLMAN,E.C.	NATURE OF INSTINCT	PRV	23 20/200
2-	TOLMAN,E.C.	BEHAVIORISTIC ACCOUNT OF EMOTION	PRV	23 30/217
9-	TOLMAN,E.C.	UNDERLEARNING ON RETENTION	JEXP	23 6/466
9-	TOLMAN,E.C.	INHERITANCE OF MAZE-LRNG ABILITY	JCP	24 4/ 1
2-	TOLMAN,E.C.	BEHAVIORISM AND PURPOSE	JPH	25 22/ 36
9-	TOLMAN,E.C.	PURPOSE AND COGNITION	PRV	25 32/285
4-	TOLMAN,E.C.	NATURE OF FUNDAMENTAL DRIVES	JASP	26 5/349
9-	TOLMAN,E.C.	BEHAVIORISTIC THEORY OF IDEAS	PRV	26 33/352
9-	TOLMAN,E.C.	HABIT AND HIGHER MENTAL PROCESSES	PBL	27 24/ 1
9-	TOLMAN,E.C.	BEHAVIORISTIC DEF OF CONSCIOUSNESS	PRV	27 34/433
9-	TOLMAN,E.C.	HABIT AND HIGHER MENTAL PROCESSES	PBL	28 25/ 24
2-	TOLMAN,E.C.	PURPOSIVE BEHAVIOR	PRV	28 35/524
9-	TOLMAN,E.C.	MAZE PERF AND MOTIVATION	JGNP	30 4/338
2+ 44	TOLMAN,E.C.	PURPOSIVE BEHAVIOR		32 CENTRY
9-	TOLMAN,E.C.	LEWIN-S CONCEPT OF VECTORS	JGNP	32 7/ 3
9-393	TOLMAN,E.C.	LAWS--EMPHASIS, MOTIV, DISRUPTION	JEXP	32 15/601
3-	TOLMAN,E.C.	SIGN-GESTALT OR CONDITIONED REFLEX	PRV	33 40/246
3-	TOLMAN,E.C.	GESTALT AND SIGN-GESTALT	PRV	33 40/391
3-	TOLMAN,E.C.	A REPLY TO MR. KOFFKA	PB1	33 30/459
3-	TOLMAN,E.C.	THE LAW OF EFFECT	JEXP	33 16/463
9-	TOLMAN,E.C.	SUCCESSIVE DISCRIM HABITS	UCPP	34 6/145
1-	TOLMAN,E.C.	THEORIES OF LEARNING (MOSS)		34 P-HALL
9-	TOLMAN,E.C.	PSYCHOLOGY VS IMMEDIATE EXPERIENCE	PHSC	35 2/356
9-	TOLMAN,E.C.	OPERATIONAL BEHAVIORISM		36 U SCAL
9-	TOLMAN,E.C.	DEMANDS AND CONFLICTS	PRV	37 44/158
3-	TOLMAN,E.C.	STRING-PULLING BY RATS	PRV	37 44/195
9-394	TOLMAN,E.C.	BEHAVIOR AT A CHOICE POINT	PRV	38 45/ 1
9-	TOLMAN,E.C.	PHYSIOLOGY, PSYCHOLOGY, SOCIOLOGY	PRV	38 45/228
3-	TOLMAN,E.C.	DISCUSSION OF LAW OF EFFECT	PRV	38 45/200
3-	TOLMAN,E.C.	A REPLY TO PROFESSOR GUTHRIE	PRV	38 45/163
5-179	TOLMAN,E.C.	PREDICTION OF VTE/SCHEMATIC SOWBUG	PRV	39 46/318
9-	TOLMAN,E.C.	SPATIAL ANGLE AND VTE	JCP	40 30/129
5-	TOLMAN,E.C.	DISCRIM LEARNING, SCHEMATIC SOWBUG	PRV	41 48/367
9-	TOLMAN,E.C.	PSYCHOLOGICAL MAN	JSP	41 13/205
4-	TOLMAN,E.C.	A DRIVE-CONVERSION DIAGRAM	PRV	43 50/503
2-	TOLMAN,E.C.	EXPECTANCY NEED-CATHEXIS PSYCH	SC	45 01/160
3+ 66	TOLMAN,E.C.	COGNITIVE MAPS IN RATS AND MEN	PRV	48 55/189
3-	TOLMAN,E.C.	MORE THAN ONE KIND OF LEARNING	PRV	49 56/144
1-	TOLMAN,E.C.	NATURE AND FUNCTIONING OF WANTS	PRV	49 56/357
4-130	TOLMAN,E.C.	PSYCHOLOGICAL MODEL (PARSONS)		51 HARVRD
1-	TOLMAN,E.C.	COLLECTED PAPERS		51 U CAL
4-	TOLMAN,E.C.	COGNITION MOTIVATION MODEL	PRV	52 59/389
9-	TOLMAN,E.C.	FREEDOM AND THE COGNITIVE NEED	AMP	54 9/536
5+ 44	TOLMAN,E.C.	PRINCIPLES OF PERFORMANCE	PRV	55 62/315
1-	TOLMAN,E.C.	BEHAVIOR AND PSYCHOLOGICAL MAN		58 U CAL
9-	TOLMAN,E.C.	PERFORMANCE VECTORS	AMP	59 14/ 1
1-	TOLMAN,E.C.	PRINCIPLES OF PURPOSIVE BEH (KOCH)		59 MCG-H
1-	TOLMAN,E.C.BRUNSWIK	CAUSAL TEXTURE OF THE ENVIRONMENT	PRV	35 42/ 43
9-	TOLMAN,E.C.DAVIS	CORRELATION BETWEEN TWO MAZES	JCP	24 4/125
9-	TOLMAN,E.C.GEIER	GOAL GRADIENT OF ACTIVITY	JCP	43 35/197

	Author	Title	Journal	Yr	Vol/Pg
9-	TOLMAN,E.C.GLEITMAN	MOTIVATION ON RESP/PLACE LRNG	JEXP	49	39/653
6-	TOLMAN,E.C.GLEITMAN	EQUAL REINF AND SHOCK IN ONE GOAL	JEXP	49	39/810
9-	TOLMAN,E.C.HONZIK	INSIGHT IN RATS	UCPP	30	4/215
9-	TOLMAN,E.C.HONZIK	HUNGER AND REWARD ON MAZE LRNG	UCPP	30	4/241
3+ 77	TOLMAN,E.C.HONZIK	INTRODUCTION AND REMOVAL OF REWARD	UCPP	30	4/257
9-	TOLMAN,E.C.HONZIK	PERCEPTION OF SPATIAL RELATIONS	JCP	36	22/287
9-	TOLMAN,E.C.KRECHEVSKY	MEANS-END READINESS AND HYPOTHESIS	PRV	33	40/ 60
9-	TOLMAN,E.C.MINIUM	OVERLEARNING AND DIFFICULTY ON VTE	JCP	42	34/301
9-	TOLMAN,E.C.NYSWANDER	RELIABILITY/VALIDITY OF MAZE	JCP	27	7/425
1-	TOLMAN,E.C.POSTMAN	LEARNING	ARVP	54	5/ 27
9-	TOLMAN,E.C.RITCHIE	VTE IN MAZE AND VISUAL DISCRIM	JCP	43	36/ 91
9-	TOLMAN,E.C.SAMS	TIME DISCRIM IN WHITE RATS	JCP	25	5/255
9-	TOLMAN,E.C.WHITE	ELIMINATION OF LONG/SHORT BLINDS	JCP	23	3/327
9-	TOLMAN,E.C.ETAL	HUNGER ON ORDER OF ELIM BLINDS	UCPP	30	4/189
3-	TOLMAN,E.C.ETAL	DISPROOF OF THE LAW OF EFFECT	JEXP	32	15/601
9-	TOLMAN,E.C.ETAL	INDIV DIFF IN VTE AND DISCRIM	CPMG	41	17/ 3
9-	TOLMAN,E.C.ETAL	ORIENTATION AND THE SHORT-CUT	JEXP	46	36/ 13
3+ 68	TOLMAN,E.C.ETAL	SPATIAL LEARNING	JEXP	46	36/221
9-	TOLMAN,E.C.ETAL	TRANSFER OF PLACE LEARNING	JEXP	47	37/ 39
9-	TOLMAN,E.C.ETAL	NONCORRECTION ON RESP/PLACE LRNG	JEXP	47	37/285
8-	TOLMAN,E.C.ETAL	TEST OF INNATE SIGN STIMULUS	JCPP	55	48/278
7-	TOMBAUGH,T.N.	RESISTANCE TO EXTINCTION AND DELAY	PRP	66	19/791
8-	TRAPOLD,M.A.	REVERSAL OF OPERANT DISCRIMINATION	PSC	66	4/247
7-	TRAPOLD,M.A.DOREN	NONCONTINGENT PARTIAL REINF	JEXP	66	71/424
7-	TRAPOLD,M.A.HOLDEN	NONCONTINGENT PARTIAL REINF	PSC	66	5/449
5-	TRAPOLD,M.A.OVERMIER	SECOND LEARNING PROCESS (BLACK)		72	A-C-C
5+205	TROWILL,J.A.PANKSEPP	INCENTIVE IN BRAIN STIMULATION	PRV	69	76/264
9-393	TRYON,R.D.	GENETICS OF LEARNING ABILITY	UCPP	29	4/ 71
9-	TURBEVILLE,J.R.ETAL	RELATIONAL/CONFIGURATIONAL LRNG	AMJP	52	65/424
8-	TURNER,C.MACKINTOSH	IRRELEVANT STIM IN DISCRIM LRNG	JCPP	72	78/ 1
2-	TURNER,M.	PHILOSOPHY AND SCIENCE OF BEHAVIOR		67	A-C-C
9-	TVERSKY,A.	INTRANSITIVITY OF PREFERENCES	PRV	69	76/ 31
9-	TVERSKY,A.	CHOICE BY ELIMINATION OF ASPECTS	PRV	72	79/281
4-	TYLER,D.W.	EXTINCTION WITH CONTROL SEC REINF	AMJP	56	69/359
7-	TYLER,D.W.ETAL	RANDOM/ALTERNATING PARTIAL REINF	AMJP	53	66/ 57
9-	UHL,C.N.	OVERTRAIN ON REVERSAL/NONREVERSAL	P+MS	64	19/927
8-	UHL,C.N.ETAL	OVERLAPPING CUES IN DISCRIM LRNG	JEXP	64	67/ 91
9-	UHL,C.N.ETAL	OVERTRAIN ON REVERSAL/NONREVERSAL	P+MS	67	24/ 75
6-	ULRICH,R.E.AZRIN	REFLEXIVE FIGHTING TO AVERSIVE S	JEAB	62	5/511
1-	UNDERWOOD,B.J.	EXPERIMENTAL PSYCHOLOGY		49	A-C
2-	UNDERWOOD,B.J.	INDIVIDUAL DIFFERENCES IN THEORIES	AMP	75	30/128
9-	UNDERWOOD,B.J.KEPPEL	ONE-TRIAL LEARNING	VLVB	62	1/ 1
4-	VACHER,J.M.SHAFER	SEC REINF AND STIMULUS CHANGE	PRP	64	15/883
8-	VAUGHT,G.M.ELLINGER	FIELD-DEPENDENCE AND FORM DISCRIM	PSC	66	6/357
5-149	VERPLANCK,W.S.	OVERSTATEMENTS OF PHENOMENOLOGY	PRV	71	21/481
4-118	VERPLANCK,W.S.HAYES	EATING AND DRINKING	JCPP	53	46/327
8-	VETTER,E.H.HEARST	GEN/DISCRIM OF SHAPE ORIENTATION	JEAB	68	11/753
4-	VINEY,W.ETAL	RANDOM INTERMIT STIM ON EXTINCTION	PRP	64	14/403
3-	VOEKS,V.W.	STRENGTH OR NUMBER S-R CONNECTIONS	JP	55	39/289
7-	VOGEL,J.R.ETAL	EXTINCTION AND DEPRESSION EFFECT	JEXP	66	72/ 51
5-185	VONNEUMANN,J.MORGENSTERN	THEORY OF GAMES		47	PRINCN
8-	VON SALL,W.JENKINS	BLOCKING STIMULUS CONTROL	PL+M	70	1/ 56
4-117	WAGMAN,W.ALLEN	COND POS REINF BASED ON SHOCK TERM	PSC	64	1/363
7-270	WAGNER,A.R.	EFFECTS OF AMOUNT/PERCENT REINF	JEXP	61	62/234
4-117	WAGNER,A.R.	COND FRUSTRATION AS LEARNED DRIVE	JEXP	63	66/142
8+343	WAGNER,A.R.	ST VALIDITY/SELECTION (MACKINTOSH)		69	DALHSE
8-	WAGNER,A.R.	INCIDENTAL STIM AND DISC (GILBERT)		69	ACAD P
8-333	WAGNER,A.R.	MODIFIED CONTINUITY THEORY	PL+M	69	3/ 1
8-350	WAGNER,A.R.	ELEMENTARY ASSOCIATIONS (KENDLER)		71	A-C-C
3-	WAGNER,A.R.LOGAN	CHOICE BEHAVIOR/DISTRIBUTION REINF	AMJP	63	76/480
8-	WAGNER,A.R.RESCORLA	INHIBITION IN COND (BOAKES)		72	ACAD P
8-346	WAGNER,A.R.ETAL	STIM SELECTION IN DISCRIM LEARNING	JEXP	68	76/171
8-	WALDER,L.O.	INCIDENTAL CUE ON GENERALIZATION	JEXP	61	61/178

4-	WALKER,E.L.	DRIVE SPECIFICITY AND LEARNING	JEXP	48	38/ 39
9-390	WALKER,E.L.	COURSE OF REACTION DECREMENT	JCPP	56	49/167
1-	WALKER,E.L.	COND AND INSTRUMENTAL LEARNING		68	B-COLE
4-	WALKER,K.C.	DISCRIM S TRANS TO UNASSOCIATED R	JEXP	42	31/312
8-	WALL,A.M.	DISCRETE-TRIAL ANALYSIS OF FI DISC	JCPP	65	60/ 70
7-293	WALLER,T.G.	EFFECT OF REWARD CONSISTENCY	JCPP	73	83/120
6-242	WALTERS,G.C.GLAZER	PUNISHMENT OF INSTINCTIVE BEHAVIOR	JCPP	71	75/331
6-238	WARDEN,C.J.AYLESWORTH	REL VALUE OF REWARD AND PUNISHMENT	JCP	27	7/117
8-	WARREN,J.M.	ADDITIVITY OF CUES IN PATTERN DISC	JCPP	53	46/484
9-	WARREN,J.M.	OBJECT AND POSITION DISCRIM	JCPP	59	52/ 92
9-	WARREN,J.M.	STIM PERSEVERATION IN DISCRIM LRNG	JCPP	59	52/ 99
9-	WARREN,J.M.	TRANSFER RELATIONS IN DISCRIM LRNG	JCPP	59	52/336
9-	WARREN,J.M.	ODDITY LEARNING SET IN A CAT	JCPP	60	53/433
9-	WARREN,J.M.	ADDITIVITY OF CUES IN DISCRIM LRNG	JCPP	64	58/124
9-	WARREN,J.M.BARON	LEARNING SETS BY CATS	JCPP	56	49/227
9-	WARREN J.M.BECH	VISUAL PROBABILITY LRNG BY CATS	JCPP	66	61/316
8-	WARREN,J.M.BROOKSHIRE	STIM GENERALIZATION AND DISCRIM	JEXP	59	58/348
8-	WARREN,J.M.MCGONIGLE	ATTENTION THEORY + DISC (GILBERT)		69	ACAD P
8-	WARREN,J.M.WARREN	TWO-CUE DISCRIM LRNG BY MONKEYS	JCPP	69	69/688
1-	WATSON,J.B.	PSYCH--STANDPOINT OF BEHAVIORIST		19	LIPPIN
2-	WATSON,R.I.	GREAT PSYCHOLOGISTS		68	LIPPIN
4-106	WEBB,W.B.	MOTIVATION OF IRRELEVANT DRIVE	JEXP	49	39/ 1
9-	WEBB,W.B.	RELATIONAL/SPECIFIC STIM DISC LRNG	JCPP	50	43/ 70
4-	WEBB,W.B.NOLAN	CUES FOR DISCRIM AS REINF	JCPP	53	46/180
8-	WEGENER,J.G.	CROSS-MODAL TRANSFER IN MONKEYS	JCPP	65	59/450
6-220	WEGNER,N.ZEAMAN	VARYING US DURATIONS	PRV	58	65/238
4-	WEINSTOCK,R.B.	MAINT SCHEDULE AND HUNGER DRIVE	PBL	72	78/311
7+295	WEINSTOCK,S.	PARTIAL REINF/WIDELY SPACED TRIALS	JCPP	54	47/314
7-295	WEINSTOCK,S.	PARTIAL REINF AT 24-HR ITI	JEXP	58	56/151
8-	WEISE,P.BITTERMAN	RESP SELECTION IN DISC LRNG	PRV	51	58/185
8-	WEISMAN,R.E.	INHIBITORY STIMULUS CONTROL	JEAB	69	12/443
8-	WEISMAN,R.E.PALMER	PRIOR NON DIFF REINF ON DISCRIM	JEAB	69	12/229
4-	WEISMAN,R.G.LITNER	POSITIVE COND REINF/SIDMAN AVOID	JCPP	69	68/597
6-	WEISMAN,R.G.LITNER	EXCITATION AND INHIBITION OF FEAR	JCPP	69	69/667
7-269	WEISS,B.	TRANSITION STATES (SCHOENFELD)		70	A-C-C
8-	WEISS,K.M.	COND SUPPRESSION AND OPERANT DISCR	JEAB	68	11/767
8-	WEISS,S.J.	COMPOUNDING OF VI AND LOW RATE	JEAB	67	10/535
8-	WEISS,S.J.	STIMULUS COMPOUNDING	PBL	72	78/189
8-	WEISS,S.J.	IRTS IN HIGH/LOW RATE DISCRIM	L+M	72	3/469
4-	WEISS,S.J.LAWSON	SEC REINF SUPRESS OPERANT RATE	JCPP	62	55/ 16
6-	WEISSMAN,A.	NONDISCRIM AVOIDANCE BEHAVIOR	PRP	26	10/591
7-278	WENDT,G.R.	INHIBITION OR COMPETITION	PRV	36	43/258
4-	WENRICH,W.W.CAHOON	SEC REINF USING DISCRIM STIM	PRP	65	16/242
4-	WENRICH,W.W.ETAL	POS REINF BY DISCRIM STIM IN AVERS	PSC	65	3/383
4-110	WHALEN,R.E.	SEXUAL BEHAVIOR AND LEARNING	JCPP	61	54/409
8-352	WICKENS,D.D.	TRANSFER TO ANTAGONISTIC MUSCLES	JEXP	38	22/101
3-	WICKENS,D.D.	RESPONSE GENERALIZATION IN COND	JEXP	43	33/221
8-	WICKENS,D.D.	CONDITIONING TO COMPLEX STIMULI	AMP	59	14/180
7-	WICKENS,D.D.SNIDE	NONREINF COMPONENT OF COMPLEX STIM	JEXP	55	49/257
4-	WIKE,E.L.	SECONDARY REINFORCEMENT		66	HARPER
4-	WIKE,E.L.BARRIENTOS	SEC REINF AND MULT DRIVE REDUCTION	JCPP	58	51/640
4-	WIKE,E.L.CASEY	SEC REINF OF FOOD FOR THIRSTY RAT	JCPP	54	47/240
4-	WIKE,E.L.CASEY	SEC REWARD OF FOOD SATIATED RATS	JCPP	54	47/441
4-118	WIKE,E.L.FARROW	DRIVE INTENSITY ON SEC REINF	JCPP	62	55/ 20
4-119	WIKE,E.L.MCNAMARA	QUEST FOR GENERALIZED COND REINF	PRP	55	1/ 83
4-	WIKE,E.L.MCNAMARA	SOME COND AFFECTING SEC REINF	JCPP	57	50/345
4-	WIKE,E.L.PLATT	REINF SCHEDULES AND BAR PRESSING	PRC	62	12/273
4-	WIKE,E.L.ETAL	REWARD OF GETTING OUT OF START BOX	PRC	62	12/397
4-	WIKE,E.L.ETAL	DRIVE AND SECONDARY REINFORCEMENT	PRC	63	13/ 45
4-	WIKES,W.P.CROWDER	SEC REINF CONTROL FOR RESP FACIL	JP	60	49/ 83
8-	WILCOX,J.M.ROSS	CS INTENSITY ON DIFF CLASS COND	JEXP	69	82/272
8-	WILLIAMS,D.I.	TRANSFER ALONG A CONTINUUM	JCPP	68	65/369
9-	WILLIAMS,D.L.	OVERTRAINING REVERSAL EFFECT	PSC	67	7/261

7-	WILLIAMS,D.R.	CLASS COND AND INCENTIVE (PROKASY)		65	A-C-C
4-	WILLIAMS,D.R.WILLIAMS	AUTO-MAINTENANCE/NONREINFORCEMENT	JEAB	69	12/511
4-	WILLIAMS,K.A.	REWARD VALUE OF A CONDITIONED STIM	JCPP	29	4/ 31
6-	WILSON,G.T.	EXTINCTION OF AVOIDANCE RESPONDING	JCPP	73	82/105
7-	WILSON,J.J.	PRE/GOAL BOX MOVEMENTS	JCPP	64	57/211
9-	WILSON,M.ETAL	FORMATION OF TACTUAL LEARNING SETS	JCPP	63	56/732
7-	WILSON,W.ETAL	TESTS OF SHEFFIELD HYPOTHESIS	JEXP	55	50/ 51
8-	WILTON,R.N.GAY	BEHAVIOR CONTRAST IN CHAINED SCHED	JEAB	69	12/905
4-	WINER,H.	EFFECTS OF RESPONSE COST	JEAB	62	5/201
6-226	WINOGRAD,E.	SHOCK INTENSITY ON ESCAPE BEHAVIOR	JEAB	65	8/117
9-	WISCHNER,G.J.	PUNISH IN DISCRIM,NON-CORRECTION	JEXP	47	37/271
9-	WISCHNER,G.J.	REPLY TO MUENZINGER ON NONCORRECT	JEXP	48	38/203
9-	WISCHNER,G.J.	COMBINATIONS OF FOOD AND SHOCK	JEXP	64	67/ 48
9-	WISCHNER,G.J.FOWLER	DURATION OF SHOCK RIGHT/WRONG	PSC	64	1/239
9-	WISCHNER,G.J.ETAL	STRENGTH OF SHOCK RIGHT/WRONG	JEXP	63	65/131
9-	WITKIN,H.A.	HYPOTHESES IN RATS	JCP	41	31/303
9-	WITKIN,H.A.	HYPOTHESES IN RATS	PRV	42	49/541
9-	WODINSKY,J.BITTERMAN	COMPOUND/CONFIGURATION IN DISCRIM	AMJP	52	65/563
4-	WOLFE,J.B.	EFFECTIVENESS OF TOKEN REWARDS	CPMG	36	12/ 60
9-398	WOLFF,J.L.	CONCEPT SHIFT AND REVERSAL	PBL	67	68/369
9-	WOLFLE,D.L.	ABSOLUTE BRIGHTNESS DISCRIM	JCP	37	24/ 59
9-	WOLFORD,G.BOWER	CONTINUITY THEORY REVISITED	PRV	69	76/515
2-	WOODS,P.J.	TAXONOMY OF INSTRUMENTAL COND	AMP	74	29/584
1-	WOODWORTH,R.S.	CONTEMPORARY SCHOOLS OF PSYCHOLOGY		31	RONALD
1-	WOODWORTH,R.S.	CONTEMPORARY SCHOOLS OF PSYCHOLOGY		48	RONALD
1-	WOODWORTH,R.S.SCHLOSBERG	EXPERIMENTAL PSYCHOLOGY		54	HOLT
1-	WOODWORTH,R.S.SHEEHAN	CONTEMPORARY SCHOOLS OF PSYCHOLOGY		64	RONALD
9-	WRIGHT,P.L.ETAL	LEARNING SETS IN RATS	JCPP	63	56/200
4-	WUNDERLICH,R.A.	GENERALIZED SECONDARY REINF	JEXP	61	62/409
9-	WUNDERLICH,R.A.DORFF	CONTIGUITY OF S, R, REINF IN DISCR	JCPP	65	59/147
8-	WYCKOFF,L.B.	OBSERVING RESP IN DISCRIM LRNG	PRV	52	59/431
4-121	WYCKOFF,L.B.	QUANTITATIVE THEORY OF SEC REINF	PRV	59	66/ 68
4-121	WYCKOFF,L.B.ETAL	SEC REINF AND CUE EFFECTS OF STIM	JCPP	58	51/103
8-	YARCZOWER,M.ETAL	DISCRIM WITH EQUATED FREQ OF REINF	JEAB	68	11/415
8-	YEHLE,A.L.	THREE-TONE CLASSICAL DISCRIM COND	JEXP	68	77/468
7-	YELEN,R.D.	REWARD MAGNITUDE AND AFTEREFFECTS	PSC	67	8/301
9-	YOSHIOKA,J.G.	POSITION HABITS WITH RATS	JCP	28	8/429
7-277	YOUNG,A.G.	RESISTANCE TO EXTINCTION/EFFORT	JEXP	66	72/610
9-	YOUNG,M.L.HARLOW	WEIGL PRINCIPLE AND ODDITY METHOD	JCP	43	35/205
9-	YOUNG,M.L.HARLOW	GENERALIZATION OF WEIGL PRINCIPLE	JCP	43	36/201
1-	YOUNG,P.T.	MOTIVATION OF BEHAVIOR		36	WILEY
1-	YOUNG,P.T.	HEDONIC PROCESSES IN MOTIV (JONES)		55	U NEBR
4-	YOUNG,P.T.	AFFECTIVE PROCESSES IN LRNG/MOTIV	PRV	59	66/104
4-	YOUNG,P.T.	MOTIVATION AND EMOTION		61	WILEY
9-	ZABLE,M.HARLOW	REVERSAL OF OBJECT/POSITION DISCR	JCP	46	39/ 13
5-167	ZEAMAN,D.	LATENCY AND AMOUNT OF REINF	JEXP	49	39/566
7-	ZEAMAN,D.	RESP LATENCY AND AMOUNT OF REINF	JEXP	49	39/466
9-	ZEIGLER,H.P.	LEARNING SET FORMATION IN PIGEONS	JCPP	61	54/252
9-	ZEIGLER,H.P.WYCKOFF	OBSERVING RESP AND DISCRIM LRNG	QJEP	61	13/129
9-	ZEILER,M.D.	RATIO THEORY OF INTERMEDIATE SIZE	PRV	63	70/516
9-	ZEILER,M.D.	INTERMEDIATE SIZE BY PIGEONS	JEAB	64	8/263
9-	ZEILER,M.D.	STIM IN INTERMEDIATE SIZE PROBLEM	PRV	66	73/257
8-	ZEILER,M.D.	S CONTROL DURING MULTIPLE DISCRIM	JEAB	68	11/549
8-	ZEILER,M.D.PRICE	DISCRIM WITH VI AND CRF SCHEDULES	PSC	65	3/ 31
7-278	ZENER,K.	THEORIES OF CONDITIONED RESPONSE	AMJP	37	50/384
4-	ZIMMERMAN,D.W.	DURABLE SEC REINF/METHOD + THEORY	PRV	57	64/373
4-122	ZIMMERMAN,D.W.	SUSTAINED PERF BASED ON SEC REINF	JCPP	59	52/353
4-	ZIMMERMAN,D.W.	DEP AND SATIATION ON SEC REINF	JGTP	61	99/139
4-	ZIMMERMAN,D.W.	S COND ON STRENGTH OF SEC REINF	PRP	63	13/135
4-	ZIMMERMAN,D.W.	CONDITIONS OF REINF ON SEC REINF	PRP	63	13/747
4-123	ZIMMERMAN,D.W.	SUSTAINED BEHAVIOR WITH COND REINF	SC	63	42/682

ABSTRACT CREDITS

480

INDEX

Numbers in *italics* indicate terms defined in the glossary.